# ENGLISH GRAMMAR
## PAST AND PRESENT

# ENGLISH GRAMMAR
## PAST AND PRESENT

**WITH APPENDICES ON PROSODY, SYNONYMS, AND OTHER OUTLYING SUBJECTS.**

**IN THREE PARTS**

**BY**

**J. C. NESFIELD, M.A.**

GYAN

*Published by*

GYAN

Gyan Publishing House
5, Ansari Road
Daryaganj, New Delhi-110002
Phone: 011-47034999, 9811692060
E-mail: books@gyanbooks.com

*Distribution Network*
gyanbooks.com
India, USA, Canada, UK, Australia



ISBN: 978-93-6208-601-3 (HB)
First Published, 1898

2nd Impression 2024

*Printed at:* Gyan Press, Delhi.



**ENGLISH GRAMMAR PAST AND PRESENT**
Author: J. C. NESFIELD

# ENGLISH GRAMMAR
# PAST AND PRESENT

IN THREE PARTS

PART I.—MODERN ENGLISH GRAMMAR.
II.—IDIOM AND CONSTRUCTION.
III.—HISTORICAL ENGLISH: WORD-BUILDING AND DERIVATION.

WITH APPENDICES ON PROSODY, SYNONYMS, AND OTHER OUTLYING SUBJECTS.

BY

J. C. NESFIELD, M.A.

LATE DIRECTOR OF PUBLIC INSTRUCTION, NORTH-WESTERN PROVINCES AND OUDH, INDIA

MACMILLAN & CO., LIMITED
ST. MARTIN'S STREET, LONDON
NEW YORK: THE MACMILLAN COMPANY
1898

# PREFACE

The plan that has been followed in preparing this book is to carry the student's mind gradually forward from the more easy to the less easy, from the better known to the less known or the unknown.

Accordingly, Part I. deals with "Modern English Grammar," covering the more familiar ground of Accidence, Analysis, Syntax, and Punctuation.

Part II. discusses the idiomatic uses of the different Parts of Speech, explaining these, when necessary, by reference to idioms that were in force in the earlier stages of our language.

Part III. deals solely with the subject of "Historical English and Derivation." On account of the greater complexity of this subject and the increasing importance ascribed to it, this Part has been made to cover about as much space as the other two Parts combined.

The Appendices deal with certain outlying subjects, such as Prosody, Figures of Rhetoric, Synonyms, etc., which do not belong to Grammar proper. Amongst them there is a valuable Note on the "Names of Vocalic Sounds" by Professor Skeat, which has been printed in this book with his permission.

The graduated method here described was suggested to the writer by an experience extending over many years, most of which were spent in an eastern country, where English is studied with extraordinary keenness, and every effort is made to find out the best means of teaching it. In fact, the present book is not an entirely new one, but an adaptation of a manual prepared by the same author a few years ago in India, while he was still living there. In adapting this manual to English use, he has adhered to the original method, because he believes that for England no less than for India it is best to assume that the average student does not know very much to start with, and that every student must be well versed in the principles of Modern English, before he can be qualified to begin the much more difficult task of tracing these to their sources.

The writer is glad to find that in following the plan thus suggested by his own experience and judgment, he was undesignedly acting up to the spirit of the directions given in the London Matriculation Directory, which run as follows:—"The English Language papers may roughly be divided into three parts: first, modern grammar, including, of course, parsing and analysis; second, historical grammar and philology, including the history of the apparent solecisms of modern grammar, and especially of the traces of *flexion* that Modern English still shows; third, subjects that come under neither of these heads, such as the correct use and meaning of words and the discrimination of synonyms, the metrical characteristics of English verse, etc. . . . From the above survey of the scope of the papers, it will be evident that the first essential of a sound and complete preparation will be a thorough grounding in the elements of English grammar."

The grounding here prescribed as "the first essential" to the matriculation-course is precisely what the writer has attempted to supply in Part I. of the present book. In fact, his own method is so closely analagous to that laid down by the University, that after reading through all the questions set for the last eighteen years by the London Matriculation examiners, he was able to distribute them under three different headings, answering respectively to Part I. on "Modern English Grammar," Part II. on "Idiom and Construction," and Part III. on "Historical English and Derivation." Each set of questions has been reprinted at the close of the Part to which it relates, so that the student may be able to test his own knowledge as he advances. The student who desires to avail himself of the opportunity thus offered will find, as the writer believes, that there is scarcely any question relating to these three branches of English Grammar, which cannot be answered from information furnished in the text of the book.

Three rather lengthy chapters have been given to the history of Sounds, Spellings, and Accents,—subjects about which very little is said in current text-books intended for School use. A fuller treatment of such subjects appeared to the writer to be indispensable, if something like a complete outline of the history of our language is to be placed before the student.

It is hoped that this book may be of some use at Ladies' Colleges and any other institutions where Historical as well as Modern English is made an object of study.

The names of the authorities consulted by the writer in dealing with Historical English can be seen from the references given in the footnotes. But he may here state that Professor Skeat is the authority from whom he has derived most help, and this not merely from the study of his books, which (it is needless to add) are in the vanguard of research, but still more from the conversations and correspondence that he was privileged to have with that gentleman, whenever he found it necessary to refer to him on any doubtful or difficult point. The writer cannot be too grateful for the help so ungrudgingly given. At the same time it must be understood that, if any mistakes occur in the course of this book, no one but the author himself is responsible. Whatever errors may be found, they are all his own.

The writer must also tender his thanks to Rev. J. Sephton, M.A., Cambridge, Reader in Icelandic at University College, Liverpool, for having read the proofs of Part III. and made such suggestions as struck him in the course of doing so.

J. C. N.

EALING, 1*st October* 1897.

# CONTENTS

## PART I.—MODERN ENGLISH GRAMMAR.


| CHAP. | | PAGE |
|---|---|---|
| 1. | ANALYTICAL OUTLINE: GENERAL DEFINITIONS | 1 |
| 2. | NOUNS | 8 |
| | Section 1.—The kinds of Nouns | 8 |
| | ,, 2.—Substitutes for a Noun | 12 |
| | ,, 3.—Gender | 12 |
| | ,, 4.—Case | 16 |
| | ,, 5.—Number | 18 |
| 3. | ADJECTIVES | 25 |
| | Section 1.—The kinds of Adjectives | 25 |
| | ,, 2.—The two Uses of Adjectives | 29 |
| | ,, 3.—Substitutes for Adjectives | 30 |
| | ,, 4.—Comparison of Adjectives | 30 |
| 4. | PRONOUNS | 33 |
| | Section 1.—Personal Pronouns | 34 |
| | ,, 2.—Demonstrative Pronouns | 37 |
| | ,, 3.—Relative or Conjunctive Pronouns | 41 |
| | ,, 4.—Interrogative Pronouns | 44 |
| 5. | VERBS | 45 |
| | Section 1.—The kinds of Verbs | 45 |
| | ,, 2.—Transitive Verbs | 46 |
| | ,, 3.—Intransitive Verbs | 49 |
| | ,, 4.—Auxiliary Verbs | 53 |
| | ,, 5.—Active and Passive Voices | 55 |
| | ,, 6.—Mood, Tense, Number, and Person | 57 |
| | ,, 7.—Indicative Mood | 58 |
| | ,, 8.—Imperative Mood | 62 |
| | ,, 9.—Subjunctive Mood | 63 |
| | ,, 10.—Infinitive Mood | 66 |
| | ,, 11.—Participles | 69 |
| | ,, 12.—Gerunds and Verbal Nouns | 72 |
| | ,, 13.—The Conjugation of Verbs | 75 |
| | ,, 14.—Auxiliary, Defective, and Anomalous Verbs | 81 |
| 6. | ADVERBS | 87 |
| | Section 1.—The Functions of Adverbs | 87 |
| | ,, 2.—The kinds of Adverbs | 89 |
| | ,, 3.—Comparison of Adverbs | 91 |
| | ,, 4.—Verbs compounded with Adverbs | 92 |
| | ,, 5.—The two Uses of Adverbs | 92 |
| 7. | PREPOSITIONS | 93 |

| CHAP. | | PAGE |
|---|---|---|
| 8. | CONJUNCTIONS | 95 |
| | Section 1.—Co-ordinative Conjunctions | 96 |
| | " 2.—Subordinative Conjunctions | 97 |
| 9. | INTERJECTIONS | 101 |
| 10. | ANALYSIS OF SENTENCES | 102 |
| | Section 1.—Analysis of Simple Sentences | 102 |
| | " 2.—Analysis of Compound Sentences | 106 |
| | " 3.—Analysis of Complex Sentences | 110 |
| 11. | THE SAME WORD USED AS DIFFERENT PARTS OF SPEECH | 118 |
| 12. | SYNTAX | 121 |
| 13. | PUNCTUATION, OR THE RIGHT USE OF STOPS | 131 |
| | QUESTIONS ON MODERN ENGLISH GRAMMAR | 138 |


## PART II.—IDIOM AND CONSTRUCTION.


| | | |
|---|---|---|
| 14. | NOUNS AND PRONOUNS | 147 |
| | Section 1.—Cases of Nouns and Pronouns | 147 |
| | " 2.—Uses of Pronouns, Past and Present | 150 |
| 15. | ADJECTIVES | 155 |
| | Section 1.—Uses of the Various kinds of Adjectives | 155 |
| | " 2.—The Uses of Articles | 159 |
| | " 3.—Adjectives used as Nouns | 161 |
| | " 4.—Degrees of Comparison | 163 |
| 16. | VERBS | 166 |
| | Section 1.—Uses of Tenses | 166 |
| | " 2.—Further Uses of the Infinitive | 168 |
| | " 3.—Sequence of Tenses | 170 |
| 17. | ADVERBS | 173 |
| | Section 1.—Position of Adverbs | 173 |
| | " 2.—Adverbs qualifying Prepositions | 175 |
| 18. | PREPOSITIONS | 177 |
| 19. | CONJUNCTIONS AND CONJUNCTIONAL PHRASES | 189 |
| 20. | MISCELLANEOUS WORDS, PHRASES, AND CONSTRUCTIONS | 193 |
| | NOTES ON CERTAIN GRAMMATICAL TERMS | 213 |
| | QUESTIONS ON IDIOM AND CONSTRUCTION | 217 |


## PART III.—HISTORICAL ENGLISH: WORD-BUILDING AND DERIVATION.


| | | |
|---|---|---|
| 21. | HISTORICAL OUTLINE | 221 |
| | Section 1.—English and Cognate Languages | 221 |
| | " 2.—Old English | 227 |
| | " 3.—Middle English | 232 |
| | " 4.—Modern English | 243 |
| 22. | BORROWINGS | 246 |
| | Section 1.—Celtic | 246 |
| | " 2.—Danish or Later Scandian | 248 |
| | " 3.—Dutch | 250 |
| | " 4.—Latin | 251 |

| CHAP. | | PAGE |
|---|---|---|
| 22. | Section 5.—French | 255 |
| | ,, 6.—Greek | 261 |
| | ,, 7.—Modern Borrowings: Miscellaneous | 262 |
| 23. | SOUNDS AND SYMBOLS | 266 |
| | Section 1.—Alphabet, Present and Past | 266 |
| | ,, 2.—Consonants | 268 |
| | ,, 3.—Vowels and Diphthongs | 277 |
| 24. | SPELLINGS | 291 |
| | Section 1.—History of English Spelling | 291 |
| | ,, 2.—Summary of English Spellings | 296 |
| 25. | ACCENTUATION, SYLLABIC DIVISION | 301 |
| | Section 1.—Words of Native or Teutonic Origin | 301 |
| | ,, 2.—Words of French or Latin Origin | 304 |
| | ,, 3.—Syllabic Division | 308 |
| 26. | ACCIDENCE | 309 |
| | Section 1.—The Forms of Nouns | 309 |
| | ,, 2.—The Forms of Adjectives | 322 |
| | ,, 3.—The Forms of Pronouns | 330 |
| | ,, 4.—The Forms of Verbs | 336 |
| | ,, 5.—The Forms of Adverbs | 358 |
| | ,, 6.—The Forms of Prepositions | 364 |
| | ,, 7.—The Forms of Conjunctions | 368 |
| 27. | COMPOUND WORDS | 369 |
| | Section 1.—Unrelated or Juxta-positional Compounds | 369 |
| | ,, 2.—Related or Syntactical Compounds | 370 |
| | ,, 3.—Disguised Compounds | 372 |
| | ,, 4.—Mistaken or Apparent Compounds | 375 |
| | ,, 5.—Hybrid Compounds | 377 |
| 28. | TEUTONIC PREFIXES AND SUFFIXES | 378 |
| | Section 1.—Prefixes | 379 |
| | ,, 2.—Suffixes | 382 |
| 29. | ROMANIC PREFIXES AND SUFFIXES | 391 |
| | Section 1.—Prefixes | 391 |
| | ,, 2.—Suffixes | 396 |
| 30. | GREEK PREFIXES AND SUFFIXES | 408 |
| | Section 1.—Prefixes | 408 |
| | ,, 2.—Suffixes | 409 |
| 31. | SUMMARY OF RESULTS IN PREFIXES AND SUFFIXES | 411 |
| 32. | BILINGUALISM, DOUBLETS, GRIMM'S LAW, VERNER'S LAW | 417 |
| | QUESTIONS ON HISTORICAL ENGLISH | 423 |
| APPENDIX | I. PROSODY AND POETRY | 425 |
| ,, | II. FIGURES OF RHETORIC | 445 |
| ,, | III. SYNONYMS | 447 |
| ,, | IV. CHANGES OF MEANING | 448 |
| ,, | V. NOTE ON VOCALIC SOUNDS BY PROF. SKEAT | 457 |
| INDEX | I. OF SUBJECTS | 462 |
| ,, | II. OF SELECTED WORDS AND PHRASES | 467 |

# PART I.—MODERN ENGLISH GRAMMAR.

## CHAPTER I.

### ANALYTICAL OUTLINE: GENERAL DEFINITIONS.

1. **A Sentence.**—A combination of words that makes a *complete* sense is called a **Sentence.** The sense is not complete, unless something is *said* about something else.

A ship went out to sea.

*Note.*—There are five different kinds of sentences:—

(*a*) **Assertive,** affirming or denying. (*Indic. Mood.*)
A man's success depends chiefly on himself. (*Affirmative.*)
He did not get much help from others. (*Negative.*)

(*b*) **Imperative,** command or prohibition. (*Imper. Mood.*)
Rely chiefly on your own efforts. (*Command* or *Advice.*)
Do not rely much on the help of others. (*Prohibition.*)

(*c*) **Interrogative,** asking a question. (*Indic. Mood.*)
Have you finished that task?

(*d*) **Optative,** expressing a wish. (*Subjunct. Mood.*)
God save the queen.

(*e*) **Exclamatory,** surprise, joy, sorrow, etc. (*Indic. Mood.*)
What a foolish fellow you have been!

2. **Subject and Predicate.**—The word or words denoting the person or thing about which something is said are called the **Subject** of the sentence.

A *ship* went out to sea.

The word or words which say something about the person or thing denoted by the Subject, as "*went out*," are called the **Predicate.**[1]

---

[1] The student must therefore guard against such definitions as "The subject is what we speak about"; or "The subject is that concerning which something is asserted." In point of fact, we make no assertion con-

Hence no sentence can be made without a Subject and a Predicate. These two things are necessary to make a *complete* sense.

But the subject may be understood as in *go*, and in almost all other Imper. sentences. In such a sentence as "*Companion, hence!*" (Shaks.), both the verb and the subject are understood.

3. **A Phrase.**—A combination of words that make sense, but not a *complete* sense, is called a **Phrase.**

On the river. Through thick and thin. A bird in the hand.

The student will therefore understand that a phrase *cannot contain a Predicate* either expressed or understood.

4. **A Clause.**—A sentence which is *part of a larger sentence* is called a **Clause.**

This is the house | where we live.

Here "where we live" is a sentence, because it has a subject "we" and a predicate "live." Similarly "this is the house" is a sentence, having "this" for its subject and "is" for its predicate. But both are *parts of a larger sentence*, and hence each of them is called a clause.

5. **Nouns.**—If we give a name to some person or thing, such as *man, house, ship*, we call the word used for this purpose a **Noun.** Hence a noun is the *naming* word.

6. **Pronouns.**—If instead of mentioning or repeating a noun we use some other word which will show what noun we are referring to, we call the word so used a **Pronoun.**

A ship went to sea, and *she* had all her sails up.

Here the pronoun "she" is used instead of the noun "ship," and saves its being mentioned twice. Hence a pronoun is a *substitute* word, and its chief use is *to save the mentioning or repetition of a noun.*

7. **Adjectives.**—If we wish to restrict the application of a noun by adding something to its meaning, we call the word used for this purpose an **Adjective.** More briefly, the adjective is said to *qualify* the noun.

*A fine* ship went out to sea.

The word *Adjective* means "adding," and is so called because it adds something to the meaning of a noun. In the above sentence we do not speak of any kind of ship, but only of *a fine* ship.

8. **Verbs.**—If we wish to *say* something about something else, we call the word used for saying it a **Verb.**

A fine ship *went out* to sea.

---

cerning the Subject, but only about the *person or thing denoted* by the Subject. If we say, "The ox is dead," we make no assertion about the *noun* "ox"—the subject, but about the *thing* or *animal* "ox" denoted by the noun.

Here the word which predicates or says something about a ship is "went out." This is therefore a verb; and thus *the predicate of a sentence must be a verb*, or it must at least contain one.

**9. Preposition with its Object.**—In the phrase "to sea," the word "to" is called a **Preposition**. This word expresses the relation in which the thing denoted by "sea" stands to the event denoted by "went out."

The noun, pronoun, or other noun-equivalent that follows the preposition is called its **Object**.

The use of a preposition, then, is *to show the relation in which the person or thing denoted by its Object stands to something else.*[1]

**10. Conjunctions.**—A Conjunction is a *joining* word. It joins words and phrases to one another, or one sentence to another sentence.

(*a*) He made himself mean *and* of no reputation.
(*b*) May he live long *and* (may he) die happily.

In (*a*) the adjective "mean" is joined to the phrase "of no reputation" by the conjunction "and."

In (*b*) the sentence "may he live long" is joined by the same conjunction to the sentence "may he die happily."

**11. Adverbs.**—These, like adjectives, are *qualifying* words. An adjective, as we have shown, qualifies a *noun;* an adverb qualifies *anything except a noun or pronoun.*[2]

That *very* fine ship has *already* sailed *half* through the Channel.

Here "very" is an adverb qualifying the adjective "fine"; "already" is an adverb qualifying the verb "has sailed"; and "half" is an adverb qualifying the preposition "through."

**12. Interjections.**—If we wish to express some feeling or emotion by a single word, and without using a whole sentence for the purpose, we call the word so used an **Interjection.**

My son, *alas!* is not industrious.

Here "alas" is a sound thrown into the sentence to express regret. Observe that the word *alas!* is not syntactically connected with the rest of the sentence, but is a mere sound thrown into it (Lat. *inter*,

---

[1] The student must guard against such a definition as "A Preposition joins a noun to a word, indicating some relation between the noun and the word thus joined with it." In point of fact, *all* Parts of Speech (excepting interjections), and not merely prepositions, indicate relations between *words*. The peculiar function of a preposition is that it indicates a relation between *things*, that is, between the things denoted by words, and not between the words themselves.

[2] An Adverb is generally defined to be a "word used to qualify verbs, adjectives, or other adverbs." The inadequacy of this definition, which excludes Prepositions and Conjunctions from the qualifying power of adverbs, is further shown in § 216.

between, *jactus*, thrown). In this respect it stands on a different footing from all other parts of speech.

**13. The Parts of Speech defined.**—Words are classified according to the purpose that they are used for, and every such class is called a **Part of Speech**. (Hence, in *parsing* a word, the first thing to do is to say what *part* (quae *pars*) of speech it belongs to.) The Parts of Speech can be thus defined :—

(1) A Noun is a word used for naming some person or thing.

(2) A Pronoun is a word used instead of a noun or noun-equivalent.

(3) An Adjective is a word used to qualify a noun.

(4) A Verb is a word used for saying something about some person or thing.

(5) A Preposition is a word placed before a noun or noun-equivalent to show in what relation the person or thing denoted by the noun stands to something else.

(6) A Conjunction is a word used to join words or phrases together, or one clause to another clause.

(7) An Adverb is a word used to qualify any part of speech except a noun or pronoun.

(8) An Interjection is a word or sound thrown into a sentence to express some feeling of the mind.

*Note.*—Observe that the Part of Speech to which a word belongs depends on *the purpose that the word is used for* in that particular context, and that the same word may be of a different Part of Speech in a different context. Thus *man* is a noun in "The *man* has come"; but a verb in "*Man* the lifeboat."

**14. The Articles.**—The words "a" and "the" are called **Articles.** "The" is called the *Definite* Article, because it particularises a noun. "A" or "an" is called the *Indefinite*, because it does not particularise a noun, but generalises it.

The articles are not a distinct part of speech, but merely adjectives. "A" or "an" is an abbreviated form of the adjective "one"; while "the" is the root form of "this," "that," "these," "those."

**15. Finite Verb : Number and Person.**—Any part of a verb that can be used *as the Predicate of a sentence* is called **Finite.**

The word "*finite*" means "limited." A finite verb is so called, because it is limited to the same **Person** (*First*, *Second*, or *Third*) and to the same **Number** (*Singular* or *Plural*) as its Subject.

(*a*) I *see* him. (*b*) They *see* him.

In both sentences the form of the verb "see" is the same. But in (*a*) the verb is in the First person, because its Subject "I" is in the First person, and in the Singular number, because its Subject is Singular. Similarly in (*b*) the verb is in the Third person, because its Subject "they" is in the Third person, and plural, because its Subject is Plural.

**16. Parts of a Verb not finite.**—There are some parts of a verb which are not finite, that is, are not limited to any particular Number or Person, because they cannot be used with a Subject or be made the Predicates of a sentence.

Such parts are three in number:—(1) the **Infinitive** mood, as "I wish *to retire*"; (2) a **Participle,** as "a *retired* officer"; (3) a **Gerund,** as "I think of *retiring*."

*Note.*—These, though they are parts of a verb, have lost what is most essential in the verb-character; that is, they do not enable us to *say* something about something else.

**17. Double Parts of Speech.**—Besides the eight parts of speech shown in § 13, there are four more which must be called double, or two parts of speech combined in one:—

(1) A **Participle.**—This is a verb and adjective combined.

A *retired* officer lives next door.

The word "retired" is a verb, because it is part of the verb "retire." It is also an adjective, because it qualifies the noun "officer." Hence a participle may be called a verbal adjective.

(2) A **Gerund.**—This is a verb and noun combined.

I think of *retiring* soon from service.

Here "retiring" is a verb, because it is part of the verb "retire." It is also a noun, because it is the object to the preposition "of."

(3) An **Infinitive.**—This too is a verb and noun combined.

I wish *to return* that book.

Here *to return* is a verb, because it is part of the verb "return." It is also a noun, because it is object (see § 22) to the verb "wish."

(4) A **Relative Pronoun** or **Adverb.**—A Relative pronoun, such as *who, which,* etc., or a Relative adverb, such as *where, when,* etc., has the character of a pronoun or adverb combined with that of a conjunction.

This is the house *where* we live.

Here "where" is an adverb, because it qualifies the verb "lives." It is also a conjunction, because it joins the two sentences. Hence, relative adverbs have been sometimes called conjunctive adverbs. Similarly, relative pronouns have been called conjunctive pronouns.

**18. Apposition of Noun with Noun.**—A noun is said to be in apposition with another noun, or with a pronoun, when it refers to the same person or thing:—

*Noun.*—Philip, *king* of Macedon, was father to Alexander the Great.
*Pronoun.*—I, the *man* you were looking for, am here.

**19. Apposition of Sentence with Noun.**—Whenever a sentence is in apposition with a noun, the sentence must be introduced by the conjunction "that."

The rumour *that you were coming* was generally believed.

**20. Apposition of Noun with Sentence.**—A noun can be in apposition with a sentence or with some implied noun, which (if it were expressed) would denote the action of the verb.

He killed his prisoners,—*a barbarous act.* (Here "act" is in apposition with the implied noun, the *killing* of prisoners.)

**21. Forms of Subject.**—The Subject to a sentence must be either a noun or a noun-equivalent. The principal forms in which a Subject can be expressed are as follows :—

(*a*) Noun : A *ship* went out to sea.
(*b*) Pronoun : *He* (some one previously named) was convicted.
(*c*) Infinitive : *To err* (=error or proneness to error) is human.
(*d*) Gerund : *Sleeping* is necessary to health.
(*e*) Phrase : *How to do this* puzzles all of us.
(*f*) Clause : *Whoever was caught* was sent to jail.

**22. Transitive Verbs : Verb and Object.**—A verb is **Transitive,** if the action or feeling denoted by the verb does not stop with itself, but is directed towards some person or thing. The word or words denoting such person or thing are called the **Object** to the verb.

That snake bit *the man.*

**23. Forms of Object.**—The various forms in which the Object can be expressed are the same as those in which the Subject can be expressed. See § 21.

(*a*) Noun : That snake bit *the man.*
(*b*) Pronoun : That snake bit *him.*
(*c*) Infinitive : We desire *to succeed* (=success).
(*d*) Gerund : He loves *riding.*
(*e*) Phrase : We do not know *how to do this.*
(*f*) Clause : We do not know *what he wants.*

**24. Factitive Verbs : Complement.**—Those Transitive verbs which require not only an Object (as all Transitive verbs do), but also some other word or words to make the predication complete, are called **Factitive.** They are, in fact, **Transitive verbs of Incomplete predication.**

The word or words that complete the predication (that is, complete what the verb left unsaid) are called the **Complement.**

He put the school (object) *into good order* (complement).
That grief drove him (object) *mad* (complement).
They made him (object) *laugh* (complement).

There is no sense in saying "he put the school," "that grief drove him," "they made him"; hence each verb must have a Complement.

**25. Intransitive Verbs.**—A verb is **Intransitive,** if the action or feeling denoted by the verb stops with itself, and is not directed towards anything else.

Fish *swim*. Rivers *flow*. All animals *die*.

**26. Intransitive Verbs with Complement.**—But Intransitive verbs, though they do not require an Object, may require a Complement, as some Transitive verbs also do.

Such verbs are called **Intransitive Verbs of Incomplete Predication.**

He became *a good scholar*. Sleep is *necessary to health*.

*Note.*—Such verbs, when the complement is in the form of a noun, can be called copulative. The word "copulative" is less suitable, however, when the complement is in some form other than that of a noun. They have been called copulative, because they couple two nouns together in the same case.

**27. Absolute use of Verbs.**—A verb is said to be used absolutely, when it is not grammatically related to the rest of the sentence:—

(*a*) **Participle** (further explained in § 284).

*The sun having set*, all went home. (*With Noun.*)
*Supposing* we are late, the door will be locked. (*Without Noun.*)

(*b*) **Infinitive Mood** (further explained in § 191 and § 192):—

*To think* that he should have told a lie! (*Simple.*)
I am,—*to speak* plainly,—much displeased with you. (*Gerundial.*)

(*c*) **Imperative Mood** (further explained in § 180):—

A few men,—*say* twelve,—may be expected shortly.

**28. Introductory Adverb.**—When the subject to an *Intransitive* verb is placed *after* its verb, the verb is usually introduced by the adverb "*there*." In this relation "*there*" does not signify "in that place," but merely serves *to introduce the verb*. It has no signification whatever.

*There* are *some men* (subject) who never drink wine.
*There* came a *maiden* (subject) to my door.

**29. Kinds of Phrases.**—The following kinds of phrases should be distinguished from one another:—

(*a*) **Adverbial** phrase, or one which does the work of an adverb:—

I hope you will work better *in future*.
Bind him *hand and foot*, and take him away.

(*b*) **Prepositional** phrase, or one which does the work of a preposition. (Such phrases end in a simple preposition.)

*In the event of* our father's death, we shall be left poor.
He worked hard *for the sake of* a prize.

(*c*) **Conjunctional** phrase, or one which does the work of a conjunction. (Such phrases end in a simple conjunction.)

I am tired *as well as* hungry.
He took medicine *in order that* he might recover.

(*d*) **Absolute Participial** phrase; see § 284.

*The sun having set,* they all went home.

(*e*) **Interjectional** or exclamatory phrase; see § 241.

*Well to be sure! For shame! Good heavens!*

## CHAPTER II.—NOUNS.

### SECTION 1.—THE KINDS OF NOUNS.

**30. Noun defined.**—A Noun is a word used for naming some person or thing (§ 13).

**31.** Nouns are of five different kinds:—

| | | |
|---|---|---|
| I. Concrete | Proper | 1 |
| | Common | 2 |
| | Collective | 3 |
| | Material | 4 |
| II. Abstract | | 5 |

#### *Proper Nouns.*

**32.** A **Proper Noun** denotes *one particular* person or thing as distinct from every other; as *James* (a person), *Kenilworth* (a book), *Paris* (a city), *France* (a country).

*Note* 1.—The writing of a Proper noun should always be commenced with a capital letter.

*Note* 2.—A word or phrase is sometimes added to a proper noun to prevent ambiguity of reference. Thus we say, "Alexander *the Great,*" or "*St.* Paul," or "Boston *in America,*" to show which Alexander, or which Paul, or which Boston is meant: for many different persons or places might be called by these names.

*Note.* 3.—A large number of nouns now Proper were originally Common. A common name, as Brown, Smith, Baker, Clark (clerc), Shepherd, Butcher, Parson, Mason, etc., being frequently applied to some individual by way of distinction, was eventually restricted to that individual and his family, and so the Common name becomes a Proper name. Words, such as Father, Mother, Baby, Granny, though really Common names, are in most families used as Proper names, to denote certain individuals; as when a man says to his child, "Where is Mother?" Proper names of rivers, such as *Avon* (Celtic), *Congo* (African), were once common names for "river."

*Note* 4.—The name Proper is from Lat. *proprius,* one's own. Hence a Proper name means *one's own individual name*, as distinct from a Common name, that can be given to a class of individuals.

*Common Nouns.*

33. A **Common Noun** denotes no one person or thing in particular, but is *common to any and every person or thing of the same kind;* as "man," "book," "country."

Thus, *man* does not point out any particular man, such as James, but can be used for any and every man. *Book* does not point out any particular book, such as *Kenilworth*, but can be used for any and every book. *Country* does not point out any particular country, such as *France*, but can be used for any country in any part of the world.

*Note.*—The name *Common* is from the Lat. *communis,* and means that which is shared by several different individuals possessing some common characteristic, in virtue of which the name can be given to any and all of them.

34. A **Proper Noun** is said to be "*used as a Common Noun,*" when it denotes (*a*) some rank or office, or (*b*) some class of persons or things.

(*a*) Such words as *Cæsar, Caliph, Sultan, Khedive, Czar,* etc., are used as Common nouns, because they denote persons holding a certain rank or office: thus we can speak of "the twelve Cæsars," "the first four Caliphs," "the Sultan of Turkey," "the Czar of Russia."

(*b*) A Proper noun becomes a Common noun, when it denotes a class of persons or things and is used in a descriptive sense. "He is *the Newton* of the age,"—that is, the greatest astronomer of the age.

*Collective Nouns.*

35. A **Collective Noun** denotes a *group* or *collection* of *similar individuals,* considered as one complete whole.

For instance, there may be *many sheep* in a field, but only *one flock.* Here "sheep" is a Common noun, because it may stand for any and every sheep; but "flock" is a Collective noun, because it stands for all the sheep at once, and not for any one sheep taken separately.

36. Every Collective Noun is also a kind of Common Noun.

Thus the term "flock" may stand for many different flocks (or groups of sheep); "class" for many classes (or groups of students).

37. **Nouns of Multitude.**—A distinction is made between a Collective Noun and a Noun of Multitude:—

(*a*) A Collective noun denotes *one undivided whole;* and hence the verb following is singular (§ 15).

The jury *consists* of twelve persons.

(*b*) A noun of Multitude denotes the *individuals* of the group; and hence the verb is plural, although the noun is singular (§ 15).

The jury (the men on the jury) *were* divided in their opinions.

### *Nouns of Material.*

**38.** A noun of **Material** denotes some particular kind of *matter* or *substance.*

Thus "sheep" is a Common noun; but "mutton" (or the flesh of sheep) is a Material noun.

**39.** The same word can be a Material noun or a Common noun according to the sense.

*Fish* live in water. *Fish* is good for food.

In the first sentence the noun denotes individual fish or fishes, and is therefore a Common noun. In the second it denotes the matter of which the bodies of fish are made, and is therefore a Material noun.

### *Abstract Nouns.*

**40.** An **Abstract Noun** denotes some *quality, state,* or *action,* apart from anything possessing the quality, etc.

*Quality*—Cleverness, height, humility, roguery, colour.
*State*—Poverty, manhood, bondage, pleasure, youth.
*Action*—Laughter, movement, flight, choice, revenge.

The four kinds of nouns previously described all relate to objects *of sense,* that is, to things which can be seen, touched, heard, smelt, or tasted; and all such nouns are called **Concrete** nouns. But an abstract noun relates to *qualities, states,* etc., which cannot be seen or touched, etc., and which are thought of *apart from* any object of sense.

*For example:* We know that a stone is *hard.* We also know that iron is *hard.* We also know that a brick is *hard.* We can therefore speak of *hardness* apart from stone, or iron, or brick, or any other object having the same quality. "Abstract" means "drawn off" (abstracted in thought) from the object. Hence *hardness* is an abstract noun; while *stone* or *brick* or *iron* is a concrete noun.

**41.** The same word may be an Abstract noun or a Common noun, according to the purpose for which it is used.

When an Abstract noun is "*used as a Common or Concrete noun,*" it may denote (*a*) the *person* possessing the quality, or (*b*) the *thing* to which the action, state, or quality belongs:[1]—

[1] The conversion of Abstract nouns to Concrete or Common nouns is due to the fact that it is much easier to think of some person or thing than to think of an abstract quality apart from any person or thing. Hence we are naturally disposed to transfer the name of the quality to the name of the person or thing possessing the quality.

*(a) Examples of Persons.*

| | | |
|---|---|---|
| *Justice* | 1. The quality of being just . . | *Abstract* |
| | 2. A judge, or one who administers justice | *Concrete* |
| *Beauty* | 1. The quality or state of being beautiful | *Abstract* |
| | 2. A person possessing beauty . . | *Concrete* |
| *Authority* | 1. The power or right to command . . | *Abstract* |
| | 2. A person possessing authority . | *Concrete* |
| *Nobility* | 1. The quality of being noble . . . | *Abstract* |
| | 2. Those who are of the class of nobles . | *Concrete* |
| *Witness* | 1. Evidence or testimony . . . | *Abstract* |
| | 2. One who gives the evidence . . | *Concrete* |

*(b) Examples of Things.*

| | | |
|---|---|---|
| *Judgment* | 1. The act or quality of judging . . | *Abstract* |
| | 2. The verdict given by the judge . . | *Concrete* |
| *Sight* | 1. The art or faculty of seeing . . | *Abstract* |
| | 2. The thing seen: "a fine sight" . . | *Concrete* |
| *Speech* | 1. The faculty of speaking . . . | *Abstract* |
| | 2. The speech delivered: the word spoken | *Concrete* |
| *Wonder* | 1. The feeling of wonder or surprise . | *Abstract* |
| | 2. The wonderful event or object . . | *Concrete* |
| *Kindness* | 1. The quality of being kind . . . | *Abstract* |
| | 2. The kind thing done . . . . | *Concrete* |

**42.** The Gerunds and the Simple Infinitives of verbs (§ 188) are in fact, though not in form, kinds of Abstract nouns. The following sentences all mean the same thing:—

*Service* is better than idleness. (*Abstract Noun.*)
*Serving* is better than idleness. (*Gerund.*)
*To serve* is better than idleness. (*Infinitive Mood.*)

**43.** An Abstract noun is used as a Proper noun, when it is **personified,**—that is, when it is spoken of as an individual person. It must then be commenced with a capital letter, as Proper nouns are.

He is the favoured child of *Fortune.*
Let not *Ambition* mock their useful toil.

**44.** There are two ways in which a Proper, Material, or Abstract noun can be used as (or changed into) a Common noun :—(*a*) by putting an article ("a" or "the") before it; (*b*) by putting it into the plural number.

| *Proper Noun.* | *Common Nouns.* |
|---|---|
| *Daniel* was a learned Jew. | *A Daniel* come to judgment.<br>There are more *Daniels* than one. |
| *Material Noun.* | |
| *Pear* is my favourite fruit. | Give me *the pear* in your hand.<br>Give me one of your *pears.* |
| *Abstract Noun.* | |
| *Justice* is a noble quality. | He is *a justice* of the peace.<br>There are four *justices* present. |

*Point out the kind or use of each of the nouns occurring below:—*

Alexander the Great, king of Macedon, was conqueror of Persia. A man ignorant of the arts of reading, writing, and ciphering is, in point of knowledge, more like a child than a man. The proper study of mankind is man. Cows are as fond of grass as men are of milk, or bears of honey. Health is one of the greatest blessings that a man or woman can hope to enjoy in this bodily existence. The Czar of Russia, although he is lord of the eastern half of Europe and the northern half of Asia, besides being master of a huge army and a large fleet, cannot live in peace and safety with his own subjects, and cannot leave his own palace without fear.

## SECTION 2.—SUBSTITUTES FOR A NOUN.

**45.** The following kinds of words or combinations of words can be used as substitutes for a Noun; see §§ 21, 23:—

(*a*) A Pronoun:—

Your horse is white; mine is a black *one* (=horse).

(*b*) An Adjective used as a Noun or with some noun understood:—

*The blind* (=blind men) receive their sight.
*The just* (=justice) is higher than *the expedient* (=expediency).

(*c*) A Verb in the Infinitive mood:—

He desires *to succeed* (=success).

(*d*) A Gerund:—

He was fond of *sleeping* (=sleep).

(*e*) A Phrase:—

No one knew *how to do this* (=the method of doing this).

(*f*) A Noun-clause; that is, a clause which does the work of a noun; (for the definition of "clause" see § 4).

*Who steals my purse* (=the stealer of my purse) steals trash.

## SECTION 3.—GENDER.

**46. Gender.**—In the grammar of Modern English, difference of Gender coincides with difference of sex or with the absence of sex:[1]—

(1) **Masculine**: *male* animals: *bull, horse, hog.*
(2) **Feminine**: *female* animals: *cow, mare, sow.*
(3) **Common**: animals of *either* sex: *parent, child.*

[1] In the proper sense of the word, this is not gender at all, since it is not based on *the form of the word.*

(4) **Neuter**: things of *neither* sex, that is, things without life: *box, flock, pain.*

*Note.*—We often take no account of the sex of young children or of lower animals; so in speaking of them we use Neuter pronouns:—

The *child* is asleep; let *it* sleep on.
Have you a *horse?* will you let me ride *it?*

**47. Modes of denoting Gender.**—There are three different ways in which the gender or sex of living beings is indicated.—

I. By a change of word; as *bull, cow.*

II. By adding a word; as *he-goat, she-goat.*

III. By adding *ess* to the Masculine; as *priest, priestess.*

I. *By a change of word:*

| *Masculine.* | *Feminine.* | *Masculine.* | *Feminine.* |
|---|---|---|---|
| Bachelor | maid (or spinster) | Horse (or stallion) | mare |
| Boar | sow | Husband | wife |
| Boy | girl | King | queen |
| Brother | sister | Lord | lady |
| Buck | doe | Man | woman |
| Bull (or ox) | cow | Milter (fish) | spawner |
| Bullock (or steer) | heifer | Nephew | niece |
| Cock | hen | Papa | mamma |
| Colt | filly | Ram (or wether) | ewe |
| Dog | bitch (or slut) | Sir | madam (or dame) |
| Drake | duck | Sire (father of colt) | dam (mother of colt) |
| Drone | bee | Sloven | slut |
| Earl | countess | Son | daughter |
| Father | mother | Stag | hind |
| Friar (or monk) | nun | Swain | nymph |
| Gander | goose | Uncle | aunt |
| Gentleman | lady | Wizard | witch |
| Hart | roe | | |

*Note.*—There are some Feminine nouns which have no corresponding Masculine:—*blonde, brunette, coquette, dowager, dowdy, drab, jilt, prude, shrew, siren, termagant, virago.*

II. *By adding a word:*

| *Masculine.* | *Feminine.* | *Masculine.* | *Feminine.* |
|---|---|---|---|
| Billy-goat | nanny-goat | Grand-father | grand-mother |
| Buck-rabbit | doe-rabbit | Tom-cat | tib-cat |
| Cock-sparrow | hen-sparrow | Land-lord | land-lady |
| He-goat | she-goat | Pea-cock | pea-hen |
| Jack-ass | she-ass | Bull-calf | cow-calf |
| Man-servant | maid-servant | Washer-man | washer-woman |

*Note.*—The Masculine "roe-buck" has no corresponding Feminine; and the Feminine "ewe-lamb" has no corresponding Masculine.

### III. *By adding* ess *to the Masculine:*

(*a*) By adding *ess* to the Masculine without any change in the form of the Masculine :—

| *Masculine.* | *Feminine.* | *Masculine.* | *Feminine.* |
|---|---|---|---|
| Author | author-ess | Patron | patron-ess |
| Baron | baron-ess | Peer | peer-ess |
| Count | count-ess | Poet | poet-ess |
| Giant | giant-ess | Priest | priest-ess |
| God | godd-ess | Prince | princ-ess |
| Heir | heir-ess | Prior | prior-ess |
| Host | host-ess | Prophet | prophet-ess |
| Jew | Jew-ess | Shepherd | shepherd-ess |
| Lion | lion-ess | Viscount | viscount-ess |

(*b*) By adding *ess*, and omitting the vowel of the last syllable of the Masculine :—

| *Masculine.* | *Feminine.* | *Masculine.* | *Feminine.* |
|---|---|---|---|
| Actor | actr-ess | Negro | negr-ess |
| Benefactor | benefactr-ess | Porter | portr-ess |
| Conductor | conductr-ess | Songster | songstr-ess |
| Director | directr-ess | Tempter | temptr-ess |
| Enchanter | enchantr-ess | Tiger | tigr-ess |
| Hunter | huntr-ess | Traitor | traitr-ess |
| Instructor | instructr-ess | Votary | votar-ess |

(*c*) By adding *ess* to the Masculine in a less regular way :—

| *Masculine.* | *Feminine.* | *Masculine.* | *Feminine.* |
|---|---|---|---|
| Abbot | abbess | Master (boy) | miss (girl) |
| Duke | duchess | Mr. | Mrs. |
| Emperor | empress | Marquis / Marquess | marchioness |
| Governor | governess | | |
| Lad | lass | Murderer | murderess |
| Master (teacher, etc.) | mistress | Sorcerer | sorceress |

**48.** The following modes of distinction between Masculine and Feminine are exceptional :—

| *Masculine.* | *Feminine.* | *Masculine.* | *Feminine.* |
|---|---|---|---|
| Bridegroom | bride | Fox | vixen |
| Widower | widow | ("Vixen" as Fem. of "fox" is now obsolete.) | |

**49.** Foreign Feminines :—

| *Masculine.* | *Feminine.* | *Masculine.* | *Feminine.* |
|---|---|---|---|
| Administrator | administratrix | Hero | heroine |
| Beau | belle | Prosecutor | prosecutrix |
| Czar | czarina | Signor | signora |
| Don | donna | Sultan | sultana |
| Executor | executrix | Testator | testatrix |

**50. Double Feminines.**—The two examples of this are *songstress* and *seamstress.*

Originally *ster* was a Feminine suffix, as it still is in "spinster." But the Feminine force of *ster* in "songster" and "seamster" has been lost, and so the Feminine form is now shown by changing *er* into *ress.*

**51.** The following are examples of Nouns in the **Common** gender :—

Parent—father or mother.
Relation—male or female.
Friend—enemy—male or female.
Cousin—male or female cousin.
Bird—cock or hen.
Peafowl—peacock or peahen.
Flirt—man or maid.
Fowl—cock or hen.
Child—son or daughter.
Deer—stag or hind.
Fallow-deer—buck or doe.
Baby—male or female.
Servant—man or maid.
Monarch—king or queen.
Person—man or woman.
Pupil—boy or girl.
Orphan—male or female.
Pig—boar or sow.
Sheep—ram or ewe.
Elephant—male or female.
Cat—male or female.
Rat—male or female.
Mouse—male or female.
Fox—male or female.
Spouse—husband or wife.
Foal—colt or filly.
Calf—bullock or heifer.

*Note.*—Some Masculine nouns, as *colt, dog, horse,* and some Feminine nouns, as *duck, bee, goose,* are used to denote either sex, provided that no question arises as to whether the animal named is a male or a female.

That is a fine little *colt.*
That *horse* of yours is a splendid stepper.
A *goose* is a much bigger bird than a *duck.*

**52. Gender of Personified Things.**—Things without life, when they are personified, are regarded as male or female ; and so, in speaking of them, we use Masculine or Feminine pronouns.

*Masculines.*—The stronger forces and more striking objects in nature (Winds, Rivers, Mountains, the Ocean, Storm, Thunder, the Sun, Summer, Autumn, Winter) ; the violent passions (Love, Fear, Anger, Despair, etc.) ; violent actions (Murder, War, etc.) ; Time, Day, Sleep, Death, the Grave.

*Feminines.*—The gentler forces and objects (as the Moon) ; whatever implies fertility or claims attachment (the Church, Nature, the Earth, the Mother-country, Countries, Universities, Ships, Cities, the season of Spring) ; the gentler feelings (Hope, Concord, Justice, Mercy, Charity, Faith, Humility, Modesty, etc.) ; the inferior passions (Jealousy, Pride, Anger, Revenge) ; the Arts and Sciences ; Fame, Liberty, Victory, Religion, Philosophy, Adversity, Prosperity, Fortune, Night, Morning.

A ship, though it is not commenced with a capital letter, is always spoken of as *she.* The same is often said of a railway train. We speak of a *sister*-ship, a *sister*-institution, a *sister*-gun.

## SECTION 4.—CASE.

**53. Case defined.**—The *relation* in which a noun stands to some other word, or the *change of form* (if any) by which this relation is indicated, is called its **Case.**[1]

**54.** There are three Cases in modern English,—the *Nominative*, the *Possessive*, and the *Objective*.

But the Possessive is the only case that is *now* indicated by a case-ending or *change of form*. The other cases have lost their case-endings, and are indicated only by grammatical relation.

**55.** When a noun is used as the *subject* to a verb or for the sake of *address*, it is said to be in the **Nominative** case.

*Rain* falls. (*Nominative of Subject.*)
Are you coming, my *friend?* (*Nominative of Address.*)

**56.** When a noun is the *object* to a verb or to a preposition, it is said to be in the **Objective** case.

The man killed a *rat*. (*Object to Verb.*)
The earth is moistened by *rain*. (*Obj. to Prep.*)

**57.** The **Possessive** case is so called, because it usually denotes the *possessor* or owner. It is formed by adding *'s* (which is called *apostrophe s*) to the noun; as—

*Singular*—man's. | *Plural*—men's.

*N.B.*—The old inflection for the Possessive case was *es*. When the *e* was omitted, as it now always is, the absence of the *e* was indicated by the comma or apostrophe; as *moon, moones, moon's*.

**58. Omission of "apostrophe s."**—There are three kinds of instances in which the apostrophe *s* is omitted:—

(*a*) After all plural nouns ending in *s*; as—

*Horses'* tails; the *birds'* nests; the *dogs'* kennels.

(*b*) Whenever the last syllable of a Singular noun begins and ends with *s*; as—

*Moses'* laws. (But we must say *Venus's* beauty; *James's* hat, etc.)

(*c*) Whenever the last syllable of a Singular noun ends with *s* or *ce*, and the noun is followed by "sake"; as—

*Conscience'* sake; for *goodness'* sake. (But we must say—a *mouse's* skin; *James's* smile.)

---

[1] *Case* lit. means "falling" (Lat. *cas-us*). The Nom. was considered the upright or perpendicular, and the other cases were said to fall off to one side of it, and were hence called *oblique* or slanting. Since English nouns have lost every case-ending but one (the Possessive), the term "case" is etymologically inappropriate. We retain it, however, to denote grammatical relation as well as change of form.

*Note.*—In poetry the omission of apostrophe *s* is common in words ending with *s*. Poets are guided simply by the metre :—

As thick as *Ajax*' seven-fold shield.—BUTLER.

In prose we should say and write *Ajax's*.

**59. Rare use of Possessive.**—The Possessive case was once used with any kind of noun; but it is now restricted to such examples as those shown below :—

(1) Nouns denoting *persons;* as—

*Henry's* book; a *man's* foot. (But we cannot say "a library's book," "the mountain's foot," since "library and "mountain" are inanimate objects.)

(2) Nouns denoting any kind of *living* thing other than man; as—

A *cat's* tail; a *horse's* head; a *bird's* feathers.

(3) Nouns denoting *personified* things; as—

*Fortune's* favourite; *Sorrow's* tears; *England's* heroes.

(4) Nouns denoting time, space, or weight; as—

**Time.**—A *day's* journey; a *month's* holiday; three *weeks*' leave; a *year's* absence; at six *months*' sight; three *days*' grace.
**Space.**—A *boat's* length; a *hand's* breadth; a *hair's* breadth; a *razor's* edge; a *stone's* throw; a *needle's* point.
**Weight.**—A *pound's* weight; a *ton's* weight.

(5) Nouns signifying certain dignified objects; as—

The *court's* decree; the *sun's* rays; the *moon's* crescent; *nature's* works; the *earth's* axis; the *soul's* delight; *heaven's* will; the *law's* delays; *truth's* triumph; the *mind's* eye; the *ocean's* roar; *duty's* call; the *country's* good.

Let all the ends thou aim'st at be thy *country's*,
Thy *God's*, and *truth's*.—*Hen. VIII.* iii. 2.

*Note.*—The Possessive is also used in a few familiar phrases, in which it has been retained for the sake of shortness—

Out of *harm's* way; at his *wit's* end; for *mercy's* sake; he did it to his *heart's* content; the *ship's* passengers; at his *fingers*' ends; he got to his *journey's* end; the *boat's* crew.

**60. Possessive Case in Apposition.**—When one Possessive case is in Apposition with another (§ 18), the apostrophe *s* is added only to that noun which is mentioned last.

Herod married his *brother* Philip's wife.

*Note.*—In such a sentence as the following, however, it is the first noun that has the apostrophe *s* :—

He called at *Smith's*, the *grocer*.

**61. Possessive Case in Phrases.**—The '*s* may be added to the last word of a phrase, when the phrase is regarded as a Compound noun and denotes some person or persons.

My son-in-law's house.
The Duke of Sutherland's death.

## SECTION 5.—NUMBER.

**62.** The form assumed by a noun to show whether it denotes one thing or more than one is called its Number.

When *one* thing is spoken of, the noun is *Singular;* when *two* or *more* things are spoken of, the noun is *Plural.*

The only kinds of nouns that (strictly speaking) admit of being pluralised are Common and Collective nouns.

But Proper, Material, and Abstract nouns can also be put in the Plural number, when they are used as Common nouns (§ 44).

**63.** The general rule for forming the Plural number of a noun is by adding *s* to the Singular; as—

| *Singular.* | *Plural.* | *Singular.* | *Plural.* |
|---|---|---|---|
| Hand | hands | House | houses |

But if the noun ends in *s, x, z, sh,* or *ch,* the Plural is formed by adding *es* to the Singular; as—

| *Singular.* | *Plural.* | *Singular.* | *Plural.* |
|---|---|---|---|
| Glass | glass-es | Brush | brush-es |
| Box | box-es | Bench | bench-es |

**64.** If the noun ends in *y* and the *y* is preceded by a *consonant,* the Plural takes the form of *-ies.* (In proper names, however, we simply add the *s* to the Singular, as *Mary, Marys.*)

| *Singular.* | *Plural.* | *Singular.* | *Plural.* |
|---|---|---|---|
| Duty | duties | Army | armies |
| Fly | flies | Lady | ladies |

*Note.*—In older English, however, the Singular was spelt as *dutie.* Hence the Plural is really formed according to the rule given in § 63, and it is the Singular that has changed.

But if the final *y* is preceded by a *vowel,* the Plural is formed by simply adding *s* to the Singular:—

| *Singular.* | *Plural.* | *Singular.* | *Plural.* |
|---|---|---|---|
| Day | days | Monkey | monkeys |
| Play | plays | Toy | toys |
| Key | keys | Boy | boys |

*Note.*—Nouns ending in *quy* form the Plural in *ies,* because in such words the *u* does not make a diphthong with *y,* but the *qu* (=*kw*) is regarded as a double consonant; as, *colloquy, colloquies.*

**65.** If the noun ends in *o,* and the *o* is preceded by a *consonant,* the Plural is generally formed by adding *es:*—

| *Singular.* | *Plural.* | *Singular.* | *Plural.* |
|---|---|---|---|
| Cargo | cargoes | Mango | mangoes |
| Hero | heroes | Potato | potatoes |
| Buffalo | buffaloes | Echo | echoes |
| Motto | mottoes | Tornado | tornadoes |
| Negro | negroes | Volcano | volcanoes |

But all nouns ending in *o* preceded by a vowel, and some ending in *o* preceded by a consonant, form the Plural in *s*, and not in *es*:—

| *Singular.* | *Plural.* | *Singular.* | *Plural.* |
|---|---|---|---|
| Bamboo | bamboos | Grotto | grottos |
| Cuckoo | cuckoos | Halo | halos |
| Portfolio | portfolios | Memento | mementos |
| Embryo | embryos | Proviso | provisos |
| Cameo | cameos | Tiro | tiros |
| Seraglio | seraglios | Piano | pianos |
| Hindoo | Hindoos | Canto | cantos |
| Curio | curios | Solo | solos |

There are a few nouns ending in *o*, which form the Plural both in *s* and *es*:—

| *Singular.* | *Plural.* |
|---|---|
| Calico | calicos or calicoes |
| Mosquito | mosquitos or mosquitoes |
| Portico | porticos or porticoes |

**66.** If the noun ends in *f* or *fe*, the Plural is generally formed by changing *f* or *fe* into *ves*:—

| *Singular.* | *Plural.* | *Singular.* | *Plural.* |
|---|---|---|---|
| Wife | wives | Calf | calves |
| Knife | knives | Half | halves |
| Life | lives | Myself | ourselves |
| Sheaf | sheaves | Shelf | shelves |
| Leaf | leaves | Wolf | wolves |
| Thief | thieves | Beef | beeves |

But there are some nouns ending in *f* which form the Plural by simply adding *s* (in accordance with the general rule given in § 63):—

| *Singular.* | *Plural.* | *Singular.* | *Plural.* |
|---|---|---|---|
| Reef | reefs | Wharf | wharfs |
| Chief | chiefs | Dwarf | dwarfs |
| Roof | roofs | Turf | turfs |
| Hoof | hoofs | Gulf | gulfs |
| Proof | proofs | Cliff | cliffs |
| Scarf | scarfs | Grief | griefs |

There are at least three nouns ending in *fe* which form the Plural by simply adding *s*:—

Safe—safes ; strife—strifes ; fife—fifes.

**67.** There are eight nouns which form the Plural by a change of the inside vowel :—

| *Singular.* | *Plural.* | *Singular.* | *Plural.* |
|---|---|---|---|
| Man | men | Tooth | teeth |
| Woman | women | Louse | lice |
| Foot | feet | Mouse | mice |
| Goose | geese | Dormouse | dormice |

There are four nouns which form the Plural in *en* or *ne* :—

| *Singular.* | *Plural.* | *Singular.* | *Plural.* |
|---|---|---|---|
| Ox | oxen | Brother | brethren |
| Child | children | Cow | kine (or cows) |

**68.** A compound noun forms the Plural by adding *s* to the principal word :—

| *Singular.* | *Plural.* | *Singular.* | *Plural.* |
|---|---|---|---|
| Father-in-law | fathers-in-law | Maid-servant | maid-servants |
| Son-in-law | sons-in-law | Foot-man | foot-men |
| Mother-in-law | mothers-in-law | Washer-man | washer-men |
| Daughter-in-law | daughters-in-law | Knight-errant | knights-errant |
| Step-son | step-sons | Coat-of-mail | coats-of-mail |
| Step-daughter | step-daughters | Court-martial | courts-martial |
| Hanger-on | hangers-on | Commander-in-chief | commanders-in-chief |
| Looker-on | lookers-on | | |
| Passer-by | passers-by | | |

In the above examples the distinguishing word or phrase is sometimes placed first, as in *step-son*, and sometimes last as in *father-in-law.* In either case it is not the distinguishing word or phrase that receives the suffix *s*, but the noun qualified by it. This rule applies to all of the above examples.

*Note.*—*Castaway* and nouns like *handful* are rather peculiar. *Castaway* is a compound participle used as a noun, which therefore takes the *s* at the end of the word, as *castaways. Handful,* though originally "a hand full," or enough to fill a hand, has become a compound noun, which forms its plural as *handfuls.*

There are four compound nouns which take a double Plural :—

| *Singular.* | *Plural.* | *Singular.* | *Plural.* |
|---|---|---|---|
| Man-servant | men-servants | Lord-justice | lords-justices |
| Woman-servant | women-servants | Knight-Templar | Knights-Templars |

Here two nouns are in apposition, the distinguishing noun being placed first to qualify or restrict the second. The second noun is the only one that could *claim* the plural suffix ; cf. *maid-servants, washermen.* The first noun is pluralised by attraction.

In a phrase like "Miss Brown" two different forms are used for the plural. We may either say "the Miss Browns" or "the Misses Brown." The latter is the more correct, but it is considered pedantic.

**69. Foreign Plurals.**—These are some Plurals which have been borrowed direct from foreign nouns :—

(Latin)

| *Singular.* | *Plural.* |
|---|---|
| Agendum | agenda |
| Addendum | addenda |
| Datum | data |
| Dictum | dicta |
| Effluvian | effluvia |
| Ovum | ova |
| Erratum | errata |
| Memorandum | memoranda |
| Medium | media |
| Stratum | strata (or stratums) |
| Alumnus | alumni |
| Focus | foci (or focuses) |
| Fungus | fungi |
| Genius | genii |
| Radius | radii |
| Terminus | termini (or terminuses) |
| Formula | formulæ (or formulas) |
| Genus | genera |
| Stamen | stamina |
| Axis | axes |
| Index | indices |
| Appendix | appendices |
| Series | series |
| Species | species |
| Apparatus | apparatus |

(Greek)

| *Singular.* | *Plural.* |
|---|---|
| Analysis | analyses |
| Basis | bases |
| Crisis | crises |
| Hypothesis | hypotheses |
| Oasis | oases |
| Parenthesis | parentheses |
| Thesis | theses |
| Phenomenon | phenomena |
| Criterion | criteria |

(Italian)

| *Singular.* | *Plural.* |
|---|---|
| Bandit | banditti (or bandits) |
| Virtuoso | virtuosi |
| Dilettante | dilettanti |

(French)

| *Singular.* | *Plural.* |
|---|---|
| Beau | beaux |
| Bureau | bureaux |
| Monsieur | messieurs |
| Madam | mesdames |

(Hebrew)

| *Singular.* | *Plural.* |
|---|---|
| Cherub | cherubim (or cherubs) |
| Seraph | seraphim (or seraphs) |

**70.** Some nouns, Sing. in *form*, are used only in a Plural sense. These are nouns of Multitude (§ 37).

*Poultry.*—The poultry are doing well.
*Cattle.*—These cattle are mine.
*Vermin.*—These vermin do much harm.
*People.*—These people have returned home.
*Gentry.*—These gentry are expected to-day.

*Note.*—When "people" is used in the sense of "nation," the Plural is "peoples."

**71.** Some nouns have the same form in both numbers.

*Living beings.*—Deer, sheep, fish (rarely fishes), swine, grouse, salmon, trout, cod, heathen.

*Collective numerals.*—Yoke (of oxen), brace (of birds), dozen, score, gross.

*Measure of weight.*—Stone, hundredweight.

This deer, these *deer*. That sheep, those *sheep*. That fish, those *fish* (rarely *fishes*). Those *heathen*. Nine *brace* of birds. Four *yoke* of oxen. Ten *dozen* books. He weighs ten *stone* and a half. That box weighs three *hundredweight*. Four *swine*. Ten *gross* of pens.

**72.** Some nouns, which take the Plural form at ordinary times, use the Singular instead of the Plural to express some specific quantity or number.

A twelve-*month*. A three-*foot* rule. An eight-*day* clock. A six-*year*-old horse. A fort-*night* (which is a contraction of "fourteen nights"). Forty *head* of cattle. Twelve *pound* weight. Ten *sail* of the line. Five *fathom* deep. A six-*penny* piece.

**73.** There are some nouns which have two forms in the Plural,—each form with a separate meaning of its own.

| | | |
|---|---|---|
| *Brother* | Brothers, | *sons of the same mother.* |
| | Brethren, | *members of the same society.* |
| *Cherub* | Cherubim, | *angels of a certain rank.* |
| | Cherubs, | *images or models of a cherub.* |
| *Cloth* | Cloths, | *kinds or pieces of cloth* (Distributive). |
| | Clothes, | *articles of dress* (Collective). |
| *Cow* | Cows, | *individual cows* (Distributive). |
| | Kine, | *cattle* (Collective). |
| *Die* | Dies, | *stamps for coining* (Distributive). |
| | Dice, | *small cubes used in games* (Collective). |
| *Genius* | Geniuses, | *men of genius or talent.* |
| | Genii, | *fabulous spirits of the air.* |
| *Index* | Indexes, | *tables of contents.* |
| | Indices, | *signs used in algebra.* |
| *Pea* | Peas, | (Distributive). |
| | Pease, | (Collective). |
| *Penny* | Pennies, | =*penny-pieces* (Distributive). |
| | Pence, | (sometimes Collective).[1] |
| *Staff* | Staves, | *sticks or poles.* |
| | Staffs, | *departments in the army.* |
| *Stamen* | Stamens, | *male organs of flowers* (Distributive). |
| | Stamina, | *endurance, vigour*, lit. *threads* (Collective). |
| *Shot* | Shot, | *little balls discharged from a gun.* |
| | Shots, | *discharges; as, "he had two shots."* |

**74.** Nouns which have one meaning in the Singular and another in the Plural:—

| *Singular.* | *Plural.* |
|---|---|
| *Advice*, counsel. | *Advices*, information. |
| *Air*, atmosphere. | *Airs*, demeanour. |
| *Ban*, a curse (under a *ban*). | *Banns*, announcement (*banns* of marriage). |
| *Beef*, flesh of ox. | *Beeves*, cattle, bulls and cows. |
| *Compass*, range or extent. | *Compasses*, an instrument. |
| *Copper*, a metal. | *Coppers*, pennies. |
| *Domino*, a kind of mask. | *Dominoes*, the game so-called. |

---

[1] Hence *six-pence* has a Collective sense, denoting a single coin, which makes the noun appear to be Singular, so that we say *a sixpence* (Singular), *sixpences* (Plural).

| *Singular.* | *Plural.* |
|---|---|
| *Force*, strength or energy. | *Forces*, army. |
| *Good*, benefit. | *Goods*, movable property. |
| *Iron*, a metal. | *Irons*, fetters made of iron. |
| *Minute*, of time. | *Minutes*, of a meeting. |
| *Physic*, medicine. | *Physics*, natural science. |
| *Return*, coming back. | *Returns*, statistics. |
| *Salt*, seasoning substance. | *Salts*, smelling salts. |
| *Sand*, a kind of matter. | *Sands*, a tract of sandy land. |
| *Vapour*, invisible steam. | *Vapours*, dejection. |
| *Vesper*, evening. | *Vespers*, evening prayers. |
| *Water*, the element. | *Waters*, springs. |

**75.** Nouns which have two meanings in the Plural against one in the Singular :—

| *Singular.* | | *Plural.* | |
|---|---|---|---|
| *Colour*, | colours. | *Colours* | 1. Kinds of colour.<br>2. Flag of regiment. |
| *Custom*, | habits. | *Customs* | 1. Habits.<br>2. *Toll* or *tax*. |
| *Element*, | simple substance. | *Elements* | 1. Simple substances.<br>2. Conditions of the air. |
| *Effect*, | result. | *Effects* | 1. Results.<br>2. *Goods and chattels.* |
| *Letter*, | 1. Of alphabet.<br>2. Epistle. | *Letters* | 1. Of alphabet.<br>2. Epistles.<br>3. *Learning.* |
| *Manner*, | mode or way. | *Manners* | 1. Modes, ways.<br>2. *Behaviour.* |
| *Number*, | as in counting. | *Numbers* | 1. As in counting.<br>2. *Poetry.* |
| *Pain*, | suffering. | *Pains* | 1. Sufferings.<br>2. *Trouble, care.* |
| *Part*, | portion. | *Parts* | 1. Portions.<br>2. *Abilities.* |
| *Premise*, | a statement or proposition. | *Premises* | 1. Propositions.<br>2. *Buildings.* |
| *Quarter*, | a fourth part. | *Quarters* | 1. Fourth parts.<br>2. *Lodgings.* |
| *Spectacle*, | anything seen. | *Spectacles* | 1. Things seen.<br>2. *Eye-glasses.* |

**76.** Nouns which have two meanings in the Singular against one in the Plural :—

| *Singular.* | | *Plural.* | |
|---|---|---|---|
| *Abuse* | 1. Wrong use.<br>2. Reproaches. | *Abuses*, | wrong uses. |
| *Foot* | 1. Part of body.<br>2. Infantry. | *Feet*, | parts of body. |
| *Horse* | 1. A quadruped.<br>2. Cavalry. | *Horses*, | quadrupeds. |

| | Singular. | | Plural. |
|---|---|---|---|
| *Issue* | 1. Result.<br>2. Offspring. | *Issues,* | results. |
| *Light* | 1. A lamp.<br>2. Radiance. | *Lights,* | lamps. |
| *People* | 1. A nation.<br>2. Persons. | *Peoples,* | nations. |
| *Powder* | 1. A medicinal mixture.<br>2. Gunpowder. | *Powders,* | medicinal mixtures. |
| *Practice* | 1. Habitual act.<br>2. Professional connection. | *Practices,* | habitual acts. |
| *Stone* | 1. A piece of rock.<br>2. Fourteen pounds. | *Stones,* | pieces of rock. |
| *Wood* | 1. A forest.<br>2. Timber. | *Woods,* | forests. |

**77. True Singulars used as Plurals.**—By a "True Singular" we mean that the final *s* is part of the original Singular noun, and not a sign of the Plural.

Such nouns, though Singular by etymology, are liable to be considered Plural on account of the final *s*; and all except the first of these named below are now always used as if they were Plural.

*Summons* (Fr. *semonce*).—This noun is still correctly used as a Singular; as "I received *a* summons to attend"; "*This* summons reached me to-day." The plural form is *summonses.*

*Alms* (A.S. *ælmesse*).—"He asked *an alms*" (New Testament). But now the word is generally used as if it were Plural; as, "I gave alms to the beggar, and for *these* he thanked me."

*Eaves* (A.S. *efese*).—The edge or lower borders of the roof of a house. The word is now always used as a Plural; as, "The eaves *are* not yet finished."

*Riches* (Fr. *richesse*).—This too is really a Singular; as, "In one hour is so great riches come to naught" (New Testament); but now, on account of the final *s*, this noun is always used as a Plural; as, "Riches *do* not last for ever."

**78. True Plurals used as Singulars.**—In such nouns the final *s* is really a sign of the Plural.

*Amends.*—This is sometimes used as a Singular and sometimes as a Plural; as, "*An* honourable amends" (Addison).

*Means.*—This is now almost always used as a Singular; as, "By *this* means."

*News.*—This is now almost always used as a Singular; as, "Ill news *runs* apace."

*Innings.*—This is a word used in cricket to denote the turn for going in and using the bat. It is *always* used as a Singular; as, "We have not yet had *an* innings"; "Our eleven beat the other by *an* innings and ten runs."

*Gallows.*—The frame-work from which criminals are hanged. This noun is used as a Singular; as, "They fixed up *a* gallows."

*Odds.*—A word used in betting, to denote the difference of one wager against another. "We gave him *a* heavy odds against ourselves."

**79.** There are some nouns which are never used in the Singular. These are for the most part names of things, which imply plurality or consist of more parts than one:—

(*a*) Instruments or tools:—*arms* (weapons), *bellows, fetters, pincers, scissors, tongs, shears, snuffers, tweezers.*

(*b*) Articles of dress:—*breeks* or *breeches, drawers, pantaloons, trappings, trousers.*

(*c*) Kinds of disease:—*measles, mumps, staggers, small-pox* (originally spelt as *small-pocks*).

(*d*) Parts of the body:—*bowels, entrails, intestines, giblets.*

(*e*) The names of sciences or subjects ending in *ics*; such as *physics, optics, acoustics, phonetics, politics, ethics, metaphysics*, etc.

(These nouns are Plural, because the corresponding Greek words, from which they have been translated, are Plural.)

(*f*) Miscellaneous words; such as *ashes, annals, assets, cates, gallows, dregs, embers, chattels, lees, nuptials, obsequies, shambles, statistics, victuals, hustings, proceeds, thanks, tidings, downs, suds, wages, chaps, auspices, billiards, environs, thews, mews, contents, credentials*, etc.

## CHAPTER III.—ADJECTIVES.

### SECTION 1.—THE KINDS OF ADJECTIVES.

**80. Adjective defined.**—An adjective is a word used to qualify a noun (§ 13).

In parsing an adjective this is the definition invariably used, and it is therefore convenient to retain it. But it needs explanation. An adjective, as we know, denotes a property of some kind or other. When we say that it qualifies or modifies a noun, we mean that it *restricts* the application of the noun to such persons or things as possess the property denoted by the adjective.

Every adjective, therefore, has a *restrictive* force; and it might be defined as "*a word used to restrict the application of a noun by adding something to its meaning.*"[1]

**81.** There are altogether six different kinds of Adjectives:[2]—

---

[1] This is an abridged form of the definition given by Mason, who, in *English Grammar*, p. 37, § 88, defines an adjective thus:—"An adjective is a word which may limit (=restrict) the application of a noun to that which has the quality, the quantity, or the relation which the adjective denotes."

[2] In Mason's *English Grammar*, p. 38, § 89, Adjectives are arranged in three classes,—Qualitative or Descriptive, Quantitative (which includes Numeral), and Demonstrative. This arrangement omits Proper and Distributive.

(1) **Proper**: describing a thing by some *Proper noun.*
(2) **Descriptive**: showing *of what quality* or *in what state* a thing is.
(3) **Quantitative**: showing *how much of* a thing is meant.
(4) **Numeral**: showing *how many* things or *in what order.*
(5) **Demonstrative**: showing *which* or *what* thing is meant.
(6) **Distributive**: showing that things are taken *separately* or *in separate lots.*

*Proper Adjectives.*

**82.** Proper Adjectives restrict the application of a noun to such persons or things as are included within the scope of some Proper name. (A Proper adjective must begin with a capital letter.)

The *Indian* plains = the plains of India.
A *Portuguese* sailor = a sailor from Portugal.
The *Turkish* empire = the empire of the Turks.
The *Gangetic* plain = the plain watered by the Ganges.
The *English* language = the language of England.

*Note.*—Proper adjectives, like Proper nouns, may be used in a descriptive sense; as, *French* leave; *British* pluck (pluck like that of a Briton).

*Descriptive Adjectives:—Quality or State.*

**83.** Descriptive Adjectives restrict the application of a noun to such persons or things as possess the *quality* or *state* denoted by the adjective.

A *brave* boy; a *sick* lion; a *tame* cat; a *large* field; a *black* horse; an *industrious* student; a *careful* workman.

*Quantitative Adjectives:—Quantity or Degree.*

**84.** Quantitative Adjectives restrict the application of a noun to such things as are of the *quantity* or *degree* denoted by the adjective.

The chief adjectives of this class are—*Much, little; no* or *none; some, any; enough* or *sufficient; all* or *whole, half.*

He ate *much* (a large quantity of) bread.
He ate *little* (a small quantity of) bread.
He ate *no* bread. I had *none.*
He ate *some* (a certain quantity of) bread.
He did not eat *any* (any quantity of) bread.
He ate *enough* or *sufficient* bread.
He ate *all* the (the *whole* quantity of) bread.
A *half* holiday is better than *none.*

*Note.*—"No" is used when the noun that it qualifies is expressed. "None" is used when no noun is expressed after it.

**85.** Adjectives of Quantity are always followed by a *Singular* noun; and this noun must always be either a noun of *Material* or an *Abstract* noun; as "much bread" (noun of Material); "much pain" (a high degree of pain, Abstract noun).

*Note.*—It is idiomatic to speak of a *quantity* of matter (Material noun), and a *degree* of some quality (Abstract noun). Hence adjectives of Quantity have also been called adjectives of Degree.

### *Numeral Adjectives.*

**86.** Numeral Adjectives restrict the application of a noun to such persons or things as are of the *number* or *serial order* denoted by the adjective.

Numeral Adjectives are subdivided into two main classes:—

I. Definite. II. Indefinite.

**87. Definite** numerals denote some *exact* number.

Those which show *how many* things there are (as one, two, three, four, etc.) are called **Cardinals.**

Those which show the *serial order* in which a thing stands (as first, second, third, etc.) are called **Ordinals.**

Those which show *how often* a thing is *repeated* are called **Multiplicative.**

| *Cardinals.* | *Ordinals.* | *Multiplicatives.* |
|---|---|---|
| One | first | one only, single, simple |
| Two | second | twofold, double |
| Three | third | threefold, treble, triple |
| Four | fourth | fourfold, quadruple (four times one) |
| Six | sixth | sixfold (six times one) |
| Seven | seventh | sevenfold (seven times one) |

**88. Indefinite** numerals denote number of some kind without saying precisely what the number is:—

*All, some, enough, no* or *none; many, few; several, sundry.*

*All* men are mortal. *Some* men die young.
*No* men were present. Ten men will be *enough.*
*Many* men are poor. *Few* men are rich.
*Several* men came. *Sundry* men went away.

A Definite numeral can be made Indefinite by placing the word *some* or *about* before it:—

*Some* twenty men (=*about* twenty men, twenty men *more or less*) were present.

**89.** The words "some," "enough," "all," "no *or* none," are adjectives of *Number* or adjectives of *Quantity*, according to the sense.

If the noun qualified by such words is a Material or Abstract noun, the adjective belongs to the class of Quantity, as has been explained in § 85. But if the noun is a Common noun (or one used as a Common noun), and capable therefore of being in the Plural number, the adjective belongs to the class of Numeral :—

| *Quantitatives.* | *Numerals.* |
|---|---|
| *Much ;* he had much bread. | *Many ;* he had many loaves. |
| *Little ;* he had little bread. | *Few ;* he had few loaves. |
| *Enough ;* he had enough bread. | *Enough ;* he had loaves enough. |
| *Some ;* he had some bread. | *Some ;* he had some loaves. |
| *No ;* he had no bread. | *No ;* he had no loaves. |
| *All ;* he had all the bread. | *All ;* he had all the loaves. |
| *Any ;* have you had any bread ? | *Any ;* did you bring any loaves ? |

*Demonstrative Adjectives.*

**90.** Demonstrative Adjectives restrict the application of a noun to those persons or things that are intended to be *pointed out* by the adjective.

The word *Demonstrative* means "pointing out."

**91.** Adjectives of this kind are subdivided (as Numeral adjectives are) into two main classes :—

I. Definite. II. Indefinite.

When a person or thing is pointed out *exactly*, as "this man," the adjective is called a **Definite** Demonstrative.

When it is pointed out in a certain sense, but *not exactly*, it is called an **Indefinite** Demonstrative.

| *Definite.* | | *Indefinite.* | |
|---|---|---|---|
| *Singular.* | *Plural.* | *Singular.* | *Plural.* |
| The | the | A, an | *nil.* |
| This | these | One, any | any |
| That, yon, yonder | those, yon, yonder | A certain | certain |
| Such | such | Such | such |
| The same, or self-same | the same, or self-same | Some | some |
| The other | the other | Another, any other | other, any other |

Demonstrative adjectives are few in number, and all of them are given in the above list.

**92.** The adjective "*the*" is sometimes called the **Definite Article**, and "*a*" or "*an*" is called the **Indefinite Article.**

**An** is used before the sound of an open vowel or silent *h ;* as—

*An* apple ; *an h*eir ; *an h*our ; *an h*onest man.

**A** is used before a consonant, before *u* or *ew* or *eu* sounded as *yoo*, and before *o* sounded as *wu :*—

*A* kite ; *a* cart ; *a* bottle ; *a u*seful thing ; *a o*ne-eyed man ; *a* European ; *a* ewer ; *an u*nusual, but *a u*nique case.

We say "*a* his'-to-ry," because here the accent is on the *first* syllable "*his*," and the *h* is distinctly sounded; but we say "*an* his-tor'-i-cal account," because here the accent is on the *second* syllable "*tor*," and the *h* is practically silent.[1]

*Distributive Adjectives.*

**93.** Distributive Adjectives restrict the application of a noun by showing that the persons or things denoted by the noun are taken *singly*, or *in separate lots.*

**94.** There are four Adjectives of this class:—*each*, *every*, *either*, *neither*.

(*a*) **Each.**—This means one of *two* things or one of any number *exceeding two*:—

The *two* men had *each* a gun.
The *twenty* men had *each* a gun.

(*b*) **Every.**—This is never used for one of two, but always for some number *exceeding two*:—

*Every* man (out of the *twenty present*) had a gun.

*Note.*—"Every" is a stronger word than "each," and means "*each without exception*":—"*all* the individuals of a group, taken *singly*."

**"Every six hours"** and similar expressions.—This means every *period or space of six hours*, six hours being taken collectively as *one* period of time:—

He came *every five hours* (=at the close of every space of five hours).

**"Every other."**—This means *every second* or *each alternate*; as—

He was attacked with fever *every other day* (=on every second day).

(*c*) **Either.**—This has two meanings—(1) *one of two*, or (2) *each of two*,—that is, *both*.

(1) You can take *either* side; that is, one side or the other.
(2) The river overflowed on *either* side; that is, on both sides.

(*d*) **Neither.**—This is the negative of "either," and signifies "neither the one nor the other":—

"You should take *neither* side"; that is, neither this side nor that, neither the one side nor the other.

## SECTION 2.—THE TWO USES OF ADJECTIVES.

**95.** There are two different ways in which an Adjective can be used—(*a*) the Attributive, and (*b*) the Predicative.[2]

---

[1] The student will see from the above that the only purpose for which the *n* is required is to separate the vowel *a* from the initial vowel-sound of the word following. Sometimes the *n* of the article has glued itself to the word following: thus *an ewt* has become *a newt; an eke-name* has become *a nick-name; an ingot* has become *a ningot* or *a nugget.* The converse process is seen in *an adder* from *a nadder*, *an apron* from *a napron*, *an auger* from *a nauger*, *an orange* from *a naring* or *a norange.*

[2] We would not go so far, however, as to say (as Mr. Mason does in *English Grammar*, p. 37, § 87) "that all true adjectives can be used in

(*a*) *Attributive use.*—An adjective is used attributively, when it qualifies its noun *directly*, so as to make a kind of compound noun :—

A *lame* horse. A *noble* character.

All true adjectives can be used attributively. But we cannot say "an asleep man," because "asleep" and similar words are not adjectives, but adverbs.

(*b*) *Predicative use.*—An adjective is used predicatively, when it qualifies its noun *indirectly*—through the verb or predicate going before.

That horse went *lame*. His character is *noble*.

An adjective so used is a form of *Complement* to the verb going before (§ 24), because it *completes* what the verb left unsaid.

## Section 3.—Substitutes for Adjectives.

**96.** Words that restrict a noun in the same way as an adjective would restrict it, are substitutes for an adjective :—

(1) A Participle (or Verbal adjective, § 17) :—

A *fading* flower. A *fallen* tree.

(2) An Adverb with some participle understood :—

The *then* (reigning) king. The *down* (going) train.

(3) A Noun or Gerund used as an Adjective :—

A *river* fish (=a fish living in rivers).
A *bathing* place (=a place used for bathing).

(4) A Noun or Pronoun in the Possessive case :—

*My* book. *Their* friendship. My *son's* teacher.

(5) A Verb in the Infinitive mood :—

A chair *to sit on*. Water *to drink*. A house *to let*.

(6) A Preposition with its object :—

A bird *in the hand* (=a bird *caught*).

(7) An Adjective clause; (see clause defined in § 4).

The book *that you lent me* will not be lost.

## Section 4.—Comparison of Adjectives.

**97.** Most adjectives of Quality, two adjectives of Quantity, viz. *much* and *little*, and two adjectives of Number, viz. *many* and *few*, have degrees of comparison.

---

both ways." A Distributive adjective cannot be used predicatively. For instance, we can say "every man," but we cannot say "man is every," Again, Quantitatives cannot in all cases be used predicatively. We can say "some bread," but we cannot say "bread is some."

Adjectives which cannot be compared may be classified thus :—
(1) Quantitative, all except *much, little.*
(2) Numeral, all except *many, few.*
(3) Proper, as *English, African,* etc.
(4) Demonstrative, as *this, that, other,* etc.
(5) Distributive, as *either, every,* etc.
(6) Descriptive, when they denote qualities which from the nature of their meaning cannot be more or less.
(*a*) Shape, as *round, square, oblong, triangular, four-footed,* etc.
(*b*) Material, as *golden, milky, vegetable,* etc.
(*c*) Time, as *weekly, monthly, annual,* etc.
(*d*) Place, as *Kentish, American, insular,* etc.
(*e*) Natural objects, as *solar, lunar, sidereal,* etc.
(*f*) Qualities in the highest degree, as *eternal, perpetual, perfect,* etc.
Qualities in a moderate degree, as *pal-ish, redd-ish.*

Such a phrase as "more perfect" is a short, but inaccurate, way of saying "more nearly approaching perfection."

**98.** The degrees of comparison are three in number,—the Positive, the Comparative, and the Superlative.

The **Positive** denotes the simple quality; as, "a *beautiful* horse."
The **Comparative** denotes a higher degree of the quality; as, "a *more beautiful* horse." This is used when *two* things are compared with reference to some quality. Comparatives are followed by "than."
The **Superlative** denotes the highest degree of the quality; as, "the *most beautiful* horse." This is used when *one* thing is compared with *all other* things of the same kind. "Superlative" means "lifting above."

**99.** In all adjectives of *more than two syllables,* and in most adjectives of two syllables, the Comparative is formed by adding "*more*" and the Superlative by adding "*most,*" as in the examples already given.[1]

**100.** But adjectives of one syllable and some adjectives of two syllables can also form the Comparative by adding *er* or *r,* and the Superlative by adding *est* or *st.*

(*a*) If the Positive ends in *two consonants,* or in *a single* consonant preceded by *two vowels, er* and *est* are added :—

| | | |
|---|---|---|
| Small | smaller | smallest |
| Thick | thicker | thickest |
| Great | greater | greatest |
| Deep | deeper | deepest |

(*b*) If the Positive ends in *one* consonant, and the consonant

[1] This is called the *Analytical* mode of comparing adjectives, as distinct from the *Synthetical* or *flexional* mode, which consists in adding the suffixes *-er* and *-est* to the root.

is preceded by a *short vowel*, the final consonant is doubled when *er* and *est* are added :—

| | | |
|---|---|---|
| Thin | thinner | thinnest |
| Fat | fatter | fattest |
| Hot | hotter | hottest |
| Wet | wetter | wettest |

(*c*) If the Positive ends in *e*, only *r* and *st* are added, and not *er* and *est* :—

| | | |
|---|---|---|
| Brave | braver | bravest |
| Wise | wiser | wisest |
| True | truer | truest |

(*d*) If the Positive ends in *y*, and the *y* is preceded by a *consonant*, the *y* is changed into *i*, when *er* and *est* are added :—

| | | |
|---|---|---|
| Happy | happier | happiest |
| Dry | drier | driest |

(*e*) If the *y* is preceded by a *vowel*, the *y* is not changed into *i* :—

| | | |
|---|---|---|
| Gay | gayer | gayest |
| Grey | greyer | greyest |

*Note.*—We cannot use the forms *-er*, *-est* with adjectives ending in such suffixes as *-al*, *-ed*, *-ful*, *-ic*, *-ile*, *-ine*, *-ose*, *-ous*, and others. Thus we cannot say, *frug-al-er*, *learn-ed-er*, *cheer-ful-er*, *com-ic-er*, *puer-il-er*, *furt-iv-er*, *verb-os-er*, *fam-ous-er*. We add *more* or *most* to such adjectives, to show that what we are comparing is the quality implied by the stem of the word, and not the suffix added to the stem.

**101. Irregular Comparisons.**—The Positives marked below with an asterisk have borrowed their comparatives and superlatives from other roots. Such Positives are therefore *defective*, because they have no Comp. or Superl. of their own. The Comp. and Superl. are also defective, because they have no Positive of their own. In all the other examples the Comp. and Superl. are *irregular*, but formed from a single root.

| | | |
|---|---|---|
| Bad, ill, evil* | worse* | worst* |
| Fore | former | foremost, first |
| Good* | better* | best* |
| Hind | hinder | hindmost |
| Late | later, latter | latest, last |
| Little* | less* | least* |
| Much (quantity)* | more* | most* |
| Many (number)* | more* | most* |
| Nigh | nigher | nighest, next |
| Old | older, elder | oldest, eldest |

**102.** There are six words which are adverbs in the Positive degree, but adjectives in the Comparative and Superlative :—

| | | |
|---|---|---|
| Fore | further | furthest |
| Far | farther | farthest |
| In | inner | innermost, inmost |
| Out | outer, utter | uttermost, utmost |
| Be-neath | nether | nethermost |
| Up | upper | uppermost |

**103. Latin Comparatives.**—All of these end in *or*, and not in *er;* and all are followed by *to* instead of *than.*

| | | | |
|---|---|---|---|
| His strength | is | *superior to* | (greater than) mine. |
| His strength | is | *inferior to* | (less than) mine. |
| This event | is | *anterior to* } | (earlier than) that. |
| This event | is | *prior to* } | (earlier than) that. |
| This event | is | *posterior to* | (later than) that. |
| This man | is | *senior to* | (older than) that. |
| This man | is | *junior to* | (younger than) that. |

## CHAPTER IV.—PRONOUNS.

**104. Pronoun defined.**—A Pronoun is a word used instead of a noun or noun-equivalent (§ 6).

A pronoun is a *substitute* word. If instead of mentioning or repeating a noun we use some other word, which will show what noun (expressed or understood) we are referring to, that word is a pronoun. Thus if some one says, "*I* am here," the word "I" is a substitute for the speaker's name, which otherwise would have to be mentioned. If we say, "*He* is here," the word *he* is a substitute for the name of some person mentioned already.

Hence it has been well said:—"Pronouns denote persons or things without being names for them." This is a suitable definition.

The usefulness of pronouns is best seen by trying to do without them:—

John saw a snake in the garden, *this snake John* thought would hurt *John*, unless *John* killed *the snake* with a stick, *this stick John* had in *John's* hand.

The nouns in italics can all be replaced by pronouns, and the sentence can be much better expressed as follows:—

John saw a snake in the garden, *which he* thought would hurt *him*, unless *he* killed *it* with a stick *which he* had in *his* hand.

**105.** Two facts follow from the above definition:—

(*a*) Since a pronoun is used instead of a noun, it must itself be of the nature of a noun, and not of an adjective.

(*b*) Since a pronoun is used instead of a noun, it must be of the same number, gender, and person as the noun it stands for.

**106.** There are four different kinds of Pronouns:[1]—

(1) **Personal**; as, *I*, *thou*, *he*, *she*, etc.

(2) **Demonstrative**; as, *this*, *that*, *such*, *one*, etc.

(3) **Relative**; as, *which*, *who*, *that*, *as*, etc.

(4) **Interrogative**; as, *who? which? what?*

This classification excludes all words that are *adjectives*, and all words that are not *substitutes for nouns*. It is explained below in § 113 that *this*, *that*, *such* are not here adjectives, but substitutes for nouns.

### SECTION I.—PERSONAL PRONOUNS.

**107.** The **Personal Pronouns** are so called, because they stand for the three persons, viz.—

(*a*) The First, which denotes the person *speaking*; as *I*, *we*, *myself*:—

I (*the person now speaking*) will do all I can to win a prize at the end of the year.

(*b*) The Second, which denotes the person *spoken to*; as, *thou*, *you*, *thyself*:—

You (*the person now spoken to*) should leave off this habit of idleness.

(*c*) The Third, which denotes the person or thing *spoken of*; as, *he*, *she*, *it*, *himself*, *herself*, *itself*:—

He (*the person already mentioned*) did a good day's work with his tutor.

**108. Forms of Personal Pronouns.**—Personal Pronouns have the same differences of gender, number, and case that nouns have:—

---

[1] A different classification of Pronouns is given in Mason's *English Grammar*, p. 48, ed. 1891. After giving eight classes of Pronouns, he subdivides each class, wherever this is possible, into two columns, one for Substantive pronouns, and the other for Adjective pronouns. Under Adjective pronouns he includes Distributive and Demonstrative adjectives, which in this book have already been disposed of in the chapter on Adjectives. It is difficult to see how such adjectives as "every," "each," "some," "other," "any," etc., or, in fact, any adjective, can be correctly called a Pronoun. A Pronoun is a *substitute* word,—a word used *for* another word. But "every," "each," "some," "other," "any" are simply *qualifying* words. They are not *substitute* words. There are no other words for which they are used as substitutes, and therefore they are not pronouns. The same author has a class of pronouns which he calls **Indefinite**, and subdivides into Substantives (*one*, *aught*, *naught*) and Adjectives (*any*, *other*, *some*, *no*). We have already shown that the last four are not pronouns at all. *Aught* and *naught* are not pronouns either, because they are not *substitutes* for any other words. *One* is a pronoun in certain contexts, as shown below in §§ 117, 119.

I. *The First Person, Masculine or Feminine.*

| Case. | Singular. | Plural. |
|---|---|---|
| *Nominative* . . | I | We |
| *Possessive* . . | My, mine | Our, ours |
| *Objective* . . . | Me | Us |

II. *The Second Person, Masculine or Feminine.*

| Case. | Singular. | Plural. |
|---|---|---|
| *Nominative* . . | Thou | Ye or you |
| *Possessive* . . | Thy, thine | Your, yours |
| *Objective* . . . | Thee | You |

III. *The Third Person, of all Genders.*

| Case. | Singular. | | | Plural. |
|---|---|---|---|---|
| | Masculine. | Feminine. | Neuter. | All Genders. |
| *Nominative* . | He | She | It | They |
| *Possessive* . | His | Her or hers | Its | Their or theirs |
| *Objective* . | Him | Her | It | Them |

**109. Two Forms of Possessive.**—Most of the Personal pronouns have two forms for the Possessive :—

| Singular. | | | | Plural. | | |
|---|---|---|---|---|---|---|
| *First Form* . | My | Thy | Her | Our | Your | Their |
| *Second* ,, . | Mine | Thine | Hers | Ours | Yours | Theirs |

The first is used, when the Possessive is placed *before* its noun. It qualifies the noun like an adjective.

This is *my* book. That is *their* house.

The second is used—(*a*) when the Possessive is separated from the qualified noun by a verb coming between ; (*b*) when the qualified noun is not expressed ; (*c*) when the Possessive is preceded by "of" :—

(*a*) This book is *mine*. That house is *theirs*.
(*b*) My horse and *yours* (your horse) are both tired.
(*c*) That horse *of yours* is tired.

*Note* 1.—"Hers," "ours," "yours," "theirs" are in fact **Double Possessives**, the "*r*" being one sign of the Possessive and the "*s*" another. The meaning of "*of*" in such a phrase as "of yours" is discussed below in § 304.

*Note* 2.—In poetry "mine" and "thine" are sometimes placed *before* their nouns, when the noun following begins with a vowel. This is done to separate the sounds of the two vowels :—

Look through *mine eyes* with thine.—TENNYSON.

*Note* 3.—In poetry "mine" can be placed after its noun; as "mother mine" instead of "my mother."

*Note* 4.—*Mine* and *thine* are the older forms. *My* and *thy* are merely contractions of these.

**110. Reflexive Personal Pronouns.**—These are formed by adding "self" or "own" to a Personal pronoun.[1]

I. *The First Person.*

| Case. | Singular. | Plural. |
|---|---|---|
| *Nom. or Obj.* . . | Myself | Ourselves |
| *Possessive* . . | My or mine own | Our own |

II. *The Second Person.*

| Case. | Singular. | Plural. |
|---|---|---|
| *Nom. or Obj.* . . | Thyself | Yourselves |
| *Possessive* . . | Thy or thine own | Your own |

III. *The Third Person.*

| Case. | Singular. | | | Plural. |
|---|---|---|---|---|
| | Masculine. | Feminine. | Neuter. | All Genders. |
| *Nom. or Obj.* | Himself | Herself | Itself | Themselves |
| *Possessive* . | His own | Her own | Its own | Their own |

[1] The student will afterwards find the origin of *self* and *own* discussed in § 311.

**111. Uses of Reflexive Forms.**—The Reflexive forms of Personal pronouns are used for two purposes—(*a*) to show that the person (or thing) does something to himself (or itself); (*b*) to make the pronouns more emphatic.

*Examples of* (*a*).

| *Singular.* | *Plural.* |
|---|---|
| I hid myself. | We hid ourselves. |
| I hit my own head. | We hit our own heads. |
| Thou lovest thine own work. | You love your own work. |

*Examples of* (*b*).

| *Singular.* | *Plural.* |
|---|---|
| I myself saw the horse. | We ourselves saw it. |
| He himself (or she herself) saw it. | They themselves saw it. |
| The wall itself fell. | The walls themselves fell. |

*Note.*—An emphatic personal pronoun can never be the subject of a sentence. We cannot say, "myself saw it," "himself saw it," etc.

SECTION 2.—DEMONSTRATIVE PRONOUNS.

**112.** A **Demonstrative Pronoun** is one that *points to* some noun going before, and is used instead of it. This noun is called the Antecedent.

**113.** The chief pronouns of this class are:—*this, that, these, those; one, ones, none; such.*

The student will have observed that these words have appeared already in the list of Demonstrative *Adjectives.* Where, then, is the difference?

*When they are followed by a noun, or require some noun to be understood after them, they are* **Adjectives.**

*When they are used as substitutes for some noun expressed or understood, and cannot have any noun either expressed or understood after them, they are* **Pronouns.**

(*a*) He came to my house *one* day.

Here *one* is an adjective (Indefinite Demonstrative) qualifying its noun "day."

(*b*) Your coat is black; mine is a white *one.*

Here *one* is a pronoun, which is used as a substitute for the previously-mentioned noun "coat," and is qualified by the adjective "white."

**114. He, she, it, they.**—The simplest forms of Demonstrative pronouns are *he, she, it, they.*

These have been hitherto called "Personal pronouns," partly because they exemplify the Third person as distinct from the First and Second, and partly because "he" and "she," and sometimes "they," do actually relate to *persons,* and not to things.

Yet it is equally correct to call them Demonstrative pronouns, since they *point to* some noun going before, and are *substituted* for it.

They might well be called "**Demonstrative pronouns of the Third person.**"

(1) My father has gone; we saw *him* start a short time ago. (Here *him* is a Demonstrative pronoun used as a substitute for its Antecedent noun "father.")

(2) My mother came yesterday; we were glad to see *her*. (Here *her* is a Demonstrative pronoun used as a substitute for its Antecedent noun "mother.")

(3) The sun has risen; *it* shines brightly. (Here *it* is a Demonstrative pronoun used as a substitute for the noun "sun.")

(4) The travellers fell asleep as soon as *they* arrived. (Here *they* is a Demonstrative pronoun substituted for the noun "travellers.")

**115. It.**—This pronoun has three distinct modes of reference:—

(*a*) To a *noun* going before. In this sense it is merely a Demonstrative pronoun used in the ordinary way:—

The sun has risen; *it* (=the sun) shines brightly.

(*b*) To a *clause* going before:—

I have treated him as he deserved; and he knows *it*. (Here "it" points to the clause "I have treated him as he deserved.")

(*c*) To a *phrase* or *clause* coming after:—

*It* is sad *to hear such bad news*. (*Phrase.*)
It—viz. "to hear such bad news"—is sad.

*It* is probable *that it will rain to-day*. (*Clause.*)
It—viz. "that it will rain to-day"—is probable.

**116. This, that, these, those.**—The uses of these words as *pronouns*, and not as *adjectives*, are as follows:—

(*a*) When two nouns have been mentioned in a previous sentence or clause, "**this**" has reference to the *latter* and "**that**" to the *former*:—

(1) Work and play are both necessary to health; *this* (=play) gives us rest, and *that* (=work) gives us energy.

(2) Dogs are more faithful animals than cats; *these* (=cats) attach themselves to places, and *those* (=dogs) to persons.

Observe that in the first of these sentences "*this*" does not specify *which* or *what* play is meant, and therefore it is not a Demonstrative Adjective. It is simply put as a *substitute* for the noun "play," and therefore it is a Demonstrative Pronoun.

A similar explanation holds good for the other example.

(*b*) The word "**that**," together with its plural form "**those**," is used as substitute for a single noun previously mentioned:—

(1) The air of hills is cooler than *that* (=the air) of plains.

(2) The houses of the rich are larger than *those* (=the houses) of the poor.

Observe the word "that" in the first example does not qualify the noun "air" by saying *which* air or *what* air, and therefore it is not an Adjective. It stands for "air" in general, and is a *substitute* for the noun "air"; and therefore it is a Pronoun.

(c) The words "**this**" or "**that**" can be used as substitutes for a *clause* or *sentence* previously mentioned :—

(1) I studied Greek and Latin when I was young, and *that* (=I studied Greek and Latin) at Oxford.

Here by using the pronoun "*that*" as a substitute for the sentence "I studied Greek and Latin," we not only avoid repeating this sentence a second time, but we give some emphasis to the words "at Oxford."

(2) Make the best use of your time at school; *that*'s a wise boy.

Here "*that*" = "one who makes the best use of his time at school." All this repetition is avoided by using the pronoun "*that*" as a substitute for the implied sentence.

(3) You paid your debts; and *this* (=the payment of your debts) is quite sufficient to prove your honesty.

**117. One, ones, none.**—When the antecedent noun is in the Singular number, we use "*one*"; but when the antecedent noun is Plural, we use "*ones*."

(1) He gained a prize last year; but he did not gain *one* (=a prize) this term. (*Singular.*)

(2) There were six lazy boys and four industrious *ones* (=boys) in our class. (*Plural.*)

**None** is properly a contraction of *no-one*, and was originally used only as a Singular. It was so used by Dryden :—

*None* but the brave *deserves* the fair.

But "none" was also used in the sense of *not any*, and in this sense could have a Plural meaning. In fact, the plural sense is now equally or more common :—

Bring me some *pence;* I have *none.*
*None have* gone away yet.

**118. Such, so.**—"Such" can be substituted for a noun in either number :—

(1) He is the judge appointed to hear this case, and as *such* (=as the appointed judge) you must not speak to him before the trial. (*Singular.*)

(2) Kings are constituted *such* (=kings) by law, and should be obeyed. (*Plural.*)

"So" is sometimes used in places where we could also use "such"; but "so" is a Demonstrative *Adverb*, and not a Demonstrative *Pronoun* :—

My business is urgent, and I hope you will treat it *so* (=as urgent).
Is he an enemy? He is *so* (=an enemy).

*Examples for Practice.*

*Show whether the words printed in italics are Demonstrative* **Adjectives** *or Demonstrative* **Pronouns** :—

*This* horse is stronger than *that.*

Health is of more value than money; *this* cannot give such true happiness as *that.*

I prefer a white horse to a black *one.*

You will repent of this *one* day, when it is too late.

You have kept your promise; *this* was all that I asked for.

The faithfulness of a dog is greater than *that* of a cat.

*One* Mr. B. helped his friend in need; *that* was a true friend.

Return to your work, and *that* immediately.

Bring me *that* book, and leave *this* where it is.

The step you have taken is *one* of much risk.

*Such* a book as yours deserves to be well read.

Prosperous men are much exposed to flattery; for *such* alone can be made to pay for it.

Prosperous men are not always more happy than unlucky *ones.*

A pale light, like *that* of the rising moon, begins to fringe the horizon.

Will you ride *this* horse or *that?*

A stranger could not be received twice as *such* in the same house.

The plan you have chosen does not seem to me to be a wise *one.*

*One* man says *this,* another *that;* whom should I believe?

**119. Indefinite Demonstrative Pronouns.**—Sometimes Demonstrative Pronouns are used *indefinitely;* that is, they are not used as substitutes for some noun previously mentioned, but for some noun understood or implied.

All Indefinite pronouns are in the Third person. *I* and *you* cannot be indefinite, because we cannot help knowing who is speaking or who is spoken to.

(*a*) **They.**—This pronoun is sometimes used for *men in general,* or some person whose name is purposely concealed:—

(1) *They* say (=men in general say) that truth and honesty is the best policy.

(2) *They* told me (=some person or persons, whom I do not wish to name, told me) that you were guilty of theft.

*Note.*—In such examples the Indef. Demons. pronoun is really equivalent to a noun signifying "person." Compare the following:—

What is *he* (=the man) at the gate?—SHAKSPEARE.
*He* (=the being) of the bottomless pit.—MILTON.

(*b*) **One.**—This pronoun is often used in the sense of *any person* or *every person:*—

*One* should take care of *one's* health.
=*A man* (any and every man) should take care of *his* health.

*Note.*—Whenever "one" is the subject to a verb, it must be followed by "one" and not by "he." Thus we cannot say, "*one* must take care of *his* health."

(c) **It.**—The indefinite use of this pronoun is against all rules of number, person, and gender.[1]

Who is *it?* *It* is I. Is *it* you? No; *it* is he.

In such phrases as those shown below, "*it*" gives **emphasis** to the noun or pronoun following:—

*It* was I who told you that. *It* is the men who work hardest, not the women. *It* was the queen who died yesterday. *It* is little things that chiefly disturb the mind.

Sometimes the noun, for which the word "*it*" is used, can be understood from the context:—

*It* is raining=rain is raining or falling.
*It* is blowing hard=the wind is blowing hard.
*It* is fine to-day=the weather is fine to-day.
*It* is hot=the air is hot. *It* is cold=the air is cold.
*It* is still early=the hour is still early.
*It* is two miles from here=the distance is two miles.
*It* was autumn=the season of the year was autumn.

Sometimes the word "*it*" is used instead of some Personal pronoun to express endearment or contempt:—

What a pretty little girl *it* is (=she is)! (*Endearment.*)
What an ass *it* is (=that man is)! (*Contempt.*)

## SECTION 3.—RELATIVE OR CONJUNCTIVE PRONOUNS.

**120.** A **Relative Pronoun** not only refers to some noun going before (as a Demonstrative pronoun does), but it also *joins two sentences together* (which a Demonstrative pronoun does not do). It would therefore be more fitly called a *Conjunctive* pronoun (§ 17).

This is a good house; I live in *it.* (*Demonstrative Pronoun.*)
The house in *which* I live is a good one. (*Relative Pronoun.*)

**121. Who, which.**—These are declined as follows for Singular and Plural alike:—

| | | |
|---|---|---|
| *Nom.* | Who, . . . | which. |
| *Poss.* | Whose, . . . | (of which). |
| *Obj.* | Whom, . . . | which. |

The forms *who, whose, whom* are used for persons only. The form *which* is now used for things without life and for any kinds of animal except men and women.

[1] An explanation, however, will be found below in § 319.

In poetry, and occasionally in prose, *whose* can be used as the Possessive form of *which* :—

The tree, under *whose* shade we are sitting.

**122. Forms of Antecedent.**—The antecedent may take the form of a noun, or any kind of noun-equivalent (§ 45).

*You have paid your debts,* which (=the fact that you have paid your debts) is a clear proof of your honesty. (*Clause.*)

**123. Antecedent understood.**—When the antecedent is understood, the neuter Relative takes the form of "**what,**" while the Masculine and Feminine retain the form of "who."

(*a*) *Who = he who,* or *she who,* or *they who.*

*Who* (=he who) steals my purse, steals trash.—SHAKSPEARE.
*Whom* (=those persons whom) the gods love, die young.—*Proverb.*

(*b*) *What = the thing which,* or *the things which.*

I cannot tell you now *what* (=the thing which) then happened.
The laws are *what* (=the things which) you say they are.

(*c*) *So, ever,* or *soever* added to the Relative pronoun or to Relative adverbs gives the meaning of totality:—

*Whosoever* (=any and every person who) breaks this law will be punished, *wherever* (in any and every place where) he may live.

*Note* 1.—"**What**" has been called a "Compound Relative," because the antecedent is said to be contained in it. But this is not correct; for the antecedent is sometimes expressed, either (*a*) in a subsequent clause, or (*b*) immediately after the Relative itself:—

(*a*) *What* I tell you in darkness, *that* speak ye in the light.
(*b*) Take *what* (or *whatever*) *help* you can get.

*Note* 2.—Whenever the antecedent is placed after the Relative, as in example (*b*), the relative is not a *substitute* word, and therefore not a true pronoun, but an adjective.

Take *whichever book* (=that book of all others which) you prefer.

**124. That.**—The word "*that*" is often used for "who," "whom," or "which," but never for "whose":—

This is the house *that* (=which) Jack built.
The man *that* (=whom) we were looking for has come.

*Note.*—Whenever "that" is the object to a preposition, the preposition is invariably placed after the verb of its sentence, and never before its own object:—

The house *that* we live *in.*

**125. As.**—The word "as" can be used for a Relative pronoun, provided it is preceded by "such," or "as," or "the same." It may be in the Nominative or the Objective case, but not in the Possessive.

This is not *such* a good book *as* I expected.
*As* many men *as* came were caught.
Yours is not *the same* book *as* mine (is).

After "such" and "as" the word "*as*" is always used. But after "the same" it is not less common to use "*that*."

This is *the same* story *that* (=which) I heard ten years ago.
This is *the same* man *that* (=whom) I saw yesterday.

*Note.*—The use of "*that*" or "*as*" after "the same" is guided by the following rules:—(1) When a verb is *expressed* after it, we generally use "*that*"; (2) When the verb is *understood*, we always use "*as*":—

(1) This is the same man *that* came yesterday. (*Verb expressed.*)
(2) This is not the same book *as* mine (is). (*Verb understood.*)

**126. But.**—The conjunction "but," *when some Demonstrative pronoun is understood after it*, is used in the sense of "who not" or "which not."

There was no one present, *but* saw (=but *he* saw=*who* did *not* see) the deed.
There is no vice so simple, *but* may (=but *it* may=*which* may *not*) become serious in time.

*Note.*—The student must avoid the common mistake of saying that *but* is a "negative relative." It is simply an Adversative conjunction with some Demonstrative pronoun understood after it. This pronoun is sometimes expressed, as in the common saying—

It never rains, *but it* pours.

*The uses of Who and Which.*

**127. Restrictive, Continuative.**—These words denote two distinct uses of "who" or "which":—

(*a*) *Restrict.*—The man *who lived there* died yesterday.
(*b*) *Contin.*—I have seen my friend, *who recognised* me at once.

In (*a*) the Relative clause does the work of an *adjective* to the noun "man," because it *restricts* the application of this noun to that particular man who is said to have "lived there."

In (*b*) the Relative clause "who recognised me at once" has no restrictive force on the noun "friend." It simply *continues* what was said in the previous clause:—"I found my friend, *and he* (=who) recognised me at once."

*Note.*—Besides the Restrictive and the Continuative, there are two more senses of "who" and "which,"—one implying a **Cause**, and the other a **Purpose**:—

(*c*) *Cause.* { Balbus, *who* had been found guilty, was hanged.
=Balbus, *because he* had been found guilty, was hanged.

(*d*) *Purpose.* { Envoys were sent, *who* should sue for peace.
=Envoys were sent, *that they* might sue for peace.

In (*c*) and (*d*) the Relative clause in neither Restrictive nor Continuative, since (*c*) implies the *cause* of something already done, and (*d*) the *purpose* for which something is going to be done.

**128. Who, that.**—"Who" and "which" are the only Relatives that are ever used in the sense of Continuation, Cause, or Purpose. The other, viz. "that," is invariably used in a Restrictive sense, and much more commonly so than "who" or "which."

"That" is strictly the *defining, limiting,* or *distinguishing* Relative. Hence if its antecedent has been defined already by some other word, we do not use *that* after it. Thus we do not say, "*My* father, *that*," etc.; but only, "My father, *who* or *whom*," because the antecedent *father* is already defined by the Possessive *my*.

### SECTION 4.—INTERROGATIVE PRONOUNS.

**129.** An **Interrogative Pronoun** is one that asks a question.

An Interrogative pronoun has been well described as a Relative in search of an antecedent, and hence in English, as in many other languages, there has been a resemblance of form between Interrogatives and Relatives:—

*Who* gained the prize? *John.*
It was *John who* gained the prize.

**130. Forms of Interrogatives.**—The Interrogative pronoun has five different forms.

*Who* spoke? (Nominative to the verb.)
Of *whom* did he speak? (Objective after preposition.)
*What* did he say? (Objective after verb "say.")
*Whose* book is that? (Possessive Case.)
*Which* of these boys will win the prize?

**131. Which, what, who.**—(*a*) "Which" is used in a *selective* sense; (*b*) "who" or "what" is used in a *general* sense:—

(*a*) *Which* of these books do you prefer?
(*b*) *What* is the name of that book? *Who* wrote it?
(*c*) *What* book is that? *Which* book do you like best?

In the examples in (*c*) "*what*" and "*which*," since they are followed by nouns, are Interrogative adjectives, in the same way as a Demonstrative can be either an adjective or a pronoun (see § 113) according to the context.

Similarly, if we use *what* in an exclamatory sense, as, "What folly!" *what* is not a substitute word, but an adjective qualifying "folly."

**132.** The student should observe the different meanings of the Interrogatives used in the following sentences:—

(*a*) *Who* is he?
(*b*) *What* is he?
(*c*) *Which* is he?

In (*a*) the "who" inquires about the name or parentage of some person that has been named.

In (*b*) the "what" inquires about his calling or social status. "What is he?" A tailor.

In (c) the "which" inquires about some particular person out of a definite group of persons. "The man who stole my purse is among the prisoners here present: which is he? Point him out."

**133. Whether.**—The word "*whether*," when it signifies one of two persons or things, is now almost obsolete.

*Whether* of them twain (=*which* of these two men) did the will of his father?—*New Testament.*

## CHAPTER V.—VERBS.

### SECTION 1.—THE KINDS OF VERBS.

**134. Verb defined.**—A Verb is a word used for *saying* something about some person or thing[1] (§ 13).

The most important item in this definition is "*saying.*" "Verb" is the English rendering of Lat. *verbum*, which signifies merely "word." "Verb" has thus acquired the dignity of being pre-eminently *the word.* Why is this? Because of all Parts of Speech it holds the highest rank, higher even than a noun. It is the *saying* something about something else which makes a *sentence*, and this cannot be done without a verb.

**135. The Kinds of Verbs.**—Verbs are subdivided into three main classes:—

I. Transitive. II. Intransitive. III. Auxiliary.

*Note* 1.—Verbs which are not used in all the moods and tenses are called "Defective." But the student must not suppose from this that "Defective" constitutes a separate or fourth class of verb. This is not at all the case. *Quoth*, for example, is a Defective verb, but also Intransitive. Again "wit" is a Defective verb, but also Transitive. Again, "may" is a Defective verb, but also Auxiliary.

*Note* 2.—Verbs are distinguished into Strong and Weak according to *conjugation*; see below, § 210.

**136.** *A verb is* **Transitive,** *if the action does not stop with the agent, but passes from the agent to something else.* (The word "Transitive" means "passing over.")

(1) The man killed *a snake.*
(2) I do not know *whether he has come.*

---

[1] The definition given in several current books is: "A verb makes an assertion." This is of questionable accuracy, because a verb cannot make an assertion without its subject. It is the sentence as a whole, and not merely the verb of the sentence, that makes an assertion. We guard against this error (as Mason does) by defining a verb to be "a word used for saying something about something else." Here, of course, "say" is meant to include all the Finite moods,—Indicative, Imperative, and Subjunctive,—and to exclude the Infinitive, Participle, and Gerund, which, though formed from verbs, have lost their verb-character and become equivalent to nouns or adjectives.

The word or words denoting that person or thing, to which the action of the verb is directed, are called the **Object** to the verb.

*Note.*—A shorter, and yet more suitable definition of Transitive is this :—**A verb that requires an object.** This is more suitable because it covers the ground of such Transitive verbs as *know, hold, possess, own, have, retain, inherit*, etc., in which no *action* is implied, but rather some state or condition.

**137.** *A verb is* **Intransitive,** *when the action stops with the agent, and does not pass from the agent to anything else.*

Men sleep to preserve life.

Sleep what? This is nonsense. No word or words can be placed as object to such a verb as "sleep."

*Note.*—Here, as in the case of Transitive, the verb may denote state or condition, and not merely action; and hence verbs which denote the former have been sometimes called by the distinctive name of Neuter. Thus "he runs" implies action; "he sleeps" implies condition.

**138.** An **Auxiliary** verb is one which (*a*) *helps* to form a tense, or a mood, of some other verb, and (*b*) *forgoes its signification as a Principal verb* for that purpose.

A merchant buys that he *may* sell.

Here *may* is not used either in its early sense of "power" or in its present sense of "permission."

I *have* come from home to-day.

Here *have* forgoes its proper signification—"possession," and helps the verb "come" to form a Present Perfect tense.

The verb that is helped by the Auxiliary is called the **Principal** verb. Thus "sell" (in the first of the above examples) is the Principal verb, and "may" is the Auxiliary.

## Section 2.—Transitive Verbs.

**139. Forms of the Object.**—Most Transitive verbs take a *single* object. The object to a verb may be expressed in various different forms, the chief of which are the following (§ 23):—

(*a*) **Noun** :—The man killed a *snake* with his stick.
(*b*) **Pronoun** :—The man lifted *me* up out of the water.
(*c*) **Infinitive** :—He desires *to leave* us to-morrow.
(*d*) **Gerund** :—He disliked *sleeping* in the daytime.
(*e*) **Phrase** :—No one knew *how to make a beginning*.
(*f*) **Clause** :—We do not know *who has come*.

**140. Position of the Object.**—A noun denoting the object to a verb is usually placed *after* the verb to which it belongs. But when the object is a Relative or Interrogative pronoun, or when the emphasis is thrown on the noun used as object, the object is placed not after, but before the verb.

**Relative.**—The man *whom* I saw yesterday has come back to-day.
**Interrogative.**—*What* did you say? *Whom* were you looking for?
**Emphasis.**—*Silver and gold* have I none; but *what* I have give I unto thee.—*New Testament.*

**141. The Double Object.**—Some Transitive verbs take two objects after them, one of which is usually the name of some *thing*, and the other of some *person or other animal.*

The *thing* named is called the **Direct** object; the *person or other animal* named is called the **Indirect**.

I forgave him (*Indirect*) his faults (*Direct*).

Another way of distinguishing the two objects is by observing that the Indirect object always stands first. If the Indirect is placed after the Direct, it must be preceded by the preposition "*for*" or "*to*":—

He taught Euclid (*Direct*) *to* his sons (*Indirect*).

This mode of showing the Indirect object suggests what is the fact, that the noun or pronoun denoting the Indirect object was originally in the *Dative* case,—a name that is still retained in some books. In Mod. Eng., however, it is better to call this case by the name of Objective, since the Indirect Object no less than the Direct can be made the Subject to the verb, when the voice is changed from Active to Passive; see below, § 163 (*a*).

**142. Factitive Verbs.**—Those Transitive verbs which take *one* object only, but still require some word or words to make the predication *complete*, are called **Factitive** (§ 24).

The additional word or words by which the predication is made complete are called the **Complement**.

**143. Forms of the Complement.**—A Complement may be in seven different forms:—a noun, an adjective, a participle, a preposition with its object, an Infinitive, an adverb, or a noun-clause:—

| | *Subject.* | *Verb.* | *Object.* | *Complement.* |
|---|---|---|---|---|
| *Noun*:— | They | made | him | king. |
| *Adjective*:— | The judge | set | the prisoner | free. |
| *Participle*:— | They | found | her | still weeping. |
| *Prep. with Object:* | This plot | filled | us all | with terror. |
| *Infinitive*:— | I | like | a rascal | to be punished. |
| *Adverb*:— | They | found | the man | asleep. |
| *Clause*:— | We | have made | him | what he is. |

*Note* 1.—The necessity of adding a Complement to certain verbs, in order to make the predication complete, can be seen at once from the example, "I like a rascal to be punished." If you merely say, "I like a rascal," you are saying the opposite to what you intended: for you do not like a rascal, but a rascal *to be punished*, or the *punishment* of a rascal.

*Note* 2.—Observe that when Factitive verbs are used, the complement must be separated from the verb by the object. This is required not only by idiom or custom, but to avoid a possible ambiguity. Thus "to make public confessions" would not convey the same sense as "to make confessions public."

*Note* 3.—In some grammars we hear of the term *Factitive object*. Such a term cannot be used for any kind of complement but nouns; and therefore it is better to include all kinds of complements under a name (Complement) which will apply equally well to all.

**144. Omission of the Relative as Object.**—This occurs in two kinds of sentences—(*a*) When the verb is Transitive; (*b*) when the verb is Intransitive, but followed by a preposition.

This never occurs, however, when the Relative is used in a Continuative sense (see § 127).

(*a*) The books I bought cost ten shillings.
(*b*) The house we lived in has fallen down.

**145. Transitive Verbs used Intransitively.**—There are two ways in which Transitives can become Intransitive:—

(*a*) When the verb is used in such a general sense that no object or objects are thought of in connection with it:—

Men *eat* to preserve life.
A new-born child *sees*, but a kitten is born blind.
He *writes* well (Intr.). He *writes* a good letter (Trans.).

(*b*) When the Reflexive pronoun is omitted:—

He *drew* (himself) near me. He *made* (himself) merry.

The following are common examples of Transitive verbs which have acquired an Intransitive counterpart by omitting the Reflexive pronoun:—

| *Transitive Verb.* | *Intransitive Counterpart.* |
|---|---|
| *Get* you (yourself) gone. | *Get* out of my way. |
| *Give* him a penny. | The shoe *gives*. |
| He *obtained* a place. | This doctrine *obtained* (maintained itself) for a long time. |
| The fire *burnt* up the house. | He *burnt* with rage. |
| Do not *stop* me. | Let us *stop* here a little. |
| They *open* the doors at nine. | School *opens* at ten o'clock. |
| A man *breaks* stones with a hammer. | The day *breaks* at six. |
| The ox *drew* this cart. | He *drew* near to me. |
| *Move* away this stone. | *Move* on a little faster. |
| He *broke up* the meeting. | School *broke up* at three. |
| The mouse *steals* food. | The mouse *steals* into its hole. |

| *Transitive Verb.* | *Intransitive Counterpart.* |
|---|---|
| They *bathed* the child. | Let us *bathe* here. |
| He *rolls* a ball down the hill. | The ball *rolls* down the hill. |
| He *burst* the door open. | The monsoon has *burst.* |
| Bad men *hide* their faults. | Bats *hide* during the day. |
| He *turned* me out of the room. | He *turned* to me and spoke. |
| They *drop* the boat into the water. | Rain *drops* from the sky. |
| They *keep* the boat on the left bank. | The boat *keeps* on the left bank. |
| He *sets* the school in order. | The sun *sets* at six P.M. |
| He must *refrain* his tongue. | He must *refrain* from tears. |
| He *feeds* the horse on grain. | Many men *feed* on rice. |
| He *rested* his horse. | The horse *rested* in the stable. |
| He *lengthened* his journey. | The days begin to *lengthen.* |
| He *spread* his garment. | The mist *spreads* over the earth. |
| The shepherd *gathered* the sheep. | The sheep *gathered* round their shepherd. |
| The wind *dispersed* the clouds. | The clouds *have dispersed* from the sky. |
| He *closed* the business. | The day *closed* at six P.M. |
| The sun *melts* the snow. | The snow *melts* in the sun. |
| He *dashed* down the cup. | He *dashed* out of the room. |

### SECTION 3.—INTRANSITIVE VERBS.

**146. Intransitive Verbs of Complete Predication.**—This is the name given to any Intransitive verb, which makes a complete sense by itself, and does not require any word or words to be added to it for this purpose:—

Rivers *flow.* Winds *blow.* Horses *run,* or *walk,* or *graze,* or *lie down.* Birds *fly.* All animals *sleep.* All animals *die.*

**147. Intransitive Verbs of Incomplete Predication.**—This is the name given to those Intransitive verbs, which do not make a complete sense by themselves, but require a **Complement** to supply what the verb left unsaid (§ 26). (Such verbs are sometimes called Copulative, because they couple one idea with another.)

The Complement to Intransitive verbs may be in the same kinds of form as the Complement to Factitive verbs:—

| | *Subject.* | *Verb.* | *Complement.* |
|---|---|---|---|
| *Noun* | A horse | is | a four-legged animal. |
| | That beggar | turned out | a thief. |
| *Adjective* | The man | has fallen | sick. |
| | The dog | went | mad. |
| *Participle* | The man | appears | pleased. |
| | The stag | continued | running and jumping. |
| *Prep. with Object* | Your coat | is | of many colours. |
| | That book | proved | of no use. |

| | Subject. | Verb. | Complement. |
|---|---|---|---|
| *Infinitive* | The flower | seems | to be fading. |
| | You | appear | to have forgotten me. |
| *Adverb* . | The man | has fallen | asleep. |
| *Clause* . | The results | are | what we expected. |

*Note* 1.—When the Complement comes after an Intransitive verb, it is called a **Subjective Complement**, because it relates to the Subject.

But when it comes after a Factitive verb in the *Active* voice, it is called an **Objective Complement**, because it relates to the Object.

*Note* 2.—The Complement usually stands *after* its verb, but for the sake of emphasis it may be placed *before* it:—

*Strait* is the gate, and *narrow* is the way that leadeth unto life, and *few* there be that find it.—*New Testament.*

*Note* 3.—The same verb, whether Transitive or Intransitive, may in different connections be used either as complete or incomplete predicates:—

| | |
|---|---|
| The world *is* (exists) | (*Comp.*) |
| The world *is round* | (*Incomp.*) |
| They *made* a snow-man | (*Comp.*) |
| They *made* him *king* | (*Incomp.*) |
| The tree *is growing* | (*Comp.*) |
| He *is growing strong*. | (*Incomp.*) |
| The water *filled* the pipe | (*Comp.*) |
| They *filled* the pipe *with water* | (*Incomp.*) |

**148. The Cognate Object.**—An Intransitive verb, though it is never followed by a noun denoting an *outside* or foreign object, may sometimes be followed by a noun *already implied more or less in the verb itself.*

Thus we can say "he has lived a sad *life*," where the noun *life* is implied already in the verb "lived," and is in fact part of its meaning. Such objects are called **cognate** or "kindred," because the noun denoting them is of kindred meaning to that of the verb itself.

There are five different forms of Cognate object:—

(*a*) *Cognate noun formed directly from the verb.*

| | |
|---|---|
| He laughed a hearty *laugh*. | He slept a sound *sleep*. |
| He died a sad *death*. | He prayed an earnest *prayer*. |
| He lived a long *life*. | He sighed a deep *sigh*. |
| He fought a good *fight*. | He sang a fine *song*. |

(*b*) *Cognate noun of similar meaning.*

| | |
|---|---|
| He went a long *way*. | He ran his own *course*. |
| He fought a good *battle*. | It blows a brisk *gale*. |
| He struck a deadly *blow*. | The bells ring a merry *peal*. |

(*c*) *A noun descriptive of the Cognate noun understood.*

They shouted *applause* = they shouted a *shout* of applause.
He served his *apprenticeship* = he served his *service* as an apprentice.
He ran a great *risk* = he ran a *course* of great risk.

He played *the fool* = he played the *part* of a fool.
He looked *daggers* at me = he looked me a *look* of daggers.

(*d*) *An adjective qualifying the Cognate noun understood.*

He shouted his loudest (shout). He ran his fastest (run or pace). He fought his best (fight). She sang her sweetest (song). He breathed his last (breath). He tried his hardest (trial or attempt).

(*e*) *Cognate noun expressed by "it."*

We must fight *it* (= the fight) out to the end.
We have no horse; so we must foot *it* (that is, go the distance on foot).
Lord Angelo dukes *it* (= acts the part of a duke) well.—SHAKSPEARE.

**149. The Reflexive Object.**—In older English, Intransitive verbs were often followed by a Personal pronoun, either reflexive or used reflexively, in the objective case.

A few such examples still occur:—

Hie *thee* home. Fare *thee* well. Haste *thee* away. They sat *them* down. He over-ate *himself*. To over-sleep *oneself*. Vaulting ambition which o'erleaps *itself*.—SHAKSPEARE.

In § 306 it is explained that what we here for convenience' sake called a Reflexive object was in reality a pronoun in the Dative case, like the Indirect object described in § 141, *Note*.

**150. Intransitive Verbs in a Causal sense.**—If an Intransitive verb is used in the sense of causing a thing to be done, it becomes Transitive. Of these there are only a few examples in English:—

| *Intransitive.* | *Causal.* |
|---|---|
| The horse trotted out. | They trotted out the horse (= caused it to trot out). |
| Water boils. | He boils the water. |
| The prisoners walk out. | He walks out the prisoners. |
| A thorn ran into his hand. | He ran a thorn into his hand. |
| That horse will starve. | Do not starve the horse. |
| Drinking freely. | Drinking himself drunk (= making himself drunk by drinking).—1 *Kings* 16, 9. |
| The bell rang twice. | Ring the bell. |
| The kite flew into the air. | He flew the kite. |
| The soldiers march out. | He marches out the soldiers. |
| Wheat grows in the field. | He grows wheat in the field. |
| The boat floated. | He floated the boat. |
| He talks hoarsely. | He talks himself hoarse (= he makes himself hoarse by talking). |

151. There are a few Intransitive verbs, in which the causal sense is indicated by *some change of vowel*.

| *Intransitive.* | *Transitive or Causal.* |
| --- | --- |
| The tree *falls.* | He *fells* the tree with an axe. |
| The sun will *rise* at six. | I cannot *raise* this box. |
| The cow *lies* on the grass. | The man *lays* down his coat. |
| We must not *sit* here. | He *set* the books in order. |
| He will *fare* well. | He will *ferry* me over. |
| The enemy *quails.* | He *quells* the enemy. |

**152. Prepositional Verbs.**—An Intransitive verb can be made Transitive by having a preposition added to it.

Such verbs may be considered to be real Transitives, provided they can be used in the Passive voice.

{We *act on* this rule. (*Active.*)
{This rule is *acted on* by us. (*Passive.*)
{No one *relies on* his word. (*Active.*)
{His word cannot be *relied on.*[1] (*Passive.*)

Observe that when the verb is in the Passive voice, the *on* cannot be parsed as a preposition, since there is no object to it. It must therefore be parsed as part of the verb itself.

*Note* 1.—In prepositional verbs, the preposition is almost always placed after the verb; but "*with*" and "*over*" are often placed before it:—

He *withstood* (stood against, endured) the attack.
He was *overcome* (defeated) by the enemy.
The banks were *overflowed* (inundated) with water.
The field is *overgrown* (covered) with weeds.
The boundary has been *overstepped* (transgressed).

All these verbs, when they are used apart from the preposition, are Intransitive. It is the *preposition which makes them Transitive.*

*Note* 2.—It sometimes happens that the preposition after the Intransitive verb is not expressed, but the verb is none the less followed by an object:—

They *laughed* (at) *him* to scorn.
He *looked* (at) *me* in the face.
Leonidas *fought* (against) *the Persians* at Thermopylæ.
I cannot *sit* (on) that horse.
I cannot *stand* (with-stand) your impertinence.

**153. Summary.**—There are thus two ways in which an Intransitive verb can become Transitive—(1) when it is used in a Causal sense (§ 150); (2) when it is connected with a preposition so closely that the verb, compounded with the preposition, can be made Passive (§ 152).

Similarly, there are two kinds of objects that can come after an Intransitive verb, although the verb itself continues to be Intransitive—(1) the Cognate object (§ 148); (2) the Reflexive or Personal object (§ 149).

---

[1] The phrase *reliable* for *reliable on* has become common. But it is indefensible on any ground but that of custom.

## SECTION 4.—AUXILIARY VERBS.

**154. Auxiliary and Notional Verbs.**—Verbs have usually been subdivided into *two* classes, Transitive and Intransitive, and not, as is done in this book, into *three*, the third of which is Auxiliary. The last is an entirely distinct class.

A Notional verb (Transitive or Intransitive) is one used as a Principal verb to express a full meaning of its own:—

(1) He *has* ten horses.

Here *has* is a Transitive verb, and is used to express the notion of "possession." Now look at the following:—

(2) He *has* been ill to-day.

Here *has* is neither Transitive nor Intransitive, but merely a *tense-forming*, that is, an Auxiliary verb. It has, for the time being, *discarded its proper sense* of "possession," in order to *help* the verb "be" to form a Present Perfect tense. It is not notional, but merely modifies the notion expressed by "be."

The classification of verbs might therefore be restated as follows:—

| | | |
|---|---|---|
| Notional or Principal | Transitive . . | Class I. |
| | Intransitive . . | Class II. |
| Auxiliary . . . . . . | | Class III. |

**155. Uses of Auxiliary Verbs classified.**—The uses of Auxiliary verbs may be classified under two separate headings: (*a*) Tense-forming; (*b*) Mood-forming. It should be understood, however, that the same verb may be used for different auxiliary purposes at different times, just as the same verb may be used Transitively at one time and Intransitively at another.

(*a*) *Tense-forming.*—"*Shall*" and "*will*" are used for forming the **Future** tenses; as "I *shall* go," "he *will* go." "*Be*" is used for forming the **Continuous** (or Imperfect) tenses; as "I *am* going," "I *was* going." "*Have*" is used for forming the **Perfect** tenses; as "I *have* gone," "I *had* gone." "*Have*" and "*be*" together are used for forming the **Perfect Continuous** tenses; as "I *have been* going," "I *had been* going." "*Do*" and "*did*" are used for forming a special kind of **Present** and **Past** tense; as "I *do* not go," "I *did* not go."

(*b*) *Mood-forming.*—"*Do*" is used for forming the **Imperative** mood, when the sentence is negative, as "*do* not come." (Out of this has grown the emphatic affirmative form "*do* come," used colloquially.) "*May*" and "*might*," "*should*," "*would*," are used for making certain forms of the **Subjunctive** mood; as "that he *may* go," "he *should* go," "he *would* go." "*Shall*," "*will*," "*have*," "*be*," "*do*," as has been shown under (*a*), are used for forming various tenses of the **Indicative** mood.

The verb "*be*," assisted by "*have*," "*shall*," "*will*," "*may*," is used for forming the tenses and moods of the *Passive* voice.

*Note.*—From the above it will be seen that Auxiliary verbs not only help Principal verbs, but also help one another. Thus in the Perfect Continuous (Active voice), "I *have been* going," we have two Auxiliaries helping each other to form a single tense. In the Future Perfect Continuous, "I *shall have been* going," we have three Auxiliaries helping one another to form a single tense.

**156. List of Auxiliary Verbs.**—The Auxiliary verbs make up a very small class. If our definition of Auxiliary (viz. a verb that (1) *helps* a Principal verb to form some tense, mood, or voice; and (2) *forgoes its own sense as a Principal verb* for that purpose) is adhered to, the following list is exhaustive:—*have, be, shall, will, may, do*,—only six, all told.

But the smallness of their number is amply compensated by the frequency of their use; for no Transitive or Intransitive verb can be conjugated without them, except in two tenses, the Present and Past Indefinite. In Old as in Mod. English the Present and Past are the only two tenses that are formed by inflexion.

*Note.*—*Can* and *must*, though Defective, are Principal verbs. They are not Auxiliary—(*a*) because they do not help to form any tense, mood, or voice; and (*b*) because they do not discard their meanings as Principal verbs for auxiliary purposes. They are merely Principal verbs very defective in form.

**157.—Auxiliary and Principal.**—The same verb may be an Auxiliary at one time and a Principal at another. This is implied already in the definition, according to which an Auxiliary verb is one that "forgoes its proper sense as a Notional or Principal verb for the purpose of becoming Auxiliary."

To make this point perfectly clear, we will take each of the six verbs named above *seriatim*:—

| | | |
|---|---|---|
| **Have** | I *had* a fine horse . . . . . . . | (*Principal.*) |
| | I *had* gone away . . . . . . . | (*Auxiliary.*) |
| **Be** | The earth *is* (exists). A horse *is* a quadruped | (*Principal.*) |
| | He *was* going. He *is* loved . . . . . | (*Auxiliary.*) |
| **Shall** | You *shall* leave the house (Command, Authority) | (*Principal.*) |
| | I *shall* leave the house (Simple Futurity) . | (*Auxiliary.*) |
| **Will** | I *will* go to-day (Determination) . . . | (*Principal.*) |
| | You *will* go to-day (Simple Futurity) . . | (*Auxiliary.*) |
| **May** | I *may* go (=am permitted to go) . . . | (*Principal.*) |
| | He works that he *may* live (Purpose) . . | (*Auxiliary.*) |

Do { You *did* that work well . . . . (*Principal.*)
{ You *did* indeed work hard . . . . (*Auxiliary.*)

### SECTION 5.—ACTIVE AND PASSIVE VOICES.

**158.** A *Transitive* verb has two voices, the **Active** and the **Passive.**

In the Active voice the person or thing denoted by the Subject is said to *do something to* something else:—

Tom *kills* a snake. (Here the person denoted by the Subject, namely Tom, *does something to* a snake.)

In the Passive voice the person or thing is said to *suffer something from* something else:—

A snake *is killed* by Tom. (Here the thing denoted by the Subject, namely a snake, *suffers something from* Tom.)

Hence Voice may be defined as that form of a Transitive verb which shows whether the agent *does* something to something else, or *suffers* something from something else.

**159.** An *Intransitive* verb is not used in the Passive voice, unless it takes a Cognate object in the Active:—

I have fought the good fight. (*Active.*)
The good fight has been fought by me. (*Passive.*)

Here the subject "fight" does not really *suffer* anything. Hence an Intransitive verb, when it takes a Passive form, is merely aping the Passive voice.

**160.** When a sentence is changed from the Active form to the Passive, the object to the Active verb becomes the subject to the Passive verb.

| *Object to Active Verb.* | *Subject to Passive Verb.* |
|---|---|
| Brutes cannot make *tools.* | *Tools* cannot be made by brutes. |
| Brutes do not possess *hands.* | *Hands* are not possessed by brutes. |

**161. Retained Object.**—Verbs that take *two* objects after them in the Active voice (§ 141) can still retain *one* in the Passive. This object may be either—

(*a*) The Indirect object of the Active verb; as—

| *Active Verb.* | *Passive Verb.* |
|---|---|
| I forgave *him* his fault. | The fault was forgiven *him* by me. |
| We allowed *him* two pounds. | Two pounds were allowed *him* by us. |

Or (*b*) the Direct object of the Active verb; as—

| *Active Verb.* | *Passive Verb.* |
|---|---|
| I forgave him *his fault.* | He was forgiven *his fault* by me. |
| We allowed him *two pounds.* | He was allowed *two pounds* by us. |

*Note.*—It has now been shown that there are five different kinds of objects which can be used with verbs :—

(1) **Direct** (with Trans. verbs).—He taught *Euclid* (§ 141).
(2) **Indirect** (with Trans. verbs).—He taught *his sons* Euclid (§ 141).
(3) **Retained** (with Pass. verbs).—His sons were taught *Euclid* (§ 161).
(4) **Cognate** (with Intrans. verbs).—The fever must run its *course* (§ 148).
(5) **Reflexive** (with Intrans. verbs).—He sat *himself* down (§ 149).

*Note.*—Among these observe that (1) and (4) are Direct objects ; (2) and (5) are Indirect ; (3) is Direct or Indirect, according as the noun or pronoun was Direct or Indirect with the Active verb. "He sat himself down," when grammatically analysed, means "He sat down *for himself*." Avoid the mistake of considering that *sat* is used in a Causal sense—"He *caused himself* to sit down." In Old Eng. the Indirect object was in the Dative case, the Direct in the Accusative.

**162.** Whenever a Factitive verb is changed from the Active voice to the Passive, the Objective Complement becomes a Subjective one.

| *Active voice : Complement to Object.* | *Passive voice : Complement to Subject.* |
|---|---|
| They proclaimed him *king*. | He was proclaimed *king* by them. |
| They did not crown him *king*. | He was not crowned *king* by them. |

**163. Verbs Active in form, but Passive in sense.**—Transitive verbs are sometimes used in a Passive sense without being put into the Passive voice :—

(*a*) Verbs with a Complement :—

The stone *feels* rough (is rough when it is felt).
Honey *tastes* sweet (is sweet when it is tasted).
The milk *smells* sour (is sour when it is smelt).
Your blame *counts* for nothing (is worth nothing when it is counted).
Your composition *reads* well (sounds well when it is read).
The house *does* not *let* (is not taken when it is meant to be let).
The horse *does* not *sell* (is not taken when it is meant to be sold).
That cloth will *wear* thin (will become thin when it is worn).

(*b*) Verbs without a Complement :—

The house *is building* (=is in a state of being built).
The trumpets *are sounding* (=are being sounded).
The cannons *are firing* (=are being fired).
The drums *are beating* (=are being beaten).
The house *is finishing* (=is being finished).
The book *is printing* (=is being printed).
The cows *are milking* (=are being milked).

*Note.*—The generally received and best supported opinion regarding this construction is that what looks like a present participle is, in reality, a gerund, with the preposition *on* or *in* omitted.

This house was three years in *building* (=being built).

Others, however, think that it is a real Active participle used in a Passive sense, like the verbs in examples (*a*).[1]

### SECTION 6.—MOOD, TENSE, NUMBER, AND PERSON.

**164. Mood defined.**—Mood is the form assumed by a verb (either by inflection or with the help of Auxiliaries) for indicating the *mode* or manner in which the action or state denoted by the verb is conceived by the mind.

**165. Names of the Moods.**—There are four Moods, three Finite and one Infinitive :—

(*a*) Three Finite moods :—

1. Indicative, or the mood of **Fact.**
2. Imperative, or the mood of **Volition.**
3. Subjunctive, or the mood of **Supposition.**

(*b*) Infinitive mood.

**166. Characters of the Moods.**—In the Indicative mood we *assert* or *inquire* about something as a *fact ;* as, "he comes," "he came," "he will come," "will he come ?"

In the Imperative mood we *command* or *advise* an action ; as, "come thou," or "come."

In the Subjunctive mood we *suppose* an action ; as, "if he come or should come."

The Infinitive mood expresses some action or state without reference to number or person ; as, "to come."

"Infinitive" means unlimited,—not limited by number or person.

**167. Number and Person.**—The number and person of a Finite verb depend upon the nature of its Subject.

| | |
|---|---|
| *Number* | If the subject is Singular, the verb must be Singular ; as, Rain *is* falling.<br>If the subject is Plural, the verb must be Plural ; as, Raindrops *are* falling. |
| *Person* | If the subject is in the First person, the verb must be in the First person ; as, I love. We come.<br>If the subject is in the Second person, the verb must be in the Second person ; as, Thou lovest. You come.<br>If the subjeet is in the Third person, the verb must be in the Third person ; as, He loves. The teacher *has* come. |

---

[1] The word ending in *-ing* must certainly be a participle in such colloquialisms as "I want a button *sewing on.*" In such a sentence as "The wall is rapidly building," *building* must certainly be parsed as a participle, as otherwise the adverb *rapidly* could not be parsed.

Hence arises the following rule:—*A Finite verb must be in the same number and person as its Subject.*

*Note.*—All nouns and noun-equivalents take verbs in the Third person. All pronouns excepting the First Personal and the Second Personal take verbs in the Third person.

**168. Tense defined.**—Tense is the form assumed by a verb (either by inflection or with the help of Auxiliary verbs) for indicating either (*a*) the *time* to which an event is referred, or (*b*) the *degree of completeness* ascribed to an event at the time of its occurrence.

The verb may tell you:—

(1) That an action *is done* at the **Present** time; as, "he sees a star."

(2) That an action *was done* in the **Past** time; as, "he saw a star."

(3) That an action *will be done* in the **Future** time; as, "he will see a star."

A verb, then, has three main times or tenses, viz. the Present, the Past, and the Future.

**169.** To each tense there are four different forms:—

I. **Indefinite**; which denotes Present, Past, or Future time in its simplest form, nothing being said as to the degree of completeness attaching to the action or state; as, "I love," "I loved," "I shall love."

II. **Continuous**; which denotes that the event (in Present, Past, or Future time) is still *continuing*, and is not yet completed; as, "I am loving," "I was loving," "I shall be loving."

*Note.*—This tense is sometimes called the **Imperfect**, because it denotes an event which is imperfect or not completed.

III. **Perfect**; which denotes that the event (in Present, Past, or Future time) is in a completed or *perfect* state; as, "I have loved," "I had loved," "I shall have loved."

IV. **Perfect Continuous**; which combines the meanings of the two preceding forms; as, "I have been loving," "I had been loving," "I shall have been loving."

## SECTION 7.—INDICATIVE MOOD.

### *Forms of the Tenses, Indicative Mood.*

**170.** The three Tenses and twelve forms of a verb in the Indicative Mood are shown in the following table:—

### I.—*Active Voice.*

| *Form.* | *Present Tense.* | *Past Tense.* | *Future Tense.* |
|---|---|---|---|
| 1. *Indefinite* | I love | I loved | I shall love |
| 2. *Continuous* | I am loving | I was loving | I shall be loving |
| 3. *Perfect* | I have loved | I had loved | I shall have loved |
| 4. *Perfect Continuous* | I have been loving | I had been loving | I shall have been loving |

### II.—*Passive Voice.*

| *Form.* | *Present Tense.* | *Past Tense.* | *Future Tense.* |
|---|---|---|---|
| 1. *Indefinite* | I am loved | I was loved | I shall be loved |
| 2. *Continuous* | I am being loved | I was being loved | (*Wanting*) |
| 3. *Perfect* | I have been loved | I had been loved | I shall have been loved |
| 4. *Perfect Continuous* | (*Wanting*) | (*Wanting*) | (*Wanting*) |

**171.** The Present, Past, and Future tenses (Indefinite) are declined in the following form, for all numbers and persons:—

### I.—*Active Voice.*

#### *Present Tense.*

| | *Singular.* | *Plural.* |
|---|---|---|
| 1*st Person* | I love | We love |
| 2*nd* ,, | Thou lovest | Ye or you love |
| 3*rd* ,, | He loves or loveth | They love |

#### *Past Tense.*

| | *Singular.* | *Plural.* |
|---|---|---|
| 1*st Person* | I loved | We loved |
| 2*nd* ,, | Thou lovedst | Ye or you loved |
| 3*rd* ,, | He loved | They loved |

#### *Future Tense.*

| | *Singular.* | *Plural.* |
|---|---|---|
| 1*st Person* | I shall love | We shall love |
| 2*nd* ,, | Thou wilt love | Ye or you will love |
| 3*rd* ,, | He will love | They will love |

*N.B.*—(1) The Singular forms of the Second person (thou lovest, thou lovedst, thou wilt love) are now seldom used except in poetry. They have been superseded by the Plural forms (you love, you loved, and you will love), which, though Plural in fact, are used in a Singular sense as well as in a Plural sense; as, "Have you come, my son?" "Have you," being addressed to "son," is used in a Singular sense, and may be parsed as Singular.

(2) The form "he loveth" is now seldom used except in poetry.

### II.—*Passive Voice.*

#### *Present Tense.*

| | *Singular.* | *Plural.* |
|---|---|---|
| 1*st Person* | I am loved | We are loved |
| 2*nd* ,, | Thou art loved | Ye or you are loved |
| 3*rd* ,, | He is loved | They are loved |

*Past Tense.*

| | *Singular.* | *Plural.* |
|---|---|---|
| 1*st Person* | I was loved | We were loved |
| 2*nd* ,, | Thou wast loved | Ye or you were loved |
| 3*rd* ,, | He was loved | They were loved |

*Future Tense.*

| | *Singular.* | *Plural.* |
|---|---|---|
| 1*st Person* | I shall be loved | We shall be loved |
| 2*nd* ,, | Thou wilt be loved | Ye or you will be loved |
| 3*rd* ,, | He will be loved | They will be loved |

**172. Do** and **Did.**—The Present Indefinite in the Active voice can also be formed by "*do*," and the Past by "*did*."

*Present Tense.*

| | *Singular.* | *Plural.* |
|---|---|---|
| 1*st Person* | I do love | We do love |
| 2*nd* ,, | Thou dost love | Ye or you do love |
| 3*rd* ,, | He does love | They do love |

*Past Tense.*

| | *Singular.* | *Plural.* |
|---|---|---|
| 1*st Person* | I did love | We did love |
| 2*nd* ,, | Thou didst love | Ye or you did love |
| 3*rd* ,, | He did love | They did love |

This form is used for three different purposes:—

(*a*) For the sake of emphasis; as, "I *do* love," "I *did* love."

(*b*) For the sake of bringing in the word "not"; as "I *do not* love" (which is better than saying "I love not"), "I *did not* love" (which is better than saying "I loved not").

(*c*) For the sake of asking a question; as, "*Does* he love?" "Why *did* he love?" "*Did* he not love?"

**173. Has come, is come.**—These two forms appear to be merely different, and at the same time equivalent, ways of expressing a Present Perfect tense. But they are not quite equivalent in sense. In the former *the time of the action* is prominent; in the latter *the state of the agent.* The former alone gives a Present Perfect tense.

"The flower *is* faded."[1] In what state is the flower? Faded. No prominence is given to *the time of the fading.* The verb "is" is here not an Auxiliary, but an Intransitive verb of Incomplete Predication, to which the participle "faded" is complement.

"The flower *has* faded." By what time was the fading of the flower completed? By the present time.[1] The verb "has"

[1] It is therefore incorrect to say (as is commonly done) that "has come" and "is come" are equivalent, and that the use of "is" and "was" for "has" and "had" is limited to verbs of motion. In the Tudor period

is here an Auxiliary, which with the word "faded" helps to form the Present Perfect tense of the verb "to fade."

**174. Shall and Will.**—These (as the student has learnt already) are the two Auxiliary verbs by means of which the Future tense is formed in both voices.

One of the puzzles in English to a beginner is to know when to use "*shall*" and when to use "*will*."

With a view to clearing up this matter it should be understood that there are *three* senses in which the future tense can be used :—

(*a*) To express *merely future time*, and nothing more.
(*b*) To combine future time with an implied *command*.
(*c*) To combine future time with an implied *intention*.

(*a*) *Merely future time.*

When nothing but future time is intended—*mere futurity*, without any idea of command or intention being mixed up with it—*shall* must be used for the *First* person, and *will* for the *Second* and *Third* persons, as below :—

| | *Singular.* | *Plural.* |
|---|---|---|
| 1*st Person* | I *shall* go | We *shall* go |
| 2*nd* ,, | Thou *wilt* go | You *will* go |
| 3*rd* ,, | He *will* go | They *will* go |

In these persons *shall* and *will* are strictly *tense-forming*, that is, Auxiliary verbs (see §§ 155, 157).

(*b*) *An Implied Command, Promise, or Threat.*

Whenever we desire to express, not merely future time, but some *command*, or *promise*, or *threat* in addition, *shall* is put for *will* in the Second and Third persons ;[1] as—

You *shall* be hanged (by some one's command).
You *shall* receive your prize to-morrow (promise).
If you do this, you *shall* be hanged (threat).

In these examples, the *shall* is not a tense-forming or Auxiliary verb, but a Principal one (see §§ 155, 157).

(*c*) *An Implied Intention.*

When the speaker wishes to express some intention of his own, then *will* is put for *shall* in the First person :—

I *will* call on you to-day, and I *shall* then say good-bye.

---

the use of the verb *to be* with Past participles was much more common than it is now. Shakspeare has such phrases as—"Is stolen away," "are marched forth," "are rid," "is entered into."

[1] In Old. Eng. *sceal* (shall) means "I must," "I owe," "I am liable for" ; and this sense is maintained, wherever this verb is used in the Second and Third persons. *Will* in Old Eng. means to intend or desire ; and this sense is maintained, whenever this verb is used in the First person. But these senses are not maintained, when *shall* is used in the First person, and *will* in the Second and Third. The verbs have then become Auxiliary, that is, they have discarded their original meanings in order to help other verbs to express future time.

Here *will* denotes the *intention* of calling, while *shall* denotes *merely future time.* Therefore *will* is a Principal verb, and *shall* is an Auxiliary.

## SECTION 8.—IMPERATIVE MOOD.

**175.** The **Imperative** mood is used only in the Present tense, and only in the Second person :—

| *Singular.* | *Plural.* |
|---|---|
| Speak, or speak thou. | Speak, or speak you, or speak ye. |

**176.** To express our will in connection with the *First* or *Third* person we either (*a*) use the Transitive verb *let*, which is itself the Second person (Singular or Plural) of the Imperative mood of the verb "to let," or (*b*) we employ the Subjunctive mood :—

| | | *Singular.* | *Plural.* |
|---|---|---|---|
| (*a*) | 1*st Person* | Let me speak | Let us speak |
| | 3*rd* ,, | Let him speak | Let them speak. |

(*b*) Every soldier *kill* his prisoners.—SHAKSPEARE.
Thither our path lies ; *wind we* up the height.—BROWNING.

The Third person of the Subjunctive occurs in the common phrase *suffice it*, which means "let it suffice," "let it be sufficient" :—

*Suffice it* to say that all the prisoners were acquitted.

**177.** The chief uses of the Imperative mood are to express (*a*) *command*, (*b*) *precept*, or (*c*) *entreaty* :—

(*a*) *Command* :—

*Speak*,—or I fire.
*Awake*, *arise*, or *be* for ever fallen.—MILTON.

(*b*) *Precept* or *Invitation* :—

*Go* to the ant, thou sluggard ; *consider* her ways and *be* wise.
—*Old Testament.*

(*c*) *Entreaty* or *Prayer* :—

*Give* us this day our daily bread, and *forgive* us our trespasses, as we forgive them that trespass against us.—*Lord's Prayer.*

**178.** When the verb is negative, that is, prohibitive, the Imperative is now formed by the Auxiliary "*do*."

| *Older Form.* | *Present Form.* |
|---|---|
| Fear not. | *Do* not fear. |
| Taste not that food. | *Do* not taste that food. |

*Note.*—Sometimes, even when the verb is affirmative, the Imperative is formed by "do," in order to give more emphasis to an entreaty. This, however, occurs only in colloquial English.

*Do* leave off making that noise.
*Do* help me to lift this box.

**179.** The Imperative mood is sometimes used to express a **Supposition**:—

*Take care* of the pence, and the pounds will take care of themselves (=If you take care of the pence, the pounds will, etc.).
*Resist* the devil, and he will flee from you (=If you resist the devil, he will flee, etc.).

**180.** Sometimes, but very rarely, the Imperative mood is used **absolutely**; see § 27 (*c*).

A large number of men, *say* a hundred, are working on the railroad.
*Behold*, this dreamer cometh.—*Old Testament.*

## SECTION 9.—SUBJUNCTIVE MOOD.

**181.** The **Subjunctive** mood is so called, because it is generally *subjoined* to some other sentence, and seldom stands alone.

*Note.*—It stands alone, only when it expresses a *wish*; see below, § 186 (2). It cannot be used either to assert a fact or to inquire about one; that is, it cannot take the place of the Indicative mood. The Indicative, however (according to the idiom now in force), can, and frequently does, take the place of the Subjunctive. In fact, the tendency of Modern English is to get rid of the Subjunctive.

**182.** The Present, Past, and Future tenses (Indefinite) are declined as follows in the Active voice:—

*Present Tense.*

| | *Singular.* | *Plural.* |
|---|---|---|
| 1*st Person* | If I love | If we love |
| 2*nd* ,, | If thou love (*not lovest*) | If you love |
| 3*rd* ,, | If he love (*not loves*) | If they love |

*Past Tense.*

| | *Singular.* | *Plural.* |
|---|---|---|
| 1*st Person* | If I loved | If we loved |
| 2*nd* ,, | If thou lovedst | If you loved |
| 3*rd* ,, | If he loved | If they loved |

*Future Tense.*

| | *Singular.* | *Plural.* |
|---|---|---|
| 1*st Person* | If I should love | If we should love |
| 2*nd* ,, | If thou shouldst love | If ye or you should love |
| 3*rd* ,, | If he should love | If they should love |

But the forms *thou love, he love* are getting more and more out of use; and the forms of the Indicative mood are now generally used in their place; as, "if thou lovest" (instead of "*if thou love*"); "if he loves" (instead of "*if he love*").

**183.** The verb "*to be*" takes the following forms in the Subjunctive mood:—

*Present Tense.*

| | *Singular.* | *Plural.* |
|---|---|---|
| 1*st Person* | If I be | If we be |
| 2*nd* ,, | If thou be | If ye or you be |
| 3*rd* ,, | If he be | If they be |

*Past Tense.*

| | *Singular.* | *Plural.* |
|---|---|---|
| 1*st Person* | If I were | If we were |
| 2*nd* ,, | If thou wert | If ye or you were |
| 3*rd* ,, | If he were | If they were |

*Future Tense.*

| | *Singular.* | *Plural.* |
|---|---|---|
| 1*st Person* | If I should be | If we should be |
| 2*nd* ,, | If thou shouldst be | If ye or you should be |
| 3*rd* ,, | If he should be | If they should be |

The forms of the Past and Future tenses are still in common use. The forms of the Present tense are not so common, and those of the Indicative mood are sometimes used instead of them.

**184.** The forms for the Continuous and Perfect tenses in the Active voice are shown below :—

| | *Continuous.* | *Perfect.* |
|---|---|---|
| *Present* | If I be loving | If I have loved |
| *Past* | If I were loving | If I had loved |
| *Future* | If I should be loving | If I should have loved |

**185.** In the Passive voice the Indefinite and the Perfect are the only tenses of the Subjunctive mood which are in ordinary use :—

| | *Indefinite.* | *Perfect.* |
|---|---|---|
| *Present* | If I be loved | If I have been loved |
| *Past* | If I were loved | If I had been loved |
| *Future* | If I should be loved | If I should have been loved |

*The Uses of the Subjunctive Mood.*

**186.** The Indicative mood expresses *a fact;* the Imperative mood expresses *an order;* the Subjunctive mood expresses *a purpose, a wish, a condition,* or *a doubt,* anything rather than a fact.

(1) *A Purpose.*

In this case the verb in the Subjunctive mood is preceded by the conjunction *that* or *lest* (lest = that not). The Auxiliary verbs "*may*" and "*might*" are used after "*that,*" and "*should*" after "*lest.*"

| | *Indicative.* | *Subjunctive: Purpose.* |
|---|---|---|
| *Present* or *Future* | I give you a prize, . . | that you *may work* well again. |
| | I shall keep your book, . | lest you *should lose* it. / that you *may* not *lose* it. |
| *Past* | I gave you a prize, . . | that you *might work* well again. |
| | I kept your book, . . | lest you *should lose* it. / that you *might* not *lose* it. |

*Note.*—In the Tudor period, and somewhat beyond it, the Subjunctive was commonly expressed without the help of an Auxiliary:—

Love not sleep, lest thou *come* to poverty.—*Old Testament.*
See that all *be* present, when he comes.
Buy us a little food, that we *die* not.—*Old Testament.*
Speak to my brother, that he *divide* the inheritance with me.—*New Testament.*

### (2) *A Wish or Order.*

Thy kingdom *come*, thy will *be* done.
*May* he live long and see not the grave!
I wish that he *were* as clever as his sister.
God *save* the queen. Long *live* the king.
Far *be* it from me to say anything false.
My sentence is that the prisoner *be* hanged.

### (3) *Condition and its Consequence.*

When the verb expresses a *condition*, it is generally preceded by the conjunction "*if.*" The verb denoting the *consequence* is expressed by the auxiliary "*would.*"

| | *First Sentence: Condition.* | *Second Sentence: Consequence.* |
|---|---|---|
| *Present* or *Future* | If he *should meet* me, | he *would know* me at once. |
| | If I *were* in his place, | I *would* or *should pay* the money. |
| *Past* | If he *had met* me, | he *would have known* me. |
| | If I *had been* in his place, | I *would have paid* the money. |

Sometimes the *if* is left out. In this case the *should*, or the *had*, or the *were* must be placed before its subject:—

| | | |
|---|---|---|
| *Present* or *Future* | *Should* he *meet* me, | he *would know* me at once. |
| | *Were* I in his place, | I *would pay* the money. |
| *Past* | *Had* he *met* me, | he *would have known* me. |
| | *Had* I *been* in his place, | I *would have paid* the money. |

Sometimes the Conditional sentence is left out or understood, and only the Consequent sentence is expressed:—

He *would* never agree to that ("if you asked him," understood).
He *would* be very thankful to you for this kindness ("if you were to do him the kindness," understood).

### (4) *A Doubt or Supposition.*

A verb in the Subjunctive mood, preceded by some conjunction or conjunctive pronoun, implies some *doubt* or *supposition.*

I will not let thee go, except thou *bless* me.—*Old Test.*
Murder, *though* it *have* no tongue, will speak.
When I ask her if she *love* me.—TENNYSON.
Blow till thou *burst* thy wind.—SHAKSPEARE.
*Whether* he *allow* me or not, I will go to him.
*Provided* he *confess* his fault, I will pardon him.
*Unless* he *consent*, we can do nothing.
Whoever he *be*, he shall not go unpunished.

*Note.*—The Subjunctive mood is not always preceded by a conjunction to express a doubt:—

"*Come* weal, *come* woe, by Bruce's side,"
Replied the chief, "will Donald bide."

## Section 10.—Infinitive Mood.

**187. Infinitive defined.**—The Infinitive is that part of a verb which names the action, without reference to any doer, and is therefore not limited by person or by number.

It is called Infinitive or Infinite, because it is not finite, that is, not limited by person or number. It cannot be attached to a subject, so as to make an assertion or sentence.

It is a mistake, however, to say that the Infinitive is "unlimited by time"; for it has separate forms for denoting past and present:—

(1) *Present* or *Indefinite.*—He seems *to work* hard.
(2) *Past* or *Perfect.*—He seems *to have worked* hard.

**188. The use of "to."**—In Old English there were two separate forms:—

The Simple or Noun-Infinitive—*drinc-an.*
The Dative or Gerundial Infinitive—*tō drinc-anne.*

As time went on, both the suffixes (*-an* and *-anne*) dropped off, and the "*to*" (a prep. followed by a Dative), which originally belonged only to the Gerundial Infinitive, was given to the Simple also. So we have now one form for both uses:—

Simple or Noun-Infinitive—*to drink.*
Gerundial Infinitive—*to drink.*

**189. Infinitive without "to."**—The preposition "to" is not an essential part of the Infinitive; for in Old English the Noun-Infinitive was formed without it. Nor is "to" even now a necessary sign of the Infinitive; for it is not used in the following contexts:—

(*a*) After verbs denoting some kind of perception:—*hear, see, feel, know, watch, behold, observe, perceive:*—

I heard him *speak.* I saw him *come.* I felt his hand *touch* me. I have known him *laugh.* I watched him *go.* I beheld, or observed, or perceived the fish *rise.*

(*b*) After the verbs *do, may, shall, will,* when they are used as Auxiliaries:—

He did not *go.* He works that he may *live.* I shall *go.* He will *go.* Do not *go* away.

(*c*) After the verbs *may, shall, will,* when they are used as

Principal verbs, and after the Principal verbs—*can*, *must*, *please*, *let*, *dare*, *need*, *make*, *bid* :—

You may *go*. He shall *be* punished. I will *see* you once more. You can *go*. You must *go*. Please *come* here. He let me *go*. I dare not *go*. You need not *go*. He made me *laugh*. He bids me *come*.

*Note.*—The "to" is expressed after *dare*, when the sentence is affirmative: "He dares to disobey me."

(*d*) The "to" can be left out after the adjective "better":—

Better *be* with the dead.—SHAKSPEARE.
(= *To be* with the dead (would be) better.)
Better *dwell* in the midst of alarms.—COWPER.

(*e*) The "*to*" is also left out after the verb "had," in such phrases as "had better," "had rather," "had sooner," "had as soon . . . as."

You had better not *remain* here.
I had rather *take* this than that.
I had sooner *run* than *walk*.
I had as soon *run* as *walk*.

*Note.*—"Had" is here used in a Subjunctive sense = would have. "I had better not remain here," means "I would have (it) better not to remain here"; that is, "It would be better for me not to remain."

(*f*) The "*to*" is left out after the conjunction "than," especially when it can be supplied from another clause:—

He is better able *to walk* than *run*.

(*g*) The "*to*" is left out after the prepositions "but" and "than,"[1] provided it is preceded by the verb "*do*":—

He *did* nothing but *laugh* (= to laugh).
He *did* nothing else than *laugh*.

*The two kinds of Infinitive.*

**190.** There are, as we have shown in § 188, two kinds of Infinitive, the forms of which are identical, though their uses are so different as to represent different parts of speech:—

I. The Noun-Infinitive (sometimes called the Simple).

II. The Gerundial or Qualifying Infinitive.

*Note.*—If we look only to the *form* of the Infinitive, the name "Simple" is limited to those Infinitives which are not preceded by "*to*." But if we look to the *syntactical value*, the name "Simple" must be extended to all Infinitives, whether preceded by "*to*" or not, that do the work of a *noun*; and the name "Gerundial" must be given only to those that do the work of an Adjective or Adverb.

**191.** The Noun-Infinitive may be used for any purpose for which an ordinary noun is used, viz. (*a*) as Subject to a verb;

---

[1] The prepositional character of *than* is shown below in § 231.

(*b*) as Object to a verb; (*c*) as Complement to a verb; (*d*) as Object to certain prepositions (rare); or (*e*) as a form of exclamation. It has hence been called, though not very commonly, "the Substantive Mood."

(*a*) Subject to a verb:—

*To err* (=error) is human; *to forgive* (=forgiveness) is divine.

(*b*) Object to a verb:—

They expect *to succeed* (=success).
A good man does not fear *to die* (=death).

(*c*) Complement to a verb:—

He appears *to be* a wise man. (*Intransitive.*)
They ordered him *to be punished*. (*Factitive.*)

*Note.*—Most grammarians hold that such a verb as *ordered* is Factitive, and *to be punished* its Complement. It would be equally correct, however, to say that *ordered* is not Factitive, but merely Transitive, having *to be punished* as its Direct object and *him* as the Indirect. The sentence thus parsed would be, "They ordered punishment for him."

(*d*) Object to the prepositions named below:—

He was *about* (=near) *to die* (=death).
They came *for to see* (=for seeing) the sport.
They desired nothing *except* or *but to succeed* (=success).
He did nothing else *than laugh*.

*Note.*—Such a phrase as "for to see" is now obsolete, though it occurs in the New Testament. The "for" is now always omitted, and the Noun-Infinitive then becomes the Gerundial.[1]

(*e*) As a form of exclamation:—

Foolish fellow! *to suppose* that he could be pardoned!

*Note.*—In this construction the Infinitive is absolute (§ 27, *b*).

**192.** The Dative or Gerundial Infinitive can be used (*a*) to qualify a verb, (*b*) to qualify a noun, (*c*) to qualify an adjective, (*d*) to introduce a parenthesis:—

(*a*) To qualify a verb, in the sense of *purpose*, *cause*, *occasion*, or *result*:—

He came *to see* (for the purpose of seeing) the sport. (*Purpose.*)
He wept *to see* (because of seeing) that sight. (*Cause.*)
I shall be interested *to hear* what is decided. (*Occasion.*)
He worked hard only *to be* (with the result of being) defeated at last. (*Result.*)

*Note.*—This Infinitive is also used in the sense of purpose for forming a periphrastic future with the help of the verb *go*.

I am *going to have* my dinner=I *shall* now *have* my dinner.

---

[1] The phrase "for to see" came into use during the Middle period of English, in imitation of the French idiom "pour" (=for), followed by an Infinitive.

(*b*) To qualify a noun, in the sense of *purpose*, or *simple futurity* :—

*Purpose* :—

A house *to let*. (*Attributive use.* See § 95.)
This house is *to let*. This house (is) to let. (*Predicative use.*)

Give him a chair *to sit on*. (*Attributive use.*)
Your condition is *to be pitied*. (*Predicative use.*)

*Note.*—Whenever the verb is Intransitive, as "*sit*," it must always be followed by a preposition. We cannot say "a chair *to sit*." In the phrase "a chair to sit on" the pronoun *it* is understood after *on* as its object.

*Simple futurity* :—

He will be rewarded in the world *to come*.
Those days have passed, never *to return*.
This house is *to be let* from Monday next.

*Note.*—Here *to be let* is not equivalent in meaning to *to let*. The former has a distinctly future sense. The latter merely indicates purpose. Cf. the line in Pope :—

Man never is, but always *to be* blest.

(*c*) To qualify an adjective, in the sense of *respect* or *purpose* :—

Quick *to hear* and slow *to speak*.

'Quick" in what respect or for what purpose? To hear. "Slow" in what respect or for what purpose? To speak.

(*d*) To introduce a **Parenthesis**; that is, a phrase thrust into the middle of a sentence by way of comment on something said :—

I am,—*to tell* you the truth,—quite tired of this work.
They were thunderstruck,—so *to speak*,—on hearing this news.

*Note.*—In (*a*) and (*c*) the Gerundial Infinitive does the work of an adverb. In (*b*) it does the work of an adjective. In (*d*) it is absolute (see § 27, *b*).

### SECTION 11.—PARTICIPLES.

**193.** The forms of the different Participles are as shown below :—

*Transitive Verbs.*

| | *Active Voice.* | *Passive Voice.* |
|---|---|---|
| *Present or Continuous* | Loving | Being loved |
| *Past Indefinite* . . | (*Wanting*) | Loved |
| *Past Perfect* . . | Having loved | Having been loved |

*Intransitive Verbs.*

| | |
|---|---|
| *Present or Continuous* . . | Fading |
| *Past Indefinite* . . . . | Faded |
| *Past Perfect* . . . . | Having faded |

*Note* 1.—The form *loving* stands for both Present and Continuous participles. These are not the same in meaning :—

(*a*) *Hearing* this he was much surprised. (*Pres.*)
(*b*) He went away *sorrowing*. (*Cont.*)

In (*a*) the action is completed, not continuous. In (*b*) it is continuous.

*Note* 2.—There is no Future Participle in English. Futurity can be expressed by the Gerundial Infinitive, as "the world *to come*" (see § 192, *b*), or by a periphrasis, as "about (*prep.*) to fall" (*Noun Infin.*), "going to see" (*Gerund. Infin.*), "going to be beaten" (*Ger. Infin.*).

**194. Double Character of Participles.**—A Participle has two distinct functions, and can be defined as that part of a verb which may be used either (*a*) for helping to form a tense, or (*b*) as an adjective for qualifying some noun or noun-equivalent.

I. *As part of a tense.*

**195.** The student will have seen already that many of the tenses of English verbs are formed with the help of the Past or Present Participle.

Thus all the tenses of the Passive voice are formed out of the verb "to be" followed by the Past Participle; as, "I am loved," "I was loved," "I shall be loved."

Again, all the Continuous tenses in the Active voice are formed out of the verb "to be," followed by the Present Participle; as, "I am loving," "I was loving," "I shall be loving."

Again, the Perfect tenses in the Active voice are formed out of the verb "to have," followed by the Past Participle; as, "I have loved," "I had loved," "I shall have loved."

II. *As an Adjective.*[1]

**196.** A Participle, when it is an adjective, belongs to the class of Descriptive (§ 83). Like other such adjectives, it can (*a*) qualify a noun, (*b*) be qualified by an adverb, (*c*) admit of degrees of comparison, (*d*) be used as a noun:—

(*a*) *Being tired* of work, *the men* went home.
(*b*) The man was picked up in an *almost dying* state.
(*c*) This flower is *more faded* than that.
(*d*) { I am much pleased with my *surroundings*.
None are so soon forgotten as *the dead*. }

**197.** Since a Participle is a verb as well as an adjective, it can take an Object, which may be of five kinds (§ 161):—

[1] To show how completely a Participle can assume the function of an adjective, there are instances in which it forgoes its verb-character altogether.

*Astonishing* to any one. *Disturbing* to any one. *Surprising* to any one.

When the words italicised are used as verbs, they are Transitive, and do not allow the prep. *to* to come between them and their object. We could not say, "This astonishes *to* me, or disturbs *to* me, or surprises *to* me."

Having shot *the tiger*, he returned home. (*Direct Obj.*)
He is busy, teaching *his sons* Greek. (*Indirect Obj.*)
Having been taught *Greek*, he was a good scholar. (*Retained Obj.*)
We saw him fighting a hard *battle*. (*Cognate Obj.*)
Having sat *himself* down, he began to eat. (*Reflexive Obj.*)

**198. Past Indefinite.**—The use of such participles depends upon whether the verb is Transitive or Intransitive :—

(*a*) If the verb is *Transitive*, the Past Indefinite Participle is never used in the Active voice, but only in the Passive :—

This much-*praised* man proved to be a rogue.
Gold is a metal *dug* out of the earth.

(*b*) If the verb is *Intransitive*, the Past Indefinite is not used at all in most verbs. But whenever it is used—(a matter depending entirely on custom), it must *precede* its noun, and not follow it :—

The *faded* rose. A *failed* candidate. A *retired* officer. The *returned* soldier. The *fallen* city. The *risen* sun. A *withered* flower. A *departed* guest.

If the speaker or writer desires to place the Past Participle of an Intransitive verb *after* its noun, he must insert the Relative pronoun and change the participle into a Finite verb; as—

The horse of Mr. A., *proceeded* to America, is for sale. (This is wrong. The sentence should be—"The horse of Mr. A., *who has proceeded* to America, is for sale.")

But the Past Participle of an Intransitive verb is sometimes put *after* its noun *in poetry*.

A Daniel *come* to judgment.—SHAKSPEARE.
With Atë by his side *come* hot from hell.—SHAKSPEARE.
Mourn for the brave—the brave that are no more,
All *sunk* beneath the wave, hard by their native shore.—COWPER.

Even in prose the Past Participle of an Intransitive verb is sometimes, *but very rarely*, placed after its noun :—

In times *past*=in times which have passed.
He is a man *descended* from a high family.

**199.** The Past Participle of verbs is sometimes used to express some *permanent habit*, *state*, or *character* :—

A well-*read* man=a man who has read much and read well.
A well-*behaved* man=a man whose habitual behaviour is good.
An out-*spoken* man=a man who habitually speaks out his mind.
A *retired* man=a man who dislikes appearing in public.
A *mistaken* man=one who errs by habit or in some specific case.

From this use of the Past Participle has arisen a large class of Adjectives, which are formed from nouns by adding "*ed*" to the end of the noun.

An evil-*heart*-ed man. A *talent*-ed man. A *land*-ed proprietor. A long-*tail*-ed ape. A smooth-*skin*-ned cat. His *saint*-ed mother. A red-*colour*-ed rose. A rough-*face*-d youth. A *hood*-ed snake. A long-*leg*-ged spider. A purple-*crest*-ed helmet. A many-*page*-d book. A long-*arm*-ed monkey. A thickly *wood*-ed hill. A noble-*mind*-ed man. A warm-*blood*-ed animal.

**200. Meanings implied in Participles.**—Participles must be parsed as Verbal Adjectives qualifying their nouns. But sometimes there is a further *meaning* implied in them, which can be more fully expressed by changing the participial phrase into a clause.

The implied meanings are (*a*) Time, (*b*) Cause or Reason, (*c*) Condition, (*d*) Concession or Contrast.

(*a*) *Time.*

*Walking* along the street (=*while* I was walking), I met a friend.
*Having met* my friend (=*after* I had met my friend), I went back with him to his house.

(*b*) *Cause or Reason.*

*Being* tired with the toil (=*because* he was tired), he sat down to rest.
The letter, *having been addressed* (=*because* it was addressed) to the wrong house, never reached me.

(*c*) *Condition.*

*Turning* to the left (=*if* you turn to the left), you will find the place you want.

(*d*) *Concession or Contrast* (rare).

*Admitting* (=though I admit) what you say, I still think that you made a mistake.
He *being* dead (=although he is dead), yet speaketh.—*New Testament.*

## SECTION 12.—GERUNDS AND VERBAL NOUNS.

**201.** A **Gerund** has four forms—two for the Active voice and two for the Passive.

| | *Active.* | *Passive.* |
|---|---|---|
| *Present or Continuous* | Loving | Being loved |
| *Perfect* . . . | Having loved | Having been loved |

**202.** The *forms* of a Gerund, then, are the same as those of a Participle, and both are parts of a verb. What, then, is the difference? A Gerund is a kind of *Noun;* but a Participle is a kind of *Adjective.* So in spite of the resemblance in *form,* they are quite distinct in *nature.*[1]

[1] In some books the Gerund is called a Participial noun. This name should be avoided, since a Noun is one part of speech and a Participle is another.

The reason of the resemblance in form is a matter of history. In Old English the *forms* of the Verbal Adjective and Verbal Noun were quite distinct. The suffix *-ing* originally belonged to the latter only.

Participle . . . *Writ-ende*, or *-inde*, or *-and*.
Verbal noun . . *Writ-ung*, or *writ-ing*.

In later English the suffix *-inde* took the form of *-ing*, while *-ende* and *-and* died out; and *-ung* became obsolete. Hence we have now only one form instead of two for the two parts of speech.

Participle . . . . . . *Writing*.
Verbal noun . . . . . *Writing*.

**203. Gerund defined.**—A Gerund is that part of a verb which, if the verb is Intransitive, has the function of a noun only, but if the verb is Transitive, retains the function of a verb also, and can be followed by an object in the same way as if it were a Finite verb:—

Fond of *sleeping* . . . (*Noun-function only.*)
Fond of *hunting* foxes . . (*Noun- and verb-function combined.*)

In point of *function* there is no difference between a Gerund and an Infinitive. Either may be correctly defined as "that part of a verb which names the action, without naming the doer." Both are Abstract nouns. The difference between them is not in function, but in *form*; observe the suffix *-ing*. They differ also in syntactical usage; for a Gerund can be preceded or followed by any kind of preposition, and it can be preceded by the Def. Art. *the*; the same cannot be said of Infinitives.

Subsequently the other forms of Gerund, such as *being loved*, *having loved*, *having been loved*, were developed in modern English, on the analogy of corresponding participles.

**204. Gerund as Noun.**—Since a Gerund is a *kind of noun*, it must be the subject to some verb (Transitive or Intransitive); or the object to some verb (Transitive); or the complement to some verb (Intransitive or Factitive); or the object to some preposition; as—

*Subject to a verb.*—*Sleeping* is necessary to life.
*Object to a verb.*—He enjoyed *sleeping* in the open air.
*Complement to a verb.*—His almost constant habit was *sleeping*.
*Object to a preposition.*—He was fond of *sleeping*.

*In the following sentences say whether the words noted below are Gerunds or Participles:*—

The rice will grow well in the *coming* rains. We heard of his *coming* back to-day. Did you hear of his *having won* a prize? The boy *having won* a prize was much praised. She was fond of *being admired*. *Being admired* by all she was much pleased. The cow *having been killed* by a tiger yesterday could not be found. The boy was ashamed of *having been beaten* in class by his sister. I am tired of *doing* this work. *Doing* this work every day you will soon improve.

*Spelling* is more difficult than *writing*. He was in the habit of *boasting* of his cleverness. A *boasting* man is much despised.

*Note.*—In such phrases as "a hunting whip," "a drinking fountain," the words *hunting* and *drinking* are Gerunds, not participles; "a whip for hunting," "a fountain for drinking." The Gerund or noun is here used as a substitute for an adjective; see § 96 (3).

**205. Gerund as a Verb.**—Since the Gerund of a Transitive verb retains its verb-character (§ 203), the object by which it is followed may be of any of the five kinds shown in § 161, *Note.*

**Direct** (with Trans.).—He is clever at teaching *Euclid.*
**Indirect** (with Trans.).—He is clever at teaching *his sons* Euclid.
**Retained** (with Passive).—He is pleased at being taught *Euclid.*
**Cognate** (with Intrans.).—He is proud of having fought a good *fight.*
**Reflexive** (with Intrans.).—He is in the habit of oversleeping *himself.*

**206. Gerund with Possessives.**—A noun or pronoun, provided it denotes a person or other animal, is usually in the Possessive case, when it is placed before a Gerund:—

I was pleased at *his* coming to-day.
He was displeased at the *barber's* not coming.

*Note* 1.—The following use of a Gerund preceded by a Possessive noun or pronoun sometimes occurs:—

This was a work *of my doing* (=done by me).

*Note* 2.—Sometimes the letter "*a*" (an abbreviation of "*on*") is placed before a Gerund in a prepositional sense:—

This set him *a* (=on) *thinking.*

*Note* 3.—The Possessive "*its*," even though its antecedent denotes an *inanimate* object, should be used with a Gerund.

The *wall* fell; I am vexed at *its* having fallen.

**207. Gerundive use of Participles.**—Such participles are not Gerunds, but participles used in a Gerundive sense:—

I depend on the wall *being built* immediately.

How are we to parse "being built" in such a connection? It is not enough to say that it is an ordinary participle; for it does more than qualify the noun "wall." The sentence does not mean "I depend on the wall that was being built," or "the wall when it was being built"; but "I depend on the *wall-being-built* immediately," that is, "on the immediate *building of* the wall." There is therefore a gerund or verbal noun implied in the participle "being built," and hence such participles can be called Gerundive Participles. The subject is more fully dealt with in chap. xx. (79).

**208.** A Verbal noun is the same thing at bottom as a Gerund, but a distinction has been drawn between them.

A Verbal noun is preceded by the Definite article and followed by the preposition "*of*"; whereas a Gerund has no article preceding it and no preposition following it:—

(*a*) I am engaged in *the* reading *of* a book. (*Verbal Noun.*)
(*b*) I am engaged in reading a book. (*Gerund.*)

In (*a*) the word "reading" is a *single* part of speech,—a noun and nothing more. In (*b*) "reading" is a *double* part of speech,—a noun and verb combined.

This distinction holds good only when the verb is Transitive.

## SECTION 13.—THE CONJUGATION OF VERBS.

**209.** To "conjugate" a verb is to show its chief parts.

*Note.*—The term "conjugation" is sometimes used in a wider sense to denote *all* the inflexions and combinations that are employed to indicate Voice, Mood, Tense, Number, and Person. The word lit. means a yoking together (Lat. *con*, together, and *jug-are, jugat*-um, to yoke).

The chief parts of a verb in English are the Present tense, the Past tense, and the Past Participle: all the other parts, Active and Passive, can be easily formed from these three.

**210.** There are two main kinds of Conjugation:[1]—

I. The *Strong*, which forms the Past tense by changing *the inside vowel* of the Present, and without adding the suffix *-d*, or *-t*, or *-ed* for this purpose; as, *rise, rose.*

II. The *Weak*, which forms the Past tense and Past Participle by adding *-d*, or *-t*, or *-ed* to the stem of the Present, with or without a change of inside vowel; as, *love, loved; buy, bought.*

---

[1] Some grammarians distinguish verbs into Regular and Irregular. The Regular answer to the Weak, and the Irregular to the Strong. But these names are misleading; for in point of fact the Strong conjugation is, in its own way, not less regular than the Weak. (It would be more appropriate to apply the term *Irregular* to such a verb as *can* or *dare*, which leaves out the *s* in the Third pers. Sing., or to such a tense as *could*, which has admitted an *l* against rule, or to such a tense as *had*, which has discarded the *v* of the present.)

The Strong conjugation contains no verbs but such as are of the primary Anglo-Saxon stock. All the verbs belonging to this conjugation (except a few that have had a prefix added to them) are monosyllabic.

Perhaps the reason why the Weak conjugation is so called is because it has no inherent strength for forming its Past tense, but requires the help of a suffix.

The Weak conjugation, however, is the *living* one. The Strong has long been dead, and now numbers only about 110, all told; even this total includes several verbs which have lost either a Strong past tense or a Strong past participle. All borrowed verbs are Weak, and all newly coined ones. Our new verb *to boycott* has *boycott-ed* for its Past tense. Borrowed or coined verbs did not originally possess, and were never able to acquire, the power of changing the inside vowel; and that is why the Weak conjugation is the living one.

The student will therefore observe that vowel-change in the Past tense is not the decisive mark of the Strong conjugation, but the absence of a suffix to form the Past tense. Even this mark (the adding or not adding of a suffix to form the Past tense) is not always conclusive in modern English, because in Weak verbs ending in *d* or *t*, the addition of *d* or *t* is latent, and must be understood; see examples in § 215.

*The Strong Conjugation.*

**211.** The Strong verbs are conjugated by internal changes, the nature of which is too various to be reduced to a single rule.

The most general process consists in (1) changing the inside vowel for the Past tense, and (2) adding *en*, *n*, or *ne* for the Past Participle, with or without change of inside vowel.

**212.** Formerly *all* verbs of the Strong Conjugation formed the Past Participle by adding *en*, *n*, *ne;* but many of them have now laid aside this suffix.

Hence the Strong verbs, as they now exist, fall into two main groups:—

(1) Those which have retained } the *en*, *n*, or *ne* in the
(2) Those which have lost } Past Participle.

Besides these there is a third group, consisting of *Mixed* verbs, that have become Weak either in the Past tense or the Past Participle, but not in both. These are, however, classed among Strong verbs, because they have retained at least one mark of the Strong Conjugation.

*Group I.* (50 *verbs*).

| *Present Tense.* | *Past Tense.* | *Past Part.* | *Present Tense.* | *Past Tense.* | *Past Part.* |
|---|---|---|---|---|---|
| Arise | arose | arisen | Draw | drew | drawn |
| Bear (produce) | bore | born | Drink | drank | *drunken, drunk |
| Bear (carry) | bore | borne | Drive | drove, drave | driven |
| Beget | begot, begat | begotten, begot | Eat | ate | eaten |
| | | | Fall | fell | fallen |
| Bid | bade, bid | bidden, bid | Fly | flew | flown |
| Bind | bound | *bounden, bound | Forbear | forbore | forborne |
| | | | Forget | forgot | forgotten |
| Bite | bit | bitten, bit | Forsake | forsook | forsaken |
| Blow | blew | blown | Freeze | froze | frozen |
| Break | broke | broken | Get | got | *gotten, got |
| Chide | chid | chidden, chid | Give | gave | given |
| | | | Go, wend | went | gone |
| Choose | chose | chosen | Grow | grew | grown |

| *Present Tense.* | *Past Tense.* | *Past Part.* | *Present Tense.* | *Past Tense.* | *Past Part.* |
|---|---|---|---|---|---|
| Hide | hid | *hidden, hid | Speak | spoke | spoken |
| | | | Steal | stole | stolen |
| Know | knew | known | Stride | strode | stridden |
| Lie | lay | lain | Strike | struck | *stricken, struck |
| Ride | rode | ridden | | | |
| Rise | rose | risen | Strive | strove | striven |
| See | saw | seen | Swear | swore | sworn |
| Shake | shook | shaken | Take | took | taken |
| Shrink | shrank | *shrunken, shrunk | Tear | tore | torn |
| | | | Throw | threw | thrown |
| Sink | sank | *sunken, sunk | Tread | trod | trodden, trod |
| Slay | slew | slain | Wear | wore | worn |
| Slide | slid | slidden, slid | Weave | wove | woven |
| Smite | smote | smitten, smit | Write | wrote | written |

*Note.*—The seven participles marked * are now chiefly used as verbal adjectives only, and not as parts of some tense :—

| *Verbal Adjective.* | *Part of some Tense.* |
|---|---|
| Our *bounden* duty. | He was *bound* by his promise. |
| A *drunken* man. | He had *drunk* much wine. |
| A *sunken* ship. | The ship had *sunk* under the water. |
| A *stricken* deer. | The deer was *struck* with an arrow. |
| The *shrunken* stream. | The stream has *shrunk* in its bed. |
| Ill-*gotten* wealth. | He *got* his wealth by ill means. |
| A *hidden* meaning. | The meaning is *hid* or hidden. |

*Group II.* (32 *verbs*).

| *Present Tense.* | *Past Tense.* | *Past Part.* | *Present Tense.* | *Past Tense.* | *Past Part.* |
|---|---|---|---|---|---|
| Abide | abode | abode | Sing | sang | sung |
| Awake | awoke | awoke | Sit | sat | sat |
| Become | became | become | Sling | slung | slung |
| Begin | began | begun | Slink | slunk | slunk |
| Behold | beheld | beheld, beholden[1] | Spin | spun | spun |
| | | | Spring | sprang | sprung |
| Cling | clung | clung | Stand | stood | stood |
| Come | came | come | Stick | stuck | stuck |
| Dig | dug | dug | Sting | stung | stung |
| Fight | fought | fought | Stink | stank | stunk |
| Find | found | found | String | strung | strung |
| Fling | flung | flung | Swim | swam | swum |
| Grind | ground | ground | Swing | swung | swung |
| Hold | held | held | Win | won | won |
| Ring | rang | rung | Wind | wound | wound |
| Run | ran | run | Wring | wrung | wrung |
| Shine | shone | shone | | | |

[1] "Beholden" means "indebted."

*Group III.—Mixed or Strong-Weak Verbs* (28 *in number*).

| *Present Tense.* | *Past Tense.* | *Past Participle.* |
|---|---|---|
| Beat | beat | beaten |
| Cleave (split) | clave, cleft | *cloven, cleft |
| Climb | clomb, climbed | climbed |
| Crow | crew, crowed | crowed, crown (rare) |
| Do | did | done |
| Grave | graved | *graven, graved |
| Hang [1] | hung, hanged | hung, hanged |
| Hew | hewed | *hewn, hewed |
| Lade | laded | laden |
| Melt | melted | *molten, melted |
| Mow | mowed | mown |
| Prove | proved | †proven, proved |
| Rive | rived | riven |
| Rot | rotted | *rotten, rotted |
| Saw | sawed | sawn |
| Seethe | seethed | *sodden, seethed |
| Sew | sewed | *sewn, sewed |
| Shape | shaped | †shapen, shaped |
| Shave | shaved | shaven |
| Shear | sheared | *shorn, sheared |
| Show | showed | shown |
| Sow | sowed | sown |
| Stave | stove, staved | stove, staved |
| Strew | strewed | strewn or strown |
| Swell | swelled | swollen |
| Thrive | throve, thrived. | thriven, thrived |
| Wash | washed | *washen, washed |
| Writhe | writhed | †writhen, writhed |

*Note* 1.—The participles marked * are now chiefly used as Verbal adjectives, and not as parts of some tense :—

| *Verbal Adjective.* | *Part of some Tense.* |
|---|---|
| A *graven* image. | The image was *engraved* with letters. |
| A *molten* image. | The image was *melted* with heat. |
| A *rotten* plank. | The plank was *rotted* by water. |
| The *sodden* flesh. | The flesh was *seethed* in hot water. |
| A well-*sewn* cloth. | I have *sewed* or *sewn* it. |
| Un-*washen* hands. | I have *washed* my hands. |
| A *shorn* lamb. | The lamb was *sheared* to-day. |
| A *hewn* log. | The log is *hewed* or *hewn*. |

*Note* 2.—The participles marked † are now seldom seen except in poetry.

### *The Weak Conjugation.*

**213.** The mode of adding the suffix of the Past tense is not uniform ; and the two rules given below should be observed :—

[1] The Intransitive verb is conjugated in the Strong form only. The Transitive verb is conjugated in both forms. *Hanged* means "killed by hanging" ; as, "The man was *hanged*." *Hung* is used in a general sense ; as, "He *hung* up his coat."

(1) If the verb ends in *e*, then *d* only is added; as—

*Live, lived* (not *liveed*).
*Clothe, clothed* (not *clotheed*).

To this rule there is no exception.

(2) The final consonant is doubled before *ed*, provided (*a*) that the final consonant is *single*, (*b*) that it is *accented* or *monosyllabic*, (*c*) that it is preceded by a *single vowel;* as—

*Fan, fanned* (not *faned*); *drop, dropped* (not *droped*).
*Compel, compelled; control, controlled.*

But in a verb like *lengthen*, where the accent is not on the last syllable, the Past tense is *lengthened;* in a verb like *boil*, where the vowel is not single, the Past tense is *boiled;* and in a verb like *fold*, where the last consonant is not single, the Past tense is *folded.*

To this rule there are very few exceptions. One exception occurs in the final *l*. The final *l* is doubled, even when it is not accented; as, travel, trav*elled* (not trav*eled*). But the final *l* is not doubled, if it has two vowels going before it; as, *travail, travailed* (not *travailled*).

**214.** (*a*) Some verbs of the Weak Conjugation form the Past tense in "*t*," and if the vowel of the Present is a long one, they shorten it:—

| *Present Tense.* | *Past Tense.* | *Past Part.* | *Present Tense.* | *Past Tense.* | *Past Part.* |
|---|---|---|---|---|---|
| Creep | crept | crept | Feel | felt | felt |
| Sleep | slept | slept | Kneel | knelt | knelt |
| Sweep | swept | swept | Smell | smelt | smelt |
| Keep | kept | kept | Spell | spelt | spelt |
| Weep | wept | wept | Lean (lēn) | lĕant or leaned | lĕant or leaned |
| Burn | burnt | burnt | Mean (mēn) | mĕant | mĕant |
| Deal (dēl) | dĕalt | dĕalt | Spill | spilt | spilt |
| Dream (drēm) | drĕamt or dreamed | drĕamt or dreamed | Spoil | spoilt or spoiled | spoilt or spoiled |
| Dwell | dwelt | dwelt | | | |

*Exceptional Verbs.*—Make, made, made. Have, had, had. Hear, heard, heard. Leave, left, left. Cleave, cleft, cleft. Lose, lost, lost. Shoe, shod, shod. Flee, fled, fled. Say, said, said. Lay, laid, laid. Pay, paid, paid.

(*b*) Some Weak verbs undergo a change of inside vowel. This, however, does not make them Strong verbs. They are Weak without any doubt, because they form the Past tense with the suffix *-d* or *-t* (see § 210).

| *Present Tense.* | *Past Tense.* | *Past Part.* | *Present Tense.* | *Past Tense.* | *Past Part.* |
|---|---|---|---|---|---|
| Beseech | besought | besought | Seek | sought | sought |
| Bring | brought | brought | Sell | sold | sold |
| Buy | bought | bought | Teach | taught | taught |
| Catch | caught | caught | Tell | told | told |

| *Present Tense.* | *Past Tense.* | *Past Part.* | *Present Tense.* | *Past Tense.* | *Past Part.* |
|---|---|---|---|---|---|
| Think | thought | thought | Can | could | (*Wanting*) |
| Work | wrought, worked | wrought, worked | Shall | should | (*Wanting*) |
| | | | Will | would | (*Wanting*) |
| Owe | ought, owed | owed | May | might | (*Wanting*) |
| Dare | durst or dared | dared | | | |

**215.** Verbs ending in *d* or *t* in the Present tense have discarded the suffix of the Past tense, to avoid the repetition of *d* or *t*.

(*a*) Some verbs in this group have the three forms (Present tense, Past tense, and Past Participle) all exactly alike :—

| *Present Tense.* | *Past Tense.* | *Past Part.* | *Present Tense.* | *Past Tense.* | *Past Part.* |
|---|---|---|---|---|---|
| Burst | burst | burst | Slit | slit | slit |
| Cast | cast | cast | Spit | spit or spat | spit |
| Cost | cost | cost | | | |
| Cut | cut | cut | Split | split | split |
| Hit | hit | hit | Spread | spread | spread |
| Hurt | hurt | hurt | Sweat | sweat | sweat |
| Let | let | let | Thrust | thrust | thrust |
| Put | put | put | Bet | bet | bet |
| Rid | rid | rid | Quit | quit or quitted | quit or quitted |
| Set | set | set | | | |
| Shed | shed | shed | Knit | knit or knitted | knit or knitted |
| Shred | shred | shred | | | |
| Shut | shut | shut | | | |

*Note.*—"Spit" is a Weak verb, although it has a form *spat* for the Past tense. In Anglo-Saxon the Present had two forms also.

(*b*) Other verbs in this group end in *d* in the Present tense, but form the Past tense and Past Participle by changing *d* into *t*. (There are at least nine such verbs in English.)

| *Present Tense.* | *Past Tense.* | *Past Part.* | *Present Tense.* | *Past Tense.* | *Past Part.* |
|---|---|---|---|---|---|
| Bend | bent | bent | Rend | rent | rent |
| Build | built | built | Send | sent | sent |
| Gild | gilt, gilded | gilt | Spend | spent | spent |
| Gird | girt, girded | girt | Wend | went | (*Wanting*) |
| Lend | lent | lent | | | |

*Exceptions* :—end-ed, mend-ed, blend-ed or blent, defend-ed.

(*c*) Other verbs of this group have the three forms all alike except that they shorten the vowel in the Past forms :—

| *Present Tense.* | *Past Tense.* | *Past Part.* | *Present Tense.* | *Past Tense.* | *Past Part.* |
|---|---|---|---|---|---|
| Bleed | bled | bled | Lead | led | led |
| Breed | bred | bred | Read | read | read |
| Feed | fed | fed | Light | lit, lighted | lit, lighted |
| Speed | sped | sped | Shoot | shot | shot |
| Meet | met | met | | | |

## Section 14.—Auxiliary, Defective, and Anomalous Verbs.

### (1) Be.

This verb is a patchwork of parts formed from three different roots, *es* (cf. Lat. *sum*, *es*, *est*), *béo* (cf. Lat. *fi-o*), and *wes*.

| | | Singular. | | | Plural. |
|---|---|---|---|---|---|
| | | 1 | 2 | 3 | 1 2 3 |
| Present | *Indicative* | am | art | is | are |
| | *Subjunctive* | be | be | be | be |
| Past | *Indicative* | was | wast[1] | was | were |
| | *Subjunctive* | were | wert | were | were |

| Infinitive. | Imperative. | Present Participle. | Perfect Participle. |
|---|---|---|---|
| To be | be | being | having been |

This verb has two different uses:—

(1) As an Intransitive verb (*a*) of Complete, (*b*) of Incomplete Predication:—

(*a*) There *are* some who, etc.—*Complete Predication.*
(*b*) His coat *is* of many colours.—*Incomplete Predication.*

(2) As an Auxiliary verb:—

All the tenses in Passive verbs and all the Continuous tenses in Active ones are formed by the help of the verb *to be.*

### (2) Have.

| | | Singular. | | | Plural. |
|---|---|---|---|---|---|
| | | 1 | 2 | 3 | 1 2 3 |
| Present | *Indicative* | have | hast | has | have |
| | *Subjunctive* | have | have | have | have |
| Past | *Indicative* | had | hadst | had | had |
| | *Subjunctive* | had | hadst | had | had |

| Infinitive. | Imperative. | Present Participle. | Perfect Participle. |
|---|---|---|---|
| To have | have | having | having had |

[1] *Wert* is also found in Milton and elsewhere; but it was inaccurate from the first, and is now obsolete.

This verb has two different uses :—

(1) As a Transitive verb, denoting possession.

We have (=we possess) four cows and twenty sheep.

(2) As an Auxiliary verb :—

All the Perfect tenses, in all the Moods, Active and Passive, are formed by the help of this verb.

## (3) Shall.

| | Singular. | | | Plural. |
|---|---|---|---|---|
| | 1 | 2 | 3 | 1 2 3 |
| *Present* . . | shall | shalt | shall | shall |
| *Past* . . | should | shouldst | should | should |

This verb has two different uses :—

(1) As a Principal verb (Transitive, with an Infinitive as object) in the sense (*a*) of command, (*b*) of duty :—

(*a*) Thou *shalt* not steal.
(*b*) He *should* do it at once.

*Note.*—In the following sentence "*should*" is used in the sense of inference, rather than in that of duty ;—

He *should* have arrived by this time.

That is, "It may be inferred, according to the ordinary course of events, that he has arrived by this time."

(2) As an Auxiliary verb (*a*) for the First person Future, (*b*) for any person Subjunctive :—

(*a*) I *shall* go away to-day.
(*b*) He worked hard lest he *should* fail.

## (4) Will.

| | Singular. | | | Plural. |
|---|---|---|---|---|
| | 1 | 2 | 2 | 1 2 3 |
| *Present* . . | will | wilt | will | will |
| *Past* . . | would<br>willed | wouldst<br>willedst | would<br>willed | would<br>willed |

| Infinitive. | Imperative. | Present Participle. | Perfect Participle. |
|---|---|---|---|
| To will | ... | willing | having willed |

This verb has two different uses :—

(1) As a Principal verb (*a*) Transitive (with an Infinitive as object), in the sense of intention or habit; (*b*) Transitive, in the sense of leaving property by will or testament :—

(*a*) I *will* not do so again. (*Intention.*)
The dog *would* come every day to the door. (*Habit.*)
(*b*) He *willed* that all he had should go to his son.

*Note.*—The phrase "*would-be*" is elliptical, and is used as an adjective :—

A would-be murderer (a man who wished or intended to be a murderer, but was prevented).

(2) As an Auxiliary verb (*a*) for the Second and Third persons Future, (*b*) for any person of the Subjunctive :—

(*a*) He *will* return to-morrow.
(*b*) He *would* know me, if he saw me.

### (5) Do.

| | Singular. | | | Plural. |
|---|---|---|---|---|
| | 1 | 2 | 3 | 1 2 3 |
| *Present* . . | do | dost | does | do |
| *Past* . . | did | didst | did | did |

| Infinitive. | Imperative. | Present Participle. | Perfect Participle. |
|---|---|---|---|
| To do | do | doing | having done |

This verb has three different uses :—

(1) As a Principal verb (Transitive) signifying "perform" :—

I am now *doing* what you *have done* already.

*Note.*—It once had the sense of "cause," as in the phrase "I *do* you to wit"=I cause you to know, I give you to understand.

(2) As an Auxiliary, only in the Present and Past tenses :—

I *did* not speak. *Do* be quiet. How *do* you do? (Here the second "do" is Principal, in imitation of the French *faire.*)

(3) As a Pro-verb or Substitute-verb, Trans. or Intrans. :—

He sings well, and so *do* you. (*Intrans.*)
He caught a worse cold than you *did.* (*Trans.*)

### (6) May.

| | Singular. | | | Plural. |
|---|---|---|---|---|
| | 1 | 2 | 3 | 1 2 3 |
| *Present* . . | may | mayest | may | may |
| *Past* . . | might | mightest | might | might |

This verb has two different uses :—

(1) As a Principal verb, Transitive, with Infin. as object :—

It *may* be true. (*Possibility.*)
You *may* now go. (*Permission.*)

(2) As an Auxiliary, for forming the Subjunctive :—

He works that he *may* live. (*Purpose.*)
*May* heaven protect thee ! (*Wish.*)

### (7) Let.

The six verbs hitherto named are the only ones that can be used as Auxiliaries. The special use of "*let*" is to express by a periphrasis the First and Third persons Imperative, as, "*let* him go." "Let" is here the Second person Imperative of the Transitive verb *to let*, followed by a Direct object "go," and by an Indirect object "him." Its conjugation is quite regular.

### (8) Can.

| | Singular. | | | Plural. |
|---|---|---|---|---|
| | 1 | 2 | 3 | 1 2 3 |
| *Present* . . | can | canst | can | can |
| *Past* . . | could | couldst | could | could |

This is a Defective verb, Transitive, followed by an Infinitive as object. (Never Auxiliary, always Principal.)

You *can* (=are permitted to) go or not, as you like.
He *cannot* (=is unable to) run as fast as you.

In Old English this verb signified "to know."

### (9) Ought.

| | Singular. | | | Plural. |
|---|---|---|---|---|
| | 1 | 2 | 3 | 1 2 3 |
| *Present* or *Past* . | ought | oughtest | ought | ought |

This verb is, in its origin, the Past tense of the verb *owe;* as, "you *ought*" (= *owed*) him a thousand pounds." In modern English the form "ought" is used only in the sense of *duty.* It is a Transitive verb, followed by a Noun-Infinitive as object.

*Present.*—You ought *to do* this; (it is your duty to do it).
*Past.*—You ought *to have done* this; (but you did not do it).

### (10) Must.

This verb has now no varieties of form.

It is, in its origin, the Past tense of an old verb *motan,* which is now obsolete. The Infinitive following is its object.

(*a*) What *must* come, *must.* (*Necessity.*)
(*b*) He *must* be dead by this time. (*Inference.*)
(*c*) We *must* pay our debts. (*Obligation.*)

### (11) Dare.

| | Singular. | | | Plural. |
|---|---|---|---|---|
| | 1 | 2 | 3 | 1 2 3 |
| *Present* . . | dare | darest | dares / dare | dare |
| *Past.* . . | durst / dared | durst / daredst | durst / dared | durst / dared |

| Infinitive. | Imperative. | Present Participle. | Perfect Participle. |
|---|---|---|---|
| To dare | dare | daring | having dared |

This verb is used in two senses:—

(*a*) A Transitive verb in the sense of *having courage,* with Infinitive as object. In this sense the Third present Singular is "dare," and not "dares," provided it is followed by a Negative:—

He *dare* not (= has not the courage to) leave the room. (*Negative.*)
He *dares* to leave the room. (*Affirmative.*)

In the Past tense, provided it is followed by a Negative, "durst" is used, and sometimes "dared":—

He *durst* not (or *dared* not) leave the room.

But if the verb is affirmative, we use "dared" and not "durst." The idiom "I dare say" simply means "perhaps." The verb *dare* has here lost most of its force.

(*b*) A Transitive verb in the sense of *challenging:* declined regularly in all the moods and tenses:—

He *dares* me (= challenges me) to fight.

### (12) Quoth.

This verb is the Past tense of an old verb, which is now obsolete except in the compound form of *be-queath*.

It means "says" or "said," and therefore stands equally for Past and Present time. It is used only in the *First* and *Third* persons, and only in the *Singular* number. It always stands *before* its subject:—

"Let me not live," *quoth* he.—SHAKSPEARE.

### (13) Need.

A Transitive verb, signifying "require," "want." As such it is declined regularly in all its moods and tenses.

The Third person Singular is *need*, and not *needs*, just as *dare* is used for *dares*, provided it is followed by a Negative:—

He *need* not (=is under no necessity to) do any more work.

In such a phrase as "he must *needs* do this," *needs* is really a Possessive case, with the apostrophe before the *s* omitted. So *needs* =need's=of need=of necessity=necessarily: an Adverb.

### (14) Worth.

This verb occurs in such a phrase as "woe *worth* the day"= "woe be to the day." Here "day" is in the Objective case.

*Worth* is here the Subjunctive mood (in the sense of wish, see § 186, 2) of an old verb signifying "to become."

### (15) Wit.

This verb signifies "to know." Only a few of its forms have survived; the rest have become obsolete.

(*a*) The Infinitive form *to wit*, in the sense of "namely," is much used in legal documents at the present day:—

He left me by will all his land, *to wit*, the three farms.

(*b*) The Present Participle has survived in the negative adverbial form of *unwittingly*, which means "unknowingly."

You cannot blame him for this, since he did it *unwittingly*.

(*c*) Two forms of the Indicative have survived, but are rare:—

*Present.*—He *wot* neither what he babbles nor what he means.—TYNDALL.

*Past.*—They *wist* not what had become of him.—*New Testament*.

### (16) Beware.

This is compounded of *be*+*ware*. "Ware" is an old form of the adjective "wary," and is complement to the verb "be."

The form "*beware*" is the only one used. It can be preceded by Auxiliary verbs, or by "to," as "to beware."

### (17) Wont.

This is the Past Participle of an obsolete verb, which signified "to continue." Hence "wont" means "accustomed."

### (18) Hight.

The Past Participle of an obsolete verb, which signified "to call or name."

### (19) Yclept.

The Past Participle of the obsolete verb "clepe," to call or name. The *y* prefix is from Anglo-Saxon *ge.*

### (20) Impersonal Verbs.

Verbs are said to be **Impersonal**, or to be used impersonally, when they take "it" for their subject, and are followed by some Personal pronoun in the Objective case, which in Personal verbs would be the Subject in the Nom. case:—

*It* shames *me* to hear this = I am ashamed to hear this.
*It* repents *me* of my folly = I repent of my folly.
*It* behoves *me* to do this = I ought to do this.

There are three instances in which the *it* is omitted, and the pronoun in the Objective case is placed *before* the verb instead of after it:—

*Methinks* = it seems to me.
*Meseems* = it seems to me.
*Melists* = it seems to me, or it pleases me.

*Note.*—In Modern English there is no difference of spelling between *thinks* Impersonal and *think* Transitive. But in Old Eng. the former was *thync-an* (to seem) and the latter *thenc-an* (to think.)

The following phrase is elliptical:—

So *please* your Majesty.—SHAKSPEARE.

This means, "If *it* so please your Majesty"; that is, "If your Majesty so please or so desire."

## CHAPTER VI.—ADVERBS.

### SECTION 1.—THE FUNCTIONS OF ADVERBS.

**216. Adverb defined.**—An Adverb is a word used to qualify any part of speech except a noun or pronoun (§ 11). (The etymology, Lat. *ad verbum*, would imply that an Adverb qualifies a verb only; and probably this was the earliest use of Adverbs.)

*Note.*—The definition usually given is:—"An adverb is a word used to qualify a verb, adjective, or other adverb."[1]

But this is evidently wrong, since an adverb may, and very often does, qualify Prepositions and Conjunctions :—

(*a*) **Prepositions** :—

The bird flew *exactly over* the sleeper's head.
He paid the money *quite up* to date.
This mistake was made *entirely through* your fault.
He was sitting *almost outside* the door.
He arrived *long before* the time.
He wept *partly through* sorrow and *partly through* anger.

(*b*) **Conjunctions** :—

A man is truly happy *only when* he is in sound health.
I dislike this place *simply because* the air is too hot.
I wish to know *precisely how* it happened.
They locked the door *shortly before* the thieves came.
The watch was found *long after* the thieves had been caught.
He has been ill *ever since* he left us.

It is immaterial whether we say that the adverb qualifies the *Preposition only* or *the entire phrase* introduced by the preposition. Similarly, we could say with equal truth that the adverb qualifies the *Conjunction only* or *the entire clause* that follows it.

*Note.*—If for an adverb proper we substitute an adverbial phrase, we find that such a phrase can qualify a preposition or a conjunction in the same way as an adverb proper does :—

**Preposition.**—He arrived *a few hours after* midnight.
**Conjunction.**—He recovered *ten days after* he had been taken ill.

**217.** An Adverb can qualify not merely individual words, but an entire Assertive sentence (§ 1, *a*). *In this case it must stand first in the sentence.*

*Unfortunately* the thief was not caught.
*Evidently* you were much distressed at the news.

We could rewrite these sentences in the following form :—

*It is unfortunate that* the thief was not caught.
*It was evident that* you were much distressed.

**218.** *Adverbs do not qualify Nouns or Pronouns.* This is the work of adjectives.

The apparent exceptions to the above rule can all be explained :—

(*a*) I am *sincerely yours.* That book is *certainly mine.*

---

[1] Angus and Bain both admit that the qualifying power of adverbs is not limited to adjectives, verbs, and other adverbs; but both have none the less adhered to the old definition. The same admission, but without any departure from the old definition, is made by Mason, who in a footnote to page 105 of *English Grammar*, ed. 1891, points out that "an adverb sometimes modifies a preposition." Since the old definition is admittedly wrong, it is better to put a more accurate one in its place.

Here the words "yours" and "mine" are the Possessive forms of "you" and "I," and are therefore equivalent to *adjectives.*

(*b*) A by-path; a fore-taste; an out-house.

Here the adverbs do not qualify the several nouns, but are *compounded* with them, so that each compound makes a *single* word.

(*c*) In the following examples the adverb that precedes the noun does not qualify the noun, but some participle or adjective understood:—

*The then* king = the king then *reigning.*
*The late* king = the king lately *reigning.*
*The above* account = the account *given* above.
*A far* country = a country far *distant.*
*An up* mail = an up-*going* mail.

(*d*) In the following example the adverb "almost" does not qualify the noun "drunkard," but the verb "is":—

He is *almost* a drunkard.

To say, "He is an almost drunkard," would be incorrect.

*Note.*—A slovenly practice is springing up, however, by which the adverb "quite" is made to qualify nouns:—

*Quite a panic* (= a serious panic) was caused.
This is *quite an item* (= a considerable item).

Very often in such sentences the word *quite* is superfluous. If for the sake of such ungainly phrases we are to say that adverbs qualify nouns also, then what distinction between Adjective and Adverb would remain?

## Section 2.—The Kinds of Adverbs.

**219.** Adverbs are subdivided into three distinct classes:—

I. Simple. II. Interrogative. III. Relative.

**220. Simple Adverbs.**—These can be distinguished from one another according to their meaning:—

(1) **Time**:—

He did this *before,* and you have done it *since.* He will *soon* arrive. He was taken ill *yesterday.*

The chief adverbs of this class are:—*Now, then, before, since, ago, already, soon, presently, immediately, instantly, early, late, afterwards, yesterday, to-day, to-morrow.*

(2) **Place**:—

We must rest *here,* and not *there.*

The chief adverbs of this class are:—*Here, there; hence, thence; hither, thither; in, out; within, without; above, below; inside, outside; far, near,* etc.

(3) **Number**:—

He did this *once,* but he will not do it *again.*

The chief adverbs of this class are:—*Once, twice, thrice, again, seldom, never, sometimes, always, often, firstly, secondly, thirdly,* etc.

(4) **Manner, Quality,** or **State** :—

He did his work *slowly*, but *surely*.

To this class of adverb belong :—*Thus, so, well, ill, amiss, badly, probably, certainly, conveniently, asleep* (=in sleep, in a state of sleep).

(5) **Quantity, Extent,** or **Degree** :—

He is *almost*, but not *quite*, the cleverest boy in the class.

To this class of adverb belong :—*Very, much, the, too, quite, almost, little, a little, rather, somewhat, half, partly, wholly, so*, etc.

*Note.*—The adverb "the" is quite distinct from the Definite article. It represents the Instrumental case (*thī*) of the Demonstrative, and is never used except before an adjective or adverb in the *Comparative* degree.

(6) **Affirming** or **Denying** :—

He did *not* come after all.

Examples :—*Yes, no, not, perhaps, undoubtedly, not at all, by all means*, etc.

**Substitute-Adverbs.**—This is the most suitable name for the Adverbs (1) *yes* (Affirm.), and (2) *no* (Negat.).

(1) Did he come? Yes (=He did come). *Affirm.*
(2) Did he come? No (=He did not come). *Negat.*

These can be fitly called *substitute*-adverbs, because in (1) *yes* is substitute for an entire affirmative sentence, and in (2) *no* is a substitute for an entire negative sentence. They might be called **pro-sentence** adverbs. Just as pro-nouns save the repetition of a noun, so do these adverbs save the repetition of a sentence. Cf. *do* in page 83 (5), where *do* is shown to be a *pro-verb* or *substitute-verb*.

*Note.*—In some books a 7th class is added, viz. adverbs of Cause or Consequence :—*Therefore, then, consequently, because, for*. It appears, however, that these words do not so much modify any word or words in a sentence, but are rather conjunctions combining the sense of one sentence with that of another by way of inference. They have therefore been included amongst Conjunctions in this book. But there would be nothing illogical in regarding them as Adverbs also; for a word may be of more than one part of speech, according to the point of view from which we look at it.

**221. Interrogative Adverbs.**—This is the name given to those adverbs that are used for asking questions :—

(*a*) **Time** :—

*When* did he *come?* *How long* will he remain here.

(*b*) **Place** :—

*Where* did he stop? *Whence* has he come? *Whither* is he going?

(*c*) **Number** :—

*How often* did the dog bark?

(*d*) **Manner, Quality,** or **State** :—

*How* did he do this? *How* (in what state of health) is he to-day?

(*e*) **Quantity** or **Degree** :—

*How far* (to what extent) was that report true?

(*f*) **Cause** or **Reason** :—

*Why* (for what reason) did he do this? *Wherefore* did she weep?

**222.** The adverb "*how*" is sometimes used in an exclamatory sense :—

*How* kind of you to do that!
*How* often have you been cautioned!

"*What*," in the sense of quantity or degree, is similarly used in an exclamatory sense :—

*What* a foolish fellow you are!
*What* clever sons you have!

**223. Relative Adverbs.**—These are the same in *form* as Interrogative adverbs; but instead of asking questions, they join two sentences together. Hence a Relative adverb is a double part of speech,—an adverb and conjunction combined, as was pointed out in § 17 (4).

(*a*) *The antecedent understood.*

This is *where* (=the place in which) we dwell.
Let me know *when* (=the time by which) you will come.

(*b*) *The antecedent expressed.*

This is the place *where* we dwell.
Let me know the time *when* you will come.

*Note.*—A list of Relative adverbs, with examples, will be found in § 239.

## SECTION 3.—COMPARISON OF ADVERBS.

**224.** Adverbs of Quality have degrees of comparison, which are formed in the same way as those of adjectives :—

(*a*) If the Adverb is a word of *one* syllable, the Comparative is formed by adding *er* and the Superlative by adding *est* :—

| | | | | | |
|---|---|---|---|---|---|
| Fast | faster | fastest | Loud | louder | loudest |
| Hard | harder | hardest | Late | later | latest or last |
| Soon | sooner | soonest | Forth | further | furthest |
| Near | nearer | nearest | Far | farther | farthest |
| Long | longer | longest | Rathe | rather | ... |

Till *rathe* (=early) she rose, half cheated in the thought.—TENNYSON.

(*b*) Some Adverbs have had a Comparative and Superlative allotted to them from another root :—

| | | | | | |
|---|---|---|---|---|---|
| Well | better | best | Much | more | most |
| Ill or badly | worse | worst | Little | less | least |

(c) Adverbs ending in *ly* form the Comparative by adding *more* and the Superlative by adding *most* :—

| | | |
|---|---|---|
| Wisely | more wisely | most wisely |
| Beautifully | more beautifully | most beautifully |

*Note.*—The adverb "*early*," however, has "*earlier*" for its Comparative.

### SECTION 4.—VERBS COMPOUNDED WITH ADVERBS.

**225.** A Verb is said to be compounded with an Adverb, when the two words are so habitually used together, that one is considered to be a part of the other.

Such Adverbs are almost always (except in poetry) placed *after* the verb; as "speak out," "rise up." Here the *out* should be parsed as part of the verb "speak"; and *up* as part of the verb "rise."

But in forming the corresponding noun, the adverb is put first :—

| *Verb.* | *Noun.* |
|---|---|
| The crops will *come out* well. | The *outcome* was a good crop. |
| No profits will *come in.* | His *income* is small. |
| Cholera did not *break out.* | There was no *outbreak* of cholera. |
| He *set out* on his journey. | He had no trouble at the *outset.* |

Similar instances are :—*Set off* (verb), *offset* (noun); *put out* (verb), *output* (noun); *fit out* (verb), *outfit* (noun); *shoot off* (verb), *offshoot* (noun); *spring off* (verb), *offspring* (noun); *shoot up* (verb), *upshot* (noun); *turn out* (verb), *outturn* (noun); *cast out* (verb), *outcast* (noun); *set on* (verb), *onset* (noun); *lay out* (verb), *outlay* (noun); *look-out* (verb), *outlook* (noun); *draw in* (verb), *indraught* (noun); *let out* (verb), *outlet* (noun); *let in* (verb), *inlet* (noun).

*Note.*—"Set-off," "turn-out," and a few more are also used as nouns.

### SECTION 5.—THE TWO USES OF ADVERBS.

**226.** As in the case of Adjectives (see § 95), there are two different ways in which Adverbs can be used, viz. (*a*) the Attributive, (*b*) the Predicative.

(*a*) *Attributive use.*—An Adverb is used attributively, when it qualifies the word associated with it in the ordinary way,—that is, when it is placed as close as possible before it or after it :—

He is *entirely wrong.* He *shouted loudly.* He *did* his work *very badly. Half through* the door. I dislike him *only because* he is lazy.

(*b*) *Predicative use.*—An Adverb is used predicatively, when it is made part of the Predicate of a sentence, or in other words, when it is used as the Complement of the verb going before it :[1]—

---

[1] We cannot endorse what is said in Mason's *English Grammar*, p. 157, ed. 1891: "The complement may consist of any Attributive adjunct; *but an Adverb or adverbial phrase never forms the complement of a predicate.*" The examples given in the text show how very common the predicative use of Adverbs is.

| *Subject.* | *Verb.* | *Complement*, etc. |
|---|---|---|
| My son | is | *well* (in good health) to-day. |
| He | will be | *better* (in better health) soon. |
| He | was turned | *adrift* (to go where he could). |
| The two boys | are | much *alike* (like to each other). |
| The bear | was caught | *alive* (in a living state). |
| Those men | are | *aware* (conscious) of their faults. |
| The game | is | *over* (finished). |
| Some money | was | still *over* (remaining). |
| The results | are | *out* (published). |
| The stars | are | *out* (visible). |
| He | was heard | *out* (to the very end). |
| The bargain | is | *off* (cancelled). |
| The train | is | *off* (started). |
| He | is | *well off* (in good circumstances). |
| Our side | is | *in* (having their innings). |
| The late minister | is | *in* (holding office) again. |

## CHAPTER VII.—PREPOSITIONS.

**227. Preposition defined.**—A Preposition is a word placed before a noun or noun-equivalent to show in what relation the person or thing denoted thereby stands to something else (§ 13). The noun or noun-equivalent is called the Object.[1]

I place my hand *on* the table.

Here if the word "on" is omitted there is no sense. The hand might be placed *on* the table, or *under* the table, or *above* the table. Until some preposition has been inserted, the relation between the hand and the table is not known.

**228. Kinds of Objects.**—Besides nouns and pronouns, we sometimes have adverbs, Infinitives, phrases, and clauses as objects to a preposition:—

(*a*) *Adverbs*:—

We must be ready by *then* (=that time). By *far* the best.
He has worked hard from *then* to *now*.
He walks about from *here* to *there*.
I have heard of worse things being done before *now*.
Until *now* it has not ceased raining.
Many strange things may happen between *now* and *then*.
You must go at *once*. This will last for *ever*.

(*b*) *Infinitives*; see § 191 (*d*):—

He was about *to die*.
He desired nothing but *to succeed*.

---

[1] A preposition is so called, because it is *placed before* (*prae*, before; *positus*, placed) a noun or noun-equivalent.

(*c*) *Phrases* :—

The day-spring from *on-high* hath visited us.
He has come from *beyond-the-seas.*
He did not return till *about-ten-days-afterwards.*
He did not see her till *within-a-few-weeks-of-his-death.*
These books are sold at *over-one-shilling* each.
I bought this for *under-half-its-value.*
He will not return till *after-the-holidays.*
The question of *how-to-do-this* is difficult.

(*d*) *Clauses* :—

This depends upon | whether-he-will-consent-or-not.
He told every one of | what-he-had-heard.
Go whenever you like except | that-you must-not-go-in-the-rain.
In | that-he-died | he died unto sin once.—*New Testament.*

**229. Omission of Object.**—There are two cases of this :—

**Relative Pronoun.**—The man (*whom* or *that*) we were looking for.
**Demons. Pronoun.**—A chair to sit on (*it*). (See § 192, *b*, *Note*.)

**230. Disguised Prepositions.**—"*On*" is changed into "*a*" in such phrases as "to go *a fishing*."

Similarly "*of*" can be changed into "*o*," as in "four o'clock," "Jack o' lantern," etc.

To the same class belong such phrases as the following :—

Flour sells at tenpence *a pound.*
He called to see me once *a week.*
He gave the men four shillings *a piece.*

The "a" *looks* so much like the Indefinite Article, that by a false analogy "the" is sometimes used in its place ; as—

Flour sells at tenpence *the pound.*

**231. Than.**—This word has been used as a Preposition by the best English writers :—

No mightier than thyself or *me* . . . . SHAKSPEARE.
A stone is heavy, and the sand weighty ; but a fool's wrath is heavier than *them* both . . *Old Testament.*
She suffers hourly more than *me*. . . . SWIFT.
You are a much greater loser than *me* . . SWIFT.
Lined with giants deadlier than *them* all . . POPE.
For thou art a girl as much brighter than *her*
As he was a poet sublimer than *me* . . . PRIOR.
Thou hast been wiser all the while than *me* . SOUTHEY.

The prepositional use of *than* is common in current journalistic literature. For instance, in *Time*, July 1883, p. 83, we find :—

She should look worse than *him.*

Even so far back as Caxton, the first English printer, we find *than* used as a preposition :—

For ther is nothyng more suspecte to evyl people than *them*, whom they know to be wyse and trewe.—*The Curial*, 4, 18.

But in current books on Grammar its prepositional character is denied.[1] The best course to take is to parse it as a Conjunction, whenever it is possible to do so by adding a clause after it :—

No animal is larger than a whale.
No animal is larger than a whale (is large).

But in such constructions as the following "than" must still be parsed as a Preposition, because there is no omitted clause which could make it a Conjunction :—

| | *Kind of Object.* |
|---|---|
| I will not take less than *ten shillings* . . . | *Noun.* |
| No one other than a *graduate* need apply . . | *Noun.* |
| Here is my son, than *whom* a better does not exist | *Rel. Pron.* |
| He did nothing else than *laugh* . . . . | *Noun-Infin.* |
| I will suffer myself rather than (that) *he should suffer* . . . . . . . | *Noun-clause.* |
| He got more *than* (what) he asked for . . . | *Noun-clause.* |
| He has said so more than *once* . . . . | *Adverb* (§ 228). |

**232. But.**—In such examples as the following "but" must be parsed as a Preposition. Otherwise it is a Conjunction.

All *but* (except) one fulfilled their promises.

He was all *but* (=everything except) ruined. (Here "ruined" is an elliptical form of the Gerund "being ruined"; and this Gerund is the object of the preposition "but.")

*But* for your help (=except on account of your help=if you had not helped me) I should have been ruined. (Here the phrase "for your help" is object to the preposition.)

I cannot *but* fear (=I cannot do anything except fear) that you are ill. (Hear the Noun-Infinitive "fear" is the object.)

## CHAPTER VIII.—CONJUNCTIONS.

233. A **Conjunction** is a word used for *joining*, and for no other purpose.

A Conjunction is never associated with an *object*, as a preposition is.

A Conjunction never *qualifies* a word, as an adverb does.

It simply *joins* words or sentences.

Hence the same word can be an adverb in one place, a preposition in another, and a conjunction in another :—

[1] For example, in Mason's *English Grammar*, p. 177, ed. 1891, we are told that "no *syntactical* explanation can be given of the relative *whom* after *than*." The syntax, however, is very simple, if we parse *than* as a preposition. There is ample analogy for the use of "than" as a preposition, besides ample authority. "Superior *to* mine" = "better *than* mine." If *to* is a preposition, why not *than*? The Scotch say, "He is taller *be* (=*by*) onie o' thaim." If *by* is a preposition, why not *than*? Again, there is the analogy of the French *que* (=than) followed by *lui* (Objective case) = "than *him*."

I have seen this man *before*. (*Adverb.*)
He stood *before* the door. (*Preposition.*)
The rain fell *before* we reached home. (*Conjunction.*)

**234.** Conjunctions are subdivided into two main classes :—

I. **Co-ordinative,** which join sentences of co-ordinate (that is, of *equal*) rank, or words that stand in the same relation to some other word in the sentence.[1]

II. **Subordinative,** which join a *subordinate* or dependent sentence to a *principal* sentence (that is, to a sentence of *higher* rank).

### Section 1.—Co-ordinative Conjunctions.

**235.** *Sentences are said to be of* **Co-ordinate** *or* **equal** *rank, when one is not dependent on the other, nor enters in any way into its construction.*

**236.** Sentences of equal rank can be combined together in four different ways, and this gives rise to four different kinds of Co-ordinative Conjunctions :—

(*a*) **Cumulative.**—By these one statement of fact is simply *added* to another.

(*b*) **Alternative.**—By these an alternative or *choice* is offered between one statement and another.

(*c*) **Adversative.**—By these conjunctions one statement of fact is *contrasted* with or set against another.

(*d*) **Illative.**—By these conjunctions one statement of fact is *inferred* or proved from another.

#### (*a*) **Cumulative** (addition).

**And.**—The one received a prize, *and* the other was promoted.
**Both . . . and.**—He was *both* degraded *and* expelled.
**Also.**—He is guilty, and you *also.*
**Too.**—He is an idler, and a gambler *too.*

---

[1] Conjunctions for the most part join sentences, not words. "The single exception," says Mr. Mason, "is the conjunction *and*, which, besides uniting one sentence to another, may unite words which stand in the same relation to some other word in the sentence, as, Two and three make five." It appears to be incorrect, however, to say that *and* is the only exception. Another example is *but* in such a sentence as the following :—"I admire the character of a poor, *but* honest, man." Here we cannot possibly split up "but honest" into a separate and independent clause. *Poor* and *honest* stand in the same relation to *man*, for they both qualify the same noun. In fact, *and* and *but* necessarily stand on the same footing ; for *but* is the disjunctive or adversative counterpart of the cumulative or conjunctive *and*. *But* unites the words *poor* and *honest*, while at the same time it disjoins or contrasts their meanings.

**As well as.**—He *as well as* you is guilty.
**No less than.**—He *no less than* you is guilty.
**Not only . . . but also.**—He was *not only* accused, *but also* convicted.
**Now.**—They preferred Barabbas to Jesus ; *now*, Barabbas was a robber.
**Well.**—You have done the work very skilfully ; *well*, I did not expect it of you.

### (*b*) **Alternative** (choice).

**Either . . . or.**—*Either* this man sinned *or* his parents.
**Neither . . . nor.**—He was *neither* an idler *nor* a gambler.
**Otherwise, else, or.**—Leave the room, *or* you will be caught.

### (*c*) **Adversative** (contrast).

**But.**—He is sad, *but* hopeful.
**Still, yet.**—He is very rich, *still* or *yet* he is not contented.
**Nevertheless.**—All men were against him ; *nevertheless* he persevered.
**However.**—All men were against him ; he stuck, *however*, to his point.
**Whereas, while.**—Wise men love truth ; *whereas* or *while* fools shun it.
**Only.**—Go where you like ; *only* do not stay here.

### (*d*) **Illative** (inference).

**Therefore.**—He was found guilty, and *therefore* he was hanged.
**Then, so, so then.**—It is time to go ; *so* or *so then* let us start, or let us start *then*.
**For.**—He will die some day ; *for* all men are mortal.

## Section 2.—Subordinative Conjunctions.

**237.** One sentence is said to be *subordinate* to another, when it depends upon the other, that is, enters into its construction with the force of a noun, adjective, or adverb.

That sentence on which the subordinate sentence depends is called the **Principal** sentence.

| *Principal.* | *Conj.* | *Dependent.* |
|---|---|---|
| I will read that book, | if | you advise me. (*Adverb.*) |
| We still hope | that | you may get well. (*Noun.*) |

**238.** The chief modes of dependence are nine in number :—

(*a*) Apposition, (*b*) Causation, (*c*) Effect, (*d*) Purpose, (*e*) Condition, (*f*) Concession or Contrast, (*g*) Comparison, (*h*) Extent or Manner, (*i*) Time.

(*a*) **Apposition**, or in a merely **Introductory** sense:[1]—

| *Principal.* | *Dependent.* |
|---|---|
| He told us (the fact), | *that* rain had fallen. |
| He wrote to us (to the effect), | *that* he had arrived safely. |
| He made a promise, | *that* he would return soon. |

The Dependent sentence in the above examples is in apposition with the noun in brackets, which may be either omitted or expressed.

(*b*) **Cause** or **Reason**:—

| *Principal.* | *Dependent.* |
|---|---|
| He will succeed, | *because* he has worked hard. |
| I will do this, | *since* you desire it. |
| Let us go to bed, | *as* it is now late. |

(*c*) **Effect**:—

| *Principal.* | *Dependent.* |
|---|---|
| He talked so much, | *that* he made himself hoarse. |

(*d*) **Purpose**:—

| *Principal.* | *Dependent.* |
|---|---|
| Men work, | *that* they may earn a living. |
| He took medicine, | *in order that* he might recover. |
| He took medicine, | *so that* he might recover. |
| He walked with a cane, | *lest* he should stumble. |

(*e*) **Condition**:—

| *Principal.* | *Dependent.* |
|---|---|
| I will do this, | *if* I am allowed. |
| They threatened to beat him, | *unless* he confessed (=if he did not confess). |
| I agree to these terms, | *provided* or *provided that* you will sign your name. |
| He gave a sudden start, | *as if* he had been shot (=as he would have done, if he had been shot). |
| You must leave the room, | *whether* you wish it *or no* (=you must leave the room under any condition whatever). |

---

[1] The word "*that*," if we look to its origin, is simply the neuter Demonstrative pronoun.

"*That*" was originally the neuter pronoun used to point to the fact stated in some previous clause or sentence. "It was good; he saw *that*." By inverting the order of the clauses, we get: "He saw *that* (namely) it was good." The primary clause has thus become a secondary or subordinate one; and "*that*" has become a subordinative conjunction.

Mr. Mason calls it "the Simple Conjunction of Subordination,"—a longer and less convenient name than "Apposition."

Dr. Abbott, in p. 257 of *How to Parse*, calls it the conjunction of "Apposition."

When no noun stands before it for the purpose of apposition, it might be called the *Introductory* conjunction, because it is used to introduce a noun-clause.

**(*f*) Concession or Contrast:—**

| *Principal.* | *Dependent.* |
|---|---|
| He is an honest man, | *though* or *although* he is poor. |
| He will never succeed, | *however* much he may try. |
| He was not contented, | *however* rich he became. |
| He was not refreshed, | *notwithstanding that* he slept long. |

*Note.*—The conjunction "however," when it is *co-ordinative*, stands alone, and is seldom placed at the beginning of its sentence. But when it is *subordinative*, it must be attached to some adverb as "much," or to some adjective as "rich," and is always placed at the beginning of its sentence:—

| *Dependent.* | *Principal.* |
|---|---|
| 1. *Though* he punish me, | *yet* will I trust in him. |
| 2. Hot *as* the sun is, | we must go out. |

Observe that whenever "*as*" is used in a Concessive or Contrasting sense, it is invariably *preceded* by some adjective, adverb, or participle, which stands as Complement to the verb following:—

Hot as the sun is = however hot the sun is.

*Note.*—Sometimes no conjunction is used:—

*Be* it a trifle, it ought to be done well.
*Were* I as rich as Crœsus, I would not buy that.

**(*g*) Comparison—(i.) Of equal degrees:—**

*The same Quality Compared.*

He is *as* clever *as* I (am).
He likes you *as much as* I (like you).
He likes you *as much as* me (he likes me).

*Different Qualities Compared.*

The sea is *as* deep *as* the mountains are high.
He is *as* good *as* he is wise (= He is no less good than he is wise).

**(ii.) Of unequal degrees.**

*The same Quality Compared.*

He is more (or less) clever *than* I (am).
He likes you more (or less) *than* I (like you).
He likes you more (or less) *than* me (he likes me).

*Different Qualities Compared.*

The sea is deeper *than* the mountains are high.
He is more wise *than* (he is) good.
He is less good *than* (he is) wise.

**(*h*) Extent or Manner:—**

| *Principal.* | *Dependent.* |
|---|---|
| Men will reap | *as* (= to what extent or in what manner) they sow. |
| This is not true, | *so far as* I can find out. |
| He chose the men, | *according as* they were fit. |

| *Dependent.* | *Principal.* |
|---|---|
| *As* men sow, | *so* will they also reap. |

(*i*) **Time** :—

*Time simultaneous.*

| *Principal.* | *Dependent.* |
|---|---|
| He called at the house, | *as* the clock struck four. |
| I will leave the room, | *as soon as* you open the door. |
| You can hold the horse, | *while* I bring the saddle. |

*Time before.*

| *Principal.* | *Dependent.* |
|---|---|
| He worked very hard, | *before* he succeeded. |
| You have much to do, | *ere* you can gain your end. |
| He remained a minor, | *until* he was seventeen years old. |

*Time after.*

| *Principal.* | *Dependent.* |
|---|---|
| He returned home, | *after* he had done the work. |
| He has been very weak, | *since* he was taken sick. |

*Time how long.*

| *Principal.* | *Dependent.* |
|---|---|
| The sun will rise, | *while* the world lasts. |
| No one can harm us, | *so long as* we remain friends. |

*Relative and Interrogative Adverbs.*

**239.** It was explained in § 17 that a Relative adverb is a *double* part of speech,—a conjunction and adverb combined in one.

The same is true of Interrogative adverbs, when they are used as conjunctions :—

Let me ask you *how* you did this.

There is no difference in *form* between a Relative and an Interrogative adverb. The former qualifies some noun expressed or understood in the Principal sentence. The latter is preceded by some verb that signifies *asking* or *inquiring.*

Relative and Interrogative adverbs, so far as they join sentences, constitute a special class of Subordinative conjunctions.

**Time.**

| *Principal.* | | *Dependent.* |
|---|---|---|
| He remained silent, | *when* | (=as soon as) he heard that. |
| He feels sad, | *whenever* | (=at any time in which) he thinks of his lost friend. |
| My friend inquired | *when* | I should return. |

**Purpose, Cause,** or **Reason.**

| *Principal.* | | *Dependent.* |
|---|---|---|
| We never understood | *why* | (=the reason for which) he acted so. |

### Place.

| *Principal.* | | *Dependent.* |
|---|---|---|
| We find flowers, | *where* | (=in a place in which) we expected only weeds. |
| We find flowers, | *wherever* | (=in any place in which) we wander. |
| He did not tell us | *whence* | (=the place from which) he had come. |

### Respect.

| *Principal.* | | *Dependent.* |
|---|---|---|
| He did not tell us | *where* | (=in what point) we were wrong. |
| We cannot perceive | *where* | (=in what respect) the difference lies. |

### Manner or Means.

| *Principal.* | | *Dependent.* |
|---|---|---|
| Let me ask you, | *how* | (=by what means or in what manner) you did this. |

### State or Condition.

| *Principal.* | | *Dependent.* |
|---|---|---|
| Let me ask you, | *how* | (=in what state of health) you are to-day. |

### Doubt.

| *Principal.* | | *Dependent.* |
|---|---|---|
| He wished to know | *whether* | (or if) he was ready to start. |

*Note.*—A Relative adverb can often be substituted for a Relative pronoun, as in the following examples :—

{ Ten o'clock is the hour *when* we must start.
{ Ten o'clock is the hour *at which* we must start.

{ Tell me the reason *why* you left us.
{ Tell me the reason *for which* you left us.

{ This is the house *where* we once lived.
{ This is the house *in which* we once lived.

## CHAPTER IX.—INTERJECTIONS.

**240.** An Interjection is not a true Part of Speech, since it does not enter into the construction of a sentence.

It is merely an *exclamatory sound*, thrown into a sentence to denote some strong feeling or emotion (see §§ 12 and 13):—

*Joy.*—Hurrah ! huzza !
*Grief.*—Oh ! ah ! alas ! alack !
*Amusement.*—Ha ! ha !
*Approval.* Bravo !
*Weariness.* Heigh-ho !
*Attention.*—Lo! hark! hush! hist!
*Reproof.*—Fie ! fie !
*Contempt* or *ridicule* { Stuff! bosh! tut-tut! pooh! pish! pshaw! tush !
*To call some one.*—Ho ! holloa !

*Note.*—*Alas* is from Lat. *ah*, and *lassus*, wearied. *Alack* is from Middle Eng. *a! lak* (loss) !

**241**. There are certain **phrases** which are used like Interjections to express some strong feeling or emotion :—

*Ah me*, or *ay me! Woe is me!*
*For shame* (=alas, on account of shame!)
*Alack-a-day* (=ah, lack or loss on the day!)
*Hail, all hail* (=be hale or healthy!) *Welcome! Well done!*
*Good-bye* (=*God be with ye!*) *Adieu* (*à Dieu*, I commend you to God!) *Farewell* (may you fare well!)
*Bad luck to it! O dear me* (=O dear or costly for me!)
*Good gracious! Good heavens! Well to be sure!* (Surprise.)
*Zounds* (God's wounds). *'Sdeath* (God's death). *'Snails* (God's nails). *Marry* (Mary). *Parbleu*, Fr. (for *par Dieu*, by God).
*Wellaway*, A.S., wá lá wá, woe! lo! woe! corrupted also to *welladay*.

*Note* 1.—It will thus be seen that there are two different ways in which interjections may arise: (1) From sounds that naturally express the feelings, as most of the monosyllables given in § 240; as *heigh-ho* (which is like the sound of yawning), *ah* (which is like the sound of sighing), *ha, ha* (which resembles the sound of laughing). (2) From phrases that have been worn down to single words, the origin of which is disguised; as *alas, zounds, 'snails, parbleu, alackaday*, etc.

*Note* 2.—From *a-lack-a-day* we get the adj. *lackadaisical*, and the corruption *lauk-a-daisy*.

**242**. There are certain moods of verbs and parts of speech which can be used for an exclamatory or Interjectional purpose:—

(*a*) *Noun-Infinitive.—To think* that he should have died! (§ 191, *e*.)
(*b*) *Subjunctive.—Would* that I had gained that prize! (*Wish*.)
(*c*) *Imperative.—Hear! hear!* (*Applause*.)
(*d*) *Noun.*—Dreadful *sight!* Foolish *fellow! Fool! Dunce!*
(*e*) *Adjective* (with some noun understood).—*Strange! Shocking!*
(*f*) *Adverb.—How* very kind of you! *How* wonderful!
(*g*) *Pronoun.—What* a sad thing it is!
(*h*) *Conjunction.—If* I could only see him once more!

**243**. Sometimes in a rapid or exclamatory sentence an Auxiliary verb with its subject is left out, and only the main verb is expressed:—

Why dream and wait for him longer?—LONGFELLOW.
(=Why *dost thou* or why *do we* wait for him longer?)

## CHAPTER X.—ANALYSIS OF SENTENCES.

### SECTION 1.—ANALYSIS OF SIMPLE SENTENCES.

**244**. A sentence which has only *one* Finite verb (expressed or understood) is called a Simple sentence; as—

| *Subject.* | *Finite Verb.* |
|---|---|
| Rain . . . . | falls. |

The word "Simple" means *single*. The sentence is called *single* (or simple), because it has only *one* Finite verb in it.

**245.** A sentence that has *more than one* Finite verb expressed or understood is either Compound or Complex.

Thus:—"If I see him to-day, I will invite him to my house." This is not a Simple sentence, because it has *two* Finite verbs, viz. "see" and "will invite."

Again:—"He was well received and (was) listened to with respect, whenever he spoke." This is not a Simple sentence, because it has *three* Finite verbs, viz. "*was*" expressed, "*was*" understood, and "*spoke.*"

**246.** There are four distinct parts or elements of which a Simple sentence can be composed; and the analysis of a sentence consists in *decomposing* it (that is, in analysing or breaking it up) into these several parts:—

§ 1.—The Subject.
§ 2.—Adjuncts to the Subject, *if any.*
§ 3.—The Predicate.
§ 4.—Adjuncts to the Predicate-verb, *if any.*

Of these four elements the first and third (viz. the Subject and the Predicate) are essential to the sentence,—that is, the sentence could not exist without them (see § 2). But the second and fourth (viz. the Adjuncts to the Subject or to the Predicate-verb) are not essential. They are mere additions, which may or may not be present, and could be removed without destroying the sentence.

The chief use of Analysis is that it is an aid to Syntax, by showing the relations in which words stand to one another in a sentence. In a language like English, that has very few inflexions left, the best guide we can have as to the relations of words to one another is Analysis. Another use of Analysis is that it brings into prominence the *logical* side of grammar. It shows, for example, that an entire clause can be the subject to a verb, and thus logically equivalent to a noun.

**247.** I. The Subject must be either a *Noun* or something that has the force of a Noun.

II. The additions or Adjuncts to the Subject (if there are any) must be either *Adjectives* or words that have the force of an Adjective. They have hence been called Attributive Adjuncts. (They are sometimes also called the Enlargement of the Subject.)

III. The Predicate must either be a *Finite verb* or it must contain one.

IV. The additions or Adjuncts to the Predicate-verb (if there are any) must be either *Adverbs* or words that have the force of an Adverb. They have hence been called Adverbial Adjuncts.

(Sometimes also they have been called the Extension of the Predicate.)

| I. Subject. | II. Attributive Adjuncts (to Subject). | III. Predicate-verb. | IV. Adverbial Adjuncts (to Predicate). |
|---|---|---|---|
| A tiger | fierce | was shot | to-day. |
| The horse | tired | will sleep | soundly. |

*The Subject.*

**248. Forms of the Subject**; as shown below :—

| | | *Subject.* | *Predicate.* |
|---|---|---|---|
| (*a*) | *A Noun* . . . | Rain | is falling. |
| | *A Noun understood* | The virtuous (men) | will prosper. |
| (*b*) | *A Pronoun* . . . | We | must go. |
| (*c*) | *A Noun-Infinitive* . | To work | is healthy. |
| (*d*) | *A Gerund* . . | Working | is healthy. |
| (*e*) | *A Phrase* . . | How to do this | is doubtful. |

*Note* 1.—The above list of forms tallies with that given in § 21, except that (*f*) *a Clause* has been omitted. A clause belongs to Complex and Compound sentences, not to simple ones.

*Note* 2.—When a Noun-Infinitive is used as Subject, it is sometimes placed after the Predicate, and is in apposition to the pronoun "it."

It is sad to see this = It—viz. to see this—is sad.

*Attributive Adjuncts (to the Subject).*

**249. Forms of Attributive Adjunct**; as shown below :—

(*a*) *Adjective.*—A *heavy* shower fell to-day.
(*b*) *Participle.*—A *fertilising* shower fell to-day.
(*c*) *Gerundial Infinitive.*—Water *to drink* is scarce in this place.
(*d*) *Possessive Noun or Pronoun.*—*My son's* teacher called here to-day.
(*e*) *Noun used as Adjective.*—The *village* school has met.
(*f*) *Gerund used as Adjective.*—*Drinking* water is scarce here.
(*g*) *Noun in Apposition.*—Philip, *King* of Macedon, perished.
(*h*) *Preposition with Object.*—A man *of virtue* will not tell a lie.
(*i*) *Adverb with Participle understood.*—The *then* king = the then (reigning) king.

*Note.*—The articles go with the noun ; though they are adjectives in fact, they are not worth counting as Attributive Adjuncts.

*The Predicate.*

**250.** The Predicate must be either a Finite verb or it must contain one. If the verb is of such a nature, that it cannot by itself make a *complete* sense (as required by the definition given in § 1), but must have some word or words placed after it for this purpose, any such word or words must be considered parts of the predicate. All possible forms of a Predicate are shown in the following scheme:—

| Subject. | Predicate. | | |
|---|---|---|---|
| | Finite verb. | Object with qualifying words. | Complement with qualifying words. |
| 1. { A hog | grunts. | ... | ... |
| The snake | was killed. | ... | ... |
| 2. { My son | became | ... | a good scholar. |
| The thief | was ordered | ... | to be severely punished. |
| 3. { The gardener | killed | that poisonous snake. | ... |
| The teacher | will teach | (*a*) my sons (*b*) Euclid. | ... |
| 4. They | found | the weary man | sound asleep. |

In (1) we have first an Intransitive verb of Complete Predication (see § 146), and then a Transitive verb in the Passive voice. Neither of these requires either an Object or a Complement. So the verb alone makes up the Predicate.

In (2) we have first an Intransitive verb of Incomplete Predication (see § 147), and then a Factitive verb in the Passive voice (see § 162). Each of these requires a Complement to make the predication complete.

In (3) we have first a Transitive verb with a single Object (see § 139), and then a Transitive verb with a double Object (see § 141). Each of these requires the Object (single or double) to be expressed, before the predication can be complete.

In (4) we have a Factitive verb in the Active voice, which therefore requires both an Object and a Complement (see § 142).

*Note* 1.—If the Object or Complement has any qualifying words attached to it, these can be mentioned with it in the same column.

Thus in the complement "a good scholar," there is no need to make a separate column for the qualifying adjective "good."

Again, in the complement "to be severely punished," there is no need of a separate column for the qualifying adverb "severely."

Again, in stating the object "that poisonous snake," there is no need of a separate column for the qualifying adjectives "that" and "poisonous."

*Note* 2.—An Auxiliary verb may be put in the same column with the Principal verb. Thus in stating "will teach," we need not give one column for "will" and another for "teach." We may deal in the same way with the verbs *can* and *must*.

*Adverbial Adjuncts (to Verb of Predicate).*

**251. The Forms of Adverbial Adjunct** are shown below:—

(*a*) *Adverb.*—He sleeps ***soundly.***
(*b*) *Adverbial Phrase.*—They walked ***side by side.***
(*c*) *Adjective.*—He went away ***sad.*** He stood ***alone.***
(*d*) *Participle.*—He went away ***vexed*** and ***disappointed.***
(*e*) *Gerundial Infinitive.*—He came ***to see*** the horse.
(*f*) *Adverbial Objective.*—He walked ***all day.*** He walked ***ten miles.***
(*g*) *Preposition with Object.*—He fell ***into a deep well.***
(*h*) *Absolute Phrase.*—We all started, ***he remaining behind.***

*Examples for Analysis.*

1. A merchant, travelling through Tartary, having arrived at the town of Balkh, entered the king's palace by mistake, thinking it to be a public inn.

2. My father taught all his sons Euclid with much success.

3. Alexander, the King of Macedon, was surnamed the Great after his conquest of the Persian Empire.

4. The man employed for this purpose caught the thief stealing a watch.

5. The merchant, having much property to sell, caused all his goods to be conveyed on camels, there being no railway in that particular part of the country.

6. A gentleman of wealth and position, living in London, some sixty years ago, had a country seat in Kent, some forty miles from the metropolis.

(*These are worked out in tabular form on page* 107.)

SECTION 2.—ANALYSIS OF COMPOUND SENTENCES.

**252.** A **Compound** *sentence is one made up of two or more* **Co-ordinate** (*that is, equal or independent*) *clauses.*

The clauses of a Compound sentence are joined together by any of the *Co-ordinative Conjunctions* described in § 235.

(1) The sun rose with power, *and* the fog dispersed. (*Cumulative.*)
(2) Either he must leave the house *or* I (must leave the house). (*Alternative.*)
(3) He called at my house, *but* I did not see him. (*Adversitive.*)
(4) He came back tired ; *for* he had walked all day. (*Illative.*)

**253.** Co-ordinate clauses can also be joined together by a Relative pronoun or adverb, provided it is used in a **Continuative,** and not in a Restrictive sense (see § 127).

| I. Subject. | II. Attributive Adjuncts (to Subject). | III. Predicate. | | | IV. Adverbial Adjuncts (to Verb of Predicate). |
|---|---|---|---|---|---|
| | | Finite Verb. | Object with qualifying words. | Complement with qualifying words. | |
| 1. A merchant | (*a*) travelling through Tartary<br>(*b*) having arrived at the town of Balkh | entered | the king's palace | ... | (*a*) by mistake<br>(*b*) thinking it to be a public inn. |
| 2. Father | my | taught | (*a*) all his sons<br>(*b*) Euclid | ... | with much success. |
| 3. Alexander | the King of Macedon | was surnamed | ... | the Great | after the conquest of the Persian Empire. |
| 4. The man | employed for the purpose | caught | the thief | stealing a watch. | ... |
| 5. The merchant | having much property to sell | caused | all his goods | to be conveyed on camels | there being no railway in that particular part of the country. |
| 6. A gentleman | (*a*) of wealth and position<br>(*b*) living in London<br>(*c*) some sixty years ago | had | a country seat | ... | (*a*) in Kent<br>(*b*) some forty miles from the metropolis. |

He slew all the prisoners, *which* (=and this) was a very barbarous act.
He is clever at planting young trees; for *which* purpose (=and for this purpose) every one is glad to employ him.
He went to London, *where* (and there) he stayed ten days.

**254. Contracted Sentences.**—Compound sentences often appear in a contracted or shortened form, so as to avoid the needless repetition of the same word:—

(*a*) When there are *two Predicates to the same Subject*:—

(1) The sun *rose* and (the sun) *filled* the sky with light.
(2) He *called* at my house, but (he) *left* soon after.

(*b*) When there are *two Subjects to the same Predicate*:—

(1) *He* as well as *you* is guilty (=He is guilty as well as you are guilty). (*Cumulative.*)
(2) Either *this man* sinned or his *parents* (sinned). (*Alternative.*)
(3) He is poor, but (he is) honest. (*Adversative.*)
(4) He is diligent, and therefore (he is) prosperous. (*Illative.*)

*Note* 1.—When two nouns are joined by "*and*," they may be treated, not as separate subjects to the same verb, but as *one* compound subject to the Plural verb following:—

The dog-and-its-master *are* gone.

In some instances, such as the following, the two Subjects united by "*and*" are inseparable:—

He and I are great friends.
Youth and experience seldom exist together.

*Note* 2.—The phrase *as well as* can be used as a Subordinative conjunction, but of course in a different sense from that belonging to it as a Co-ordinative conjunction. This is explained in § 375 (2).

*Examples.*

(1) His greatest enemy, as well as his best friends, repeatedly declared him to be innocent of the fault laid to his charge.

*A.* His greatest enemy repeatedly declared him to be innocent of the fault laid to his charge.

*B.* His best friends repeatedly declared him to be innocent of the fault laid to his charge.

*Connective*:—As well as.

(2) Either you or your son must sign his name.

*A.* You must sign your name.
*B.* Your son must sign his name.

*Connectives*:—Either . . . or.

(3) He, not I, is certainly the author of that plan.

*A.* He is certainly the author of that plan.
*B.* I am certainly not the author of that plan.

*Connective*:—(*nil*). Here no connective is required.

| | The Clauses. | Connective. | I. Subject. | II. Attributive Adjuncts (to Subject). | III. Predicate. Finite Verb. | Object with qualifying words. | Complement with qualifying words. | IV. Adverbial Adjuncts (to Verb of Predicate.) |
|---|---|---|---|---|---|---|---|---|
| Example (1) | A. His greatest enemy repeatedly declared him to be innocent of the fault, etc. | ... | enemy | his greatest | declared | him | to be innocent of the fault laid to his charge | repeatedly. |
| | B. His best friends declared him to be innocent of the fault, etc. | as well as | friends | his best | declared | him | to be innocent of the fault, etc. | repeatedly. |
| Example (2) | A. You must sign your name at once on that paper. | either | you | *nil* | must sign | your name | *nil* | (*a*) at once (*b*) on that paper. |
| | B. Your son must sign his name at once on that paper. | or | your son | *nil* | must sign | his name | *nil* | (*a*) at once (*b*) on that paper. |
| Example (3) | A. He is certainly the author of that plan. | ... | He | *nil* | is | *nil* | the author of that plan | certainly. |
| | B. I am certainly not the author of that plan. | *nil* | I | *nil* | am not | *nil* | the author of that plan | certainly. |

## SECTION 3.—ANALYSIS OF COMPLEX SENTENCES.

**255.** A **Complex** *sentence consists of a Principal clause with one or more* **Subordinate** *clauses depending on it.*

The clause which contains *the main verb* of the entire complex sentence is called the **Principal** clause.

*Note.*—It has been said that the Principal clause is that which contains "the principal *subject* and predicate."[1] But this is not true; for sometimes there is no principal subject, the subject itself being a Subordinate clause :—

| *Subject (Subord. clause).* | *Predicate (Prin. verb).* |
|---|---|
| Who steals my purse | steals trash. |

**256. Subordinate and Co-ordinate Clauses.**—A Subordinate clause is a *component part* of some other clause, in which it does the work (without possessing the form) of a Noun, Adjective, or Adverb.

A Co-ordinate clause is not a component part of any other clause, but forms a *complete grammatical whole* by itself.

**257.** There are three kinds of Subordinate clauses,—the **Noun**-Clause, the **Adjective**-Clause, and the **Adverb**-Clause; and these are defined as follows :—

I. *A Noun-Clause is one which does the work of a Noun in relation to some other clause.*

II. *An Adjective-Clause is one which does the work of an Adjective in relation to some other clause.*

III. *An Adverb-Clause is one which does the work of an Adverb in relation to some other clause.*

*Note.*—The same clause may be a Noun-clause in one sentence, an Adjective-clause in another, and an Adverb-clause in another. This entirely depends on the context :—

*Where Moses was buried* is still unknown . . *Noun-clause.*
No one has seen the place *where Moses was buried* *Adj.-clause.*
They encamped *where Moses was buried* without knowing it . . . . . . . . *Adv.-clause.*

### I. *The Noun-Clause.*

**258.** There are three kinds of connectives, by which a Noun-Clause can be introduced :—

(1) The Conjunction "*that*" used in the sense of Apposition, or in a merely Introductory sense (see § 238, *a*) :—

We did not know *that* he would leave us so soon.

---

[1] See for example Mason's *English Grammar*, page 160.

(2) A Relative or Interrogative adverb, provided that no Antecedent is expressed :—

*Where* he is going is not known to any one. (*Relat.*)
Let us inquire *whether* he will go to-day. (*Interrog.*)

*Note.*—The conjunction "*if*" can be used for "*whether*" as an Interrogative adverb—

Let us inquire *if* (=*whether*) he will go to-day.

(3) A Relative or Interrogative pronoun, provided that no Antecedent is expressed :—

*Who* steals my purse steals trash. (*Relat.*)
I beg to inquire *who* came here to-day. (*Interrog.*)

**259.** The Noun-Clause, since it does the work of a Noun, can be—

(*a*) The Subject to a Verb.
(*b*) The Object to a Verb.
(*c*) The Object to a Preposition.
(*d*) The Complement to a Verb.
(*e*) In Apposition to a Noun.

(*a*) **Subject to a Verb**; see § 21 (*f*):—

*Where he is going* is not known to any one.
*That he will come back soon* is certain.
*Whom the gods love* die young.—*Proverb.*

(*b*) **Object to a Verb**; see § 23 (*f*):—

He promised *that he would soon pay back the debt.*
I shall be glad to know *when he will pay it.*
Perceiving *what a mistake he had made*, he yielded.

(*c*) **Object to a Preposition**; see § 228 (*d*):—

My success in future depends upon *who is placed over me.*
This book will sell for *what it is worth.*
Except *that he speaks too fast* he is an excellent teacher.

(*d*) **Complement to a Verb**; see § 143 and § 147 :—

This is exactly *what I expected.*
His teachers have made him *what he is.*

(*e*) **In Apposition to a Noun**; see § 19 :—

The news *that he intended to come* gave us much pleasure.
The reason *why he was so sad* is unknown to me.

**260.** The conjunction "*that*" (in the sense of apposition) is often left out after a *verb*, provided that the noun with which the clause is in apposition is not expressed :—

It seems (that) *he is not clever.*

*N.B.*—The conjunction "*that*" is never left out *when the noun is expressed.* Such a sentence as the following is inadmissible :—

The *fact he is not clever* gives us much pain.

**261.** A sentence consisting of the very words spoken by any one may be the Subject or Object to a verb, and must therefore be considered as an example of a Noun-Clause :—

"I have seen this man before," was the only thing that he said.
The sleeper started up from his bed, shouting, "I am bitten."

### *Examples of the Noun-Clause.*

*Pick out the Noun-Clause and say whether it is the Subject to some Verb, or the Object to some Verb, or the Object to some Preposition, or the Complement to some Verb, or in Apposition to some noun expressed. Supply the Conjunction* "that" *wherever it has been left out :—*

1. No one knows when he will come, or whether he will come at all, or whether he is even alive.
2. How this came to pass is not known to any one.
3. What is sauce for the goose is sauce for the gander.
4. It is quite evident rain will fall to-day.
5. The Equator shows where days and nights are of equal length.
6. What is one man's meat is another man's poison.
7. You must know that the air is never quite at rest.
8. I think I shall never clearly understand this.
9. We heard the school would open in ten days' time.
10. The name "Volcano" indicates the belief of the ancient Greeks, that the burning hills of the Mediterranean were the workshops of the divine blacksmith, Vulcan.
11. Even a feather shows which way the wind is blowing.
12. Whatever faculty man has is improved by use.
13. The fool hath said in his heart, "There is no God."
14. "Know thyself," was the advice given us by a Greek sage.
15. He did not know that his father had been shot.
16. The fact that you have not signed your name to a letter shows that you lack moral courage.
17. It will be easily understood how useful even the simplest weapons were to the first dwellers on the earth.
18. The question first occurring to the mind of a savage is how is fire to be made.
19. Common sense soon taught him that fire could be produced by rubbing two sticks together.
20. In chipping their flint weapons men must have seen that fire occasionally flashed out.
21. We learn from travellers that savages can produce fire in a few seconds.
22. He shouted out to the thief, "Leave this house."
23. We cannot rely on what he says.
24. It is quite evident you have made a mistake.
25. It was very unfortunate that you were taken ill.
26. He was a man of fine character except that he was rather timid.

### II. *The Adjective-Clause.*

**262.** An Adjective-Clause does the work of an Adjective to some noun or noun-equivalent in some other clause.

The only kind of connective word by which an Adjective-Clause can be introduced is a Relative pronoun or Relative adverb, and then only when the Relative is used in a **Restrictive** sense (see § 127).

If the Relative is used in a **Continuative** sense, the sentence is Compound, and not Complex (see § 253).

1. Among the men, *who came here to-day,* not one turned out to be honest.

Here the italicised clause qualifies or restricts "*men.*"

2. We found the wolf lying dead in the very place *where* (=*in which*) *it was shot.*

Here the italicised clause qualifies or restricts "*place.*"

**263.** The Relative pronoun, provided it would be in the Objective case, and provided its sense is Restrictive, and not Continuative, is often left out (see § 144).

The food he needed (=*which* or *that* he needed) was not procured without a great deal of trouble.

*Pick out the Adjective-Clause or Clauses in each of the following examples, and point out the noun or pronoun qualified by it in some other clause. If the Relative pronoun has been omitted anywhere, supply it:—*

1. Man has the power of making instruments, which bring into view stars, whose light has taken a thousand years to reach the earth.
2. The first thing that man needed was some sharp-edged tool.
3. The exact time when the theft was committed was never found out.
4. The man by whom the theft was committed has been caught.
5. The house we lived in has fallen down.
6. This is the same story that I heard ten years ago.
7. It's an ill wind that blows no one any good.
8. This is not such a book as I should have chosen.
9. He made his living by the presents he received from the men he served.
10. All that glitters is not gold.
11. In ponds from which but a week before the wind blew clouds of dust, men now catch the re-animated fish.
12. A river is joined at places by tributaries that swell its waters.
13. Of what use is a knowledge of books to him who fails to practise virtue?
14. Fortune selects him for her lord, who reflects before acting.
15. Springs are fed by rain, which has percolated through the rocks or soil.
16. Nuncoomar prepared to die with that quiet fortitude with

which the Bengalee, so backward, as a rule, in personal conflict, often encounters calamities for which there is no remedy.

17. I have seen the house where Shakspeare was born.
18. The plan you acted on has answered well.
19. They accepted every plan we proposed.
20. Surely the story you are telling me is not true.
21. Thrice is he armed that hath his quarrel just.
22. The night is long that never finds the day.
23. He travelled home by the way his father showed him.
24. There are times when every one feels a little sad.
25. Such men as are false to their friends should always be avoided.
26. I forgot to tell you the time when I shall return.

### III. *The Adverb-Clause.*

**264.** An Adverb-Clause does the work of an Adverb to some verb, adjective, or adverb in some other clause.

An Adverb-Clause can be introduced by any of the *Subordinative* conjunctions, excepting the conjunction "*that*," when it is used in the sense of Apposition.

| *Principal Clause.* | *Adverb-Clause.* | *Subord. Conjunc.* |
|---|---|---|
| He will succeed, | *because* he works hard . | *Cause.* |
| He worked *so* hard, | *that* he was quite tired . | *Effect.* |
| He took medicine | *that* he might get well . | *Purpose.* |
| I will do this, | *if* I am allowed . . . | *Condition.* |
| He is honest, | *although* he is poor . . | *Contrast.* |
| He likes you *more* | *than* (he likes) me . . | *Comparison.* |
| Men will reap | *as* they sow . . . . | *Extent or Manner.* |
| The sun will rise, | *so long as* the world lasts . | *Time.* |

*Note.*—The Subordinative conjunctions have been described and enumerated in § 238. Besides these there is the class of Subordinative connectives, which in § 239 are enumerated under the name of Relative and Interrogative adverbs. These can be used for Noun-clauses and Adjective-clauses as well as for Adverb-clauses.

**265.** After the conjunctions *though, when, unless, till, if, whether . . . or*, and *while*, the Predicate-verb "**to be**" is often understood. This must be supplied in the Analysis.

{ Though much alarmed at the news, he did not lose all hope.
{ Though *he was* much alarmed, etc., he did not lose all hope.
{ He sprained his foot, while walking in the dark.
{ He sprained his foot, while *he was* walking in the dark.
{ His opinion, whether right or wrong, does not concern me.
{ His opinion, whether *it is* right or wrong, does not concern me.
This must be kept, till (*it is*) called for.

**266.** When an Adverb-Clause is introduced by "**than,**" its Predicate-verb is not always expressed; it must therefore be borrowed from the clause on which it depends:—

He loves you better than (he loves) me.
He loves you better than I (love you).

**267.** The Relative "**who**" or "**which**" makes an Adverb-Clause, whenever it is substituted for a Subordinative conjunction signifying Cause or Purpose. (See § 127, *Note.*)

*Cause.*—They should pardon my son, *who* (=*because he*) has never committed such a fault before.

*Purpose.*—A man was sent, *who* should deliver (=*that he* might deliver) the message.

*Note.*—The student can now therefore take note that four different kinds of clauses can be introduced by the Relative "who" or "which":—(1) A *Co-ordinate* Clause, where the Relative is used in a **Continuative** sense. This belongs to Compound sentences. (2) A *Noun*-Clause, where no Antecedent to the Relative is expressed. This belongs to Complex sentences. (3) An *Adjective*-Clause, where the Relative is used in a **Restrictive** sense. This belongs to Complex sentences. (4) An *Adverb*-Clause, where the Relative is used in the sense of **Cause** or **Purpose.** This also belongs to Complex sentences.

*Pick out the Adverb-Clause or Clauses in the following. Show what word or phrase is qualified by every such clause, and what Adverbial relation is denoted thereby:—*

1. He will succeed, because he has worked hard.
2. Men engage in some work, that they may earn a living.
3. He threatened to beat him, unless he confessed.
4. He was always honest, though he was poor.
5. This is not true, so far as I can tell.
6. He likes you as much as I do.
7. He tried for a long time before he succeeded.
8. Let us go to bed, as it is now late.
9. He walked with care, lest he should stumble.
10. I agree to this, provided you sign your name.
11. Though he punish me, yet will I trust in him.
12. He returned home, after he had finished the work.
13. Prove a friend, before you trust him.
14. When the cat's away, the mice will play.
15. He persevered so steadily, that he succeeded at last.
16. I will let off this man, who has been well punished already.
17. He sees very well, considering that he is sixty years of age.
18. I gave him a prize, that he might work harder next year.
19. They deserted their former associate, who had become poor and unfortunate.
20. As the tree falls, so will it lie.
21. Ever since we left the house, it has not ceased raining.
22. I would be glad to lend you that money, if I had as much in my own pocket.
23. Murder, though it have no tongue, will yet speak.
24. Unless you leave the house at once, I will send for a policeman.
25. A jackal, while prowling about the suburbs of a town, slipped into an indigo tank; and not being able to get out he laid himself down, so that he might be taken for dead.

26. The owner of the tank, when he beheld what seemed to be a dead jackal, carried the body into the jungle and there flung it down.

27. This one fact, if closely examined, proves the man to be guilty.

28. He is an honest man, though poor; and industrious, though old and rather infirm.

29. Better to reign in hell than serve in heaven.—MILTON.

30. If the trunk of a tree, when young and pliable, is not made to grow straight, it cannot be straightened afterwards, when old and stiff.

31. A rabbit cannot run so swiftly as a hare; but it is more skilful than a hare in digging the ground and boring holes under the earth.

32. The wild grey rabbit is not so large as the tame rabbit kept in a cage.

*Example of a mixed sentence analysed.*

*The governor of the town, who was present, called out with a loud voice and ordered Androcles to explain how a savage beast could have so forgotten its innate disposition all of a sudden, that it became converted into a harmless animal, which preferred rather to spare its victim than to devour him.*

(*This is worked out in tabular form in page* 117.)

**268.** The analysis of the last example might be shown as follows:—

*A.* "The governor of the town cried out with a loud voice":—

(*a*) *Relation to other clauses:* principal
(*b*) *Subject:* the governor
(*c*) *Enlargement of Subj.:* of the town
(*d*) *Predicate-verb with complement:* cried out
(*e*) *Extension of Pred.:* with a loud voice.

*B.* "Who was present":—

(*a*) *Relation to other clauses:* co-ordinate to A.
(*b*) *Subject:* who
(*c*) *Enlargement of Subj.:* nil
(*d*) *Predicate-verb with complement:* was present
(*e*) *Extension of Pred.:* nil.

*C.* "And (the governor of the town) ordered Androcles to explain":—

(*a*) *Relation to other clauses:* co-ordinate to A.
(*b*) *Subject:* the governor
(*c*) *Enlargement of Subj.:* of the town
(*d*) *Predicate-verb with complement:* ordered to explain
(*e*) *Extension of Pred.:* nil
(*f*) *Object:* Androcles
(*g*) *Enlargement of Obj.:* nil.

*D.* "How a savage beast could have so forgotten its innate disposition all of a sudden":—

(*a*) *Relation to other clauses:* Noun-clause; object to "explain"
(*b*) *Subject:* a beast

| The Clause. | Kind of Clause. | Connective. | I. Subject. | II. Attributive Adjuncts (to Subject). | III. Predicate. | | | IV. Adverbial Adjuncts (to Verb of Predicate). |
|---|---|---|---|---|---|---|---|---|
| | | | | | Finite Verb. | Object with qualifying words. | Complement with qualifying words. | |
| A. The governor of the town cried out with a loud voice, | Principal Clause. | .. | the governor | of the town | cried out | *nil* | *nil* | with a loud voice, |
| B. Who was present, | Co-ordinate to A. (§ 253). | who | who | *nil* | was | *nil* | present, | *nil* |
| C. And ordered Androcles to explain | Co-ordinate to A. | and | (the governor) | *nil* | ordered | Androcles | to explain, etc. | *nil* |
| D. How a savage beast could have so forgotten its innate disposition all of a sudden, | Noun-Clause, object to *explain* in C. | how | a beast | savage | could have forgotten | its innate disposition | *nil* | (*a*) all of a sudden, (*b*) so that, etc. |
| E. That it became converted into a harmless animal, | Adverb-Clause in continuation of *so* in D. | that | it | *nil* | became | *nil* | converted into a harmless animal, which, etc. | *nil* |
| F. Which preferred rather to spare its victim | Adject.-Clause to *animal* in E. | which | which | *nil* | preferred | to spare its victim | *nil* | rather than, etc. |
| G. Than devour him. | Adverb-Clause in continuation of *rather* in F. | than | (it) | *nil* | (preferred) | to devour him. | *nil* | *nil* |

(c) *Enlargement of Subj.:* savage
(d) *Predicate-verb with complement:* could have forgotten
(e) *Extension of Pred.:* (1) so, (2) all of a sudden
(f) *Object:* disposition
(g) *Enlargement of Obj.:* (1) its, (2) innate.

*E.* "That it became converted into a harmless animal":—

(a) *Relation to other clauses:* Adverb-clause to "forgotten"
(b) *Subject:* it
(c) *Enlargement of Subj.:* nil
(d) *Predicate-verb with complement:* became converted into a harmless animal
(e) *Extension of Pred.:* nil.

*F.* "Which preferred rather to spare its victim":—

(a) *Relation to other clauses:* Adjective-clause to animal"
(b) *Subject:* which
(c) *Enlargement of Subj.:* nil
(d) *Predicate-verb with complement:* preferred
(e) *Extension of Pred.:* rather
(f) *Object:* to spare its victim
(g) *Enlargement of Obj.:* nil.

*G.* "Than (it preferred to) devour him":—

(a) *Relation to other clauses:* Adverb-clause to "preferred"
(b) *Subject:* it
(c) *Enlargement of Subj.:* nil
(d) *Predicate-verb with complement:* preferred
(e) *Extension of Pred.:* nil
(f) *Object:* to devour him
(g) *Enlargement of Obj.:* nil.

## CHAPTER XI.

### THE SAME WORD USED AS DIFFERENT PARTS OF SPEECH

**A.** *Indef. Article.* The sportsman shot *a* tiger.
*Prep.* He has gone *a*-hunting.

**All.** *Adj. of Quantity.* He ate *all* the bread.
*Indef. Num. Adj.* We must *all* die some day.
*Adj. used as Noun.* We lost our *all* on that day.
*Adv.* *All* bloodless lay the untrodden snow.

**Any.** *Adj. of Quantity.* Have you *any* bread?
*Adv. of Qu.* We must stop and rest before going *any* farther.
*Indef. Num. Adjective.* Did you bring *any* loaves?
*Indef. Dem. Adjective.* Take *any* book that you like best.

**As.** (a) *Relative pronoun*:—
He is not such a fool *as* he looks.
As many men *as* came were caught.
Yours is not the same book *as* mine.

(*b*) *Relative adverb* (or subordinative conjunction):—
*Time.* He trembled *as* (at what time) he spoke.
*Manner.* Do not act *as* (in what manner) he did.
*State.* He took it just *as* (in what state) it was.
*Extent.* He is not as (to that extent) clever *as* (to what extent) you are.
Hot *as* (to whatever extent) the sun is (= however hot the sun is), we must go out in it.
*Reason.* The air is now cool, *as* (for what reason or for the reason that) the rain has fallen.

(*c*) *In Elliptical Phrases*:—all of these imply "extent."
I condemn you *as* a judge (to what extent or so far as I am a judge), but *as* a man (to what extent I am a man), I pity you.
I will inquire again *as* to (to what extent the question relates to) that matter.
*As* regards this journey (to what extent the question regards this journey), we can now decide nothing.

**Better.** *Comp. Adj.* My book is a *better one* than yours.
*Comp. Adv.* You are working *better* to-day.
*Adj. used as Noun.* Do not despise your *betters.*

**Both.** *Def. Num. Adj.* *Both* the men have arrived.
*Conj. Co-ord.* He is *both* a fool and a knave.

**But.** *Adv.* There is *but* (only) one man present.
*Prep.* Who could have done this *but* (except) him?
I cannot *but* believe that you are lost. (I cannot believe anything *except* that, etc.)
*Conj. Co-ord.* He is a man of common sense, *but* not learned in books.
*Conj. Subord.* There was no one present, *but* (he) pitied (= who did not pity) the lame horse.
Perdition catch my soul, *but* I love thee.—SHAKSPEARE. (May perdition catch my soul, *if* I do *not* love thee.)

**Either.** *Distrib. Adj.* He is ruined in *either* case.
*Conj. Co-ord.* He is *either* a fool or a knave.

**Else.** *Adv.* We could not catch any one *else.*
*Conj. Co-ord.* He has some real sorrow; *else* he would not weep as he does.

**Enough.** *Adj. of Quantity.* He has eaten *enough* bread.
*Adj. of Number.* We have *enough* loaves.
*Adj. used as Noun.* He had *enough* to do.

**Half.** *Adj. of Quantity.* *Half* measures do not succeed.
*Adj. used as Noun.* One *half* of his task is now done.
*Adv. of Quantity.* He was *half* dead with fear.

**Little.** *Adj. of Quality.* A *little* blow may give much pain.
*Adj. of Quantity.* He has eaten *a little* bread.
*Adv. of Quantity.* Let us wait here *a little.*
*Adj. used as Noun.* Man wants but *little* here below.

**More.** *Adj. of Quantity.* He eats *more* bread than you.
*Adj. used as Noun.* *More* is done than was expected.
*Adv. of Quantity.* I like him *more* than (I like) you.
*Adj. of Number.* *More* men came to-day than yesterday.
*Adv. of Number.* I saw him once *more*.

**Much.** *Adj. of Quantity.* He has wasted *much* time.
*Adv. of Quantity.* I am *much* pleased with your son.
*Adj. used as Noun.* You will not get *much* from me.

**Neither.** *Adj. Distrib.* I agree with *neither* side.
*Conj. Co-ord.* *Neither* you nor I can do that.

**Near.** *Adv.* Stand *near*, while I speak to you.
*Prep.* There is a fine tree *near* our house.
*Adj.* He is a *near* relative of mine.

**Needs.** *Verb.* The earth is very dry and *needs* rain.
*Adv.* He must *needs* know the reason of this.
*Noun.* Our *needs* or wants are few.

**One.** *Def. Num. Adj.* There is but *one* shilling left.
*Indef. Dem. Adj.* He came here *one* day.
*Indef. Dem. Pron.* *One* is apt to waste *one's* time.
*Def. Dem. Pron.* Your horse is white; mine is a black *one*.

**Only.** *Adj.* The *only* dog I had was stolen.
*Adv.* I heard of this *only* yesterday.
*Conj. Co-ord.* Do what you like; *only* (=but whatever else you may do) keep silence.

**Round.** *Adj.* A square thing does not fit into a *round* hole.
*Prep.* Draw a circle *round* a given centre.
*Adv.* The flies are flying *round* and *round*.
*Verb.* Gama was the first to *round* the Cape of Good Hope.
*Noun.* Men must go their daily *round* of duty.

**Since.** *Prep.* I have not seen him *since* Monday last.
*Adv.* I took this house four weeks *since*.
*Conj. Subord.* We must trust you, *since* you are speaking in earnest

**Single.** *Verb.* *Single* out the best.
*Adj.* He is a *single* (unmarried) man.

**Such.** *Def. Dem. Adj.* He is not *such* a man *as* I expected.
*Indef. Dem. Adj.* He came to me on *such* a day.
*Def. Dem. Pron.* You are a coward; I am not *such*.

**That.** *Def. Dem. Adj.* I am no admirer of *that* book.
*Def. Dem. Pron.* The light of the sun is brighter than *that* of the moon.
*Relat. Pron.* The book *that* you gave me is lost.
*Conj.* { *Effect.* He aimed *so* well *that* he hit the mark.
*Apposit.* He heard *that* you had come.
*Purpose.* We must eat *that* we may live. }

**Than.** *Conj. Subord.* I like this more *than* (I like) that.
*Prep.* { These workmen, *than* whom I have never seen men more industrious, have left me.
He was fond of any drink other *than* wine. }

**Then.** *Adv. of Time.* He was better *then* than he is now.
*Conj. Co-ord.* I see, *then*, we ought to start at once.

**The.** *Def. Article.* *The* ass is a dull animal.
*Adv. of Quantity.* *The* more, *the* merrier.

**Too.** *Adv. of Quantity.* He is *too* fond of play.
*Conj. Co-ord.* We *too* must expect to die some day.

**Well.** *Adv. of Quality.* He has done the work very *well.*
*Adv. used as Noun.* Leave *well* alone.
*Conj. Co-ord.* He has finished his work in time ; *well,* I did not expect it of such a lazy man.

**What.** *Inter. Pron.* *What* did you say ? *What* house is that ?
*Rel. Pron.* I do not know *what* you mean, § 123 (*b*).
*Indef. Demons.* I tell you *what* (=something) ; see § 315.
*Adverb.* *What* with illness and *what* with losses, the poor man is almost ruined (see chap. xx. 76).

**While.** *Noun.* Stop a little *while.*
*Conj.* *While* the cat's away, the mice play.

**Yet.** *Conj. Co-ord.* I have called ; *yet* no one answers.
*Adv. of Time.* You may *yet* (=even now, still) find him.

## CHAPTER XII.—SYNTAX.

### Parsing Chart.

#### I. *Nouns.*

| Kind of Noun. | Gender. | Number. | Case. |
|---|---|---|---|
| Proper<br>Common<br>Collective<br>Material<br>Abstract | Masculine<br>Feminine<br>Common<br>Neuter | Singular<br>Plural | Nominative<br>Possessive<br>Objective |

#### II. *Pronouns.*

| Kind of Pronoun. | Gender. | Number. | Person. | Case. |
|---|---|---|---|---|
| Pers. { Simple<br>Reflexive<br>Demons. { Definite<br>Indefinite | Masculine<br>Feminine<br>Common<br>Neuter | Singular<br>Plural | 1st<br>2nd<br>3rd | Nominative<br>Possessive<br>Objective |
| Relative<br>Interrogative | Agreeing in Gender, Number, and Person with its antecedent. | | | |

### III. *The Cases of Nouns or Pronouns.*

| | | |
|---|---|---|
| *Nom.* to Verb.<br>,, as Compl. to Verb<br>,, in Apposition<br>,, of Address<br>,, Absolute<br>*Possessive* | *Obj.* to Verb Direct<br>,, ,, Indirect<br>,, ,, Retained<br>,, ,, Cognate<br>,, ,, Reflexive<br>,, as Compl. to Verb | *Obj.* in Apposition<br>,, to Preposition<br>,, Adverbial<br>,, after certain Adjectives<br>,, Interjectional |

### IV. *Adjectives.*

| The Kind of Adjective. | | Degree. | Use. |
|---|---|---|---|
| Proper.<br>Of Quality.<br>Of Quantity.<br>Distributive. | Numer. { Def. Indef.<br>Demons. { Def. Indef. | Positive<br>Comparative<br>Superlative | Attributive<br>Predicative |

### V. *Adverbs.*

| Kind. | Degree. | Use. | Attributive Uses. |
|---|---|---|---|
| Simple<br>Relative<br>Interrogative | Positive<br>Comparative<br>Superlative | Attributive<br>Predicative | To qualify Verb<br>,, ,, Adjective<br>,, ,, Adverb<br>,, ,, Preposition<br>,, ,, Conjunction<br>,, ,, Sentence |

### VI. *Finite Verbs.*

| Kind of Verb. | Person. | Number. | Tense. | Form. |
|---|---|---|---|---|
| { Transitive<br>Intransitive<br>Auxiliary | 1st<br>2nd<br>3rd | Singular<br>Plural | Present<br>Past<br>Future | { Indefinite<br>Continuous<br>Perfect<br>Perf. Contin. |

| Mood. | Voice. | |
|---|---|---|
| Indicative<br>Imperative<br>Subjunctive | Active<br>Passive | Agreeing with its subject or subjects, expressed or understood.<br>Governing its object or objects, expressed or understood. |

### VII. *Infinitive.*

| Form. | (*a*) Use as Noun-Inf. | (*b*) Use as Gerundial Inf. |
|---|---|---|
| Indefinite<br>Continuous<br>Perfect<br>Perf. Contin. | Subject to Verb<br>Object to Verb<br>Complement to Verb<br>Object to Preposition<br>Exclamatory | To qualify—<br>,, a Verb<br>,, a Noun { Attributively<br>Predicatively<br>,, an Adjective<br>To introduce a Parenthesis |

### VIII. *Participle or Verbal Adjective.*

| Form. | Voice. | Kind of Verb. | Use. |
|---|---|---|---|
| Present<br>Past<br>Perfect | Active<br>Passive | Transitive<br>Intransitive | Attributive<br>Predicative { Complement<br>Absolute<br>Gerundive |

### IX. *Gerund.*

| Form. | Voice. | Kind of Verb. |
|---|---|---|
| Present<br>Perfect | Active<br>Passive | Transitive<br>Intransitive |

### X. *Conjunctions.*

| Co-ordinative. | Subordinative. |
|---|---|

*Most of the following rules have been incidentally given already in different places. They are here collected and summarised; and others not given before have been added, so as to make the account more complete.*

**269. Nominative case.**—See No. III. of Parsing Chart.

(1) As Subject to a verb (see § 55):—

*I* did this. *Rain* is falling. *You* are tired.

(2) As *Subjective* Complement to a verb (see § 147):—

I am *the man*. Cæsar was declared *emperor*.

*Note.*—An Infinitive can come between the verb and the noun:—

He appeared *to be* a wise man.

(3) In Apposition with a noun or pronoun in the Nominative case (see § 18):—

John, *the carpenter*, has succeeded well in business.

(4) For purposes of Address (see § 55):—

How art thou fallen, *O Cæsar!*

(5) In the Absolute construction (see § 27, *a*):—

(*a*) *With Participle*, in **past** or **present** sense:—

Off we started, he *remaining behind*.
Off we started, he *having given* the signal.

*Note.*—Without altering the sense, we could substitute the clause "while he remained behind" for the phrase "he remaining behind." In the absolute construction the noun or pronoun is in the Nominative case, because (as we see from this) it is *the Subject to the Finite verb that is implied in the Participle.*

(*b*) *With Gerundial Infinitive*, in **future** sense; § 192 (*b*).

The caul was put up in a raffle, *the winner to pay* five shillings.—DICKENS, *David Copperfield.*

The estate has been divided between us, *you to have* two-thirds of it, and *I* one-third.

**270. Possessive case.**—See No. III. of Parsing Chart. (*a*) A noun or pronoun in the Possessive case qualifies Nouns and Gerunds as an adjective would do (§ 96, 4):—

*My* son. The *barber's* shop. The *tiger's* claw.—*Noun.*
I was displeased at *his* going away without leave. } *Gerund*
This was a plan of *your* contriving. } (§ 206).

(*b*) When two Possessive nouns are in apposition with each other, or are connected by "*and*," the apostrophe *s* is not added to the noun that stands *first* (see § 60):—

Herod married his *brother* Philip's wife.
*Maple* and Company's firm.

*Note.*—Sometimes, however, the *s* is given to the noun that stands first:—

For the *queen's* sake, his sister.—BYRON.

(*c*) A noun or pronoun in the Possessive case can be the Complement to a verb; (for Pronouns, see § 109, *a*):—

That book is *mine*, not *yours*.
This shop seems to be *a barber's*.

**271. Objective case.**—See No. III. of Parsing Chart.

(1) As Object to verb (§ 161, *Note*):—

(*a*) The master teaches *Euclid*. (*Direct.*)
(*b*) He teaches *his sons* Euclid. (*Indirect.*)
(*c*) His sons were taught *Euclid*. (*Retained.*)

(*d*) The fever will run its *course*. (*Cognate.*)[1]
(*e*) He sat *himself* down. (*Reflexive.*)

(2) As Objective Complement to a verb (§ 147):—

The citizens made him their *king*.

*Note.*—An Infinitive can come between the verb and the noun:—

The people considered him *to be* a wise man.

(3) In Apposition with a noun or pronoun in the Objective case (§ 18):—

The people of England beheaded Charles I., their *king*.

(4) As Object to a preposition (§ 56):—

He fought against *me*. A house built on *sand*.

(5) Adverbial Objective:—so called because such phrases qualify words as an adverb would do:—

He lived ten *years* (Time). He walked ten *miles* (Space). This cost ten *shillings* (Price). That box weighs ten *pounds* (Weight). The air is a *trifle* hotter to-day (Degree). Bind him *hand* and *foot* (Attendant circumstance).

(6) Objective after the adjectives "like" or "unlike," "near," "next." (This has probably arisen from the omission of the preposition "*to*," which is still sometimes used after these adjectives):—

No man could bend the bow *like him*.
The house *nearest the grove* is the one that I prefer.

(7) Objective after Interjections or in exclamatory phrases:—

Woe is *me!* Oh unhappy *man!* Oh dear *me!*
Foolish *fellow!* to have wasted his time as he has done!

**272. The two uses of Adjectives.**—See No. IV. of Parsing Chart.

(*a*) Attributive use (§ 95):—

An *industrious* student will generally succeed.

(*b*) Predicative use (§ 95):—

He was *industrious*, and therefore he succeeded.

**273. Noun or Gerund used as an Adjective** (§ 96, 3). A noun or gerund can be used attributively for an adjective, but not predicatively:—

---

[1] It is maintained in Mason's *English Grammar*, p. 150, ed. 1891, that "the cognate objective should more properly be classed among the Adverbial Adjuncts," that is, as an Adverbial objective, see § 271 under (5). This we cannot admit, because when the verb of the sentence is changed from Active to Passive, as "He fought a good fight," "A good fight was fought by him," the Cognate object becomes the Subject; whereas if the cognate object were adverbial, it would remain adverbial.

A *village* watchman. *Drinking* water.
A *sea* captain. *Marble* halls. A *bathing* place.

**274. Adjective substituted for Adverb.**—An adverb qualifying a *verb* can be changed into an adjective qualifying the *subject* to the verb. The adjective in this case does the work of an "adverbial adjunct" to the verb (§ 251, *c*):—

The stars are shining *bright*.
And *furious* every charger neighed.—CAMPBELL.
*Dark* lowers the tempest overhead.—LONGFELLOW.
And *fearless* there the lowly sleep.—MRS. HEMANS.
They neither toil nor spin, but *careless* grow.—THOMSON.
*Slow* rises worth, by poverty depressed.—JOHNSON.

*Note* 1.—When the adverb qualifies *any part of speech except a verb*, we cannot substitute an adjective for it. Thus we cannot say "He is *immense* clever" for "He is *immensely* clever."

*Note*. 2.—In poetry an adjective and adverb are sometimes coupled together by "*and*" when the adjective qualifies the subject to the verb, and the adverb qualifies the verb itself:—

When *faint* and *wearily* he drags
Along his noontide way.—SOUTHEY.
Trip it *deft* and *merrily*.—SCOTT.
But Sir Richard bore in hand
All the sick men from the land
Very *carefully* and *slow*.—TENNYSON.

**275. Pronoun and Antecedent.**—See Nos. II. and III. of Parsing Chart.

(*a*) A Pronoun must be in the same case, number, and gender as its Antecedent; but in case it depends upon its own sentence. (This is called a Concord or Agreement.)

After Cæsar was declared *emperor* (Nominative), they slew *him* (Objective).

You must return the *book* (Objective), *which* (Nominative) was lent.

*Note*.—To prevent any doubt as to what word is meant to be the antecedent, the antecedent should be placed as close as possible to the relative following.

(*b*) A Relative Pronoun, if it has two Antecedents, and these are not of the same person, agrees in person with the Antecedent *nearest to it*:—

You are the man who *is* (not *are*) chosen.

**276. The two uses of Adverbs.**—See No. V. of Parsing Chart.

(*a*) Attributive use (§ 226). An adverb, used attributively, may qualify anything except a noun or pronoun:—

(1) *Adjective.*—He is *remarkably clever*.
(2) *Verb.*—*Act decisively*, if you act at all.

(3) *Other Adverb.*—He explained his views *remarkably well.*
(4) *Preposition.*—The sun stood *exactly over* our heads.
(5) *Conjunction.*—You may go *only if* you promise to return.
(6) *Sentence.*—*Fortunately*, all the thieves were caught.

(*b*) Predicative use (§ 226). Here the adverb is Complement to the verb going before :—

(1) *Subjective.*—The results will soon be *out* (=published).
(2) *Objective.*—We found him *quite well* (=in perfect health).

**277. Verb and Subject.**—See No. VI. of Parsing Chart as to Number and Person.

A Finite Verb must be in the same number and person as its Subject (§ 167). (This is another Concord or Agreement.)

*Note.*—Avoid such a mistake as "The man with his dog *have* just come." Such a mistake arises from confounding "*with*" with "*and.*"

**278. The Third Person of Verbs.**—A verb is invariably in the Third person, except when the Subject is a Personal pronoun in the First or Second person (§ 21) :—

(*a*) *Noun.*—A *snake* is crawling through the grass.
(*b*) *Pronoun.*—*He* returns to us to-morrow.
(*c*) *Infinitive.*—*To err* is human.
(*d*) *Gerund.*—*Sleeping* gives rest to the body.
(*e*) *Phrase.*—*How to do this* was unknown to every one.
(*f*) *Clause.*—*That we must all die* is certain.

**279. Subjects not of the same Person.**—(*a*) When two or more Subjects, not of the same Person, are joined by "*and,*" the verb is in the First person rather than the Second, and in the Second rather than the Third; and *the First person should be mentioned last* :—

James and I *are* (=we are) great friends.

(*b*) When two Subjects are joined by "*or*" or "*nor,*" the verb agrees in person with the Subject nearest to it :—

Either James or I *am* at the top of the class.
Either you or James *has* done it.
Neither James nor you *were* present.

It would be better, however, to repeat the verb for each Subject. The sentences would then be re-written as follows :—

Either James *is* at the top of the class, or I *am.*
Either you *have* done it, or James *has.*
Neither James *was* present, nor *were* you.

(*c*) When two Subjects are joined by "as well as," the verb agrees in number and person with the *first* one :—

My comrades as well as I myself *were* caught.

The reason of this rule is that "My comrades were caught" is the Principal clause, to which the other clause introduced by "as well as" is Co-ordinate.

**280. Two Singular Subjects with Plural Verb.**—Two or more Singular nouns, when they are joined by "*and*," require a verb in the Plural.

> A man and his wife *have* come here asking for work.
> Your horse and mine (=my horse) *are* both at the door.

To this rule there are two exceptions :—

(*a*) If the two nouns joined by "*and*" refer to the same person or thing, the verb is Singular, and not Plural ; as—

> The great scholar and poet *is* dead.

Here "scholar" and "poet" refer to the same man, and the sentence might have been written :—

> The man, who was a great scholar and a great poet, is dead.

*Note.*—When the article is mentioned *only once*, as in the sentence "*the* great scholar and poet," it stands for *both the nouns*. This shows that *only one* person (and not two) is intended, and that hence the verb must be singular.

But if the article is mentioned twice, as in the sentence "*the* scholar and *the* poet," then two distinct persons are intended, and the verb following must be in the plural number ; as—

> The scholar and the poet *are* dead.

(*b*) If the two nouns joined by "*and*" are regarded as denoting *a single object or notion*, the verb is Singular ; as—

> Truth and honesty *is* the best policy. Curry and rice *was* his favourite food. Slow and steady *wins* the race.

Here "truth and honesty" = the practice of truth and honesty, and hence the verb following is singular. Similarly, "curry and rice" = the food consisting of curry and rice, or the mixture of curry and rice. "Slow and steady" = the plan of being slow and steady.

**281. One Singular Subject with Plural Verb.**—A noun of *Multitude* (as distinct from a *Collective* noun, see § 37) is followed by a Plural verb :—

> The jury (*i.e.* the individual jurors) *were* divided in *their* opinions, and could not agree as to the verdict.
> The jury (as one body) selected *its* speaker.

> The multitude (individual men and women) *rise* from *their* seats and shout applause.
> This multitude (as one body) *is* too large to be contained in so small a building.

**282. The Simple or Noun-Infinitive.**—See No. VII. of the Parsing Chart.

The Simple or Noun-Infinitive may be (*a*) the Subject to a verb, (*b*) the Object to a verb, (*c*) the Complement to a verb, (*d*) the Object to a preposition (although this is very uncommon), (*e*) a form of exclamation (see § 191) :—

(*a*) *Subj. to Verb.*—*To sleep* is necessary to health.
(*b*) *Obj. to Verb.*—We desire *to improve.*
(*c*) *Compl. to Verb.*—He appears *to be clever.*
(*d*) *Obj. to Prepos.*—Your cow is about (=near) *to die* (=death).
(*e*) *Form of Exclam.*—*To think* that he should have deceived me!

**283. The Gerundial or Qualifying Infinitive.**—See No. VII. of the Parsing Chart.

The Gerundial or Qualifying Infinitive may be used—(*a*) to qualify a verb, in which case it does the work of an adverb; (*b*) to qualify a noun, in which case it does the work of an adjective; (*c*) to qualify an adjective, in which case it does the work of an adverb; (*d*) to introduce a parenthesis, in which case it is absolute (see § 192):—

(*a*) *Verb.*—They went out *to see* the sport.
(*b*) *Noun* { A house *to let.* (*Attributive.*)
This house is *to let.* (*Predicative.*)
(*c*) *Adjective.*—Be quick *to hear* and slow *to speak.*
(*d*) *Parenthesis.*—He is,—*to speak* plainly,—a thief.

*Note.*—In qualifying a *noun*, the Infinitive is sometimes used in the Passive voice. No rule, however, can be given as to when the Active voice is the more idiomatic and when the Passive:—

A man *to be admired.* (*Attributive.*)
That man is *to be admired.* (*Predicative.*)

**284. The three uses of Participles.**—See No. VIII. of the Parsing Chart.

(*a*) Attributive use (see § 95 for Adjectives):—

A *willing* horse. A *fallen* tree. A *withered* flower.

(*b*) Predicative use.—This may occur either (1) when the Participle is Complement to some verb (see § 95 again), or (2) when the Participle is used absolutely with some noun going before (see §§ 27 (*a*) and 269, 5):—

(1) { We found him *sleeping.* (*Object. Complem.*)
He became *alarmed.* (*Subject. Complem.*)
(2) Our pace was slow, the horse *being tired.* (*Absolute.*)

*Note* 1.—That the Participle is predicative in the Absolute construction is clear from the fact that an absolute *phrase* can be easily rewritten in the form of a subordinate *clause*, in which a Finite verb or predicate is substituted for the Participle:—

{ Our pace was slow, the horse *being tired.*
Our pace was slow, *because* the horse *was tired.*

*Note* 2.—When no noun or pronoun is expressed, the Participle is called an **Impersonal Absolute.**

*Supposing* this to be true, you are certainly guilty.

(*c*) Gerundive use (§ 207).—Here the Participle denotes something that could be equally well expressed by a Gerund or Verbal noun :[1]—

{ This prevented the letter *being sent* ;=
{ This prevented *the sending of* the letter.

### *Note on Concord and Government.*

The plan adopted in some books on English Grammar is to subdivide the subject of Syntax under two main headings :—

I. Concord or Agreement. II. Government.

In a highly inflected language, such as Latin, Greek, or the Old English, a subdivision of that kind is useful, since the inflexions of words depend chiefly on their mutual concord or agreement and on the extent to which they govern or are governed by one another.

In Modern English, however, in which very few of the old inflexions have been retained, the subdivision of Syntax into rules of Concord and rules of Government is of scarcely any use ; for it leaves the greater part of the ground untouched. The only points on which these principles are seen at work are the following :—

### *Concord or Agreement.*

(1) The verb must agree with its subject in Number and Person. (This, together with the apparent exceptions thereto, has been set forth in § 277.)

(2) The Demonstrative adjective "this" or "that" must be of the same number as the noun it qualifies. (These are the only two adjectives that have one form for the Singular and another for the Plural.)

(3) A pronoun must be of the same Number, Gender, and Person as its antecedent. (So far as inflexion is concerned, this applies only to the Demonstrative pronouns of the Third person (§ 114), and to the Relative pronoun "who" or "which" (§ 121).

(4) A noun in apposition with a pronoun or other noun must be in the same case. (This is shown in § 269 (3) and § 271 (3). The only case that is now indicated by an inflexion is the Possessive, and even this case drops its inflexion when it is in apposition with another Possessive. See § 270.)

### *Government.*

All that we can say on this point is that certain Verbs, two or three Adjectives, and all Prepositions govern a noun or pronoun in the Objective case.

---

[1] The student will find this subject more fully dealt with in chap. xx. (79).

# CHAPTER XIII.

## PUNCTUATION, OR THE RIGHT USE OF STOPS.

**285.** Punctuation divides one sentence or one part of a sentence from another, to help the reader's eye.

**286.** The names of the different points, stops, or marks used for this purpose are :—

| | | | |
|---|---|---|---|
| Comma, indicated by | , | Note of exclamation, indicated by | ! |
| Semicolon, indicated by | ; | Brackets, indicated by | () or [] |
| Colon, indicated by | : | Dash, indicated by | — |
| Full stop or period, indicated by | . | Hyphen, indicated by | - |
| Note of Interrogation, indicated by | ? | Inverted commas, indicated by | " " |
| Apostrophe, indicated by | ' | | |

*The Comma.*

**287.** The comma represents the shortest pause. Its chief uses in a **simple** sentence are the following :—

(*a*) Between nouns or pronouns in apposition ; as—

Alexander, the *son* of Philip, *king* of Macedon.

(*b*) Between three or more words of the same Part of Speech, when only the last two are connected by "*and*."

Greece, Italy, and Spain are the peninsulas of Southern Europe. (*Nouns.*)

We should live soberly, prudently, and industriously at all times. (*Adverbs.*)

Early to bed and early to rise
Makes a man healthy, wealthy, and wise. (*Adjectives.*)

(*c*) After the Nominative of address :—

Friends, Romans, countrymen, lend me your ears.

(*d*) After an absolute construction :—

The sun having set, we all went home.

(*e*) When words of the same class or rank go together in pairs, each pair is separated by a comma :—

By night or by day, at home or abroad, asleep or awake, he is a constant source of anxiety to his father.

(*f*) After an adverbial phrase at the commencement of a sentence. (Here, however, the comma can be put in or not, at the option of the writer.)

In fact, his poetry is no better than prose. At last, he has gained his point.

(*g*) Before and after a participial phrase, provided that the participle might be expanded into a sentence, and is not used in a merely qualifying sense (see § 200) :—

Cæsar, having defeated the Gauls, led his army into Britain.
(Here "having defeated" means "after he had defeated.")
Convinced of the accuracy of his facts, he stuck to his opinion.
(Here "convinced" means "because he was convinced.")

But when the participle qualifies the noun so as merely to *restrict* its meaning, as an adjective would do, the comma should not be used :—

A dog lying asleep on a public road is likely to be run over.
A man convinced against his will is of the same opinion still.

(*h*) Explanatory phrases are separated by commas :—

The field was oblong, 60 yards in length, 40 in breadth.

(*i*) Before and after gerundial Infinitives used in an explanatory or parenthetical sense :—

I am, to tell you the truth, thoroughly sick of work.
To sum up, the man was convicted of three charges.

(*j*) A comma is sometimes used to introduce a sentence quoted in Direct Narration. The sentence so quoted must be commenced with a capital letter :—

What I say unto you, I say unto all, Watch.—*New Testament.*

(*k*) A comma is sometimes inserted to mark the omission and save the repetition of a verb :—

My regiment is bound for India ; yours, for Gibraltar.

**288.** (*a*) In a **compound** sentence the co-ordinate clauses, when they are expressed at full length, are generally separated by a comma :—

His vanity is greater than his ignorance, and what he lacks in knowledge is supplied by impudence.

But when the two sentences are not expressed at full length or are very closely allied, the comma is omitted :—

I made haste and caught him.
I took up a stone and threw it at the mad dog.

(*b*) When the conjunction is omitted between co-ordinate clauses, these must be separated (1) by a comma, when they are short ; or (2) by a semicolon, when they are long :—

(1) Steam propels, elevates, lowers, pumps, drains, pulls, etc.
(2) Between fame and true honour there is much difference ; the former is blind applause ; the latter is an internal and more silent homage.

**289.** In **complex** sentences the following rules regarding the use of commas should be noted :—

(*a*) A Noun-clause is not usually separated by a comma from the Principal clause :—

It is generally allowed that the art of teaching is difficult.
No one knows when he will come.
His being pardoned depends upon whether he will confess his fault or not.

But Noun-clauses must be separated from each other by commas, when they are objects or subjects to the same verb :—

No one knows when he will come, or whether he will come at all, or whether he is even alive.
Who he was, or why he came, or what he intends to do, will all be found out in time.

(*b*) An Adjective-clause is not separated from the Principal clause by a comma, unless it (the Adjective-clause) is rather lengthy :—

The man *we saw* yesterday has come again to-day.
Fortune selects him for her lord, *who reflects before acting.*

(*c*) An Adverb-clause is separated by a comma from the Principal clause :—

He will succeed, because he works hard.
I will gladly do this, if I am allowed.

The comma is never omitted, unless the Adverb-clause is either very short or expressed elliptically :—

He likes you better than me.
Send me word before you start.

*Insert commas, where necessary, in the following sentences :—*

The triple alliance consists of Germany Austria and Italy. My son so far from being blamed for his conduct was commended and even rewarded. The roof of the house having caught fire the inmates fled and remained outside the house until the fire was put out. Towns villages and hamlets were all alike attacked with the epidemic of cholera. I shall be happy to make the attempt that you speak of if I am permitted. From morning till noon from noon to evening from evening to midnight this same grief never leaves him. Early this morning when we had just left the house we met the man that we had been looking for. He found as I expected he would that the house he had lately purchased was a bad one. What was the cause of so much grief to him was never known to any of us. I hope my friend that you will come and spend at least a week with us. He has now grown so old that he spends most of his time in sleeping taking his food or sitting in an easy-chair. I remain my dear sir yours faithfully William Matthews. I shall not leave home for business unless you set the example. Example as the proverb says is the sincerest form of precept. To tell you the plain truth I should be glad to retire from business altogether considering that I am now past sixty years of age and have a son to succeed me. The boatman shouted to a man on shore throw out the rope. A snake sleeping in the grass will bite if any one treads upon it. The prisoner having been convicted of the crime of which he was accused must make up his mind to suffer the penalty. The building is a noble structure of red brick and comprises a reading-room a library a room for writing letters and a room for refreshments. It is quite true that this fine building was erected by private subscriptions. In fact of all that was subscribed L. gave the largest amount in cash but M. was not less liberal because he gave the land on which the building was erected. A dog barking at nothing is a nuisance.

### *The Semicolon.*

**290.** The **Semicolon** is used, when a greater pause is required than is indicated by the comma.

Its chief uses are as follows :—

(*a*) To separate *longer* clauses from one another. Here a greater pause is necessary to prevent the sentences from being confused together :—

> Honesty of purpose in worldly affairs has many advantages over deceit ; it is a safer way of dealing with men ; it is an easier mode of despatching business ; it inspires men with greater confidence ; it acquires more and more confidence in itself, while deceit becomes more and more diffident.

(*b*) To give greater emphasis to different clauses, so that the mind may dwell longer on each of them in succession :—

> As Cæsar loved me, I weep for him ; as he was fortunate, I rejoice at it ; as he was valiant, I honour him ; but as he was ambitious, I slew him. So there is tears for his love ; joy for his fortune ; honour for his valour ; and death for his ambition.—SHAKSPEARE.

(*c*) To divide clauses, which are connected by some Alternative or Illative conjunction. (Here a greater pause is required, because the mind requires a little more time to perceive the alternative or the inference) :—

> I met him as he was leaving his house ; *otherwise* I should not have known where he lived.
>
> I refused to do what he asked me to do ; *for* I was convinced that he had been misinformed of the facts.

### *The Colon.*

**291.** The **Colon** may be used at the writer's discretion, if he thinks that the pause is not sufficiently marked by a semicolon. On this point no fixed rules can be given.

The main uses of the colon are the following :—

(*a*) To introduce an additional remark in explanation or in confirmation of a previous one :—

Strive above all things, in whatever station of life you may be, to preserve health : there is no happiness in life without it.

(*b*) To introduce a quotation. In this case it is usually followed by a dash :—

Then Peter stood forth and said :—"Of a truth I perceive that God is no respecter of persons," etc.

(*c*) To recapitulate a series of co-ordinate clauses. Here, too, the colon must be followed by a dash :—

The storm had passed ; the sun was shining on the green leaves of the trees ; the streams were dancing around the rocks ; the birds hopped about him, as they chirped their cheerful notes :—such were the pleasant scenes and sounds that welcomed the wanderer back to his home.

(*d*) To introduce a series of co-ordinate clauses. Here, again, the colon is followed by a dash :—

You must now hear what I have to say about the uses of iron :—we sleep on iron ; we travel on iron ; we float on iron ; we plough the fields with iron ; we shoot with iron ; we chop down trees with iron :—in fact, there is scarcely anything that we can do without the help of this wonderful metal.

(*e*) To introduce an example of some rule. Here, again, the colon is followed by a dash :—

The Indefinite article has sometimes the force of a Numeral adjective, signifying *one* :—as, "A stitch in time saves nine."

*Insert commas, colons, or semicolons, where necessary, in the following sentences* :—

1. According to an old belief if a sick man sneezes it is a sure sign of recovery but when a man is going on a journey or about to commence some business should any one about him sneeze the sneeze indicates that the object in which he is interested will not be accomplished.

2. In Rome the army was the nation no citizen could take office unless he had served in ten campaigns.

3. The drill was unremitting at all times so long as a man continued to be a soldier when the troops were in winter quarters sheds were erected in which the soldiers fenced with swords buttoned at the points or hurled javelins also buttoned at the points at one another.

4. The Carthaginian army was composed entirely of mercenary troops Africa Spain and Gaul were their recruiting grounds and these countries were an inexhaustible treasury of warriors as long as the money lasted which the recruits received as pay.

5. While I was still wondering at my sudden deliverance a man came suddenly forward and said my good sir there is nothing to be surprised at I was sent here to find you and rescue you from these

robbers well I have succeeded in finding you and so I have accomplished what I was sent for as you now see.

6. Whenever you hesitate about beginning to do something which must be done eventually remember the maxim a thing begun is half done.

*The Full Stop or Period.*

**292.** The **Full Stop** or **Period** indicates the close of a complete sentence. The sentence following must invariably be commenced with a capital letter.

The full stop is also used after abbreviations; as, A.D. (for Anno Domini); B.L. (for Bachelor of Law); Bart. (for Baronet); the Hon. (for the Honourable).

*Inverted Commas.*

**293. Inverted Commas** are used for indicating the beginning and end of a quotation, or of the actual words used by a speaker.

The councillors stood up, and with one voice exclaimed :—"Death before dishonour."

"Wine is a mocker," said the wise king.

Campbell was the author of the following stanza :—

"The more we live, more brief appear
Our life's succeeding stages;
A week to childhood seems a year,
A year like passing ages."

*Note of Exclamation.*

**294.** A **Note of Exclamation** is used after words or sentences which express emotion.

How are the mighty fallen in the midst of the battle! I am distressed for thee, my brother Jonathan!
Nonsense! How can you talk such rubbish?
What a conceited fellow you are! Be silent.
"Land ahead!" shouted the delighted crew.

*The Apostrophe.*

**295.** The **Apostrophe** (') is inserted to show that some letter or letters have been omitted.

The Hon'ble (for *Honourable*); e'en (for *even*); 'tis (for *it is*); ta'en (for *taken*); don't (for *do not*); shan't (for *shall not*); won't (for *will not*); tho' (for *though*); an ox's head (for *oxes head*); and all other instances of the Possessive case.

*Note of Interrogation.*

**296.** A **Note of Interrogation** is used after sentences which ask questions. The sentence following must be commenced with a capital.

Where was he born? When did he die?

*Insert the proper stops and capitals, where necessary, in the following sentences:—*

Whats the matter Thomas ist that old pain of yours again no its not that at all said he but something a good deal better would you believe it my poor old uncle is dead and he has left me five thousand pounds that was very good of him she replied but its come too late why he inquired because she answered you are now old and broken in health what a pity it is that he did not die twenty years ago or give you the money while he was still alive.

*Dashes.*

**297.** The **Dash** has four main uses:—

(*a*) To mark a break or abrupt turn in a sentence:—

Here lies the great—false marble where ?
Nothing but sordid dust lies here.

(*b*) To mark words in apposition or in explanation:—

They plucked the seated hills with all their loads—
Rocks, waters, woods—and by the shaggy tops
Uplifting bore them in their hands.

(*c*) To introduce a quotation, a first clause, or a final clause; but in this case it must be preceded by a colon. (For examples, see § 291.)

(*d*) To insert a parenthetical phrase or sentence in the middle of a main sentence. Here *two* dashes are required.

At the age of ten—such is the power of genius—he could read Greek with facility.

*Brackets.*

**298. Brackets** are used like a couple of dashes in (*d*), as just explained, for inserting a parenthetical sentence in the middle of a main sentence.

At the age of ten (such is the power of genius) he could read Greek with facility.

*The Hyphen.*

**299.** A **Hyphen** is used for joining the parts of a compound word; as "bathing-place."

*Note.*—A hyphen, like the dash, is formed by the horizontal line. But the line is shorter.

*Insert a dash, hyphen, or brackets, wherever necessary, in the following sentences, and add any other appropriate stops:—*

England and Russia the two greatest empires on the face of the earth have no real cause of enmity. I could tell you all about my but perhaps you have heard enough by this time. My dog such is the power of jealousy attacked its rival whenever they met. This is very uphill work. If you read without spectacles and I believe you can be so good as to read out the contents of this letter. When I took my degree and this was twelve years ago I had good prospects before me. I will never but I need not finish my sentence for you know already what I was going to say.

*Diæresis.*

**300. Diæresis** (separation) consists of two dots placed over the second of two vowels, to show that they are to be sounded separately :—

Coöperation = co-operation.

*Asterisks.*

**301. Asterisks** denote that some words or clauses have been omitted :—

The Jews * * * * * had to pay heavy taxes to the Norman kings.

---

## QUESTIONS ON MODERN ENGLISH GRAMMAR.

Collected, in the order of their occurrence, from London Matriculation Papers that have been set from January 1879 to January 1897. Against each question the month and year are quoted.

1. What are the different uses of the verb *to be?* From how many roots are the different parts of this verb taken? (Jan. 1879.)

2. What are Weak verbs? Classify *bring, sing, take, seek, teach, set, bleed, eat* as Weak or Strong. Give reasons in each case, and call attention to peculiarities. (Jan. 1879.)

3. What is meant by the Infinitive mood of a verb? Explain as fully as you can the Infinitive form in the phrase, "This house *to let.*" (June 1879.)

4. What adjectives cannot properly be used in the Comparative or Superlative degree? (June 1879).

5. Write two sentences showing the same word used in one as a preposition, in the other as a conjunction; also two sentences showing the same word as a preposition and as an adverb. (June 1879.)

6. Classify the pronouns. (June 1879.) Illustrate by examples the points most worthy of attention in the Syntax of Pronouns. (Jan. 1880.)

7. Explain what is meant by *tense* and *mood* of verbs. Add a few notes on the uses of the Subjunctive. (June 1880).

8. Which are the English Auxiliary verbs properly so called? and why? (Jan. 1881.) Distinguish them from every other class of verb.

9. Distinguish between Co-ordinating and Subordinating conjunctions. What are the various uses of the word *but* in English? (Jan. 1881.)

10. Give instances of *Proper* nouns used as *Common* nouns, and *vice versa.* (Jan. 1881.)

11. State clearly the rules of English Accidence with regard to the use of *shall* and *will* in Assertive sentences. (Jan. 1881.)

12. What is a verb? What is meant by the Infinitive mood? Tell what you know of the past and present use of *to* in the Infinitive. (June 1881.)

13. What is an adverb? Classify the adverbs. Tell what you can of the grammatical use of the words *yes, no.* (June 1881.)

14. Classify the conjunctions, and point out which of them are used in forming co-ordinate sentences. (June 1881.)

15. Explain and give examples of the difference between subordinate and co-ordinate sentences, between extension and completion of the predicate, and between a direct and an indirect object. (June 1881.)

16. Point out and answer the chief questions that may arise as to the application of the rule that a verb should agree with its subject in number and person. (June 1881.)

17. Enumerate the elements of flexion in the Verb. What is the use of the Subjunctive mood? (Jan. 1882.)

18. What part of speech is the Infinitive? What is meant by the Dative Infinitive and the Simple Infinitive? Show the origin of the suffixes in "the hang*ing* crane," "the hang*ing* of the crane." (Jan. 1882.)

19. How is the future indefinite tense expressed in English? Illustrate your answer by an examination of the original meaning of the Auxiliaries employed for the purpose. Explain the term "Imperfect Continuous" tense. (Jan. 1882.)

20. Discuss the origin and grammatical use of the Gerundial Infinitive. (June 1882.)

21. What are the chief rules for the use, in punctuation, of the comma, the colon, and the semicolon? (June 1882.)

22. What is exactly meant by the phrase—*part of speech?* What by the term *parse?* Classify the words *pen, petition, long, that, wire.* (June 1883.)

23. Point out the grammatical difference between *the* in such a phrase as, "He did his duty, and was *the* happier for it"; and *the* in, "He was *the* happier of the two." (June 1883.)

24. Explain the terms *Strong* and *Weak* as applied to verbs, also the term *conjugation.* To which conjugation do you assign *teach, fight, work, do, fly, flow, flee, tell, till, toll?* (June 1883.)

25. What is the force of *run* in such a phrase as "to run wild"; of *wear* in "the day wears"; of *give* in "the shoe gives"; of *obtain* in "this doctrine obtained"? Mention any noticeable uses of *to taste, ring, sit, stand.* (June 1883.)

26. Give examples of verbs that are used both as "complete" and as "incomplete predicates," and explain these terms. (June 1883.)

27. What is an *Indefinite pronoun?* Write a list of the Indefinite pronouns, and exemplify their uses. (Jan. 1884.)

28. Write eight sentences giving four examples of the use of the same verb transitively and intransitively. Rewrite the four sentences containing transitive verbs with change of voice from Active to Passive. (Jan. 1884.)

29. Give the fullest subdivision of an English verb into tenses that you have met with in any grammar. Which of these are distinguished by inflexions? (Jan. 1884.)

30. What are the marks of a Strong verb? About how many of such verbs have we still in use? To which conjugation belong *shall, buy, fight, reach, touch?* (June 1884.)

31. Parse all the words ending in *-ing* in this sentence:—Darkling, we went singing on our way, with our walking sticks in our hands, weary of toiling in town. (June 1884.)

32. Define a sentence, a phrase, and a clause, and give instances of each. (Jan. 1885.)

33. To which conjugation do the following verbs severally belong—*see, saw, say, sow, sew, sue, sit, seethe, sell?* Write down the past tense and past part. of each, noticing any peculiarity. (June 1885.)

34. Mention some nouns (i.) with two plural forms; (ii.) with no plural form; (iii.) with only a plural form; (iv.) of plural form which are treated as singulars; (v.) of singular form which are treated as plurals. (Jan. 1886.)

35. Explain the term *preposition.* How does a preposition differ from a conjunction? Mention some prepositions that have become conjunctions. (Jan. 1886.)

36. Classify our words. Show that to some extent the form of a word indicates its class. Why only "to some extent?" To what class or classes belong *that, ink, after, stand, parallel, good?* (June 1886.)

37. What is the use of the Analysis of sentences? What shapes may the subject of a sentence assume? and in what ways may it be extended? (June 1886.)

38. Analyse:—

(*a*) I saw them run.
(*b*) He can make it go.
(*c*) Let her depart.
(*d*) Who is it?
(*e*) He was crowned king.
(*f*) He was hanged,—a well-deserved punishment. (June 1886.)

39. Write a sentence containing three extensions of the predicate, one of them a clause, and let this clause contain a subject with two extensions. (June 1886.)

40. Write down the plural form of *wharf, colloquy, potato, Mary, Knight-Templar,* and *canto,* and state and discuss the rule you go by in each case. Mention some words in which the *s* of the stem has been mistaken for the plural flexion. (Jan. 1887.)

41. Illustrate our habit of using nouns as adjectives both with and without change of form, and also of using adverbs as adjectives. (Jan. 1887.)

42. What form of the indefinite article do you use before the words—*history, historical, European, usual, humble, ever?* Give reasons for your answers. Can you mention any instances of the transference of the *n* of the indefinite article to the beginning of the following noun? (Jan. 1887.)

43. Repeat and criticise the current definitions of a verb. Which seems to you the least unsatisfactory, and why? (Jan. 1887.)

44. What are the characteristic marks of the Strong conjugation? Make a list of some half-dozen Weak verbs that have vowel-change in the

Past tense; also of half a dozen that have no change there; also of half a dozen that do change, but not in the way of addition. (Jan. 1887.)

45. Parse the italicised words and phrases:—

(a) *Down* with it!

(b) His *having been beaten* once only made him *the* more determined to succeed.

(c) *Seeing* is *believing*.

(d) The *hearing* ear and the *seeing* eye, the Lord hath made *even* both of them. (Jan. 1887.)

46. In what two ways may Adjectives be compared? How do there come to be two ways? By what terms would you denote them? State the general rule as to their use. (June 1887.)

47. Discuss the ordinary definition of a pronoun. What other definition has been suggested? Distinguish between the forms *my* and *mine*. Which is the older form? What similar pairs are there? (June 1887.)

48. Explain the terms *voice, mood, infinitive.* Show by what means, in English, transitive verbs are used intransitively, and *vice versa.* Mention some Causative verbs. (June 1887.)

49. By what other names than Weak and Strong are the two conjugations known? Which is the living one? To which do these verbs belong—*fight, think, bare, bear, catch, teach, reach, beseech, hang, fly*? (June 1887.)

50. What adjectives cannot be compared? Write down those adjectives that are defective in their comparison? (Jan. 1888.)

51. What English nouns make no change in the plural, and why? (Jan. 1888.)

52. Describe fully, with examples, English verbs of Incomplete Predication, and the different forms that the Complement may assume. (Jan. 1888.)

53. State the correct modern usage of *shall* and *will*; and show by reference to the etymology of the words how that usage is to be accounted for. (Jan. 1888.)

54. Define *infinitive, gerund, present participle,* and *past participle,* giving examples of each. (Jan. 1888.)

55. Explain the different uses of the verbal form which terminates in *-ing*, and show in what cases it is properly a participle. (June 1888.)

56. What principle would you adopt in classifying nouns in English? Explain fully the basis of the classification that you adopt. (Jan. 1889.)

57. Frame a sentence showing by subordinate clauses the use of the comma, semicolon, and colon. (Jan. 1889.)

58. State what is meant by a Part of Speech; and illustrate your statement by a sentence, in which the same word shall successively be of various Parts of Speech. (June 1889.)

59. Classify the pronouns, giving explanations where necessary. (June 1889.)

60. Explain the primitive meaning of each of the Auxiliary verbs, and show how that meaning has been modified in modern usage. (June 1889.)

61. Distinguish between an *adverb* and a *relative adverb*, and give a list of the relative adverbs. (June 1889.)

62. Define, giving examples, a simple sentence, a complex sentence, and a compound sentence. (June 1889.)

63. How are words grouped with reference to their grammatical usage? In which group or groups do you place *than*, *but*, *divine*, *single*, *that*, *while*? (Jan. 1890.)

64. Give instances of nouns that can be used as verbs, and of verbs that can be used as nouns. How is it that such transferences are so commonly possible in English? (Jan. 1890.)

65. Prove that vowel-change is not the decisive mark of the Strong conjugation. To which conjugation belong these verbs—*bring*, *fight*, *read*, *hang*, *beseech*, *go*? (Jan. 1890.)

66. Show that the Weak is our living conjugation. Why is it called the Weak? What other names for it are suggested? (Jan. 1890.)

67. In what ways are Adjectives compared? Discuss *perfect*, *golden*, *lunar*, and *French*. (June 1890.)

68. Discriminate, giving examples, between verbs of Incomplete Predication, Transitive verbs, Intransitive verbs, and Impersonal verbs. (June 1890.)

69. Distinguish between the Infinitive and the Gerund in modern English; and discuss the forms in *-ing* in the following sentence:—

John and two *fishing* friends started off early this morning, with their *fishing* rods, to the river *a-fishing*; but the *fishing* to-day has been unsuccessful. (June 1890.)

70. What is meant by the *case* of a noun? How did the word come to be used in such a sense? (Jan. 1891.)

71. Give instances of verbs that can be used both Transitively and Intransitively; also of some that can be used both as complete predicates and as incomplete; also of some that can be used both as Auxiliaries and Principals. (Jan. 1891.)

72. Mention some Strong verbs in which the *n* of the Past participle has dropped off; some in which the preterite has come to be used as the Past participle; and some which have two forms of the preterite. (Jan. 1891.)

73. Show from still familiar forms that *melt*, *show*, *shave*, *swell*, *grave* were once of the Strong conjugation; and write down the past participles of *shoe*, *light*, *work*, *knit*, *speed*. (Jan. 1891.)

74. Show how the addition of the Plural sign *-s* altogether alters the meanings of many English nouns. (June 1891.)

75. The Infinitive is sometimes called the Substantive mood. Explain this, and give some examples of the different parts which the Infin. may play in English sentences. What is the Gerundial Infin., and how was it distinguished in Old English? (June 1891.)

76. Write down the plural of *gallows*, *topaz*, *solo*, *who*, *Mary*. Mention some words about whose plural form there is variety of usage, and some that have been wrongly taken for plurals, though really singular. (Jan. 1892.)

77. How would you describe the number of the following words—*alms*, *banns*, *heronries*, *optics*, *poultry*, *pride*, *salmon*, *scissors*, *sheep*, *sixpences*, *thanks*, *wheat*? (June 1892.)

78. Give a list of Double plurals of English nouns, in which one form has the Collective idea, and the other the Distributive. (June 1892.)

79. What is meant by saying that there is no future tense in our lan-

guage? Indicate how we express the ideas of simple futurity, of intention, and of compulsion. How do we express a future participle?
(June 1892.)

80. Specify as many as you can of the shades of meaning of *one*, with an illustration of each; and explain as far as you can how they arose.
(Jan. 1893 and Jan. 1894.)

81. Are the following words properly of the Singular or the Plural number?—*eaves, tidings, alms, news, riches, means.* Are there any words that have only a Singular form, and any that have only a Plural?
(June 1893.)

82. What should be meant by a "mixed conjugation"? Is there such a thing? Prove that such verbs as *teach, seek,* and *tell* have certainly no mixture in their conjugation. (June 1893.)

83. Give examples of Defective verbs. Write down the Second Sing. Pret. of *am*. What other form is found? (June 1893.)

84. Give instances of the conversion of abstract nouns into concrete, proper into common, common into proper, and try to explain why each of these conversions should occur. (Jan. 1894.)

85. In what various ways may Interjections arise? (Jan. 1894.)

86. Give an account of the signs of number in Modern English. Indicate and explain cases where (1) a plural sense is found without a plural inflexion; (2) a plural inflexion without a plural sense. (June 1894.)

87. Define a sentence. How would you deal with the following:—*go; hence! does it rain? yes; let us return.* (June 1894.)

88. Distinguish carefully the use of the word *riding* in the following:—

(*a*) He is very fond of *riding*.
(*b*) He is always happy when *riding*.
(*c*) He has capital *riding* horses. (June 1894.)

89. Give all the grammatical forms in use of the verbs *can, shall, will, ought, must,* showing (1) how far, if at all, each has deviated from its original meaning; (2) how the place of the wanting forms is supplied.
(June 1894.)

90. Supply the plural to each of the following, accounting for any apparent irregularity in its formation:—*man-servant, maid-servant, man-of-all-work, passer-by, looker-on, castaway, prince-consort, lord-lieutenant, camel-driver.* (June 1894.)

91. Defend or criticise the following sentences, suggesting where you can the *explanation* of what you think grammatically anomalous:—

(*a*) With selfish people, the frequency of imposture, together with the inadequacy of present arrangements, serve as an excuse for not giving at all.
(*b*) Nothing but dreary dykes, muddy and straight, guarded by the ghosts of suicidal pollards, occur to break the monotony of the landscape.
(*c*) Twice one are two.
(*d*) Between every stitch she would look up to see what was going on in the street. (June 1894.)

92. Define *Infinitive, Strong verbs, Weak verbs, Present participle, Verbal noun, Auxiliary verb.* Explain carefully what is meant by (i.) Irregular, and (ii.) Defective verbs. Give examples throughout.
(Jan. 1895.)

93. Distinguish and account for the force of the words italicised in each of the following:—

(*a*) I *did* say so, though I thought I *did* not.
(*b*) *Do* go.
(*c*) *Do* not go.
(*d*) I *dare* not say he did.
(*e*) I *dare* say he did.

(June 1895.)

94. Illustrate and explain the different uses of (i.) the Infinitive, and (ii.) the various verbal forms in *-ing*. Tell the history of *-ing* as the ending of the present participle. (Jan. 1896.)

95. Classify nouns according to their meaning, and illustrate the passage of nouns from one class to another. (June 1896.)

96. Define Mood, Voice, Auxiliary verb, Strong-Weak verb.

(Jan. 1897.)

*Correct or justify the following.*[1] *Point out the error, if any.*

1. I am verily a man who am a Jew.
2. Too great a variety of studies distract the mind.
3. Who do you speak to?
4. The river has overflown its banks.
5. Man never is, but always to be blest.
6. Neither our virtues or our vices are all our own.
7. If I were old enough to be married, I am old enough to manage my husband's house.
8. I am to blame, not you.
9. Art thou proud yet? Ay, that I am not thee.
10. Whoever the king favours
The cardinal will find employment for.
11. Here you may see that visions are to dread.
12. Nothing but wailings was heard.
13. Neither of them are remarkable for precision.
14. I cannot tell if it be wise or no.
15. It must be confessed that a lampoon or a satire do not carry in them robbery or murder.
16. Whose own example strengthens all his laws,
And is himself the great sublime he draws.
17. They were both fond of one another.
18. Thersites's body is as good as Ajax, when neither are alive.
19. Thou art much older than thy looks.
20. There were no less than five persons concerned.
21. Recite the first six lines of *Paradise Lost.*
22. Neither he nor we are disengaged.
23. One of the best books that has been written on the subject.
24. I like it better than any.
25. And since I never dare to write
As funny as I can.
26. Laying the suspicion on some one, I know not who.
27. Well is him that hath found prudence!
28. Neither he nor I have any doubt of his success.

---

[1] Reprinted from London Matriculation Papers set from Jan. 1879 to Jan. 1897.

29. One of the best treatises that has been written on the subject.

30. I am one of those who cannot describe what I do not see.

31. The country was divided into counties, and the counties placed under magistrates.

32. Nobody ever put so much of themselves into their work.

33. He hath given away above half his fortune to the Lord knows who.

34. Friendships which we once hoped and believed would never grow cold.

35. Nepos answered him, Celsus replied, and neither of them were sparing of censures on each other.

36. Such are a few of the many paradoxes one would cite from his writings, and which are now before me.

37. The largest circulation of any Liberal newspaper.

38. Injustice springs only from three causes. . . . Neither of these can be found in a being wise, powerful, and benevolent.

39. This dedication may serve almost for any book that has, is, or shall be published.

40. In the best countries a rise in rents and wages has been found to go together.

41. He belongs to one caste, and the hewers of wood and drawers of water to another.

42. The second assault was met by Buckingham by a counter attack on the Earl of Bristol, whom he knew would be the chief witness against him.

43. And many a holy text around she strews,
That teach the rustic moralist to die.

44. This view has been maintained by one of the greatest writers that has appeared in this country.

45. The administration of so many various interests, and of districts so remote, demand no common capacity and vigour.

46. He having none but them, they having none but he.

47. Breaking a constitution by the very same errors that so many have been broke before.

48. They are not only the most charitable of any other nation, but most judicious in distinguishing the properest objects of compassion.

49. The part of this reed used by the Indians is from 10 to 11 feet long, and no tapering can be perceived, one end being as thick as another.

50. If he had writ one word by the next post, this had been just and civil.

51. Thou lovest, but ne'er knew love's sad satiety.

52. *Macbeth.* There's blood upon thy face.
*Murd.* 'Tis Banquo's then.
*Macb.* 'Tis better thee without than he within.

53. This is he, my master said,
Despised the Athenian maid.

54. Luckily the monks have recently given away a couple of dogs which were returned to them, or the breed would have been lost.

55. It was the most amiable, although the least dignified, of all the party squabbles by which it had been preceded.

56. Having perceived the weakness of his poems, they now reappear to us under new titles.

57. Neither you nor I am right.

L

58. I am one of those who cannot describe what I feel.

59. Whom they were I really cannot specify.

60. Whom do you say that I am?

61. His is a poem, one of the completest works that exists in any language.

62. He was shot by a secretary under notice to quit, with whom he was finding fault,—very fortunately without effect.

63. It is characteristic of them to appear but to one person, and he the most likely to be deluded.

64. I think it may assist the reader by placing them before him in chronological order.

65. Few people learn anything that is worth learning easily.

66. My resolution is to spare no expense in education; it is a bad calculation, because it is the only advantage over which circumstances have no control.

67. Image after image, phrase after phrase, starts out vivid, harsh, and emphatic.

68. Books that we can at a glance carry off what is in them are worse than useless for discipline.

69. He preferred to know the worst than to dream the best.

70. Humanity seldom or ever shows itself in inferior minds.

71. You have already been informed of the sale of Ford's theatre, where Mr. Lincoln was assassinated, for religious purposes.

72. The Moor, seizing a bolster, full of rage and jealousy, smothers her.

73. Nor do I know any one with whom I can converse more pleasantly or I would prefer as my companion.

74. They drowned the black and white kittens.

75. The then Ministry were in favour of the bill.

76. The people is one; they have all one language.

77. George and myself went up the mountain together.

78. The Duke of Wellington is one of those who never interfere with matters over which he has no control.

79. Her voice was ever soft, gentle, and low; an excellent thing in woman.

80. Peter the Hermit's diet was abstemious, his prayers long and fervent.

81. I shall have great pleasure in accepting your invitation.

82. Each of the girls went to their separate rooms to rest and calm themselves.

83. Being early killed, I sent a party in search of his mangled body.

# PART II.—IDIOM AND CONSTRUCTION.

## CHAPTER XIV.—NOUNS AND PRONOUNS.

### SECTION 1.—CASES OF NOUNS AND PRONOUNS.

**302. Genitive or Possessive.**—The meanings denoted by this case can be distinguished into (*a*) Subjective, (*b*) Objective, (*c*) Descriptive. In one point, however, they all agree: they all have the power of an Adjective, that is, they all qualify or restrict the noun following.

(*a*) *Subjective*:—

*England's* power is very great. (*Possession.*)
A good son will repay his *father's* benefits. (*Origin.*)
*Shakspeare's* plays are excellent. (*Agency.*)
His friendship (the friendship felt by him) is sincere. (*Subject.*)

(*b*) *Objective* (now rather scarce):—

His friendship (the friendship for him) must be given up.
My *friend's* praises were heard everywhere.
*Cæsar's* murderers were conquered at Philippi.

(*c*) *Descriptive*, equivalent to a Descriptive adjective, § 81:—

I'll knock your *knave's* (=knavish) pate.—SHAKSPEARE.
The *mother's* (=motherly) nature of Althæa.—LOWELL.

**303. Familiar "your" and "my."**—These possessives are used indefinitely, and with some implication of contempt:—

*Your* worm is *your* only emperor for diet; *your* fat king and *your* lean beggar is but variable service.—*Hamlet*, iv. 3, 24.

When he entered the room, on seeing a servant coming towards him to order him out, up goes *my* grave Impudence (=the grave-faced, impudent fellow whom I was watching) to the maid, etc.—*Tatler*.

He saw more than *your* fool of a tourist generally sees.—MRS. WARD.

**304. "Of" followed by a Possessive.**—This occurs in such phrases as "that book *of James's*," "that handsome face *of my father's*," "that book *of yours*."

Three explanations have been offered—all conceivable:—

(1) "Of my father's" is an ellipse for "of my father's faces." Here "faces" is the Object to "of" used in a Partitive sense. This is good grammar, but it makes nonsense, since "my father" cannot have more than one face. But it is defensible on grounds of analogy with instances where it makes sense, as in "That book of my father's (books)."

(2) "Of my father's" is a Double Possessive. This explanation is the most natural, and seems to be the right one.

(3) The "of" merely denotes apposition, as in "the continent *of* Asia," which means "the continent, *namely* Asia." Similarly, the phrase "that face *of* my father's" can mean "that face, *namely* my father's (face)."

*Note.*—The ambiguity of the preposition "of" is sometimes removed by placing a Possessive noun after it. Thus, "a picture of the Queen" means a picture consisting of a likeness of the Queen. But "a picture of the *Queen's*" means a picture of which the Queen is owner.

The construction by which "of" is placed before a Possessive is not a modern idiom, but is frequently met with so far back as Chaucer, and has continued in constant use up to the present day:—

> An old felawe (fellow, partner) *of youres.*—*Pardoner's Tale.*
> A trusty frende *of Sir Tristram's.*—MALORY (15th cent.).

**305. Personal Genitives.**—In Old English *mine*, *thine*, *our*, and *your* (=A.S. *mīn*, *thīn*, *ūre*, *eówer*) had two distinct functions—(1) as independent pronouns, where we now have to say *of me*, *of thee*, *of you*, *of us*; (2) as adjectives, declined in A.S. like other adjectives, so as to be in the same number, gender, and case as the noun following.

In Mod. Eng. function (1) is obsolete; yet some traces of it can be seen in such examples as the following:—

(1) Having heard of A.'s death, *my* mind was much disturbed.

Here *my*=*of me*, and the implied *me* is qualified by the participle "having heard."

(2) Poor is *our* sacrifice, whose eyes
Are lighted from above.—NEWMAN.

Here *our*=*of us*, and *us* is the antecedent to "whose."

(3) Have I not *all their* letters to meet me in arms?—1 *Hen. IV.* ii. 3, 28.

Here *all their letters* mean "letters from them all"; and *all* qualifies the pronoun *them*.

(4) At *your only* choice (=at the choice of you only).—*Coriol.* i. 9, 36.

(5) I took *her* leave (=leave of her) at Court.—*All's Well that Ends Well*, v. 3, 79.

(6) But I have sworn to frustrate *both their* hopes (= the hopes of both of them).—MARLOWE.

(7) Tell her 'tis *all our* ways (= the ways of all of us); it runs in the family.—SHERIDAN.

The common phrase "*in my despite*" means "in spite of me"; cf. the obsolete phrase "maugre myn," which in the Middle period of English meant the same thing. (*Maugre* is from Old French *maugré*, Mid. Fr. *malgré*, ill-will.)

**306. Dative case.**—In Old English there was a Dative case distinct from the Objective. What we now call the Indirect Object was then a Dative. Other examples of what in Old English was a Dative are given below:—

(*a*) **Dative of Interest.**—The Jew ate *me* (to my astonishment) a whole ham of bacon.—ADDISON.

"Archers," he cried, "send *me* (for my satisfaction) an arrow through yon monk's frock."—SCOTT.

Knock *me* this gate, and rap *me* well.—SHAKSPEARE.

(*b*) **Reflexive Dative** (see § 149).—Fare *thee* well (=fare well *for thyself*).

He overslept *him*self (slept too long *for himself*).

But hear *thee*, Gratiano;
Thou art too wild, too rude, and bold of voice.
*Merchant of Venice*, ii. 2, 189.

(*c*) **With Impersonal Verbs.**—*Me*thinks; *me*seems; it likes *us* well.—SHAKSPEARE.

(*d*) **With the Verbs "be," "worth."**—

Woe worth *the day!*
Woe is *me!*

(*e*) **As Indirect object to a Transitive verb** (see § 141).—He taught *my sons* Euclid.

I hope you will do *me* this favour.

**307. Dative Absolute.**—In Old English the noun or pronoun in such constructions was in the Dative case; cf. the Ablative in Latin and the Genitive in Greek.

Eów slǽpendum = you sleeping. (Here *slǽp-end-um* is the Dative plural of the present participle; and *eów* is the Dative plural of the Second Personal pronoun.)

They have stolen away the body, *us* sleeping.—*Wyclif's Bible.*

The modern substitutes for the Dative Absolute are:—

(*a*) The Nominative, common even in Chaucer's time:[1]—

And *he* continuyng ever in stourdynesse.—*Clerke's Tale*, iv. 9.

---

[1] In Milton we meet with such phrases as "*me* overthrown," "*us* dispossessed," "*him* destroyed." It would be wrong to infer from this that the Dative Absolute of Old English was lingering in use up to Milton's

(*b*) The use of the preposition "with" in connection with a noun or participle following:—

Besides, *with the enemy invading* our country, it was my duty to go in the campaign.—THACKERAY.

**308. Cognate Accusative.**—This construction (see § 148) occurs in the oldest English, and has been in constant use ever since:—

{Thá leof-od-on heora líf.—*Anglo-Saxon.*
{They lived their life.
{He had bled so mychel blood.
{He had bled so much blood.—*Middle English.*

SECTION 2.—USES OF PRONOUNS, PAST AND PRESENT.

**309. "Ye" supplanted by "you."**—In Old English, and in the English Bible, *ye* (=A.S. *gé*) is a Nominative, and *you* (=A.S. *eów*) is an Accusative or Dative:—

*Ye* have not chosen me, but I have chosen *you*.—*John* xv. 16.

But prior to the date of the first Authorised Version some confusion had already been springing up in profane literature. Hence in the Elizabethan dramatists and later, when our language was still in some respects unsettled, we find *ye* and *you* apparently used indiscriminately, as if there were no difference between them:—

I do beseech *ye*, if *you* bear me hard.—*Julius Cæsar*, iii. 1, 157.
His wrath, which one day will destroy *ye* both.—*Par. Lost*, ii. 734.

*Note.*—*Ye* took the place of *you* in such examples as the above, because the unaccented *you* was pronounced as *y'*,—a sound very unlike that of the accented *you*. It was written as *ye*, because this spelling, though far from suitable, made a nearer approach to the sound of *y'* than the spelling of *you* did. We still say colloquially, "look *ee* here" for "look *ye* or *you* here."

**310. "Thou" and "thee" supplanted by "you."**—In the fourteenth century, and throughout the Tudor period, *you* was the more formal, distant, and respectful mode of address, and *thou* the more familiar, such as a father could use to a son, but not a son to a father: [1]—

---

time. The poet was merely adopting, or attempting to reintroduce, the Latin idiom—in which attempt he met with no followers.

We say "reintroduce" advisedly, because even in Old English the Dative absolute was not a true Teutonic idiom, but a mere imitation of the Latin Ablative absolute.

[1] This question is worked out very fully by Prof. Skeat in *William of Palerne*, preface, p. xli. The results are embodied in Abbott's *Shakspearian Grammar*, pp. 153-158.

(1) *Grat.* I have a suit to *you.*
*Bass.* *You* have obtained it.
*Grat.* *You* must not deny me. I must go with *you* to Belmont.
*Bass.* Why, then *you* must. But hear *thee*, Gratiano;
*Thou* art too wild, too rude, and bold of voice.
*Merchant of Venice*, ii. 2, 187-190.

So long as the two friends are talking to each other in a formal way on a matter of business, they adopt the respectful and more distant *you*. But as soon as the one begins to address the other in a more confidential and intimate tone, he at once uses the more familiar *thee* and *thou.*

(2) All that Lord Cobham did was at *thy* instigation, *thou* viper! for I *thou* thee, *thou* traitor.

This language was used at Sir Walter Raleigh's trial (A.D. 1603), when Coke, finding that argument and evidence were wanting, insulted the illustrious prisoner by applying to him the familiar "*thou.*"

*Note* 1.—"Thou" is retained in poetry and in addresses to the Deity, in both of which archaicisms are suitable.

*Note* 2.—Quakers used to address every one as *thou*, because (it is presumed) all men in their view were or ought to be friends and equals. They disowned the tone of distance and superiority implied by the more formal *you.*

### 311. Self, my-self, him-self, etc.

When "self" is added to a pronoun of the *First* or *Second* person, it is preceded by the *Possessive* case. But when it is added to a pronoun of the *Third* person, it is preceded by a pronoun in the *Objective* case. Thus we have:—

*First and Second Persons.*—My-self, our-selves. Thy-self, your-selves.

*Third Person.*—Him-self, her-self, it-self, them-selves.

How is this to be explained? The word "self" was originally an adjective signifying "same," "actual," "identical." In Old Eng. it was declined with the preceding pronoun:—*Ic self* (Nom. "I self or the same"), *mín selfes* (Gen. "of me the same"), *mé selfne* (Accus. "me the same"), etc.

On these *self* (= identical) hills.—RALEIGH.
To shoot another arrow that *self* (= same) way
Which thou didst shoot at first.—SHAKSPEARE.
At that *self* (= same) moment enters Palamon.—DRYDEN.
His servant was healed in the *self-same* hour.—*Matt.* viii. 13.

But in later English "self" came to be also used as a noun, as we still see it used in such phrases as "a man's better *self*" (= the better side of his character); "she was beauty's self" (= a personification of beauty). Here the noun "self" is very correctly qualified by a noun in the Possessive case. Similarly in the First and Second persons we have "*my*-self," "*your*-self," etc., where the noun "self" is correctly qualified by the Possessives "my" and "your." The same construction occurs in what have now become provincial phrases, "his self," "their selves," in which "self" has been pluralised as a noun on the analogy of "shelf, shelves." "Self" is commonly used as a noun with the Third Personal pronoun in the Authorised Version of 1611:—

> Who *his* own *self* bare our sins.—1 *Peter* ii. 24.
> He may make *his-self* easy.—DICKENS.

But since the Tudor period "self" has retained its original function as an *adjective*, whenever it is compounded with the Third Personal pronoun:—

(1) He hurt *him*-self.
(2) He did it by *him*-self.
(3) He *him*-self did it.
(4) They *them*-selves did it.

In (1) and (2) there is no difficulty. In (3) and (4) we have the objectives *him* and *them* in what seems to be apposition with *he* and *they* respectively. But the apposition is apparent, not real. The construction is merely a survival of the Old English Dative, denoting agency. If these phrases were literally translated into Mod. Eng., they would be "*by* him-self," "*by* them-self," just as we still say sometimes, "He did it by himself," "They did it by themselves." But in Mod. Eng. the *by* is usually omitted, and the Reflexive or Emphatic pronoun is placed immediately after the subject to the verb, as if it were in apposition with it.

In the phrase "they them-*selves*," there is a confusion between "self" as a noun and "self" as an adjective; and since adjectives have now no plural forms, the phrase would be more correctly worded "they them-self." But it has been assimilated to the phrase "We our-*selves*." The latter is quite correct; for here "selves," Plural noun, is in apposition to "we," Plural pronoun, and is qualified by the Possessive pronoun "our."

**312. Own.**—This adjective is placed after the Possessive forms of personal pronouns in all persons alike:—

My own, mine own. Thy own, thine own. His own, her own, its own. Our own, your own, their own.

"Own" is never placed after *double* Possessives, like "ours," "yours," "theirs." It means literally "possessed," and was originally spelt *ágen*, the p.p. of *ág-an* (A.S.), to possess.

Sometimes we have the doubly emphatic phrases, "my own self," "your own self," etc.

**313. Which.**—(*a*) as Interrogative; (*b*) as Relative:—

(*a*) According to present idiom, "which" as an Interrogative is used in a *selective* sense, and "who" or "what" in a *general* sense (see § 131). A similar distinction prevailed in Old English also. *Hwá* (who) was used in a general sense; *hwilc* or *hwylc* (which) in a more special one. *Hwi-lc* is short for *hwí-lic*, "why or how like," "what sort of": cf. Lat. *qua-lis.*

*Hwylc* (of what sort) is mín módor (my mother?)—*Matt.* xii. 48.

(*b*) "Which" as a Relative is now used only for Neuter (sex-less) antecedents, or for the names of young children and lower animals, when no question of sex arises about them. This restriction, however, is of recent date; for "who" *in the Nom. case* did not come into use at all as a *Relative* pronoun till the sixteenth century. Before this the Nom. had been used exclusively as an *Interrogative*, though the other cases were used as Relatives at a much earlier date:—

Our Father, *which* art in heaven.—*New Test.*<br>
Then Warwick disannuls great John of Gaunt,<br>
*Which* did subdue the greatest part of Spain.—3 *Hen. VI.* iii. 1.

**314. "The whom," "the whose," "the which,"** etc.—In Middle English we find the Relative particularised by the Def. article. But modern idiom is against it, even in poetry:—

*The whose* power as now is falle.—GOWER.<br>
Your mistress, from *the whom* I see<br>
There's no disjunction.—*Winter's Tale,* iv. 4.<br>
'Twas a foolish quest,<br>
*The which* to gain and keep he sacrificed all rest.—BYRON.

**315. "Who," "what," as Indefinite Demonstratives.**—The Indefinite use of "who," "what," in the sense of *some one* or *something* dates back to Old English. Though modern idiom is against it, it has survived in the common word "somewhat" = something, and in the phrase "as who should say":—

Love is bought for litil *what.*—GOWER.<br>
Come down and learn the little *what*<br>
That Thomalin can sayne.—SPENSER.<br>
With promise of his sister and *what* else.—SHAKSPEARE.<br>
The cloudy messenger turns me his back<br>
And hums, as *who* should say, You'll rue the time<br>
That clogs me with this answer.—*Macbeth,* iii. 6.

**316. "That" for "who" or "which."**—It has been shown in § 128 that "that" is pre-eminently the *Restrictive* relative, and "who" or "which" the *Continuative.*

This use of "that" as an indeclinable Relative pronoun is

by no means modern. In Old Eng. the indeclinable Relative was *the*, the place of which was taken by *that* in Mid. Eng. In the Tudor period and later the Relative "that" yielded to the influence of "who" and "which" (both of which during the period named could be fortified, if necessary, by the Def. art. "the"), and almost disappeared. About Addison's time it again came into fashion, and has held its ground ever since as the Restrictive Relative.

Addison, however, who was evidently not acquainted with the history of our language, protested against the change. In his "Humble Petition of 'Who' and 'Which'" he makes the petitioners say:—"We are descended of ancient families, and kept up our dignity and honour many years, till the Jack Sprat *that* supplanted us."

**317. "That" for "what" or "that which."**—This use of "that" has become archaic. It arose merely from the loss of Rel. *that* following the Demonstrative *that*. In A.S. the phrase was *that the* or *that that* (= that which):—

> We speak *that* (what) we do know, and testify *that* we have seen.—*New Test.*
>
> I am possessed of *that* is mine.—SHAKSPEARE.

**318. "It" with Impersonal verbs.**—Verbs used in the *third* person only, and without having a *personal* subject, are called Impersonal.

(*a*) Impersonal verbs denoting *physical* events were used with "it" in Old English, as now, and were not less common:—

> *Hit* rínth = *it* rains. *Hit* fréoseth = *it* freezes.

(*b*) But verbs denoting *mental feelings* have undergone an important change. The Dative of the person (§ 306, *c*) has become the Subject, in the Nominative case. The change was gradual, and Impersonal verbs were more common in Shakspeare's time than now:[1]—

> It yearns me not.—*Hen. V.* iv. 3.
>
> It dislikes me.—*Othel.* ii. 3, 49.
>
> It likes us well.—*Hamlet*, i. 2, 81.
>
> Where it thinks best unto your royal self.[2]—*Rich. III.* iii. 1, 63.

---

[1] "An abundance of Impersonal verbs is a mark of a very early stage in a language, denoting that a speaker has not yet arrived so far in his development as to trace his own actions and feelings to his own agency."—ABBOTT, *Shakspearian Grammar*, p. 208.

[2] "Thinks," the Impersonal verb, means "seems," and is derived from A.S. *thync-*; but the Personal verb "think" comes from A.S. *thenc-*; and *thenc* is allied to *thanc*, "thank," a kindly remembrance.

**319. It is I.**—In Old and Mid. Eng. the phrase was "it am I," out of which the Mod. Eng. "it is I" has been developed:—

*Old English:* "I it am."

Ic sylf hit eom<br>*I* self *it am* } =it is myself.—*Luke* xxiv. 39.

*Mid. Eng.:* "it am I."

I am thy mortel foo (=foe), and *it am I*<br>That loveth so hoote (=hotly) Emelye the brighte.—CHAUCER, *Knight's Tale.*

*Mod. Eng.:* "it is I."

*It is* not *he* that slew the man, *hit is I.*—*Gest. Rom.*

Thus in Old and Mid. Eng. "it" is the *complement* to the verb "am"; while in Mod. Eng. it has become the *subject.* Hence any pronoun of any number or person can now be placed after "it is" as complement: "it is we," "it is you," "it is they," etc., instead of "it are we," "it are you," etc.

**320. "It is," "it was," for giving emphasis.**—This device is found in Old English. In Mid. Eng. it was equally common.

In the tyme bitwene Abraham and Moyses *it was* that men come verst (first) to Engelond.—ROBERT OF GLOUCESTER.

# CHAPTER XV.—ADJECTIVES.

## SECTION 1.—USES OF THE VARIOUS KINDS OF ADJECTIVES.

### *Quantitative.*

**321. Some, any.**—These are used as follows:—

(*a*) **Some** is used in *affirmative* sentences; as—

"He has procured *some* bread." We cannot say, "He has procured *any* bread."

(*b*) **Any** is used in *negative* sentences; as—

"He has *not* procured *any* bread." We cannot say, "He has not procured *some* bread."

(*c*) **Any** and **some** can both be used in *interrogative* sentences:—

Has he procured *any* bread?<br>Has he procured *some* bread?

But in such sentences "any" is more commonly used than "some," and is to be preferred to it.

**322. Little, a little, the little.**—Each of these expressions has a distinct meaning of its own:—

(*a*) **Little** is a *negative* adjective, and means "not much."

He had *little* money=(not much money).

(*b*) **A little** is an *affirmative* adjective, and means "some at least":—a certain quantity, however little.

He had *a little* money=(some money at least, although the amount was small).

(*c*) **The little** implies two statements—one *negative*, and the other *affirmative*.

He spent *the little* (or *what little*) money he had.
That is—(1) The money he had was not much. (*Negative.*)
(2) He spent all the money that he had. (*Affirmative.*)

*Note.*—When "little" and "a little" are used as Adverbs, the same distinction holds good:—

I *little* expected (=did not expect) such treatment.
I am *a little* (rather, slightly) tired.

*Numeral Adjectives.*

323. **Few, a few, the few.**—Each of these expressions has a distinct meaning of its own:—

(*a*) **Few** is a *Negative* adjective, and signifies "not many."

He read *few* books (he did *not* read *many* books).

(*b*) **A few** is an *Affirmative* adjective, and signifies "some at least":—a certain number, however few.

He read *a few* books (that is, he read *some* books *at least*, though the number was small).

(*c*) **The few** implies two statements, *one Negative* and *the other Affirmative.*

He read *the few* (or *what few*) books he had.
That is (1) The books he had were not many. (*Negative.*)
(2) He read all the books he had. (*Affirmative.*)

324. **Many a, a many.**—The former phrase is followed by *Singular* nouns, and the latter by *Plural* ones:—

(*a*) **Many a.**—Here "a"="one"; "many a man" means "many times one man," or "many men." Hence "many" has here the force of a Multiplicative numeral:—

*Many a* youth and *many a* maid
Dancing 'neath the greenwood shade.—MILTON.

It is interesting to notice that this construction is met with in our language so far back as the beginning of the thirteenth century:—

*Moni enne* (=many a) thing.—LAYAMON.

(*b*) **A many.**—Here "many" has the force of a *Collective noun*, and "*of*" is understood after it:—

They have not shed *a many tears*,
Dear eyes, since first I knew them well.—TENNYSON.

*A many of* our bodies.—SHAKSPEARE, *Hen. V.* iv. 3.
*A many of* us were called together.—LATIMER.
*This many* summers on a sea of glory.—*Hen. VIII.*

In prose it is more common to put in the word "great" between *a* and *many*. "A great many men" means "a large number *of* men," the "*of*" being understood, and *many* being a Collective noun. Similarly in such a phrase as "a few books," we might regard *a few* as a Collective noun, the "*of*" being understood after it.

*Note.*—In Old English "menigu" was a Collective *Noun*, signifying "a multitude or large number," and "manig" was an Indefinite Numeral *Adjective*, signifying "many." In Modern English the same word "many" stands for both; for it is equivalent to "menigu" in the phrase *a many*, and to "manig" in the phrase *many a* or simply *many*.[1]

**325.** Definite Numeral Quantities are sometimes Collective nouns, where "*of*" must be understood after them in Mod. Eng. In Mid. Eng. the sense of *of* was expressed by the Gen. Plural. Similarly, in A.S. *twelf scéapa* means "twelve of sheep." All numerals in A.S. governed Genitives plural.

*A dozen* (of) sheep; *a million* (of) apples.
*A hundred* (of) years; *a thousand* (of) years.
*A hundred-thousand* (of) years.

### *Demonstrative Adjectives.*

**326. Definite Demonstratives** are used as follows:—

(*a*) **This, these**: point to something *near*:—

*This* tree; *these* trees.
*These* eyes (=my own eyes) saw the deed.

(*b*) **That, those, yon, yonder.**[2]—These point to something *farther off*; as—

*That* tree; *those* trees; *yon* tree, or the tree *yonder*.

---

[1] This explanation, however, contains only half the truth. The English "many" became mixed up with the Norman *meinee* (Old Fr. *meisnee*, Low Lat. *mansionata*), which meant a household, a company. In Mid. Eng. *a gret meinee* (="a great many" in Mod. Eng.) meant "a great company of men," and this commonly used phrase was largely instrumental in producing confusion. It occurs in the ballad of "Chevy Chase" in the sense of "household troop":—

The Percy out of Northumberland came,
With him *a great meinee*.

Out of the noun *meinee* we get the adj. *meni-al*, pertaining to household work; which therefore has no connection, as has been supposed, with the word "manual," pertaining to the hand (*manus*).

[2] "Yon" (A.S. *geon*) was an adjective signifying "distant." "Yonder" was an adverb formed from it. Hence the phrase *the tree yonder* means "the tree there." In Mod. Eng., however, the distinction is not always observed.

(*c*) **Such.**—This refers either (1) to something just mentioned, or (2) to something just going to be mentioned :—

(1) His praise of me was not sincere : I do not like *such* a man.
(2) *Such* food as we get here does not suit me.

"Such" can also be used as an *Indefinite* Demonstrative :—.

He called at my house on *such a* day (=some day or other), and I gave *such and such* an answer (some answer or other) to his questions.

*Note.*—The adverb *so* can also be used Indefinitely :—

A week or *so* (that is, a week more or less).

**327. Indefinite Demonstratives** are used thus :—

(*a*) **One.**—This word is properly a Numeral adjective ; but it may also be used as an Indefinite Demonstrative :—

He came *one* day (on a certain day which I cannot remember) to see me.

*One* Mr. James (a certain man whom I do not know, but who is called Mr. James) came to see me.

*Note.*—This use of "one" is by no means of recent date :—

*Oon Grecus* that reigned there some tyme.—TREVISA.

(*b*) **Any.**—This is more emphatic than "a" or "an," and can be used with Plural as well as Singular nouns :—

*Any* man (that is, any and every man) could do that.

You may take *any* books (no books in particular, but any books) that you like best.

(*c*) **Some.**—This is used in two senses—(1) as showing that no person or thing in particular is specified ; (2) for making a Definite number Indefinite (see § 88).

(1) *Some* man (I do not know who he was) called here to-day.
(2) He owes me *some* 20 pounds (*about* 20 pounds).

(*d*) **Other than.**—This means "different from" :—

He has no books *other than* English ones.

This is better than saying, "he has no other books than English." "Than" is here a preposition. "Other" was originally a Comparative adj., and hence it takes "than" after it.

(*e*) **The other day.**—In spite of the Definite article, "the other" is here Indefinite,—some day a little before the present.

He came here *the other* day (a day of recent date).

*Note.*—An explanation of this phrase is offered in chap. xx (69).

**328. Some, any.**—It depends upon the sense whether these are *Demonstrative*, *Quantitative*, or *Numeral* :—

| | | |
|---|---|---|
| *Some* | (1) *Some* man called here to-day . | *Indef. Demons.* |
| | (2) Give me *some* bread . . . . | ,, *Quant.* |
| | (3) Give me *some* loaves of bread . | ,, *Number.* |

*Any*
- (1) Take *any* book that you like best *Indef. Demons.*
- (2) He has not had *any* bread . . ,, *Quant.*
- (3) Did you bring *any* loaves ? . ,, *Number.*

Both of these adjectives are Indefinite; but, as may be seen from the following examples, "some" is the least Indefinite of the two :—

Did *any* man call here to-day? Yes; *some* man did call.
Take *any* books that you like; but you must take *some*.
Can you come at *some* hour to-day? Yes, at *any* hour you like.

*Distributive Adjectives and Phrases.*

**329. Each other, one another.**—In these phrases we have a Distributive adjective (*each*, *one*) combined with a Demonstrative adjective (*other* or *another*). *Each* is Nom., *other* is *Accus.*; cf. Lat. "alius alium."

(*a*) "**Each other**" is used for *two* persons :—

The two men struck *each other* (that is, *each* man struck the *other* man).

(*b*) "**One another**" is used for *more than two* persons :—

They all loved *one another* (that is, each man loved every other man).

**330.** The drift of a Distributive adjective can also be expressed in the following ways :—

(*a*) They went out two *by* two, or *by twos* (in separate pairs).
(*b*) They went out *two and two* (in separate pairs).
(*c*) They went out *two at a time* (in separate pairs).
(*d*) The twenty men had a gun *a piece* (had each a gun).
(*e*) They went to their *respective* homes (each to his own).

## SECTION 2.—THE USES OF ARTICLES.

**331. Origin and Character of the Articles.**—The articles are adjectives, and not a separate part of speech. This is proved by their origin.

In Old English the Nom. masculine and feminine singular of the demonstrative adjective (which was chiefly used as a definite article) was derived from a base *sa*; but the Nom. neuter singular, and all the other cases, whether singular or plural, in all genders were formed from a base *tha*. Out of this base "*tha*" was formed the indeclinable A.S. relative *the*, which in course of time took the place of the A.S. def. article, and has remained the Def. article ever since.

The Indefinite article comes from A.S. *án* (one), a Numeral adjective, that was declined throughout the Singular in all genders. In the Middle period of English *án* was differentiated into a regular Indefinite article by the loss of its accent and consequent shortening of the vowel. Thus *án* becomes *an*, as in Modern English; while the numeral *án* took the form of *ón*, which in Modern English is *one*. *A* is merely an abridgment of *an*.

*Note.*—It is therefore opposed to history as well as to reason to consider the Articles to be a distinct part of speech. It is opposed to reason, because whenever they are used they discharge, as their origin would imply, the function of Adjectives in limiting or defining the application of a noun. The universality of their use gives them an exceptional character, which distinguishes them from ordinary Adjectives; but this does not make them distinct parts of speech.

**332. Uses of Articles.**—These are exemplified as follows:—

(*a*) If we wish to *particularise* the noun, we use the *Definite* article for either number:—

Let us go and bathe in *the* river (that is, the river near our house, or the river where we usually bathe).

This settles *the* matter (that is, the matter in which we are engaged).

(*b*) If we wish to *generalise* the noun, we use the *Indefinite* article for the Singular and none for the Plural:—

*A* tiger is a fierce animal (that is, any tiger; or tigers generally).

Cats are not so faithful as dogs.

*Note.*—Since "*a*" has arisen from "*one*" it is still sometimes used in the sense of "one."

*A* stitch (=one stitch) in time saves nine.

Two of *a* trade (=of the same trade) should live apart.

**333.** An article is not used with a Proper, Material, or Abstract noun, except to make it a Common noun:—

He is *the Nestor* (=the oldest man) of the service.—*Proper.*

Sugar-cane is one of *the grasses* (=kinds of grass).—*Material.*

He is *a justice* of the peace.—*Abstract.*

*Note* 1.—"The" may, however, be placed before an Abstract noun, to show the particular connection in which the quality named by the noun stands:—

*The injustice* of the world. *The shortness* of life. *The love* of money. *The faithfulness* of a dog.

*Note* 2.—The Definite article is placed before (1) names of rivers, as *the Thames;* (2) mountain-ranges, as *the Alps;* (3) groups of islands, as *the Hebrides.* Before other geographical Proper names the article is not used.

**334.** "*The*" is sometimes used to indicate a *class* or *kind*:—

*The lion* is a noble beast=
*A lion* is a noble beast=
*Lions* are noble beasts.

**335.** When "*the*" is placed before a *Common* noun, it sometimes gives it the meaning of an *Abstract* noun:—

He felt *the patriot* (the patriotic spirit or feeling) rise within his breast.
He acted *the lord* (the lordly character) wherever he went.

**336. Omission of Article.**—There are some stock phrases in which no article is used :—

| | | | |
|---|---|---|---|
| strike root | take breath | in fact | on demand |
| leave school | follow suit | at school | for love |
| give ear | do penance | in bed | for money |
| send word | by land | by day | at anchor |
| set foot | by water | by night | at ease |
| shake hands | at sea | in debt | at sight |
| keep house | on board ship | in trouble | at interest |
| give battle | at home | at daybreak | at dinner |
| give place | under ground | at sunset | in hand |
| cast anchor | in jail | at fault | on earth |
| set sail | out of doors | in court | over head and |
| catch fire | by name | in demand | ears |

Compare *to-day*, *in-deed*, etc., where the words are fused into one.

The article can also be omitted in such colloquialisms, as "Father is gone out," when the Common noun denotes a well-known individual, and is used as a Proper noun. See § 32, *Note* 3.

## Section 3.—Adjectives used as Nouns.

**337.** The change from Adjective to Noun is complete, when the word can be used in the Plural number or in the Possessive case. The change is complete, because Adjectives as such have neither case nor number.

> *Nobles*=noble men or noblemen.
> A *noble's* house=a nobleman's house.
> I have told you many *secrets*=secret things.

*Note.*—In using a Proper adjective to denote some language, no article is placed before it, and no noun is expressed:—

> The grammar of *English* is simpler than that of *Greek*.

**338.** Some adjectives are used as nouns in the Singular only, some in the Plural only, and some in both :—

(*a*) *Singular only :*—

Our all. The whole. Our best. Our worst. Much (as, Much has been done). More (as, More has been done). Little (as, Little has been done). Less (as, Less has been done).

(*b*) *Plural only :*—

Opposites. Morals. Contraries. Particulars (=details). Movables. Eatables. Drinkables. Valuables. Greens (=green vegetables). Sweets and bitters (=the sweet and bitter contingencies of life). Our betters (=men better than ourselves). Our equals. The ancients. The moderns. The Commons. The actuals.

*Note.*—"These presents" (that is, *present letters*, *literæ præsentes*, the present writing) is a legal term borrowed from Anglo-French. "News" was formed on the analogy of Fr. *nouvelles,* plural of Old Fr. *novel,* adj. new. "Means" is plural of the adj. "mean" used as a noun.[1]

(*c*) *Singular and Plural*:—

A secret; secrets. A liquid; liquids. A solid; solids. A total; totals. A capital; capitals. An elder; elders. A senior; seniors. A junior; juniors. A native; natives. A mortal; mortals. An inferior; inferiors. A superior; superiors. A criminal; criminals. Another; others. A divine (theological teacher); divines.

**339.** Participles (which, in fact, are Verbal adjectives, see § 17) are sometimes used as Plural nouns:—

Belongings, surroundings, bygones, hangings, beings.

In Old English, two nouns were formed from Pres. participles:—

*Feó-nd* (=fiend): Pres. part. of *feón* (to hate).
*Freó-nd* (=friend): Pres. part. of *freón* (to love).

**340.** There are certain phrases in which adjectives go in pairs, some noun being understood after them:—

*From bad to worse*=from a bad state to a worse one.
*The long and short*=the sum and substance of the matter.
*In black and white*=written with black ink on white paper.
*Through thick and thin*=through thick or difficult obstacles and through thin or easy ones. (This occurs in Chaucer.)
*From first to last*=from the beginning to the end.
*At sixes and sevens*=in a state of disorder.
*High and low*=in high places and low ones, everywhere, up and down.
*Right or wrong*=whether the act is right or not.
*For better, for worse*=for any good or evil that may happen.
*Fast and loose*=with a tight or loose hold, as he may prefer; that is, at random, recklessly.
*Black and blue.* "He beat them black and blue" (so as to bring out black and blue marks on the skin).
*Right and left.* "He struck out right and left" (to this side and that side).
*Slow and steady.* "Slow and steady (patient and steady progress) wins the race."
*For good, for good and all*=finally, permanently; for all future contingencies, good or evil.

**341. Adjectives preceded by "the."**—When an adjective is preceded by the Definite article, it can be used as a Noun in the three senses shown below:—

(1) As a Common noun (*Plural*) denoting *Persons*:—

---

[1] "Mean" in the sense of "intermediate" is from Anglo-French *meien,* Late Lat. *medianus.* "Mean" in the sense of "common" is from Anglo-Saxon *ge-mǽne.* The plural *means* is from the former.

None but *the brave* (=those men who are brave) deserves the fair.
To *the pure* (=those persons who are pure) all things are pure.

*Note.*—In earlier English this construction was common in a *Singular* sense also, and the article was sometimes omitted :—

For he nought helpeth *needful* in *his* neede.—CHAUCER.

(2) As an Abstract noun (*Singular*) :—

*The good*=that quality which is good, =goodness in general.
*The beautiful*=that quality which is beautiful, =beauty in general.
All the motions of his nature were towards *the true*, *the natural*, *the sweet*, *the gentle*.—DE QUINCEY.

(3) As a name for some particular part of a thing :—

*The white* (=the white part) of the eye.
*The vitals* (=the most vital parts) of the body.
*The thick* (=the thickest parts) of the forest.
*The wilds* (=the wild parts) of a country.
*The interior* (=the inside parts) of a house.
*The exterior* (=the outside parts) of a house.
*The middle* (=the middle part) of a river.
*The small* (=the smallest part) of the back.

**342.** In poetry, adjectives are sometimes used as nouns, without having an article placed before them :—

*Fair* is foul, and *foul* is fair.—SHAKSPEARE.
O'er *rough* and *smooth* she trips along.—WORDSWORTH.
And fold me in the riches of thy *fair*.—GREEN.
And sudden *pale* usurps her cheeks.—SHAKSPEARE.
Say what you can, my *false* o'erweighs your *true*.—SHAKSPEARE.
My *earthly* by his *heavenly* overpowered.—MILTON.
From *grave* to *gay*, from *lively* to *severe*.—POPE.

**343.** There are several adverbial phrases, made up of a preposition and an adjective, in which some noun is understood after the adjective :—

**Extent.**—On the whole, in the main, in general, in particular, at the full or in full, at all, not at all, at most, at large, in short, a little.

**Time.**—At last, at the latest, at first, at the first, to the last, at present, for the present, in the past, in future, for the future, once for all, before long, for long.

**Place.**—On the right (hand), on the left (hand), on high, in the open (air).

**Manner.**—In the right (on the true or right side of the question), in the wrong (on the wrong side of the question), in the dark, in common, on the loose.

**State.**—At best, for the best, at worst, on the alert.

## SECTION 4.—DEGREES OF COMPARISON.

**344. Positive Degree.**—When two persons or things are said to be *equal* in respect of some quality, we use the *Positive* degree with *as . . . as*; or we can use the Comparative adverb (*less* or *more*) with "not":—

This boy is *as* clever *as* that.
This boy is *no less* clever *than* that.
That boy is *not more* clever *than* this.

**345. Comparative Degree.**—When *two* persons or things are said to be *unequal* in respect of some quality, we use the *Comparative* degree:—

(*a*) This boy is more clever or cleverer *than* that.
(*b*) This boy is *the* cleverer *of the two.*

*Note* 1.—Forms (*a*) and (*b*) do not mean entirely the same thing. Form (*a*) merely denotes *superiority*. Form (*b*) denotes the *selection* of the one in preference to the other.

*Note* 2.—Observe that whenever the Comparative degree is used in the (*b*) or *selective* sense, it must be preceded by the Definite article, as might be expected; for the proper function of this article is to particularise or select, see § 332 (*a*).

**346. Superlative Degree.**—When one person or thing is said to surpass all other persons or things of the same kind, we use the *Superlative* degree with *the . . . of*.

Chaucer was *the* greatest *of* all the poets of his age.

The same thing can be expressed by the Comparative degree followed by *all others*, or *all the others*:—

Chaucer was greater than *all the other* poets of his age.

*Note* 1.—Care must be taken not to omit the word *other*. To say, "Chaucer was greater than all the poets of his age" makes nonsense: for this can only mean that Chaucer was greater than himself.

*Note* 2.—Milton, by a poetical license, and in imitation of a Greek idiom, confounds the Comp. with the Superl. in the following lines:—

Adam, the goodliest man of men since born,
His sons; the fairest of her daughters, Eve.

**347. Comparatives which have lost their force**:—(*a*) Latin Comparatives:—*interior, exterior, ulterior, major, minor.* These are now never followed by "*to*":—

A fact of *minor* (secondary) importance.
He had an *ulterior* (further) purpose in doing this.
The *interior* (inside) parts of a building.

Some can be used as nouns:—

He is a *minor* (a person under age).
He is a *major* (in the military rank).
The *interior* of the room was well furnished.

(*b*) English Comparatives:—*former, latter, elder, hinder, inner, outer* or *utter, upper, nether*, and the Double Comparative *lesser.* These are now never followed by *than*:—

The *former* and the *latter* rain.—*Old Testament.*
The *inner* meaning; the *outer* surface.
The *upper* and the *nether* mill-stones.
He talks *utter* nonsense.

The words *elder* and *elders* can also be used as nouns, to denote some person or persons of dignified rank or age; as "the village elders."

**348. Distinctions of Meaning**: between (a) *eldest* and *oldest*; (b) *farther* and *further*; (c) *later* and *latter*; (d) *nearest* and *next*; (e) *outer* and *utter*; (f) *foremost* and *first*.

(*a*) { My *eldest* son died at the age of twelve.
He is the *oldest* of my surviving sons.

Here "eldest" means first-born, and is applied only to *persons*. 'Oldest" is applied to things as well as to persons, and denotes the greatest age. "That is the *oldest* tree in the grove." In the Comparative degree the same distinction of meaning holds good; and besides this, *older* has retained its Comparative force, while *elder* has lost it.

(*b*) { Liverpool is *farther* from London than Dover is.
The *further* end of the room. A *further* reason exists.

The word "farther" (comparative of "far") denotes a greater distance between two points. The word "further" (comparative of *fore*) denotes something additional or something more in advance.[1]

(*c*) { This is the *latest* news.
This is the *last* boy in the class.

The words "later" and "latest" denote time; the words "latter" and "last" denote position.

(*d*) { This street is the *nearest* to my house.
This house is *next* to mine.

The word "nearest" denotes space or distance; ("this street is at a less distance from my house than any other street"). But "next" denotes order or position; ("no other house stands between this house and mine").

(*e*) The *outer* surface. An *utter* failure. An *utter* fool.

"Outer" means that which is outside; "utter" means extreme or complete, in a bad sense.

(*f*) { The *first* occasion. The *first* student in the class.
That struck the *foremost* man in all this world.—SHAKSPEARE.

"First" means standing first in order of time or first in position. "Foremost" means most prominent, most distinguished, most conspicuous. The quotation from Shakspeare refers to Julius Cæsar, who at the time of his murder was the most conspicuous man in the world. Both are Superlatives of "fore."

[1] Avoid the mistake of supposing that "further" is the Comparative of *forth*. In *far-ther* and *fur-ther* the Comparative suffix is *-ther*, as also in *o-ther*. The real Positive of "further" is *fore*, which afterwards acquired the extended form of *forth*.

## CHAPTER XVI.—VERBS.

### SECTION 1.—USES OF TENSES.

**349. The Present Indefinite** can be used to denote :—

(*a*) What is always and necessarily true :—

The sun *shines* by day and the moon by night.
Things equal to the same thing *are* equal to one another.

(*b*) What is habitual in life or character :—

He *keeps* his promises. He *has* good health.

(*c*) What is present, if this is helped by the context :—

I *understand* what you *say*.
The door *is* open : no one had shut it.

(*d*) What is future, if this is helped by the context :—

He *comes* (= will come) in a few days' time.
When *do* you (= will you) start for Edinburgh ?

(*e*) What is past, provided that the event is known to be past. (This is called the Historic or Graphic present.)

Báber *now leads* (= then led) his men through the Kyber pass, and *enters* (= entered) the plains of India.

**350. The Past Indefinite.**—The special use of this tense is to state something *that was true once*, but is now past and gone. *It excludes absolutely all reference to* **present** *time*.

Vasco da Gama *was* the first man from Europe who *rounded* the Cape of Good Hope.

**351. The Present Perfect.**—This tense connects a *completed* event in some sense or other with *the present time*.

I *have lived* twenty years in London (that is, *I am living there still*, and I began to live there twenty years ago).

The lamp *has gone out* (that is, it has just gone out, and we are *now* left in darkness).

*Note.*—The Present Perfect can be used in reference to a past event, provided the state of things arising out of that event is *still present*.

The British Empire in India *has succeeded* to the Mogul.

The series of events by which the British Empire superseded the Mogul took place more than a century ago. The events are therefore long past. Yet it is quite correct to use the *Present* Perfect tense "*has* succeeded," because the state of things arising out of these past events is *still present :* the British Empire *still exists*, and pertains to *present time* no less than to past time.

**352. The Past Perfect** (also called the Pluperfect).—This is used whenever we wish to say that *some action had been completed before another was commenced.*

The verb expressing the *previous* action is put into the Past Perfect or Pluperfect tense. The verb expressing the *subsequent* action is put into the Past Indefinite.

| (a) *Previous Action.* | *Subsequent Action.* |
|---|---|
| *Past Perfect.* | *Past Indefinite.* |
| He *had been* ill two days, | when the doctor *was sent for.* |
| He *had seen* many foreign cities, | before he *returned* home. |

| (b) *Subsequent Action.* | *Previous Action.* |
|---|---|
| *Past Indefinite.* | *Past Perfect.* |
| The boat *was sunk* by a hurricane, | which *had* suddenly sprung up. |
| The sheep *fled* in great haste; | for a wolf *had entered* the field. |

**353. The Future Perfect.**—This tense denotes the completion of some event (*a*) in *future* time, (*b*) in *past* time.[1]

(*a*) He *will have* reached home, before the rain sets in. (The reaching of home will be completed, before the setting in of rain commences.)

(*b*) You *will have* heard (must have heard in some past time) this news already; so I need not repeat it.

**354. Shall** and **will** in Interrogative sentences:—

In Assertive sentences, *merely future time* is denoted by "shall" in the First person, and by "will" in the Second and Third; a *command* is denoted by "shall" in the Second and Third persons; an *intention* is denoted by "will" in the First person (see § 174).

In interrogative sentences, however, the change of situation from asserting a fact to asking a question modifies to some extent the uses of "shall" and "will." All possible meanings of "shall" and "will," when they are used interrogatively, are shown in the following examples:—

**Shall I.**
- (*a*) *Shall I* be sixteen years old to-morrow? (Here the "shall" merely inquires after something future.)
- (*b*) *Shall I* post that letter for you? (Here the "shall" inquires about a command. Do you command or desire me to post that letter for you?)

**Will I.** (This is not used at all, because "will" in the First person would imply intention, and it would be foolish to ask another person about one's own intentions.)

[1] It seems like a contradiction to make a *future* tense have reference to *past* time. But the future here implies an inference regarding something which is believed to have passed rather than past time itself. "You will have heard" = I infer or believe that you have heard.

**Shall you.** *Shall you* return home to-day? (This merely inquires about something future. Here the "shall" cannot imply command, because it would be foolish to inquire of any one whether he commands himself to do so and so.)

**Will you.** *Will you* do me this favour? (Here the "will" denotes willingness or intention. Are you *willing* or do you *intend* to do me this favour? Hence "will you" is the form used for asking a favour.)

**Shall he.** *Shall he* call for the doctor? (Here the "shall" implies a command. Do you desire or command him to call for the doctor?)

**Will he.** *Will he* be fourteen years old to-morrow? (Here the "will" merely inquires about something future.)

*Note* 1.—"Will I" might be used for the moment as an answer to "will you."

Will you lend me your umbrella for a few minutes?
*Answer.—Will I?* Of course I will.

*Note* 2.—It might be questioned whether "shall" or "will" is the more correct in the following sentences:—

(*a*) James and I *shall* be very happy to see you.
(*b*) James and I *will* be very happy to see you.

The "shall" is demanded by "I," and the "will" by "James," according to the rule given in § 174. Both therefore might be used, but (*b*) is the more common of the two.

All doubt could be removed by rewriting the sentences as follows:—

James *will* be very happy to see you, and so *shall* I.
I *shall* be very happy to see you, and so *will* James.

*Rewrite the following sentences, so as to bring out the full force of "shall" and "will":—*

1. You shall not go home until you have finished your lesson. 2. Shall I send the horse at four o'clock? 3. I will give you your pay in due course. 4. Will you assist me in this matter? 5. Shall he carry your box for you? 6. An idle man shall not enter my service. 7. I will not grant you a certificate. 8. Will you punish me, if I leave the room without your consent? 9. By what time of the day shall I have your dinner ready? 10. He shall not ride that horse, till he has acquired a better seat.

### Section 2.—Further Uses of the Infinitive.

**355.** The two main forms of the Infinitive are—(*a*) the Indefinite, "to love," and (*b*) the Perfect, "to have loved."

When should the one be used, and when the other?

**356. The Indefinite form** can be used after *any and every tense* of the preceding Finite verb. In fact, the tense of the preceding verb has no effect whatever on the tense of the Infinitive following it:—

| | *Finite verb in all tenses.* | *Infinitive (Indefinite).* |
|---|---|---|
| *Present* | I expect<br>I am expecting<br>I have expected<br>I have been expecting | to meet you. |
| *Past* | I expected<br>I was expecting<br>I had expected<br>I had been expecting | |
| *Future* | I shall expect<br>I shall be expecting<br>I shall have expected<br>I shall have been expecting | |

**357. The Perfect form** is used in the following ways:—

(*a*) After the *Past* tenses of verbs expressing wish, intention, hope, duty, etc., it shows that the wish, intention, hope, or duty *did not* (for some reason or other) *take effect*:[1]—

| | |
|---|---|
| He wished *to have come;*<br>He intended *to have come;*<br>He hoped *to have come;*<br>He expected *to have come;* | but something prevented him from coming. |
| He should *have come;*<br>He ought *to have come;* | but he neglected to do so. |

*Note.*—If we substitute the Indefinite form of the Infinitive for the Perfect form, nothing is implied as to whether the desire, etc., was fulfilled or not:—

| | |
|---|---|
| He wished *to come;*<br>He intended *to come;*<br>He hoped *to come;*<br>He expected *to come;*<br>He should *come;*<br>He ought *to come;* | but whether he came or not is an open question, on which the form of the Infinitive throws no light. |

(*b*) After verbs of seeming, appearing, etc., the Perfect form shows that the event denoted by the Infinitive took place at some time *previous* to that denoted by the Finite verb:—

| | | |
|---|---|---|
| *Present.* | He seems | to have worked hard (that is, at some previous time). |
| *Past.* | He seemed | |
| *Future.* | He will seem | |

---

[1] It has been represented, and this very erroneously, that the Perfect form of the Infinitive ought not to be used. But it is sanctioned by authority as well as by idiom, and was common in Elizabethan English:—

I thought thy bride-bed *to have decked*, sweet maid.—*Hamlet*, v. 1, 268.

We retain the idiom in the very common expression:—"I would (intended to) *have done* it." This construction invariably implies that the intention was not carried out. In the quotation from *Hamlet*, "thought" means "hoped," "expected."

*Note* 1.—If we substitute the Indefinite form of the Infinitive for the Perfect, the tense or time denoted by the Infinitive verb is the same as that denoted by the Finite verb.

*Present.* He seems }
*Past.* He seemed } to work hard.
*Future.* He will seem }

*Note* 2.—The Perfect form of the Infinitive is frequently used in a *past* sense after verbs of saying in the Passive voice :—

He is said *to have done* this = It is said that he *did* this.

**358. Infinitive after Relative Adverbs.**—The Infinitive is placed after Relative adverbs in such phrases as "*how to write*," "*when to come*," "*where to begin*," etc.

He did not know *how to write* (=the way to write).
He was not told *when to come* (=the time for coming).
I wish I knew *where to begin* (=the place for beginning).

Here the Relative adverb stands for the corresponding noun denoting manner, time, place, etc.

**359. Infinitive after Relative Pronouns.**—This occurs in such sentences as :—

(*a*) He had no money *with which to buy* food.

This is equivalent to "He had no money to buy food *with it*"; or "He had no money to buy food *with*" (§ 229).

(*b*) He is not such a fool *as to say* that.

Here the construction is elliptical. "He is not such a fool as *he would be* a fool to say (=for saying, or if he said) that."

**360. For to.**—At one time the Preposition "for" was often used before the Infinitive (see § 191, *d*), as in the phrase "for to see." Hence has arisen the common idiom of inserting a noun or pronoun between the preposition and the Infinitive.

There was too much noise *for any one to hear.*
The railway is the quickest way *for men or goods to be conveyed* from place to place.

## SECTION 3.—SEQUENCE OF TENSES.

**361.** When two sentences are joined together by some Subordinative conjunction, or by some Relative (or Interrogative) pronoun or adverb, one of them is called the **Principal** and the other the **Dependent** sentence (§ 234 and § 255) :—

| *Principal.* | *Dependent.* |
|---|---|
| I will let you know | *when* I shall start. |

**362.** There are two main rules about the Sequence of Tenses, and all special rules centre round these two.

RULE I.—*If there is a* **Past** *tense in the principal sentence, it must be followed by a* **Past** *tense in the dependent sentence* :—

| *Principal Sentence.* (*Past Tense.*) | *Dependent Sentence.* (*Past Tense.*) |
|---|---|
| It *was* settled, | that I *should* do this. |
| He *would* come, | if you *wished* it. |
| He *was* honest, | although he *was* poor. |
| He *asked* me, | whether I *had seen* his dog. |
| He *was* informed, | that I *had been helping* him. |
| We never *understood*, | how or why he *did* that. |
| He *did* not leave off, | till he *had succeeded*. |
| I *was inquiring*, | what you *had heard*. |
| He *succeeded*, | because he *worked* hard. |
| He *remained* silent, | as soon as he *heard* that. |
| I *would* do this, | if I *were* allowed. |
| He *walked* so far, | that he *tired* himself. |

RULE II.—*If there is a* **Present** *or* **Future** *tense in the principal sentence, it can be followed by* **any tense whatever** *in the dependent sentence.*

*Examples of Rule II.*

| Principal | Dependent | *Any tense whatever.* |
|---|---|---|
| *Present* or *Future.* I know or I shall know | that he reads a book.<br>that he is reading.<br>that he has read.<br>that he has been reading. | The four forms of the Present tense. |
| | that he will read.<br>that he will be reading.<br>that he will have read.<br>that he will have been reading. | The four forms of the Future tense. |
| | that he read.<br>that he was reading.<br>that he had read.<br>that he had been reading. | The four forms of the Past tense. |

**363. Exception to Rule I.**—There is one exception to Rule I. The **Past** tense in the principal sentence can be followed by a **Present Indefinite** in the dependent sentence, to express some *universal* or *habitual* fact :—

| *Principal Sentence.* (*Past Tense.*) | *Dependent Sentence.* (*Present Tense.*) |
|---|---|
| They *learnt* at school, | that honesty *is* the best policy. |
| The students *were* taught, | that the earth *moves* round the sun. |
| His illness *showed* him, | that all men *are* mortal. |
| He *was* glad to hear, | that his brother *is* industrious. |
| They *were* sorry to hear, | that he *has* a bad temper. |

**364. Conjunctions of Purpose.**—When the dependent sentence is introduced by a Conjunction of *purpose* (§ 238, *d*), the two following rules must be observed :—

(*a*) If the verb in the principal sentence is in the **Present** or **Future** tense, the verb in the dependent sentence must be expressed by "may" (**Present** tense).

(*b*) If the verb in the principal sentence is in the **Past** tense, the verb in the dependent sentence must (in accordance with Rule I.) be expressed by "might" (**Past** tense).

| | | *Principal Sentence.* | *Dependent Sentence.* |
|---|---|---|---|
| Present | *Indef.* | He comes, | *Present tense.* that he *may* see me. |
| | *Contin.* | He is coming, | |
| | *Perfect* | He has come, | |
| | *Perf. Cont.* | He has been coming, | |
| Future | *Indef.* | He will come, | that he *may* see me. |
| | *Contin.* | He will be coming, | |
| | *Perfect* | He will have come, | |
| | *Perf. Cont.* | He will have been coming, | |
| Past | *Indef.* | He came, | *Past tense.* that he *might* see me. |
| | *Contin.* | He was coming, | |
| | *Perfect* | He had come, | |
| | *Perf. Cont.* | He had been coming, | |

*Note.*—The word "lest" = "that not." The *only* Auxiliary verb that can be used after "lest" is *should*, whatever may be the tense of the verb in the principal sentence :—

| | *Principal Sentence.* | *Dependent Sentence.* |
|---|---|---|
| Present . . | He goes, | lest he *should* see me. or that he *may* not see me. |
| Future . . | He will go, | lest he *should* see me. or that he *may* not see me. |
| Past . . . | He went, | lest he *should* see me. or that he *might* not see me. |

365. **Conjunctions of Comparison.**—When the dependent sentence is introduced by some Conjunction of Comparison, Rule I. has no existence whatever. *Any tense can be followed by any tense.*

| *Principal Sentence.* | *Dependent Sentence.* |
|---|---|
| He *likes* you better, | than he *liked* me. |
| He *liked* you better, | than he *likes* me. |
| He *will like* you better, | than he *has liked* me. |
| He *has liked* you better, | than he *liked* me. |
| He *liked* you better, | than he *is liking* me. |
| He *will like* you better, | than he *was liking* me, etc. |

*Note* 1.—If the comparison is expressed by "as well as" instead of "than," the same rule holds good. Any tense may be followed by any tense, according to the sense intended by the speaker.

He *likes* you as well as he *liked* me.
He *will like* you as well as he *has liked* me, etc.

*Note* 2.—If no verb is expressed after "*than*" or after "*as well as*," the tense of the verb *understood* in the dependent sentence is the same as that of the verb *expressed* in the principal sentence.

He *liked* you better than (*he liked*) me.
He *will like* you as well as (*he will like*) me.

## CHAPTER XVII.—ADVERBS.

### SECTION 1.—POSITION OF ADVERBS.

**366.** If the word to be qualified is an Adjective, or an Adverb, or a Preposition, or a Conjunction, the qualifying Adverb is placed immediately *before it.*

| | |
|---|---|
| *Adjective* or *Participle* | We are *half* pleased and *half* sorry.<br>The orange you brought was *quite* ripe.<br>Your pay is *too* high for your work. |
| *Adverb* | A snake creeps *very* silently.<br>He stood *far* apart from me.<br>He seized my hand *rather* eagerly. |
| *Preposition* | He arrived *long* before the time.<br>We sat *almost* in the shade.<br>He stood *exactly* behind me. |
| *Conjunction* | Tell me *precisely* how it happened.<br>I like an orange *only* when it is ripe.<br>He did this *merely* because he was ordered. |

*Note.*—There is one exception to the above rule. The word "enough" (when it is an Adverb and not an Adjective) is placed *after* the word it qualifies:—

He spoke highly *enough* of what you had done.

**367** (*a*). If the verb to be qualified is *Intransitive*, the qualifying Adverb is placed immediately *after* it:—

He lived *well* and died *happily*.
He laughed *heartily* at that joke.
He spoke *foolishly* about his own merits.

*Note.*—To this rule there are eight or nine exceptions:—

The Adverbs *always*, *never*, *scarcely ever*, *often*, *sometimes*, *generally*, *usually*, *rarely*, and *seldom* are usually placed *before*, and not *after*, the verb they qualify.

He *always* laughed at a good joke.
He *never* spoke about his own merits.
He *often* came here to see me.
He *sometimes* slept in my house.
He *seldom* stayed with me for long.

But they are usually placed after the verb "to be":—

He is *seldom* absent. He is *always* attentive.

(*b*) If the verb to be qualified is *Transitive*, the qualifying Adverb must not be allowed to separate the verb and its object.

The Adverb must therefore be placed either *before the verb* or *after the object*; but it is more commonly placed after the object:—

He bore his losses *cheerfully*.
He *briefly* explained his meaning.

Sometimes, however, if the object is qualified by a clause, or consists of a good many words, the adverb may come between the verb and its object:—

He rewarded *liberally* all those who had served him well.

But this is scarcely so idiomatic as, "He liberally rewarded," etc.

**368.** If the tense of the verb is formed by an Auxiliary verb, the adverb is generally placed *between* the Auxiliary verb and the Principal verb: the latter may be either Trans. or Intrans.:—

The wind has *suddenly* risen. Your son will *soon* return.
I have *quite* understood you. He is *almost* dying, I fear.
We have *not* seen him since Monday last. (*Neg. Adverb.*)

*Note.*—This, however, does not justify the objectionable habit, that has been springing up lately, of inserting an adverb between "*to*" and the verb following:—

It is my duty to *plainly* tell you, etc.

**369.** An Adverb is placed first in a sentence—(*a*) when it is intended to qualify *the whole sentence*, (*b*) when it is used *very emphatically*.

(*a*) *Luckily* no one was inside, when the roof fell in.
(*b*) *Down* went the Royal George with all her crew complete.
COWPER.

The meaning of the two sentences given below depends entirely on the position of the adverb:—

(1) *Happily* he did not die.
(2) He did not die *happily*.

In (1) the adverb qualifies the entire sentence, because it stands first (as just explained). In (2) it qualifies the Intransitive verb "die," because it is placed immediately after it; see § 367. So (1) means, "It was a happy result that he did not die"; and (2) means, "He did not die a happy death."

**370. Only.**—The meaning of a sentence depends upon the position of this word, which may be either an Adj. or an Adv.:—

(*a*) *Only* he promised to read the first chapter of that book.

Here "only" is an Adjective, qualifying the pronoun "he."

He alone, and no one else, promised to read the first chapter, etc.

(*b*) He *only* promised to read the first chapter of that book.

Here "only" is an Adverb qualifying the verb "promised"; and the meaning is that he merely or only promised, but did not perform the promise.

(*c*) He promised *only* to read the first chapter of that book.

That is, he did not promise to study, analyse, or remember, but *only to read.* Here "only" is an Adverb qualifying the word "read."

(*d*) He promised to read *only* the first chapter of that book.

That is, he promised to read nothing more than the *first* chapter. Here "only" is an Adverb qualifying the adjective "the first."

(*e*) He promised to read the first chapter of that book *only* (or, *only* of that book).

That is, he promised to read the first chapter of no other book but that. Here "only" is an Adverb qualifying the phrase "of that book."

### SECTION 2.—ADVERBS QUALIFYING PREPOSITIONS.

**371.** A few more examples are here given of Adverbs qualifying prepositions, as the point stated in § 216 (*a*) has hardly yet been sufficiently recognised:—

**A little.**

We have gone *a little beyond* a mile.
The crow flew *a little above* his head.
He is *a little under* fourteen years of age.

**Almost.**

A sword was hanging *almost over* his head.
It fell *almost on* his head.

**Along.**

He went to London *along with* his friend.

It was *all along of* (entirely owing to) your idleness that you were plucked. (Here the adverb "all" qualifies the prepositional phrase "along of." The phrase is colloquial and rather vulgar.)

**All.**

His horse sprang forward *all of* a sudden.
I have looked *all through* that book.
Your efforts were *all to* no purpose.
Such conduct is *all of* a piece (thoroughly consistent) with his character.

**Altogether.**

He married *altogether below* his station.

**Apart.**

*Apart from* his imprudence (without taking his imprudence into account), he has been very unfortunate.

**Away.**

He is never happy, *away from* home.

**Close.**

He is *close upon* fourteen (very nearly fourteen) years of age.
He came and sat *close beside* me.

**Decidedly.**

Your son's industry is *decidedly above* the average.

**Distinctly.**

His abilities are *distinctly above* the average.

**Down.**

They lived *down in* a valley.
They made him pay his debt *down to* the last farthing.

**Entirely.**

It was *entirely through* your neglect that we were late.
He took his hat *entirely off* his head.

**Exactly.**

The house stands *exactly on* the top of the hill.
Every word was copied out *exactly to* the letter.
Your quarters are *exactly under* mine.

**Far.**

Your work is *far below* the proper mark.
My house stands *far beyond* the river.
*Far from* despising that man, I greatly respect him.

**Greatly.**

*Greatly to* his credit, he came out first.

**Hard.**

The cottage stood *hard by* the river.

**Half.**

By this time we had sailed *half across* the Atlantic.

**Immediately.**

He went to bed *immediately after* his arrival.
*Immediately on* his beginning to speak, every one was silent.

**Long.**

He arrived *long after* twelve o'clock.

**Much.**

His work is *much below* the mark.
*Much to* his surprise he was plucked.

**Out.**

That was all done *out of* envy.
I am *out of* patience with that man.

**Partly.**

He wept *partly through* sorrow, and *partly through* anger.
The fog is *partly above* and *partly below* us.

**Precisely.**

It was *precisely on* that point that we differed.
He arrived *precisely at* four o'clock.

**Quite.**

We walked *quite through* that forest (through its entire breadth).
He held his head *quite below* the water.
I am *quite of* the same opinion as yourself.

**Right.**

He was leaning *right against* the wall.
The sun was *right above* our heads.

**Shortly.**

He reached home *shortly before* four o'clock.

**Soon.**

I managed to get back *soon after* six.

**Up.**

Your work is not *up to* date.

**Well.**

I am sure I am *well within* the mark.

**Together.**

He *together with* his accomplice has cheated me.

## CHAPTER XVIII.—PREPOSITIONS.

**372. Relations denoted by Prepositions.**—The more important are shown in the following list:—

(1) **"Of" in the sense of Apposition**; see § 304, (3). This can be traced back as far as the fifteenth century:—

He was a ryght good knight *of a yonge man*.
MALORY (15th cent.).

There was in the castell a vii score prisoners *of Frenchmen*.
BERNERS (16th cent.).

The frail sepulchre *of our flesh*.—SHAKSPEARE.

Compare the modern phrases "a fool *of a man*"; "the two *of us*" (=we two); "he made an ass *of himself*"; "he made a great success *of it*" (=made it a great success); "the sum *of* 40 *pounds*."

The use of "*of*" in an appositional sense is common before Proper names:—

The island *of* Ceylon. The province *of* Ulster. The city *of* Paris. The continent *of* Asia. The county *of* Kent. The lake *of* Geneva. The title *of* colonel. The name *of* Brighton.

On the other hand, we cannot place "*of*" before the Proper names of rivers, mountains, or capes. Thus we cannot say "the river *of* Thames"; "the mountain *of* Blanc"; "the Cape *of* St. Vincent."

(2) **Against**: denotes opposition of place or aim, comparison or contrast, and provision to meet some expected event:—

1. He is leaning *against* the wall . *Place.*
2. He is acting *against* my interests . *Aim.*
3. Four boys left this term *against* three last term . . . . *Comparison.*
4. Be ready *against* the day of battle . *Provision for.*

The conjunctional use of *against* has become a vulgarism :—

I shall have everything ready *against* you come.

(3) **At**: denotes proximity, with actual or intended contact; hence proximity of value, valuation; direction, consequence, dependence :—

| | | |
|---|---|---|
| 1. | He is not *at* home just now . . | *Place.* |
| 2. | He was there *at* four o'clock . . | *Time.* |
| 3. | He is now quite *at* his ease . . | *State.* |
| 4. | *At* what price is this sold ? . . | *Valuation.* |
| 5. | He laughed *at* me. Take a shot *at* it | *Direction.* |
| 6. | He plays well *at* cricket . . . | *Action.* |
| 7. | Stand up *at* the word of command . | *Time and consequence.* |
| 8. | He remains here *at* my pleasure . | *Dependence.* |

(4) **By**: denotes originally nearness of place; hence time, agency, instrumentality, manner, amount, adjuration :—

| | | |
|---|---|---|
| 1. | Come and sit *by* me . . . | *Proximity in place.* |
| 2. | Always get up *by* sunrise . . | *Proximity in time.* |
| 3. | {He did his duty *by* his children . / Do to others as you would be done *by*} | *About, towards.* |
| 4. | He was fairly treated *by* me . . | *Agency.* |
| 5. | Seize him *by* the neck . . . | *Instrumentality.* |
| 6. | Cleverer than you *by* a good deal . | *Amount.* |
| 7. | They sell corn *by* the bushel . . | *Unit of measurement.* |
| 8. | He swore *by* heaven . . . | *Adjuration.* |

*Note.*—Such a phrase as occurs in, "He went away *by himself*," is an example of (7), and means "He went away *alone*, himself at a time." The phrase "He came *by* a large fortune" is an example of (1): "He came into the possession of," etc.

(5) **For**: its chief uses are shown below :—

| | | |
|---|---|---|
| 1. | He will soon start *for* home . . | *Direction in space.* |
| 2. | He was imprisoned *for* life . . | *Direction in time.* |
| 3. | *For* what offence was he imprisoned ? | *Cause or reason.* |
| 4. | *For* all his learning, he has no sense | *In spite of.* |
| 5. | He sold his horse *for* a small sum . | *Exchange.* |
| 6. | He fought hard *for* his friends . | *On behalf of.* |
| 7. | Do not translate word *for* word . | *Conformity.* |
| 8. | This stuff is not fit *for* food . . | *Purpose.* |

(6) **Of**: its main sense is "proceeding from," or "pertaining to"; its detailed uses are shown below :—

| | | |
|---|---|---|
| 1. | What did he die *of?* . . . | *Cause.* |
| 2. | *Of* what family is he sprung ? . . | *Source.* |
| 3. | He was despised and rejected *of* men | *Agency* (rare). |
| 4. | He was deprived *of* his appointment | *Separation.* |
| 5. | He is a man *of* strong will . . | *Quality.* |
| 6. | He sent me a box *of* books . . | *Contents.* |
| 7. | This box is made *of* leather . . | *Material.* |
| 8. | He lived in the house *of* his father . | *Possession.* |

9. He received the sum *of* 100 rupees . *Apposition.*
10. What are you thinking *of* . . *Concerning.*
11. The horse is lame *of* one leg . . *Point of reference.*
12. He gave us *of* his best . . . *Partition.*
13. The love *of* parents (parents' love for child) . . . . . . . *Subject.*
14. The love *of* parents (child's love for parents) . . . . . . *Object.*
15. He used to come here *of* an evening *Time.*

(7) **With**: denotes "by," "near," "among"; also "against," as in Anglo-Saxon. Its uses are enumerated below :—

1. He lives *with* his mother . . *Union in place.*
2. Frogs begin to croak *with* the rainfall *Union in time.*
3. His views do not accord *with* mine. *Agreement.*
4. One king fought *with* another . *Opposition.*
5. I parted *with* my friend yesterday . *Separation.*
6. He is not popular *with* his pupils . *Point of reference.*
7. *With* all his wealth he is discontented . . . . . . *In spite of.*
8. He killed the snake *with* a stone . *Instrument.*
9. He looked upon them *with* anger . *Manner.*

(8) **On** or **upon**: the main sense is "rest on the outside side of a thing" :—

1. I place my hand *on* the table. . *Place.*
2. I came here *on* Saturday last. . *Time.*
3. He lives *on* his father . . . . *Dependence.*
4. He was appointed *on* these terms . *Condition or basis.*
5. They made an attack *on* my house. *Direction.*
6. He spoke for over an hour *on* that subject . . . . . . *Concerning.*

(9) **To**: literally motion towards anything; hence purpose, limit, etc. :—

1. He has returned *to* his father's house *Place.*
2. You must go back *to*-night . . *Time.*
3. *To* all appearances he is tired. . *Adaptation.*
4. The chances are three *to* one . . *Proportion.*
5. They fought *to* the last man . . *Limit.*
6. *To* their utter disgust they were beaten . . . . . . *Effect.*
7. { They will come *to* dinner . . / He came *to* see us (Gerund. Infin.) } *Purpose.*

*Note.*—The prep. "*to*" is often used as an alternative to "*of*" in such sentences as, "He is a cousin *to* me," for "He is a cousin *of* mine."

(10) **From**: literally motion or rest apart from anything :—

1. He had gone *from* home . . *Space.*
2. You must begin *from* daybreak . *Time.*
3. He is sprung *from* noble ancestors. *Descent.*
4. *From* all we hear he is mad . . *Inference.*

5. This was done *from* spite . . *Motive.*
6. A wise man is easily known *from* a fool . . . . . . *Discrimination.*

**373. Prepositions compared.**—The following peculiarities should be noted:—

(*a*) **At, in.**—"*At*" relates to a *small* extent of space or time; "*in*" to a *wider* extent:—

He will start *at* six o'clock *in* the morning.
The end is *at* hand (=very close).
The work is *in* hand (=in a state of progress).

(*b*) **With, by.**—"*With*" relates to the *instrument* employed for doing anything; "*by*" to the agent or doer:—

This book was written *by* me *with* a quill pen.

(*c*) **Between, among.**—The first (A.S. *be-twéon-um*, in pairs) denotes "in the middle of two"; the second (A.S. *on mang*, in a mixture or crowd) "in the middle of more than two":—

Those two men quarrelled *between* themselves.
Those three men quarrelled *among* themselves.

(*d*) **Beside, besides.**—The former means *by the side of*, and hence sometimes *outside of.* The latter means *in addition to*:—

He came and sat *beside* me (=by my side).
Your answer is *beside* (=outside of, irrelevant to) the question.
*Besides* (=in addition to) advising he gave them some money.

(*e*) **By, since, before.**—These are all used for a *point* of time,—not for a *period* or *space* of time:—

You must be back *by* four o'clock.
He has been here *since* four o'clock.
He did not get back *before* four o'clock.

(*f*) **In, into.**—The preposition "*in*" denotes position or rest inside anything; while "*into*" denotes motion towards the inside of anything:—

The frog is *in* the well. (*Rest.*)
The frog fell *into* the well. (*Motion.*)

(*g*) **In, within.**—"In" denotes the close of some period; "within" denotes some time *short of the close*:—

He will return *in* (=at the close of) a week's time.
He will return *within* (=in less than) a week's time.

(*h*) **Since, from.**—Both of these denote a *point* of time, not a space or period. But "since" is preceded by a verb in some Perfect tense, and "from" by a verb in some Indefinite tense. Another difference is that "since" can be used only in reference to *past* time, whereas "from" is used for *present* and *future* time as well as for past:—

He *has been* ill *since* Thursday last.
{ He *begins* work *from* six o'clock daily. (*Present.*)
He *began* work from six o'clock in the morning. (*Past.*)
He *will begin* work *from* to-morrow. (*Future.*)

(*i*) **Before, for.**—"For" is used with *negative* sentences, to denote a *space* of *future* time.

"Before" is used in negative and affirmative sentences alike, to denote a *point* of *future* time.

{ The sun will *not* rise *for* an hour.
(We could not say "before an hour," because "before" is used for a point of time, and not for a space of time.)

{ The sun will rise (*affirmative*)
The sun will not rise (*negative*) } *before* six o'clock.

*Insert appropriate prepositions in the places left blank*:—

1. I was brought up —— Italy —— Rome. 2. The moon rose —— twelve o'clock —— the night. 3. We knew him —— a glance as soon as he came —— sight. 4. He lives —— Tonbridge —— the county of Kent. 5. The boat was tied to the shore —— a sailor —— a rope. 6. The field was ploughed up —— a peasant —— a pair of oxen. 7. The work must be done —— twelve o'clock. 8. You must be back —— a week from the present time. 9. No one has seen him —— Thursday last. 10. I have not seen him —— his last birthday. 11. He will not get home —— sunset. 12. I shall be ready to start —— two or three hours. 13. Take care to be back —— mid-day. 14. I shall not be back —— the end of the week. 15. He has been absent from home —— Friday last, and I do not think he will return —— the 30th of next month. 16. Let me see you again —— an hour's time. 17. I shall have completed my task —— to-morrow evening. 18. The train will start —— forty minutes from now. 19. I have lived —— London —— 1st March. 20. I do not expect that he will be here —— a week, and I am certain that he will not be here —— sunset to-day.

(*j*) **Participial prepositions.**—In addition to the simpler prepositions described already, there are some of participial or adjectival origin, which were once used absolutely:—

He went *past* the house (the house having been past).
All *except* two (two being excepted).
*During* two weeks (two weeks (en)during or continuing).
All *save* three (three being safe, saved, or reserved).
*Notwithstanding* his age (his age not-withstanding or not preventing).

There are other prepositions that have come from participles in the present tense used as Impersonal Absolutes; see § 284 (*b*), *Note* 2.

*Regarding* this matter, what is your opinion?
*Considering* his age, he has done well.

Compare *touching*, *owing to*, *concerning*, *respecting*, etc.

**374. Words followed by Prepositions.**—Particular words are followed by particular prepositions, although there may be several other prepositions that have the same meaning. This is purely a matter of idiom. For instance, out of the numerous prepositions or prepositional phrases signifying cause, the verb "die" has somehow or other selected "of" for denoting the illness which was the cause of death, and declines to be followed by any other. Thus we say, "He died *of* fever." We do not say, "He died *through* fever, or *by* fever, or *from* fever, or *owing to* fever, or *on account* of fever, or *with* fever." Yet in other connections all of these prepositions may be used to denote cause.

Again, though we always say "die *of* fever," we never say "sick *of* fever," but always "sick *with* fever," where "with" and "of" are both used in the sense of cause.

(*a*) *Nouns followed by Prepositions.*

Abatement *of* the fever.
,, *from* the price asked.
Admission *to* a person.
,, *into* a place.
(To take) advantage *of* some one's mistake.
(To gain) an advantage *over* some one.
(To have) the advantage *of* a man.
Analogy of one thing *with* another.
,, *between* two things.
Antidote *to* some poison.
,, *against* infection.
Antipathy *to* some animal or some taste.
Arrival *at* a place.
,, *in* a country.
Attendance *on* a person.
,, *at* a place.
Authority *over* a person.
,, *on* a subject.
,, *for* saying or doing.
Aversion *to* a person or thing.

Beneficence *to* the poor.
Benevolence *towards* the poor.

Charge *of* murder (*noun*).
,, *with* murder (*verb*).
Claim *on* or *against* some one.
,, *to* something.
Connivance *at* any one's faults.
Contemporary (*noun*) *of* some one.
,, (*adj.*) *with* some one.
(A) contrast *to* a person or thing.
(In) contrast *with* a person or thing.
Contribution *to* a fund.
,, *towards* some project.

Decision *on* some case.
,, *of* some dispute.
Disagreement *with* a person.
Disgust *at* meanness.
Dislike *to* a person or thing.
Distrust *of* a person or thing.
,, *in* a person or thing.
Doubt *of* or *about* a thing.

Encroachment *on* one's rights.
Endeavour *after* happiness.
Envy *at* another's success.
Evasion *of* a rule.
Exception *to* a rule.
(Make) an exception *of* some person or thing.
Experience *of* a thing.
,, *in* doing something.

Failure *of* a plan.
,, *of* a person *in* something.

(Has) a genius *for* mathematics.
(Is) a genius *in* mathematics.
Glance *at* a person or thing.

Glance *over* a wide surface.
Gratitude *for* a thing.
,, *to* a person.

Hatred *of* or *for* a person.
,, *of* a thing.

Imputation *of* guilt.
,, *against* some one.
Influence *over* or *with* a person.
,, *on* a man's action.
Innovation *upon* former practice.
Interest *in* a subject.
,, *with* a person.

Jest *at* a man's bad luck.
Joy *in* his good luck.
Justification *of* or *for* crime.

Key *to* a mystery.

Libel *on* a person.
,, *against* his character.
Likeness *to* a person or thing.
Liking *for* a person or thing.
Longing *for* or *after* a thing.

Match *for* a person.

Need *for* assistance.
(In) need *of* assistance.
Neglect *of* duty.
,, *in* doing a thing.

Offence *against* morality.
,, *at* something done.

Parody *on* or *of* a poem.
Popularity *with* neighbours.
Premium *on* gold.
Pride *in* his wealth (*noun*).
Prides himself *on* his wealth (*verb*).

Proof *of* guilt.
,, *against* temptation.
(In) pursuance *of* an object.

Quarrel *with* another person.
,, *between* two persons.

Readiness *at* figures.
,, *in* answering.
,, *for* a journey.
Reflections *on* a man's honesty.
Regard *for* a man's feelings.
(In) regard *to* that matter.
Relevancy *to* a question.
Reputation *for* honesty.
(In) respect *of* some quality.
(With) respect (*to*) a matter.
Rupture *with* a friend.
,, *between* two persons.

Search *for* or *after* wealth.
(In) search *of* wealth.
(A) slave *to* avarice.
(The) slave *of* avarice.
Sneer *at* good men.
Stain *on* one's character.
Subsistence *on* rice.

Taste (experience) *of* hard work.
,, (liking) *for* hard work.

Umbrage *at* his behaviour.
(We have no) use *for* that.
(What is the) use *of* that?
(There is no) use *in* that.

(At) variance *with* a person.
(A) victim *to* oppression.
(The) victim *of* oppression.

Witness *of* or *to* an event.

### (*b*) *Adjectives and Participles followed by Prepositions.*

Abhorrent *to* his feelings.
Abounding *in* or *with* fish.
Accompanied *with* his luggage.
,, *by* his dog.
Accountable *to* a person.
,, *for* a thing.
Adapted *to* his tastes.
,, *for* an occupation.

Aggravated *at* a thing.
,, *with* a person.
Alien *to* his character.
Alienated *from* a friend.
Amenable *to* reason.
Amused *at* a joke.
Angry *at* a thing.
,, *with* a person.

Annoyed *at* a thing.
,, *with* a person *for* saying or doing something.
Answerable *to* a person.
,, *for* his conduct.
Anxious *for* his safety.
,, *about* the result.
Apprised *of* a fact.
Apt (expert) *in* mathematics.
,, *for* a purpose.

Beholden *to* a person.
Betrayed *to* the enemy.
,, *into* the enemy's hands.
Blessed *with* good health.
,, *in* his children.
Blind *to* his own faults.
,, *of* one eye.
Bound *in* honour.
,, *by* a contract.
(Ship) bound *for* England.

Careful *of* his money.
,, *about* his dress.
Charged *to* his account.
,, (loaded) *with* a bullet.
,, *with* (accused of) a crime.
Clothed *in* purple.
,, *with* shame.
Cognisant *of* a fact.
Complaisant *to* a person.
Compliant *with* one's wishes.
Concerned *at* or *about* some mishap.
,, *for* a person's welfare.
,, *in* some business.
Consequent *on* some cause.
Conspicuous *for* honesty.
Contingent (conditional) *on* success.
Covetous *of* other men's goods.

Deaf *to* entreaties.
Debited *with* a sum of money.
Deficient *in* energy.
Determined *on* doing a thing.
Disappointed *of* a thing not obtained.
,, *in* a thing obtained.
,, *with* a person.
Disgusted *with* a thing.
,, *at* or *with* a person.
Displeased *with* a person.

Disqualified *for* a post.
,, *from* competing.

Eager *for* distinction.
,, *in* the pursuit of knowledge.
Easy *of* access.
Economical *of* time.
Emulous *of* fame.
Engaged *to* some person.
,, *in* some business.

False *of* heart.
,, *to* his friends.
Familiar *with* a language.
,, (well known) *to* a person.
Favourable *to* his prospects.
,, *for* action.
Fruitful *in* resources.
Fruitless *of* results.

Glad *of* his assistance.
,, *at* a result.
Good *for* nothing.
,, *at* cricket.

Hardened *against* pity.
,, *to* misfortune.

Ill *with* fever.
Impatient *of* reproof.
,, *at* an event.
,, *for* food.
Impervious *to* water.
Indebted *to* a person.
,, *for* some kindness.
,, *in* a large sum.
Indignant *at* something done.
,, *with* a person.
Indulgent *in* wine.
,, *to* his children.
Inspired *with* hope.
Introduced *to* a person.
,, *into* a place.
Irrespective *of* consequences.

Jealous *of* his reputation.

Lavish *of* money.
,, *in* his expenditure.
Liable *to* error.
,, *for* payment.

Mad *with* disappointment.
Moved *to* tears.
,, *with* pity.
,, *at* the sight.
,, *by* entreaties.

Negligent *of* duty.
,, *in* his work.

Obliged *to* a person.
,, *for* some kindness.
Occupied *with* some work.
,, *in* reading a book.
Offended *with* a person.
,, *at* something done.

Parallel *to* or *with* anything.
Paramount *to* everything else.
Popular *with* schoolfellows.
,, *for* his pluck.
Possessed *of* wealth.
,, *with* a notion.
Preferable *to* something else.
Preventive *to* fever (*adj.*).
(A) preventive *of* fever (*noun*).
Profuse *of* his money.
,, *in* his offers.
Provident *of* his money.
,, *for* his children.
Pursuant *to* an inquiry.

Quick *of* understanding.
,, *at* mathematics.

Ready *for* action.
,, *at* accounts.
,, *in* his answers.
Receptive *of* advice.
Reconciled *to* a position.
Reconciled *with* an opponent.
Requisite *to* happiness.
,, *for* a purpose.
Resolved *into* its elements.
,, *on* doing a thing.
Responsible *to* a person.
,, *for* his actions.
Revenge *on* a person *for* doing something.

Satisfied *of* (concerning) a fact.
,, *with* his income.
Secure *from* harm.
,, *against* an attack.
Sensible *of* kindness.
Sick *of* waiting.
,, *with* fever.
Significant *of* his intentions.
Slow *of* hearing.
,, *in* making up his mind.
,, *at* accounts.
Subversive *of* discipline.
Suitable *to* his income.
,, *for* his purpose.
Suited *to* the occasion.
,, *for* a post.

Tired *of* doing nothing.
,, *with* his exertions.

Vexed *with* a person *for* doing something.
,, *at* a thing.

Weak *of* understanding.
,, *in* his head.

Zealous *for* improvement.
,, *in* a cause.

(c) *Verbs followed by Prepositions.*

Abide *by* a promise.
Absolve *of* or *from* a charge.
Accord *with* or *to* a thing.
Admit *of* an excuse.
,, *to* or *into* a secret.
Agree *to* a proposal.
,, *with* a person.
Answer *to* a person.
,, *for* conduct.
Apologise *to* a person.
,, *for* rudeness.
Appeal *to* a person.
,, *for* redress or help.
,, *against* a sentence.
Apply *to* a person *for* a thing.
Ask *for* a thing.
,, *of* or *from* a person.
Aspire *after* worldly greatness.
,, *to* some particular object.
Attend *to* a book or speaker.
,, *on* a person.

Bear *with* a man's impatience.
Beat *against* the rocks (the waves).
,, *on* one's head (the sun).
Beg pardon *of* a person.
,, a person *to* do a thing.
Blush *at* one's own faults.
,, *for* any one who is at fault.
Borrow *of* or *from* a person.
Break *into* a house (thieves).
,, oneself *of* a habit.
,, *through* restraint.
,, ill news *to* a person.
,, (dissolve partnership) *with* a person.
Bring a thing *to* light.
,, ,, *under* notice.
Burst *into* a rage.
,, *upon* (suddenly invade) a country.
Buy a thing *of* a person.
,, ,, *from* a shop.

Call *on* a person (visit him at his house).
,, *to* (shout to) a person.
,, *for* (require) punishment.
Charge a man *with* a crime.
Come *across* (accidentally meet) any one.
,, *into* fashion.
,, *by* (obtain) a thing.
,, *of* (result from) something.
,, *to* (amount to) forty.
Communicate a thing *to* a person.
,, *with* a person *on* a subject.
Compare similars *with* similars—as one fruit *with* another:
,, things dissimilar, by way of illustration — as genius *to* a lightning flash.
Complain *of* some annoyance *to* a person.
,, *against* a person.
Confer (*Trans.*) a thing *on* any one.
,, (*Intrans.*) *with* a person *about* something.
Confide (*Trans.*) a secret *to* any one.
,, (*Intrans.*) *in* one's honour.

Conform *to* (follow) a rule.
,, *with* one's views.
Confront a man *with* his accusers.
Consist (made up) *of* materials.
,, (have its character) *in* hypocrisy, falsehood, charity.
Correspond *with* a person (write).
,, *to* something (agree).
Count *on* a thing (confidently expect).
,, *for* nothing.

Deal well or ill *by* a person.
,, *in* (trade in) cloth, tea, spices, etc.
,, *with* a person (have dealings in trade, etc.).
,, *with* a subject (write about it).
Descant *on* a subject.
Die *of* a disease.
,, *from* some cause, as overwork.
,, *by* violence.
Differ *with* a person *on* a subject.
,, *from* anything (to be unlike).
Divide *in* half, *into* four parts.
Draw money *on* a bank.
Drop *off* a tree.
,, *out of* the ranks.

Embark *on* board ship.
,, *in* business.
Encroach *on* one's authority.
Enter *upon* a career.
,, *into* one's plans.
Entrust any one *with* a thing.
,, a thing *to* any one.
Err *on the side of* leniency.
Exchange one thing *for* another.
,, *with* a person.
Excuse a person *from* coming.

Fail *in* an attempt.
,, *of* a purpose.
Fall *among* thieves.
,, *in love with* a person.
,, *in with* one's views.
,, *on* the enemy (attack).
,, *into* a mistake.
,, *under* some one's displeasure.

Feed (*Intrans.*) *on* grass.
,, (*Trans.*) a cow *with* grass.
Fill *with* anything.
(*full of* something). (*Adject.*)
Fly *at* (attack) a dog.
,, *into* a rage.
Furnish a person *with* a thing.

Gain *on* some one in a race.
Get *at* (find out) the facts.
,, *over* (recover from) an illness.
,, *on with* a person (live or work smoothly with him).
,, *out of* doubt.
,, *to* a journey's end.
Glance *at* an object.
,, *over* a letter.
Grieve *at* or *for* or *about* an event.
,, *for* a person.
Grow *upon* one=(a habit grows on, etc.).

Impose *on* (deceive) a person.
Impress an idea *on* a person.
,, a person *with* an idea.
Indent *on* an office *for* stamps.
Indict a person *for* a crime.
Indulge *in* wine.
,, oneself *with* wine.
Inquire *into* a matter.
,, *of* a person *about* or *concerning* some matter.
Intrude *on* one's leisure.
,, *into* one's house.
Intrust a person *with* a thing.
,, a thing *to* a person.
Invest money *in* some project.
,, a man *with* authority.

Jump *at* (eagerly accept) an offer.
,, *to* a conclusion.

Kick *against* (resist) authority.
,, *at* a thing (scornfully reject).

Labour *under* a misapprehension.
,, *for* the public good.
,, *in* a good cause.
,, *at* some work.
Lay facts *before* a person.
,, a sin *to* one's charge.
,, a person *under* an obligation.
Lean *against* a wall.
Lean *on* a staff.
,, *to* a certain opinion.
Live *for* riches or fame.
,, *by* honest labour.
,, *on* a small income.
,, *within* one's means.
Look *after* (watch) some business.
,, *at* a person or thing.
,, *into* (closely examine) a matter.
,, *for* something lost.
,, *over* (examine cursorily) an account.
,, *through* (examine carefully) an account.
,, *out of* a window.

Make *away with* (purloin) money.
,, *for* (conduce to) happiness.
,, *up to* (approach) a person.
,, some meaning *of* a thing.
March *with* (border on) a boundary.

Operate *on* a patient.
Originate *in* a thing or place.
,, *with* a person.

Pass *from* one thing *into* another.
,, *for* a clever man.
,, *over* (omit) a page.
,, *by* a man's door.
Perish *by* the sword.
,, *with* cold.
Play *at* cricket.
,, *upon* the guitar.
,, tricks (trifle) *with* one's health.
Point *at* a person.
,, *to* some result.
Prepare *for* the worst.
,, *against* disaster.
Preside *at* a meeting.
,, *over* a meeting.
Prevail *on* (persuade) a person to do something.
,, *against* or *over* an adversary.
,, *with* a person (have more influence than anything else).
Proceed *with* a business already commenced.

Proceed *to* a business not yet commenced.
,, *from* one point *to* another.
,, *against* (prosecute) a person.

Reckon *on* (confidently expect) something.
,, *with* (settle accounts with) a person.
Reconcile *to* a loss.
,, *with* an adversary.
Reflect credit *on* a person.
,, (*Intrans.*) *on* a man's conduct (discreditably).
Rejoice *at* the success of another.
,, *in* one's own success.
Repose (*Intrans.*) *on* a bed.
,, confidence *in* a person.
Rest *on* a couch, *on* facts, etc.
(It) rests *with* a person to do, etc.
Result *from* a cause.
,, *in* a consequence.
Run *after* (eagerly follow) new fashions.
,, *at* (attack) a cat.
,, *into* debt.
,, *over* (read rapidly) an account.
,, *through* (squander) his money.

See *about* (consider) a matter.
,, *into* (investigate) a matter.
,, *through* (understand) his meaning.
,, *to* (attend to) a matter.
Set *about* (begin working at) a business.
,, a person *over* (in charge of) a business.
,, *upon* (attack) a traveller.
Sit *over* a fire.
,, *under* an imputation.
Smile *at* (deride) a person's threats.
,, *on* (favour) a person.

Speak *of* a subject (briefly).
,, *on* a subject (at greater length).
Speculate *in* shares.
,, *on* a possible future.
Stand *against* (resist) an enemy.
,, *by* (support) a friend.
,, *on* one's dignity.
,, *to* (maintain) one's opinion.
Stare *at* a person.
,, a person *in* the face.
Stick *at* nothing.
,, *to* his point.
Succeed *to* a property.
,, *in* an undertaking.
Supply a thing *to* a person.
,, a person *with* a thing.

Take *after* (resemble) his father.
,, a person *for* a spy.
,, *to* (commence the habit of) gambling.
,, *upon* oneself to do a thing.
Talk *of* or *about* an event.
,, *over* (discuss) a matter.
,, *to* or *with* a person.
Think *of* or *about* anything.
,, *over* (consider) a matter.
Touch *at* Gibraltar (ships).
,, *upon* (briefly allude to) a subject.
Trespass *against* rules.
,, *on* a man's time.
,, *in* a man's house.
Trust *in* a person. } (*Intr.*)
,, *to* a man's honesty. } (*Intr.*)
,, a man *with* money. (*Trans.*)
Turn verse *into* prose.
,, *to* a friend *for* help.
,, *upon* (hinge on) evidence.

Wait *at* table.
,, *for* a person or thing.
,, *on* (attend) a person.
Warn a person *of* danger.
,, ,, *against* a fault.

### (*d*) *Adverbs followed by Prepositions.*

*Note.*—Adverbs are followed by the same prepositions as the corresponding adjectives.

Adversely *to* one's interests.
Agreeably *to* one's wishes.
Amenably *to* reason.
Angrily *with* a person.
Anxiously *for* one's safety.
Appropriately *to* an occasion.

Compatibly *with* reason.
Conditionally *on* some event.
Conformably *to* reason.
Consistently *with* reason.
Contentedly *with* one's lot.
Effectively *for* a purpose.
Favourably *to* one's interests.
Fortunately *for* a person.
Independently *of* persons or things.
Irrelevantly *to* a question.
Irrespectively *of* consequences.
Loyally *to* one's rulers.
Obstructively *to* happiness.
Offensively *to* a person.
Prejudicially *to* one's interests.
Previously *to* some event.
Profitably *to* oneself.
Proportionately *to* anything.
Simultaneously *with* some event.
Subsequently *to* some event.
Sufficiently *for* the purpose.

## CHAPTER XIX.—CONJUNCTIONS AND CONJUNCTIONAL PHRASES.

**375.** The distinction between Co-ordinative and Subordinative Conjunctions has been shown already in chapter viii. The present chapter shows how individual Conjunctions or Conjunctional phrases can be idiomatically used :—

(1) **Both . . . and.**—This is an emphatic way of expressing the union of two facts, without giving priority to either :—

He is *both* a fool *and* a knave. (He is not a fool only, not a knave only, but both at once, one as much as the other.)

*Note.*—If, however, one fact is more important than the other, the more important one should be mentioned last :—

He was *both* degraded from his class, *and* expelled for one year from the school.

(2) **As well as.**—This conjunctional phrase is Co-ordinative in one sense and Subordinative in another :—

(*a*) *Co-ordinative.*—In adding one co-ordinate sentence to another, it gives emphasis to the *first* :—

He as well as you is guilty =
Not only you, but he also is guilty.

(*b*) *Subordinative* :—

| *Principal.* | *Dependent.* |
|---|---|
| He does not write | as well as you do |

= His writing is not as good as yours.

(3) **Not only . . . but** or **but also.**—In adding one sentence to another, these give emphasis to the *second* of the two :—

*Not only* I, *but* all other men declare this to be true.

That man was *not only* accused of the crime, *but also* convicted of it by the magistrate.

(4) **Nay.**—This has sometimes the force of "not only . . . but also": by appearing to deny the first statement, it places the second one in a stronger light :—

He was accused, *nay* convicted (accused, and what is more, convicted) of the crime by the magistrate.

(5) **Aye, yea.**—These have practically the same force as *nay*, although *nay* is the negative form of *aye.* They mean "more than this," and are used to mark the introduction of a more specific or more emphatic clause :—

I therein do rejoice, *yea,* and will rejoice.—*Phil.* i. 18.

Sometimes they are used to introduce a clause with the sense of "indeed," "truly," "verily."

*Aye,* call it holy ground.—MRS. HEMANS.
*Yea,* hath God said, Ye shall not eat of every tree of the garden? —*Genesis,* iii. 1.

(6) **Or rather.**—This has very much the same force as "nay." It corrects the first statement in order to place the second one in a stronger light :—

He was injured, *or rather* ruined altogether, by the failure of that bank.

(7) **Now.**—This Conjunction (which must not be confounded with the adverb of time) introduces a new remark in *explanation* (not simply in continuation) of a previous one :—

And Pilate said unto them, "Will ye have this man or Barabbas?" They answered, "Not this man, but Barabbas." *Now* Barabbas was a robber.—*New Testament.*

(8) **Well.**—This word (when it is used as a Conjunction, that is, as a Conjunctive and not a Simple adverb) introduces a new remark implying satisfaction, regret, surprise, or any other feeling of the mind suggested by the previous remark :—

You have finished the work that was given you ;—*well,* you have done a good deal better than you usually do, and I am much pleased with your improvement.

(9) **Or.**—This conjunction has four different meanings :—

(*a*) An alternative or exclusive sense (§ 236, *b*) :—

Either this man sinned *or* his parents.

(*b*) An inclusive or non-alternative sense. Here the "or" is nearly equivalent to "and."

Such trades as those of leather, *or* carpentry, *or* smith's work flourish best in large cities.

(*c*) To indicate that one word is synonymous or nearly synonymous with another :—

The tribes *or* castes of India are very numerous.

(*d*) As an equivalent to "otherwise" (§ 236, *b*) :—

You must work hard ; or (=otherwise=if you do not work hard) you will lose your place in the class.

(10) **If.**—This conjunction has three different uses :—

(*a*) For asking a question in the Indirect form of narration :—

I asked him *if* (=whether) he would return soon.

(*b*) For expressing a condition or supposition :—

*If* you return to us to-morrow (=in case you return, or in the event of your returning), we shall be glad to see you.

(*c*) For making an admission or concession. (Here the verb must be Indicative, because it concedes something as a *fact*) :—

*If* I *am* dull (=though I admit that I am dull), I am at least industrious. (I am dull *indeed*, *but* nevertheless industrious.)

Considering how ill I was, it is no wonder *if* (=that) I made some mistakes yesterday.

(11) **But.**—The uses of this word as a Preposition have been shown already in § 232. Its uses as a Conjunction and as an Adverb have still to be shown.

(*a*) As a Subordinative conjunction :—

(1) It never rains *but* it pours.—*Proverb.*
(It never rains *except that* it pours, or It never rains without pouring.)

(2) I found no one *but* he was true to me.—SHAKSPEARE.
(I found no one who was not true to me.)

(3) Perdition catch my soul, *but* I love thee.—SHAKSPEARE.
(Perdition catch my soul *if* I do *not* love thee.)

(4) It cannot be *but* Nature hath some Director of infinite power. —HOOKER.
(It cannot be, or it is impossible, *that* Nature hath *not* a Director, etc.)

(5) No one saw that sight *but* went away shocked.
(No one saw that sight *except that* he went away, or *who* did *not* go away, shocked.)

*Note* 1.—In (5) the Demonstrative *he* is understood after "but"; see § 126.

*Note* 2.—The above use of "but" as a Subordinative conjunction has arisen from the omission of the conjunction "that." If "that" were expressed, "but" would retain its original character as a preposition signifying "except," and the Noun-clause following it would be its object.

(*b*) As an Adversative conjunction of the Co-ordinative class :—

He is rich, *but* discontented.

(*c*) As an Adverb in the sense of "only" :—

There is *but* (=only) a plank between us and death.
We can *but* die (nothing worse than death can befall us).

(12) **While** or **whilst.**—"While" is properly a noun signifying "time." The conjunction "while" is an abridged form

of the phrase "the while that," etc., and in this phrase the noun "while" is an Adverbial objective (see § 271).

The Conjunction "while" has three different uses:—

(*a*) To denote the *simultaneity* of two events:—

You can sit down, *while* (at the same time that) I stand.

(*b*) To denote *indefinite duration*:—

*While* (so long as) the world lasts, human nature will remain what it is.

(*c*) To denote some kind of antithesis or contrast:—

Men of understanding seek after truth; *while* (= whereas) fools despise knowledge.

(13) **Lest.**—This in the Tudor period was followed by the present Subjunctive:—

Take heed, *lest* you *fall* =
Take heed, *that* you may *not* fall.

In the later Modern English the tense and mood following this conjunction is formed by the Auxiliary verb "should":—

He worked hard, *lest* he *should* fail =
He worked hard, *that* he *might* not fail.

(14) **As.**—Since this word is a Relative adverb, it is also a Conjunction (see § 17, 4).

Its uses and meanings as a Conjunction can be seen from the following examples:—

(*a*) *Time*:—

He trembled *as* (= at what time, or while) he spoke.

(*b*) *Manner*:—

Do not act *as* (= in what manner) he did.

(*c*) *State* or *Condition*:—

He took it just *as* (= in what state) it was.

(*d*) *Extent*:—

He is not so clever *as* (to what extent) you are.

(*e*) *Contrast* or *Concession* resulting from the sense of extent:—

Hot *as* the sun is (to whatever extent the sun is hot), we must leave the house =
However hot the sun is, we must leave the house =
Although the sun is ever so hot, we must leave the house.

(*f*) *Cause*:—

*As* (from what cause or for the reason that) rain has fallen, the air is cooler.

(15) **However.**—This is a Co-ordinative conjunction, when it stands alone; but Subordinative, when it qualifies some adjective or adverb.

(*a*) Co-ordinative :—

All men were against him ; he kept his courage, *however*, to the last.

(*b*) Subordinative :—

*However* poor a man is, he need not be dishonest.

*However* well you may work, you cannot demand more that your stipulated pay.

(16) **When, where.**—These conjunctions or Relative adverbs (in the same way as the Relative pronouns "who" or "which") can be used in two very distinct senses :—

(*a*) The Restrictive or qualifying (§ 127) :—

The house where (= in which) we lived has fallen down.
The hour *when* (= at which) you arrived was four P.M.

(*b*) The Continuative or simply connective :—

On 24th January we reached Paris, *where* (= and there) we stayed a fortnight.

We stayed at Paris for two weeks, *when* (= and then) I received a letter which compelled me to return to London.

(17) **Though, but.**—Both of these conjunctions (the first Subordinative, the second Co-ordinative) denote concession or contrast :—

(*a*) He is honest, *though* poor.
(*b*) He is poor, *but* honest.

These two sentences mean precisely the same thing, because in (*a*) "He is honest" is the *Principal* clause, and in (*b*) the Co-ordinate clause, "but he is honest," is more *emphatic* than the clause preceding it ; see (3) in this chapter. Thus the Principal clause and the Emphatic clause are the same.

If, however, we rewrite the two sentences thus :—

(*a*) He is honest, though poor ;
(*b*) He is honest, but poor,

the two sentences are not equivalent. The first emphasises the fact that he is honest in spite of his poverty. The second emphasises the fact that he is poor in spite of his honesty.

## CHAPTER XX.—MISCELLANEOUS WORDS, PHRASES, AND CONSTRUCTIONS.

(1) **All of them, both of them** :—

All of them (= they all) consented.
Both of them (= they both) consented.

In phrases like "some of them," "one of them," "two of them," the "*of*" has a partitive sense. Such a sense is, however, impossible where "all" or "both" are concerned. We must therefore conclude that phrases like "all of them," "both of them," have come into use by analogy.

(2) **"Am," "have," with Infinitive**:—

I am or was to go.
I have or had to go.

These two sentences mean much the same thing. The Infinitive in both expresses future time, combined sometimes with a sense of duty. The Infinitive is Gerundial. See § 192 (*b*), and § 269 (5), (*b*). It is interesting to note that both constructions have come down to us from Old English [1]:—

Hé is *tó cumenne* } = Lat. Ille venturus est.
He is to come } = Eng. He is about-to-come.

Thone calic the ic *tó drinccnne* hæbbe } = The cup that I am
The cup that I *to drink* have } = about-to-drink.

From these examples it will be observed that in Old English the verb "*be*" was used when the verb following was *Intransitive*, and "*have*" when the verb following was *Transitive*. The syntactical propriety of such distinction (which has been lost in Mod. English) is obvious.

*Note.*—It should be observed, however, that the Perfect Infinitive cannot be used after *have*, but only after the verb *be*. We can say, "I *was* to have gone" (that is, it was settled for me to go, only something prevented me); but we cannot say, "I *had* to have gone," nor can we say, "I *had* to have drunk."

(3) **An if**:—this is a reduplication = if if. *An* is a contraction of *and*, which in the Northern dialect of English meant "if":—

But *and if* that evil servant shall say.—*Matt.* xxiv. 48.
Now *an* thou dalliest, then I am thy foe.—BEN JONSON.

When the old meaning of *an* or *and* was forgotten, the *if* was placed after it to remove any doubt as to its meaning.

(4) **And** in Interrogative sentences:—

And art thou cold and lowly laid?—SCOTT.

In such sentences the "and" does not join its own sentence to a previous one, but introduces a form of exclamation:—"Can it be true that thou art cold and lowly laid?"

(5) **And all**:—

The soldiers had decamped, horses *and all*.
The strawberry-runners have been planted out, soil *and all*.

"And all" appears to be a more inclusive and more emphatic

---

[1] Sweet's *Short Historical English Grammar*, ed. 1892, p. 130.

phrase than *et cetera* (=and the rest), and to have been formed on the same type. The first sentence means, "The soldiers had decamped, with their horses and everything else belonging to them." The second means, "The runners have been planted out, with their own soil."

(6) **As**, before a noun :—

> (*a*) This box will serve us *as* a table.
> (*b*) We will not have this man *as* our chief.

The ellipses can be filled up as follows :—

(*a*) This box will serve us *as* a table (would serve us, if we had a table).

(*b*) We will not have this man *as* (in the way in which we would have) our chief.

(7) **As**, before an adjective :—

> He considered the report *as* false.

That is, "He considered the report *as* (he would consider it, if it were) false."

(8) **As**, before "*if*" and "*though*" :—

> (*a*) He clung to it *as if* his life depended on it.
> (*b*) He clung to it *as though* his life depended on it.

That is, (*a*) "He clung to it, as (he would have clung to it), if his life depended on it." (*b*) "He clung to it as (fast as he could have clung to it, for he could not have clung to it faster) though his life depended on it."

(9) **As thee, as me** :—

> The nations not so blest as *thee*.—THOMSON.
> Even such weak minister as *me*
> May the oppressor bruise.—SCOTT.

These uses of the Objective case, if we consider "*as*" to be here a conjunction, are grammatical blunders; for the right construction would be "not so blest as *thou* (art blest)," and "such weak minister as *I* (am weak)." But it has been suggested by one writer that "*as*" might perhaps be here regarded as a preposition of comparison followed by a pronoun in the Objective case. In colloquial English this use of "as" is common; but careful writers avoid a phrase of such doubtful accuracy.

(10) **As to** :—

> I have heard nothing more *as to* that matter.

This phrase is of French origin = *quant à*, an elliptical phrase denoting "as far as relates to," etc. It has been explained in the same way in chapter xi.

(11) **As usual**:—

He came at four o'clock, *as usual.*

"As" is here used as a Relative for "which," and the verb "*is*" is understood after it:—"He came at four o'clock, which (his coming at four) is or was usual (with him)."

(12) **At best, at its best**, or **at the best**:—

*At best* he is only a moderate speaker.
He was *at his best* this morning.

In Superlative phrases of very frequent occurrence, such as "at best," "at worst," "at first," "at last," "at most," "at least," no pronoun or article is placed between the preposition and the adjective, unless we wish to particularise.

But in similar phrases that are of less frequent occurrence, a pronoun or the Definite article should be inserted:—

The wind is *at its loudest* or *the loudest.* The storm is *at its fiercest.* To-day the patient is *at his weakest.* The season is now *at its loveliest.* The air is now *at its hottest.*

(13) **At ten years old, at four miles distant**:—

(1) My son was *ten years old* when he died.
(2) My son died *at ten years of age.*
(3) My son died *at ten years old.*

(1) My house is *four miles distant* from the sea.
(2) My house is *at four miles' distance* from the sea.
(3) My house is *at four miles distant* from the sea.

Sentences (1) and (2) in both sets of examples are quite correct. Sentence (3) has arisen from a confusion between the constructions in (1) and (2). This mixed construction is not grammatically correct; and, though it is used by some writers and speakers, it is best to avoid it.

(14) **Away** (after Intrans. verbs):—

Fight *away,* my men.

This adverb is a contraction for "on-way." It denotes continuity ("go on, continue fighting") and sometimes intensity ("fight hard"), because such action implies movement on the way, not rest or inactivity. After verbs of motion it generally means "off," as "go *away,*" "send him *away.*"

(15) **Bid fair to**, etc.:—

This institution *bids fair* (=makes a fair or good promise) to flourish for many years to come.

Here the adjective "fair" qualifies some noun implied in the verb "bid": "bids a fair bidding or promise."

(16) **But he, but they.**—(Old Eng. *bútan*, by-out).

What stays (=supports) had I *but they*?—SHAKSPEARE.
And was he not the earl? 'Twas none but *he*.—WILLIAM TAYLOR.
The boy stood on the burning deck,
Whence all but *he* had fled.—MRS. HEMANS.

The Nominative after "but" appears to have arisen from a confusion between "but" as an Adversative conjunction of the Co-ordinative class and "but" as a preposition. "Whence all had fled, *but he* had not fled,"—that is, all had fled except him.

On *but* as a preposition, see § 232; as a conjunction, § 375 (11). In the curious phrase "*But* me no *buts*" (Shaks.), *but* is used as a verb in the Imperative mood, and *buts* as a noun in the Plural number. *Me* is the Dative or indirect object. *Buts* is the direct object. Compare the following in Scott:—"*Woman* me no more than I *woman* you: I have not been called Mistress to be *womaned* by you."—*Peveril of the Peak.*

(17) **But what**:—

(*a*) I cannot say *but what* you may be right.
(*b*) Not *but what* he did his best.

Here "what" has come into use as a substitute for "that." In both sentences "but" is a preposition, to which the following Noun-clause is the object (see § 259, *c*).

(*a*) This sentence could be reworded thus:—"I cannot say anything *against* the fact that-you-are-right,"—that is, anything to the contrary of your being right.

(*b*) This sentence is elliptical. The ellipse could be filled up as follows:—"I do not say anything except that he did his best, or to the contrary of his having done his best."

*Note.*—The substitution of "*what*" for "*that*" after the preposition "but" occurs only after the verbs "say" or "believe." It does not occur after any other verbs.

(18) **By thousands, by little, by himself,** etc.:—

(*a*) The ants came streaming out *by thousands.*
(*b*) The water oozes out little *by little.*
(*c*) He went out of the room *by himself.*

From denoting cause or agency, the preposition "by" came to denote manner or number; in which sense it often does the work of a Distributive adjective (see § 330, *a*). In (*a*) "by thousands" means "in the manner or to the number of thousands,"—that is, "a thousand at a time," or "one thousand after another." In (*b*) "little by little" is elliptical for "by little and by little"; as in Pope:—

Loth to enrich me with too quick replies,
*By little and by little* (he) drops his lies.

In (*c*) the phrase "by himself," which is often used for "alone," is founded on the analogy of the above phrases :—"He went out by himself,"—that is, "he went out himself at a time," or "he went out *alone*, unaccompanied by any one else." See § 372 (4).

(19) **Came to pass, came to be considered,** etc. :—

In this construction (which is very common), the Infinitive is Gerundial, and the "to" denotes *effect* or *result*. On this use of the preposition "to" before a noun, see § 372 (9); on its use in the same sense with the Gerundial Infinitive, see § 192 (*a*).

(20) **Can but, cannot but** :—

(*a*) We *can but* die.
(*b*) We *cannot but* die.

In (*a*) the word "but" is an adverb: "We can *only* die,"—that is, we cannot come to anything worse than death. In (*b*) the word "but" retains its original character as a preposition :—"We cannot do anything *except* die." Here "die" is the Noun-Infinitive used as object to the preposition "but."

(21) **Come, go** :—

(*a*) Are you *coming* to the meeting to-day?
(*b*) Are you *going* to the meeting to-day?

In sentence (*a*) the use of the verb "*come*" implies that the questioner himself intends to be present at the meeting, and he inquires whether the person addressed will be present also. The person addressed might say in reply, "Yes I shall be there with you"; or "No, I shall not join you there."

In sentence (*b*) the use of the verb "*go*" is perfectly general; and hence the person addressed might reply :—"Yes, I am going to the meeting; are you?" or "No, I am not going; are you?"

"*Come*" means motion *towards* a person or place; "*go*" means motion *from* a person or place. Thus we say, "The sun is *coming* up," or "the sun is *going* down"; "The plant is *coming* into *flower*," or "the plant is *going* to *seed*,"—that is, it has passed its prime, and is beginning to fade or pass away.

He has *come* to grief.
He has *gone* to the dogs.

These colloquial phrases mean almost the same thing. There is no saying why "come" is used in one and "go" in the other.

(22) **Dare, dares, dared, durst** :—

(*a*) For I know thou darest,
But this thing (Trinculo, the jester) *dare* not!—SHAKSPEARE.

(*b*) Here boldly spread thy hands; no venomed weed
*Dares* blister them, no slimy snail *dare* creep.
BEAUMONT AND FLETCHER.

(c) That man hath yet a soul, and *dare* be free.—CAMPBELL.
(d) Why then did not the ministers use their new law? Because they *durst* not.—MACAULAY.

It has been clearly proved that *dare* is one of the verbs which use an old past tense for a present, and that "he *dares*" is grammatically as bad as "he *shalls*," "he *mays*," "he *cans*." Nevertheless in the fifteenth century a practice began to spring up of using *dares* for *dare* in the Third Person Sing.; and the example quoted in (*b*) shows that in the Tudor period the two forms could be used promiscuously.

It is also well known that *durst* is a Weak past tense formed by adding the suffix *-te* to the stem *dors*: thus in A.S. the form is *dors-te.* Historically this is the proper past tense, as in example (*d*). Nevertheless a new form *dared* has also come into use.

As often happens in Modern English, when there are double forms, they are differentiated in use; cf. the double forms *is come*, *has come*, the different uses of which are described above in § 173; cf. also *elder, older; later, latter; nearest, next; outer, utter; foremost, first;* see § 348.

The following are the uses of *dare, dares, dared*, and *durst* that appear to be getting more and more established in current idiom:—

*Dare* is used for the Third Person Sing. whenever the sentence is negative, *or* whenever the Infin. following is unaccompanied by *to*:—

He dare not *go*.
He dare *be* free. See example (*c*).

*Dares* is used, whenever the sentence is affirmative, *and* whenever the Infin. following is accompanied by *to*:—

He dares *to* insult me.

*Dares* is also used, whenever the verb is followed by a personal object, in the sense of challenge:—

He *dares* me to my face.

*Dared* is much used with reference to direct assertions, and *durst not* with reference to hypothetical ones:—

He durst not do it = He would not dare to do it.

Another point of idiom is that *durst* is not used in affirmative sentences. We do not say, "He durst do it," but "He dared to do it."

(23) **Dependent on, independent of**:—

I am wholly dependent *on* your help.
I am quite independent *of* your help.

Why is the same preposition not used with both adjectives? "On" is used after "dependent," because this preposition denotes "rest," "support," as on some foundation. "Of" is used after "independent," because this preposition denotes "separation," and the same meaning is implied in the adjective "independent."

(24) **Doubt that, doubt but** :—

(*a*) I do not doubt *that* he is ill.
(*b*) I do not doubt *but* or *but that* he is ill.

These two sentences amount to the same thing. They might be rewritten as follows :—

(*a*) I do not doubt (=question) the fact that he is ill.
(*b*) I do not doubt anything *against* the fact that he is ill.

In (*b*) the word "but" is a preposition, and the Noun-clause "that he is ill" is its object; or if "that" is omitted after "but," the "but" is a Subordinative conjunction.

(25) **Even** (as an adverb) :—

(*a*) The hearing ear and the seeing eye, the Lord hath made *even* both of them (not merely one, but both alike).
(*b*) *Even* so (just in the same way) did the Gauls occupy the coast.
(*c*) Thou wast a soldier *even* to Cato's wish (fully up to the level of Cato's wish).
(*d*) I have debated *even* in my soul (in my very soul, to my level best).

We thus see that *even* is an intensifying adverb, signifying "so much as," "fully up to the mark."

In A.S. *efn*, the adjective, means "level. The adverbial counterpart is from A.S. *efn-e*, which has become *even*.

(26) **Excuse, excuse not** :—

(*a*) I hope you will excuse my coming here to-day.
(*b*) I hope you will excuse my *not* coming here to-day.

These two sentences amount to the same thing, and could be rewritten as follows :—

(*a*) I hope you will excuse (=dispense with, not insist on) my coming here to-day.
(*b*) I hope you will excuse (=pardon) my *not* coming (my neglect to come) here to-day.

Observe that the verb "excuse" is used in a different sense in each sentence.

*Note.*—Owing to the ambiguity of the verb "excuse," sentence (*a*) might mean "I hope you will excuse or *pardon* the fact of my having come here to-day." So it is best to avoid construction (*a*).

(27) **Far from, anything but** :—

His manners are *far from* pleasant.
His manners are *anything but* pleasant.

The phrase "far from" is equivalent to "anything but":—"His manners are anything *but* (=except) being pleasant." Here "being pleasant" is the object to the preposition "but." "The quality of being pleasant is not merely absent from his manners, but *far* distant *from* them."

(28) **First importance, last importance :—**

(*a*) This is a matter of the *first* importance.
(*b*) This is a matter of the *last* importance..

Though "first" and "last" are usually of opposite meanings, yet in the above phrases their meaning is the same. In (*a*) "first" denotes "foremost,"—taking precedence of everything else. In (*b*) "last" denotes "utmost," "greatest,"—which comes to the same thing as "foremost."

The opposite phrase to "of the first or of the last importance" is "of the least importance":—

This is a matter of the least importance (=of little or no importance, of less importance than anything else).

(29) **Good-looking :—**

He is a *good-looking* (handsome) man.

This is a well-established phrase. Yet we cannot turn it round and say "He looks good" for "He is handsome"; and if we say "He looks *well*," this means, "He looks (or seems to be) *in good health.*"

(30) **Had as lief, had rather, had better, had as soon,** etc.—These phrases, preceded by a noun or pronoun in the Nom. and followed by a *to*-less or Simple Infinitive, are well-established idioms :—

*I had as lief* not be, as live to be
In awe of such a thing as I myself.—SHAKSPEARE.
*I had rather* be a kitten, and cry mew.—SHAKSPEARE.

But the original construction was different. What is now the subject was in the Dative case (§ 306), and some form of the verb *be* was used where we now use *had* :—

And *leever me is* be poure and trewe.—*Cursor Mundi.*
(=And it is more agreeable to me to be poor and true.)

But in the transition between the old and the present constructions we find the Dative case used with *had* instead of the Nominative, and the Nominative used with *be* instead of the Dative :—

Poor lady! *she were better* love a dream.—SHAKSPEARE.
*You were best* hang yourself.—BEAUMONT AND FLETCHER.
*Me rather had* my heart might feel your love.—SHAKSPEARE.

This is the history of the construction. But in parsing such a sentence as, "I had as lief do this as that," we must now paraphrase it into, "I should have it as agreeable to me to do this as that." *Lief* is from A.S. *léof*, dear, agreeable; cf. *love*.

(31) **He to deceive me**, and similar phrases:—

(*a*) *I* to be so foolish!
(*b*) *He* to deceive me!

These exclamatory sentences are elliptical. (*a*) "Am I a person to be so foolish!" (*b*) "Could he be a person to deceive me!" The Infinitive is here Gerundial, and qualifies the noun or pronoun going before.[1]

(32) **How do you do?**—

The first *do* is the Auxiliary, which is used for asking a question in the present or past (Indefinite) tense (§ 172).

The second *do* may be explained as an imitation, or rather translation, of the French *faire*, in the old French sentence: *Comment faites-vous?* How do you make or do?

It has been also suggested that *do* is from A.S. *dúg-an*, to prosper. But the modern sound and spelling of *dúg* would be *dow*, like *cow* from A.S. *kú*. So this idea has been given up.

(33) **I do you to wit**:—

This quaint and almost obsolete expression means "I cause you to know." In Old English the verb *dó-n* (= do) meant (amongst other things) "cause," and this was very freely used in Middle English, when our language had lost the power of forming fresh Causal verbs, like *raise* from *rise*.

(34) **That will do**:—

The explanation usually given is that this *do* is not from A.S. *do-n*, but from A.S. *dúg-an*, to avail, to be sufficient (*Intrans.*), out of which we get the Adjective *dought-y*, valiant; and that hence the sentence "That will do" is equivalent to "That will suffice." But this explanation is untenable; for as shown in (32) the modern pronunciation and spelling of *dúg*

---

[1] The construction of a Nominative case with the Gerundial Infinitive is at least as old as the fifteenth century, and is not uncommon in Shakspeare (see Kellner's *Hist. Eng. Syntax*, p. 255):—

*Thow to lye* by our moder is too muche shame for us to suffre.—MALORY.
A heavier task could not have been imposed
Than *I to speak* my griefs unspeakable.—SHAKSPEARE.

In Modern English this construction is chiefly seen (*a*) in exclamatory phrases, as shown above, and (*b*) in the absolute construction, as shown in § 269 (*b*).

would be *dow*, and not *do*. As an alternative explanation it might be said that "that will do" means "that will work," so that *do* is here a Transitive verb used Intransitively on the principle explained in § 145 (*a*). Shakspeare has "I'll *do*, I'll *do*, and I'll *do*," where the verb *do* is evidently used Intransitively (see *Macbeth*, i. 3, 10).

(35) **I beg to**, etc. :—

I *beg* to inquire whether I may go home.

This is a common ellipse for "I beg leave to," etc. It is more common to omit the noun "leave" than to insert it.

(36) **I take it** :—

You will win in that case, *I take it*.

This is a common phrase for "in my opinion."

(37) **I was given to understand** :—

If this sentence is converted from the Passive form to the Active, it becomes :—"Some one gave or caused me to understand." Here "me" is the Indirect object, and "to understand" (Noun-Infinitive) is the Direct. By the rule given in § 161, a verb which has two objects in the Active voice can retain one in the Passive. Hence in the sentence "I was given to understand," the Noun-Infinitive is *Retained object* to the Passive verb "was given."

(38) **If you like** :—

You can do this, *if you like*.

We now regard *you* as the subject to the verb *like*, to which *it* is the object understood. But originally the phrase was, "If (it) like you," *i.e.* if it is agreeable to you. Cf. what Shakspeare says in *Hamlet*, "It *likes us* well." Here *like* or *likes* is an Impersonal verb, followed by *you* or *us*, which in Old English was in the Dative case; see above, § 306 (*c*). *Like* is, of course, the Third Person Sing. *Subjunctive*, not Indicative.

(39) **In respect of, with respect to** :—

He is senior to me *in respect of* service.
We must have a talk *with respect to* that subject.

These phrases are not identical in meaning. "In respect of" means "in point of" some quality, and is preceded by an adjective. "With respect to" means "concerning," and qualifies some verb or noun : we should not say, "We must have a talk in respect of that subject."

(40) **In that** :—

*In that* he died, he died unto sin once.—*New Testament*.

The words "in that" might be called a conjunctional phrase. But strictly speaking *in* is a preposition, having as its object the noun-clause "that he died." Here *that* is the Introductory conjunction, or if we say, "In the fact that," it is the conjunction of Apposition. See § 238 (*a*).

(41) **In thorough working-order**:—

Here "thorough" is an adjective qualifying the compound noun "working-order" (that kind of order which is suitable for working). It does not qualify either *working* or *order*, but the compound noun made up of both.

(42) **It's me, that's him**:—

These phrases are condemned by grammarians, because "me" and "him" are Subjective complements to the verb "is," and such complements must be in the same case as the Subject,—that is, in the Nominative case (see § 269, 2).

Nothing can be said in defence of the vulgarism "that's him."

But the phrase "it's me" has been defended on two grounds: (1) because it is the counterpart and exact translation of the French "*c'est moi*," which is recognised as an established idiom by the best French writers; (2) because "me" is an adopted or borrowed objective of "I," and might be used as a complement, though not as a subject. It is best, however, not to use it.

(43) **Lesser, less.**—"Lesser" is a Double Comparative, which is used for euphony to balance the sound of "greater":—

> The *greater* light to rule the day, and the *lesser* light to rule the night.—*Old Testament.*

*Note.*—Observe "lesser" is always an adjective. But "less" may be either an adjective or an adverb.

(44) **Methinks, I think**:—

The two verbs, though spelt alike in Modern English, are from different roots. *Methinks* = it seems to me; the *me* is in the Dative case (see § 306, *c*), and the *thinks* (impersonal) is from A.S. *thync-an*, to seem. The *personal* verb exemplified in "I think" is from A.S. *thenc-an*.

(45) **More than**, with adjectives and verbs:—

(*a*) It is *more than* probable that he will fail. (*With Adj.*)
(*b*) He *more than* hesitated to promise that. (*With Verb.*)

The construction is elliptical. The two sentences could be written at greater length as follows:—

(*a*) It is not only probable, but more than this,—it is practically certain, that, etc.

(*b*) He *did* more than *hesitate* (that is, he refused) to promise. (Here the Noun-infinitive "hesitate" is object to "than"; § 231.)

(46) **Mutual friend** :—

The word "mutual" implies reciprocity; as "our friendship is mutual,"—that is, "I love you, and you love me in return." But the phrase "a mutual friend" has come into vogue in a sense quite different from that of reciprocity. "I made his acquaintance through a *mutual* friend,"—that is, a *common* friend, some one who was a friend to myself as well as a friend to him. The use of the word "mutual" in this particular phrase is anomalous, but sanctioned by usage. We could not speak of two persons having "mutual ancestors."

(47) **Never so, ever so** :—

(*a*) He refuseth to hear the voice of the charmer, charm he *never so* wisely.—*Old Testament.*

(*b*) He refuseth to hear the voice of the charmer, charm he *ever so* wisely.

These two phrases mean the same thing. In (*a*) the dependent clause written out in full would be, "although he charm *so* wisely as he *never* charmed before." In (*b*) the clause can be rewritten "however wisely he may charm." The phrase "*ever so*" is the one now used; "*never so*" was used in the sixteenth century.

*Note.*—The phrase *ever so* is sometimes used as follows :—

*Ever so* many persons called here to-day.

Here "ever so many" means a larger number than usual, or a larger number than I care to count. Here *ever* is a mistake for "never"; and the sentence written in full would be—

Never so many persons called here before (as called here) to-day.

(48) "**No**," "**none**," as adverbs :—

(*a*) He is *no* scholar.
(*b*) He is *none* the wiser for all his experience.

In (*a*) the word "no" = in no respect. In (*b*) "none" = in no degree. "None" is used in this adverbial sense, only when it is followed by such a phrase as "the wiser,"—that is, by "the" and a Comparative. Similarly we can say "*all* the better," where "all," like "none," is used adverbially.

(49) **No more** :—

I will do *no more* than I can help.

After a Transitive verb, like *do*, we must look for an object. We find one implied in *no more*. But the construction is not strictly grammatical; for the adjective *no* is never used as a noun, and *more* is here an adjective in the Comparative degree, since it is followed by *than*; and hence it is not used as a noun. We must explain the construction by saying that *no* is here used for *nothing*.

But *more* can be used as a noun when it is not followed by *than*, in the same way as *much* can; see below (70).

Let knowledge grow from *more to more*.—TENNYSON.

(50) **None of them** :—

None of them *were* present.

"None," when it is used as a Subject, is properly a Singular = not one, or no one. But the phrase "none of them," when it is used as a Subject, takes a Plural verb by attraction:—"they none." Or the Plural may be explained by analogy to the phrases "all of them," "some of them," etc. See above (1).

(51) **Odds and ends**, scraps, leavings. Here *odds* is for *ords*, beginnings (A.S. *ord*, beginning), not for *orts*, leavings.

(52) **One more . . . and** :—

(*a*) *One more* whistle, *and* the train started.
(*b*) *One more* such loss, *and* we shall be ruined.

In each of these sentences there is an ellipsis of some verb in the Principal clause. (*a*) "*There was* one more whistle, and the train started,"—that is, *after* one more whistle, the train started. (*b*) "*We must incur* one more such loss, and then we shall be ruined,"—that is, *if we incur* one more such loss, we shall be ruined. This sentence therefore expresses a condition and its consequence.

(53) **One to another, to one another, to each other** :—

(*a*) They shouted *one to another*.
(*b*) They shouted *to one another*.

The phrase in (*a*) is grammatically correct, while that in (*b*) is grammatically wrong, since "one" is in the Nominative case in apposition with "they":—"They shouted—one shouted to another." Nevertheless the phrase "*to one another*" has become established by usage, and is now the more idiomatic of the two.

If we use the phrase "each other," we could not say "they shouted each to other"; but we should have to say "they shouted each to *the other*," because "each other" is used for two persons, whereas "one another" is used for more than two (see § 329). "Each to the other" is, however, an awkward phrase, and far less idiomatic than "to each other."

(54) **Or, nor,** in Negative sentences:—

He was not a clever man in books *or* in business.

The question has been raised whether "or" is correct in such sentences, or whether "nor" should be written in the place of it. The answer is that the "or" is correct. The sentence, however, is elliptical; and the ellipse would be filled up as follows:—

He was not clever *either* in books *or* in business.

If "nor" is used instead of "or," the sentence must be rewritten in the following form, which, however, is awkward and cumbersome:—

He was not clever in books, *nor* was he clever in business.

(55) **Or ere, or ever**:—

Would I had met my dearest foe in heaven, *or ever* I had seen that day, Horatio.—SHAKSPEARE.

It is generally explained that *or* is a corruption of *ere*. Hence the phrase *or ere* is merely a reduplication. "Or ever" (=ere ever) has been compared to such compound conjunctions as *whenever*, *wherever*, *however*, etc. Some, however, think that *ever* has been confounded with *ere*, misspelt as *e'er*. In this case the phrase *or ever* would be another instance of reduplication.

(56) **Other than, other besides**:—

(*a*) No person *other than* a graduate need apply.
(*b*) No other person *besides* my friend applied.

In (*a*) "other than" means "different from," "except," "but":—"No one *except* a graduate, no *other* person *but* a graduate." The word "than" is here a preposition (not a conjunction), which compares or distinguishes a graduate from other men. In (*b*) "other besides" means "other in addition to":—"No one besides or in addition to my friend applied."

(57) **Out, out and out**:—

(*a*) *Out*, brief candle!
(*b*) He was quite *out* of it.
(*c*) *Out* upon it!
(*d*) He was beaten *out and out*.
(*e*) He proved to be an *out and out* deceiver.

In (*a*) *out* is an adverb compounded with some verb "go" understood. In (*b*) *out* is an adverb qualifying the preposition *of*; § 371. In (*c*) some verb is understood, as in (*a*), before the adverb *out*. The phrase is exclamatory, and used to express indignation. In (*d*) the adverb is repeated for the sake of intensifying it: the reduplicated adverb means "utterly." In (*e*) some participle is understood with the reduplicated adverb, which gives it the force of an adjective signifying "utter"; see § 96 (2).

(58) **Out of temper, in a temper**:—

(*a*) He is *out of temper* (angry).
(*b*) He is *in a temper* (angry).

These phrases mean the same thing, and written in full would be, (*a*) out of his *ordinary* or *good* temper, (*b*) in a *bad* temper.

(59) **Please,** followed by an Imperative:—

*Please* write more legibly.

This is elliptical. The full sentence would be, "*If it please you*, write more legibly." It is a very polite way of making a request.

(60) **Prevent being, prevent from being**:—

(*a*) The delay *prevented* your letter *being* sent.
(*b*) The delay *prevented* your letter *from being* sent.

These two sentences mean the same thing, and both are correct. But in (*a*) "being sent" is a Passive Participle *used gerundively*, while in (*b*) "being sent" is not a participle at all, but a Passive gerund or noun used as object to the preposition "from."

In (*a*) the Gerundive Participle (see § 207 and § 284, *c*) contains an implied noun, and the words "prevented your letter *being sent*" are equivalent to "prevented *the sending of* your letter."

(61) **Save he, save we,** etc.:—

There was no stranger in the house save *we* two.—*Old Testament.*
No man hath seen the Father, save *he* which is of God.—*New Test.*
All the conspirators, save only *he*.—SHAKSPEARE.
None shall be mistress of it save *I* alone.—SHAKSPEARE.

This Nominative (which is now gradually going out of use) is a survival of the Nominative Absolute, which was used when "save" was still an Adjective used absolutely, and had not been changed into a Preposition. On Participial prepositions see § 373 (*j*).

(62) **Several people, several persons**:—

*Several people* think that the winter is over.

The phrase "several people," though common, is not so correct as "several persons," because "several" has a distributive force and denotes individuals, while "people" is a Collective noun.

(63) **Shortly, briefly**:—

I will write *shortly* (=in a short time).
I will write *briefly* (=in few words).

The adverb "shortly" is used to denote shortness only of *time*, and only of *future* time. We cannot say "He went away *shortly*" (a short time ago); nor can we say "He lived there *shortly*" (for a short time). The adverb "briefly" is used only in the sense of shortness in *language*.

(64) **So and so, or so, so so, and so on** :—

(*a*) He asked what I meant, and I told him *so and so*.
(*b*) I shall return in a week *or so*.
(*c*) *So so* it works: now, mistress, sit you fast.—DRYDEN.
(*d*) He disliked dances, plays, picnics, *and so on*.

In (*a*) "so and so" is the adverbial form of the Indefinite adjective "such and such." "I told him *so and so*," might be rewritten "I gave him *such and such* an answer" (see § 326, *c*). These expressions are used, when the speaker does not think it necessary or does not desire to enter into particulars.

In (*b*) "or so" is also used Indefinitely, and the sentence might be rewritten, "I shall return in a week or such-like,"—that is, a week more or less (see § 326, *c*).

In (*c*) "so so" means "fairly well," and is used when the speaker does not wish to say anything definite. When the phrase is preceded by "but," it means something less than "well." "His leg is but *so so*" (Shakspeare),—that is, "his leg is in rather a worse state than usual."

In (*d*) the phrase "and so on" means "and such-like," or "etc." (*et cetera*). The adverb "on" means "forward,"—that is, to the end of the list:—"He disliked dances, plays, picnics, and such-like amusements to the end of the list."

(65) **So as to**, etc. :—

I got up at six A.M. *so as to be* certain of being in time.

This construction is elliptical, and the ellipse should be filled up as follows:—"I got up at six A.M. *so* (= in such a way) *as* (= in which way I should get up) to be certain," etc. The Infinitive in such phrases is Gerundial.

(66) **So kind as to**, and similar phrases :—

He was *so* kind *as to* take me into his house.

"He was so (to that extent) kind as (to which extent a man would be kind) to take me (for taking me)," etc. Here too the Infinitive is Gerundial. The sentence is equivalent to "He was kind *enough* to take me."

(67) **Somehow or other, anyhow** :—

He managed *somehow or other* to pay off his debts.

Here "how" has been substituted for the corresponding

noun. "He managed some how or other how = in some *way* or other (way) to pay off his debts."

(68) **Thank you.**—This is merely an ellipse for "I thank you."

(69) **The other day.**—In § 327 (*e*) it has been pointed out that this phrase is Indefinite,—some day a little preceding the present, that is, a few days ago. Perhaps *the other day* meant "the second day," that is, two days from now, two or three days ago; for in Old English "other" meant "second." Shakspeare has *this other day* as an equivalent to *the other day.* The same explanation suits this phrase equally well:—"This is the second day that has passed since such and such a thing happened."

(70) **This much, so much, so much for**:—

(*a*) *This much* at least we can promise.
(*b*) He is now *so much* better that we need not be alarmed.
(*c*) *So much for* his courage; now as to his honesty.

In (*a*) "much" is used as a noun: "this much" is equivalent to "this amount," "this quantity."

In (*b*) "much" is an adverb qualifying the adjective "better"; and "so" is another adverb qualifying "much."

In (*c*) the first clause written out in full would be:—"As *for* (= regarding) his courage, *so much* has been or can be said." Here there is a confusion between "this much" as a noun and "so much" as an adverb. The phrase "so much" is used in this place as a noun to some verb understood. It is generally used when the speaker or writer is ridiculing something. "This is all that can be said about his courage; now let us see what can be said about his honesty."

(71) **To be mistaken**:—

(*a*) You will find that you *were mistaken.*
(*b*) You will find that you *mistook it.*

The form of the verb in (*a*) is according to idiom; and this must be adhered to. The form in (*b*) is what we should have expected from the meaning of the verb "mistake," which is "to misapprehend, or to misunderstand." But the form of the verb in (*b*) is against idiom, and should therefore not be used.

*Note.*—The origin of this use of the word "mistaken" is explained in § 199. Past participles are sometimes used to denote state or character; see examples in § 199. Shakspeare has—

The *ravined* salt-sea shark (*Macbeth*).

where ravined means "addicted to ravining,"—that is, ravenous. If this explanation is correct, the only peculiarity about *mistaken* is that the word denotes a special act of mistaking something as well as a habit of mistaking things. "Mistaken" is often used in the sense of habit; as, "He was a very *mistaken* man," a man who had formed many false opinions, and was accustomed to act on them.[1]

(72) **To be sure**:—

Shall you go? *To be sure* I shall.

Here "to be" is the Gerundial Infinitive, and the phrase "to be sure" signifies "certainly." The phrase, "Well, to be sure!" is a form of exclamation denoting astonishment.

(73) **To boot**:—

I give you this *to boot.*

I give you this by way of an extra. "To boot" means "in addition," "over and above." "Boot" has always meant profit; and is of the same root as the first syllable in *better.* The prep. *to* is here used in the sense of purpose; § 372 (9).

(74) **What not**:—

When this phrase is used, it stands after a string of nouns or verbs, and denotes that many more might be added, but there is no need to mention them:—

Steam propels, lowers, elevates, pumps, drains, pulls, and what not (what else does it not do?).

Persians, Copts, Tartars, Medes, Syrians, and what not (=several other nations that I need not name) were brought under the dominion of Alexander the Great.

(75) **What was, what was not**:—

(*a*) *What was* my astonishment on seeing this!
(*b*) *What was not* my astonishment on seeing this!

These two sentences come to the same thing, in spite of the "not." The first means "How great was my astonishment," etc.; the second means "No astonishment could be greater than mine was," etc.

(76) **What with, somewhat**:—

The phrase "what with," repeated before two or more nouns, is sometimes used for enumerating a series of things:—

*What with* the cunning of his methods, *what with* the flattery of his tongue, and *what with* the influence of his money, he soon became the leading man in the town.

It might be supposed that "what with" is an elliptical phrase for "what *he effected* with cunning," etc. But more probably "what" is here an Indefinite Demonstrative adjective (§ 315) used as an adverb in the sense of "partly." The com-

[1] The word "drunken" is used in the same way. Among the *dramatis personæ* of the *Tempest* we have "Stephano, a *drunken* butler."

pound word "somewhat" is still used sometimes as a noun signifying "something," and sometimes as an adverb signifying "to some extent" or "partly":—"I am *somewhat* tired of this book." In colloquial English we still say, "I tell you what," which means "I tell you something," or "I have something to tell you." In Shakspeare we have:—

> I tell you *what* (=something), Antonio.

(77) **Who**, in the phrase "*as who should say*," where *who* is used as an Indefinite demonstrative pronoun.

One example has been given from Shakspeare in § 315.

But the expression is still common:—

> "Is the present generation of young men at Oxford affected to any appreciable degree by the traditions of the place?"
> "Oh, yes," replied my host, *as who should say*, "We haven't altogether gone to the dogs."—*Quiver*, May 1894.

(78) **Write you, write to you**:—

> I will *write you* a letter on this matter.
> I will *write to you* soon.

We can use the phrase "*write you*," when "you" is the Indirect object to the verb and is followed by a Direct object. But if there is no Direct object and the verb "write" is used Intransitively (§ 145, *a*), we must say "*write to you*."

(79) **Gerundive use of Participles.**—In this construction a Participle is used instead of Gerund, and denotes what would otherwise be expressed by a Gerund; see § 207 and § 284 (*c*).

> To-janes (=at the time) tho *sunne risindde* (of the sun rising).—*Old English Miscellany*.
> After the *sunne goying* down.—WYCLIFF.
> Moost humblie besechyng my sayd lorde to take no displaysir on *me* so *presumyng*.—CAXTON.
> We have no right to be hurt at a *girl telling* me what my faults are.—THACKERAY.
> There is always danger of this *disease appearing* in the sound eye.—HUGH CONWAY.
> Don't fear *me being* any hindrance to you.—DICKENS.
> I ask where there could be pictures at Compton Green without *me knowing* it.—BESANT AND RICE.
> Would you mind *me asking* you a few questions?—STEVENSON.[1]

[1] This and the seven previous examples are all taken from Kellner's *Historical English Syntax*, pp. 262-264, where the subject is very fully and ably discussed. The subject is also discussed in Abbott's *How to Parse*, pp. 234, 235, where he says, "These are not exactly participles." This is quite true; they are examples of the Gerundive use of participles.

In the first of the following sentences "*being sent*" is a participle used Gerundively; in the second it is an actual Gerund:—

(1) This prevented the letter *being sent.*
(2) This prevented the letter from *being sent.* See (60).

*Note.*—It may be pointed out, however, that a Participle used Gerundively does not always convey quite the same sense as the corresponding Gerund would do.

(*a*) What do you think of my *horse running* to-day? That is, "What do you think of the plan or proposal that my horse *shall run* to-day?" Here then the participle denotes future time.

(*b*) What do you think of my *horse's running* to-day? That is, "What do you think of the pace at which my horse *ran* to-day?" Here then the Gerund denotes *past* time.

(80) **Phrases and words suggested by French:—**

(*a*) "How do you *do?*" See (32), where it is shown that *do* is a translation of the French *faire.*

(*b*) "It's *me.*" A translation of Fr. "c'est *moi*"; see (42).

(*c*) "The window *gives* upon the street." Here *gives* is a translation of the Fr. *donne,* which, though lit. "gives," means *looks, abuts.* Here we must parse *gives* as a Transitive verb used Intransitively on the principle shown in § 145 (*b*).

(*d*) "That goes *without saying.*" A translation of Fr. *sans dire;* so evident that there is no need to mention it.

(*e*) "That subject came *upon the carpet.*" A translation of Fr. *sur le tapis;* we often say "on the *tapis,*" that is, on the tablecloth, before the meeting. "Carpet" once meant a covering of any kind, a tablecloth as much as a floorcloth.

(*f*) "*As to,*" followed by a noun: "I am indifferent *as to* his success." A translation of Fr. *quant à,* as much as relates to. See explanation in chap. xi. The phrase *as to* is at least as old as Wycliff.

(*g*) "*Solidarity* of interests." A phrase lately borrowed from French Communists. Entire union of interests.

(*h*) "He *affects* the latest fashion." Translation of Fr. *affect-er,* follows, adopts.

(*i*) "To *exploit* a new invention." From Fr. *exploit-er,* to make the most of for the sake of trade, to utilise to the utmost.

---

## NOTES ON CERTAIN GRAMMATICAL TERMS.

**Absolute Construction.** Any construction may be called absolute, in which a word or phrase is independent of the rest of the sentence; § 27.

**Accidence** (Lat. *accidentia,* Neut. Plur., "things which befall"): the collective name for all those changes of form that are incidental to certain Parts of Speech.

**Analysis** (Gr. *ana*, up; *lysis*, loosening or breaking). Analysis means "breaking up" a whole into its component parts. Grammatically, this term admits of several applications, such as (*a*) the breaking up of a compound letter into its parts, as *x* into *ks*, or the vowel ī into *a*+*i*; (*b*) the breaking up of a syllable into its letters; (*c*) the breaking up of a word into its prefixes, stem, and suffixes; (*d*) the breaking up of a Compound or Complex sentence into its component clauses; (*e*) the breaking up of a clause into its component parts,—the subject, attributive adjuncts, predicate, and adverbial adjuncts.

**Anomaly,** a solitary or very uncommon deviation from accidence, syntax, or idiom: (Greek word, *anōmalia*, unevenness of ground).

**Apposition** (Lat. *ad*, *posit-*, placed): the placing of one noun or sentence against another for the purpose of explanation; see §§ 18-20.

**Archaism** (Gr. *archai-os*, ancient): the use of a word that was once common, but is now out of ordinary use, as *clomb* for *climbed*, *meseems* for *it seems to me*, *eyen* for *eyes*.

**Assimilation** (Lat. *ad*, to, *similis*, like): the process by which a consonant is made to take the form of another consonant through the influence of contact, as in the word *as*(=*ad*)*similation*.

**Defective**: deficient in certain forms. This term can be applied to (1) verbs that are wanting in certain parts; (2) adjectives that have no comparative or superlative of their own, but borrow them from other roots; (3) nouns which have a singular but no plural, or a plural but no singular.

**Dialect** (Gr. *dia-lect-ik-e*, the art of conversation): a local or provincial form of speech characterised by some peculiarities of accent, pronunciation, or grammatical usage, which distinguish it from the standard speech of the nation, such as the Yorkshire dialect or the Dorsetshire dialect. Until some standard has become established, the different local varieties of kindred speech are dialects of coequal rank. But when a standard speech has been formed, the dialects or local varieties fall into a lower rank and are regarded as the speech of the unlearned.

**Ellipsis** (Gr. *en*, in, and *leipsis*, leaving): an omission (allowed by idiom or custom) of a word or words, which must be mentally supplied in order to make the phrase or sentence grammatical, as, "It is *more than certain* that," etc.—that is, "it is not only certain, but something more, that," etc.

**Etymology** (Gr. *etymos*, true, *logos*, word): that branch of philology which traces the origin or true beginning of a word. Sometimes, however, the word is used for a synonym for Accidence.

**Euphony** (Gr. *eu*, well, and *phon-e*, a sound): the pleasing effect produced on the ear by pronouncing or grouping words in a particular way.

**Good English.** This implies five things at least: (1) the choice of suitable words—see **Impropriety** below; (2) correct syntax and accidence: no bad grammar—see *bad grammar* below under **Grammar**; (3) correct order of words, as, for example, that the antecedent must be placed as close as possible to its Relative—see § 275 (*a*) *Note;* (4) correct idiom—see *phraseological idiom* under **Idiom** below; (5) absence of verbiage—see **Verbiage** below.

**Grammar** (Gr. *gramma*, a letter; Old Fr. *gramaire*): an exposition, partly practical and partly theoretical, of the various forms and methods employed in any given language for the expression of thought.

The above definition, since it makes no reference to time, is wide enough to include the forms and methods formerly used (Historical Grammar) as well as those in present use (Modern Grammar). Grammar includes Accidence and Syntax, the order of words as well as the relations of words to one another, phraseological idiom as well as the principles of more regular construction, the sounds and symbols used in word-making, the prefixes and suffixes by which words are built up, the clauses of which a compound or complex sentence consists.

The subjects of punctuation, prosody, rhetoric, poetic diction, and the derivations of words, though closely allied to Grammar, do not come within the scope of Grammar proper.

When we say that a phrase or sentence is in "bad grammar" we generally mean that it is a violation of Accidence or Syntax.

**Homonym** (Gr. *homos*, the same, and *onoma*, a name): a word spelt and pronounced exactly in the same way as another, but having an entirely distinct meaning and a distinct etymology; as *bear*, verb (A.S. *ber-an*; Sanskrit, *bhar*), *bear*, noun (A.S. *ber-a*; Sanskrit, *bhal-a*).

**Idiom** (Gr. *idiom-a*, peculiarity) is used in two senses:—(*a*) Grammatical idiom, viz. whatever pertains to the structure of a language in its accidence and syntax; (*b*) Phraseological idiom, viz. some particular combination of words that is not strictly in accordance with the general structure of a language, and therefore requires a specific explanation or exposition. The latter is the sense in which "idiom" is chiefly used.

*Note.*—In this book, Part I. deals chiefly with Grammatical idiom, and Part II. with Phraseological.

**Impropriety** (Lat. *in*, not, *proprius*, proper): the using of a word in a sense that does not properly belong to it, as "to *perpetrate* a virtuous action." (*Perpetrate* is always used in reference to something bad, although etymologically it means simply "to perform.")

**Inflexion** (Lat. *in*, and *flexum*, to bend or change). "By inflexion we understand an addition to a whole class of words, expressing some grammatical function, or a meaning so general as not to constitute a new word. Thus the inflexion *s* is added to *tree* to express the meaning of plurality, this meaning being so general that we feel *trees* to be essentially the same word as the uninflected singular *tree*."—SWEET.

**Neologism** (Gr. *neos*, new, and *logos*, speech): the use of a new word suitable and sanctioned by authority, but not thoroughly established in general use and therefore still rather uncommon; as *altruism*, to denote the habit of living for others in contrast with selfishness; *solidarity*, to denote entire union of aims, duties, and interests.

**Paronym** (Gr. *para*, beside, *onoma*, name): a word pronounced in the same way as another, but differently spelt, as *hair, hare; air, heir; were, ware, wear; mare, mayor; one, won.*

**Parse** (Lat. quæ *pars* orationis): to parse a word is to show (1) to what part of speech it belongs; (2) to account for its inflexions, if it has any; (3) to show in what relation it stands to any other word or words in the same sentence.

**Philology** (Gr. *philos*, friend, *logos*, word or speech): the study of words; but usually in the more specific sense,—the comparative study of kindred languages, such as the Teutonic group, or the still wider Aryan group.

**Phonetics** (Gr. *phonetica*, things pertaining to the voice): that branch of grammar that deals with speech-sounds.

**Pleonasm** (Gr. *pleion*, more): redundancy—see below **Tautology.**

**Poetic license.** A license or liberty allowed to poets, but not allowed to writers of prose; such as the use of uncommon or archaic words, the use of uncommon constructions or phrases, etc.

Poets, however, are prohibited the use of solecisms (see this word defined below), that is, blunders. For instance, we cannot tolerate Byron's "There let him *lay*," but we can tolerate such a phrase as "Trip it *deft and merrily*," because the conjoining of an adverb to an adjective, though rare, admits of syntactical explanation (see § 274).

**Purity** (Lat. *puritas*): the use of words sanctioned by the best modern writers. This excludes (*a*) the use of obsolete words, (*b*) the use of foreign words or phrases when suitable English ones exist, such as saying Lat. *de die in diem*, for "from day to day," or Fr. *à propos*, for "with reference to."

**Slang** (Sc. *sleng*): a mode of speaking peculiar to some particular place or calling; as stockbrokers' slang, schoolboys' slang, the slang of sailors, soldiers, the theatre, the university. Sometimes a slang word rises into general acceptance as part of the national speech, as *donkey, dunce, a jingo, to boycott, whig, tory.*

**Solecism** (Gr. *Soloikos*, a dweller at Soloi, a town notorious for speaking bad Greek): this word denotes (*a*) a violation of accidence or syntax, that is, a grammatical blunder, or (*b*) a violation of idiom; as,

(*a*) *Whom* do men say that I am (*whom* for *who*).
(*b*) He died *with* fever (*with* for *of*).

**Style** (Lat. *stilus*, an instrument for writing); such use of words in the expression of thought as distinguishes one writer or speaker from another. Thus a style may be terse or diffuse; pithy or pointless; obscure or perspicuous; explicit or vague; simple or rhetorical; spirited or tame; light or ponderous, etc.

**Synonym** (Gr. *syn*, with, *onoma*, name): a word having the same or nearly the same meaning as another, and capable of being used in the same or nearly the same context, as *unlikely, improbable.*

*Note.*—We are obliged to introduce the word *nearly*, as there are few, if any, examples of *perfect* synonyms. *Unlikely* and *improbable* are as nearly perfect synonyms as any other pair of words that we could easily find. Yet we could hardly substitute "*improbable* to happen" for "*unlikely* to happen."

**Syntax** (Gr. *syn*, with, *taxis*, arrangement): that part of Grammar that deals with the order of words in a sentence, and with their relations to one another in its construction.

**Synthesis** (Gr. *syn*, with, *thesis*, placing). Analysis means "breaking up"; synthesis means "adding on." The one is in all possible applications (see those given under **Analysis**) the converse of the other.

A language is said to be in the *Synthetic* stage, when the different parts of a word are formed by adding inflexions to the stem. A language is in the *Analytical* stage, when it has discarded most of its inflexions, and makes a very frequent use of auxiliary words.

**Tautology** (Gr. *to auto*, the same, *logos*, word): repeating the same word without necessity, or the same sense by means of another word.

**Technology** (Gr. *techne*, art or science, *logos*, word): an explanation of technical terms, as when a word has some specific meaning in connection with some art or science, different from that in general use. Thus *elbow* has one sense in architecture, another in navigation, and another in ordinary use.

**Verbiage** (Lat. *verbum*): a needless profusion of words. It includes pleonasm or tautology together with other forms of verbosity.

---

## QUESTIONS ON IDIOM AND CONSTRUCTION.

Collected from London Matriculation Papers set from January 1879 to January 1897.

1. Explain the construction of *self*. What part of speech is it? Trace its history. (Jan. 1879.)

2. Correct or justify:

(*a*) That's him.
(*b*) Many a day.
(*c*) I expected to have found him better. (Jan. 1879.)

3. State clearly the rules of English accidence regarding the use of *will* and *shall* in Interrogative sentences. (Jan. 1880.)

4. Discuss, with reference to the history of their usage, the words *ye* and *you*, *that* and *which* (as Relatives). (June 1880.)

5. Tell what you know of the origin and present use of *a* and *the*. How would you place them among the parts of speech, and why? (June 1881.)

6. What is a Relative pronoun? Point out and explain the different uses of *that*, *what*, *which*, *whether*. (June 1881.)

7. What is the real power of the Genitive case? (Jan. 1882.) Distinguish its uses according to meaning.

8. Tell the history of the forms *a* and *an*, and discuss their grammatical use. (Jan. 1883.)

9. Take six of our common English prepositions, and show in what way each has been taken to represent different relations of place, time, and causality. (Jan. 1883.)

10. Discuss the syntax of the following:—

(*a*) I meant to have written to you.
(*b*) I heard of him running away.
(*c*) It's me. (Jan. 1883.)

11. Explain how you would classify the words *aye*, *yea*, *yes*, *no*, *nay* among the parts of speech. (June 1883.)

12. How do you classify pronouns? Parse the word *what* in the sentences:—

(*a*) I will tell you *what*.
(*b*) He was some*what* weary.
(*c*) *What* o'clock is it?
(*d*) *What* man is this?
(*e*) *What* with the wind, and *what* with the rain, it was not easy to get on. (June 1884.)

13. Explain and parse the following phrases:—*methinks*; *woe is me*; *I had as lief*. (Jan. 1885.)

14. Define the terms *inflexion*, *analysis*, *synthetic*, *interjection*; *strong* and *weak* as applied to verbs; *abstract* and *concrete* as applied to nouns; *simple* and *complex* as applied to sentences. (June 1885.)

15. What exactly is meant by a *Pronoun*? What by a *Relative pronoun*? Mention any differences in usage between *who* and *that*. (June 1885.)

16. Write some short sentences to show the various meanings of the prepositions *at*, *with*, *if*, *from*, *against*. Explain:—

(*a*) He did his duty *by* him.
(*b*) *Under* these circumstances.
(*c*) Ten *to* one it is not so.
(*d*) Add ten *to* one.
(*e*) Keep up *for* my sake. (June 1885.)

17. Parse *after* and *out* in each of the following:—

(*a*) *After* him then, and bring him back.
(*b*) *After* he came, all went wrong.
(*c*) You go first, and I will come *after*.
(*d*) *After* that I will say no more.
(*e*) *Out*, brief candle.
(*f*) He was quite *out* of it.
(*g*) *Out* upon it!
(*h*) He was beaten *out and out*.
(*i*) He proved an *out and out* deceiver. (June 1885.)

18. Parse each of the four words, *But me no buts*. What other parts of speech may *but* be? Would you say, *They all ran away but me*, or *They all ran away but I*? (Jan. 1886.)

19. What is meant by an *idiom*? Mention two or three English idioms, and try to explain them. (Jan. 1886.)

20. Point out what is idiomatic in these phrases:—

(*a*) There came a letter.
(*b*) Let me fight it out.
(*c*) We spoke to each other.
(*d*) Many a man would flee.
(*e*) What an angel of a girl!
(*f*) What with this, and what with that, I could not get on. (June 1886.)

21. What errors have crept into these phrases:—

(*a*) Ever so many.
(*b*) To do no more than one can help.
(*c*) These sort of things.

Suggest some explanation of "*of*" in such phrases as "a friend *of* mine." (June 1886.)

22. Parse the italicised words and phrases:—

(*a*) *Down* with it!
(*b*) His *having been beaten* once only made him the more determined to succeed.
(*c*) *Seeing* is *believing*.

(*d*) The *hearing* ear and the *seeing* eye, the Lord hath made *even* both of them.
(*e*) *Whatever* sceptic could inquire for,
For every *why*, he had a *wherefore*.
(*f*) *Let* knowledge grow from *more* to more. (Jan. 1887.)

23. Distinguish between *farther* and *further*, *gladder and gladlier*, *nearest* and *next*, *latest* and *last*, *peas* and *pease*, *genii* and *geniuses*. (Jan. 1887.)

24. Give instances of common nouns becoming proper, and of proper becoming common. How does the possessive of personal pronouns differ from the genitive? (June 1887.)

25. Discuss these phrases:—

(*a*) He found them *fled*, horses *and all*.
(*b*) Fight *away*, my men.
(*c*) Get *you* gone.
(*d*) I give him this *to boot*.
(*e*) He overslept *himself*.
(*f*) How did he come *by* such a fortune? (June 1887.)

26. Define the words *grammar*, *etymology*, *syntax*, *gender*, *number*, *case*, *mood*, and *tense*. (Jan. 1888.)

27. Correct or justify:—

(*a*) Thinking of them, my pen tarries as I write.
(*b*) It's me.
(*c*) I intended to have written to him. (Jan. 1888.)

28. Give the sources of the following expressions, pointing out the objection to their use as English idioms, and showing how the meaning might in each case be properly conveyed:—

(*a*) That window *gives* upon the street.
(*b*) That affair came *upon the carpet*.
(*c*) That goes *without saying*.
(*d*) He is feeble *as to* his mind.
(*e*) *Solidarity* of interests.
(*f*) He *affected* the latest fashion.
(*g*) To *exploit* a new invention. (June 1888.)

29. Notice any differences in usage between the relatives, *that*, *who*, *which*. (Jan. 1890.)

30. Point out any grammatical errors that are common in ordinary colloquial speech. State exactly what you understand by "good English." (Jan. 1890.)

31. Write several sentences illustrating the correct modern usage of *shall* and *will* in Interrogative sentences, giving any explanations that appear to be necessary. (June 1890.)

32. Why are Prepositions so called? Discuss the use of *past* in "He went *past* the house"; of *of* in "The island *of* Great Britain"; of *by* in "Do your duty *by* the University." (Jan. 1891.)

33. What do you understand by a Pronoun? What by a Reflexive pronoun? Point out the inconsistency of saying *I myself*, and yet *He himself*, and account for it. (Jan. 1892.)

34. Give the meaning and origin of the following prepositions:—

*maugre*, *but*, *between*, *notwithstanding*, *during*. And mention as many as you can of the various senses in which *by*, *to*, *with* are used. (Jan. 1892.)

35. Explain and illustrate the terms *inflexion*, *assimilation*, *etymology*, *phonetics*, and *accidence*. (June 1892.)

36. Discuss the verbal forms in italics :—

(*a*) How *do* you *do*? (*b*) I *do* you *to wit*.
(*c*) Woe *worth* the day. (*d*) *Seeing* is *believing*.
(*e*) He that hath ears to *hear*, let him *hear*.
(*f*) The hawthorn bush, with seats beneath the shade,
For *talking* age and *whispering* lovers made. (June 1892.)

37. Parse the words italicised in the following :—

(*a*) *Please* write clearly. (*b*) *Thank* you.
(*c*) If you *like*. (*d*) From *bad* to worse.
(*e*) Get *you* gone. (*f*) He was accused of *having run* away. (June 1893.)

38. Discuss carefully these words and ways of speaking :—*talented ; a friend of mine ; reliable ; neither he nor she are at hand ; they all hoped to have succeeded.* (June 1893.)

39. Define and illustrate the terms :—*dialect*, *slang*, *technology*, *archaism*, *neologism*, *solecism*. (Jan. 1894.)

40. Parse *but* in the following sentences, and explain carefully its idiomatic usage in each case, with reference to its original meaning :—

(*a*) There is none here *but* hates me.
(*b*) And was not this the earl? 'Twas none *but* he.
(*c*) He would have died *but* for me.
(*d*) He is all *but* perfect.
(*e*) There's not the smallest orb which thou behold'st,
*But* in his motion like an angel sings.
(*f*) He is *but* a madman. (Jan. 1895.)

41. Distinguish between the comparative degree of an adjective and an adjective with comparative force. To which class belong—*former*, *inferior*, *older*, *elder*, *outer*, *utter*. (June 1895.)

42. Point out any defects in the grammar or style of the following :—

(*a*) Homer was not only the maker of a nation, but of a language.
(*b*) He is better versed in theology than any living man.
(*c*) Shakspeare frequently has passages in a strain quite false, and which are entirely unworthy of him.
(*d*) Nothing can hinder this treatise from being one of the most considerable books which has appeared for the last half-century.
(*e*) A statute inflicting the punishment of death may be and ought to be repealed, if it be in any way expedient. (June 1896.)

43. Differentiate the following as regards usage :—*further*, *farther ; late*, *latter ; older*, *elder ; outer*, *utter ; foremost*, *first.* (Jan. 1897.)

# PART III.—HISTORICAL ENGLISH: WORD-BUILDING AND DERIVATION.

## CHAPTER XXI.—HISTORICAL OUTLINE.

### SECTION 1.—ENGLISH AND COGNATE LANGUAGES.

**376. Languages first spoken in Britain.**—The English language was not native to Britain. It was preceded by Celtic, and to some extent by Latin, before the occupation of the island by English settlers from the Continent.

*Celtic.*—The language spoken by the ancient Britons was a form of Celtic, similar to what was spoken by kindred tribes in Wales and Cornwall. The English, when they came, paid no attention to this Celtic speech, though they picked up a few words accidentally; but after their conversion to Christianity they adopted the same forms of the Roman letters as those used by the conquered Britons.

*Latin.*—So long as Britain was a Roman province, Latin was the language of the camps and of the ruling class, and during the last two centuries of the Roman occupation it was the language of the Church also. In the neighbourhood of the forts and monasteries, wherever Roman influence was dominant, a popular form of Latin was already springing up. Had it been left to run its course, it would in time have overspread the island, as it did Gaul and Spain and other continental provinces of the Roman empire. But three events occurred, that rendered this impossible and gave an exceptional character to the future language of Britain: (1) in A.D. 409 the Romans withdrew every garrison from the island and never again returned to it; (2) the heathen Picts and Scots from North Britain overran the provinces which the Romans had left, and destroyed every trace of Roman culture that came in their way; (3) forty years later a new race of heathen, still more formidable, poured into

Britain by way of the North Sea and the Channel, in a series of invasions that spread over at least 100 years, and made their own language the current speech of the best part of the island.

**377. Introduction of English.**—The new language thus violently thrust into Britain was English, a member of the **Teutonic** group of languages, very different from those that preceded it, and yet, as will be presently shown, remotely cognate.

The invaders came from the low-lying lands about the estuaries and lower courses of the Rhine, the Weser, and the Elbe, and some way up the western coast of Denmark. From the year 449, and for about 100 years in succession, they poured into the island in large flat-bottomed boats, many of which were driven with fifty oars at least, and were capacious enough to carry women and children besides the rowers. A tribe called Angles settled in the country north of the Humber, and as far north as the Highlands of Scotland; Frisians for the most part in the country between the Humber and the Thames; and Saxons in the country south of the Thames. The only territory that remained to the Celtic-speaking natives was the Scotch Highlands, Strathclyde (the land south of the Firth of Clyde), Cumbria or Cumberland (the land of the Cymry or Welsh), Wales proper, and Cornwall.

**378. The Aryan family of Languages.**—Thus far we have referred to three separate classes of language,—the Celtic, the Latin, and the Teutonic. These, though quite distinct, are found on closer inspection to possess certain points in common sufficiently marked to show that they belong, with others still to be named, to one large family called the Aryan,[1] which is subdivided as follows:—

A. *The Asiatic or East-Aryan Group.*

(*a*) **Sanskrit**, and the neo-Sanskrit languages of India, such as Bengali, Hindi, Punjábi, etc.
(*b*) **Zend**, or old Persian; modern Persian.
(*c*) **Armenian**, ancient and modern.

B. *The European or West-Aryan Group.*

(*d*) **Greek**, ancient and modern.
(*e*) **Romanic**, including Latin and the neo-Latin languages,—Italian,

[1] Other, but less suitable, names are Indo-European and Indo-Germanic. *Indo-* is too narrow for A, the Asiatic group; and *Germanic* is too narrow for B, the European. "Indo-Germanic," however, has now become the most usual name through the influence of German scholars.

French, Provençal, Spanish, Portuguese, Romansch of the Engadine, and Roumanian of Eastern Europe.

(*f*) **Lettic**: Old Prussian (dead); Lithuanian, still spoken in Eastern Prussia; and Livonian.

(*g*) **Slavonic**: Old Russian; modern Russian; Polish; Bohemian; Bulgarian; Servian.

(*h*) **Celtic**: Welsh or Cymric; Cornish (dead, but not extinct); Gaelic (Highland Scotch); Erse or Irish; Manx (in the Isle of Man); Breton (of Brittany in France).

(*i*) **Teutonic**:[1] Low German (including English); High German.

*Note* 1.—There are two points of distinction between Teutonic and the other Aryan languages: (1) the Teutonic languages have shifted certain consonantal sounds of the Dental, Labial, and Guttural series in the manner described in § 586, and no other Aryan language has done the same. (2) No Aryan language except the Teutonic has formed a Past tense by a dental suffix, *d* or *t* (the Weak conjugation).[2]

*Note* 2.—From the above sketch the student can see what languages are spoken in the British Isles at the present day, viz. English in the whole of England itself, and (in its Scotch dialectal form) in the lower half of Scotland; Cymric or Welsh in Wales; Gaelic in the Highlands of Scotland; Erse in some parts of Ireland; and Manx in the Isle of Man. The four last named are all Celtic.

*Note* 3.—**Cognate, Derived.**—The student can also understand from the above sketch the difference between cognate words and derived words. Words are *cognate* to one another when they have some root that is found in other languages of the same family: thus we have Gothic *fadar* (father), Anglo-Sax. *fæder*, Icelandic *fathir*, Dutch *vader*, Swed. *fader*, Germ. *vater*. All these are cognate within the Teutonic family. Looking to a still wider group, the Aryan, we find *pater* in Latin, *pater* in Greek, *pidar* in Persian, and *pitar* in Sanskrit. These, therefore, are all cognate words with the Teutonic ones. At the bottom of all of them we find a common root *pa*, to feed or protect, and a common suffix *-ter*, which denotes agent. They are all collateral, co-equal, co-radical, or cognate. We cannot say that any one is *derived* from any other.

*Derived* words are on an entirely different footing, and are of two main varieties. (*a*) Those derived from some internal source, as *tell* from *tale* by vowel-mutation, § 452; *timely* from A.S. *tíma* (time), to which the A.S. suffix *-lic* (ly) has been added. (*b*) Those derived from some external or foreign source, as *manual*, from Lat. *manu-s* (hand), to which the Latin suffix *-alis* (al) has been added.

---

[1] The name *Teutonic* is borrowed from Lat. *Teutonicus*. A tribe which the Romans called *Teutoni* invaded Italy in ancient times. The Modern German name is *Deutsch*, which we have Anglicised to *Dutch*. In North America immigrants from any part of Germany are still called *Dutchmen*.

[2] But the *past participial* suffix *-d*, as in "love-*d*," is identical with that of Lat. "ama-*tus*," and is found in many other Aryan languages. This Aryan suffix is called *-to* in Skeat's *Princ. Eng. Etym.* series i. § 253, ed. 1892. It has no connection with the Teutonic suffix *-d* (A.S. *-de*), with which the Past tenses of Weak verbs are formed.

**379. The Teutonic Languages classified.**—These are classified under two main headings,—the Low German and the High German.

### A. *Low German.*

I. **Gothic** or **South-eastern**: the oldest of the extant Teutonic languages, and the most perfect in its inflexional forms: the language or dialect once spoken by the Goths on the lower Danube. The chief work extant in Gothic is a translation of parts of the Bible made in A.D. 350, while the Roman Empire still existed, by Wulfila (better known as Ulphilas), bishop and missionary of the Goths.

II. **Scandian** or **North-eastern**: represented (1) on the *Continent* by the languages of Denmark, Norway, and Sweden, the native homes of the Norse; (2) in *Britain* by the Anglian or *early* Scandian dialect imported by the Angles, who, in the fifth century A.D., colonised the country north of the Humber up to the Highlands of Scotland; (3) in *Britain* again by the Danish or *later* Scandian imported by the Danes, who in the ninth and tenth centuries overspread Northumbria, besides settling in many parts of the eastern side of England to the south of the Humber; (4) in *Iceland*, where the earliest forms of Scandian have been better preserved than elsewhere through the secure and isolated position of that remote island.

III. **Frisio-Saxon** or **Western**: covering the area now known as Holland and Belgium, situated along the lower courses and estuaries of the Elbe, the Weser, and the Rhine.

(*a*) *Saxon:* represented (1) on the *Continent* by Old Saxon, preserved in the "Heliand" (Healer or Saviour), a poem of the ninth century; (2) in *Britain*, by the Wessex dialect, generally known as Anglo-Saxon, that is, the Saxon dialect of the South of England as distinct from the Saxon of the Continent: it has an older and much more abundant literature than its continental sister.

(*b*) *Friesic:* represented (1) on the *Continent* by Old Friesic, of which nothing is now extant earlier than the thirteenth century, though the forms of the language even at this late date are often very archaic; (2) in *Britain* (as has been inferred), by the Old Mercian dialect (so-called from the kingdom of Mercia), spoken between the Humber and the Thames, of which a few much earlier specimens are extant. Of all the languages of the Continent modern Frisian is most like modern English.

(*c*) *Dutch:* the language of Holland; and closely allied to it, the *Flemish* of Flanders and the dialect of Bremen. These are not represented by any dialect in Great Britain, but are near akin to Saxon and Friesic.

*Note.*—Another Low German dialect is the Pomeranian, spoken along the southern coast of the Baltic. Even Old Lombardic was Low German, and in its oldest form very like Anglo-Saxon.

### B. *High German.*

**German.**—High German as distinct from Low German is represented solely by what is known as "German,"—the language of Luther, and the official and literary language of the German Empire. It is called High, because it first appeared in the interior and higher parts of Germany. In many districts of Germany, where High German has become the language of the educated classes, Low German is still spoken by the masses. On the difference between Low German and High, see *Note* 1 to § 380.

**380. Low German origin of English.**—*All* the conquerors of Britain, including (*a*) the Angles, Frisians, and Saxons of the first invasions, (*b*) the Danes and Norse of the later invasions (*c*) the Danes or Normans of the last invasion, were of the Low German stock. Not one of them ever spoke High German. All except the last helped to form the Teutonic portion of the English tongue. The last would have done the same; but it happened that before coming to England they had lived for five or six generations on the north-west coast of France, where they forgot their mother tongue, and became French in speech, though not in blood: hence they contributed very largely towards the Romanic element, which is now numerically greater than the Teutonic, though the words are in less frequent use.

Low German is much more ancient than High. High German was Low German once, and did not begin to exist as a separate branch of the Teutonic languages till after the beginning of the eighth century. But on the Continent of Europe it has now become the more important of the two, and has for several centuries been gaining on its northern rival.

If Low German has lost ground on the Continent of Europe, it has been more than compensated by the great importance of English and its extension to new countries and continents,—America, Australia, India, and South Africa.

*Note* 1.—The shifting of consonants from the Low German to the High is dealt with in § 586, under the heading of **Grimm's Law**. It is there shown that Low German,—the class to which English belongs,—holds an intermediate place between the Aryan or Classical languages (Sanskrit, Latin, Greek, etc.) on the one side, and High German, its modern offshoot, on the other. The notion (not unfrequently expressed) that English is derived from German is putting the cart before the horse, and is in direct opposition to Grimm's Law. We have borrowed only about twenty-four words from German, and of these less than a quarter are in common use: the most common are *swindler*, *plunder*, *meerschaum*, *poodle*, *waltz*.

*Note* 2.—From what has been said in § 379, English is a *mixed* Low German language, mainly based on the Frisian, Mercian, or Midland speech, but at the same time much indebted to the Scandian dialect of the North and the Saxon dialect of the South.

**381. Origin of the names "English" and "England."**—It was among the Angles of Northumbria, especially in York, its capital, that a high standard of literary culture first sprang up in Great Britain; for though Kent became Christian a little earlier and started schools of its own, the small size of the kingdom, and its disastrous wars with Mercia and Wessex, appear to have checked its intellectual growth.

In York, as elsewhere, Latin, or *Læden*, as the Angles called it, was the language of the learned. But books began to be written in the vernacular also; and this vernacular was called *Ænglisc* (or English),—that is, the language of the Angles. Our first poet, Cædmon, the cowherd of Whitby, wrote his poems in *Ænglisc;* and before his death the Venerable Bede translated the Gospel of St. John into the same language.

From the example thus set "English" came to be a general name for all the Teutonic dialects of Britain as distinct from Latin. Even the Wessex or Saxon dialect, in spite of its marked differences from the Anglian and the reputation it received from the hands of Alfred the Great, was often called *Ænglisc* by Alfred himself.

In political as well as literary pre-eminence the Anglian kingdom of Northumbria was the first to come to the front. The first Bretwalda was an Anglian king. Hence the island as a whole was called Ængla-land or England, and the people English.

**382. Periods in the Growth of English.**—The name "English," taken in its widest sense, denotes the language used by the English people from their first settlement in Britain up to the present time, in whatever parts of the world they may have settled since. It has been growing for the last 1400 years, and is now so unlike its earliest forms, that most persons would probably find it harder to learn Anglo-Saxon than to learn French. Yet we must call Anglo-Saxon a form of English, unless we are prepared to deny the name of Englishman to Alfred the Great; for that was the language that he wrote and spoke. Moreover, there are many words that have never altered their form within the historical period, such as *corn*, *lamb*, *nest*, *ram*, *wind*, *hand*, *spell*, *under*, *his*, *him*, *word*, *in*, *bill* (axe), *twist*, *bed*, *gold*, *can*, *blind*, *storm*, *is*, which were so spelt in the seventh century.

The growth of English has been subdivided into three main periods, to each of which approximate dates have been assigned,[1]

[1] Sweet's *Short Historical English Grammar*, p. 1, ed. 1892.

—approximate, because changes in language cannot be other than gradual and continuous:—

I. Old English; from A.D. 450 to about 1200.
II. Middle English; from A.D. 1200 to about 1500.
III. Modern English; from A.D. 1500 to the present time.

Old Eng. has been called the period of *full* endings, Mid. Eng. of *levelled* endings, and Mod. Eng. of *lost* endings.

| | | | | | |
|---|---|---|---|---|---|
| OLD. | leorn-*ian*, | món-*a*, | sun-*ne*, | sun-*u*, | stán-*as*. |
| MID. | lern-*en*, | mon-*e*, | sun-*ne*, | sun-*e*, | ston-*es*. |
| MOD. | learn, | moon, | sun, | son, | stones. |

By *levelled* endings is meant that the vowels *a*, *o*, *u* are all changed or levelled to *e*. By *lost* endings is meant that only a very few of them have remained, and these few have mostly become non-syllabic. Thus *stán-as* (two syllables) has become *stones* (one syllable), and *luf-o-de* or *luf-o-den* (three syllables) has become *loved* (one syllable). In *stones* the *e* is written, not so much for the preservation of the vowel in the levelled suffix *-es*, as because the retention of the *e* was found convenient for giving length to the vowel going before.

## SECTION 2.—OLD ENGLISH.

**383. Dialects of Old English.**—The name "Old English" is simply a general name for the three main dialects which came into literary use in our island, and of which the extant specimens are sufficient to show their respective characteristics.

(1) The **Northumbrian** dialect, spoken north of the Humber, and imported by *Anglian* tribes, who came from what is now called the Duchy of Schleswig; it was afterwards reinforced, but modified, by the language of the *Danes*, a fresh batch of invaders of the same stock as the Angles, viz. Scandinavian. Most of its early literature is lost.

*Note.*—One of the marked peculiarities of this dialect is the retention of its original gutturals. Thus Northerners to this day say *kirk*, *brig*, *rig*, while Midlanders and Southerners say *church*, *bridge*, *ridge*; and the lower classes in Northumberland and Scotland never drop the letter *h* at the beginning of a word. This letter, however, is dropped in Lancashire and Yorkshire, where the Northern dialect has been less perfectly preserved.

(2) The **Mercian** dialect, probably to a large extent of *Frisian* origin, spoken between the Humber and the Thames. On the Continent the Frisians were overlapped by Saxons on the west

and by Angles on the north and east; in England they were overlapped by Angles on the north and by Saxons on the south. This dialect in its most ancient form was more akin to Saxon than to Anglian, though there may have been from the first some northern elements as well as southern in this somewhat mixed dialect. Mercian is the great ancestor of modern standard English, and to this extent is of more importance than either of the other two. Unfortunately, however, most of its early literature is lost.[1]

(3) The **Wessex** dialect, spoken south of the Thames, and imported by *Saxon* tribes, who crossed the Channel from the lower courses of the Rhine and Weser. This was the mother-tongue of Alfred the Great; and an abundant literature has survived. In the *Old* period of English, but not in the Middle, this dialect holds the most prominent place. It had ceased to be used for literary purposes before the Modern period commenced.

*Note.*—There was a fourth dialect of less importance,—the Kentish, very similar to the Wessex dialect,—that is, of a distinctly Southern character,[2] neither Mercian nor Northumbrian.

**384. Frisian Origin of Mercian.**—This point does not rest upon the direct testimony of ancient records, but partly upon the evidence of language, and partly upon the general probabilities of the case.

(*a*) Procopius,[3] an historian of the sixth century A.D., says that in his time Britain was inhabited by three tribes,—Angles, Frisians, and Britons; so that he evidently included Saxons among Frisians. On the other hand, Bede (A.D. 673-735) says that Angles were sprung from Frisians. Frisians, then, were the intermediate tribe, and formed a large contingent of the first

---

[1] It was called *Mercian*, rather than Frisian, from the old kingdom of Mercia which the Frisians founded in England. The name "Mercia" gradually overspread a much larger area than that of the original kingdom. It was derived from the *marches* or borders by which this inland kingdom was surrounded on all sides.

[2] This point is enforced by the author of the article on "English Language" in *Encyclopædia Britannica.* According to Bede, who wrote in Latin, the kingdom of Kent was founded by a tribe called *Geātas.* These have been rashly identified with the Jutes of Jutland, a sub-tribe of Anglians. But the Kentish dialect was not at all Anglian in character. Hence we must suppose either that the identification is wrong, or, if right, that the Anglian dialect in Kent was afterwards so thickly overlaid with Saxon as to have been submerged and lost.

[3] *De Bello Gothico*, iv. 20.

invaders,[1] by whom the foundations of English were laid in this island.

(*b*) "In England, Mercia lies between the Anglian (north of the Humber) and the Saxon (south of the Thames). Abroad, Friesland lies between Scandinavia and Holland. It was only natural that in crossing the sea the Scandinavians (then known as Angles) should make for the north of England, the Saxons (from the coast of Holland) should go southward, while groups of Frisians or East Saxons would make for Essex" (Skeat).[2]

(*c*) The Old Friesic of the Continent resembled the Mercian of England more nearly than it did either the Saxon or the Anglian, as is shown by the extant remains.[3] "At the present day," says another writer, "the most English dialects of the Continent are those of the North Frisian islands of Amrom and Sylt on the west coast of Schleswig."[4] This is corroborative testimony to the fact that the kingdom of Mercia was founded by Frisians, whose dialect (called Mercian after the name of their kingdom) was the forerunner of our Midland dialect, and through this of modern standard English. There is a well-known couplet, every word of which is said to be both Friesic (of the Continent) and English:—

Good butter and good cheese
Is good English and good Fries.

(*d*) Trevisa, a Cornishman who lived in A.D. 1387, says:— "Englishmen *from the beginning* had three manners of speech, Southern, Northern, and Middle speech, as they came of *three manners of people* of Germany."[5] The Southern speech, we know, came from Saxons; the Northern from Angles; the Midland, as we infer, came from Frisians. Evidently there was a long-standing tradition concerning some specific tribe, which gave to the Midland dialect "from the beginning" its specific characteristics of speech. It is certain that by the founders of the "*Middle* speech" he could not have meant the Geātas of Bede, who lived in *Kent*, and whose speech like his own was *Southern*.

---

[1] Freeman, in *Old English History*, pp. 37-39, admits his inability to say how the kingdom of Mercia was founded. To say, as he does, that it was "probably" founded by Angles is mere guessing, and opposed to the testimony of language.

[2] Letter to the Academy, of 14th March 1896.

[3] Examples are given in the Letter to the Academy by Professor Skeat.

[4] *Ency. Brit.*: article on "English Language."

[5] Quoted from Trevisa's *Polychronicon*, in Skeat's *Princ. Eng. Etym.* series i. p. 31, ed. 1892.

*Note.*—Some basis for the fact alleged by Trevisa, that "the Middle" or Mercian speech was founded by a distinct "manner of people from the beginning," may be found in the letter that Canute, the Danish King of England (1016-1035), wrote to his subjects from Rome, in which he prescribes that "the *West Saxons*, the *Mercians*, and the *Danes* are all to keep their own customs."[1] Amongst Danes he evidently included their near kinsmen, the Angles, who with the Danes occupied East Anglia and Northumbria; by the West Saxons he evidently meant the Saxons who lived to the south of the Thames and founded the kingdom of Wessex; by the Mercians he must have meant a people who were *neither Saxons nor Anglo-Danes.* We can best fill up this gap by the hypothesis that they were Frisians, whose tribal name, however, was superseded by that of the great kingdom (Mercia) which they founded.

**385. Anglo-Saxon not convertible with Old English.**—Anglo-Saxon is merely another name for the Wessex dialect, and might conveniently be considered to mean *the Saxon of England* as distinct from *the Saxon of the Continent.*[2] The term is often used, however, as if it were convertible with Old English. But this is a mistake. The Wessex dialect is merely a third part of Old English, and not the whole of it. There are instances in which it fails to give any clue to the origin of modern English words. For example, the Mod. Eng. "*are*" is not derived from A.S. or Wessex "*sindon,*" but from the Mercian "*arun,*" which was itself borrowed from the Northumbrian dialect.

It is worth noticing, too, that the oldest extant specimen of English is in this Northumbrian dialect, and consists of some lines taken from the original Cædmon (see § 381), and preserved in a fly-leaf of the Cambridge MS. of Bede's *Church History.*

The Wessex or A.S. dialect owes its importance to three causes:—(1) The unification of England under Egbert and his successors, whose capital, Winchester, in the kingdom of Wessex, became the capital of England; (2) the influence and example of Alfred the Great, whose books were written in the Wessex dialect; (3) the preservation of a large part of the Wessex literature, while most of the Mercian and Northumbrian literature

---

[1] Freeman's *Old English History*, p. 244.

[2] The name, unless it is so interpreted, is unsuitable and misleading, because it would tend to confound the Anglian dialect with the Saxon. It was first applied to the Wessex dialect by scholars in the sixteenth century, who wished to revive the study of the language used by Alfred the Great. As Alfred the Great called himself *Anglo-Saxonum rex,*—that is, "king of the Angles and Saxons," they called his language *Anglo-Saxon* also; but no such name was ever given to it by Alfred himself or by any other ancient writer.

has been lost. For the earliest forms of most of our English words we have nothing but Anglo-Saxon to go to.

**386. Periods of Anglo-Saxon.**—The Anglo-Saxon literature has been so well preserved, that it is possible to subdivide it into periods:[1]—

| | A.D. A.D. |
|---|---|
| **Early A.S.** (the language of Alfred) . . | 700–900 |
| **Late A.S.** (the language of Ælfric) . . . | 900–1100 |
| **Transitional period** (the language of Layamon)[2] | 1100–1200 |

Alfred the Great, born in 849, superintended the translation into Saxon of the *History of the World* by Orosius, the *Church History* by Bede, the *Consolations of Philosophy* by Boethius, and the *Pastorals* of St. Gregory (all written in Latin). He also superintended the compilation of the early portions of the *Old English Chronicle*.

Ælfric, abbot of Ensham, Oxon, wrote a collection of *Homilies*, the *Lives of the Saints*, and the *Colloquium*, or conversation in Latin with interlinear Saxon.[3] In the Late A.S. the inflexions were not so perfectly preserved as in the Early.

Layamon, a monk who lived near the Severn, wrote a very lengthy poem of some 56,000 lines, called *Brut*, on the kings of Britain, which was not completed till the year 1205 A.D.

**387. Old and Modern English compared.**—Old English is distinguished from Modern by two chief characteristics.

(*a*) It was in the main a *Synthetical* language,—that is, it had a large number of inflexions which Modern English has discarded. "Synthesis" (a word borrowed from Greek) means "adding on." A language is said to be in the Synthetical stage when it expresses the grammatical relations of words by adding some flexional suffix to the stems of Nouns, Adjectives, Pronouns, and Verbs. A language that discards such endings as much as possible, and in their place makes a freer use of prepositions and other auxiliary words, is said to be in the *Analytical* stage. This is the character of Modern English.

(*b*) It was in the main a *pure* language,—that is, it contained very few words that were not of Teutonic origin; whereas Mod. Eng. is extremely composite, much more than half its vocabulary being non-Teutonic. Layamon's *Brut*, though it was written a century and a half after the Norman Conquest, and contains some 56,000 lines, has scarcely 150 French words in it. The number of Latin words admitted before this date

[1] Sweet's *Short Historical English Grammar*, p. 1.

[2] Many call this Transitional period by the name of *Early English*, and connect the two preceding ones under the common name *Old English*.

[3] Earle's *Anglo-Saxon Literature*, pp. 217-222.

amounted to less than 200; and the number of Celtic borrowings did not come to 15.

To show the difference between Old and Modern English, we may compare Genesis ix. 1, as translated by Ælfric, who wrote late in the tenth century, with the authorised translation published in 1611:—

(1) God blets-*o-de* Noe and his sun-*a*, and cwæth hem tó:
(*God blessed Noah and his sons, and quoth them to:*
Weax-*ath* and bé-*oth* gemenigfil-*de* and á-fyll-*ath* th-*á*
*Wax* (ye) *and be* (ye) *manifolded and fill* (ye) *the*
eorth-*an*.
*earth.*)

(2) God bless-ed Noah and his son-s, and said unto them, Be fruitful and multiply, and replenish the earth.

Observe that in (1) every word (barring the Hebrew name *Noe*) is Teutonic; whereas in (2) there are two Romanic words, *multiply* and *replenish*, and one Hybrid or mixed word, *fruitful*. Observe also that in (1) the verbs, adjectives, and nouns have inflexions, which Modern English has discarded.

## SECTION 3.—MIDDLE ENGLISH.

(*Approximate dates*, A.D. 1200-1500.)

**388. Character of Middle English.**—In its Middle period English went through three kinds of change:—

(*a*) The Mercian dialect, or Midland, as we should now call it, became eventually predominant in the place of the Wessex or Southern, which up to the Norman Conquest and for two centuries afterwards had held the first place.

(*b*) Many of the vowel sounds were changed; those of the old inflexions that were not lost were "levelled" (§ 382); the lost inflexions were replaced by a freer use of form-words,—prepositions and auxiliary verbs; many Strong verbs were replaced by Weak ones.

(*c*) A very great addition was made to the vocabulary. A large number of French words, which for about 200 years had been used only by the clergy and the upper classes and in the law courts, filtrated at last into the native speech, where much of it became permanently fixed as part of our English vocabulary. The absorption of all this French facilitated the introduction of fresh relays of Latin, which throughout the Middle Ages continued to be the language of the learned and of the Church.

**389. Dialects of Middle English.**—The three main dialects were the same as in the Old period; but instead of calling them Northumbrian, Mercian, and Wessex (or Anglo-Saxon), it is now more appropriate to call them Northern, Midland, and Southern.

One good test for distinguishing the three dialects is the ending of the Present Plural Indicative. The Northern had *-es*, as sing-*es* (we, you, or they sing); the Southern had *-eth*, as sing-*eth* (we, you, or they sing); the Midland had *-en* or *-e*, as sing-*en* or sing-*e* (we, you, or they sing). Another flexional test lies in the form of the Pres. Part.; the Northern had *-and*, the Midland *-ende*, the Southern *-inde*, the last of which was eventually changed to *-ing*, and superseded the other two.

Another characteristic point of difference between the three dialects is that the Northern was the most tenacious of the old *sounds* and the Southern of the old *inflexions*. The Northern, for example, stuck, and still sticks, to the old guttural *k* or *g*, which in the Southern became *ch* or *j*, as in *church*, *bridge*, for the earlier *kirk*, *brig*. The Midland followed the South in discarding some of the earlier consonantal sounds, and the North in discarding the earlier inflexions.

**390. Literary decline of the Southern Dialect.** — The Southern dialect lost, through the Norman Conquest, though not till some time after, the political and literary supremacy that it had enjoyed under kings of its own race; and Winchester, the old capital of England, fell into the second rank. The last book of any importance written in the Southern dialect was Trevisa's translation of the *Polychronicon*, made in A.D. 1387 (alluded to in § 384).

As a *spoken* language the Southern dialect is not even now extinct among the peasantry. The rustic dialect that may still be heard in the south of England is the modernised descendant of King Alfred's "Wessex." A few years ago an attempt was made to revive it in the *Dorsetshire Poems* by William Barnes.

**391. The Northern Dialect.**—The Danish Conquest, which north of the Humber was more complete than anywhere to the south of it excepting in East Anglia, did much to unsettle the inflexions of this dialect, just as the Norman Conquest did those of the other two dialects later on. In and before the twelfth century the final *-n* of the Infinitive was dropping off; the *-eth* of the third person Singular was assuming its modern form *-es*; the final *-e* at the end of nouns (which was syllabic in the

Midland dialect) was becoming mute or disappearing. In fact, by the thirteenth century the Northern dialect had become almost as flexionless as Modern English.

A few more peculiarities of the Northern dialect may here be mentioned, in addition to those given in § 383 (1), *Note* :—

(1) It very rarely employed the suffix *-n* or *-en* for forming the Plurals of nouns, whereas in the Southern this was the commonest form of all. The Northern had only about four such Plurals—*eghen* (eyes), *hosen*, *oxen*, and *schoon* (shoes).

(2) On the other hand, it preserved with great care the final *-en* of the Past Part. of Strong verbs': thus *broke* for *broken*, though common in the Midland dialect, is hardly ever found in the Northern.

(3) It employed only the suffix *-s* (as in Modern English) for forming the Genitive Singular of nouns of any gender, whereas the Southern dialect kept up for a long time the use of the suffix *-e* for forming the Genitive of Feminine nouns.

(4) It formed the Pres. Part. in *-and*, while the Midland formed it in *-ende*, and the Southern in *-inde* (see § 389).

(5) It never used the prefix *ge* (softened down to *i* or *y* in the Middle English period) for forming the Past Participle of verbs, whereas the Southern dialect long continued to use it, as in *y-broke* or *y-broken*.

(6) The Northern dialect used the preposition *at* before the Gerundial Infinitive, while the Southern used *to*. Our noun *a-do* (=at do) is a relic of this.

On those peculiarities of the Northern dialect which have been traced to Danish influence, see § 393.

What is called the Lowland Scotch is the best living representative of the Northern dialect; and the poems of Burns, written not much more than 100 years ago, are its best literary specimen in modern times. The same dialect, but in a less marked form, is still spoken in the northern counties of England. Not many years since it was reproduced as a literary curiosity in Tennyson's "Northern Farmer"; and still more recently by Mary Beaumont in *Joan Seaton*, a story of Yorkshire dales, written in the North Riding dialect.

A line of Scotch poets, commencing with James I. (of Scotland), A.D. 1394-1437, and ending with Sir David Lyndsay, who died in A.D. 1555, was largely influenced by our great Midland poet, Chaucer (§ 392), from whom they borrowed not only their metres, but many peculiarities of phraseology and style, and even of grammar; see *Note* to § 403.

**392. The Midland Dialect.**—What is now the language of the British Empire is not the descendant of the language of Alfred the Great nor of that of Bede the Northumbrian, but of the Mercian or Midland dialect spoken between the Humber and the Thames. The predominance of this dialect was determined by several causes:—

(*a*) London, the city of ships floating on its broad river, was marked out by nature to be the capital of England. However cultivated Winchester or York might be, the literary life of the nation would eventually centre round the capital. "It is a curious reflection," says Professor Skeat, "that if London had been built on the south side of the river, the speech of the British Empire and of the greater part of North America would probably have been very different from what it is."[1] The Midland or London dialect was the language of the supreme law-courts and of the political and commercial activity of the nation. The last two chapters of the *Old English Chronicle*, which was commenced by King Alfred in his own (the Wessex) dialect, were written up to A.D. 1154 at Peterborough, within the Midland area, and in the Midland dialect. In this dialect was issued, in the reign of Henry III. (A.D. 1258), a proclamation for summoning a parliament from all the counties of England — the first occasion since the Conquest on which English was officially used in preference to French. This was the language in which Wycliff wrote his translation of the Bible, and in which Chaucer, himself a Londoner, raised English poetry to a height of excellence that has hardly been surpassed since. The Universities of Oxford and Cambridge lay within the Midland area. All dialects met in towns like Oxford, Cambridge, and London; and hence the Midland dialect has borrowed from both the others. Thus the phrase "they are" is of Northern origin; the phrase "he hath" is of Southern. The Midland adopted both.

(*b*) Apart from the advantages of its position and the great influence exercised by the writings of Chaucer and Wycliff, the

[1] *Princ. Eng. Etym.* series i. p. 29, ed. 1892. Opinions differ as to what was the dialect *first* spoken in London. Mr. Oliphant (see *Standard English*) thinks that it was originally a form of Saxon or Southern dialect; and that the East Midland dialect, after taking hold of Oxford and Cambridge, crept down to the south, conquering all the dialects on its way, and finally seized on London, where it absorbed and superseded the original Saxon. This opinion appears to be based on the hypothesis that London, being situated in Middle-*sex*, must have had at first a *Saxon* dialect. But it has been shown in § 384 that the *East Saxons* and *Middle Saxons* may have been a tribe of Frisians, speaking a Mercian or Midland dialect from the first.

Midland dialect possessed certain linguistic peculiarities sufficient to suggest the probability of its ultimate ascendancy. (1) It contained fewer Scandian or Danish words than the Northern, but more than the Southern. (2) Its grammar, though more complex than that of the Northern, was less complex than that of the Southern. (3) It received a much larger number of French words than the Northern; and no dialect that aimed at becoming the national standard for speaking and writing could dispense with French, which for more than 200 years had been the language of the court and the government. (4) Being the intermediate dialect, it was intelligible to Northerners and Southerners alike, when these were often not intelligible to each other. "The Mercians," says Trevisa, A.D. 1387, "who are men of the Middle of England, being as it were partners with the extremities, better understand the side-languages, Northern and Southern, than Northern and Southern understand each other."

(*c*) Near the close of the Middle period, the Mercian or Midland dialect was the only one patronised by the printing presses,—the new appliance which Caxton introduced into England in 1477. Henceforth any Englishman who thought he could write something worth reading wrote it in the Midland dialect, which had now become the literary language of the nation and was destined to become that of the empire.

*Note* 1.—The Midland dialect exhibited two sub-dialects, the Eastern and the Western. It is from the former rather than the latter that Mod. Eng. has chiefly sprung. The Eastern sub-dialect borrowed freely from the Northern Dialect spoken in East Anglia and eventually superseded it there, and its area included the important cities of Oxford, Cambridge, and London.

*Note* 2.—The stages of the Midland dialect have been roughly subdivided into three periods as follows:[1]—

| | A.D. |
|---|---|
| **Early**: (Orm's *Ormulum*) . . . . . | 1200–1300 |
| **Late**: (Robert of Brunne, Mandeville, Wycliff, Chaucer, who died in 1400) . . . | 1300–1400 |
| **Transitional period**: (Malory, Caxton) . . | 1400–1500 |

Compare the three periods of Old English in § 386, and the three periods of English as a whole in § 382.

**393. Danish Influence.**—The Danes, as the student is aware (§ 379, II.), were of the same stock as the Angles,—Scandinavian, not Frisian or Saxon. But they settled in

[1] Sweet's *Short Historical English Grammar*, p. 1, ed. 1892. The influence of Caxton on Mod. Eng. has hardly been sufficiently recognised.

England about 500 years later than their Anglian kinsmen, and they came from a different part of Scandinavia,[1]—both of which facts would tend to account for some variation of dialect. Thus when Danes settled as they did in great force in East Anglia, and in still greater force north of the Humber, the Angles, in their intercourse with Danes, lost some of the inflexions of their own dialect. Since the stems of the words were the same on either side, the men of one tribe could make themselves better understood by those of the other if they dropped their inflexions than if they retained them. Thus out of the Anglian *sun-u* and the Danish *sun-r* the more simple word *son-e* (now pronounced as *sun*) was formed. The same kind of process is now going forward in the United States, where German immigrants, settled among English-speaking people, find it convenient to strip their German words of their inflexions, so as to adapt them more easily to English speech. This accounts for the early date at which the Northern dialect of English became almost flexionless; see § 391. After about 1250 A.D., the Midland dialect, which in its original Frisian or Mercian form was more like the Saxon spoken south of the Thames, borrowed more from the Northern than from the Southern. The Danish conquests of Mercia and East Anglia must have materially helped to assimilate the Midland to the Northern speech. The following are examples of Northern influence:—

**Same.**—In the Northern and Midland this took the place of the Southern *thilke*.

**Are.**—In the Northern and Midland this took the place of the Southern *sindon*.

**They, their, them.**—All these came from the Northern dialect, and were adopted by the Midland, in preference to *hi*, *heora*, *hem*, the old Plurals of *he*.

**Till.**—This Prep. is of Scandian origin, and was borrowed by the Midland dialect from the Northern.

*Note.*—The words *that*, *ours*, *yours*, and *she* have also been ascribed to Northern influence. But the first three are Anglo-Saxon,

---

[1] The first and earliest batch of Scandians, known in history as Angles, came from that part of the peninsula of Denmark that is nearest the Elbe.

The second batch, known in history as Danes, came from regions lying further north,—that is, from Jutland, the islands of Denmark, and South Sweden.

A third and last batch, less known in history, came from Norway, and colonised the Orkneys, the Western Islands, the Isle of Man, and parts of Lancashire, Cumberland, and Ireland.

and *scæ* (the earliest form of *she*) is found in the later chapters of the *Saxon Chronicle*, written in Peterborough in the Midland dialect; see below §§ 496, 505, and 506.

As to the effect of the Danish Conquest on our vocabulary, the two languages, the Scandian and the Saxon, were so much alike at bottom, that they melted imperceptibly into one:—

*House* is A.S., but *husband* is Scand.; *drop* (Trans.) is A.S., but *drip* (Intrans.) is Scand.; *shoot* is A.S., but *scud* and *scuttle* are Scand.; *blow* (with *blossom*) is A.S., but *bloom* is Scand.; *sit* is A.S., but *seat* is Scand.; *woe* is A.S., but *wail* is Scand.; *bite* is A.S., but *bait* (its Causal form) is Scand.; *ride* is A.S., but *raid* is Scand., and yet *road* (another noun-form) is A.S.; *true* is A.S., but *trust* and *tryst* are Scand., while *truth* (another noun-form) is A.S.; *weigh* is A.S., but *wag* is Scand., and yet *wain* is A.S.; *rise* is A.S., but *raise* (a Causal form) is Scand.; *knee* is A.S., but *kneel* is Scand.; *gird* and *girdle* are A.S., but *girth* is Scand.; *slay* is A.S., but *slaughter* is Scand.; *strike* (in the sense of "go") is A.S., but *streak* is Scand.; *gleam* is A.S., but *glimmer* is Scandian.

It sometimes happens that we get the *sound* of a word from Southern, and its *sense* from Northern. Thus "dream" is phonetically from A.S. *dréam* (Mid. Eng. *dreem*), which in A.S. did not signify "dream," but "joy," "happiness." But the Norse word *draumr* meant "dream" and nothing else.

**394. The Norman Conquest.**—The Norman Conquest, the greatest event in our political history, was likewise the greatest in the history of our language. For a long time the two languages, French and English, kept almost entirely apart, like a couple of rivers flowing side by side in parallel streams within the same banks. "The way in which the French-speaking Dane was so long kept apart, by the mere accident of language, from his English cousin, is one of the most curious facts in history" (Skeat). The English of A.D. 1200 is almost as free from French words as that of 1050.

It was not till after 1300 that French words began to be incorporated in large numbers. But by this time English had made itself the daily speech of the upper classes, as it always had been of the lower, while French was going more and more out of daily use. The incorporation was very complete. Such words as *grace*, *peace*, *fame*, *beef*, *ease* (all of French origin) appear now to be as much a part of our original language as *kindness*, *rest*, *shame*, *ox*, *care*, all of which are native words that were in common use in the time of Alfred the Great.

Though English had some sounds unknown to French and *vice versâ*, yet most of the vowels and consonants common to both were at that time pronounced in the same way; and this made the fusion of the two languages all the more easy and complete.

**395. Struggle between French and English.**—English, in spite of the degradation that it received from the Norman Conquest, never ceased to be used as a literary language. Books continued to be written in English as before, and the stream of literature never ran dry. In the Monastery of Peterborough the *Old English Chronicle* (commenced in about 879 under the direction of Alfred the Great) was written up by two successive hands to the death of Stephen in 1154. "Within two generations after the Conquest, faithful pens were at work transliterating the old *Homilies* of Ælfric into the neglected idiom of his posterity" (*Ency. Brit.*). The huge poem of 56,000 lines, known as Layamon's *Brut*, was not completed before the year 1205.

In 1204 the loss of Normandy, by separating England from France, broke the connection between the French and the Anglo-Norman aristocracies. In 1215 a combination of English and Norman barons forced King John to sign the Magna Charta. In 1258 English was officially used for the first time since the Conquest, in the celebrated proclamation issued in the name of Henry III. for summoning a parliament of *barons* from all parts of England; which shows that French had ceased to be the only language spoken and read by the Anglo-Norman nobles. In 1349, three years after the victory at Crecy, it was ruled that Latin should be no longer taught in England through the medium of French. In 1362 it was ruled that all pleadings in the law courts should be conducted in English, for the reason (as stated in the preamble to the Act), "that French has become much unknown in the realm." We may safely say that by the year 1400 French was not much spoken in England. A vast English literature had sprung up in the interim, which was as popular in the halls of nobles as in the humbler dwellings of knights and burgesses.

**396. French Influence on English Grammar.**—The only influence of French on English grammar was to accelerate the change from Synthetical to Analytical; in fact, it did for the Midland and Southern dialects what the Danish language had already done for the Northern. We say *accelerate* designedly; for the change would have come in any case, though possibly neither so rapidly nor so completely as it did, without the help of French. Symptoms of the change had shown themselves clearly enough before French influence had begun to work, and even to some extent before the Conquest. In Layamon's *Brut*, which shows no signs of French influence and contains *very few* words of French origin, the "levelled" inflexions of the Middle period begin to be seen side by side with the full inflexions of Old English. The growing tendency of English was to strengthen the accent on the *first* syllable, so that the last syllable, containing the inflexion, was slurred over or lightly sounded. Thus, forms like *nam-a* (name), *sun-u* (son), became *nam-e*, *sun-e*. In the same way all unaccented vowels in the final syllable excepting *i* were "levelled" or assimilated to *e*, so that *-an*, *-as*, *-ath*, *-on*, *-od* became *-en*, *-es*, *-eth*, *-en*, and *-ed*. Adjectives of French origin seldom took English inflexions, which helped English adjectives to discard theirs.

*Note.*—For some time past there has been a traditional tendency to ascribe our plural suffix *-es* partly, if not principally, to French influence, in supersession of the A.S. *-an*. Even this, however, cannot now be conceded. "It is quite true that the *as* was originally only the plural of *one* declension of *Masc.* nouns, and that the A.S. suffix *-an* was originally rather more common. But the extension of *-as* (which became *-es*) to some of the other declensions set in rather early, say before 1100, at any rate before French had produced any effect on our language. We have now abundant evidence to show (and Prof. Napier has shown it) that the plural in *-es* was overwhelmingly common by 1200. It was pre-eminently common in the Midland dialect, as seen in the later chapters of the *Saxon Chronicle*, that were written in Peterborough up to the death of Stephen. It had nothing whatever to do with French, as we were all taught to believe. Very likely French influence drove the nail home; but it did not put the nail in its place, nor give the initial blows" (Skeat). See also Sweet's *English Grammar*, § 989.

**397. Teutonic Preponderance in English Grammar.**—The grammatical structure of our language was as strictly Teutonic by the close of the Middle period as it had been before the Conquest, notwithstanding the shock that it had received in the interim. The Teutonic elements are noted below:—

(*a*) *Grammatical forms*:—

(1) Noun-inflexions; the possessive *-'s*, plural in *-en*, plural in *-s*.

(2) All pronoun-inflexions.

(3) All verb-inflexions; the personal endings *-st*, *-th*, and *-s*; tense endings *-d* and *-t*; participial endings *-en* and *-ing*; gerundial ending *-ing*.

(4) Adjective suffixes *-er* and *-est* marking degrees of comparison; and the auxiliary words *more* and *most* used for the same purpose.

(5) All the suffixes used for forming adverbs, and many of those used for forming verbs.

(*b*) *Grammatical words*:—

(1) All nouns forming the Plural by vowel-change.

(2) Almost all nouns having the same form for the Plural as for the Singular.

(3) All the pronouns,—Personal, Demonstrative, Relative, and Interrogative.

(4) All the Demonstrative adjectives,—*the, this, that, other, such,* etc.

(5) All the Numerals except *second, dozen, million, billion, trillion.*

(6) All the Distributive adjectives.

(7) All adjectives of irregular comparison.

(8) All Strong verbs (except *strive* and possibly one or two more).

(9) All Weak verbs, excepting *catch*, that have different vowels in the Pres. and Past tenses.

(10) All Auxiliary verbs.

(11) All Defective and Anomalous verbs.

(12) The old Causative verbs, viz. those formed by vowel-change.

(13) Almost all the prepositions.

(14) Almost all the conjunctions.

(15) Most of the adverbs of Time and Place.

(16) All pronominal adverbs.

It is easy to make sentences on ordinary subjects without using a single word of French or Latin origin. But it is very difficult to make the shortest English sentence out of French or Latin words, and wherever such words are used, they are forced to submit to all the duties and liabilities of English ones.

**398. French Influence on the English Vocabulary.**—The Norman Conquest established in England a foreign court, a foreign aristocracy, and a foreign hierarchy. The French language, in its Norman dialect, became for a time the only polite medium of intercourse. The native tongue, at first despised as the language of a subject race, was left for a time to the use of boors and serfs. Words denoting the commonest and most familiar objects,[1] such as the elements, the seasons, divisions of

[1] But it is possible to underrate the influence of French in furnishing names even for common and familiar objects. Elements: *air* is French. Seasons: *autumn* is Latin. Divisions of time: *hour, minute, second* are French. Natural scenery: *valley, mountain, gravel, river, torrent, fountain* are French. Kinship: *uncle, aunt, nephew, niece* are French; and *grandfather, grandmother* are half French. Parts of a house: *brick, lintel, storey, attic, ceiling, tile,* etc., are French; and *door-post* is half French. Food: *beef, mutton, veal, venison,* etc., are French. Clothing: *gown, coat, chemise, trousers,* etc., are French. Agricultural implements: *hatchet, hoe, coulter* are French. Agricultural processes: "*turn* the *soil,*" *manure, fruit, herb, vegetable, cole, cauli-flower, cabbage, grain, granary, stable, car* are French. Trees and plants: *damson, chestnut, almond, laurel, bay, mustard,* etc., are French. Colours: *blue, violet, lake, crimson, carmine, mauve* are French.

time, natural scenery, soils and metals, the closest kinds of kinship, parts of a house, food and clothing, agricultural implements and processes, trees and plants, quadrupeds, birds, water animals, insects, parts of the body, actions and postures, etc., are to this day, in a large number of instances (though not by any means exclusively), of Teutonic origin.

A few generations after the Conquest, when English began to be used for general literature in the place of French, most of the terms at hand to express ideas above those of daily life were to be found in the French of the privileged and learned classes, who, for the past two centuries, had had the chief control of art, science, and law. Hence each successive literary effort of the reviving English tongue shows a large adoption of French words to supply the place of the forgotten native ones. Thus in general literature we have *ancestors* for *fore-elders*, *beauty* for *fair-hood*, *caution* for *fore-wit*, *conscience* for *in-wit*, *library* for *book-hoard*, *obstructive* for *hindersome*, *remorse* for *ayen-bite* (=again-bite), etc. (For examples of borrowings in Law, Government, Feudalism, etc., see below in § 418.)

Another effect of French on the English vocabulary was to give it a dualistic or *bilingual* character. Thus nouns or adjectives often go in pairs; as *foe, enemy; hostile, inimical; home, domicile; homely, domestic; unlikely, improbable; bold, courageous*, etc. Sometimes a Romanic adjective is given to a Teutonic noun; as *bovine, ox; oval, egg; human, man*, etc. Verbs, too, often go in pairs; as *cast out, eject; be, exist; buy back, redeem*, etc.

At one time there seems to have been a habit of using words in pairs, one Teutonic and the other Romanic. Thus, at the beginning of the Prayer-book we have "*acknowledge* and *confess*"; "*sins* and *wickedness*"; "not *dissemble* nor *cloke*"; "*humble, lowly*"; "*assemble* and *meet together*"; "*pray* and *beseech*." All these pairs of words mean the same thing; and in each pair one is Teutonic and the other Romanic.

**399. Other Results of French Influence.**—To French influence combined with Latin we owe certain other effects besides those already named:—

(*a*) *Word-building.*—We owe to this influence a very large number of prefixes and suffixes, many of which are still in living use for forming new words. Our Romanic suffixes are even more numerous than our Teutonic ones. The French fem. suffix *-ess* superseded the Teutonic *-ster*. We have also many hybrid words, in which Teutonic and Romanic elements are compounded; as *cott-age* (from A.S. *cote*, "hut," + *age*, Fr. suffix). Our language thus gained in wealth as much as it lost in purity.

(*b*) *Spelling.*—The chief, perhaps the only, harm that French did to our language was to disturb the phonetic spelling that it possessed in its earliest form. (Some account of this will be found in §§ 456, 457.) It is to French that we owe the unnecessary compound *qu* (the function of which was served equally well by our own *cw* in A.S.), the sibilant sound of *c* before the vowels *e* and *i*, the sound of *g* as *j* before the same vowels, and the use of the letter *i* as a consonant to denote the sound now expressed by *j*. Thus almost all words containing a *j* are of French or other foreign origin.

### SECTION 4.—MODERN ENGLISH.

**400. Commencement of the Modern Period.**—The period of Modern English begins somewhere about A.D. 1500, or a little later. The commencement of this period was preceded or accompanied by several great events, which, in other countries besides England, mark the commencement of Modern as distinct from Medieval history. The art of printing was introduced into England in 1477 by Caxton, who learnt it from the Dutch. Columbus discovered the West Indies in 1492, which led to the discovery of the American continent soon after. Vasco de Gama rounded the Cape of Good Hope in 1497, which brought Southern Asia in touch for the first time with the western nations of Europe. The Renaissance or Revival of Learning opened up new fields of research; and in 1497 Erasmus, the Dutchman, one of the foremost champions of the new learning, visited England, and took up his residence here for a time. Greek began to be studied for the first time in the English Universities. Luther had just begun to lecture in Germany, when Henry VII., the first of our Tudor kings, died on 21st April A.D. 1509.

**401. Characteristics of Modern English.**—The Modern form of English is distinguished from those that preceded it by two main characteristics:—

(*a*) Our language has now become almost entirely *analytical*; as analytical, in fact, as it is ever likely to be, and more analytical than any other modern language in Europe. All the Old English and Middle English inflexions, excepting the few that still remain, have disappeared. Final *e*, which in the Middle period was syllabic, has either disappeared or is retained to give length to the preceding vowel. The plural and genitive suffixes of nouns have ceased to be syllabic, except when the preceding consonant happens to be of such a kind as to compel the sounding of the final *-es*. Ben Jonson, the dramatist, who wrote a treatise on English grammar, lamented the loss of the plural suffix *-en* in verbs (see § 389, where it is shown that *-en* was the Plural inflexion of the Midland dialect). But the lamentation was in vain; for the suffix had gone beyond recovery. The fact that this suffix, together with the suffix *e* (levelled from *a*, *o*, *u*, see § 382), disappeared *after* Anglo-French had ceased to operate, shows that the tendency to discard inflexions was inherent in the language itself, and was merely accelerated, not produced, by foreign influences.[1]

(*b*) The Modern period is marked by a large number of new borrowings, and these from a great variety of sources. The study of Greek, introduced into England with the revival of learning, led to the influx of a considerable number of Greek words, in addition to such as had been previously borrowed through the medium of Latin. "Surrey, Wiat, and others introduced a knowledge of Italian literature, which soon had a great effect, especially on the drama. Several Italian words came in through this and other influences, either directly or through the medium of French. The discoveries of Columbus and the opening up of the New World brought us into contact with Spanish, and many names of things obtained from the West Indies came to us in a Spanish form. The English victories in India, beginning with the battle of Plassy in 1757, made us acquainted with numerous East Indian words; and English maritime adventure has brought us words from nearly all parts of the world. During the resistance of the Netherlands to Spain, in the time of Elizabeth, English borrowed several words from Dutch: it was not uncommon for English volunteers to go over to Holland to

---

[1] Two proofs have now been given that French influence on English grammar even *indirectly* was really very little,—much less than it has been represented:—(1) In the *Note* to § 396, it has been shown that the plural inflexion *-es* (traditionally ascribed to a large extent to French influence) had begun to take possession of English nouns and oust other plural inflexions *before* French influence had begun to work. In fact, it was our English *-es* that compelled French nouns to change their *-s* into *-es*, so as to bring them into conformity with our own (see below, § 483, *Note* 1). (2) In § 401 it has been shown that the inflexions of Middle English did not begin to drop off until *after* French influence had ceased to operate.

aid in the repulse of the Spaniards. English has also borrowed, chiefly in very recent times, from German, and even from remote continental languages, including Russian, and even Turkish and Hungarian. In fact, there are few languages from which we have failed to borrow words either directly or indirectly. It often requires a little patience to discover from what foreign language a word has been borrowed, and at what period. It is some help to remember that most of the words taken from remote and somewhat unlikely sources have been borrowed during the Modern period, *i.e.* since 1500" (Skeat).

**402. Subdivisions of the Modern Period.**—The Modern period can be subdivided into three stages or periods:—

I. Tudor English, from about 1500 to 1625, the date of the death of James I. Speaking roughly, its literature may be called that of the sixteenth century, though it goes some twenty-five years beyond it.

II. The English of the remainder of the seventeenth century, which comes to an end with Dryden, who died in A.D. 1700. The language of Milton abounds in Latinisms and other idioms, which are not now admissible. The age of Dryden is marked by a large number of borrowings from Modern French, a good deal of which is not even yet fully assimilated. It is also marked by the thorough establishment for the first time of "*its*" as the Possessive form of "*it*."

III. The remaining period up to the present day. One main difference between the two centuries represented by I. and II. on the one hand, and the two which have succeeded it on the other, is that "the former is the period of experiment and comparative licence both in the importation of new words and in the formation of idioms and grammatical constructions. The latter period, on the other hand, is marked by selection and organisation" (Sweet). The grammar of Shakspeare is in some points so unlike that of the present day that it has been found necessary for a modern scholar (Dr. Abbott) to publish a "Shakspearian Grammar" explaining its peculiarities. The forms and inflexions used by Shakspeare and his contemporaries are, however, strictly modern.

Another marked difference consists in the great change in the vowel-sounds which took place in the sixteenth and seventeenth centuries. This change, however, has been completely disguised by the absence of a corresponding change in the spelling (see Chapter xxiii.). If one of Shakspeare's plays were now acted with the pronunciation that was current in his own day, it would be difficult, if not impossible, for the audience to understand it.

**403. Decay of Dialects.**—In Old and Middle English we were forced to recognise three distinct literary dialects,—the Anglian, the Mercian, and the Wessex in the Old period, answering to the Northern, the Midland, and the Southern in the Middle period.

In Modern English, owing to the complete ascendancy of the Midland dialect, which before the close of the Middle period had left no rivals in the field, we recognise only one language, viz. that of Modern English literature.

Provincial dialects still exist in different parts of England. We may still hear *housen* for *houses* in Wiltshire and Dorsetshire, *brig* for *bridge* in some parts of Yorkshire. But such dialects are no longer literary, or are revived merely as literary curiosities, as in Barnes's *Dorsetshire Poems*, or Tennyson's "Northern Farmer" in imitation of the Lincolnshire dialect.

The only English dialect that survived for some time longer in literary form was what we now call Lowland Scotch, though this is really nothing but a modern form of the old Northern dialect (see § 391). Burns's poetry is mostly written in this dialect, and is its best modern representative.

*Note.*—From 1422 to 1555 there were three Scotch poets who wrote under the influence of our great Midland poet Chaucer, and under this influence introduced some of the peculiarities of the Midland dialect into their own Northern. James I. (of Scotland) was a prisoner in England for nineteen years. Here he wrote his great poem the *King's Quair* (the quire or book of the king), in close imitation of Chaucer, whose seven-lined stanza has been called the "Rime Royal" after the use made of it by the Scotch king. When the king returned to his own country, his example was followed by Henryson (1480-1508), who wrote a poem called *Testament of Cresseid*, intended to be a continuation of Chaucer's *Troilus.* (It was followed, but to a less degree, by Dunbar, 1465-1529, and by Gavin Douglas, 1474-1522.) Lastly, Sir David Lyndsay (1490-1555), wrote a poem called the *Dreme* in the manner of our old English poet. All these poems contain some Chaucerisms, which influenced not only the phraseology, but the grammar of the Northern dialect.

## CHAPTER XXII.—BORROWINGS.

### SECTION 1.—CELTIC.

**404. Fewness of Celtic borrowings.**—The Celtic borrowings were *very few*, much fewer than has been supposed. Those Britons who were not killed or ousted by the invading English were so completely conquered, that they had every motive for acquiring the new speech and forgetting their own. We are not even sure whether the bulk of them still spoke Celtic; for many had come to speak a rustic kind of Latin, as in Gaul.

Most of the words supposed to have been borrowed by English from Celtic, and still quoted as Celtic in some books, are now known to have been borrowed the other way.[1] The following are a few examples of these mistaken etymologies:[2]—

Balderdash (origin doubtful, certainly not Celtic).
Barrow (A.S. *beorg*, hill).
Bill (A.S. *bill*, axe).
Chine (Fr. *échine*, backbone).
Cower (Sc. *kúr-a*, to doze).
Crimp (Du. *krimp-en*).
Crisp (A.S. *crisp*; Lat. *crisp-us*, curled).
Cudgel (A.S. *cycgel*).
Dainty (O. Fr. *daintie*; Lat. *dignitat-em*).
Filly (Sc. *fylja*, female foal).
Flaw (Sc. *flag-a*, a crack).
Fleam (Fr. *flamme*; Gr. *phlebotomia*, blood-letting).
Frieze (Fr. *frize*, called after Friesland).
Fudge (Low Germ. *futsch*).
Funnel (Breton *founil*; Lat. *infundibul-um*).

**405. Geographical Names** of Celtic origin:—

**Avon** (river).—There are said to be fourteen rivers in Great Britain bearing the name of *Avon*.

**Exe, Esk, Axe, Ux** (river).—In Scotland there are said to be eight rivers called *Esk*. In England we have *Ex*-eter, *Ax*-minster, *Ux*-bridge, and the river *Ouse*, a softened form of *Usk*.

**Aber** (mouth of a river): *Aber*-deen, *Aber*-ystwith, *Aber*-gavenny, *Ber*-wick (for *Aber*-wick).

**Car, Caer** (castle): *Car*-lisle, *Car*-diff, *Caer*-narvon, *Caer*-marthen.

**Llan** (sacred enclosure): *Llan*-daff, *Lam*-peter (in Wales).

**Combe** (hollow in a hill-side): Addis-*combe*, Ilfra-*combe*, Wy-*combe*.

**Lin** (pool): *Lin*-ton, *Lin*-dale.

**Strath** (broad valley): *Strath*-clyde, *Strath*-mere.

**Pen, Ben** (mountain): *Pen*-rith, *Pen*-zance, *Ben*-Nevis, *Ben*-Lomond, *Pen*-dragon; cf. *Pen*-nine range.

**Inch** (island): *Inch*-cape.

**406. Names of Objects.**—Examples are given below:[3]—

(1) Before the Conquest:—*brock* (a badger), *crock* (hence *crockery*), *dun* (brown), *taper* (?) (a small wax candle). (Number of words very small.)

---

[1] This has been proved by Professor Rhys.

[2] Tested by Skeat's *Concise Etymological Dictionary*.

[3] Selected from Skeat's *Princ. Eng. Etym.* series i. chap. xxii. ed. 1892. Since the date of this publication the author, as he informs me, has seen reason to exclude many of the words that he then believed to be Celtic. Some of those given under (2) are still very doubtful. Further research tends to reduce more and more the number of words once supposed to be Celtic; and we must now exclude the following words, all of

(2) After the Conquest, from about 1250 A.D.:—*bald*, *bog* (quagmire), *brag*, *brat*, *bump*, *clock* (orig. a bell), *crag* (rock), *cub* (whelp), *curd* (of milk), *nook*, *plod*, *rub*, *skip*, *prop* (support), *ribbon*. (Many of these, however, are doubtful: see footnote 3 in p. 247.)

(3) From Welsh:—*cam* (crooked, *Shaks.*), *cromlech* (stone monument), *Druid*, *flannel*, *gag* (stop the mouth), *gull* (sea-bird), *hassock* (footstool), *hawk* (clear the throat), *lag* (slack, backward), *toss* (to throw), *bard* (poet).

(4) From Scotch:—*cairn*, *clan*, *claymore* (kind of sword), *galloway* (small horse), *gillie* (a boy, page), *pibroch* (martial tune), *plaid*, *reel* (Highland dance), *whiskey*.

(5) From Irish:—*brogue* (wooden shoe), *colleen* (a little girl), *fun*, *mug* (cup), *shamrock* (a trefoil), *shanty* (small mean dwelling), *tory* (a hostile pursuer, first used in a political sense in 1680).

## SECTION 2.—DANISH OR LATER SCANDIAN.

**407. Danish borrowings.**—Danish words were used in current speech long before 1250; but it was not till about 1250 or later that many of them were brought into literary use. In those days not one Saxon or Dane in a thousand could read or write, and hence changes were thoroughly established in popular speech long before they showed themselves in writing. The Danish verb "call" appears, however, in the *Battle of Maldon*, an A.S. poem written in A.D. 993. The verb "cast" appears in a Homily written in 1230. These are among the earliest examples of Danish borrowings of *verbs*.

Danish words have a tendency to resist palatalisation,—that is, the conversion of the gutturals *k* or *g* to the corresponding palatals *ch*, *j*, or *y*.[1] Many of our words beginning with *sk*, such as *skill*, *skin*, are Danish. The suffix *-sk*, as in *bu-sk* (prepare oneself), *ba-sk* (orig. to bathe oneself) is exclusively Danish, and is still used in Icelandic.

(1) Nouns of Danish origin:—*tarn* (pool), *stag*, *hustings*, *bark* (of tree), *brink*, *beck* (brook), *bulk* (size), *cleft*, *cur*, *egg*, *fell* (hill),

---

which were supposed to have come from that source:—*cart*, *cradle*, *down* (hill), *merry*, *put*, *slough*, *babe* (imitative), *basket* (Fr.), *boast*, *brisk*, *cabin* (Fr.), *dudgeon*, *lad*, *lass*, *loop*.

[1] The reason usually given for this resistance to palatalisation is that the Danes, being a Northern people and living in a cold climate, did not open their mouths wider than they could help in talking, and were consequently fond of guttural or throat sounds. We are informed, however, by Mr. Skeat that palatalisation is not in any way barred by a fondness for gutturals or a habit of keeping the mouth closed, but is due to the insertion (after *k* or *g*) of the vowel *i* and is extremely common in Swedish,—a Northern language.

*fellow* (*felági*, partner), *geysir*, *harbour*, *husband*, *kid*, *leg*, *raft*, *rein-deer*, *sister*, *skirt*, *sky*, *slaughter*, *trust*, *tryst*, *window*, *wing*.

(2) Verbs of Danish origin :—*bait*, *bask*, *busk*, *call*, *cast*, *dash*, *die*, *drip*, *droop*, *gasp*, *glint*, *glimmer*, *irk* (hence *irk-some*), *are* (Third plur. of *am*), *bark*, *raise*, *rouse*, *rush*, *skim*, *smelt*, *smile*, *take*, *thrive*, *wag*, *wail*, *whirl*, *rive*, *thrive*, etc.

(3) Adjectives and adverbs :—*both*, *bound* (for some journey), *harsh*, *ill*, *irksome*, *loose*, *same*, *scant*, *sleek*, *sly*, *their* (Poss. Pronoun), *tight*, *ugly*, *weak*, etc.[1]

(4) *Patronymics*.—The A.S. suffix for forming patronymics is *-ing*, as *Hard-ing*, *Mann-ing*, etc. The Scandian or Danish suffix is *-son*, as *Ander-son*, *Eric-son*, *Collin-son*, *Swain-son*, *Robert-son*, *David-son*, *Thom-son*, etc.

(5) Prepositions :—*till*, *fro* (a doublet of A.S. *from* or *fram*), *a* for *on* in *aloft*, etc.

(6) Pronouns : *they*, *them*, *their*.

**408. Geographical Names.**—Scandian names of places are, as we should expect, mostly to be found in the Lowlands of Scotland, the northern counties of England, and Lincolnshire, in all of which the Danes settled in great force.

**Beck** (brook) : *Beck*-ford, Hol-*beck*, Ber-*beck*, Wans-*beck* (Woden's beck).

**By** (town).—There are said to be about 600 towns or villages in Britain called after this word ; of these about 200 are in Lincolnshire, 150 in Yorkshire, and only *one* to the south of the Thames :—

Grims-*by*, Whit-*by*, Apple-*by*, Nase-*by*, Sower-*by*, Soul-*by*, etc.

**Dal** (dale) : Avon-*dale*, Scars-*dale*, Lons-*dale*, Danes-*dale*, etc.

**Fell** (hill) : Scaw-*fell*, Wilber-*fell*, Sna-*fell*.

**Force, foss** (waterfall) : *Foss*-dyke, *Foss*-way, Scale-*force*, Stockgill-*force*, *Foss*-bury.

**Frith, forth** (estuary, cf. Lat. *port*-us) : *Frith* of *Forth*.

*Note*.—There is also an A.S. word *ford*, which means a river-crossing. Hence Ox-*ford*, Twi-*ford*, etc.

**Gate** (road, way) : Rei-*gate*, Sand-*gate*, Belsay-*gate*, etc.

**Gill** (ravine, chasm) : Orms-*gill*, Cars-*gill*, Esk-*gill*, etc.

**Holm** (river-flat, or islet) : *Holm*-forth, Lang-*holm* ; cf. Stock-*holm* in Sweden. Dun-*holm* (turned by Normans to *Dur-eme*, now spelt as *Dur-ham*).

**Kirk** (church) : *Kir*(*k*)-by, *Kirk*-wall, Sel-*kirk*, etc. ; cf. Dun-*kirk* in France.

**Scar** (detached rock) : *Scar*-borough, *Scars*-dale, etc.

**Skip** (ship) : *Skip*-ton, *Skip*-with.

**Suther** (south) : *Suther*-land, *Sodor* and Man.

**Thorp** (village) : Bishop-*thorp*, Stain-*drop*.

**Thwaite** (place ; cf. A.S. *stede*, stead) : Cross-*thwaite*.

**Wich, wick** (creek or bay ; cf. *Vik*-ing, man from the creek or bay, as Saxons called the Danes) : Ips-*wich*, Green-*wich*, Sand-*wich*, *Wick*-low, etc.

[1] Compiled from Skeat's *Princ. Eng. Etym.* series i. chap. xxiii.

*Note.*—There is also an A.S. *wic*, a town or village. Hence the Norse word can be applied only to places on the sea or navigable rivers, and we cannot always be sure even of them.

It has been usual to add to this list names ending in *ness*, as *Sheer-ness*, and names ending in *ey* or *ea*, as *Jers-ey*, *Angles-ea*; but these endings are no test at all; for *ness* is also A.S., and appears in Beowulf, while Scandian *ey* is merely another form of A.S. *íg*, island. Thus Shepp-*ey* is A.S. Scép-*íg*.

## SECTION 3.—DUTCH.

**409. Two sets of Dutch borrowings.**—(*a*) In the time of Edward III. a large number of Dutch weavers were induced to settle in England, especially in Norfolk, Suffolk, Essex, and Kent. The dialects that they brought with them (Old Frisian and Old Dutch) had much in common with that brought by Frisians and Saxons many centuries before. (*b*) In the reign of Elizabeth, English soldiers, who went out to Holland as volunteers to assist the Dutch against the Duke of Parma, brought home a good many Dutch words with them. After the fall of Antwerp, about a third of its merchants and manufacturers settled on the banks of the Thames, and Dutch sailors at the same time brought some new nautical terms.[1]

(*a*) *First borrowings*:—

(1) Words connected with weaving or the sale of woven goods:—*Botch* (to repair, patch), *brake* (machine for breaking hemp), *curl* (crimple), *lash* (to join a piece and make a seam), *spool* (a reel to wind yarn on), *tuck*, *groat*, *hawker*, *huckster*, *lack* (orig. blemish).

(2) Other words in common use:—*cough*, *mud*, *muddle*, *nag*, *fop*, *loll*, *luck*, *rabble*, *scoff*, *scold*, *slot* (bolt), *slender*, *slight*, *sprout*, *tub*, *tug*, *wiseacre* (Dutch *wijs-segger*, a wise sayer, a sooth-sayer).

(*b*) *Second borrowings*:—

(1) Naval words:[2]—*deck* (of a ship), *freebooter* (pirate or sea-robber), *hoise* or *hoist*, *hold* (of a ship), *hoy* (a small vessel), *hull* (of a ship), *skipper* (mariner), *yacht*, *boom* (pole), *cruise*, *sloop*.

(2) Trade words:—*cope* (orig. to bargain with; cf. *cheap*), *dollar*, *gilder*, *hogshead* (Dutch *oxhoofd*), *holland* (Dutch linen), *ravel* (to unweave or entangle).

(3) Words picked up by volunteers, etc.:—*boor* (Dutch peasant), *burgomaster* (lit. town-master), *canakin*, *frolic*, *fumble*, *glib* (smooth, voluble), *jeer*, *leaguer* (a camp; cf. be-*leaguer*, *lair*, *lie*), *loiter*, *land-*

---

[1] Skeat's *Princ. Eng. Etym.* series i. chap. xxiv.

[2] It must not be supposed, however, that *all* or even the majority of our naval terms are from Dutch. Others are Romanic, Scandian, or Anglo-Saxon. Romanic: *anchor*, *vessel*, *navy*, *navigate*, *flotilla*, *careen*, *gally*, *hulk*, *prow*, *port*, *mariner*, *poop*, *mizzen*-(mast). Scandian: *lee*, *harbour*, *raft*. Anglo-Saxon: *ship*, *oar*, *seaman*, *sail*, *mast*, *steer*, *stern*, *helm*, *keel*, *fleet*, *yard*.

*scape*, *manakin*, *mop*, *mope*, *rover*, *ruffle*, *sniff*, *sutler*, *toy*, *trick*, *slope*, *fop*, *waggon*, etc.

(4) A few words connected with painting,[1] such as *easel*, *landscape*, *lay-figure* (Dutch *lee*-man, a jointed model of the human body that may be put up in any attitude).

*Note* 1.—Some very recent Dutch borrowings have come to us from the Boers in South Africa:—*laager* (a camp), *kraal* (a collection of huts within a stockade), *trek* or *treck* (to migrate with waggons drawn by oxen).

*Note* 2.—The diminutive suffix *-kin*, as in *bump-kin*, *mana-kin*, *manni-kin*, is usually Dutch, in which it had the form of *-ken*. The suffix *scape* occurring in *landscape* is from Dutch *schap* (shape).

## SECTION 4.—LATIN.

**410. Latin borrowings distinct from French.**—Since French is little else than a modern form of Latin, it has been usual to put the Latin and French borrowings together, and to arrange them in the following periods:—

*First Period*, A.D. 43-410:—borrowings traced to the Roman occupation of Britain or picked up on the Continent: *all Latin.*

*Second Period*, A.D. 596-1066:—words borrowed during and after the conversion of our ancestors to Christianity: *all Latin.*

*Third Period*, A.D. 1066-1480:—words borrowed on and after the Norman Conquest till the accession of Henry VII., the commencement of Modern History: *all French.*

*Fourth Period*, from A.D. 1480:—words borrowed during and after the great intellectual movement known as the Renaissance or Revival of Learning: *all Latin.*

The arrangement is faulty, because shoals of Latin borrowings came in within the third period, and shoals of French ones within the fourth. Moreover, there was a special class of French borrowings in the time of Charles II., of which no account is taken in the above arrangement. It is now known, too, that *some* French words occur in late A.S. texts *before* 1066; as *turn*, A.S. *tyrn-an*, from Old Fr. *torn-er*; *proud*, A.S. *prūd*, from Old Fr. *prud* (of which our word *prude* is the Fem.); for other examples see *Note*, § 416.

The plan followed in this book is to keep the French and the Latin borrowings apart, and to subdivide each aggregate into separate periods of its own.[2] We shall take the Latin borrowings first, as the earliest of these were fixed in English, even before the French language had begun to exist.

---

[1] On art terms borrowed from Italian see § 425, (1), (*a*).

[2] The arrangement observed in this book is in accordance with that shown in Professor Skeat's *Principles of English Etymology*, series i. and ii.

The first two periods in the new arrangement tally, as will now be shown, with the first two in the old.

**411. I. First Period: pre-Christian, up to A.D. 596.**—Some of the borrowings belonging to this list may have been picked up on the Continent by the English before they came over to Britain; but some could easily have been learnt in Britain itself from the conquered natives. These borrowings are about ten in number, and almost all of them bear testimony to the Roman occupation:—

**Caster, Chester**: A.S. *ceaster*, Lat. *castrum*, camp or fortified place; seen only in geographical names:—*Chester*, *Caster*, *Caistor*, *Chester*-field, Lan-*caster*, Don-*caster*, Dor-*chester*, Man-*chester*, Win-*chester*, Ex-*eter* (for Ex-*cester*), Lei-*cester*, etc.

**Coln**: Lat. *colonia*, military settlement; seen only in geographical names:—Lin-*coln*, *Colne*, *Col*-chester.

**Mile**: A.S. *míl*, Lat. *mille* (*passuum*), a thousand paces.

**Pine** (verb): A.S. *pín*, Lat. *pœn-a*: cf. Eng. *pain*, *pun*-ish-ment.

**Pool**: A.S. *pól*, Welsh *pwll*, Lat. *padul*-is, a marsh: cf. Hartle-*pool*, Liver-*pool*.

**Port**: A.S. *port*, Lat. *port*-us, a harbour; cf. *Por*-chester, *Ports*-mouth, *Port*-land, Devon-*port*, New-*port*, etc.

**Street**: A.S. *strǽt*, Mercian *strét*, Lat. *strāta* (*via*), a paved road; cf. *Strat*-ton (town with paved street), *Streat*-ham (South London), *Strat*-ford, *Strad*-brook, etc.

**Wall**: A.S. *weall*, Mercian *wall*, Lat. *uall*-um, a rampart; borrowed at a time when the Lat. *v* (written *u* in old MSS.) was pronounced as *w*; cf. *Wall*-bury, *Wal*-ton, etc.

**Wick, wich**: A.S. *wíc*, Lat. *uic*-us, a town or village; seen only in geographical names: *Wick*-ham, *Wig*-ton, etc.

**Wine**: A.S. *wín*, Lat. *uin*-um.

**412. II. Second Period: pre-Norman, A.D. 597-1066.**—In A.D. 597 St. Augustine with a band of forty monks landed in Kent to teach Roman Christianity to the heathen English. Their conversion brought England for the first time into connection with the Continent, and especially with Rome and Italy, and this connection brought commerce, with new words and ideas. The number of Latin borrowings during this period, however, amounts to less than 200. English was thus still an almost pure language, and showed little inclination to admit strangers (for we can hardly include Danish words under such a name) until some 200 years after the Norman Conquest, when it began to borrow on a very large scale. The following examples are given in their modern spellings:—

(1) Church terms of Latin origin:—*altar*, *candle*, *chalice*, *cowl*, *creed*, *cup*, *disciple*, *font*, *mass* (sacrificial rite), *nun*, *shrine*, *shrive*, etc.

Church terms of Greek or Hebrew origin borrowed through Latin:—*alms*, *angel*, *anthem*, *amen*, *apostle*, *bishop*, *canon*, *Christ*, *church*, *clerk*, *deacon*, *devil*, *martyr*, *minster*, *monk*, *paschal*, *pope*, *priest*, *psalm*, *school*, *stole*, etc.

(2) Trade words, articles of commerce, etc.:—*beet* (beetroot), *box* (chest), *cap*, *cheese*, *fan*, *fork*, *kettle*, *linen*, *mat*, *mint*, *mul*-(berry), *pease* (Lat. *pis*-um, from which a false singular *pea* has been formed), *pear*, *penny*, *poppy*, *pound*, *sock*, *spend* (Lat. *dis-pend*-ere), *ton*, *tun*, etc.

(3) Miscellaneous:—*ass*, *belt*, *box* (tree), *castle*, *chalk*, *coulter* (of a plough), *fever*, *fiddle*, *fennel*, *hemp*, *kiln* (Lat. *culina*), *kitchen* (Lat. *coquina*), *lake*, *lobster*, *mill*, *mount-ain*, *noon* (Lat. *nona hora*, the ninth hour), *pan*, *pillow*, *pine* (tree), *pipe*, *pit*, *pole*, *post*, *prime*, *punt*, *shambles*, *sickle*, *sole* (of foot), *tile* (Lat. *tegul*-a), *tunic*, *turtle*-(dove), *verse*, *dish* (A.S. *disc*, Lat. *disc*-us), etc.

413. III. **Third Period: pre-Classical or pre-Renaissance, A.D. 1066-1485.**—The Norman Conquest, which took place in 1066, and was the means of making about half our vocabulary French two or three centuries later, gave a great impetus to the study of Latin, from which French itself is mainly derived. When we had already borrowed from French such words as *charity*, *quality*, *quantity*, it was easy to take the Latin word *pugnacitas* and change it to *pugnacity*, although it had not been preceded by a French form *pugnacité*. It is even asserted by the great French lexicographer that the French word *pugnacité* was borrowed from the English *pugnacity*.[1]

It must be remembered, too, that during the Middle Ages, as Craik observes, "Latin was the language of all the learned professions, of law and physic as well as of divinity in all their grades. It was in Latin that the teachers in the Universities (many of whom in England were foreigners) delivered their prelections in all the sciences." The Latin borrowings during this period are much more numerous than those of the pre-Norman period.

In England one of the main sources of supply was the Vulgate Version of the Bible,—that is, the current Latin text. It was from a MS. copy of this text that Wycliff (A.D. 1324-1384) prepared his English translation of the Bible. The Vulgate was constantly quoted in the old Homilies, and it was usual to accompany the quotation with comments in English.

Words borrowed direct from Latin, as the following examples show, are more like the original Latin than the early French borrowings (A.D. 1066 to about 1350).

---

[1] Skeat's *Princ. Eng. Etym.* series ii. p. 150, chap. viii.

*Ab-brevi-ate* (Latin *brevis;* cf. Fr. *abridge*). *Ab-negat-ion* (Lat. *neg-*, *negat-;* cf. Fr. "de-*ny*"). *Ac-quiesce* (Lat. *-quiesc-ere;* cf. Fr. *ac-quit*). *Ac-quire* (Lat. *quær-ere;* cf. Fr. "con-*quer*"). *Ad-judic-ate* (Lat. *judic-*, *judicat-;* cf. Fr. "ad-*judge*"). *Ag-grav-ate* (Lat. *grav-*, *gravat-;* cf. Fr. "ag-*grieve*"). *Al-levi-ate* (Lat. *levis*, light; cf. Fr. "re-*lieve*"). *Ap-preci-ate* (Lat. *pretium*, price; cf. Fr. "ap-*praise*"). *Ap-prehend* (Lat. *prehend-;* cf. Fr. "*ap-prise*"). *Ap-proxim-ate* (Lat. *proximus;* cf. Fr. "*ap-proach*," from Lat. *prope*, near). *Dis-simul-ate* (Lat. *simul-*, *simulat-*, to pretend; cf. Fr. "*dis-semble*"). *Bene-diction* (cf. Fr. *benison*). *Male-diction* (cf. Fr. *malison*). *Cad-ence* (cf. Fr. *chance*), etc.

One of the borrowings of this period, *autumn*, has superseded *harvest*, which in A.S. denoted the season (of autumn), and is now made to denote the fruits of the season.

The great difference between the Latin borrowings of Period II. and those of Period III. is that the former were adapted to Saxon models, and the latter to French ones.

**414. IV. Fourth Period, from A.D. 1480.**—The tendency to Latinise our speech received a new and very powerful impulse from the Renaissance or Revival of *classical* learning, Greek and Latin. In the preceding period the Latin borrowings were from ecclesiastical, legal, and other medieval books. The new period was marked by the study of the poets, orators, historians, etc., whose writings make up the classical literature of ancient Greece and Rome. Latin words began to pour in by shoals, and threatened to swamp our native speech. Fortunately, however, another movement, the Reformation, set in very soon after,—a movement that in England, as elsewhere in Europe, was essentially Teutonic, and found its strength in the native element of our language and character. Hence if a large number of Latin words were borrowed at this time, an equally large number were rejected as superfluous or awkward in the next generation.

The Latin borrowings of this period, like those of the preceding, are *book*-words,—that is, they have kept their Latin shape in all but the last syllable, or have discarded the last Latin syllable altogether, as in *advent*, Lat. *advent-us*.

A writer in Queen Elizabeth's time condemns such innovations as the following, though all but the last three have held their ground:—*audacious, compatible, egregious, despicable, destruction, homicide, obsequious, ponderous, portentous, prodigious, attemptat, facundity, implete.*

Among the rejected words the following will serve as examples:—*torve, tetric, cecity, fastide, trutinate, immanity, scelestick, pervicacy, straminecous, lepid, sufflaminate, facinorous, immorigerous, stultiloquy, mulierosity, coaxation, ludibundness,*[1] etc.

It has been estimated that the total number of words which we have borrowed immediately from Latin, and not through the medium of French, is considerably above 2400.[2] This estimate includes only such words as are fairly common, and only main or primary words. If the rejected words and derivatives were included, the number would be very much greater.

It is a noticeable fact that many of the words associated with the higher culture are of Latin origin, such as *evolve, evolution, operate, cultivate, demonstrate, horticulture, inductive, educate,* etc.

Latin borrowings did not cease with the Renaissance. Whenever new words are wanted to express something new in art or science, we still borrow from Latin, and sometimes from Greek. In fact, Latin is a language from which we have borrowed at all times, from the fifth century onwards.

**415. Formation of English Verbs from Latin ones.**—English verbs have been formed out of Latin ones either (*a*) from the stem of the Present Infinitive, or (*b*) from the stem of the Past Participle. The fact that so many *verbs* have been borrowed from Latin shows the thoroughness with which the borrowings of the Third and Fourth Periods were blended with English; for in our Latin borrowings of the two earlier periods we cannot find more than four verbs, all the rest being nouns or adjectives.

(*a*) *Abs-cond* (abscond-ere); *co-erce* (coerc-ere); *con-temn* (contemn-ere); *im-bue* (imbu-ere); *in-stil* (instill-are); *lave* (lav-are); *e-mend* (emend-are, Fr. form *a-mend*); *scan(d)* (scand-ere), etc.

(*b*) *Ab-use* (abus-um); *an-nex* (annex-um); *credit* (credit-um); *fix* (fix-um); *e-dit* (edit-um); *act* (act-um); *re-lapse* (re-laps-um); *pro-mise* (promiss-um); *sug-gest* (suggest-um); *sub-stitute* (substitut-um), etc.

## SECTION 5.—FRENCH.

**416. Three sets of French borrowings.**—There are *three* different sets of French borrowings, as against the four of Latin.

I. "Words of **Anglo-French** origin, that came into the language before 1350, and belong to the good old stock, being of equal value and use with the words of native origin." It was the Norman Conquest in 1066 that set this stream flowing in

---

[1] Trench's *English Past and Present*, ed. 1877, pp. 102-110.

[2] Skeat's *Princ. Eng. Etym.* series ii. p. 250.

force, and led to the formation, in England itself, of a separate Anglo-French dialect.

II. "Words of **Central** (or Parisian) French origin, imported chiefly between **1350** and **1660**, the date of the accession of Charles II."

III. "**Late French** words (of Parisian origin), introduced into the language since **1660** or thereabouts. They are on the whole of far less value than those in the two former classes" (Skeat).[1]

*Note.*—It has been asserted by very high authorities that there was a set of French borrowings which *preceded* the Norman Conquest (see article by Kluge in *Englische Studien*, vol. xxi. p. 334):—*bat, capon, castle, cat* (North Fr.), *catchpoll* (in late A.S. *cæccpol*), *false, mantle, market, proud, pride, purse, rock, sot, targe, trail, turn.* All these appear in late A.S., and are traceable to a French origin.

**417. Popular and Learned.**—The former belong chiefly to Class I., the latter (to a large extent) to Classes II. and III.

(*a*) "Popular" French words are such as grew up orally in ancient Gaul from the intercourse of Roman soldiers and settlers with the Gauls or *people* of the province; and hence they are called *popular*—lingua Romana popularis—lip-Latin, and not book-Latin. Such words are a good deal changed from the original Latin speech. Thus *c* or *k* at the beginning of a word often becomes *ch;* as in *cantare, chant; camera, chamber; caput, chief.* *C* or *g* in the middle of a word is often left out; as in *decanus, dean; inimicus, enemy; securus, sure; regula, rule; fact-um, feat; pericul-um, peril.* *B* sometimes disappears between vowels; as in *describe, descry; subitaneus, sudden.* *P* sometimes disappears before *t;* as in *conception, conceit; compute, count.* *D* or *t* often vanishes; as in *radic-em, race; native, naive; catena, chain; amictus, amice; conduct, conduit; præda, prey; radius, ray; pallid, pale; medianus, mean; dilate, delay; fata, fay; rotundus, round,* etc. *V* between two vowels disappears; as *civit-atem, cit-y.* *Ll* between vowels becomes vocalised or disappears; as *bellitas, beauty; colloc-are, couch.* *Di* before a vowel becomes *g* or *ch* or *j;* as *prædic-are, preach; diurnata, journey;* (as)*sedi-um, siege.* *Ti* undergoes a similar change; as *viatic-um, voyage; silvatic-us, savage.* *Bi, pi, vi* before a vowel tend to become *ge* or *ch;* as *rabi-es, rage; appropi-are, approach; diluvium, deluge.* *B* or *p* becomes *v* or *f;* as *ab-ante, van; ripa-r-ius, river; prob-are, prove.* Words thus derived make up the

[1] *Princ. Eng. Etym.* series ii. chap. ix.

bulk of the vocabulary of Old French, of which our own Anglo-French dialect was a peculiar offshoot.

(*b*) "Learned" French words are such as were borrowed by French writers from the study of Latin books, and not from lip-Latin. They are merely Latin words slightly altered and put into a French dress. Central or Parisian French enriched itself with a large stock of such words. Our French borrowings of the Second Period, that is, from A.D. 1350 to about 1660, are chiefly words of this class; and we cannot always separate them from words that we borrowed direct from Latin and refashioned in the same way as if we had taken them from French (see § 413). Thus *fierce* is a word of "popular" French origin (Lat. *ferocem*). But *ferocity* (Lat. *ferocitas*) is from learned or literary French, *ferocité*.

**418. I. Anglo-French borrowings,** up to about A.D. 1350.—These are called Anglo-French, as distinct from those of every other French dialect, because this dialect was *developed in England independently of foreign influence.* At the time of the Conqueror, and for a short time afterwards, it coincided with the French of Normandy, one of the northern dialects of Old French. But being cut off from contact with France by the English Channel, and at the same time in constant contact with English, it was developed in this island in a manner peculiarly its own, until by the time of Edward III. it had become quite distinct from every form of continental French. This dialect did not die out in England, till it had produced an abundant literature and given a bilingual character to our own English speech.

One great mark of the thoroughness with which Anglo-French and Early English were blended into one homogeneous whole is the fact that we borrowed French *verbs* in large numbers, and without hesitation; whereas in our borrowings from Late French we admitted scarcely anything but nouns and adjectives.

Our Anglo-French words are on the whole quite as necessary to our language as our Anglo-Saxon ones. The word *hour,* for example, is indispensable, because A.S. *tíd* (= tide), which also meant "hour," is now used to denote the ebb and flow of the sea. Again, *second* is indispensable as the ordinal for "two," because A.S. *óðer* (= other, lit. "second") has become useful in other ways. Cf. Lat. *autumn* and A.S. *harvest* in § 413.

Examples of Anglo-French borrowings: (on the general character of such borrowings, see § 398):—

(*a*) Titles, offices, etc. :—*duke, marquis, baron, constable, count, lieutenant, mayor, prince, viscount, emperor, vicar, dean, canon, chancellor,* etc.

(*b*) Feudalism and war, etc. :—*aid, cavalry, banner, battle, captain, fealty, lance, realm, armour, arms, fief, escutcheon, homage, vassal, serjeant, serf, trumpet,* etc.

(*c*) Law : *attorney, barrister, damages, felony, larceny, fine, judge, jury, justice, estate, fee, plea, plead, plaintiff, defendant, assize, prison, suit, summons,* etc.

(*d*) Government : *people, parliament, crown, reign, treaty, council, cabinet, court, minister,* etc.

(*e*) Church : *friar, relic, tonsure, ceremony, baptism, Bible, prayer, preach, lesson, cloister, penance, homily, sermon,* etc.

(*f*) Hunting : *course, covert, falcon, leveret, quarry, rabbit, venison* (hunted flesh), *catch, chase.*

(*g*) Cookery : *beef, veal, pork, mutton, pullet, boil, roast, broil, salmon, sausage,* etc.

(*h*) Abstract terms : *sense, honour, glory, fame, colour, dignity, chivalry, piety, art, science, nature,* etc.

(*i*) Relationship : *aunt, cousin, spouse, parent, uncle, nephew, niece.*

*Note.*—Most terms expressing very close relationship are, however, Teutonic ; such as *son, daughter, father, mother.* Hybrids like *grandfather, grandmother* help to show how completely the two languages were blended.

**419.** II. **Central French borrowings,** from A.D. 1350 to about 1660.—By the middle of the fourteenth century, when English was the only language spoken, and Anglo-French had almost ceased to affect our vocabulary, we had begun to borrow from continental French, not, as before, from the French of Normandy, but from Central or Parisian French, which by this time had become the standard language of France as it still is.

As has been stated already in § 417, many of the French borrowings of this period were from literary French, that is, the French derived from book-Latin, and not that derived, as old French was, from lip-Latin.

Specimens of Central French borrowings found in Chaucer :—

*Cadence* (Lat. *cadentia,* Anglo-French *chance*), *poetry, advertence, agony, annex, ascendant, casual, complexion, composition, conservative, cordial, duration, existence, fructify, oracle, persuasion, reprehend, triumph, urn, volume, vulgar,*[1] etc.

Specimens in Lydgate, fifteenth century :—*adulation, ambiguity, artificer, combine, condign, chronicle, deception, decoction, demure, dissent, doublet, encourage, fraudulent, hospitality, immutable, inclination, influence, inspection,* etc.

The French borrowings of this period were not all book-

[1] Skeat's *Princ. Eng. Etym.* series ii. p. 153.

words. Some were names of products imported into England through France by way of Calais. The following examples are given in their modern English spelling:—

*Sugar, almonds, spicery, vermilion, figs, raisins, saffron, ivory, pepper, ginger, liquorice, sulphur, incense, pæony, anise, dates, chestnuts, olive oil, rice, turpentine, cotton, canvas, fustian,* etc.

The writings of Chaucer contain a great many French words, some of which were of Anglo-French origin, and others of Central or literary French. But it would be a mistake to suppose that Chaucer *introduced* them. Before Chaucer wrote, the English language had been deeply interpenetrated by an admixture of French. "He merely employed with great skill and with plastic effect a language that was common to himself and his contemporaries" (Skeat).

420. III. **Late French borrowings,** from A.D. 1660.—By this time the French language had entered fully upon its Modern period, and was a good deal changed from the Old French to which our Norman or Anglo-French dialect belonged, and with which it agreed in the main in pronunciation and accent.

The borrowings of this period differ from those that preceded it in three respects at least—(1) They contain scarcely any *verbs*, which shows that Modern French is to Modern English an exotic, and not a true graft; (2) they have in many instances retained the Modern French system of accentuating the last syllable, whereas the older borrowings followed the English method of throwing the accent back on the first; cf. *cap'-tain* (Old French), *cam-paign'* (Modern French); (3) they have in many instances preserved the Modern French method of pronouncing vowels and consonants; compare for example *rage* (Old French) with *rouge* (= rōōzh, Modern French). Old French, on the contrary, was pronounced in nearly the same way as English was at the time of its incorporation (see above, § 394).

Besides individual words, a large number of Modern French *phrases* (such as *à propos*, for example) became current in England at this time, and many of them are still in vogue, though we could do quite as well without them.

An affected preference for everything French came into fashion with Charles II., whose vicious reign of twenty-five years corrupted the language no less than the morals of his country. The poet Dryden (1631-1700), from a desire to please the court, fell in with the prevailing fashion, as when he needlessly substituted the French *fraicheur* for the English *freshness* :—

Hither in summer evenings you repair
To taste the *fraicheur* of the purer air.

The tide receded a little with the accession of William III., but the study of French still continued in fashion.

**421. Pronunciation of Late French words.**—Some borrowings belonging to this class have become thoroughly naturalised in sound and accent; as *foliage*, *brilliant*, *antechamber*, *console*, *corset*, *deference*, *detach*, *diversion*, etc. (Fr. *mêlée* (a hand-to-hand conflict) has been lately naturalised as *mellay* in Tennyson's *Princess.*) Others are still French, though current in English speech.

**A** sounded as ȧ : po-màde, váse, gal-lánt, spȧ, chȧ-grin.

**At** sounded as ȧ : éclat (=é-clȧ).

**E** sounded as ā : fête (fāte), écarté, soirée, levée, parterre.

**Et** sounded as ā : ball-et (băllā), val-et, cro-quet, etc.

**En** sounded as ŏn : en-core (=ŏn-core), en-nui, ren-dez-vous.

**I** sounded as ē : ré-gime, po-lice, suite, gla-cis, fa-tigue, clique, pique, in-trigue, ma-chine, qui-nine, etc.

**Ou** sounded as ōō : group, bou-quet, soup, tour, route, rou-é, etc.

**Au** sounded as ō : mauve (=mōv), haut-boy, au revoir.

**Eau** sounded as ō : beau, plat-eau, bur-eau, portmant-eau.

**Ieu** sounded as ū : lieu, pur-lieu.

**Oi** sounded as *war* : pat-ois, soi-rée, reser-voir, mem-oir.

**Eur** : liqu-eur, haut-eur, douc-eur. (In grand-*eur* and amat-*eur* the French sound has been lost.)

**On** (nasal) : coup-on, cray-on, chign-on.

**Ch** sounded as *sh* : chaise, ma-chine, chan-de-lier, cham-ois.

**Ge, j** sounded as *zh* : ré-gime, gendarme, mi-rage (=rȧzh), rouge (=rōōzh), ju-jube.

**Qu, que** sounded as *k* : bou-quet, cro-quet, brusque, marque, qua-drille, co-quette, grot-esque, etc.

**S, t** (silent) : corps, a-propos, pat-ois, trait, de-pot.

*Note.*—When a foreign word is adopted whole, without any change of spelling, as *addendum* (Lat.), *prestige* (Fr.), *analysis* (Gr.), *bazaar* (Persian), we forget that it is foreign, *provided it accepts an English pronunciation.* Such a word may be said to be "acclimatised." (On the doubtful word *prestige*, see § 422.)

**422. Accentuation of Late French words.**—In the following examples, all of which are Late French borrowings, the accent is thrown on the last syllable of dissyllables, in accordance with French usage, and in trisyllables there is rather a strong accent on the last syllable besides one on the first :—

*Dissyllables :* a-droit′, bru-nette′, ca-det′, ca-jole′, cam-paign′, caprice′, ca-ress′, (cf. older borrowing *lar′*-gess), fes-toon′, gri-mace′, gui-tar′, har-angue′, in-trigue′, gro-tesque′, etc.

*Trisyllables:* baga-telle', debau-chee', confid-ant', incomm-ode', reprim-and', refug-ee', volunt-eer', palis-ade', barric-ade', arab-esque', etc.

*Wavering words:* Among the borrowings from Late French some are quite naturalised, some are still French, others are wavering. For example, some pronounce *prestige* as *pres'-tidge*, as if it were thoroughly Anglicised. Others still sound it as *pres-tizh*, as if it were still thoroughly French.

## SECTION 6.—GREEK.

**423. Continuity of Greek borrowings.**—Greek shares with Latin, though to a much smaller degree, the distinction of having been a continuous source of supply from the fifth century down to the present day.

*All* Greek borrowings up to the Revival of Greek learning (which for England may be dated from A.D. 1540) reached us at second or third hand through Latin or French.

Since 1540 some Greek words have been borrowed direct from Greek, and are especially so borrowed at the present day, when new words are wanted for some new fact or object in art or science. Others have been borrowed through Latin or French, as before, or through Italian, Spanish, Arabic, Portuguese, or Dutch.

The form of the word borrowed seldom gives any clue as to the date of the borrowing. For instance, *hypnotism*, *theosophy*, *photograph*, *telephone*, etc. (all of Greek origin), were coined lately in England. If they had been borrowed through French many centuries ago, the form of the words would have been just what they are now. But the form of "pro-*gramme*" shows that it came through French; cf. "tele-*gram*," coined in England.

**424. Specimens of Greek borrowings:—**

(*a*) Out of the Latin borrowings (rather less than 200) of the Second Period (§ 412), at least one-third were Greek before they became Latin:—

Alms (A.S. *ælmesse*, Gr. *eleēmos-yne*); anthem (A.S. *antefn*, Gr. *anti-phona*); angel (Gr. *angel-os*); apostle (Gr. *apostol-os*); bishop (A.S. *biscop*, Gr. *episcop-os*); chest (Gr. *kist-e*); Christ (Gr. *Christ-os*); church or kirk (A.S. *cyric-e*, Gr. *kuriak-a*); clerk (Gr. *cleric-os*); devil (A.S. *déofol*, Gr. *diabol-os*); dish (A.S. *disc*, Gr. *disc-os*); imp (A.S. *imp*, Gr. *emphut-os*).

*Note.*—Words like *antiphona* and *kuriaka* were Gr. Neuter Plurals, out of which Late Latin Fem. singulars were formed.

(*b*) Greek borrowings that have come through French, having first passed into Latin:—

Blame (Fr. *blasm-er*, Lat. *blasphem-are*, Gr. *blasphem-ein*); currants (Fr. *raisins de Corinthe*, Gr. *Corinth-os*); dropsy (Fr. *hy-dropisie*, Gr. *hydropisis*); fancy (Fr. *fantasie*, Gr. *phantasia*); frenzy (Fr. *frenaisie*, Gr. *phrenesis*); govern (Fr. *govern-er*, Gr. *kubern-ān*); graft (Fr. *graffe*, Gr. *graph-ein*); ink (Fr. *enque*, Gr. *en-caust-on*); place (Fr. *place*, Gr. *plat-eia*); slander (Fr. *esclandre*, Gr. *scandal-on*); surgeon (Fr. *chirurgien*, Gr. *cheir-urg-eon*); palsy (Fr. *paralysie*, Gr. *para-lysis*); al-chemy (Arab. article *al:* Gr. *chemeia*, mingling).

(*c*) Greek borrowings coined from Greek direct:—

Analysis, hydrophobia, monopolist, telephone, anthology, demology, zoo-logy, tele-gram, epi-dem-ic, epi-lepsy, epicure, utopia, æsthetic, cosmetic, cosmo-polite, etc.

(*d*) Hybrids:—

Con-trive (Lat. prefix *con-*; Old Fr. *trov-er*, to find; Gr. *trop-os*, a turn, revolving); re-trieve (Lat. prefix *re-*, base the same as the preceding); in-toxic-ate (Lat. prefix *in-*, Gr. stem *toxic-on*, poison, Lat. suffix *-ate*), etc.

*Verbs* of Greek origin are rare. But a very large number of verbs have been formed with the Greek suffix *-ize* or *-ise*, which can be freely attached to stems of any origin whatever.[1]

### SECTION 7.—MODERN BORROWINGS: MISCELLANEOUS.

**425. Modern borrowings.**—Under this heading we include the various sources not already named, from which new words came into English within the modern period of our language,—that is, after A.D. 1500.

(1) *Italian.*—The Renaissance or Revival of Learning, which originated in Italy, led to a study of Italian literature. Dante, Tasso, Ariosto, and Petrarch were all translated into English. The poems of Surrey, Wyatt, Spenser, and Milton all show an intimate acquaintance with Italian. In the reigns of the Tudors Italian was as necessary to every courtier as French was in the time of Charles II. The Ottava Rima, Blank Verse, and the Sonnet all came from Italy. The scenes of seven of Shakspeare's plays are laid in Italy. The tide receded with the establishment of the Commonwealth, and was entirely thrown back by the overwhelming taste for French, that set in with the accession of Charles II. But the borrowings were rather numerous, while the fashion lasted.[2]

One word, and possibly two more, came from Italy at a very

[1] The spelling *-ise* is French; but this was altered to *-ize* by pedants, who knew Greek, but forgot that *-ise* came to us through Fr. *-iser*.

[2] Skeat's *Princ. Eng. Elym.* series ii. p. 315.

early period. *Pilgrim* occurs in Layamon's *Brut*, spelt as *pilegrim*, from Italian *pellegrino*. Another word is *roam*, probably derived from *Rome*, to which pilgrimages were made by Englishmen from the time of Alfred the Great to that of Chaucer's *Wife of Bath*. *Ducat*, a Venetian word, occurs in Chaucer.

(*a*) Direct from Italian :—

Balcony (It. *balcone*, a stage); bandit (It. *bandito*, outlawed); canto; comply (It. *complire*, Lat. *complere*); contraband (Lat. *contra*, against, *bannum*, a decree); ditto (a thing already said, from Lat. *dictum*, said); duel; duet; monkey (It. *monicchio*); gusto (Lat. *gust-us*, taste); fresco (of the same root as *fresh*); milliner (a dealer in *Milan* goods); isolate (It. *isolato*, detached); imbroglio; grotto; portico; quota; rebuff, etc.

*Note.*—We are indebted to Italian for many of our terms in music, poetry, and painting :—

*Music* :—concert, sonata, spinet, fugue, breve, duet, contralto, opera, piano, prima donna, quartet, quintet, solo, soprano, trio, canzonet, tremolo, falsetto, etc.

*Poetry* :—canto, sonnet, stanza, improvise, octava rima.

*Painting* :—miniature, profile, vista, model, palette, pastel, mezzotinto, amber, etc. (On painting terms derived from Dutch, see § 409.)

(*b*) Through French :—

Alert (It. *all' erta*, on the watch); arcade; artisan; bank-rupt (It. *banco*, *rotto*, afterwards changed to Lat. *rupta*); brusque (It. *brusco*); bust (It. *busto*); caprice (It. *capriccio*, a whim); canteen (It. *cantina*, a cellar); cartoon (It. *cartone*, Lat. *charta*); cavalcade (It. *cavalcata*, a troop of horsemen); cascade (It. *cascata*, a waterfall), etc.

(2) *Spanish.*—Our borrowings from Spain were not due to a study of Spanish literature, but to our commercial and political relations with Spain, and to the descriptions of the country and her colonies furnished by English travellers.[1] Spanish borrowings are almost as numerous as Italian. The *al-* prefixed to some Spanish nouns is the Arabic article, *al*.

(*a*) Direct from Spanish :—

Alligator (*al ligarto*, a lizard); armada (armed fleet); booby (*bobo*, a blockhead); buffalo; canoe (West Indian); cargo; cigar; armadillo (the little armed one, an animal); cork (*corcho*, Lat. *corticem*, bark); domino; don; filibuster (Sp. *filibuster*; corruption of Dutch *vrijbuiter*, Eng. freebooter); peccadillo (dim. of *pecado*, a sin), etc.

(*b*) Through French :—

Bizarre; calenture; cask (Fr. *casque*, Ital. *casco*); castanets (of the same root as *chestnut*); escalade; garble; parade (*parada*, a show); risk (*risco*; a steep rock), etc.

---

[1] Skeat's *Princ. Eng. Etym.* series ii. p. 339.

(3) *Portuguese.*—About four dozen words :—

Albatross, albino, apricot, caste (Indian trade-guild), corvette (small frigate), firm (mercantile association), lingo (language), marmalade, molasses, parasol, tank (cf. Lat. *stagnum*, a pool of standing water), fetish (Lat. *factitius*, artificial).

(4) *German:* that is, the High German (see § 379, B). Only about twenty-four all told; and all of these are scientific and technical terms, except the following :—

Landau (a kind of carriage), meerschaum, mesmerise, plunder, poodle, swindler, waltz, zinc, carouse (through Fr. *carous*, Germ. *gar-aus*, lit. "quite out," a bumper drunk right off).

(5) *Russian* or *Slavonic:* rather fewer than the German :—

Knout, mammoth, argosy, mazurka (Polish dance), sable (an animal), rouble, polka, slave, steppe, vampire, czar.

(6) *Persian :*—

Bazaar, bezique (a game), caravan, divan, orange (*P. naring*), check or cheque, chess, dervish, exchequer, hazard, jackal, jasmine, jujube (through French), lemon, lilac, etc.

(7) *Sanskrit :*—

Banyan (a kind of tree), camphor, chintz, crimson, ginger, hemp, indigo, jungle, loot (to plunder), etc.

(8) *Hindustâni* (Northern India) :—

Bangle (a ring bracelet), chutny (a kind of pickle), dacoit (highway robber), topee (a sunshade for the head).

(9) *Hebrew :*—

Balsam (cf. older form *balm*, through French), alphabet (through Greek), amen, bedlam (mad-house, corruption of *Bethlehem*), cinnamon, cherub, cider (through French), maudlin (corruption of *Magdalene*), jubilee, jockey (corruption of *jackey*, dim. of *Jack*, Hebrew *Jac-ob*), hallelujah (*halelû jâh*, praise ye God), seraph (coined from the plural *seraphim*), shekel, etc.

(10) *Syriac :*—

Abbess, abbot, abbey (all from *abba*, father), damask (from *Damascus*), damson (a Damascene plum), muslin (from the town *Mosul*), mammon (riches), Messiah (anointed), etc.

(11) *Arabic:* rather numerous; some have come from the Levantine trade through Greek or Italian; others by way of Spain, in which country the Arab-speaking Moors were dominant for about 700 years; others more indirectly by way of France.

Admiral (spelt by Milton as *ammiral;* Arab. *amir*, prince, with suffix *-al*, which may have arisen in various ways: see *New Eng. Dict.*), alcove (a recess), algebra, Arabesque, arsenal, artichoke, assassin, caliph, caraway (seed), cipher, coffee, cotton, garbage, garble, nadir, zenith, etc.

(12) *Turkish* :—

Bey (provincial governor), horde, bosh (nonsense), ottoman (from *Ottoman*, founder of the Turkish empire), yataghan (a dagger-like sword), janizary, horde, and a few more.

(13) *Dravidian* (Southern India) :—

Teak (a kind of timber), bandicoot, mungoose, curry, cheroot, cooly (labourer), mango (kind of fruit), tope (mango-orchard), pariah (out-caste), and a few more.

(14) *Malay* :—

Bamboo, caddy (small tea-chest), cockatoo, gong, mangrove, ourang-outang, paddy (rice), rattan (cane), sago, upas (a (fabled) poisonous tree), amuck (as in the phrase "to run amuck." Dryden treats the *a* as an article, and uses the phrase "to run *an* Indian muck." The noun *mucker* for *muck* is well fixed in colloquial speech).

(15) *Chinese* :—

China (in the sense of porcelain), tea (Ch. *tsa*, *chá*; the last, though not used in England, is universally used in India, where it became current through the Portuguese), nankeen (a kind of cloth, from *Nankin*).

(16) *Thibetan* :—

Lama (Buddhist high priest at Llassa), yak (Thib. ox).

(17) *Australian* :—

Boomerang, kangaroo, paramatta (so called from the place).

(18) *Polynesian* :—

Taboo (a prohibition), tattoo.

(19) *Egyptian* :—

Behemoth, sack (hence dim. *satchel*, and *sack-cloth*), gum, gypsy, ibis, oäsis, paper (*papyrus*).

(20) *North African* :—

Barb (a horse), morocco (from the country), fez (Moorish cap).

(21) *West African* :—

Canary, chimpanzee, guinea, gorilla, yam (sweet potato).

(22) *North American* :—

Caucus (perhaps, one who pushes on ; now, a preliminary meeting for a political purpose), moose, skunk, squaw, tobacco, tomahawk, totem (ancestral symbol), wigwam (Indian hut), opossum, raccoon.

(23) *Mexican* :—

Cocoa (orig. *cacao*), chocolate, copal, jalap, tomato.

(24) *Peruvian* :—

Alpaca, coca (whence cocaine), condor, guano, llama, pampa (a wide grassy plain in South America : cf. *prairie* in North America, and *steppe* in Russia), jerked beef (corruption of *charqui*, raw meat cut up into strips and dried in the sun), puma.

# CHAPTER XXIII.—SOUNDS AND SYMBOLS.

(Compiled chiefly from chaps. v. xvi. xviii. of Skeat's *Princ. Eng. Etym.* series i.)

## SECTION 1.—ALPHABET, PRESENT AND PAST.

**426. Modern English Alphabet.**—A letter is a visible symbol intended to represent an articulate sound. The English alphabet now consists of 26 letters, each of which has two forms, the large or capital and the small :—

| | | | | | | |
|---|---|---|---|---|---|---|
| A, a | E, e | I, i | M, m | Q, q | U, u | X, x |
| B, b | F, f | J, j | N, n | R, r | V, v | Y, y |
| C, c | G, g | K, k | O, o | S, s | W, w | Z, z |
| D, d | H, h | L, l | P, p | T, t | | |

Capitals are used for the first letter of a sentence following a full stop or a note of interrogation ; for proper names ; for the names of days and months ; for the name of the Deity ; for the pronoun "I" ; for the first letter of every line of poetry ; for titles of honour or office ; for the first letters of a quoted speech or sentence ; for the interjection "O."

*Note.*—The order of our letters is based on that of the Greek and Latin alphabets.

**427. Anglo-Saxon Alphabet.**—The Angles, Frisians, and Saxons, who colonised Britain, brought with them from the Continent their national Runic alphabet, which was founded on Latin as there used.

On their conversion to Christianity they adopted the Latin alphabet in its *British* form, which they learnt from the conquered Celts. To this they afterwards added from their own runes three new symbols—(1) þ (=th, called *thorn*) ; (2) ð (=th, called *eth*, which is merely a *d* crossed); (3) ƿ (=w, called *wén*); also the vowel *æ* (=the short sound of *a* in *cat*). (To avoid the risk of ƿ being confused with þ or *p*, editors of A.S. MSS. now use *w* for ƿ).

The A.S. alphabet had no *j*, *q*, or *v*. These were afterwards borrowed from French. *k* and *z* were rarely used.

*Note* 1.—The name *Runes* was originally given to the letters or characters belonging to the written language of the ancient Norse, but it is often applied to the letters used by any of the ancient nations of Northern Europe, whether Norse or any other branch of Teutons. The oldest runic alphabet had sixteen letters only ; the later had many more, up to twenty-four at least. The word *rune* means mystery, in allusion to the fact that the knowledge of runes was confined to a very select few, and these few chiefly wizards or sorcerers.

*Note* 2.—The symbol *j* is merely a late variant of *i*, and arose from the practice of writing the *i* with a tail, as in i, ij. This explains why the *j* is still always written with a dot.

*Note* 3.—The symbol *v* is merely another form of *u*, and was used either as a vowel or a consonant. The letter *w* is merely a double *v*, though it is called a double *u*. The Anglo-French scribes substituted *w* for the Runic ƿ.

*Note* 4.—The A.S. symbol *æ* is now entirely extinct. It must not be confounded with the Romanic *æ* and *œ*, which are sounded as *ē*, or with the Greek *æ*, as in *archæology*, where *æ* is meant to represent the Greek *ai*. The symbols *æ* and *œ* ought not to be used at all. It is much better to write *medieval* than *mediæval*, *phenomenon* than *phænomenon*, as we already write *ether*, *Egypt*, etc. (See Skeat's *Student's Pastime*, p. 223.)

**428. Values of Anglo-Saxon Letters.**—The consonants *b*, *d*, *k*, *l*, *m*, *n*, *p*, *t* had their present values. *C* was originally sounded as *k* in *all* positions, and of the two was much more commonly used: in later A.S. it became *ch* before *e* and *i*; thus A.S. *cin* gradually became *chin*. Until *qu* was brought into use by Anglo-French scribes, *cw* was used for expressing the sound of *kw* (or *qu*). Similarly *g* had originally the guttural sound of *g* in *go* before *e* and *i*; it never had the *j* sound that it can now have before these two vowels, but it sometimes had the sound of consonantal *y*, as in A.S. *gé*, sounded as *yea*, and now spelt and sounded as *ye* (pronoun). Initial *h* had the same sound that it now has, but medial and final *h* were sounded as guttural *ch*, as in the Scotch *loch* (cf. *Loch* Lomond). *S* did duty for *s* and *z*. The A.S. *z* was sounded as *ts* or *dz*, not as modern *z*. *F* did duty for *f* and *v*, and was sounded as *v* between two vowels, as in *seofon* = seven; cf. Romanic *nephew* = nevew. The letters þ and ð were used promiscuously either for the sound of *th* in "this" or for that of *th* in "thin." The letter *y* was invariably a vowel, never a consonant; and it had the sound of German *ü*, which afterwards became confused and finally identified with our own *i*. The sound of *y* consonant was denoted by *ge* or *gi*, as already shown.

The short vowels *a*, *e*, *i*, *o*, *u*, and the long or accented vowels *á*, *é*, *í*, *ó*, *ú* had the same sounds as in modern Italian. The diphthong *æ*, the most characteristic sound in Old English, had the sound of *a* in *cat*, as was stated in § 427. In the accented form *ǽ* expressed the corresponding *long* sound, and had something like the sound of *a* in *Mary*, or like that of the bleat of a sheep in *baa*.

*Note*.—In A.S. the *a* (unaccented) was more open than the *a* in *cat*; it was more like the *a* in Ger. *mann* (man).

## SECTION 2.—CONSONANTS.

**429. Vowels and Consonants.**—Those letters or symbols that are used to express the *open* sounds of a language are called vowels. In producing such sounds the emission of the breath, though it is modified by the organs of speech, is not interrupted or stopped by actual contact between any of these organs.

Consonants, on the other hand, are the symbols used to express the *closer* sounds of a language. Such sounds are produced by the contact of one organ of speech with another, whereby the stream of breath is wholly or partially stopped.[1]

An organ of speech is any part of our bodily structure which helps us to utter articulate sounds.

The chief organs are the tongue, the throat, the palate, the teeth, and the lips. By means of these organs the breath is modified as it passes through the larynx. The science that deals with speech-sounds is called *Phonetics* (from Greek *phon-e*, sound or voice).

**430. Classification of Consonants.**—Consonants can be classified according to the organ chiefly used in sounding them:—

(1) **Gutturals** (Lat. *guttur*, throat): formed by raising the *back* of the tongue against the soft palate.

(2) **Palatals** (Lat. *palatum*, palate): formed by raising the *front* of the tongue towards the *hard* palate or palate proper.

(3) **Dentals** (Lat. *dent-es*, teeth): formed by bringing the *point* of the tongue towards the teeth or upper gums.

(4) **Labials** (Lat. *labium*, lip): formed by closing the lips.

(5) **Glottal** (Gr. *glottis*, mouth of windpipe): the name given to the open throat-sound expressed by the letter *h*.

Consonantal sounds have been also subdivided into—I. **Stops** or **Mutes**, viz. Gutturals *k, g;* Dentals *t, d;* and Labials *p, b;* in forming which the breath is entirely stopped for a time, until it is released again with an explosion. II. **Continuants** or **Spirants**, viz. Palatals *ch, j;* Dentals *th*(in), *th*(is); Labials *f, v*, and *wh, w;* Sibilants *s, z*, and *sh, zh;* and the letters *h* and *y;* in forming all which the breath is not stopped, but only squeezed, so that the sound can be kept up by merely con-

---

[1] This definition, however, does not apply to the exceptional letter *h*, which is a mere breath.

tinuing the breath. III. **Liquids** or flowing letters, viz. *l*, *m*, *n*, *ng*, *r*, which are "intermediate between the Stops on the one hand and the Continuants on the other; for they partially obstruct the breath-passage, not closing it entirely like the Stops, nor leaving a free channel for it through the mouth, like the Continuants" (Miss Soames).[1]

A third subdivision is into **Voiced** and **Voiceless**, of which an explanation will be found in § 432.

The tabular statement given in p. 270 shows how our consonantal sounds, twenty-five in number, are classified with reference to the three principles of subdivision just named. These twenty-five sounds, excepting the two marked with an asterisk, are simple: *ch* and *j* are compound.[2]

On account of their hissing sound, *s*, *z*, *sh*, and *zh* are called **Sibilants** (Lat. *sibilant-es*).

*W* and *y* are called semi-vowels, because they are used sometimes as vowels and sometimes as consonants; cf. *we*, f-*ew*; *ye*-t, th-*ey*.

**431. How the Sounds are formed.**—The reader should test the accuracy of the following remarks by noting the movements of his own organs of speech in sounding each consonant:[3]—

**Stops**: The six stops are classified according to the place where the breath is stopped. "In the back-stops **k** and **g** (gutturals), it is stopped by the back of the tongue touching the soft palate; in the point-stops **t** and **d** (dentals), it is stopped by

---

[1] *Introduction to the Study of Phonetics*, p. 35.

[2] The palatal sounds represented by *ch* and *j* have been analysed by phoneticians into *t*+*sh* and *d*+*zh* respectively, and are called by Dr. Murray (*New English Dictionary*) "consonantal diphthongs." In Sanskrit, however, they are regarded as simple sounds, and are both represented by single consonants, which are named *tálabya*, that is, "palatal."

Owing to the insufficiency of our alphabet we use *digraphs* to represent the sounds of *ng*, *th*, *wh*, *sh*, and *zh*. To represent the voiced sound of *th* (viz. that of *th* in "this") a sixth digraph, *dh*, is sometimes added. These six sounds are all as simple as if they were expressed by a single letter, and not by a digraph or combination of two letters.

The sound of *zh* occurs in such words as *azure*, *leisure*, *elision*, etc.

The sound of *wh* is seldom heard except in the North of England and in Scotland. Thus *while* is usually pronounced the same as *wile*.

No mention in the table (p. 270) is made of *c*, *q*, and *x*, because *c* has the sound of either *s* or *k*; *q* has the sound of *k* in *qu*=kw; and *x* has the sound of *ks* in *ex-tra* or of *gz* in *exert*.

[3] The account given in the text is based on the description given by Miss Laura Soames in *Introduction to the Study of Phonetics*, pp. 30-39.

| | | (1) Guttural. | (2) Palatal. | | (3) Dental. | | (4) Labial. | | | (5) Glottal. |
|---|---|---|---|---|---|---|---|---|---|---|
| | | | | | (a) Dental. | (b) Inter-dental. | (a) Labial. | (b) Labio-dental. | (c) Labio-guttural. | |
| I. Stops | Voiceless | k | ... | | t | ... | p | ... | ... | ... |
| | Voiced | g | ... | | d | ... | b | ... | ... | ... |
| II. Continuants | Voiceless | ... | *ch | sh | s | th(in) | ... | f | wh | h |
| | Voiced | ... | *j, y | zh | z | th(is) | ... | v | w | ... |
| III. Liquids (all voiced) | Nasal | ng | ... | | n | ... | m | ... | ... | ... |
| | Lingual | ... | r | | l | ... | ... | ... | ... | ... |

the point of the tongue touching the upper gums; in the lip-stops **p** and **b** (labials), it is stopped by closing the lips" (Soames).

(1) **Gutturals.**—The digraph *ng* is called a nasal in the above table, because, while the back of the tongue is raised against the soft palate, the breath passes up the nose-passage and escapes through the nostrils. A cold in the head, by blocking up the nose-passage, causes the *ng* to be sounded almost as a pure guttural *g*.

(2) **Palatals.**—In sounding *ch* and *j* the front of the tongue *touches* the hard palate, whereas in sounding *y* it comes *near* the hard palate, but does not quite touch it. For the sounding of *y* the tongue is in very much the same position as in sounding *i*; and hence *i* becomes *y* before a vowel, as in *opinion* = opinyon.

*Sh* and *zh* are the sibilant palatals corresponding to *ch* and *j* respectively; and hence one is sometimes interchanged with the other; as in *chair*, *chaise* (sounded as shaise); *jujube*, sometimes sounded as *zhuzhube* (Fr.).

In sounding *r* the tongue, after almost touching the hard palate, is made to vibrate towards the upper gums. Hence *r* has been called the trilled consonant. Except in the North, however, it is never really heard as a consonant, unless it is followed by a vowel in the same or in the next word; cf. *far-ther* (sounded as *father*), *farr-ier*.

(3) **Dentals.**—In sounding *t* and *d* the point of the tongue, as has been stated already, touches the upper gums. In sounding *s* and *z* it comes very near the roots of the upper teeth, but does not quite touch them.

The sounds of *th*(in) and *th*(is) are called "inter-dental," because in forming these sounds the point of the tongue is placed *between* (Lat. *inter*) the upper and lower teeth.

In sounding *s* and *z* the point of the tongue, as we have already explained, comes very near the roots of the upper teeth. The tongue is therefore in an intermediate position between that used in sounding *t* and *d* and that used in sounding *th*(in) and *th*(is). Thus a foreigner, unable to sound the *th* in *thanks*, will say *sanks*. Similarly *bind-eth* became *bind-es* (voiceless *s*), and eventually *bind-s* (voiced *s* = *z*, through contact with voiced *d*). Eng. *water* became Ger. *wasser*.

In forming the sounds of *n* and *l* the point of the tongue touches the upper gums; but in sounding *n* the breath escapes through the nose-passage, while in sounding *l* it escapes at one side or at both sides of the tongue. Hence *n* is called a nasal dental, and *l* a lateral one. If the nose-passage is blocked by a cold, the *n* is sounded almost as *d*. *N* is sometimes (though rarely) changed to *l*, owing to the tongue being in very nearly the same position: thus *flannel* was originally *flannen*; *postern* is from Fr. *posterne* or *posterle* (Lat. *post-erula*, a little back gate).

(4) **Labials.**—In sounding *p*, *b*, and *m* the lips are closed against each other, while the tongue is left to rest on the lower jaw. The letter *m* is called a nasal labial, because, as happens in the case of *ng* and *n*, the breath escapes through the nose-passage. If this passage is blocked by a cold, the *m* is sounded almost like *b*.

In sounding *f* and *v* the edges of the upper teeth are pressed against the lower lip, while the tongue rests on the lower jaw. Hence these letters are called "labio-dentals" or lip-dentals.

In sounding *wh* and *w* the lips are rounded with the corners drawn together, while the tongue is almost in the same position as in sounding *g*. Hence these letters are called "labio-gutturals." For the same reason the letters *w* and *g* are liable to be interchanged; as in *ward*, *guard* (Fr. *garde*).

(5) **Glottal.**—"The aspirate *h* is partly an open throat-sound and partly a breath vowel-glide" (Sweet). As a voiceless Continuant it is liable to be interchanged with another voiceless Continuant, *s*; as *hemi*(sphere), *semi*(circle).

**432. Voiceless and Voiced Consonants.**—In the table of consonants given in § 430, some are said to be Voiceless and others Voiced.[1] Omitting the Liquids (all of which are Voiced) we have among Stops and Continuants nine sets of letters paired off as voiceless or voiced, which may be more conveniently shown as follows:—

| | | | | | |
|---|---|---|---|---|---|
| Guttural | k | g | Inter-dental | th(in) | th(is) |
| Palatal | ch | j | Labial | p | b |
| | sh | zh | Labio-dental | f | v |
| Dental | t | d | Labio-guttural | wh | w |
| | s | z | | | |

The distinction between voiceless and voiced can be easily verified by any one who will make the experiment on his own organs. For example, we find it very easy to sound *ka*, so long as the

[1] Other names given for Voiceless are "Surd" and "Whispered"; and for Voiced other names are "Sonant" and "Breathed." These are equally suitable. The names Hard and Soft, Sharp and Flat are also used; but they are not suitable.

*k* is followed by a vowel; but if we cut off the vowel and try to sound the *k* alone, we cannot produce an audible sound, though we are conscious of a feeling of muscular tension in the tongue. There is no *voice* or audible sound in it; and hence the consonant is said to be voiceless.

On the other hand, if we make a similar experiment with *ga*, we find that even without the assistance of the vowel it is possible to make an audible guggle. This consonant, therefore, is said to be voiced or sonant. The voiced or sonant consonants are midway between vowels and the voiceless consonants.

Since the organs of speech are the same in all races of men alike, the distinction between Voiceless and Voiced holds good in the pronunciation of *all* languages, and not only of English. The following rules are of wide application:—

*Rule* I.—Voiceless consonants are assimilated in sound to voiceless ones, and voiced to voiced.

(*a*) In monosyllables the first letter usually holds its ground, and the second one gives way to the first; as *dogs* = dogz, *cabs* = cabz, *looked* = lookt.

(*b*) In dissyllables or compound words the first letter usually gives way to the second one; as in *five-teen*, sounded and spelt as *fif-teen*; *cup-board*, sounded, but not spelt, as *cub-board*; *black-guard*, sounded, but not spelt, as *blag-guard*.

*Rule* II.—A voiceless consonant is often voiced, when it is placed in vocalic company, that is, between two vowels. Thus in *breath* the *th* is voiceless, while in *breathe* it is voiced. Again *rise* is sounded as *rize*, not as *rice*.

*Note.*—There are, however, exceptions, as in, *dose*, etc. But the voiceless sound of *s* is more commonly spelt as *c*, provided it is at the end of a syllable and followed by *e* or *i*, as in *vice*, *glance*, etc.

*Rule* III.—When a consonant of one class is *substituted*, as sometimes happens, for a consonant of another class, a voiceless consonant is replaced by a voiceless one, and a voiced by a voiced, as per Rule I. Thus *bat* (winged mammal) was spelt *bakke* in Mid. Eng., where voiceless *t* has been substituted for voiceless *k*.

*Rule* IV.—When an *intrusive* consonant (that is, one not belonging to the root) is inserted into a word, the intruder is usually of the same class as the consonant going before:—

Num-*b*-er, Lat. *num-er-us*; gen-*d*-er, Lat. *gen-er-is*; thun-*d*-er, A.S. þun-or. (Observe that the *m* and *b* are both labials, while the *n* and *d* are both dentals.)

**433. Voiced Consonants changed to Vowels.**—A voiced

or sonant consonant (which, as we have shown above, is something midway between a voiceless consonant and a vowel) sometimes loses its consonantal force and becomes vocalic,—a change which began to take effect in Anglo-Saxon times.

A good example is furnished by the letter *g*, which is sometimes vocalised, sometimes made silent, and sometimes lost.

(*a*) From *g* to *gh* (silent):—*hnǽg-(an)* becomes *neigh; weg-(an), weigh; síg-(an), sigh.*

(*b*) From *g* to *y* (vocal) or *i*:—*dæg* becomes *day; grǽg* becomes *gray; nægel* becomes *nail; stigel* becomes *stile.*

(*c*) From final *ig* to *y; ǽn-ig* becomes *any; hál-ig, holy; cear-ig, chary.* (Here the *g* fell off altogether, leaving *i*, which became *y*.)

(*d*) From *g* to *w* (vocal):—*ág-en* becomes *own* (adj.); *drag-(an), draw; fug-ol, fowl; búg-(an), bow* (verb).

(*e*) From *g* to *ow* (vocal):—*morg-(en)* becomes *morrow; furg, furrow; sorg, sorrow; holg, hollow.*

*Note.*—The examples in (*a*), (*b*), (*c*), in which the *g* became silent *gh* or *y*, or fell off altogether, are distinguished from those in (*d*) and (*e*) by the quality of the preceding vowel. In (*a*), (*b*), (*c*) the preceding vowel is palatal, viz. *æ*, *e*, or *i* (by "palatal" it is simply meant that they are sounded in the back of the throat); whereas in (*d*) the vowel is not palatal, but pure *a*, *o*, or *u*, and in (*e*) the *g* is preceded by *r* or *l*.

**434. Substitution.**—See Rule III. in § 432, by which voiceless consonants of one class can be *substituted* for those of another, and voiced for voiced; as when a child learning to speak will say *tat* for *cat*, or *frough* for *through*, or *loo* for *you*.

(1) **k, s** (ce), both voiceless:—*prank, prance; crook, cross;* Lat. *princ*-ipem (in which the *c*=*k*), Eng. *prince.*

(2) **k, t**, both voiceless:—*apricock* (older spelling), *apricot; bakke* (Mid. Eng.), *bat; milt, milk* (cf. *milter*, the male of *spawner*); Lat. *lac-tuca*, Eng. *let-tuce.*

(3) **sk, sh**, both voiceless:—A.S. *scrif*-an, *shrive;* A.S. *scín*-an, *shine;* A.S. *sco, shoe;* A.S. *scǽþ, sheath.*

(4) **k, p**, both voiceless:—Fr. *trompe* (trump or trumpet), Eng. *trunk* (of an elephant, so called from its trumpeting sound); Lat. *locusta* (locust), A.S. *lopust*, Mod. Eng. *lobster;* Lat. *quinque* (five, cf. *quinquennial*), Gr. *penta* (five, cf. *pentagon*); *sect, sept.*

(5) **p, t** (voiceless); **b, d** (voiced):—*apti-tude, attitude* (from Lat. *aptus*, fit); *crypt, grotto; verb, word; barb, beard.*

(6) **th** (as in *this*), **d**, both voiced:—*seethe* (present tense), *sodden* (past participle); *murther* (older spelling), *murder;* A.S. *byrðen*, Mod. Eng. *burden;* A.S. *cúðe*, Mod. Eng. *could* (with intrusive *l*).

(7) **th** (as in *thin*), **h, s**, all voiceless:—*cast-eth, cast-es*, and finally *cast-s; thanks, sanks* (as pronounced by foreigners, who cannot articulate *th*); Gr. *hemi* (half), Lat. *semi; hyper*-critical, *super*-fluous Gr. *hept-a* (seven, as in *heptarchy*), Lat. *sept-em* (as in *September*, the seventh month).

(8) **m** (labial nasal) goes with **p**, and **n** (dental nasal) with **t** :—A.S. *henep*, Mod. Eng. *hemp* ; A.S. *æmete*, Mod. Eng. *emmet*, or by contraction, *ant* ; *Hants*, *Hampshire*.

(9) **r**, **l** (both voiced) :—*wrap*, *lap* ; Lat. *purpura*, Eng. *purple* ; Fr. *prune*, Eng. *prune* or *plum*.

(10) **b** or **v**, **g** or **j** (all voiced) :—Lat. *rabies*, Fr. *rage* ; *abbreviate*, *abridge* ; *cave*, *cage* ; *servant*, *serjeant* ; *leger-de-main* (Old Fr. *legier de main*, in which *legier* is from Lat. *leuis*, Late Lat. *levis*).

(11) **s**, **r** (*s* is voiced to *z* before it is changed to *r*) :—*are* for *ase* (plural of *is*) ; *were* for *wese* (plural of *was*) ; A.S. *leós-an* (to lose), pp. *lor-en* (for *los-en*), Mod. Eng. *lorn* (lost) ; A.S. *isen*, Mod. Eng. *iron* ; Old Fr. *vaslet*, hence *varlet*.

> The parching air
> Burns *frore*, and cold performs the effect of fire.
> *Par. Lost*, ii. 594, 595.

Here *frore* is the A.S. *fror-en*, for which Mod. Eng. has substituted *frozen*.

(12) **w**, **g** :—A.S. *weard* (Eng. *ward*), Fr. *gard* (Eng. *guard*) ; Old High Ger. *werre* (Eng. *war*), Fr. *guerre*. (*N.B.*—As the French had no *w*, they used *gu* or *g* instead of it. Both are voiced letters.)

**435. Assimilation.**—See Rule I. (*a*) and (*b*) in § 432. This process may take place either with or without a change of spelling :—

(*a*) Without change of spelling :—*dogs*=*dogz* ; *looked*=*lookt* ; *pressed*=*prest* ; *cup-board*=*cub-board* ; *hast-en*=*hāsen* ; *ad-journ*=*aj-journ* ; *know-ledge*=*knol-ledge* (rhyming with *college*) ; *soft-en*=*soffen* ; *row-lock*=*rul-lock*.

(*b*) With change of spelling :—*hussy* or *hussif* for *house-wife* ; *lissom* for *lithe-some* ; *gossip* for *god-sib* (related in God) ; *gospel* (for *god-spell*) ; *fif-teen* for *five-teen* ; *wimen* (misspelt as *women*) for older form *wim-men*, for *wif-men* ; *Lam-mas* for *hláf-mas* (lit. the loaf-mass) ; *quag-mire* for *quake-mire* ; *an(s)-swer* for *and-swer*, etc.

In words of Romanic origin assimilation is equally common ; cf. *ac*-cept, *af*-fix, *ag*-grieve, *al*-low, *an*-nounce, *ap*-proach, *ar*-rive, *as*-sent, *at*-tend. All of these words are formed with the prefix *ad*.

**436. Metathesis**, or the change of place of adjacent consonants :—

(1) **ks**, **sk** :—A.S. *misc*-an, Mod. Eng. *mix* (=*mics*) ; A.S. *acs*-i-an, Mod. Eng. *ask*, or *ax* (vulgar) ; *task* (a duty imposed), *tax* (a payment imposed), etc.

(2) **ps**, **sp** :—A.S. *wæps*, Mod. Eng. *wasp*, or *waps* (provincial) ; Mid. Eng. *claps*-en, Mod. Eng. *clasp* ; A.S. *hæpse*, Mod. Eng. *hasp*.

(3) **r** :—A.S. *brid*, Mod. Eng. *bird* ; A.S. *þridda*, Mod. Eng. *third* ; A.S. *þurh*, Mod. Eng. *through* ; A.S. *cræt*, Mod. Eng. *cart* ; *scarp*, *scrap* ; *granary*, *garner* (Romanic).

**437. Initial "h."**—The aspirate in French was weak, in Teutonic strong. Hence, in Mid. Eng., which contained many words of French origin, we have *abit* for *habit*, *eir* for *heir*, *ost* for *host*, *ostel* for *hostel*, *onest* for *honest*, *onour* for *honour*, *umble* for *humble*, *our* for *hour*.

There are several words in Mod. Eng. that have lost their initial *h* through the weakness of the French aspirate :—

*Able* from Lat. *habilis ; arbour* from Mid. Eng. *herbere*, Lat. *herbarium ; ortolan* from Lat. *hortulan*-us (a bird of the garden) ; *ostler* for *hosteler*, due to Lat. *hospitalis ; ordure* from Fr. *ordure*, due to Lat. *horridus*, of which *ordure* is a derivative.

The habit of sounding the *h* in the wrong place or leaving it out is a very old one. Instances of it occur in the *Romance of Havelok* (reign of Edward I.), where we have *is* for *his*, *eþen* for *heþen* (hence), and *herles* for *erles* (earls); the fact being that this MS. was (as Prof. Skeat has discovered) written out by a Norman scribe. It arose, as seems probable, from the desire of the lower classes to imitate their French-speaking masters, by whom, as they saw, the letter *h* was not much patronised. "But nature being too strong for them, they were driven to preserve their *h* from destruction by sounding it in words which had no right to it; and hence the confused result" (Skeat).[1]

The *h* is almost or quite silent in English, unless its syllable is accented. The *h* in *hit* (now spelt as *it*, but not originally so) was lost through lack of emphasis: thus "*hit* rains" became "*it rains.*" When the syllable is not accented, we ought to use *an* before the *h*, and not *a* :—

*a* his′-tory ; *an* his-tor′-i-cal record.
*a* hos′-tel ; *an* ho-tel′.
*a* har′-ri-er ; *an* har-angue′.

**438. Palatalisation.**—In Modern English, Gutturals have shown a tendency to become Palatals, because Palatals can be more easily sounded; but in the Northern dialect, that is, in Northumbrian and Lowland Scotch, where the Scandinavian element has been predominant from the first (see first note to § 383), palatalisation has been usually resisted.

**k** or **c** (guttural) > **ch** : (the symbol > means *becomes*) :—

A.S. *cealc* (borrowed from Lat. *calc-em*), Mod. Eng. *chalk* ;[2] A.S. *cierr* (a turn of work), Mod. Eng. *char*-woman ; A.S. *cild*, Mod.

---

[1] *Princ. Eng. Etym.* series i. p. 360. "But," as the author has since informed me, "this explanation is not quite sufficient. It is now observed that many Dutch and Low German dialects have lost *h* altogether. The explanation in the text can only apply to the insertion of the *h* in the wrong place" (Skeat).

[2] Lat. *calc*=*kalk*. A.S. *cealc*=(1) *kialk*, and later (2) *chalk* (with the *l* sounded). The *ce* (=*ki*) is the intermediate link between *k* and *ch*, and in late A.S. it really became *ch*.

Eng. *child;* A.S. *ceós-an,* Mod. Eng. *choose;* A.S. *ceorl,* Mod. Eng. *churl;* A.S. *wicc-a* or *wicc-e,* Mod. Eng. *witch* (still preserving, however, the *k* sound in *wick-ed,* addicted to witchcraft); A.S. *cear-ig,* Mod. Eng. *char-y* (but still preserving the *k* sound in *care,* Merc. *caru*).

*Note.*—Observe that the change from *k* or *c* to *ch* takes place only when the guttural is followed by *e* or *i*.

Sometimes we have two forms of the same word, one spelt with the Guttural, and the other with the Palatal. Hence the following doublets:—

Bank, bench; dike, ditch; lurk, lurch; mark, march; shriek, screech; seek, be-seech; kirk, church, etc.

**g** > **y**, and **gg** (written **cg**) > **j**:—

A.S. *brycge,* Mod. Eng. *bridge* (still, however, pronounced as *brig* in parts of Yorkshire); A.S. *geard,* Mod. Eng. *yard;* A.S. *ge-wis,* Mod. Eng. *ywis* (also spelt as *Iwis,* and often wrongly spelt as *I wis,* as if there were two words); A.S. *gear-u* (ready), Mod. Eng. *yare;* A.S. *gearn,* Mod. Eng. *yarn;* A.S. *giern*-an, Mod. Eng. *yearn;* A.S. *gild*-an, Mod. Eng. *yield.*

*Note.*—This change, like the preceding, takes place only when the guttural is followed by *e* or *i*.

## Section 3.—Vowels and Diphthongs.

**439. Vocalic Sounds in Modern English.**—In addition to the twenty-five consonantal sounds shown in tabulated form in p. 270, there are twenty different vocalic sounds in Modern English, making a total of forty-five different sounds, out of which all English words can be articulated, whatever their spelling may be.[1]

The vowel-sounds in present use are shown in tabular form in p. 278. (This, however, does not include certain French sounds that have become current in English, of which some account has been given above in § 421.)

[1] There were eighteen vowels and vowel-sounds in Anglo-Saxon:—Seven short (a, æ, e, i, o, u, y), seven accented or long (á, ǽ, é, í, ó, ú, ý), and four diphthongs (ea, eo, éa, éo); *y* gradually took the same sound as *i*. The A.S. *a* was a little more open in sound than our modern *a* in *cat;* more like the *a* in German *mann* (man). The A.S. *æ* (unaccented) was exactly the same in sound as the *a* in *cat.* The A.S. diphthongs need not be considered, as the sounds are obsolete. The system of Mod. Eng. sounds adopted in this book is that described by Professor Skeat in the Note printed (with his permission) in Appendix V., which tallies in essential respects with that given by Miss Laura Soames in pp. 15-23 and in pp. 39-54 of *Introduction to the Study of Phonetics.*

| No. | Symbols in Dictionaries. | Examples. | Anglo-Saxon Equivalents. | Symbols by Sweet and Skeat. |
|---|---|---|---|---|
| {1 | ă | =*a* in *marry* | æ | æ |
| {2 | â | =*a* in *Mary* | ǽ | ae |
| 3 | ȧ | =*a* in *path* | á | aa |
| {4 | ĕ | =*e* in *let* | e | e |
| {5 | ā | =*a* in *late* | é | ei |
| {6 | ĭ | =*i* in *fit* | i | i |
| {7 | ē | =*ee* in *feet* | í | ii |
| {8 | ŏ | =*o* in *dog* | o | o |
| {9 | au | =*au* in *fraud* | *nil* | ao |
| {10 | *nil* | =*o* in *o-bey* | *nil* | o' |
| {11 | ō | =*o* in *note* | ó | ou |
| {12 | ŏŏ | =*oo* in *stood* | u | u |
| {13 | ōō | =*oo* in *stool* | ú | uu |
| {14 | *nil* | =*a* in *China* | *nil* | ə |
| {15 | *nil* | =*ur* in *turn* | *nil* | əə |
| 16 | ŭ | =*u* in *but* | *nil* | ɐ |
| 17 | ī | =*i* in *pine* | *nil* | ai |
| 18 | ū | =*u* in *duke* | íw | iuu |
| 19 | oi | =*oi* in *moist* | *nil* | oi |
| 20 | ou | =*ou* in *mouth* | *nil* | au |

Whenever two vowels are bracketed together in the above scheme, this is intended to show that they go together in a pair. In each pair it should be noticed that the second vowel is (*approximately* speaking) a lengthened variety of the other. Length, however, as will be shown in the sequel, is not the only difference in some of them.

No. 1. This is one of the most characteristic sounds in our language. It was expressed in A.S. by *æ;* but as this symbol has become obsolete, it is now expressed by *a*, as in *marry*. Example, A.S. *ræt*, Mod. Eng. *rat* (the same sound).

No. 2. This sound never occurs in Modern English except before the consonant *r*, and even then it is not a pure or unmixed sound, unless the *r* is trilled (*i.e.* followed by a vowel in the same or in the next word), as in *Mary, fairest.* If the *r* is untrilled (*i.e.* followed by a consonant, and not by a vowel), the *r* becomes vocalic and takes the sound of *ə* (No. 14), as in *fair* (sounded *faeə*).

No. 3. The short sound that corresponded with this vowel is extinct in Modern English. In A.S. it was expressed by *a* (unaccented), and had the sound of *a* in A.S. *mann* or German *mann* (which is rather more open than the present sound of *a* in *man*). The long sound of *a*, as in *path, ask*, was expressed in A.S. by *á* (accented).

No. 4. This is one of the very few sounds (only four all told) that are expressed by the same symbol at the present day as in Anglo-Saxon times. Example, A.S. *nest*, Mod. Eng. *nest* (the same sound).

No. 5. This sound must not be confounded with No. 2; for it is a closer sound than No. 2, *i.e.* we bring the jaws nearer together in sounding it. It pairs (approximately) with No. 4, which is also a close sound, as in *let, late.* In A.S. it was expressed by *é* (accented), the sound of which corresponded with the first *a* in *fa-tal.* (In a syllable like *late*, that ends with a consonant, there is, in our present sounding of it, a glide or slight after-sound expressed by *i*, and hence *ei* is the phonetic symbol assigned by phoneticians to No. 5.)

No. 6. This is another of the sounds expressed in Mod. Eng. by the same symbol as in A.S. Example, A.S. *wind*, Mod. Eng. *wind* (the same sound).

No. 7. This, though now expressed by *ee*, is really *ii*, that is, No. 6 doubled or lengthened, but with a difference. The short of *ii* is not the Eng. *i* in *pin*, but the less open Fr. *i* in *fini.* The sound *ii* was expressed in A.S. by *í* (accented), as in *wín* (wine), then sounded as we now sound *ween.*

No. 8. This is the third example of a sound expressed by the same symbol now as in A.S. Example, A.S. *docga*, Eng. *dog.* The sound of this *o* is quite distinct from that of *o* in *o-bey*, No. 10; for in *dog* the *o* is an open sound, and in *o-bey* a close one. If we sound *dog* with a drawl, as some do, it becomes *daug*, just as our word *not* has actually come out of a quicker and shorter pronunciation of *naught.*

No. 9. This is simply No. 8 lengthened, as has been already explained. It was unknown in A.S., and hence there was no symbol equivalent to it. The use of a digraph to express the sound does not make it anything else than a simple or pure sound. It is not diphthongal.

No. 10. This sound is always unaccented. It is never heard in monosyllables. Nor is it ever heard in polysyllabic words, unless it ends the syllable to which it belongs, as in *o-bey*, *mo-lest*, *dit-to*, *fel-low*.[1] (If it is not the last letter in the syllable, it immediately becomes something else. Thus in *ob-stacle* the sound of *o* is No. 8; while in *but-ton* it is identical with ə, No. 14, *but-tən*.) The sound of *o'* is heard more distinctly at the end of a word than at the beginning. At the beginning it is apt to be sounded like No. 14: thus a man will at one moment say *o'bey* and at another *əbey*. But at the end of a word it comes out clearly; for it is considered a vulgarism to say *fellə* for *fello'* (*fellow*).

No. 11. This is a close sound like No. 10, and not an open sound like No. 8. It therefore pairs with No. 10. It does not, however, make a perfect pair with the *o* in *note;* for in this and other syllables that end in a consonant, the sound of *o* is followed by a glide or slight after-sound expressed by *u*, and hence *ou* is the phonetic symbol assigned to it by phoneticians. When the syllable ends in a vowel, and this is the first syllable of a word and accented, as *no'-ble*, *po'-et*, no glide after the *o* is heard.

No. 12. This sound is equivalent to A.S. *u*, as in A.S. *ful*, Mod. Eng. *full* (the same sound); and might be classed with *e*, *i*, and *o* as the fourth example, in which the sound in Mod. Eng. is expressed by the same symbol as in A.S. But excepting in syllables beginning with *p*, *b*, or *f* (as in *pull*, *bull*, *full*), the sound is now usually expressed by *ŏŏ*, as in *stood*. The substitution of the digraph *oo* for A.S. *u* cannot, of course, alter the fact that the sound is single and simple as before.

---

[1] The rule, however, is not quite universal, when this vowel occurs in the final syllable. If a verb like *bellow* is augmented by some grammatical inflexion, as *bellow-s*, *bellow-ed*, the original sound of *o'* is retained, notwithstanding the final consonant. Similarly, if the plural inflexion *-s* or *-es* is added to a noun, the sound of *o'*, which occurred in the final syllable of the singular, is retained in the plural: as *hero*, *hero-es;* *window*, *window-s*.

No. 13. This is No. 12 lengthened, and was expressed in A.S. by *ú*, as in A.S. *rúm*, Mod. Eng. *room* (the same sound).

No. 14. This sound is not represented, so far as we have seen, by any symbol in the current Dictionaries; yet it is one of the commonest sounds in our language. It is called by phoneticians the Obscure, Indefinite, or Neutral vowel, and is symbolised by ə (turned *e*). It is always unaccented. It occurs in almost every variety of spelling, as in the last syllables of *China*, *button*, *sudden*, *humble*, *cupboard*, *tortoise*, *meerschaum*, in the first and last syllables of *America*, *abandon*, and in the middle syllables of *history*, *mystery*, *teachable*. This sound is so natural to human speech, that hesitating speakers use it to fill up gaps in their sentences.

No. 15. This is No. 14 doubled, but long and usually accented. It is never heard except when it is followed by an *untrilled* "*r*" or some equivalent sound, as in *kernel*, *colonel*, *burn*, *bird*, *first*, etc. It was unknown in A.S. (In the word *perturb* it is accented in the second syllable, and unaccented in the first.)

No. 16. This sound is approximately an accented form of No. 14, and is heard in such words as *but*, *one*, *flood*, *touch*, etc. It was unknown in A.S.

No. 17. This sound was not represented by anything similar in A.S. It is compounded of No. 6 preceded by the *a* of German *mann* or A.S. *mann*.

No. 18. This sound is heard in such words as *few*, *Europe*, *you*, etc. The A.S. equivalent was *íw*, as in the words *híw*, hue; *íw*, yew; in which we have made no change in the sound or sense, but only in the spelling. This sound is compounded of No. 6 and No. 13.

No. 19. This sound appears in such words as *moist*, *boy*, etc. It was unknown in A.S. It is compounded of No. 9 and No. 6.

No. 20. This sound is heard in such words as *mouth*, *now*, etc. It was unknown in A.S. It is compounded of No. 3 and No. 12.

*Note.*—Among the above pairs the most perfect are 1 and 2 (*marry*, *Mary*), 8 and 9 (*dog*, *fraud*), 12 and 13 (*stood*, *stool*), 14 and 15 (*China*, *turn*). But even in these there is some difference of quality, besides that of mere length; for the short vowel in every case is rather more open than the corresponding long one. In the three remaining pairs there are, as we have shown, other slight differences.

**440. Classification of Vocalic Sounds.**—The main classification is into Simple (*i.e.* pure, unmixed) and Compound (*i.e.* mixed or diphthongal).

The **Simple** sounds, 14 in number, are either Short or Long.

| Short (eight) | |
|---|---|
| | ă in *marry*. |
| | ĕ in *let*. |
| | ĭ in *fit*. |
| | ŏ in *dog*. |
| | o' in *o*-bey. |
| | ŏŏ in *stood*. |
| | ə in Chin-*a*. |
| | ŭ in *but*. |

| Long (six) | |
|---|---|
| | â in *Mary*. |
| | ȧ in *path*. |
| | ē in *feet*. |
| | *au* in *fraud*. |
| | ōō in *stool*. |
| | əə in *turn*. |

The **Compound** (or diphthongal) sounds are the following:—

| | |
|---|---|
| Partly diphthongal (two) | ā, made up of A.S. *é*+*i*, as in *late*, *vein*. |
| | ō, made up of A.S. *ó*+*u*, as in *note*. |
| Wholly diphthongal (four) | ī, made up of *a*+*i*, as in *pine*, *aisle*. |
| | ū, made up of A.S. *i*+*ú*, as in *duke*. |
| | *oi*, made up of *au*+*i*, as in *moist*. |
| | *ou*, made up of A.S. *á*+*u*, as in *mouth*. |

The two first, viz. ā and ō, are called *partly* diphthongal, because when they end the syllable, as in *fa*-tal, *no*-ble, they are Simple, corresponding precisely with A.S. *é* and *ó* respectively; but when they are followed by a consonant in the same syllable, as in *late*, *note*, they are compounded with a semi-vowel, which serves as a glide or slight after-sound. In the former the semi-vowel is *i*, as shown above; in the latter *u*.

The four last are on a different footing. They are *wholly* diphthongal. Here the second element is not a mere glide or semi-vowel, but a fully sounded vowel. Otherwise nothing like the compound sounds expressed by ī, ū, *oi*, *ou* can be produced. The full sounds of both vowels are fused into one, so as to make a third sound distinct from either.

In the compound ī, the first vowel is the short *a* of the German *mann*. The long *a* of *path* would give us the vocalic sound heard in *naive*, *aye*, *Isaiah*, *ayah* (Indian maid-servant), which is much more open than the ī of *pine*, *aisle*.

In the compound ū, the *i*, being placed in contact with A.S. *ú* or Eng. ōō, becomes *y*. Hence *u-nit* is sounded as *yoo-nit*.

With the help of an *untrilled* "*r*" (which has the sound of ə), five more diphthongs and four triphthongs can be expressed.

*Diphthongs*:—care, deer, drawer, mower, poor.
*Triphthongs*:—fire, pure, (de)stroyer, power.

**441. Vowel-lengthening by final "e."**—The device most commonly used for expressing the sound of a long vowel or diphthong, as distinct from that of a short one, is by adding *e* after a single consonant. How did this device come into existence?

Take the word *stone* as an example. The A.S. and Mercian form was *stán*, and in the Dative case *stán-e*. The corresponding forms in Mid. Eng. were *ston* or *stoon* (Nom.) and *stón-e* (Dat.). Now most of the prepositions in Old and Mid. Eng. were followed by the Dative case, and hence this form of noun was more frequently seen than any other. "As the use of *ston* for *stoon* made the length of the vowel in *ston* uncertain, while in the Dative case there was no such doubt, the use of a suffixed *e* after a single consonant soon came to be associated with the idea of vowel length, and it is now distinctly recognised as the usual way of representing a long sound. It is an extremely poor contrivance; but it came about naturally enough" (Skeat).[1]

In the case of words like *wrote*, *arose*, etc. (which are not nouns, but parts of a verb, and therefore not susceptible of the Dative suffix *-e*), the addition of final *e* for the purpose of vowel-lengthening was due to analogy. In A.S. the past tense of *writ'-an* (to write) was *wrát*, in Mid. Eng. *wroot*. So the word went through the same changes of sound and spelling as *stán*.

**442. Shifting of Long Vowel sounds.**—The whole of the

[1] *Princ. of Eng. Etym.* pp. 32, 33, ed. 1895. Another explanation is given in *Ency. Brit.* under art. "English Language":—"In the thirteenth century the Old Eng. short vowels in an open syllable still retained the short quantity, as *nă-ma*; but by the beginning of the fourteenth century they were lengthened to *nā-me*, a change which has also taken place in all the Teutonic and even in the Romance languages, as in *buō-no* for *bŏ-num*. The lengthening of this penultimate left the final syllable by contrast shortened or weakened, and paved the way for the disappearance of final *e* in the century following, through the stages *nā-me*, *nā-m*, *nām*, the one long syllable *nam*(*e*) being the quantitative equivalent of the two short syllables in *nă-mĕ*; and thus came the idea that mute *e* makes the preceding vowel long, the truth being that the lengthening of the vowel made the *e* mute."

These explanations are not contradictory, but supplementary, both being quite correct. The first (Mr. Skeat's) explains the case of a vowel that was always long. The second takes the case of a vowel that has been made long, but was originally short.

Long Vowel system of Anglo-Saxon sounds fell to pieces, and was replaced in the sixteenth and seventeenth centuries by a new scheme throughout; and even these sounds have since changed (without corresponding changes in symbol) to those current in our present language. (See Skeat's *Princ. Eng. Etym.* chap. v. series i.)

I. A.S. *á* as in *bath*, changed to Mod. Eng. *ō*, as in *both*.
II. A.S. *é* as in *same*, changed to Mod. Eng. *ē*, as in *seem*.
III. A.S. *í* as in *meet*, changed to Mod. Eng. *ī*, as in *mite*.
IV. A.S. *ó* as in *boat*, changed to Mod. Eng. *ōō*, as in *boot*.
V. A.S. *ú* as in *shoot*, changed to Mod. Eng. *ou*, as in *shout*.

The above scheme is interesting for one reason, if for no others,—that it explains how *oo* came to express the sound for which it is now used. One would have thought that *oo* would be intended to express a long *o*, just as *ee* is used to express a long *e*, as in *seem*. This is what *oo* did actually express for some words in Mid. Eng., when the symbol *oo* first came into use, just as *brooch* is still sounded as *brōch*. Since then, however, the sound has shifted to that of *oo* in *boot*, *shoot*, etc. The sound has changed, but the spelling has remained.

*Note.*—In Mid. Eng. the symbol *oo* had two different sounds—(1) the sound of *oa* in *broad*, Mid. Eng. *brood*; usually denoted by *au*, as in *fraud*; see table in p. 278, No. 9; and (2) the sound of *ō*, as in *hole*, *both*, *coal*; see table in p. 278, No. 11.

The shifting of the *oo* sound implies what is the fact, that there was a general shifting of the long vowel sounds all along the line, such as is shown in the scheme given above. When the A.S. *ú* ceased to express the sound of *oo* as in *shoot*, a new sound was given to it, namely, that expressed by the *ow* in *now* (A.S. *nú*).[1]

**443. I. The A.S. "á."**—In A.S. (as has been shown in line I. of § 442) this vowel was sounded as the *a* in *bath*, *father*, etc. In Mid. Eng. this was changed to *o* or *oo*, but pronounced as *au*, the *oa* in *broad*. Since the sixteenth century the sound of Mid. Eng. *au* has shifted to that of *ō*, as in *both*, *whole*, *goal*.

A.S. *wá*, Mod. Eng. *woe*; A.S. *cnáw-an*, Mod. Eng. *know*; A.S. *ná*, Mod. Eng. *no*; A.S. *cláð-ian*, Mod. Eng. *clothe*; A.S.

[1] The A.S. *ú* never became *yōō* in sound, but always *ou* or *ow*, as in *nú*, now; *cú*, cow. But the Anglo-French *u* (from Lat. *u*) did become *yōō* in sound. Hence the rule that all words having *ū* pronounced as *yōō*, if correctly spelt, came out of a Latin *u*, usually long; as *pure*, Lat. *pūrus*; *sure*, Lat. *secūrus*. (An exception is *duke*, where the *u* has been lengthened; from Lat. *dŭc-em*.)

*ðás*, Mod. Eng. *those;* A.S. *gást*, Mod. Eng. *ghost;* A.S. *sáwel*, Mod. Eng. *soul;* A.S. *stán*, Mod. Eng. *stone;* A.S. *hám*, Mod. Eng. *home;* A.S. *tá*, Mod. Eng. *toe;* A.S. *hál*, Mod. Eng. *whole;* A.S. *wrát*, Mod. Eng. (*he*) *wrote;* Scand. *lágr*, Mod. Eng. *low*, etc.

*Note.*—Here belong nearly all the words written with *oa*, or ending with *oe*.

**444.** II. **The A.S. "é."**—The sound of A.S. *é*, as has been shown in line II. of § 442, was similar to that of the former element of the *ā* (= *ei*) in *same*, but in Mod. Eng. has shifted to the sound of *ē* in *seem*.

A.S. *hé* (sounded as *hā*), Mod. Eng. *he;* A.S. *ðé*, Mod. Eng. *thee;* A.S. *wé*, Mod. Eng. *we;* A.S. *mé*, Mod. Eng. *me;* A.S. *gé*, Mod. Eng. *ye;* A.S. *hél*, Mod. Eng. *heel;* A.S. *téþ*, Mod. Eng. *teeth;* A.S. *cwén*, Mod. Eng. *queen;* A.S. *tén* (ten), Mod. Eng. *teen* (as in *thirteen*); A.S. *grén-e*, Mod. Eng. *green;* A.S. *sém-an*, Mod. Eng. *seem;* A.S. *bléd-an*, Mod. Eng. *bleed*, etc.

**445.** III. **The A.S. "í."**—The sound of A.S. *í*, as has been shown in line III. of § 442, was the same as *ē* or *ee* in *meet*, but has shifted in Mod. Eng. to the diphthongal sound of *ī* in *mite*. (In Tudor English it had the sound of *ā* in *fame* or *ei* in *vein*):—

A.S. *bí* (sounded as *bē*), Mod. Eng. *by;* A.S. *mín*, Mod. Eng. *mine;* A.S. *hwíl*, Mod. Eng. *while;* A.S. *wríð-an*, Mod. Eng. *writhe;* A.S. *ís*, Mod. Eng. *ice;* A.S. *rís-an*, Mod. Eng. *rise;* A.S. *líf*, Mod. Eng. *life;* A.S. *wíf*, Mod. Eng. *wife;* A.S. *ðín*, Mod. Eng. *thine;* A.S. *swín*, Mod. Eng. *swine;* A.S. *líc*, Mod. Eng. *like;* A.S. *rím*, Mod. Eng. *rime* (misspelt as *rhyme*); A.S. *twín*, Mod. Eng. *twine*, etc.

*Note* 1.—The original sound of *í* has survived in a shortened vowel in *women* (pronounced as *wim-men*; from A.S. *wíf* compounded with *man*), and in *stirrup* (A.S. *stí-ráp*).

*Note* 2.—In a large number of Romanic words of late introduction ending in "*i . . . e*," the final syllable is still sounded as if the vowel were *ee*:—*un-ique*, *po-lice*, *oblique*, *quin-ine*, etc. (The *ē* sound in "ob-*lige*" has now become archaic.)

> Dreading e'en fools, by flatterers besieged,
> And so obliging that he ne'er ob-*liged*.
>
> POPE, *Prol. Sat.* 208.

**446.** IV. **The A.S. "ó."**—The sound of A.S. *ó*, as has been shown in line IV. of § 442, was similar to the former element of *ō* in *boat*, but has shifted in Mod. Eng. to the sound of *ōō* in *boot:*—

A.S. *sceó*, Mod. Eng. *shoe*; A.S. *dó*, Mod. Eng. *do;* A.S. *tó*, Mod. Eng. *too* and *to;* A.S. *eów*, Mod. Eng. *you;* A.S. *bót*, Mod. Eng. *boot;* A.S. *slóh*, Mod. Eng. *slew;* A.S. *dróg*, Mod. Eng. *drew;* A.S. *mód*,

Mod. Eng. *mood;*[1] Scand. *blóm,* Mod. Eng. *bloom;* A.S. *gós,* Mod. Eng. *goose;* A.S. *tóð,* Mod. Eng. *tooth,* etc.

In the following examples the A.S. *ó* has shifted to the shorter sound "*ŏŏ*," chiefly before *k*, *t*, and *d*:—

A.S. *fót,* Mod. Eng. *fŏŏt;* A.S. *stód,* Mod. Eng. *stŏŏd;* A.S. *gód,* Mod. Eng. *gŏŏd;* A.S. *cóc,* Mod. Eng. *cŏŏk;* A.S. *bóc,* Mod. Eng. *bŏŏk;* A.S. *hóc,* Mod. Eng. *hŏŏk;* A.S. *bósm,* Mod. Eng. *bosom* (sounded as *bŏŏsom*), etc.

In the following examples the vowel sound has been still further shortened and unrounded to *ŭ:*[2]—

A.S. *óðer,* Mod. Eng. *other* (sounded as *ŭther*); A.S. *módor,* Mod. Eng. *mother;* A.S. *glóf,* Mod. Eng. *glove;* A.S. *flód,* Mod. Eng. *flood* (sounded as *flŭd*); A.S. *blód,* Mod. Eng. *blood* (sounded as *blŭd*); A.S. *móste,* Mod. Eng. *must;* A.S. *ge-nóg,* Mod. Eng. *enough,* etc.

*Note.*—In words of French origin the sound of *ŭ* is sometimes spelt as *o* and sometimes as *ou.* The former usually occurs before or after *m*, *n*, or *v*. The latter at first had the sound of *ou* in *soup* (=*sŏŏp*); *i.e.* it was at first *ú* (long), but has been shortened.

Front, on-ion, doz-en, gov-ern, com-rade, com-bat, etc.
Troub-le, doub-le, scourge, jour-ney, coup-le, etc.

**447. V. The A.S. "ú."**—The sound of A.S. *ú*, as has been shown in line V. of § 442, was the same as *ōō*, as in *shoot* or *boot*, but has shifted in Mod. Eng. to the sound of *ou* or *ow*, as in *shout*, *crowd*. In the word *un-couth* (A.S. *un-cúð*) the symbol in the second syllable has preserved its original sound.

A.S. *hú,* Mod. Eng. *how;* A.S. *ðú,* Mod. Eng. *thou;* A.S. *nú,* Mod. Eng. *now;* A.S. *cú,* Mod. Eng. *cow;* A.S. *úr-e,* Mod. Eng. *our;* A.S. *hús,* Mod. Eng. *house;* A.S. *mús,* Mod. Eng. *mouse;* A.S. *dún,* Mod. Eng. *down;* A.S. *tún,* Mod. Eng. *town;* A.S. *út-,* Mod. Eng. *out;* A.S. *ab-út-an,* Mod. Eng. *about,* etc.

**448. Two, who, one,** etc.—The vowel sounds in these three peculiar words have undergone more than one shifting.

*Two, who.*—The A.S. forms were *twá*, *hwá*, the vowel in each case being immediately preceded by *w*. The *á*, after passing through the intermediate sound of *au* as in ordinary cases, acquired in due course the sound of *ō* as shown in line I. in § 442. But instead of stopping there it passed into the

---

[1] We have another word *mood,* which is derived from Lat. *mod-us,* manner or mode. *Mode* is the usual spelling of this word; but in grammar it is spelt *mood.* A.S. *mód* and Latin *mod-us* are not cognate, and in fact have different vowels.

[2] "Rounding" means the lateral compression of the lips, so as to give a narrower passage for the vowel sound. The "unrounding" is the relaxation of this. Cf. *move* with *glove.*

sound of *ōō*, as per line IV. in § 442, owing to the influence of the *w*; and the sound of *ōō* remained, even after the *w* had become silent. (*Twá* > *twau* > *twō* > *twōō* > *tōō*.)

*One.*—The history of the sound of this word is still more peculiar. The A.S. form of the word was *án*; in Mid. Eng. it was changed to *oon*, the vowel of which was sounded as *au* in *fraud*, and afterwards as *ō* in *both* or *bone* (see line I. in § 442). In the fifteenth century a parasitic *w* prefixed itself to the vowel, which changed the spelling of *oon* to *woon*. The *woon* was still at first sounded as *wone* (cf. *bone*, *both*). But by the influence of the parasitic *w* the *ō* sound gradually shifted to the *ōō* sound (see line IV.). It was then gradually shortened to *ŏŏ*, and finally unrounded to *ŭ*, so that the word is now sounded as *wŭn*, rhyming with *bŭn*. When the *w*, that caused all this confusion, was discovered to be a parasite, it was discarded, so as to bring the spelling of the word a step nearer to the classical and cognate word *un-us* (Latin). But the pronunciation *wŭn* stuck and still sticks to the altered spelling *one*.

*Only*, *alone*, *atone*.—In these words, all of which are compounded with *one*, the earlier sound of the vowel, as in *bone*, survived, because in these compounds the syllable "one" was not corrupted by the parasitic *w*.

*Anon.*—This word was once spelt *an-oon*, being derived from the A.S. phrase *on án* (= "in or on one"). Here then the *á* shifted to *oo*, in accordance with § 443. But the *oo* or *ō* (pronounced as *au*) was gradually shortened to *ŏ*, as we now have it. Cf. *dog*, vulgarly sounded as *daug*.

*An* (Indef. Article).—This was originally the A.S. *án* (= one). But when *án* came to be used as an Indef. Article, owing to lack of stress the *á* was shortened to *ă*.

**449. The "au" sound.**—It was stated in § 443 that in Mid. Eng. the intermediate sound between the *á* of A.S. and the *ō* of Mod. Eng. was *au*, as in *fraud*, but that in Mid. Eng. it was spelt as *o* or *oo*. We have still a few words spelt with *o*, *oo*, or *ou*, in which the *au* sound has been retained, especially before *r* or after *cl*, or after *r* preceded by another consonant, as in *wrath*, *broad*:—

A.S. *cláð*, Mod. Eng. *cloth*; A.S. *wráð*, Mod. Eng. *wroth*; A.S. *gár*, Mod. Eng. *gore*; A.S. *ge-ára*, Mod. Eng. *yore*; A.S. *brád*, Mod. Eng. *broad*; A.S. *ár*, Mod. Eng. *oar*; A.S. *bár*, Mod. Eng. *boar*; A.S. *hár*, Mod. Eng. *hoar*; A.S. *sár*, Mod. Eng. *sore*; A.S. *már-a*, Mod. Eng. *more*; A.S. *lár*, lore; A.S. *rár*-ian, roar; A.S. *gán*, gone (sounded as *gaun*), etc.

In some other words spelt with *oo* or *o*, but not similarly derived, the *au* sound is still found :—

*Door, floor, loss, lost, frost, cost, soft, off, often, broth*, etc.

*Note.*—In *door* and *floor* the *au* sound is due to the *r*. In *soft*, A.S. *sóft-e*, the ō was shortened to ŏ before *ft*, so as to make *sŏft-e* (which was more easily pronounced), and afterwards (when the word became monosyllabic) it was lengthened out again. In the remaining words the original vowel was ŏ, which was lengthened to *au*, the long sound of the vowel *o* described in No. 9, p. 278.

**450. The diphthong "ea."**—It was in the Tudor period that the diphthong *ea* first came into use. It was then sounded as ā, like *ea* in *great*. But the ā sound has, with few exceptions, shifted to that of ē, as in *dream*, *beat*, etc.; cf. line II. in § 442. The change was gradual, and we find considerable variety in English poets up to a recent date :—

Here thou, great Anna, whom three realms obey,
Dost sometimes council take, and sometimes *tea*.—POPE.
The lowing herd winds slowly o'er the *lea*,
And leaves the world to darkness and to me.—GREY.
I am monarch of all I survey,
From the centre all round to the *sea*.—COWPER.
But I beneath a rougher *sea*,
And whelmed in deeper gulfs than he.—COWPER.

*Note.*—The only words in which the diphthong *ea* has retained the Tudor sound of ā are :—*Steak*, *bear* (verb), *bear* (noun), *wear*, *tear* (verb), *break*, *great*, *pear*, *swear*,—nine words in all. In every instance, except that of *steak*, the ā sound has been preserved by the influence of the following *r*, or that of the preceding *br* and *gr*. In *steak* the retention of the ā sound is perhaps due to the strong combination *st*.

**451. The diphthong "oa."**—This symbol, like the preceding, first came into use in the Tudor period, and had the sound of *au*, as in *broad*, being intended to supply the place of *oo*, which in Mid. Eng. had also the sound of *au* in some words. (See *Note* to § 442.)

We still have some words in which the *au* sound has been retained with the *oa* spelling (see examples in § 449). But there is a much larger number of words in which the *au* sound has shifted to that of ō, and the diphthong *oa* (which, when final, takes the form of *oe*) is very largely used to express this sound in Mod. Eng. spelling :—

*Boat* (A.S. *bát*); *oak* (A.S. *ác*); *loan* (A.S. *lán*); *road* (A.S. *rád*); *oath* (A.S. *áð*); *toad* (A.S. *tád*); *loaf* (A.S. *hláf*); *loath* (A.S. *láð*); *roe; toe; doe; foe*, etc.

**452. Vowel-mutation.**—The modification that a vowel

may receive, through the influence of another vowel occurring in a following suffix, is called Mutation. The first vowel is by this process modified in the direction of the second one. In almost every instance the mutating or modifying vowel is *i*. Thus *Franc-ish* became *Frenc-isc*, afterwards shortened to "French." Here the *a* is modified in the direction of *i*, the result being a new vowel intermediate to the other two.

But the *i* (though usually seen in Gothic, an older language) cannot always be detected in the extant forms of Anglo-Saxon; for it not unfrequently happened that the *i*, after having produced a mutation of the preceding vowel, dropped out of sight and was lost. This is called *concealed mutation*, examples of which are very common in English.

The kinds of examples in which concealed mutation is chiefly seen in Mod. Eng. are:—

(1) In the formation of the plurals of certain nouns, in which the final *-is* is now lost, as *foot, feet*. See below, § 486.

(2) In the formation of Causal verbs; as *set* from *sat*, Past tense of *sit*. Here the mutation is caused by the *i* of the old Infin. ending *-ian*. See below, § 454.

(3) In the formation of the Present tenses of certain Weak verbs; as *sell*, from *sale* (A.S. *sal-ian*). Here the mutation is caused by the *i* in *-ian*, as in (2). See below, § 513.

(4) In the formation of Degrees of Comparison in certain adjectives; as *old*, *elder*, *eldest* (A.S. *eald, yldra, yldesta*, through *-ira, -ista*, the more ancient forms of the suffixes *-ra, -esta*). Similarly the *o* in *fore* has been mutated to *y* or *i* in *for-ist, first* (A. S. *fyrst*). ("Older," the other form of the Comparative, is of recent date, and according to the rules of Mod. Eng. grammar has been regularly formed from *old*.)

(5) In the formation of Trans. verbs from nouns or adjectives; as *full, fill; gold, gild; hale, heal; foul, de-file*, etc. The process of change was as follows:—A.S. *ful* (adj.), *full-ian* (Causal verb, "to make full"), *fyll-an*, Mod. Eng. *fill;* A.S. *gold* (noun), *gold-ian* (Causal verb), *gyld-an*, Mod. Eng. *gild;* A.S. *hál* (whole, hale, adj.), *hál-ian* (Causal verb), *hǽl-an*, Mod. Eng. *heal;* A.S. *fúl* (foul, adj.), *fúl-ian* (Causal verb), *fýl-an*, Mod. Eng. *(de)-file*. (The forms *full-ian, hál-ian, fúl-ian* are theoretical in A.S., but are actually found in Gothic, where the radical vowels did not undergo mutation.)

(6) In nouns formed by adding certain suffixes; as *fox, vix-en* (in which the *-en* was originally *-in*); *thumb, thimb-le* (A.S. *thým-el*, from *thum-i-la*); *corn, kern-el* (A.S. *cyrn-el*, from *curn-i-la*); *long* (A.S. *lang*), *length* (for *lang-itha*); *strong* (A.S. *strang*), *strength; broad* (A.S. *brád*), *breadth*, etc.

(7) In adjectives by adding the suffix *-ish;* as *Angel* (*Angle*), *English* (*Angel-ish*); *Frank, French* (*Frank-ish*); *Wales, Welsh* (*Wal-ish*).

*Note*.—Mutation is not confined to words of Teutonic origin. Thus we have *kitchen* from Lat. *coquina* (a cook-room); *kettle* from

Lat. *catillus* (a bowl); *pit* (older form *pyt*) from Lat. *puteus*, *putius* (a well); *mill* (*miln* in Mid. Eng., *mylen* in A.S.) from Lat. *molina* (a grinder); *minster* from *monister* for Lat. *monasterium* (abode of monks).

**453. Vowel-gradation.**—Gradation must not be confounded with Mutation. It is seen, for example, in verbs of the Strong conjugation. The principal parts of a verb are the present tense, the past tense, and the past participle, as in *sing*, *sang*, *sung*. Here *sing* is in the *i* grade, *sang* in the *a* grade, and *sung* in the *u* grade. But Gradation is by no means confined to the conjugation of Strong verbs; thus we have *bind*, *bond*, *band*. These words are co-radicals,—that is, we cannot say that one is derived from another, and the only safe way to express the primitive root would be by leaving out the vowel and calling it *b*nd*. But derivatives (that is, derived words) may be formed from any grade or special form of the root.

*Band*, *band-age*, *band-y* (from A.S. *band*, pt. t. of *bind-en*, to bind); *bond*, *bond-age*; *bund-le* (from A.S. *ge-bund-en*, pp. of *bind-en*). *Abode* (from A.S. *ábád*, pt. t. of A.S. *ábíd-an*, to abide). *Strike* (verb, A.S. *stríc-an*); *streak* (Swed. *strek*, a line), *stroke* (A.S. *strác*, pt. t. of *stríc-an*). *Shov-el* (from A.S. *scof-en*, pp. of *scúf-an*, to shove); *sheaf* (from *sceáf*, pt. t. of *scúf-an*). *Bairn* (from A.S. *bǽr*, pt. t. singular of *ber-an*, to bear), *bier* (from *bǽr-on*, pt. t. plural of *ber-an*), *bur-den*, *birth* (from *bor-en*, pp. of *ber-an*).

*Note.*—The difference between vowel-gradation and vowel-mutation throws some light upon that between Cognate words and Derived words (see § 378, *Note* 3). Thus if we take the verb *bear* as an example, we find that it is cognate with Gr. *pher-o*, Lat. *fer-o*, Sanskrit *bhar-âmi*, and Goth. *bair-an*, and that in English itself it has three cognate forms, viz. *bear* (Pres.), *bare* (old Past), and *bor-en* or *bor-n* (Past Part.), all based upon the Aryan root *bher*. Each of the cognate forms last named has a vowel grade of its own, but none is derived from any other. On the other hand, *bair-n*, *bar-m*, (wheel)-*barr-ow*, *bier*, *birth*, *berth*, *burden*, are all derived words,—derived from one or other of the graded roots, the vowels of which have in some instances undergone mutation.

**454. Gradation and Mutation combined.**[1]—Both processes are exemplified in the formation of Causal or Transitive Verbs (Weak) from Intransitive (Strong). (Some, however, of the Intransitives, that were Strong in A.S., have since become Weak.)

Causal verbs were usually formed—(1) from the stem of the *Past* tense of Strong verbs (Gradation); (2) by adding an *i* to the

[1] The German names for Gradation and Mutation are *Ablaut* (off-sound) and *Umlaut* (about-sound) respectively.

stem of this tense, which produced a change in the stem-vowel (Mutation). The *i* is seen in Gothic, but rarely in Old English, in which the *i*, after producing mutation, was dropped.

| Intransitive. | | | | Transitive. | |
|---|---|---|---|---|---|
| Eng. | A.S. | Past tense by Gradation. | Causal Infinitive. | Infin. by Mutation. | English. |
| To drink | drinc-an | dranc | dranc-ian | drenc-an | to drench. |
| To sit | sitt-an | sat | sat-ian | sett-an | to set. |
| To quail | cwel-an | cwal | cwal-ian | cwell-an | to quell. |
| To lie | licg-an | lag | lag-ian | lecg-an | to lay. |
| To rise | ris-an | rás | rás-ian | rǽr-an | to rear. |
| To blink | blinc-an | blanc | blanc-ian | blenc-an | to blench. |
| To clink | clinc-an | clanc | clanc-ian | clenc-an | to clench. |
| Can | cunn-an | can | can-ian | cenn-an | to ken. |
| To bow | búg-an | béag | béag-ian | býg-an | to bow |
| To sink | sinc-an | sanc | sanc-ian | senc-an | to sink |

The two following verbs, both of Scandian or Old Norse origin, are examples of gradation without mutation, because the Old Norse *ei* is not subject to mutation :—

| Eng. | Old Norse. | Past tense by Gradation. | Causal Infinitive. | English. |
|---|---|---|---|---|
| To rise | ris-a | reis | reis-a | to raise. |
| To bite | bit-a | beit | beit-a | to bait. |

In the three following verbs the Causal forms are from the Present tense, not the Past (mutation without gradation) :—

| Eng. | A.S. | Causal Infinitive. | Infin. by Mutation. | Eng. |
|---|---|---|---|---|
| To fall | fall-an | fall-ian | fell-an | to fell. |
| To swoop | swáp-an | swáp-ian | swǽp-an | to sweep. |
| To fare | far-an | far-ian | fer-i-an | to ferry. |

*Note.*—In the verb *ferry*, the final *y* represents the *i* of the Infinitive suffix *-ian*, which was preserved in A.S., and not lost, as in the other examples, because of the preceding *r*, which required that the *i* should be retained.

## CHAPTER XXIV.—SPELLINGS.

### Section 1.—History of English Spelling.

(Compiled from chap. xvi. of Skeat's *Princ. Eng. Etym.* series i.)

**455. Phonetic Character of A.S. Alphabet.**—An alphabet is said to be strictly phonetic—(1) when every simple sound is represented by a distinct symbol, and (2) no sound is represented by more than one symbol.

Anglo-Saxon spelling was in the main phonetic. Among the consonants the chief defects were the double use of *f* for the sounds of *f* and *v*, the double use of *s* for the sounds of *s* and *z*, and the uncertain uses of þ and ð for the sounds of *th* in *this* or *thin*. Another defect was that the *k* was at first superfluous, as *c* had originally the sound of *k* in *all* positions.

The letter *h* had two distinct sounds, but these were not used at random. Initially *h* was simply an aspirate, as in *hot*. Medially and finally it had a guttural sound like that of *ch* in *Loch Lomond;* cf. A.S. *riht*, sounded as *richt*, which led to Mod. Eng. *right*, in which the guttural, though lost to the ear, is still preserved to the eye.

**456. Anglo-French Scribes.**—In the thirteenth and fourteenth centuries the English language was respelt according to the Anglo-French method by scribes who were familiar with Anglo-French, but not with Anglo-Saxon.[1] Hence the A.S. forms of the Latin letters were gradually replaced by French ones borrowed from the Continent. The change was not violent, as most of the French forms were nearly the same as those previously in use in Old English. The symbol æ (the most characteristic of all the vowels in Old English) and the mark denoting vowel-length were discarded. The letter ƿ was replaced by a French *w* similar to what we still use. The symbol ð had almost disappeared before 1300; but þ, denoting either sound of *th*, lingered on much longer. In the fifteenth century the form of þ was identified with that of *y;* so that in our early printers we find "y[e]" for *the* and "y[t]" for *that*, used, however, simply to save space, and not to indicate that *the* and *that* were to be sounded like *ye* and *yat*. Thus in Tunbridge Wells there is a street called "Ye Pantiles," a survival of the Caxton method of printing "the."

**457. Further Changes in Middle English.**—The A.S. *c* (originally sounded as *k* in all positions) was often replaced by *k;* thus the A.S. *cyn* was respelt as *kin;* and *kin* it still remains. On the other hand, the Anglo-French *c* had the sound of *s* before *e* and *i;* and was therefore used with this power in

[1] Though they were ignorant of Anglo-Saxon, they were fond of Mid. Eng., which they learnt, rewrote, studied, and in fact saved. Although in the thirteenth century they spelt English inaccurately, we find that in the fourteenth century many of their mistakes were corrected, as by that time they had acquired the pronunciation of nearly all the sounds except that of *gh*, which perished in the struggle, being dropped by common consent.

words of Anglo-French origin, such as *certain*, *city*. *Cw* was turned into *qu*, as in A.S. *cwic*, Mid. Eng. *quik*, Mod. Eng. *quick*. The vowels *u* and *y*, which in A.S. were vowels only, came to be used as consonants also, the former with the sound of *v*. The vowel *i* or its capital form *I* was made to represent the Anglo-French sound of *j* as in "joy,"—a sound unknown in Anglo-Saxon. The same scribes introduced the new diphthongs *ai* or *ay*, *au* or *aw*, *ei* or *ey*, *eu* or *ew*, *oi* or *oy*, and *ou* or *ow*, together with the consonantal combinations *ch*, *th*, and *sh*. The gutturals *c* and *g* of early A.S. were liable to be followed by a short intrusive *e*, as *ceaf*, *geard*; and this favoured the change in late A.S. of *ceaf* into *chaff*, and of *geard* into *yard*. "Gu" was never followed by a vowel in A.S.: all such words as *guard*, *guise*, *guile*, *guerdon*, *guide* are either new words introduced from French (as is the case with the words named) or new spellings of old words; as *guest* for A.S. *gæst*, and *guild* needlessly substituted for *gild*. *Hw*, which gave and still gives correctly the sound of the first letters in *which* and similar words, was changed to *wh*.

Notwithstanding all these changes, the spelling was still in the main phonetic, though less regularly so than in the A.S. period.

**458. Decay of the Phonetic System.**—The phonetic system, which characterised the earliest phases of our language, is now a thing of the past: it is lost beyond recovery. Our present spelling is chaotic. The decay of phoneticism may be briefly traced as follows:—

(1) The mixture of French words with English consequent on the Norman Conquest, the disuse of marks to denote the lengthening of vowels, the introduction of new symbols and combinations, and the investing of some of the old symbols with new sounds, weakened, though it did not greatly disturb, the phonetic system. "As the Anglo-French symbols were also Latin letters, many of which retained their Latin sounds, not much harm was done" (Skeat).

(2) As time went on, the sounds changed more rapidly than the symbols did. In about A.D. 1400, the sound of final *e* (already lost in the Northern dialect) was lost in the Midland also. When it remained, as in *base*, it no longer formed a distinct syllable, but denoted that the preceding vowel was long. But even this rule was not regularly applied; for the vowel was still short in *come*, *give*, *have*, *live*, *love*, etc. Consonants at the end of an accented syllable were doubled after a short

vowel, as in *better*. But here again the rule was not consistently acted on; as in *city*, *metal*, etc.[1] The introduction of printing in 1477 (of which "Caxton English" was the first visible result) tended to preserve symbolical forms that were not in keeping with contemporary sounds.

(3) Phonetic spelling was still aimed at even in Caxton English. But a new principle, which worked in the opposite direction, was introduced with the Revival of Learning in the sixteenth century. It was held by the scholars of that day that, whatever the demands of pronunciation might be, the spelling of a vowel ought to be made to represent *to the eye* the forms from which words were derived, especially words derived from Latin and Greek. So it came to pass that, after 1500, English spelling was governed by two conflicting principles, namely, the *phonetic*, which chiefly concerned *popular* words (*i.e.* the oldest and commonest words in popular use); and the *etymological*, which chiefly concerned *learned* words (*i.e.* words derived immediately from Latin or Greek). Thus the Mid. Eng. *vitailles* (provisions), which we borrowed from French, was respelt as *victuals*, because the root of the word could be traced back to Lat. *vict*-us, food. Similarly *dett*, borrowed from French *dette*, was respelt as *debt*; and *dout*, borrowed from French *dout*-er, was respelt as *doubt*, because the former could be traced to Lat. *debit-um*, and the latter to Lat. *dubit-o*. Similarly the Mid. Eng. *sutel* was respelt as *subtle* for the sake of the Lat. *subtilis*, although the *b* had never been admitted into Old French, from which *sutel* was borrowed.

But owing to the faulty scholarship of that age, many of the so-called etymological spellings were wrong. Thus *sythe* and *sent* were respelt as *scythe* and *scent*, because an *sc* was used in the highly classical word "science"; whereas *scythe* is from A.S. *sīðe*, and *scent* from Fr. *sent*-ir, or Lat. *sent*-ire. The Middle English *ake* (derived from A.S. *ac-an*, verb) was respelt as *ache* from a supposed connection with Greek *achos*. *Rime* (derived from A.S. *rīm* = number) was respelt as *rhyme* from a supposed connection with Greek *rhuthmos*, from which we get the entirely different word "rhythm." *Stile*, which is really derived from the Lat. *stilus*, was supposed to be derived from the Greek *stulos*, a pillar; and so it was respelt as *style*. The

---

[1] In point of fact, the final consonant is usually doubled before *e*, but seldom before other vowels: thus we have *pal'-ate*, *met'-al*, *cit'-i-zen*, *prem'-isses*, *mem'-o-ra-ble*, *hon'-our*, *pop'-u-lar*, *mod'-u-late*, etc.

Mid. Eng. *tunge* or *tonge* was respelt as *tongue*, because the absence of *u* after the *g* looked bad by the side of Fr. *langue*, Lat. *lingua*. The Mid. Eng. *iland*, derived from A.S. *īg-land* (= *īg*, an island + *land*, land), was respelt as *island*, the *s* having been inserted, because it was supposed to be derived from French *isle*, Lat. *insula*. Even words of Latin origin were wrongly respelt to make them look like Greek; thus *silvan* (from Lat. *silva*, a forest) was respelt as *sylvan*, because it was supposed to be derived from Gr. *hul-e* or *hyl-e*. The authors of these and such-like innovations, by which our spelling has been ruined, knew something (though not enough) about one portion of our language, viz. that derived from Latin and Greek, but nothing at all about the other, that derived from Anglo-Saxon.

(4) The changes in spelling since 1600 are comparatively trifling; but the changes in pronunciation, especially in the vowel-sounds (see § 442), have been very great. For instance, the symbol *oo*, which ought to express, and did once express the sound *ō* (as *ee* in *queen* does the modern sound of *ē*), now has the same sound as the A.S. *ū*, as in "fool." Again, the symbol *ou*, which in Mid. Eng. stood for A.S. *ū*, as in Mod. French, and sometimes even in Mod. Eng., as in "soup," "group," "route," is now usually sounded as in "foul," "sound." Again, the symbol *oa* (introduced in the Tudor period), which once was sounded as *au*, as it still is in *broad*, is now used to express the sound of *ō*, as in *toad*, *boat*. Again, the symbol *ea*, which in the Tudor period (when it was first introduced) expressed the modern sound of *ā* (as it still does in *great*), is now chiefly used to express the modern sound of *ē*, as in *beach*.

**459. Summary.**—The spelling of Mod. Eng. is, in fact, little better than a chaos. The main causes of confusion were—(*a*) the respelling of English by Anglo-French scribes, which, though it did not greatly disturb the phonetic system at the time, did much to weaken its powers of resistance and expose it to future inroads; (*b*) the adoption of the so-called etymological principle in the sixteenth century by men imperfectly acquainted with the Classical portion of our language and totally ignorant of the Teutonic portion; (*c*) the violent later changes in our vowel sounds, which were not accompanied by any corresponding changes in spelling. We still spell words in much the same way as they were spelt in the days of James I. "Practically we retain a Tudor system of symbols with a Victorian pronunciation" (Skeat).

## Section 2.—Summary of English Spellings.

**460. Summary of Spellings.**—In order to give a fairly complete summary of English spellings, we must first enumerate the different sounds, consonantal and vocalic, to be expressed by letters, and then the different letters or combinations of letters that are in actual use for expressing these sounds.

### I. *Consonantal Sounds and Spellings.*

From the scheme of consonants given above in § 431, it will be seen that in English as now used there are altogether twenty-five consonantal sounds, which, taking them as nearly as we can in the order of the alphabet, run as follows:—

| | | | | | | | |
|---|---|---|---|---|---|---|---|
| 1. b | 4. g | 7. k | 10. n | 13. s | 16. w | 19. ch | 22. th(in) |
| 2. d | 5. h | 8. l | 11. p | 14. t | 17. y | 20. ng | 23. sh |
| 3. f | 6. j | 9. m | 12. r | 15. v | 18. z | 21. th(is) | 24. zh |
| | | | | | | | 25. wh |

*Note.*—*Qu* (=kw) and *x* (=ks or gz) are not included.

We have now to show the different ways in which each of these sounds can be expressed or spelt:—

1. **b**: *b*ond (initial), e*bb* (final), *bu*oy, cu*pb*oard.

2. **d**: bon*d*, la*dd*er, call*ed*, hor*de*, wou*ld*.

3. **f**: *f*elt, whi*ff*, *ph*legm, lau*gh*, ha*lf*, o*ft*en, sa*pph*ire, li*eu*tenant (where *ieu* = *ef*).

4. **g**: *g*ame, e*gg*, *gh*ost, *gu*ard, ton*gue*.

5. **h**: *h*ot, *wh*o.

6. **j**: *j*ob, *g*ist, *G*eor*ge*, ju*dge*, sol*di*er, ju*dg*ment, Green*wich*, *ga*ol.

7. **k**: *k*ill, *c*all, a*cc*ount, ba*ck*, bis*cu*it, *q*uell, li*qu*or, grotes*que*, *ch*aos, a*che*, wa*lk*, Ba*cch*anal, lou*gh*.

8. **l**: *l*ake, ki*ll*, i*sl*and, ai*sle*, gaze*lle*, sera*gl*io, Wool*wi*ch, Gui*ld*ford.

9. **m**: *m*end, ha*mm*er, hy*mn*, la*mb*, program*me*, phleg*m*, psa*lm*, Ha*mp*den, dra*chm*.

10. **n**: pi*n*, i*nn*, dei*gn*, *kn*ee, *gn*aw, Jo*hn*, Linco*ln*, We*dn*esday, riba*nd*, bor*ne*, A*nne*, coig*ne*.

11. **p**: *p*lace, ha*pp*y, ste*ppe*, Cla*ph*am, hiccou*gh*.

12. **r**: *r*ain, bo*rr*ow, *rh*ythm, *wr*ite, Nor*wi*ch.

13. **s**: *s*elf, ki*ss*, den*se*, *c*ell, dan*ce*, *sc*ene, coale*sce*, *sch*ism, quart*z*, *sw*ord, ha*st*en, is*th*mus, *ps*alm, creva*sse*.

14. **t** : we*t*, ke*tt*le, gaze*tte*, *Th*ames, look*ed*, *t*wo, de*bt*, indi*ct*, recei*pt*, ya*cht*, cas*te*.

15. **v** : *v*est, ha*ve*, na*vv*y, o*f*, ne*ph*ew, hal*ve*.

16. **w** : *w*ine, *wh*en, s*u*ave, ch*o*ir.

17. **y** : *y*ield, un*i*on, hallelu*j*ah, vi*gn*ette (where *gn* = ny), cotil*l*on, mil*li*on.

18. **z** : *z*eal, fi*zz*, hi*s*, clean*se*, sci*ss*ors, *X*erxes, fur*ze*, Wedn*es*day, Chi*sw*ick, Win*ds*or, veni*s*on, *cz*ar, bu*s*iness, beau*x*.

19. **ch** : *ch*ur*ch*, ni*che*, la*tch*, na*t*ure, ques*ti*on, righ*te*ous, violin*c*ello.

20. **ng** : thi*ng*, thi*n*k, to*ngue*, ha*nd*kerchief, Birmi*ng*ham.

21. **th**(is) : *th*en, soo*the*.

22. **th**(in) : brea*th*, Ma*tth*ew.

23. **sh** : *sh*all, A*s*ia, ti*ss*ue, pen*s*ion, mousta*che*, fu*chs*ia, mi*ss*ion, fa*sh*ion, offi*c*iate, so*c*ial, o*c*ean, con*sc*ience, *sch*edule, vi*t*iate, por*t*ion, lun*che*on, *ch*aise.

24. **zh** : sei*z*ure, lei*s*ure, occa*s*ion, transi*ti*on, rou*ge*, ré*g*ime, *j*ujube (sometimes sounded as *jujube*).

25. **wh** : *wh*ile, etc. (often sounded as *w*, except in the North).

Total, 180 spellings for 25 sounds.

### *Silent Consonants.*

(1) **b** (after *m*) : lam*b*, lim*b*, dum*b*, num*b*, plum*b*, clim*b*, clom*b*, tom*b*, wom*b*, crum*b*, thum*b*, com*b*, bom*b* : (the *b* is excrescent in *crumb*, *limb*, *numb*, and *thumb* ; in the rest it is part of the root).

**b** (before *t*) : dou*b*t, de*b*t, de*b*tor.

(2) **ch** : ya*ch*t, dra*ch*m, s*ch*ism.

(3) **g** (before *n* and *m*) : *g*nat, *g*naw, *g*nash, *g*narled, *g*neiss, dei*g*n, fei*g*n, rei*g*n, champa*g*ne, campai*g*n, coi*g*ne, impu*g*n, phle*g*m.

(4) **gh** (final) : hi*gh*, nei*gh*, wei*gh*, dou*gh*, slou*gh* (mire), plou*gh*, thou*gh*, throu*gh*, bou*gh*.

**gh** (before *t*) : cau*gh*t, hau*gh*ty, frau*gh*t, fou*gh*t, nau*gh*t, thou*gh*t, sou*gh*t, bou*gh*t, tau*gh*t, mi*gh*t, ri*gh*t, etc.

(5) **h** : *h*eir, *h*our, *h*onour, *h*umour (where u = yoo), *h*onest, Jo*h*n.

*Note.*—*h* is sometimes silent in the middle of a word, as "ex*h*ibitor."

(6) **k** (before *n*) : *k*now, *k*nack, *k*nave, *k*nead, *k*nee, *k*nell, *k*night, *k*nit, *k*nob, *k*nock, *k*not, *k*nuckle, *k*nack, *k*nout, *k*noll, *k*nacker, *k*napsack, *k*nife.

(7) **l** : cou*l*d, shou*l*d, wou*l*d ; yo*l*k, fo*l*k ; wa*l*k, ta*l*k ; psa*l*m, pa*l*m ; ha*l*f, ca*l*f ; Linco*l*n.

(8) **n** (after *m*) : autum*n*, hym*n*, condem*n*, dam*n*, colum*n*, lim*n*.

(9) **s** : vi*s*count, pui*s*ne (= puny), i*s*le, i*s*land, ai*s*le.

(10) **t** (after *s* and *f* and before *l* and *n*) : has*t*en, lis*t*en, glis*t*en, mois*t*en, this*t*le, whis*t*le, wres*t*le, jos*t*le, of*t*en, sof*t*en.

(11) **w** (before *r*): *w*rap, *w*retch, *w*raith, *w*rath, *w*roth, *w*reath, *w*reck, *w*rite, *w*right, *w*rench, *w*rest, *w*rinkle, *w*riggle, *w*rist, *w*rithe, *w*rong, *w*rought, a*w*ry.

**w**: s*w*ord, ans*w*er, t*w*o, *w*ho, Kes*w*ick, Chis*w*ick.

*Note.*—The letter "r": The letter *r* in such words as *dear, deer, moor, roar, pour,* is not sounded as a consonant (unless the next word begins with a vowel), but has the sound of the Indefinite vowel ə (described in § 440), so that here it helps to make a diphthong. It is not sounded as a *consonant* except before a word or syllable beginning with a vowel. Compare "*far, farr'*-ier"; "*far, far'* away"; "*hair,* the *hair'* of a man"; "*boor,*" "a *boor*-ish man."

It also helps to form a triphthong or treble vowel-sound, in such words as *fire, pure, destroyer, bower,* unless the next word begins with a vowel, in which case the *r,* as before, is sounded as a consonant. See above, § 440.

## II. *Vocalic Sounds and Spellings.*

The different vocalic sounds, twenty in number, are shown in p. 278. We have now to give examples of the different ways in which these can be expressed:—

(1) **ă**: m*a*d, pl*ai*d, h*a*ve, s*a*lmon, thr*e*sh.

(2) **â**: M*a*ry, *ai*ry, *ae*rie, b*ea*rer, m*ayo*ralty, *Aa*ron, *ao*rist, th*e*rein.

(3) **å**: p*a*th, *a*rt, h*ea*rt, cl*e*rk, *au*nt, baz*aa*r, p*al*m, hurr*ah*, v*a*se (Fr.), pl*ai*ster, é-cl*at* (Fr.).

(4) **ĕ**: b*e*d, h*ea*d, *a*ny, s*ai*d, s*ay*s, l*eo*pard, l*ei*sure, r*ey*nard, *a*te, fr*ie*nd, Th*a*mes, b*u*ry.

(5) **ā**: f*a*t*e*, t*ai*l, pl*ay*, f*a*-tal, camp*aign*, str*aigh*t, v*ei*n, th*ey*, r*eign*, w*eigh*, st*ea*k, f*ê*te (Fr.), cong*é* (Fr.), ball*et* (Fr.), champ*ag*ne (Fr.), dem*es*ne (Fr.), g*ao*l, g*au*ge, *eh*, d*ah*lia, h*alf*penny.

(6) **ĭ**: b*i*t, n*y*mph, pr*e*tty, g*i*ve, surf*ei*t, marr*ie*d, coff*ee*, happ*y*, guin*ea*, donk*ey*, w*o*men, b*u*sy, br*ee*ches, s*ie*v*e*.

(7) **ē**: th*e*m*e*, m*e*-teor, qu*ee*n, *ea*ch, f*ie*ld, s*ei*ze,[1] *æ*sthetic, rout*i*n*e*, inval*i*d, qu*ay*, p*eo*ple, C*ai*us, B*eau*champ.

(8) **ŏ**: fr*o*m, w*a*n (after *w* or *qu*), h*ou*gh, y*ach*t, sh*o*n*e*, kn*ow*-ledge, l*au*rel.

(9) **au**: h*au*l, l*aw*, l*o*st, t*a*ll, t*al*k, p*ou*r, *ough*t, br*oa*d, s*o*r*e*, l*o*rd, w*a*r, w*a*ter, wr*a*th, V*augh*an, g*o*n*e*.

---

[1] The following is a list of all the words in which *ei* has the sound of *ē*:—*conceive, deceive, receive* (and their derivatives), *ceiling, seize, either, neither, plebeian, weir, weird, seignory, inveigle, Leigh, key.* So this spelling is by no means limited to syllables beginning with *c* or *s*, as is often asserted. See for instance Mason's *English Grammar*, p. 14.

(10) o': her-*o*, foll-*ow*, her-*oes*, foll-*owed*, fur-*lough*, de-p*ôt*, Phar-*aoh*.

(11) ō: not*e*, no-ble, b*o*th, t*oad*, t*oe*, s*ou*l, d*ough*, m*ow*, br*oo*ch, *oh*, m*au*ve (Fr.), b*eau* (Fr.), dep*ôt* (Fr.), à prop*os* (Fr.), ye*o*man, s*ew*, Co*ck*-burn.

(12) ŏŏ: h*oo*k, b*u*ll, c*ou*ld, w*o*lf.

(13) ōō: f*oo*l, t*o*mb, sh*oe*, m*ove*, s*ou*p, thr*ough*, tr*u*th, bl*ue*, j*ui*ce, sl*eu*th-hound, sl*ew*, r*u*d*e*, man*œu*vre.

(14) ə: o'-ce*a*n, Sa'-r*ah*, suf'-f*e*r, but'-t*o*n, Eu'-r*o*pe, thor'-*ough*, tor'-t*oise*, fa'-m*ou*s, meer'-sch*au*m, waist'-c*oa*t, cup'-b*oa*rd, pleas'-*ure*, mar'-t*y*r. (All in *unaccented* syllables.)

(15) ŭr: t*ur*n, c*olo*nel, h*er*d, h*ear*d, b*ir*d, bl*urr*ed, *err*ed, st*irr*ed, w*or*d.

(16) ŭ: sh*u*t, bl*oo*d, s*o*n, c*o*m*e*, t*ou*ch.

(17) ī: m*i*n*e*, *i*-dol, tr*y*, l*y*r*e*, s*ig*n, h*igh*, h*eigh*t, d*ie*, r*ye*, *is*land, *ai*sle, ch*oi*r, ind*i*ct, *eye*.

(18) ū (=yōō): t*u*n*e*, d*u*-ty, d*ue*, s*ui*t, f*eu*d, n*ew*, l*ieu*, v*iew*, imp*ug*n.

(19) oi: c*oi*l, b*oy*.

(20) ou: l*ou*d, d*ow*n.

Total, 200 spellings for 20 sounds.

Grand total of spellings for consonants and vowels, 380.

*Note*.—The number of spellings would be still further increased, if we added the five diphthongs and four triphthongs formed with the help of the letter *r*, to which allusion is made in § 440.

**461. The same Spelling with different Sounds.**

*Consonants*:—

**c**: violin*c*ello, *c*at, *c*ity.

**ch**: *ch*aos, *ch*aise, su*ch*, *ch*oir, dra*ch*m (silent).

**j**: *J*ew, *j*u*j*ube, hallelu*j*ah.

**ge**: rou*ge*, villa*ge*.

**g**: *g*ive, *g*in*g*er.

**ti**: no*ti*on, ques*ti*on, transi*ti*on.

**s**: ha*s*, ga*s*.

**sc**: *sc*ene, *sc*arce.

**sch**: *sch*eme, *sch*edule.

**si**: occa*si*on, disper*si*on.

**th**: *th*in, *th*is, *Th*ames.

**x**: bo*x*, e*x*ample (=eg*z*ample), chateau*x*, *X*enophon.

**ph**: nym*ph*, ne*ph*ew.

**gh**: *gh*ost, lau*gh*, hou*gh*.

**qu**: li*qu*or, *qu*een.

*Vowels :—*

**a** : c*a*t, t*a*ll, p*a*th, m*a*ny, m*a*de, c*a*re, w*a*s, stew*a*rd.

**a . . . e** : r*a*v*e*, h*a*v*e*, *a*r*e*.

**ai** : m*ai*d, s*ai*d, pl*ai*d, *ai*sle.

**au** : *au*nt, h*au*nt, g*au*ge, m*au*ve, meer-sch*au*m.

**e** : h*e*r, cl*e*rk, b*e*d, pr*e*tty.

**e . . . e** : w*e*r*e*, h*e*r*e*.

**ea** : h*ea*r, st*ea*k, h*ea*rt, h*ea*d.

**ei** : v*ei*n, l*ei*sure, s*ei*ze, surf*ei*t, h*ei*ght.

**ey** : *ey*e, th*ey*, k*ey*.

**ew** : n*ew*, s*ew*.

**i . . . e** : b*i*t*e*, n*i*ch*e*, pol*i*c*e*.

**ie** : f*ie*ld, d*ie*, s*ie*ve.

**o** : h*o*t, c*o*ld, w*o*lf, w*o*men, wh*o*m, s*o*n, butt*o*n, l*o*st, her-*o*.

**o . . . e** : c*o*v*e*, pr*o*v*e*, l*o*v*e*, m*o*r*e*, sh*o*n*e*.

**oa** : l*oa*d, br*oa*d, cupb*oa*rd.

**oe** : sh*oe*, t*oe*.

**oo** : h*oo*k, f*oo*l, br*oo*ch, fl*oo*d, d*oo*r.

**ou** : p*ou*r, th*ou*gh, thr*ou*gh, y*ou*ng, th*ou*.

**ough** : r*ough*, hicc*ough*, c*ough*, h*ough*, tr*ough*, b*ough*, th*ough*, thr*ough*.

*Note.*—The reasons why our vowels came to express so many different sounds are—(1) because the Anglo-French scribes discarded the marks or accents denoting vowel-length in Anglo-Saxon words (see § 456), and their example has been followed ever since; (2) because our vocalic symbols, though sufficient for the simple and pure language for which they were originally intended, are not sufficient for the very composite language that English has since become; (3) because one of the vocalic symbols (*æ*) used in A.S has disappeared in modern English, though the sounds that it expressed have remained; (4) because in the sixteenth and seventeenth centuries a general shifting of the vowel-sounds took place, which was very seldom accompanied by a change of spelling (see § 442); (5) because the sounds of certain vowels are affected by the proximity of certain consonants, the presence or absence of an accent, and by syllabic division; in short, the sound of a vowel varies with its surroundings.

For example, the vowel *a*, as shown above, is now used to express at least eight different sounds, viz. those exemplified in *cat, tall, path, many, made, care, was, steward.* (1) The sound of *a* in *cat* was represented in A.S. by the symbol *æ;* as this has become obsolete, *a* is made to do duty for it. (2) The sound of *a* in *tall* is produced by the liquid *l*, which has had the effect of prolonging the vowel and deepening its tone. (3) The sound of *a* in *path* was represented in A.S. by *á;* but as the accent has gone out of use, there is nothing but the simple *a* left to express this sound. (4) The sound of *a* in *many* (A.S. *manig*) may be ascribed to the frequent interchange of *a* and *e* in English; cf. A.S. *thenc-an*, *thank:* the sound of the *a* in *manig* has changed, but the spelling has remained. (5) The sound of *a* in *made* was represented in A.S. by *é* (very nearly); but as the sound of A.S. *é* has since shifted to that of *ee* in *seem*, the vowel *a* has been made to do duty for it. (6) The sound of *a* in *care* was represented in A.S. by *ǽ* (very nearly); but as this symbol has become obsolete, the vowel *a* followed by *re* has had to take its place. (7) The sound of *a* in *was* (=*wos*) is produced by the rounding of the lips in sounding the *w* that goes before; and in sounding the vowel *o*, the lips are somewhat rounded also. (8) The indefinite or neutral sound of *a* in *steward* arises from the want of accent on the syllable in which it stands.

To take the example of *o*. The short sound in *nŏt* is the same as the short sound in A.S. The long sound in *nō-table* was equally common in A.S., but in A.S. the vowel was accented to express this. The *au* sound of *o* in *cloth* is explained in § 449. The *oo* sound of *o* in *two* is explained in § 448. The *u* sound of *o* in *mother* (=mŭther) is explained in § 446.

## CHAPTER XXV.—ACCENTUATION, SYLLABIC DIVISION.

**462. Accent, Emphasis.**—When we lay stress upon a *single syllable*, we call it **accent**:[1]—

Sup-ply′, sim′-ply. Re-bel′ (*verb*), reb′-el (*noun*).

When we lay stress upon an *entire word*, we call it **emphasis**:—

*Silver* and *gold* have I none.
I appeal from Philip *drunk* to Philip *sober*.

*Note.*—When the mark ′ is placed against the side of a completed syllable, this is intended to show that the *whole syllable* is accented, and not merely the last letter against which the symbol is placed; as *hum′-ble*, *chil′-dren*.

### Section 1.—Words of Native or Teutonic Origin.

(Compiled from chap. xxv. of Skeat's *Princ. Eng. Etym.* series i.)

**463. Position of the English Accent.**—The modern English language delights in throwing the accent as far back as possible, and this in all words, whether of Romanic or Teutonic origin.

**464. Medial Long Vowel shortened by Accent.**—The

[1] There is, however, another meaning of accent, viz. a mark placed over a vowel to show that the vowel is long. See the seven accented vowels in A.S. described in footnote to § 439.

long vowel of an *accented* monosyllable is apt to become shortened, if an *unaccented* syllable is added to it.

The added syllable may be (*a*) a suffix, or (*b*) a word.

(*a*) *An added suffix* :—

*Gŏs'-ling* (once *goose-ling*) is from *goose*. *Heath'-er* (sounded as *hĕth'er*) is from *heath* (but in *hea'-then* the vowel of the first syllable remains long, the accented syllable being *hea'*-, and not *heath'*-). *Rŭm'-mage* (for *room-age*) is from *room*. *Saus'-age*, sounded as *sŏs'-age*. *Thrŏt'-tle* is from *throat*. *Hăr'-rier* is from *hare*. *Chĭl'-dren* is from *chīld*. *Sŏrr'-y* is from A.S. *sār*, sore. *Dăr'-ling* for *dear-ling*. *Strip'-ling* for *stripe-ling*.

*Note.*—In *thrŏttle, hărrier, chĭldren* the original short vowels of A.S. *thrŏtu, hăra,* and *cild* have been retained by the accent.

The vowel-shortening is conspicuous in forming the past tenses and past participles of some "Weak" verbs.

Thus *lead* (Mid. Eng. *lēd-en*) made the Past tense *lĕd'-de;* hence (after the elision of the final *e* in Mod. Eng.) we have the Past tense in *lĕd-d*, which was finally abbreviated to *lĕd*. From *read* we have *read* (pronounced as *rĕd*); from *hide* we have *hĭd;* from *hear* we have *heard* (pronounced as *hĕrd*); and from *feed* we have *fĕd*. In forming the past participles of such verbs a similar process has been at work.

Vowel-shortening is produced, if the added suffix contains no vowel :—

Thus *wide* gives *width;* *broad* gives *bread-th* (pronounced as brĕdth); *blithe* gives *bliss;* *bear* gives *ber-th* and *bir-th*.

(*b*) *An added word* :—

*Bŏn'-fire* from *bone+fire*. *Break'-fast* (pronounced as *brĕk-fast*) from *break+fast*. *Crăn'-berry* from *crane+berry*. *Hŭs'-band* from *house+band*. *Hŭs'-sif* or *hŭs'-sy* from *house+wife*. *Lăm'-mas* (a name for 1st August or feast of first-fruits) from A.S. *hláf+mæsse* (through spellings *hlăm-mæsse, lăm'-masse*=loaf-mass). *Wĭm'-men* (misspelt as *women*) from *wife-men*. *Fĭf'-ty* from *five-ty*. *Mĕr'-maid* from *mere+maid* (=water-maid). *Nŏs'-tril* from *nose+thirl*. *Sher'-iff* from *scīr+rēfa* (a shire-reeve). *Star'-board* from *steer+board* (Mid. Eng. *stere+bord*, later *ster+bord*). *Tăd'-pole* is from *toad-poll*, a toad which is all head or poll. *Whit'+by* from *white+by*. *Es'-sex* from *East-sex*, *Sŭs'-sex* from *South-sex*, *Sŭf'-folk* from *South-folk*. *Vĭn'-yard* from *vine-yard*. *Fore-head* is sounded as if it rhymed with *horrid*, and *know-ledge* as if it rhymed with *college*. *Shĕp'-herd* is from *sheep+herd*. *Stĭr'-rup* from *sty+rope* (A.S. *stig+rāp*, where *stig* means to climb or ascend). *Hŏl'-i-day* from *holy+day*. *Twopence, threepence, fourpence, fivepence* are sounded as if they were spelt *tŭp'-pence, thrĕp'-pence, fŏr'-pence, fĭp'-pence*. *Rowlock* sounded as *rul'-luck* (a corruption of *oar-lock*).

**465. Final Long Vowel shortened through want of Accent.**

—The vowel in the last syllable of a dissyllabic compound, though originally long, is apt to become shortened, if no accent is thrown upon it.

The *swain* in *boat'-swain, cock'-swain*, is often sounded as *s'n* (*bōs'n, cŏx'n*). The *stone* in *brim'-stone, grind'-stone* is often sounded as *s'ŭn* (*brim'-stŭn, grīnd'-stŭn*). The *bour* (originally A.S. *búr*) in *neigh'-bour* is sounded as *bŭr*. The *reeve* in *sheriff* (put for *shire-reeve*) is sounded as *rĭf*. The *rŭp* of *stir'-rup* was originally *ráp*, A.S. for *rope*. The *y* of *daisy* was once *eye*, as in *day's-eye* (the eye of day). The *bănd* of *hus'-band* was originally *bōndi* or *búandi*, dweller. The *coat* of *waist'-coat* is sounded as *cŭt*. The *dŏm* of *king'-dom* was originally *dōm*; the *lŏck* of *wed'-lock* was originally *lác*, which by § 443 should have given *loke*. The *rĕd* in *hat'-red* was originally A.S. *ræden* (mode, condition, state). The *-en* of kitt-*en* was orig. *-oun*, as in Mid. Eng. kit-*oun*. Similarly the *-er* of cat-*er* was orig. *-our*, as in Mid. Eng. cat-*our*. The *day* of *Monday, Tuesday*, etc., is sounded as *dy̆* or *dĭ*. In proper names *town* is reduced to *tŏn*, and *hám* is reduced to *hăm*, as in *Hamp-ton, Taun-ton*, etc.; *Nor-ham, Totten-ham*, etc.

**466. Short Vowel or Syllable in Dissyllables cancelled.** —In dissyllables the vowel of the unaccented syllable, if short, may disappear, and in extreme cases even the whole of the unaccented syllable.

(*a*) *Disappearance of short vowels:—*

*Heron* is sometimes written *hern; heronery* is always sounded *her'-nery*. The cancelling of the short vowel is very common in the past tense and past participle of "Weak" verbs, such as *loved* or *lov'd, looked* or *look't*. Hence we obtain the etymologies of *fond, lewd, shrewd*. *Fon-d* is for Mid. Eng. *fonn-ed*, acting like a *fonne* or fool. *Lew-d* is for Mid. Eng. *lew-ed*, unlearned, belonging to the laity. *Shrew-d* is for Mid. Eng. *schrew-ed*, wicked, lit. accursed, pp. of *schrew-en*, to accurse. *Fol-d*, occurring in the compound word "sheep-fold," has no connection with the verb "fold," to double together, but comes from A.S. *fald*, also *falod* and *falud*. In the plural and the Possessive suffixes *-es*, the *e* is generally cancelled; thus *day-es* has become *days; mann-es* (Possessive) has become *man's*. Similarly the Mid. Eng. *runn-es* has become *runs*. The A.S. word *ælmesse* (of Greek origin) passed into *almesse* (later *almes*) in Mid. Eng., and finally into *alms* in Mod. Eng. *Luf-o-de* was in three syllables in A.S., *love-de* was in two (sometimes three, *lov-e-de*) syllables in Mid. Eng., and *loved* is in one syllable in Mod. Eng.

(*b*) *Disappearance of whole syllable:—*

*Since* for *sithence*; *nor* for *nother*; *or* for *other*; *lone* for *alone; drake* for *endrake* (unless the *en* was confounded with *an*, Indef. article); *wanton* for *wan-towen* (*wan*=lacking or not, *towen*=trained or educated); *lark* (bird) for Mid. Eng. *laverk*.

**467. Short Middle Syllable in Trisyllables cancelled.—**

In trisyllables, of which the first syllable is accented, the short middle syllable sometimes disappears:—

*Four-teen-night* has become *fortnight*; *fore'-castle* is often sounded *fŏ'c'sle*. *Hō-lin-oak* (that is, the holly-oak) has become *holm-oak*; *furrow-long* has become *furlong*. *Zoet'-el-aar* (Dutch for "victualler") has become *sutler*. *Glou'-ces-ter* is sounded as *Glos'-ter*, *Dav'-en-try* as *Daintry*. The days of the week have all except Saturday lost a medial short syllable. Thus A.S. *Sunnan-dæg*, *Monan-dæg*, *Tiwes-dæg*, *Wodnes-dæg*, *Thunres-dæg*, *Frige-dæg* have become respectively *Monday*, *Tuesday*, *Wednesday* (sounded as Wens-day), *Thursday*, *Friday*.

**468. Emphasis.**—When emphasis is thrown or not thrown on a word of one syllable, it sometimes produces doublets—that is, a pair of words derived from the same elements, but differently spelt and having different meanings.

Thus *to* and *too* are distinguished by emphasis, the first being sounded as *tŏŏ* (unemphasised), and the second as *tōō* (emphasised); as, "I *too* will go *to* London." Similarly *off* (pronounced as *auf*) is the emphasised form of *of* (pronounced as *ŏv*); as, "He fell *off* his horse"; "The horse was within a mile *of* its stable."

Initial *h*, if the word is emphatic, or if the syllable is accented, is sounded; otherwise it is weak, so as to be practically silent.

Thus we sound the *h* very clearly if we say, "I saw *her*, but not *him*." But we do not sound it at all in such sentences as, "I saw *her* yesterday. I shall see *him* to-morrow." Similarly, if the first syllable of a word is accented, we are careful to sound the *h* clearly and give the indefinite article the form of *a*; as "*a* hos'-tel." But if the first syllable is not accented, we do not sound the *h*, and we give the indefinite article the form of *an*; as "*an* ho-tel'" (see § 437).

To the same cause we must ascribe the loss of *h* in the unemphatic pronoun *it*, which in A.S. was *hit*.

The absence of accent or emphasis sometimes changes or helps to change a voiceless letter into a voiced one.

Thus in the common monosyllables *with*, *thou*, *the*, *they*, etc., the *th* was originally voiceless; but now through lack of emphasis they are voiced. In plural nouns, and in the third person singular of verbs, the final *-es* in the Mid. Eng. forms was not accented. The *s* (originally voiceless) became voiced even in Mid. Eng., and is sounded as *z* after voiced consonants. Thus *day-es* has become *days* = dayz; *runn-es* has become *runs* = runz. Similarly in the common unaccented words *is* and *was*, the *s* became voiced quite early, so that *is* = *iz*, and *was* = *waz*.

## Section 2.—Words of French or Latin Origin.

(Compiled from chap. v. of Skeat's *Princ. Eng. Etym.* series ii.)

**469. French Accent.**—In an Anglo-French word the accent fell as a rule on the same syllable as that on which it fell in the corresponding Latin word. Thus the Latin accusative *ra-ti-on'-em* came into Anglo-French in the form of *re-soun'*.

But in English the accent is thrown on the first syllable of a word (§ 463). Hence when the French word *re-soun'* found its way into Middle English, there was a strong tendency to turn it into *re'-son*, and the Mod. Eng. *rea'-son* is the natural result.

In Chaucer's time the accent in this and analogous words was still unsettled; and the poet uses whichever form happens to suit his rhyme or metre best at the time:—

> Til that he knew, by grace and by *re-soun'*.—*Monk's Tale.*
> As fer as *re'-soun* axeth, hardily.—*Clerk's Prologue.*

Similarly in one line he has *hon-our'*, and in another *hon'-our*; in one line he has *for'-tune*, in another *for-tun'-e*.

The words *riches*, *duress*, and *laches* all show a shortening of the final syllable, which in French was *-esse* (accented) and not *-es* (unaccented). Hence these words are now pronounced *rich'-es*, *du'-rĕss*, *lach'-es*. The French word *pres-tige'* has with some acquired the English pronunciation of *pres'-tige*. The Italian *bal-co'-ne* is now pronounced in English as *bal'-co-ny*.

**470. Accent in Nouns and Verbs.**—Nouns are distinguished from the corresponding verbs by the position of the accent, the noun being accented on the first syllable, and the verb on the second; as *ex'-port* (noun), *ex-port'* (verb). Two causes helped to produce this result.

(1) In Old English it was the custom to accent the verb in verb-compounds, as *un-dōn'* (to undo), and the prefix in noun-compounds, as *to'-cyme* (arrival). The same practice was afterwards extended to compounds of Latin or French origin.

(2) When *nouns* were borrowed, they were made to conform in point of accent to nouns of Teutonic origin. Thus the noun *con'-vert* was accented on the same principle as the Teutonic words *fath'-om*, *moth'-er*. But when *verbs* were borrowed, they came in under different conditions; for they did not come into Middle English as dissyllables, as nouns did, but as trisyllables. Thus the Infinitive mood of the verb *convert* was *con-vert'-en*, while the past tense was *con-vert'-ed*, and the pres. part. *con-vert'-ing*. The accent, being thus thrown on the stem of the verb from the first, was retained as a convenient mode of distinguishing between two parts of speech:—

> *Ab'-stract* (noun), *ab-stract'* (verb); *ac'-cent* (noun), *ac-cent'* (verb); *af'-fix* (noun), *af-fix'* (verb); *com'-mune* (noun), *com-mune'* (verb); *com'-pound* (noun), *com-pound'* (verb), etc.

In words of three syllables, the noun, as before, has the accent on the first syllable, and the verb on the second :—

*At'-tri-bute* (noun), *at-trib'-ute* (verb) ; *en'-vel-ope* (noun), *en-vel'-op* (verb).

*Note.*—There is no difference of accent, however, in the noun *ex'-er-cise* and the verb *ex'-er-cise* ; but in the other verbal form *ex-ert'*, not only does the accent fall on the second syllable, but the absence of accent in the first has changed the sound of *x* from *ks* to *gz*.

If the contrast is between an adjective and a verb, the verb, as before, has the accent on the second syllable, and the adjective on the first :—

*Ab'-sent* (adj.), *ab-sent'* (verb) ; *fre'-quent* (adj.), *fre-quent'* (verb).

But if the question is between an adjective and a noun, the noun takes the accent on the first syllable, and the adjective on the second : [1]—

*Com'-pact* (noun), *com-pact'* (adj.) ; *in'-stinct, in-stinct'* ; *in'-val-id, in-val'-id* ; *pre'-ce-dent, pre-ce'-dent* ; *min'-ute, mi-nute'*.

Sometimes, however, there is no change of accent to distinguish one part of speech from another :—

*Con-tent'* (adj. and verb), *con-tents'* (noun). *As-say', con-sent', her'-ald, sup-port', re-spect'* (all nouns and verbs). *Con'-crete, pa'-tient* (adjectives and nouns).

*Note.*—There is now, however, a tendency to pronounce *contents* (noun) as *con'-tents*, according to the analogy of other English words.

**471. Transfer of Accent gradual.**—The process of transferring the accent (in words of French or Latin origin) from the last to the first syllable was gradual. It was very unsettled, as we have seen in Chaucer's time ; and was by no means definitely fixed in the Tudor period.

*Spenser.*—In this poet we have *cap-tive', cru-el', en-vy', for-est', pre-sage', tres-pass'* ; and *mis-chie'-vous*, which we now pronounce as *mis'-chie-vous*, though in lower life *mis-chie'-vous* is still common.

*Shakspeare.*—The nouns *con'-verse, rec'-ord, in'-crease, in'-stinct* are given as *con-verse', re-cord', in-stinct'* ; *con'-trary* is given as *con-tra'-ry*, and *ex'-tir-pate* as *ex-tir'-pate*.

*Milton.*—The following words in Milton all have their accent on the last syllable, where we now have them on the first :—*ad-verse', as-pect', com-rade', con-test'* (noun), *con-trite', e-dict', im-pulse', in-sult'* (noun), *pre-text', pro-cess', pro-duct', pro-strate', sur-face', up-roar'*.

---

[1] Probably the reason why in such adjectives the accent is on the second syllable is that in the adjective the word is nearer to its original use as a past or present participle ; i.e. *compact'-us, instinct'-us, inval'-id-us, ce'-dens, minut'-us.*

The following lines all show some peculiarity of accent, which has since been changed:—

Ne let *mis-chie'-vous* witches with their charms.—SPENSER.
Our wills and fates do so *con-tra'-ry* run.—SHAKSPEARE.
O argument *blas-phe'-mous*, false and proud.—MILTON.
In this great *ac-a-de'-my* of mankind.—BUTLER.
'Twixt that and reason what a nice *bar-rier'*.—POPE.
*Com-pens'-a-ting* his loss with added hours.—COWPER.
Perishing gloomily,
Spurred by *con-tu'-mely*.—HOOD.

**472. Transfer of Accent resisted.**—In a few instances the attempts made to throw the accent back were thwarted. Thus Dryden's *ap-os'-to-lic* has not held its ground against *ap-o-stol'-ic*; and in trisyllables the tendency to throw the accent back on the first syllable is not so strong as in dissyllables.

Ab-do'-men, a-cu'-men, ad-mon'-ish, ad-ven'-ture (but *ad'-vent*), fa-nat'-ic (but *lu'-na-tic*), re-mon'-strate (but *dem'-on-strate*), in-ter'-pret, in-ter'-stice (but *in'-ter-val*, *in'-ter-est*), so-nor'-ous, etc.

When an adjective has a negative prefix attached to it, the original accent is sometimes retained and sometimes thrown back:—

*Retained*:—doc'-ile, in-doc'-ile; du'-ly, un-du'-ly; de'-cent, in-de'-cent; no'-ble, ig-no'-ble; hon'-est, dis-hon'-est; pru'-dent, im-pru'-dent; mod'-est, im-mod'-est, etc.

*Thrown back*:—po'-tent, im'-po-tent; fa'-mous, in'-fa-mous; fi'-nite, in'-fi-nite; pi'-ous, im'-pi-ous, etc. (These words are less *felt* to be compounds than those above.)

When a new syllable is added to the end of a dissyllabic word, the accent is sometimes retained and sometimes thrown back:—

*Retained*:—ad-here', ad-he'-rent; a-vow', a-vow'-al; per-use', per-u'-sal; de-fend', de-fend'-ant; com-ply', com-pli'-ance, etc.

*Thrown back*:—de-spair', des'-pe-rate; pro-vide', prov'-i-dent; pro-test', prot'-es-tant; sub-side', sub'-si-dence; con-fide', con'-fi-dent; pho'-to-graph, pho-tog'-ra-phy; in'-cense, frank'-in-cense, etc.

**473. Disappearance of Unaccented Syllables.**—The force of the English accent is so strong that unaccented syllables run the risk of disappearing altogether. This has been exemplified already in the case of Teutonic words (see §§ 466, 467). It is no less true in the case of Romanic words also, and shows itself—(*a*) in Aphesis, or the loss of an initial *vowel*; (*b*) in Apheresis, or the loss of a longer initial syllable; (*c*) in Apocope, or the loss of a final syllable; and (*d*) in Syncope, or the loss of a medial syllable.

(*a*) Aphesis:—*mend* for *amend*; *peal* (of bells) for *appeal*; *pert* (saucy) for Fr. *apert*; *prentice* for *apprentice*; *vanguard* for Fr. *avant-garde*; *bishop* for Lat. *episcopus*; *scutcheon* for *escutcheon*; *special* for *especial*; *sterling* for *Easterling*; *squire* for *esquire*, etc.

(*b*) Apheresis:—*fray* for *affray*; *spend* from Lat. *dis-pend-ere*; *spite* for *despite*; *sport* from Lat. *dis-port* (Fr. *desport*); *gin* for *engine* (Lat. *ingenium*); *sample* for *en-sample*; *cheat* for *escheat*; *spital* for *hospital* (Lat. *hospitale*); *dropsy* for *hydropsy* (Gr. *hydropsis*).

(*c*) Apocope (the most common loss is that of final *e*, one of the marks that distinguish Modern from Middle English):—*beast* for *best-e*; *feast* for *fest-e*; *chivalry* for *chivalry-e*; *riches* for *riches-se*; *duress* for *dures-se*.

(*d*) Syncope:—*punch* for *punish*; *clerk* for *cler-ic*; *French* for *Frenc-isc* (Frankish); *but-ler* for *bot-il-ler* (one who attends to bottles); *chim-ney* for *chim-e-nee*; *laun-dress* for *lav-end-er-ess*; *crown* for *cor-one* (Lat. *corona*); *par-lous* (Shakspeare) for *per-il-ous*; *part-ner* for *parc-e-nere*; *ward-robe* for *war-* or *gar-de-robe*; *dam-sel* for *dam-o-sel*; *mar-shal* for *mar-es-chal*; *proxy* for *pro-cur-a-cy*; *pal-sy* for Mid. Eng. *pal-es-y*, Fr. *par-a-lys-ie* (Gr. *par-a-lys-is*); *sext-on* for *sa-crist-an*.

## SECTION 3.—SYLLABIC DIVISION.

**474. Rule of Syllabic Division.**—Syllabic division is ruled by accentuation, and not, as has been sometimes maintained, by etymology. "Word-division has nothing to do with etymology. From a practical point of view *im′-pu-dence* is right, being based on true phonetic principles, *i.e.* on the spoken language. It is only when we take the word to pieces that we discover that it is formed from *im-* (for *in-*), the base *pud*, and the suffix *-ence*. The practice here is one thing, and theory another. The spoken language has *pe-ruse′* at one moment, and *pe-ru′-sal* at another. It rightly regards ease of utterance, and nothing else" (Skeat).[1]

It may be added that syllabic division by etymology is impracticable for two reasons—(1) the component parts of a word are sometimes so mixed together as to be indistinguishable; as *monkey* (2 syll.) from Old Ital. *moniccio* (4 syll.); (2) the etymologies of words can be known only to those few persons who have studied the subject; whereas all men should know how a word ought to be sounded. (Cf. *banqu-et* (little bench), *ban′-quet*.)

La-ment′, lam′-en-ta′-ble; at′-om, a-tom′-ic; at′-tri-bute (noun), at-trib′-ute (verb); or′-tho-dox, or-thog′-ra-phy; pro-vide′, prov′-i-dence; tel′-e-gram, te-leg′-ra-phy; ex-pect′, ex′-pec-ta′-tion; me-chan′-ic, mech′-a-nism; do-min′-ion, dom′-i-nant; fi′-nite, fin′-ish; ta′-ble, tab′-let; nu′-mer-al, num′-ber; o′-cean, o′-ce-an′-ic, etc.

[1] *Student's Pastime*, ed. 1896, pp. 119, 120. The rules for Syllabic Division given in Miss Soames's *Introduction to the Study of Phonetics*, pp. 73, 74, are based upon the same principle.

The terminations *-cial, -cious, -cean, -sion, -gion, -tion, -tial, -tious*, since they are sounded as one syllable, should not be divided into two:—

So′-cial, o′-cean, le′-sion, le′-gion, con′-scious, mo′-tion, par′-tial, cap′-tious, fi-nan′-cial.

But in such cases as the following, the initial consonant of any of the above syllables goes with the preceding short vowel, in order to preserve the accent:—

Re-lig′-ion, con-trit′-ion, prec′-ious, con-dit′-ion, o-pin′-ion, on′-ion, ver-mil′-ion, de-cis′-ion.[1]

## CHAPTER XXVI.—ACCIDENCE.

### Section 1.—The Forms of Nouns.

#### *Gender.*

**475. Gender in Old and Modern English.**—What we call gender in Mod. Eng. is based not on a difference of words, but on one of sex. Males are said to be Masculine, females Feminine, things without life Neuter,—that is, of neither sex. From a grammatical point of view this is not gender at all.

In Old English, however (as in Lat., Greek, and to this day in Mod. German), the gender of a noun depended on the *forms* that a noun assumed in the course of its declension, not on the sex or absence of sex in the person or thing denoted.

Thus in A.S. *here* (army) was Masc.; *wynn* (joy), Fem.; *wíf* (woman), Neuter; *wíf-man* (another word for woman), Masc.; *mægden* (maiden), Neuter; *sunne* (sun) was Fem.; *móna* (moon) was Masc.

Adjectives had gender as well as nouns; and an adjective took the gender of the noun associated with it.

Gender gradually went out of use, with the general decline of the inflexional system. It was very seldom seen after the beginning of the fourteenth century.

**476. Masculine and Feminine endings in Old English.**—Three distinct sets of suffixes for expressing gender were once

---

[1] Some of these words cannot be written so as to describe the sound. Thus *religion* is really *re-ligi′-on*, and *contrition* is really *con-triti′-on*. The *gi* represents the *j*, and the *ti* the *sh*. The *g* and *t* are palatalised by the *i*, which then disappears in sound. Precisely as in the case of Umlaut (vowel-mutation, see § 452), so here the spelling represents the stage before palatalisation was completed. In words like *opinion*, *onion*, *union*, *vermilion*, the *i* in the last syllable becomes *y* through contact with the *o* following. The final syllable is therefore *-ion* = *-yon*.

common. In the following examples the grammatical gender tallied with the natural :—

| (1) *Masc.* **-a.** | *Fem.* **-e.** |
|---|---|
| wicc-*a* (sorcerer) | wicc-*e* (sorceress). |
| widuw-*a* (widower) | widuw-*e* (widow). |
| han-*a* (cock) | henn-*e* (hen). |
| (2) *Masc.* **-ere.** | *Fem.* **-estre.** |
| tæpp-*ere* (bar-man) | tæpp-*estre* (bar-woman). |
| spinn-*ere* (male spinner) | spinn-*estre* (female spinner). |
| sang-*ere* (male singer) | sang-*estre* (female singer). |
| (3) *Masc.* | *Fem.* **-en.** |
| fox (dog-fox) | fyx-*en* (bitch-fox). |
| munec (monk) | mynec-*en*-u (nun). |
| god (a god) | gyd-*en* (a goddess). |

All these marks of sex, except a few survivals, are now extinct :—

(1) "Widuw-*e*" has become "widow" by the loss of final "*e.*" "Widuw-*a*" (the old Masc.) is now "widow-*er*,"—that is, the masc. suffix *-ere*, now spelt as *-er*, has been tacked on to the stem *widuw*. The suffix *-ere* or *-er* has lost its Masculine force in all but three words, *widow-er*, *murder-er*, *sorcer-er*. The last two have the Fem. forms *murder-ess*, *sorcer-ess*. All other nouns ending in *-er* will stand for either sex; cf. *milter*, *spawner*.

(2) "Spinn-*estre*" is now spelt as "spin-*ster*," but this word does not now denote a female spinner. "Sang-*estre*" has become "song-*ster*," a noun of Common gender, out of which a hybrid Feminine "song-*str-ess*" has been formed by adding the Romanic Fem. suffix *-ess*. With the exception of *spinster*, all nouns ending in *-ster* now stand for either sex, though more commonly for a male than for a female.

(3) "Fyx-*en*" has become "vix-*en*," but this is not now used only for the feminine of "fox." This is the only word in which the fem. suffix *-en* has survived. (The change of *o* in *fox* to *i* in *vixen* is an example of mutation caused by the suffix *-en*, orig. *-in* ; see § 452, 6.)

The Teutonic suffixes *-e* and *-en* were ousted in the fourteenth century by the Romanic (French) suffix *-ess*. The suffix *-estre* or *-ster* fought the ground for some time with *-ess*, until eventually hybrids like "songstress" were formed, which showed that the original Feminine force of *-ster* was forgotten. In fact, the final *er* of *ster* was mistaken for the Masculine suffix *-er*, and so *-ess* was added to it to make it Feminine.

**477. Romanic Feminine Suffixes.**—Four kinds are seen in Mod. Eng. :—

(1) **-ess**, which is added to native as well as foreign words.
(2) **-ine**, as in hero-*ine*, Czar-*ina*, Margrav-*ine*, Landgrav-*ine*.
(3) **-a**, as in donn-*a*, in-fant-*a*, sultan-*a*, signor-*a*.
(4) **-rix**, from Lat. nouns ending in *-or*, as in testat-*or*, testat-*rix*.

The first is from Fr. *-esse*, popular Lat. *-issa*. This is the only one that became naturalised; but even this is not now used as freely as it once was; for no new Feminines (unless perhaps jocosely) are now coined with it. Thus we do not say "doctress," but "lady doctor."

In Wycliff we have:—dawnser-*esse*, neighbor-*esse*, techer-*esse*, cosyn-*esse* (female cousin), servaunt-*esse*, spous-*esse*, etc.

In the Tudor period we have:—waggon-*ess*, hero-*ess*, butler-*ess*, doctr-*ess*, foster-*ess*, champion-*ess*, vassal-*ess*, etc.

**478. Feminines in "ess" less regularly formed:—**

**Abb-ess**, Old Fr. ab-*esse;* Late Lat. abbat-*issa*.

**Duch-ess**, Old Fr. duc-*esse*, duch-*esse;* Lat. dux, duc-is.

**Mistr-ess**, not formed by adding *-ess* to *master*, but borrowed direct from Old Fr. maister-*esse*, Fem. of "maistre," Lat. magister.

**Miss**, a contraction of "mistress."

**Marchion-ess.**—The French word is *marquise*, the regular Fem. of *marquis*. "Marchion-*ess*" is from Late Lat. "marchion-*issa*," the stem of which is "marchion-," prefect of the marches or border.

**Murder-ess**, formed by adding *-ess* to the noun "murder." *Er* (the old A.S. suffix *-ere*) is added to "murder" to make the Masculine; cf. "widow-*er*."

**Sorcer-ess.**—The Masc. form is "sorcer-*er*." The stem is Old Fr. *sorc-ier*, Late Lat. *sort-iarius*, in which the suffixes *-ier*, *-arius* denote the agent. When the Fem. "sorcer-*ess*" had been formed, *-er* was substituted for *-ess* to make the Masculine.

**Empr-ess, govern-ess, nur-se.**—In these three words the suffix is from Latin *-icem*, not *-issa*. "Imperatr-*icem*," "gubernatr-*icem*," "nutr-*icem*," were shortened into French words ending in *-ice*, which in English become *-ess* or *-se*, by analogy with *-ess* from *-issa*.

**479. Different words for Masculine and Feminine.**—See list in § 47, I.:—

**Bachelor, maid.**—Old Fr. *bachelor*, Late Lat. *baccalarius*, the origin of which is not known for certain. A.S. *mægd-en* (maid or maiden), in which *-en* is a diminutive suffix.

**Boar, sow.**—A.S. *bár*, a male pig. A.S. *sugu*, a sow. "Swine" is quite a distinct word, and denotes a pig of either sex. See § 489, *Note* 3.

**Boy, girl.**—"Boy" is not found in A.S., but in Old Dutch "boef," cognate with Lat. *pup*-us, whence the diminutive form *pup*-illus, "pupil." In Mid. Eng. "boy" meant a menial, as it still does in *pot-boy*, *stable-boy*, *post-boy*, *Capeboy*, etc. In A.S. the word for "boy" was *cnafa*, which in Mod. Eng. has degenerated into *knave*. "Girl" is formed (with diminutive suffix "*l*") from Old Low Germ. *gör*, a child of either sex. In Mid. Eng. we find *cnave-girle* (that is, boy-child) for "boy."

**Brother, sister.**—A.S. *bróðor*, cognate with Lat. *frater*. Scand. *systir*, cognate with A.S. *seostor*, allied to Lat. *soror* for *sosor*.

**Buck, doe.**—A.S. *bucc-a*, a male fallow-deer. A.S. *dá*, doe.

**Bull, cow.**—"Bull" is not found in A.S. except in the diminutive form *bull-uc*, a bull-calf or bullock. "Cow" is from A.S. *cú*, sounded as *coo*, as it still is in the north of England. In A.S. the name *ox-a* (ox) stood for both. Wycliff has *shee-oxe* for "cow."

**Bullock or steer, heifer.**—A.S. *bull-uc* (not *-uca*), bullock. A.S. *steór*, steer. A.S. *heáh-fore*, heifer. (*Heáh* means high or full-grown; and *fore* is cognate with Greek *por-is*, a cow-calf or young cow.)

**Cock, hen.**—A.S. *cocc*, of imitative origin; cf. "cuckoo." A.S. *henn-e*, the Fem. counterpart of A.S. *han-a*, a cock. On the Masc. suffix *-a* and the Fem. *-e*, see § 476 (1).

**Colt or foal, filly.**—A.S. *colt*, which meant the young of any animal. In Scand. *kullt* meant "boy." *Foal* is from A.S. *fol-a*, the male young of an animal; on the suffix *-a* see § 476 (1). *Filly* is from Scand. *fyl-ja*, a female foal.

**Dog, bitch.**—A.S. *docga;* Mid. Eng. *dogge*, dog. A.S. *bicc-e*, bitch. On suffix *-e* see § 476. The *cc* has been palatalised to *tch* (§ 438).

**Drake, duck.**—No connection between these words. Mid. Eng. *dok-e, duk-e*, a bird that dives (on the Fem. suffix *-e* see § 476). *Drake* is perhaps a contraction for *ened-* or *end-rake*, and the *-en* has been confounded with *an*, the original form of the Indef. article, or lost from want of accent. *Ened* is A.S. for "duck"; but the meaning of *rake* is not known.[1]

**Drone, bee.**—A.S. *drán*, the hummer. A.S. *beó*, *bí*, bee.

**Earl, countess.**—A.S. *eorl*, a man: (its use as a title of rank is of Scand. origin). Old Fr. *cont-esse*, the fem. form of *count*.

**Father, mother.**—A.S. *fæder;* Scand. *faðir*, cognate with Lat. *pater*, lit. a feeder or supporter. A.S. *móder;* Scand. *moðir*, cognate with Lat. *mater*, which perhaps meant "measurer" or "manager."

**Friar or monk, nun.**—Old Fr. *freire*, a brother, cognate with Lat. *frater*. A.S. *munec*, Lat. *monach*-us, Gr. *monach*-os, one who lives alone. A.S. *nunn-e;* Late Lat. *nunna, nonna*, mother.

**Gaffer, gammer.**—The first is a contraction of Eng. *grandfather;* the second of Fr. *grand-mère* (grandmother).

**Gander, goose.**—A.S. *gan-d-ra* (gander), in which the *-ra* is a suffix, and the *d* is excrescent. The stem is *gan-*, cognate with Lat. *an-ser;* Gr. *chēn*. "Goose" is from A.S. *gós*, plur. *gés*, of which the root is *gan* as before. Hence "gander" and "goose" are from the same Teutonic root, *gan*.[2] (The Aryan root is *ghan*.)

**Gentleman, lady.**—Fr. *gentilhomme;* Eng. gentleman. For the origin of "lady" see "lord" below.

**Hart, roe.**—A.S. *heort*, hart. A.S. *ráh*, roe.

**Horse or stallion, mare.**—A.S. *hors*, lit. a runner (cf. Eng. *cours-er*). Fr. *estalon*, a stalled horse. A.S. *mere*, Fem. form of A.S. *mearh*, a battle-horse.

**Husband, wife.**—Scand. *hús-bóndi*, house-occupier; from Pres. Part.

---

[1] Dr. Murray (*New. Eng. Dict.*) declares himself unable to ascertain the meaning of *rake*. It has been said that *rake* means "master" (hence male) and is allied to *ric* (dominion), as in "bishop-*ric*." "But it cannot go with *ric*, as the gradation is wrong" (Skeat).

[2] The A.S. *gós* is from the form *gan-s*, in which *s* is only a suffix. *Gans* became *gons* and eventually *gós*, the *n* of *gons* having been lost through the lengthening of the *o*.

of *bûa*, to dwell in : (no connection with *bond*, *band*, or *bind*). A.S. *wîf*, a woman ; cf. "fish-wife," a fish-woman, one who sells fish.

**King, queen.**—A.S. *cyn-ing*, "one of noble kin" (*cyn*=kin, tribe). (It has been said that *cyn-ing* means "son of the tribe," but that is not the explanation now given.) A.S. *cwén*, woman. Its meaning as a title of rank is of later origin.

**Lad, lass.**—It used to be said that *lad* and *lass* were from Welsh *llawd* and *llodes.* But this is now abandoned. No one knows the etymology of either word. Possibly *lad* may mean "one led," Mid. Eng. *lad*, pp. of *led-en*, to lead.

**Lord, lady.**—A.S. *hláford*=*hláf-weard*, the loaf-keeper ; cf. A.S. "stí-weard," stykeeper or steward. A.S. *hláf-dige*, loaf-kneader, hence lady.

**Man, woman.**—A.S. *mann*, a person of either sex. A.S. *wíf-man*, a female person ; plur. A.S. *wíf-men*, late A.S. *wim-men*, the sound of which still attaches to the modern misspelling "women."

**Milter, spawner.**—"Milter" means a fish with *milt* or *milk;* the old word for soft-roe was *fiske-melk*, fish-milk. "Spawner" means a fish that scatters eggs ; Old Fr. *espandre*, to scatter.

**Nephew, niece.**—Old Fr. *neveu*, Lat. *nepot*-em, grandson or nephew. Old Fr. *niece*, Lat. *neptis*, granddaughter or niece. (The pair of words in A.S. was *nef-a* and *nef-e ;* see suffixes *-a* and *-e* in § 476 ; but "nephew" and "niece" could not have come from these words.)

**Papa, mamma.**—Fr. *papa*, Lat. *pappas ;* due to the infantile repetition of *pa, pa.* "Mamma" should have been spelt *mama*, due to the child's repetition of *ma, ma.*

**Ram or wether, ewe.**—A.S. *ram*, a male sheep. A.S. *weðer* (wether) a yearling ; from Aryan *wet*, a year. A.S. *eowu*, a female sheep ; cf. Lat. *ov*-is.

**Sir, madam or madame.**—Fr. *sire*, Lat. *senior*, older. Fr. *madame*, Lat. *mea domina*, my lady.

**Sire, dam.**—Origin as above.

**Sloven, slut.**—Etymology distinct. Teut. base *slup-*, to slip, with Mid. Eng. suffix *-ein*, Fr. *en*, gives *sloven.* "Slut" is from Mid. Eng. *slutt-e*, an untidy woman ; cf. Scand. *slöttr*, a lazy man.

**Son, daughter.**—A.S. *su-nu*, cognate with Gr. *hui-os* for *sui-os*, son. A.S. *dóhtor*, daughter. (It has been said that "daughter" meant orig. "milkmaid." But this is now disbelieved by the best authorities.)

**Stag, hind.**—"Stag" has been traced to Scand. *stig-a*, to mount ; hence "stag" would mean lit. the mounter. But this etymology is not now accepted, because the vowel is wrong. A.S. *hind*, the female of stag.

**Swain, nymph** (used in poetry for "youth" and "damsel").—Scand. *sveinn*, a lad or servant. Lat. *nymph-a*, a nymph.

**Tapster, barmaid.**—For *tapster* see § 476 (2). Orig. a feminine ; but when the final *er* in *-ster* was mistaken for the Masc. suffix *-er*, the compound *bar-maid* was formed to supply the place of a feminine.

**Uncle, aunt.**—Fr. *oncle*, Lat. *avunculus*, a little grandfather. Old Fr. *ante*, Lat. *amita*, a father's sister.

**Wizard, witch.**—A.S. *wicc-a* (Masc.), *wicc-e* (Fem.) ; see suffixes

-*a* and -*e* in § 476. "Witch" is from both forms, and was once of Common gender:—

Your honour is a *witch*.—SCOTT.

"Wizard" = *witt-ish-ard*. Old. Fr. *wisch-ard* or *guisc-art*, sagacious.

**Widower, widow**; see above, § 476.

**Bridegroom, bride.**—A.S. *brýd*, a bride. To give this stem a Masc. form, A.S. *guma* (man) was added. Hence A.S. *brýd-guma* bride-groom); but in Mid. Eng. the word *grome* (Mod. Eng. *groom*) was substituted for *guma*.

*Note.*—A reason can sometimes be shown why words of separate origin should have been selected to note the distinction of sex. (1) The function or position of the male as distinct from that of the female is sometimes denoted by the names that stand for male and female respectively: thus *father* means the supporter, feeder, *mother* the manager; *husband* means house-occupier, *wife* means woman; *king* means one of noble kin, *queen* means woman, and came to denote a king's woman or wife; *lord* means the loaf-keeper, *lady* the loaf-kneader; *milter* means the fish that carries milk or milt, *spawner* the fish that scatters eggs, —that is, the female. (2) The male or female is sometimes denoted by the etymology of the word; thus *boy* meant a male, so *girl*, which originally denoted either sex, was restricted to the female; *dog* (A.S. *docg-a*) meant originally the male, and *bitch* (A.S. *bicc-e*) the female; *earl* meant originally a male, and so the want of a noun to denote the feminine title of rank had to be supplied by a new word, *countess*; as *friar* denoted brother, a new word *nun* (*nunn-e*) was wanted to express the female counterpart; *ewe* (A.S. *eown*) denoted a female sheep, so *ram* was needed to denote the male; *sir* (from Lat. *senior*) denoted a male, so *madam* or *madame* was needed to denote the female. *Bride* (A.S. *brýd*) denoted a female, so it was necessary to add *groom* (A.S. *guma*) to the word to denote the male, "the bride's man."

### *Case.*

**480. Case in Old English.**—There were five cases: Nominative, Accusative, Genitive, Dative, Instrumental. "Case" means "falling": the Nom. was considered to be the upright form, from which the others fell to one side, and were thence called "oblique" or slanting.

All the Case-endings except that of the Genitive (which we now call Possessive) have disappeared.

The loss of -*m* and -*e* for the Dative Singular, and of -*um* for the Dative Plural, left the Dative undistinguished from the Accusative, both of which we now call by the common name "Objective." A few Dative forms, however, have survived, as in *whil-om*, *seld-om*, *who-m*, *the-m*, *hi-m*.

The Dative inflexion in -*e* appears in the written form of

many words, as in *ston-e* (§ 441); but is no longer *known* to be a Dative. Similarly a Dative form lies concealed in *meadow* (from A.S. *mǽdw-e*, Dat. of *mǽdu*) and in *shadow* (from A.S. *sceadw-e*, Dat. of *sceadu*). The Dative survives, therefore, etymologically, but not grammatically.

**481. Possessive Case-endings.**—In Old English there were various declensions, as in Latin and Greek, and for these different declensions there were different Genitive endings—(*a*) for the Singular, (*b*) for the Plural.

(*a*) The ending *-es* was originally limited to (Strong) Singular nouns, and then only to Masculines and Neuters. For (Strong) Feminine nouns, Singular, the Genitive ending was *-e:* (contrast *Lord's-day* with *Lady-day*). Another Genitive ending (Singular) for Masculine and Feminine nouns of the Strong declension was *-an*. The same was also used for Neuter nouns of the Weak declension.

Thus we have *Sun-day* (A.S. *Sunn-an* (Fem.) *dæg*, day of the Sun), *Mon-day* (A.S. *Món-an* (Masc.) *dæg*, day of the Moon), *Tues-day* (A.S. *Tiw-es* (Masc.) *dæg*, day of Tíw, the god of war), *Wednes-day* (A.S. *Wódn-es* (Masc.) *dæg*, day of Woden), *Thurs-day* (A.S. *Þunr-es* (Masc.) *dæg*, day of Thunor, thunder), *Fri-day* (A.S. *Frig-e*, the Genitive of *Frigu*, the goddess of love), *Satur-day* (A.S. *Sæter-dæg*, or *Sætern-dæg*, a compound noun, and therefore not requiring a Genitive suffix to *Sætern*, Saturn).[1]

(*b*) It was not till the fourteenth century that *-es* became the ordinary Genitive ending for the Plural as well as the Singular; and as grammatical gender became extinct at about the same time, no question arose as to whether the same ending could be given to Fem. nouns as to Masc. ones. It was therefore given henceforth to all nouns alike, in both numbers. One of the old plural suffixes was *-ena*, of which there is now one solitary example left, viz. *Wit-ena-gemót*, "the assembly of wise men," the Saxon parliament.

The ending *-es* continued for some time to be a distinct syllable. This occurs, though very rarely, in Shakspeare:—

Larger than the moon-*ës* sphere.—*Midsummer Night's Dream*, ii. 1.
To show his teeth as white as whal-*ës* bone.—*Love's Labour's Lost*, v. 2.

[1] There were two forms for "Saturday" in A.S.—(1) *Sætern-dæg*, which is simply a compound word; and (2) *Sæternes dæg*, in which the noun *Sætern* appears with a Genitive suffix *-es*. The latter form fell out of use, because it was longer and less convenient than the compound form *Sætern-dæg*, from which our *Saturday* has come. The noun *Sætern* is, of course, borrowed from Lat. *Saturnus:* whereas every other day of the week has been named after some Teutonic god or goddess.

In the place of *-es* we now always write "*'s*" (apostrophe *s*), in which the apostrophe or comma is intended to denote the elision of *e*. This in Singular nouns. In Plurals we cut out the *-es* altogether, and leave only the apostrophe, as *horses'*, unless the Plural ends in *-n*, as *men's*.

*Note.*—For the sake of uniformity, and to distinguish the Genitive Singular from the Nom. and Obj. Plural, we write the apostrophe even in nouns, in which there has been no actual elision of *e*, as *stone's*, the original form of which was A.S. *stán-es*, Mid. Eng. *stoon-es*.

**482. Substitution of "his" for "s."**—The Genitive or Possessive suffix was sometimes spelt as *-is*. As this was sometimes[1] written apart from the noun, it became confounded with *his*, through the uncertainty of initial "*h*" (§ 437).

> Argal *his* brother.—LAYAMAN, A.D. 1200.
> Decius Cæsar *his* tyme.—TREVISA, A.D. 1380.
> For Jesus Christ *his* sake.—*English Prayer-book.*

*Note.*—It was once supposed that the *his* gave rise to the Possessive suffix *-es* or *'s*. This theory is, of course, ridiculous, for two reasons—(1) the Possessive suffix *s* gave rise to the Genitive pronoun *his*, and not *vice versa*; (2) the same suffix is used with Feminine nouns, as "Jane's bonnet," and with Plural nouns, "men's work." We could never have said "Jane *his* bonnet," or "men *his* work."

### *Number.*

**483. Plural endings in Old English.**—The chief Plural endings in Anglo-Saxon were *-as*, *-an*, *-a*, *-u*.

> (1) A.S. stán-*as*, stones. (3) A.S. hand-*a*, hands.
> (2) A.S. steorr-*an*, stars. (4) A.S. lim-*u*, limbs.

Of these the most common was *-an*. Another very common one was *-as*. At first the ending *-as* could be used with nouns of only one declension, and these only of the Masculine gender; but eventually it became the plural ending of almost all English nouns; and even in A.S. it was from the first very common, because the number of nouns of that declension happened to be very large.

The 3rd and 4th died out in the twelfth century. The 1st and 2nd, which remained, took the forms of *-es* and *-en* in Mid. English.

*Note* 1.—The earlier ending in English was *-es*, not *-s*; as A.S. *cyning-as*, Mid. Eng. *king-es*, Mod. Eng. *king-s*. The rule now is to

[1] It was chiefly used (as in the examples quoted) with *foreign proper names*, which had no real genitive. So *is* was written separately, by way of denoting a genitive; and this *is* became confounded with *his*.

contract *-es*, to *-s*, wherever the pronunciation of the word allows it. In such a word as *stones* (A.S. *stán-as*) the *e* is retained, not for the sake of the *s*, but to give length to the *o*. In French, on the other hand, the plural suffix was at first *-s*, not *-es*, as Anglo-French *flur-s*. But the French *-s* was forced to conform to the Mid. Eng. *-es*, which was syllabic. Thus we have Anglo-French *flur-s*, Mid. Eng. *flour-es*, Mod. Eng. *flower-s*. See *Note* to § 396.

*Note* 2.—The Plurals in ics, as *mathematics*, *physics*, were many of them introduced with the Revival of Learning, in imitation of the Greek plurals, from which our own words were borrowed. In Gower we have *mathem-atic* (Sing.), not *mathem-atics* (Plur.).

**484. Plurals in -ies.**—It is usually said that nouns, which end in *y* in the Singular, form the Plural in *-ies*. It would be nearer the truth to say that such nouns in forming the Plural have retained the original Singular ending in *-ie* and added *-s* to it :—

Flie (=fly), flies. Citie (=city), cities.

*Note.*—*Dice* is the modern spelling of Mid. Eng. *dys*, Old Fr. *dez*, the plural of *det*. Out of this plural we have coined a Sing. *die*, the small cube on which the dice are engraved.

**485. Plurals in -ves.**—In § 66 two lists of nouns are given, in the first of which final *fe* or *f* becomes *ves* in the Plural, while in the other final *fe* or *f* remains unchanged after the addition of *-s*.

(*a*) As regards the first list it should be noted—(1) that the nouns there given are all (except the last, *beef*, *beeves*) of *Teutonic* origin ; and (2) the change from *f* to *v* occurs in the Genitive and Dative *Singular*, and all through the Plural in Mid. Eng.

| | | | |
|---|---|---|---|
| A.S. | Nom. Sing. *hláf* | Gen. Sing. *hláf-es* | Nom. Plur. *hláf-as* |
| Mid. Eng. | ,, ,, *lof* | ,, ,, *lov-es* | ,, ,, *lov-es* |
| Mod. Eng. | ,, ,, *loaf* | ,, ,, *loaf's* | ,, ,, *loaves* |

*Note.*—The changing of *f* into *v* is merely an example of the voicing of voiceless consonants, as explained in § 432, II., through the voiceless *f* being placed between two vowels. Indeed, the *f* between two vowels was sounded as *v* even in A.S.

(*b*) As regards the second list, it should be noted that the words there given are either of French origin, or they end in *f* or in *ff*, or the final *f* is preceded by *oo*. Thus in *hoof*, *roof*, *proof*, the *f* is preceded by *oo* ; and moreover *proof* is of French origin. *Chief*, *gulf*, *grief*, *safe*, *strife*, *fife* were all French before they became English. The rest all end in *rf* or in *ff*. *Reef* is merely a modern spelling of *riff*.

*Note.*—The Fr. plural ending was *-s*, and not *-es*, as in Early and Middle English. This may help to explain why the form *-s* is given to nouns of foreign origin, and *-es* to native ones.

Tennyson has *hooves*, and we sometimes, though rarely, hear *wharves, dwarves*. *Scarves*, however, is rather more common than *scarfs*.

**486. Mutation Plurals,**—that is, Plurals formed by a change of the root-vowel. The A.S. forms of these nouns, Singular and Plural, are shown below :—

| *A.S.* | | *Mod. Eng.* | | *A.S.* | | *Mod. Eng.* | |
|---|---|---|---|---|---|---|---|
| *Sing.* | *Plural.* | *Sing.* | *Plural.* | *Sing.* | *Plural.* | *Sing.* | *Plural.* |
| Mann | menn | Man | men | Fót | fét | Foot | feet |
| Mús | mýs | Mouse | mice | Tóð | téð | Tooth | teeth |
| Lús | lýs | Louse | lice | Gós | gés | Goose | geese |

The *earliest* forms of the above plurals were *mann-is*, *mús-is* (cf. Lat. *mur-es*), *lús-is*, *fót-is* (cf. Lat. *ped-es*, Gr. *pod-es*), *tóð-is* (cf. Lat. *dent-es*), and *gós-is*. The Plural, in fact, was formed by adding the ending *-is*.

The effect of the *i* in the ending *-is* was to change *mann-* into *menn-*, *mús-* into *mýs-*, *lús* into *lýs-*, *fót-* into *fét-*, *tóð-* into *téð-* and *gós-* into *gés-*; so that after the suffix *-is* had dropped off as it did even in Anglo-Saxon times, nothing but the mutation of the root-vowel was left as a mark of the Plural.

*Note* 1.—*Women*, being derived from A.S. *wíf-man*, has the same mutation plural that *man* has. The sound of the vowel in the first syllable is still as if the word were spelt *wimmen*; but the vowel in the singular has been affected by the *w*.

*Note* 2.—Several other nouns had once a form of Plural marked by a change in the root-vowel. Thus the old plural of *bóc* (book) was *béc*, which superseded a still older plural *bóc-is*, and was itself eventually superseded by the new plural *books*. Similarly *bróc* formed its plural in *bréc* (whence the modern double plural *breeks*). The same process is seen at work in *brœthr*, the Northern plural of *brother*, and in *ký*, the plural of *cow* (A.S. *cú*). All these are instances of what in § 452 is called "**Vowel-Mutation.**"

**487. Plurals in -en or -ne.**—If our literary language had remained purely Southern (that is, if our modern standard English had sprung from the Anglo-Saxon, and not from the Midland dialect), its predominant Plural suffix might possibly now be *-en*, and instead of Plurals like *steorr-an* being turned into *stars*, we might have had a borrowed noun like *art* forming its Plural in *art-en*, like *ox*, *ox-en*.

*Ox-en* is now the only noun left, in literary English, that has formed its Plural regularly in *-en*.[1] The other three words

---

[1] The word *bracken* as plural of *brake* was once included in this list. But this has been disproved in the *New English Dictionary*.

*children*, *brethren*, and *kine*, are Double Plurals, as will be shown in § 488.

Note.—The suffix *-en* died hard. *Hosen* (plural of *hose*) occurs in Old Test., Dan. iii. 21; and *shoon* (plural of *shoe*) occurs in Shakspeare. Spenser has *eyen* for *eyes*, and *foen* for *foes*. In a book written about 1420 we find *been* for *bees*, *een* for *eyes*, *fleen* for *flies*, *pesen* for *peas*, and *toon* for *toes*; and a century later *treen* for *trees*, and *sistren* for *sisters*. In villages in the south of England *housen* is still heard for *houses*, though the A.S. plural was *hús* (unchanged).

**488. Double Plurals.**—There are at least five words in common use whose Plural is formed with *two* Plural suffixes:—

**Child-re-n.**—In A.S. there was a declension in which the case-endings of the plural were preceded by an *r*. Thus the Plural of *cild* (child) was *cild-ru*.[1] In Mid. Eng. *cild-ru* became *child-re* or *child-er*, which, when a second Plural suffix was added, became *child-re-n* or *child-er-n*: (*childern* is still heard in villages, and *childer* occurs in Tudor dramatists). Similarly the old plural of *lomb* (lamb) was *lomb-ru*, of *cealf* (calf), *cealf-ru*, and of *ǽg* (egg), *ǽg-ru*. Cf. Calv*er*-ley = calves' lea or field.

**Brethre-n.**—In A.S. the singular was *bróðor*, hence our Plural *brothers*. In Icel. the Sing. was *bróðir*, which by vowel-mutation gave a plural *bræthr*. This in the fourteenth century became *brethre*, because *r* in Eng. required a vowel after it. To this *-n* was afterwards added, making the double plural *brethr-e-n*.[2]

**Kine.**—The old plural of *cú* (cow) was *cý* (see *Note* 2 to § 486). This was developed into *kine* by adding *-en* to the plural stem, making *cý-en*, *ký-en*, *kine*. (The A.S. *c* was sounded as *k*.)

**Breeks, breeches.**—In A.S. the plural of *bróc* (see *Note* 2 to § 486) was *brée*. By adding *-s* or *-es* we get *breeks* or *breeches*. (In A.S. *c* = *k*, and the *c* of *brée* was palatalised to *ch*.)

**Sixpen-ce-s.**—*Pen-ce* is one of the Plurals of *penny*.[3] "Sixpence,"

---

[1] A more complete explanation of the *r* in *children* is as follows:—"The word *cild* was a neuter in *-os*, like Gr. *gen-os*, Lat. *gen-us* (= **gen-os*). The *e-* stem corresponding to the *o-* stem in *-os* was *-es*. This appears in the genitives:—Gr. *gen-es-os* (= *gen-e-os*, the *s* having dropped out), Lat. *gen-es-es* = *gen-er-is*. So Nom. Sing. **cild-os* became **cild-oz*, **cild-o*, *cild*. But the plural was **cild-es-us*, the A.S. neut. plur. suffix *u* being added. This became *cild-er-u*, and then *cildru*" (Skeat).

[2] A more complete explanation of this mutation-plural is as follows:—"The original plur. of *bróðir* was *brǿð(i)r*, in which the *i* dropped out. But only the oldest Icel. MS. used the symbol *ǿ* = *oe*, the umlaut of *o* = A.S. *é*. The *ǿ* came to be confused with *ǽ*, and *ǽ* was wrongly written for it. That is how the *æ* came in. As the Icel. *æ* is always long, the mark denoting length was not written over it. Since this *æ* really meant *œ*, it was, of course, written *é* in English" (Skeat).

[3] *Penny* is from A.S. *pening*, later A.S. *penig*, whence Mid. Eng. *peni*, with Plur. *penies*, or (contracted form) *pens*. Our mod. Plur. *pennies* is from Mid. Eng. *penies*, and *pence* from Mid. Eng. *pens*.

though really a Plural, was regarded as a Singular Collective noun, to which the Plural suffix *-s* was added.

**489. Same form for Plural as for Singular.**—To this class belong *deer, sheep, swine, yoke, score.* In A.S. the nouns *deer, sheep, swine* were Neuter, and Neuters had the same form for Plural as for Singular, provided the vowel was long either by nature or position.

*Note* 1.—This class of noun once included many more; such as *folk, year, head* (Neut. Plur. in A.S., *héafōd-u, héafd-u*), *pound* (enclosure), *horse, night* (in A.S. Fem. Plur. *night-a,* where the Fem. suffix *-a* dropped off). A.S. *geŏe* (yoke) was also Neuter; but as the vowel was short, it formed its plural in *geŏc-u,* which by the change of *u* to *e* gives us the Mod. Plur. *yoke.* A.S. *scor-a* (score) was Feminine, not Neuter; and was a Plural already: (as a Sing. it is not found in A.S.). The change of *a* to *e* gives us its Mod. Eng. form *score,* which now stands for both numbers. To this day we say "forty *head* of cattle," "a body of 1000 *horse,*" "fort*night*" (a contracted form of "fourteen *night*"), "ten *score*" (not *scores*).

*Note* 2.—A few nouns such as *salmon* (lit. the leaper or jumper), from Lat. root *sal,* have the same form for Plural as for Singular, by the analogy of Teutonic words. To the same class belong *grouse, trout, cod, heathen, brace, dozen, gross;* these are all modern imitations, and all but *heathen* are of foreign origin. The word *stone* is very peculiar. Its proper plural is *stones* (A.S. *stán-as*). But in the sense of weight, it has the one form *stone* for both numbers.

*Note* 3.—The student must not yield to the temptation of supposing that *sow, swine* make up a pair of words analogous to *cow, kine.* "Sow" is from A.S. *sugu,* a female pig; "swine" is from A.S. *swín,* a pig of either sex, the suffix *n* being adjectival and therefore applicable to either gender.

*Sing.* { *This* foul *swine* (pig) . . . *lies* now
Near to the town of Leicester, as we learn.
SHAK., *Richard III.* v. 3.

*Plur.* All the *swine* (=pigs) were sows.
TENNYSON'S *Princess.*

Observe, too, that the derivative *swin-ish* shows that *swine* is Singular; for adjective-suffixes like *-ish* and others are added to Singulars, not to Plurals. The genitive singular *swin-es* appears in the name "Swineshead" in Huntingdonshire.

**490. Plurals that have become Singulars.**—Of this there are several examples:—

**Truce.**—In A.S. *tréowa* meant a pledge (Singular). In Mid. Eng. this word was respelt as *trew,* and had *trews* as its Plural, which in Mod. Eng. has become *truce* and is regarded as a Singular.

**Bodice.**—This is simply a respelling of *bodies,* the Plural of *body.*

**Baize.**—Coarse woollen stuff: an error for *bayes,* an old Fem. Plur. of French *bai.*

**Trace.**—A respelling of French *traits,* Plural of *trait,* a line. We now say *traces* for the straps by which a vehicle is drawn.

**Sledge.**—Apparently a respelling of *sleds*, plural of *sled*, the word still used in Canada for "sledge," from Icel. *sleði*.

**Small-pox.**—Here *pox* is the Plural of *pock*, A.S. *poc*, a pustule.

**Chess.**—The Norman plural of *check;* the original meaning of which was "king," of Persian origin. The original sense of *check* was "King! mind the king!"

**Welkin.**—In A.S. the Sing. *wolcen* (cloud) had as its Plural *wolcn-u;* see Plural suffix in § 483 (4). *Wolcn-u* became in Mid. Eng. *wolken* (clouds), which is now spelt as *welkin* and has lost its Plural force.

**A sixpence.**—"Pence" is merely another spelling of *pennies*, the Plural of *penny*. In the compound form of *sixpence* it can be pluralised as *sixpences*, since *sixpence* (the silver coin) is Singular in sense.

**491. Singulars which have become Plurals.**—There are at least nine such words, and two more about which the student should be on his guard:—

**Burials.**—Originally a Singular, from A.S. *byrgels*, a tomb; respelt in Mid. Eng. as *buriels*. When the *e* was changed to *a* in Mod. Eng., *burials* seemed to be a Plural like *victuals, vitals, trials, removals*, etc.

**Riddles.**—In A.S. the word was *rǽdelse*, which had as its Plural *rǽddels-an*. Out of *riddles* we have coined a Sing. *riddle*.

**Peas.**—In A.S. the word was *pisa*, Plur. *pis-an*. When the Plural suffix was lost, the *s* looked like a Plural, and so a Singular *pea* was formed out of the modernised *peas*. We still, however, say *pease*-pudding, not *pea*-pudding.

> The vaunting poets found nought worth *a pease*.
> SPENSER, *Shep. Calendar*.
>
> Not worth two *peas*-en.—SURREY.

**Skates.**—Dutch *schaats*, Plural *schaats-en*.

**Eaves.**—A.S. *efese*, Mid. Eng. *evese*, with Plural form *eves-es*. Though *eaves* is now always used as a Plural, no Singular *eave* was coined till very lately by Tennyson, who has given us the compound *eave-drop* for *eaves-drop*.

**Alms.**—A.S. *ælmesse*, from Gr. *eleēmosyne*, whence the adj. *eleemosynary*. No Singular *alm* has been coined, like "burial," "riddle," "pea," "skate."

> Seeing Peter and John about to go into the temple, he asked *an alms*.—*Acts* iii. 3.

**Cherry.**—This Singular has been coined from Mid. Eng. *cheris*, Old Fr. *cerise*, Lat. *ceras*-us (a cherry-tree), Gr. *keras*-os. Here, as before, the final *s* of *cheris* was wrongly taken for a Plural suffix.

**Minnows.**—This could not have arisen from A.S. *myne;* but came orig. from Old Fr. *menuise*, which gave Mid. Eng. *menuse*. The last looked like a Plural, which gave rise to a new Sing. *menu* or *menow*, from which we get our mod. Sing. *minnow*.

**Riches.**—Fr. *richesse*, richness, wealth; cf. *caress, largess*. In Mid. Eng. it was spelt, as in French, *richesse*, and had a plural *richess-es*, like our present word *caress-es*.

Against the *richesses* of this world shall they have misease of poverty.—CHAUCER.
In one hour *is* so great *riches* come to naught.—*Rev.* xviii. 17.
*Riches do* not consist in having more gold and silver.—LOCKE.

**Summons, laches.**—These words have both retained their Singular force so far; but the final *s* exposes them to danger. *Laches* is a French word parallel to *riches*, signifying "laxity," to which it is allied in root. *Summons* is from French *semonce*, and not, as has been supposed, from Lat. *sub-* or *sum-moneas*.

### *Note on the Number of Nouns.*

It has been observed that there are instances in English in which (1) a plural sense is found without a plural inflexion; (2) a plural inflexion without a plural sense. Such instances can easily be recapitulated from what has been already said.

(1) *A plural sense without a plural inflexion*:—

Examples of this can be seen in § 70, where the nouns given are nouns of Multitude, as *cattle*; in § 71 and § 489, where the nouns have the same form for the Plural as the Singular, as *sheep*; in § 72, where the noun retains a Singular form in order to denote some specific quantity, as *a twelvemonth*; and in § 491, where the nouns given were originally Singular, but have been mistaken for plurals, and thus acquired a plural sense, as *alms*.

(2) *A plural inflexion without a plural sense*:—

Examples of this can be seen in § 78, where the Plural nouns given have acquired a Singular sense, as *news* (= new things, tidings); in § 79 (*e*), where the nouns given denote a single science, but have acquired a Plural form in *-ics* in imitation of the Greek plural from which they have been translated, as *physics*; in § 490, where the words given were originally Plural, but have been mistaken for Singulars and acquired a Singular sense, as *truce*.

## SECTION 2.—THE FORMS OF ADJECTIVES.

**492. Loss of Adjective Inflexions.**—In Old English adjectives had two different modes of declension—(1) the Weak, when the adjective was preceded by a Demonstrative adjective; (2) the Strong, when it was not so preceded. Gender, number, and case had each its own set of inflexions for both. But with the gradual *levelling* of inflexions, peculiar to the Middle period of English (see § 382), the two declensions fell eventually into one, and most of the inflexions took the form of *-e*, which itself disappeared in Modern English, leaving nothing.

In Chaucer (whose death was in 1400) the Strong declension has usually no inflexion for the Singular, and the Weak has *-e* throughout. Both declensions had *-e* throughout the Plural. This, however, applies only to adjectives of *one* syllable. If the adjective was of more than one syllable, it was generally uninflected in both numbers, more especially if the adjective was of Romanic origin.

*Note.* 1.—The word *old-en* appears to contain a trace of the obsolete adjective suffix *-an*, which was a common suffix in the Weak declension, Singular and Plural.

*Note* 2.—In the word *alder-liefest* (dearest of all) Shakspeare has preserved an old genitive Plural form, which in Old English was spelt as *-ra*; A.S. *eal-ra*, Mercian *al-ra*.

With you, mine *alder*-liefest sovereign.—2 *Hen. VI.* i. 128.

*Note* 3.—The Dative and Instrumental suffix *-um* in the Plural of both declensions has survived in *seld-om*, Old Eng. *seld-um*, at rare (times).

*Note* 4.—The only flexional forms that have survived and are still in common use are *these* and *those*, both of which were originally plurals of *this*, but are now allotted to *this* and *that* respectively.

493. **Cardinals**: so called from Lat. *cardin-em*, a hinge, because on them the Ordinals were said to hinge or depend. All our Cardinals, except *dozen* and *million*, are of Teutonic origin.

**One**: A.S. *án* (cf. Lat. *un-us*), from which the Indefinite article *an* or *a* has also come. *Only* is from A.S. *án-lic* (one-like).

*Note.*—The word *aught* is from A.S. *á+wiht*, a thing or particle. From its negative form *naught* we get *not*. (Here *á* stands for *án*.)

**Two.**—A.S. *twá*, the Fem. and Neut. of *twegen*, whence *twain*, *be-tween*, *twin*. Cf. Gr. *duo*, Lat. *du-o*, whence *dual*, *duel*. The Fr. cognate is *deux*, and the German *zwei*.

**Both.**—Lit. "they two." Old Norse, *báðir*. The last syllable (*ðir*) signifies "they." For *bá* compare A.S. *bá*, Lat. am-*bo*, and Gr. am-*pho*.

**Three.**—A.S. Masc. *þrí*, Fem. and Neut. *þreó*. Our word *three* is pronounced exactly like A.S. *þrí*, but comes from *þreó*.

**Four.**—A.S. *feówer*; cf. Goth. *fidwor*, Lat. *quatuor*.

**Five.**—A.S. *fíf*; cf. Germ. *fünf*, Lat. *quinque*.

**Six.**—A.S. *six*, Lat. *sex*, Gr. *hex*.

**Seven.**—A.S. *seofon*, Lat. *septem*, Gr. *hepta*.

**Eight.**—A.S. *eahta*, Lat. *octo*, Gr. *okto*.

**Nine.**—A.S. *nigon*, Mid. Eng. *nin-e*, where the *e* is a Plural suffix; cf. Lat. *novem*.

**Ten.**—A.S. *tén*, *teón*, a contraction of A.S. **tehon*, like Goth. *taihun*; cf. Lat. *decem*, Gr. *deka*. Our English numeral has therefore lost a medial guttural. (* denotes that the form is theoretical.)

**Eleven.**—A.S. *end-lufon*, Goth. *ain-lif*, where *ain* means "one," and *lif* means "over" or "left." So "eleven" means "ten and one over."

**Twelve.**—A.S. *twelf*, Goth. *twa-lif*=ten and two over.

**Dozen.**—Old Fr. *dos-aine*, from *dose* (=twelve, Lat. *duodecim*), with suffix *-aine*.

**Thirteen—nineteen.**—All formed by adding *teen* (A.S. *tín*, sounded as *teen*) to the Cardinals.

**Twenty.**—A.S. *twen-tig*. Here *twen* is short for *twegen*, two; and *tig*=ten, cognate with Lat. *dec*-em. Thus *-teen* is added to denote addition, and *-tig* to denote multiplication.

**Score.**—A.S. *scor-a* (Plur.), a long notch cut in a stick called tally.

> Whereas our forefathers had no other books but the *score* and the *tally*, thou hast caused printing to be used.—*Henry VI.* part ii.

**Thirty—ninety.**—All formed in the same way as "twenty."

**Hundred.**—A.S. *hund* (cognate with Lat. *cent*-um), and *réd* or *rǽd*, reckoning.

**Thousand.**—A.S. *þúsend*, Scand. *þúsund*, also written *þús-hund* by a popular and false etymology. The *und* (wrongly written *hund*) does not mean "a hundred." The real sense and origin of *þúsund* are not known.

**Million.**—Fr. *million*, Lat. *million-em:* the root is *mille*.

**494. Ordinals**; from Lat. *ordin-em*, because such numerals show the *order* in which things or persons stand. All but one are of Teutonic origin.

**First.**—A.S. *fyrst*=fore-est, superlative of *fore*, in which the *o* has become *i* or *y* by the influence of *i* in *-ist*, later *-est*. See § 452 (4).

**Second.**—Lat. *secundus*, which superseded A.S. *óðer* (other), a comparative form=beyond this, second.

**Third**, for *thrid*, A.S. *thridda;* cf. Lat. *tertius*.

**Fourth**, and the remaining ordinals, are formed by adding *th* (A.S. *ta* or *ða*) to the Cardinal.

**Multiplicatives**, formed by adding either (*a*) Teutonic *fold*, or (*b*) Romanic *-ple* or *-ble:*—

*Teutonic:* two-*fold*, three-*fold*, etc. (A.S. *feald*).

*Romanic:* sim-*ple* (one-*fold*), dou-*ble*, tre-*ble*, tri-*ple*, etc. (Lat. *plex*).

*Note.—Simple* (from Lat. *simplex*) has ousted the Old English word *án-feald*, one-*fold*.

**495. Indefinite Adjectives** of Quantity or Number:—

**All.**—A.S. *eal* (Sing.), *ealle* (Plur.).

**None, no.**—A.S. *ne*+*án* (not one). "No" is short for "none."

**Many.**—Noun or Adj. See derivations given in § 324, *Note*.

**Several.**—Old Fr. *several*, Late Lat. *separale*, a thing apart.

**Some.**—A.S. *sum*.

**Enough.**—A.S. *ge-nóh* or *ge-nóg*, Mid. Eng. *inóh*, *enógh*.

**Few.**—A.S. *féa* (Sing.), *feáwe* (Plur.); Mid. Eng. *fewe*.

**Sundry.**—A.S. *syndrig;* cf. *sundr-ian* (verb), to divide or separate; hence "sunder."

**Much.**—A.S. *myc-el*; from the first syllable we get *much;* from the entire word we get the obsolescent *mickle*.

**Little.**—A.S. *lyt*, *lyt-el.* "Little" has no connection with *less.* The base *lut* means to deceive. Hence "little" still sometimes means "base," "mean," "small-minded," "narrow-minded."

**Any.**—A.S. *ǽnig*, from A.S. *án*, one.

**Whole.**—The *wh* is no longer sounded, but was substituted for *h* in the sixteenth century. A.S. *hál*, Mid. Eng. *hool*, Mod. Eng. *whole*.

**Half.**—A.S. *healf*, side. Hence "on my behalf" means "on my side," "in my interests."

## 496. Demonstrative Adjectives:—

**The.**—(*a*) Now the Definite article: A.S. *ðe*, used at first as an indeclinable Relative. It next became a Demonstrative adjective, as it now is. (In Old Eng. *se* (Masc.) and *seó* (Fem.) were used as the Def. article before Masc. and Fem. nouns.[1])

(*b*) Before Comparative adjectives or adverbs: A.S. *ðý* or *ði*, the Instrumental case, Singular; as, "*The* more, *the* merrier."

**That.**—A.S. *ðæt*, neuter Sing., Nom. and Accus. The suffix *-t* is a mark of the Neut.; cf. *i-t*, *wha-t;* Lat. *i-d*, *qui-d*, *illu-d*, etc. Before the close of the Mid. period "that" could be used with any Sing. noun in any case or gender.

**This.**—A.S. Masc. *ðes*, Fem. *ðéos*, Neut. *ðis*. Our modern "this" is most like the Neuter.

**These, those.**—A.S. *ðǽs*, *ðás;* two plural forms of *ðes*. In Mod. Eng., however, *these* has been allotted as the plural of *this*, and *those* of *that*.

**Such.**—A.S. *swylc*, from *swá* (so) and *lic* (like). Hence the modern phrase "such-like" is pleonastic.

*Note.*—The obsolescent *thilk* means "the like," from A.S. *þylc*, composed of the instrumental *þi* + *lic*. In the seventeenth century "other-like" was used for "such-like."

**Same.**—A.S. *same*, used only as an adverb. Its use as an adject. was due to Danish influence. Cf. Lat. *sim*-ul.

**Other.**—A.S. *óðer*, second, different from the first. The syllable *ðer* is a Comparative suffix; cf. Lat. "al-*ter*." "Other" means "more than this or that," hence "different from this or that."

**Yon, yonder.**—A.S. *geon* (adj.), distant. *Yonder* was an adverb derived from *yon*, and was used as such. *Yon*, though an adj., has been used adverbially:—

> I and the lad will go *yonder.*—*Old Testament.*
> Him that *yon* soars on golden wing.—MILTON.

**An** (Indef. article), the unemphatic and weaker form of A.S. *án* (one).

**Ilk.**—Originally an adjective, from A.S. *ylca*, same. Hence the phrase *of that ilk* means "of that same." It is quite a different word from *thilk*.

---

[1] In Old Eng. *se* (Masc.) and *seó* (Fem.) were used as the Def. article in the Nom. case only: all the other cases were taken from the root found in the Neuter *ðæt*.

**497. Distributive Adjectives:—**

**Each.**—A.S. *ǽlc*, for *á-ge-líc=á-gi-líc*, where the *i* in *gi* causes mutation; aye-like or ever like.

**Every.**—From A.S. *ǽfre* (ever) and *ǽlc* (each); in Mid. Eng. *ever-ich*, *ever-ilc*.

*Note.*—Thus the modern idiomatic distinction in the use of *each* and *every* (see § 94) has no foundation in etymology.

**Either . . . n-either.**—A.S. *ǽgþer*, a contraction of *ǽ-g-hwæþer*, formed from *á* (ever)+*gi* for *ge* (a prefix)+*hwæþer* (which of two). Here the vowel *á* has been mutated by the *i* in *gi*.

*Comparison of Adjectives.*

**498. Modes of expressing Comparison.**—Four different modes, as shown below, have existed in English. Of these the 1st, 3rd, and 4th are synthetic or flexional, and the 2nd is analytical.

(1) **-er, -est**: A.S. -*(i)ra* and *-ast*, *-ost*, or *-est*.[1] The *ra* is made up of -*(i)r-a*, in which the *r* is the real Comparative suffix, and the *a* is merely the Weak adjectival inflexion. The *r* stands for an original *s*, as seen in the allied languages of the Aryan speech. Cf. our own form "wor-*se*." In the Tudor period the suffixes *-er* and *-est* were attached to adjectives, which cannot now receive them. Thus we find the following:—

Inventivest, honourablest, ancienter, eminentest, eloquenter, learnedest, solemnest, famousest, virtuousest, repiningest, delectablest, movingest, unhopefullest (Shakspeare).

(2) **More, most**: A.S. *mára*, *mǽst*. Used with all adjectives that do not take *-er* and *-est*, and sometimes with those that do. This mode of comparison is first seen in the fourteenth century, and may perhaps have been partly due to French influence. Even in the Tudor period it was freely used with monosyllables:—

Ingratitude *more strong* than traitor's arms.—SHAKSPEARE.

This analytical mode of comparing adjectives is indispensable for adjectives ending with a suffix. If we attached *-er* and *-est* to a suffix, it would seem like comparing the suffix, instead of the quality denoted by the adjective.

---

[1] Philologists have traced these forms still farther back. They say that the original Teutonic suffix for expressing the comparative degree was *-iz* or *-ōz*, which stands for an Aryan or Indo-European *ies*, *iōs*. The *-iōs* appears in Latin as *-ior*, as in dur-*ior*, Gen. dur-iōr-is, the *s* being changed to *r*. The superlative *-est* is said to be compounded of the comparative suffix *-is* (weak form of *ies*), and the superlative suffix *-to*. Both appear in the Greek "meg-*is-tos*," greatest. On the Latin form *-mus*, see (4) in § 498. See Brugmann, *Comp. Gr.* ii. § 135.

(3) **-ter, -ther** (Comparative suffix): cf. Lat. "al-*ter*," "u-*ter*." In English this comparative form is seen in:—

O-*ther*, ei-*ther*, whe-*ther*, af-*ter*, un-*der*, ne-*ther*, fur-*ther*.

*Note* 1.—"Far-ther" does not strictly belong to this list. The Mid. Eng. *farr-er* was changed to *far-ther* in imitation of "fur-ther," the Comparative of *fore*.

*Note* 2.—"Other" means "beyond this," from an Aryan root *ana*, signifying "this"; cf. Lat. *al-ter*, Sansk. *an-tar*. See § 496, **Other**. The Comparative origin of *other* comes out very clearly in such a phrase as "other *than* a soldier."

(4) *-ma* (Superlative suffix): cf. Lat. *-mus*, as in *opti-mus*, *postu-mus*, etc. In Old Eng. the *-ma* sometimes stands alone, and sometimes is reinforced by the addition of *-est*, which made the double suffix *-mest*. This has been misspelt in Mod. Eng. as *most* through a confusion with the other "most" described under (2), with which, however, it must not be confounded; for in A.S. the one was spelt *mest*, and the other *mǽst*.

In-*most* (A.S. inne-*ma* or inne-*mest*), ut-*most* (A.S. úte-*ma* or úte-*mest*), hind-*most* (A.S. hinde-*ma* or hinde-*mest*), fore-*most* (A.S. for-*mest*), mid-*most* (A.S. mede-*ma* or mede-*mest*).

*Note.*—We sometimes have *most* added to nouns; as "top-*most*," "end-*most*," "head-*most*." These words probably mean "most at the top," "most at the end," etc., in which the "most" described under (2) has been confounded with that under (4).

**499. Double Comparisons.**—The doubling of Comparatives and Superlatives is not now permitted, though it was once common. We now intensify Superlatives with the help of phrases; as "*by far* the best," "the *very* worst," "the lowest *of the low*," etc.

After the *most straitest* sect of our religion I lived a Pharisee.—*Acts* xxvi. 5.
Less gifts and *lesser* gains I weigh them not.—HALL'S *Satyres*.
Let not my *worser* spirit tempt me again.—*King Lear*, iv. 6.
*More kinder. More sweeter. More corrupter.*—SHAKSPEARE.

The only double Comparatives now used are *lesser*, *nearer*. On the formation of *nearer*, see below, § 501, I.

**500. Mixed Comparisons.**—In the words *inner-most*, *upper-most*, *utter-most*, *further-most*, *hinder-most*, *nether-most*, we have what looks like the double Superl. suffix *-most* added to Compar. forms *inner-*, *upper-*, *utter-*, *farther-*, *hinder-*, *nether-*. But probably *innermost*, *uttermost*, *nethermost* are merely misspellings of A.S. *inne-mest*, *úte-mest*, *niðe-mest*; and *uppermost*, *further-most*, *hindermost* must have been formed by analogy, for they are not found in A.S.

In *former* we have the Comp. *-er* added to the Superl. *for-ma*, which was common in A.S.

In *near-est* (= nigh-er-est) we have the Superlative *-est* added to the Comparative *near* (= nigh-er), and in *near-er* we have a double Comparative, as is shown in § 501, I.

**501. Irregular Comparisons.** — These may be classified under three different headings, as below :—

I. *With change of root-vowel* :—

**Old, elder, eldest.** — A.S. *eald, yld-ra, yld-est.* (There was originally an "*i*" before the *-ra* and *-st*, which produced a change in the vowel of the positive.) The forms *older, oldest* are more recent. (On the special meaning now assigned to each pair of forms, see § 348.)

**Nigh, near, next.**—A.S. *néah* or *néh*, *neár* (short of *néah-ra* = *nigher*), *néh-st* (which in Mod. Eng. is spelt *next*). The word *near* is therefore a Comparative :—

The *near* in blood, the nearer bloody.—*Macbeth*, ii. 3.
The *nere* to the church, the ferther from God.—HEYWOOD'S *Proverbs*.

Out of the word "near" we have formed a new trio, *near* (Pos.), *near-er* (double Comp.), *near-est* (Superl. added to Comp.). On the special meanings now assigned to *next* and *nearest*, see § 348.

**Late, later, latest.**—A.S. *læt, lator, latost.* In the thirteenth century we get *late, lat-re* (hence *latt-er*), and *lat-st* (hence *last*, a contraction of *lat-st, lat-est*; cf. "best," a contraction of "bet-st," "bet-est"). On the special meaning now assigned to each pair of forms, see § 348.

II. *From obsolete roots* :—

**Good, better, best.**—*Good* is from A.S. *gód*; *better* and *best* from obsolete A.S. *bat*, from which we get the verb "batten" and the noun "boot" (profit) by gradation. *Best* is a contraction of *bet-st*, which was formed by mutation from *bat-ista*; see § 452 (4).

**Bad or evil, worse, worst.** —*Bad* is from A.S. *bæd-del*, an effeminate man; *evil* from A.S. *yfel*, and *ill* from Scand. *illr*. *Worse* is from A.S. Comparative form *wyr-sa* (in which the *-sa* or *-se* is not changed into *ra* or *re*, as usual, but retained). *Worst* is from A.S. *wyrr-est.*

**Little, less, least.**—The positive is from A.S. *lyt, lyt-el.* The Comparative and Superlative are from the root *lǽs* (adv.), which gave *lǽs-sa* (less, the *-sa* not being changed to *-ra*), and *lǽs-st* (least). *Less-er*, the double Comp. form, is a deriv. of *less*.

**Much or mickle, more, most.**—A.S. *mic-el, má-ra, mæ-st.* These are at bottom from the same root, which in A.S. was *mag-* (to be able, hence *might*), in Latin *mag-* (hence *mag-nus, magnitude*, etc.), and in Gr. *meg-* (hence Greek coinages like *meg-a-ther-i-um*). *Much* is from the first syllable of *mic-el*. *Má-ra* means more in point of size, and in Mod. Eng. is assigned as comparative of *much* or *mickle*.

**Many, more, most.**—A.S. *manig, má, mǽst.* On *many* see above,

§ 324. *Má* is not a Positive adjective,[1] but a Comparative adverb that was afterwards turned into an adjective, and made to signify "more" in point of number. There is no etymological connection between *many* and the two words that have been assigned to it as Comparative and Superlative.

III. *From adverbial roots of time and place:—*

**Far, farther, farthest.**—A.S. *feor*, *fyr-ra*, *fyrr-est*, the vowel having undergone mutation through an *i* which preceded *-ra*, as in *-ira;* see § 452 (4). In Mid. Eng. the forms were *fer*, *ferr-er*, *ferr-est*. Hence it is clear that the *th* in "farther, farthest" is intrusive, based on the analogy of "further, furthest." See § 498, *Note* 1.

**Fore, former, foremost or first.**—A.S. *fore: former* (not seen before sixteenth century) was got by adding the Comp. *-er* to the A.S. Superl. *for-ma; foremost* is a double Superl. got by adding *-est* to *for-ma*. *First* is from A.S. *fyrst* (=for-est, the regular Superl. of *fore*, in which the *o* is changed to *y* by the influence of the *i* in Teutonic *-ist*).

**Forth, further, furthest.**—These are duplicates or doublets of the preceding. *Forth* is an extension of *fore*, A.S. *forð*, from which the Comp. and Superl. are not formed. (It has been clearly proved that *ther* was a comparative suffix of *fore*, see § 498 (3); and that the Superlative *furth-est* was formed out of the Comparative *fur-ther*, mistaken for *furth-er*.)

**Ere, erst,** A.S. *ǽr*, *ǽr-ra*, *ǽr-est*.—Our mod. *ere* (which is now a conjunction only) was formed from the Positive, though it is nearer in signification to the Comparative. *Erst* is now only an adverb.

**Hind, hinder, hindmost or hindermost.**—*Hind* is from A.S. *hind-an* (adv. backwards, hence *hind*). "Hinder" in A.S. was used as a Positive adverb, and was therefore a different part of speech from our mod. Comparative adjective. Chaucer has *hinderest*, and Wycliff *hindermore*. *Hindmost* is from A.S. *hinde-ma* (to which *-est* or *-ost* has been added, making *hind-most*).

**Neath, nether, nethermost.**—*Nether* is from A.S. *ni-ðer*, in which *-ther* is a comparative suffix; see above, § 498 (3). *Nethermost*, which looks like a double Superl. *most* added to the Comparative *nether*, is more probably a corruption of A.S. *niðemest* (=ni-ðe-m-est). Here *ni* (down) is the base, *ðe-m* is the Aryan *ta-ma*, such as we see in "op-*ti-mus*," and *-est* is the usual A.S. Superlative suffix.

**Out, outer or utter, utmost or uttermost.**—A.S. *úte* or *útan*, *útor*, *úte-ma* or *úte-mest*. In *mest* there are two Superl. suffixes, *-ma* and *-est*. "Utter" and "outer" are now both used as Positives, but in

[1] The distinction between *mára* and *má* is that the former was an adjective and the latter an adverb in A.S. The *s* (the original sign of the Comparative) has become an *r* in the former word, having been preserved by the following *a*. But it dropped off in the adverb, to which no Nom. inflexion was attached, leaving only *má*. In Gothic these forms were *mai-z-a* (adjective) and *mais* (adverb). The former appears in A.S. as *má-r-a*, and the latter as *má*. The *z* in the one became *r*, and the *s* in the other was lost.

different senses, as shown in § 348. The word *út* had two Comp. forms, *úttor* and *útor*, besides a third *ýter*, which became obsolete. The first has produced the Modern English *utter* by a shortening of the first vowel from *ú* to *u*. The second has produced *outer*, by retaining the long vowel, but changing its sound from *ú* to *ou*, as explained in § 447.

**In, inner, inmost or innermost.**—A.S. *in*, *inne-ra*, *inne-mest*. The last has been contracted to *in-most* or expanded to *inner-most*.

*Note.*—Adjectives are said to be **defective** in their comparison, when they do not possess all three Degrees of Comparison complete.

To this class belongs *rathe*, *rather*. *Rathe*=early, and is now rarely used :—

> Bring the *rathe* primrose that forsaken dies.—MILTON.

*Rather* has become adverbial. *Rathest* is obsolete.

To the same class belong all those named under II. and III. Under II. we have Positives, viz. *good*, *bad*, *little*, *much*, *many*, which have no comparatives or superlatives of their own ; and Comparatives with Superlatives, viz. *better*, *best*,—*worse*, *worst*,—*less*, *least*,—and *more*, *most*, which have no positives of their own. Under III. we have a list of Comparative and Superlative adjectives to which there is no corresponding *adjective*, but only an adverb, in the Positive degree.

## SECTION 3.—THE FORMS OF PRONOUNS.

### *Forms of Pronouns of the First and Second Persons.*

**502. First and Second Personal Pronouns declined.**—In A.S. there was a dual number of the First and Second Personal Pronouns, which died out before A.D. 1300. The Singular and Plural forms are given below for purposes of reference, not for committal to memory :—

I. *First Person.*

| Case. | Singular. | | Plural. | |
|---|---|---|---|---|
| | Old Eng. | Mod. Eng. | Old Eng. | Mod. Eng. |
| *Nom.* . | Ic | I | wé | we |
| *Gen.* . . | mín | mine, my | úser, úre | our, ours |
| *Dat.* . . | mé | me | ús | us |
| *Accus.* . | mec, mé | me | úsic, ús | us |

II. *Second Person.*

| Case. | Singular. | | Plural. | |
|---|---|---|---|---|
| | Old Eng. | Mod. Eng. | Old Eng. | Mod. Eng. |
| *Nom.* . | ðú | thou | gé | ye |
| *Gen.* . . | ðín | thine, thy | eówer | your, yours |
| *Dat.* . . | ðé | thee | eów | you |
| *Accus.* . | ðec, ðé | thee | eówic, eów | you |

**503. Nominative.**—The only difference of inflexion between the Old Eng. and Mod. Eng. forms is the *c* at the end of the Nom. Sing. *ic.* This letter has dropped off, as in several parallel instances; cf. *godly* for A.S. *godlíc*, *holy* for A.S. *hálig.*

*Ich*, in the Southern dialect, is found up to the close of the Middle period :—

*Ich* am an old man.—AWDELY, A.D. 1565.

Shakspeare puts the following sentences in the mouth of Edgar, who had disguised himself as a Somersetshire peasant and assumed the peasants' dialect :—

*Ch'ill* (=Ich will=I will) not let go.
*Ch'ud* (=Ich would=I would) ha' been zwaggered.
*Ch'ill* (=Ich will=I will) pick your teeth.—*King Lear*, iv. 6.

*Note.*—On the emphatic and reflexive forms *myself*, etc., see § 311.

**504. Accusative, Dative.**—The *c* of *mec* and *ðec* (Singulars), and the *ic* of *ús-ic* and *eów-ic* (Plurals), have dropped off, like the *c* of *ic* in the Nominative. In other respects the forms in Mod. Eng. are almost the same as those in Old Eng.

The effect of the loss of these endings has been to make the Accus. form coincide with the Dative. These two cases we now call by a single name, Objective.

**505. Genitive, Possessive.**—The forms of the Genitive or Possessive can be thus accounted for :—

(1) **Mine, thine.**—These are merely modern spellings of *mín* and *thín*, a final *e* having been added to indicate the lengthening of the preceding *i*. The final *n* is or was a Genitive suffix in all the Teutonic languages. In the south of England we still hear *hisn, ourn, yourn;* see below (3).

*My* and *thy* are shortened forms of *mín* and *thín*. In the twelfth century the final *n* began to drop off before a consonant, which gave rise to the modern *my* and *thy*. In point of idiom, however, separate uses have been assigned in Mod. Eng to *mine* and *thine* on the one hand and to *my* and *thy* on the other ; see § 109.

*Note.*—The Reflexive or emphatic *own*, as in "my own," "his own," etc., is from A.S. *ágen*, p.p. of the verb *ág-an*, to possess. It therefore means literally "possessed."

(2) **Our, your.**—These are modern spellings of *úre* and *eówer*. The final *re* is a Genitive suffix (Plural) of adjectives ; cf. all-*er*, all-*re*, al-*ra*, the old Genitive plurals of "all."

(3) **Ours, yours.**—A.S. *úres*, *eówres*, both of which contain the Gen. suffix *-es* superadded to the Gen. suffix *-re*. The forms *ours*, *yours* are therefore not due to Northern influence, as has been alleged. In Mid. Eng. we sometimes find *our-en* for *ours*, and *her-en* for *theirs*. In peasant English, in the southern counties, we still hear *hisn*, *hern*, *ourn*, *yourn*, *theirn*, which, like "mine," "thine," "ours," and "yours," are used only when there is no noun expressed after them.

*Forms of the Pronoun of the Third Person.*

**506. The Third Personal Pronoun declined.**—The pronoun of the third person, which is also a Demonstrative pronoun, was declined as follows in A.S. The original stem or base of the word is **hi**.

*Singular.*

| Case. | Masculine. | | Feminine. | | Neuter. | |
|---|---|---|---|---|---|---|
| | Old Eng. | Mod. Eng. | Old Eng. | Mod. Eng. | Old Eng. | Mod. Eng. |
| *Nom.* . | hé | he | héo | she | hit | it |
| *Gen.* . | his | his | hire | her | his | its |
| *Dat.* . | him | him | hire | her | him | it |
| *Accus.* . | hine | him | hí | her | hit | it |

*Plural, all Genders.*

| Case. | Old Eng. | Mod. Eng. |
|---|---|---|
| *Nom.* . . | hig, hí | they |
| *Gen.* . . | hira, heora | their |
| *Dat.* . . | hem, heom | them |
| *Accus.* . . | hig, hí | them |

(1) **He.**—This has come to us unchanged (except in the sound of the vowel and in the loss of accent) from A.S. In Mid. Eng. we find the form *ha*, which in peasant language is now sounded as *a*. This *ha* is an unemphatic form of A.S. *hé;* cf. our use of *thə* for *the.*

> "Rah, tah, tah," would *a* say; "bounce" would *a* say; and away again would *a* go; and again would *a* come.—2 *Hen. IV.* iii. 2, 303.

(2) **His.**—This contains the Genitive suffix *s* attached to the root *hi*, and has come to us unchanged from A.S. The single form *his* does the double work, for which in the other pronouns two possessive forms exist (see § 109): (*a*) "This is *his* horse"; (*b*) "My horse is better than *his.*"

(3) **Him.**—The *m* is the Dative Singular suffix, either Masculine or Neuter, but not Feminine; cf. who-*m*. This Dative form, on account of the greater frequency of the Dative case in Old English, has superseded the accusative *hine*, and now stands for both under the single name "Objective." By Chaucer's time the old Accusative *hi-ne* had wholly disappeared from the *literary* form of the Midland dialect. But it is still used in common talk—"I saw *'un*" (sounded *ən*).

*Note.*—It is worth noticing that the Dative case in A.S. has contributed much more than any other to the shaping of nouns and pronouns in Mod. Eng. Another example of this is given in § 441.

(4) **She.**—This has replaced *héo*, the feminine form of *hé*, which lasted as late as 1387. *She* has been supposed to be an altered form of A.S. *seó*, the feminine form of the Definite article *se*. See above, § 496, under the word **The.** But it is now believed that *she* has come from the Midland *scǽ*, which occurs in the last chapter but one of the *Saxon Chronicle*, written in the twelfth century at Peterborough, within the area of the Midland dialect.

(5) **Her.**—This word in Mod. Eng. stands—(1) for the Old Eng. Genitive *hire*, which contains a Genitive feminine suffix *-re;* (2) for the Old Eng. Dative *hire*, which contains a Dative feminine suffix *-re*; (3) for the old Accusative form *hí*, which was superseded by the Dative.

(6) **Hers** is a double Possessive form, due to the analogy of *ours* and *yours*, and not (as has been alleged) to Northern influence.

(7) **It.**—The final *t* is a true Neuter suffix, as in *tha-t, wha-t*. Cf. Lat. *i-d, illu-d, quo-d*, etc. Our Modern form *it* stands for—(1) the Old Eng. Nominative *hit*, by the loss of the initial *h;* (2) the Old Eng. Dative *him* (Neuter); and (3) the Old Eng. Accusative *hit.*

(8) **Its.**—This has replaced the Old Eng. Neuter *his*, which lasted into the Tudor period :—

> No comfortable star did lend *his* light.—SHAKSPEARE.
> Put up again thy sword in *his* place.—*Matthew* xxvi. 52.

Along with the use of *his* we find, in the fourteenth century, an uninflected genitive *hit*, which in the Tudor period appears in the unemphatic form of *it*, the *h* having been lost through want of accent.

> The hedge-sparrow fed the cuckoo so long,
> That it had *it* head bit off by *it* young.—*King Lear*, i. 4.

The inflected form *its*, which is now predominant, is used only three times by Milton, A.D. 1608-1674, not once in the version of the Bible printed in 1611, and occurs in only a few passages, in Bacon and Shakspeare. Dryden is the first great authority who is quite familiar with its use.

*Note.—Its* is written without the apostrophe, because it never had one; for no such form as *it-es* ever existed, and hence there was no *e* to be elided.

(9) **They.**—It was in the north of England, and in the thirteenth century, that this word came into use in supersession of *hig, hí*, the Nominative Plural of *hé*. The earliest forms of it were *thei, tha*.

The A.S. forms *hig, hí* were retained in the Southern dialect till near the end of the fourteenth century.

*They* originally was the Nominative Plural of the Old Norse definite article, and was spelt in Norse as *their*.[1]

(10) **Their**, the Gen. Plur. of the def. art., Old Norse *þeirra* (cf. A.S. *þára*). These superseded *hira, heora*, the Genitive Plural of *hé*. All these forms contain a Genitive Plural suffix *-ra, -r*. The form **theirs** is formed in the same way as *ours, yours*, and answers the same purpose (§ 109).

(11) **Them.**—This is a Dative form, containing the Dative Plural suffix *-m*; cf. whil-*om*, seld-*om*. In A.S. the Dative Plural of the def. art. was *ðám*; in Old Norse, *þeim*. The latter replaced (*a*) *hem, heom*, the Dat. Plur. of *hé*; and (*b*) *hig, hí*, the Accus. Plur. of *hé*.

*Note* 1.—It will be seen from the above that the A.S. or Old Eng. pronoun of the Third Person was formed from a single stem, **hi** (=he); but the Mod. Eng. pronoun of this person contains forms based on three different stems, viz. **hi, sa,** and **tha.** **Hi** is the stem used throughout the Singular, except in the Nom. Fem. *she*, when **sa** is the stem used. **Tha** is the stem used throughout the Plural.

*Note* 2.—The Old Accus. Plur. *hem* is not extinct. It is seen in the dramatists in the form of *'em*. The apostrophe has been printed under the mistaken notion that *em* is a contraction of *them*; whereas it is simply a survival of *hem*, with loss of initial *h*; cf. *hit, it*. The form *em* (sounded as *əm*) is very common to this day in colloquial English.

### *Interrogative and Relative Pronouns.*

**507. Relative Pronoun in A.S.**—In A.S. the only kind of Relative was the indeclinable particle *þe* (the), which was usually joined as a suffix to some part of the declinable Demonstrative adjective *sé*.

In Mid. Eng. the Relative in ordinary use was the indeclinable *that* (see above, § 316).

**508. The Interrogative Pronoun in A.S.**—The Interro-

[1] There was a form *þá* in A.S., which became *tho*, and not *they*, and was once common.

gative Pronoun, which in A.S. answered to "who" and "what," was declined in the manner shown below. It was used only as a pronoun proper,—that is, it was not placed before a noun, as in "what man."

| Case. | Masculine and Feminine. | | Neuter. | |
|---|---|---|---|---|
| | Old Eng. | Mod. Eng. | Old Eng. | Mod. Eng. |
| *Nom.* . | hwá | who | hwæt | what |
| *Gen.* . | hwæs | whose | hwæs | whose |
| *Dat.* . | hwám, hwǽm | whom | hwǽm | what |
| *Accus.* . | hwone, hwæne | whom | hwæt | what |
| *Inst.* . | hwí | why (adv.) | hwí | why (adv.) |

(1) **Who.**—A.S. *hwá*, Masc. and Fem. This was used as an Interrogative from the earliest times. As a Relative, though found occasionally in the fourteenth and fifteenth centuries, it did not come into common use before the sixteenth, and then, as now, it was restricted to *personal* antecedents.

"Who" as a Relative is not recognised by Ben Jonson, who in his English Grammar speaks of "one Relative *which*." "Who" and "which," however, were both used in the Tudor period:—

Our Father, *which* art in heaven.—*New Test.*
God, *who* at sundry times, etc.—*New Test.*

Both forms of the Relative are found in Shakspeare. Shakspeare even uses *who* where we should now use *which*:—

A lion *who* glared.—*Julius Cæsar.*
The winds
*Who* take the ruffian billows by the tops.—2 *Hen. IV.*

(2) **Whose.**—A.S. *hwæs*, of all genders. The *s* is a true Gen. suffix; cf. hi-*s*. The "whose" of Mod. Eng. is generally limited to persons,[1] though we sometimes find it applied to things as an equivalent to "*of which*."

Nebuchadnezzar the king made an image of gold, *whose* height was threescore cubits.—*Dan.* iii. 1.

[1] This limitation may perhaps have arisen from the analogy of *his* and *its*, the former being now limited to persons and the latter to things. Our language has gained nothing but inconvenience by restricting the use of *whose* to persons, and it may be hoped that the older practice of using *whose* for all genders will be some day resumed. It is much easier to say "*whose* height" than "the height *of which*."

Of man's first disobedience and the fruit
Of that forbidden tree, *whose* mortal taste, etc.—*Par. Lost*, i. 2.

(3) **Whom.**—A.S. *hwǽm*, Dative Sing., in which the *m* is a true Dative suffix; cf. the *m* in *hi-m*.

Between the A.S. *hwǽm* and the modern *whom* two differences exist:—(1) *Hwǽm* applied to all genders, whereas *whom*, according to present idiom, applies only to Masc. and Fem., and then only to human beings, not to the lower animals. (2) *Hwǽm* was strictly a Dative, whereas *whom* is used both as a Direct and an Indirect objective, and has superseded the A.S. Accus. *hwæ-ne*, as *him* (Dative) has superseded *hi-ne* (Accus.). The old Accus. *hwæne* or *hwone* became obsolescent in the thirteenth century.

(4) **What.**—A.S. *hwæt*, originally Neuter (like A.S. *tha-t*, and Lat. *illu-d*), and never Masc. or Fem. Its present capacity of being used for all genders and both numbers commenced at the beginning of the thirteenth century, in the Northern dialect.

*What* woman is this? *What* man is that?

According to present idiom, "*what*" takes the place of "*which*," either (*a*) when no antecedent is expressed, or (*b*) when the antecedent is placed *after* the relative (see § 123, *Note* 1).

The strict observance of this distinction, however, is of recent date, as is clear from the following uses of *what*:—

I fear nothing *what* (=which) can be said against me.—*Timon of Athens*, iv. 2.

That *what* (=which) is extremely proper in one company, may be highly improper in another.—CHESTERFIELD.

*Note.*—The use of *what* in such a construction as the following has now become a vulgarism:—

A thief is a man *what* steals.

(5) **Whether.**—A.S. *hwæðer*=which of the two, has now become archaic.

God Cupid, or the keeper, I know not *whether*,
Unto my cost and charges brought you thither.
BEAUMONT AND FLETCHER.

The last syllable *-ther* is a Comparative suffix (see § 498, 3); and as the Comparative degree implies a comparison between *two* things or persons, it is from this suffix that the word "whether" acquired the sense of "which of the *two*."

(6) **Which.**—A.S. *hwilc*, short for *hwí-lic*, why-like; *hwí* is the Instrumental case of *whá*, and the origin of adv. *why*.

(7) **As.**—Short for Mid. Eng. *also;* A.S. *eal-swá* (quite so).

## SECTION 4.—THE FORMS OF VERBS.

**509. Forms of verbs in Old and Modern English.**—The parts of a verb can be formed either—(*a*) synthetically, that is, by suffixes or personal endings attached to the tense-stem; or (*b*) analytically, by the use of Auxiliary verbs in company with Participles and Infinitives.

In Old as in Modern English the conjugation of a verb was chiefly analytical; the only tenses formed synthetically were the Present and the Past, and these only in the Active voice. Hence it has been said that there are only two real tenses in English.

Future time could be expressed by the Auxiliaries "shall" or "will," followed by an Infinitive, if it was necessary to use them. But if future time was implied by the context, the Present tense did the work of a Future also; and this, in preference to the other, was the ordinary idiom.

The Perfect and Continuous tenses were then, as now, formed by the use of Auxiliaries in combination with Participles.

Then, as now, there were three Finite moods,—the Indic., the Imper., and the Subjunc.,—besides the non-Finite parts of a verb,—the Infinitive, the Participle, and the Gerund.

The tenses of the Subjunctive were usually formed synthetically in Old Eng., but the Auxiliary "should" is also met with occasionally.

The Passive voice was then, as now, conjugated analytically throughout, though the verb *weorðan* (to become) was rather more commonly used than the verb "to be."[1]

On the whole, then, the structure of a verb in Old Eng. was the same at bottom that it is in Modern. It was far less synthetical than in Latin.

**510. Old Conjugation of Strong and Weak Verbs.**—For purposes of reference, not for committal to memory, a Strong and a Weak verb are conjugated below in those parts that were formed synthetically in Old Eng.

The exclusion of *all* Plural inflexions from *all* tenses of *all* the Finite moods, and of the Simple and Dative inflexions from the Infinitive mood, is what chiefly distinguishes a Modern from an Old Eng. verb.

All those Plural inflexions which were not *-en* in Old Eng. became *-en* (and sometimes *-e*) in the Midland dialect. It was the loss of this *-en* that Ben Jonson deplored. (See § 392.)

---

[1] Even in Gothic, the oldest of all the Teutonic languages extant, only a few instances of Passive forms due to inflexions had survived. Wright's *Primer of the Gothic Language*, ed. 1892, p. 135.

A. STRONG VERB. *Nim-an*, to take.

*Present Tense.*

| Indicative. | | Subjunctive. | |
|---|---|---|---|
| *Singular.* | *Plural.* | *Singular.* | *Plural.* |
| 1. ic nim-*e* | wé nim-*ath* | ic nim-*e* | wé nim-*en* |
| 2. ðú nim-*est* | gé nim-*ath* | ðú nim-*e* | gé nim-*en* |
| 3. hé nim-(*e*)*th* | hí nim-*ath* | hé nim-*e* | hí nim-*en* |

*Past Tense.*

| Indicative. | | Subjunctive. | |
|---|---|---|---|
| *Singular.* | *Plural.* | *Singular.* | *Plural.* |
| 1. ic nam | wé nám-*on* | ic nám-*e* | wé nám-*en* |
| 2. ðú nám-*e* | gé nám-*on* | ðú nám-*e* | gé nám-*en* |
| 3. hé nam | hí nám-*on* | hé nám-*e* | hí nám-*en* |

| Imperative. | |
|---|---|
| *2nd Sing.* . . | nim |
| *2nd Plur.* . . | nim-*ath* |

| Infinitive. | |
|---|---|
| *Simple* . . | nim-*an* |
| *Dative* or *Gerundial* | tó nim-*anne* or -*enne* [1] |

| Participle. | |
|---|---|
| Pres. . . . | nim-*ende* or -*inde* [2] |
| Past or Passive . | num-*en* |

[1] The change from -*anne* to -*enne* is an example of vowel-mutation. The original form was -*anni*, the last vowel of which changed the *a* to *e*, and was itself eventually reduced to *e*.

[2] The change from -*ende* (the original form) to -*inde* took place after A.D. 1066. It is an example of the regular change from *en* to *in* as in *henge*, "hinge.

B. WEAK VERB. *Hýr-an*, to hear.

*Present Tense.*

| Indicative. | | Subjunctive. | |
|---|---|---|---|
| *Singular.* | *Plural.* | *Singular.* | *Plural.* |
| 1. ic hýr-*e* | wé hýr-*ath* | 1. ic hýr-*e* | wé hýr-*en* |
| 2. ðú hýr-*est* | gé hýr-*ath* | 2. ðú hýr-*e* | gé hýr-*en* |
| 3. hé hýr-*eth* | hí hýr-*ath* | 3. hé hýr-*e* | hí hýr-*en* |

*Past Tense.*

| Indicative. | | Subjunctive. | |
|---|---|---|---|
| *Singular.* | *Plural.* | *Singular.* | *Plural.* |
| 1. ic hýr-*de* | wé hýr-*d-on* | 1. ic hýr-*de* | wé hýr-*d-en* |
| 2. ðú hýr-*de-st* | gé hýr-*d-on* | 2. ðú hýr-*de* | gé hýr-*d-en* |
| 3. hé hýr-*de* | hí hýr-*d-on* | 3. hé hýr-*de* | hí hýr-*d-en* |

| Imperative. | |
|---|---|
| *2nd Sing.* . . | hýr |
| *2nd Plur.* . | hýr-*ath* |

| Infinitive. | |
|---|---|
| *Simple* . . | hýr-*an* |
| *Dative* or *Gerundial* | tó hýr-*enne* or -*anne* |

| Participle. | |
|---|---|
| *Pres.* . . . | hýr-*ende* or -*inde* |
| *Past* or *Passive* . | hýr-*e-d* |

**511. Strong and Weak Verbs distinguished.**—Both classes of verbs are found in Gothic, the oldest of the extant Teutonic languages. There is reason to think, however, that Strong verbs are the older of the two;[1] for few or none of our

[1] The Strong conjugation in the Teutonic languages may be compared with the 3rd conjugation in Latin, which was probably older than the

primitive or root-verbs belong to the Weak class, and examples occur in which the original root has perished and only the derivative remains.

In A.S., whenever a new verb was derived or formed from another, or from a noun, the Derivative verb always assumed the Weak form, and not the Strong. Thus we have the Weak verb *fell* (Causal) from the Strong *fall*, and the Weak verb *love* (A.S. *luf-ian*) from A.S. *lufu*, love (noun). Similarly in Mod. Eng., whenever a verb is formed from a noun or some other word, or is borrowed from some foreign source, it invariably assumes the Weak form.

In Old English the two classes of verbs were distinguished as follows :—

(1) The Past tense in *Strong* verbs was formed by vowel-*gradation* (§ 453); while in *Weak* verbs it was formed by adding the suffix *-de* or *-te* to the stem of the Present tense. (If, as sometimes happens, a vowel-change is seen in some Weak verbs also, this is the result of *Mutation*, not gradation; see § 513, *b*.) (2) In *Strong* verbs the Second Pers. Sing. of the Past tense was expressed by the suffix *-e*, while in *Weak* verbs it was expressed by adding the suffix *-st* to the suffix *-de*. (3) In *Strong* verbs the stem of the Second Pers. Sing. and of all persons in the Plural of the Past tense had not always the same vowel as the stem of the First and Third Persons Singular:[1] (observe the difference of accent in the Past tense of specimen A, § 510). (4) In *Strong* verbs the Past Part. was formed by the suffix *-en*, while in *Weak* verbs it was formed by the suffix *-d*.

In Mod. Eng. these characteristics have been preserved in the main, but with the following modifications :—

No. (1) remains as before, except that the final *e* of the Weak suffix *-de* has disappeared, leaving no distinction in Weak verbs between the form of the Past tense and that of the Past participle.

No. (2) has entirely gone. *All* verbs, whether Weak or Strong, now have *-st* or *-est* as the suffix of the Second Person Singular in the Past tense.

No. (3) has also gone, but not without leaving several traces

---

other three: for in this conjugation the past tense was sometimes formed by reduplication, as sometimes in Gothic and always in Greek, and sometimes by a change of the root-vowel, as in *ag*-o (Pres.), *ēg*-i (Past).

[1] It depends upon the conjugation whether the vowel changes or not. The verbs *fall* and *shake* kept the same vowel throughout the Past tense.

of its former existence. Thus the stem of the Plural *were* (Past tense of the Strong verb *wes-an*, with the *s* changed to *r*) has not the same vowel as that of the Singular *was*. There was once a good deal of uncertainty about the Past tenses of such verbs as *swim*, *begin*, *run*, *drink*, *shrink*, *sink*, *ring*, *sing*, *spring*, all of which now take the stem of the A.S. Past. Sing. *swam*, *began*, *ran*, etc. Yet Byron has the following:—

> The isles of Greece, the isles of Greece,
> Where burning Sappho loved and *sung*,
> Where grew the arts of war and peace,
> Where Delos rose and Phœbus *sprung*.

On the other hand, the verbs *spin*, *slink*, *stink*, *sting*, *win*, *fling*, *wring*, *cling*, *string* all now form their Past tenses in *spun*, *slunk*, *stunk*, etc., which was once the stem of the *Plural*, and not that of the Singular.

No. (4) remains as before, except that many of the Strong verbs have lost or half-lost the suffix *-en* that was once universal in the Past Participle.

**512. Strong Verbs classified: reduplicated Past.**—In Gothic (as in Latin, Greek, and other Aryan languages) Past tenses could be formed by reduplication of the root-syllable. In Gothic such verbs were a special class of the Strong conjugation; such as *hait-an* (to call), *hai-hait; ték-an* (to touch), *tai-tók*.[1]

The Strong verbs in Teutonic thus naturally fall into two main divisions—(1) reduplicative verbs; (2) gradation verbs. The first class constituted one single conjugation; the second was distinguished into six sub-classes, the peculiarities of which need not be discussed in this book.[2]

In A.S. examples of reduplication are very few, and these few were far less distinctly preserved than in Gothic. The chief examples are:—

*Héht* (Gothic *hai-hait*), pt. t. of *hát-an*, to call; which shows reduplication by the repetition of *h*.

---

[1] Gothic uses *ai* with two values, viz. *ĕ* and *ai*. In this case it has the value *ĕ*. Hence the Gothic *hai-*, *tai-* stand for *hĕ-*, *tĕ-;* and exactly correspond to the Latin and Greek reduplicative prefixes "*pe*-pendi," "*te*-tupha."

[2] The seven Strong conjugations have been called after certain typical verbs selected to represent each class. These have been put into a couplet by Professor Skeat as a help to remembering them:—

> *Drive* slowly; wisely *choose;* from *drink* for-*bear;*
> *Mete* justly; *shake* the tree; down *falls* the pear.

*Réord* (Gothic *rai-róth*), pt. t. of *rǽd-an*, to advise; which shows reduplication by the repetition of *r*.

*Léolc* (Gothic *lai-laik*), pt. t. of *lác-an*, to skip; which shows reduplication by the repetition of *l*.

*Léort* (Gothic *lai-lót*) pt. t. of *lǽt-an*, to permit; where an *r* has been substituted for the repeated *l*.

*Dréord*, pt. t. of *drǽd-an*, to dread, in which the *dr* has been reduplicated as *rd* by metathesis or change of order in the consonants.

More commonly the repeated consonant is lost, and a diphthong is substituted for the root-vowel; as Goth. *fai-fall*, A.S. *féoll*, Eng. *fell;* Goth. *hai-hald*, A.S. *héold*, Eng. *held*.[1]

In Mod. Eng. all traces of reduplication are lost, except in one, and possibly two, examples. The certain example is *hight* (the Past tense of *hát-an*, to call), which in A.S. was spelt *hé-ht*, and in Gothic *hai-hait*, as shown above. The other example that has been alleged is *did*, the Past tense of *do*. But this example is doubtful; for in A.S. the form corresponding to *did* was *dy-de*, apparently a Weak past tense formed with the suffix *-de*.[2] Some, however, believe it to be reduplicated.

**513. Weak Verbs classified.**—Weak verbs in Old English may be subdivided into two main classes—(*a*) those which had the vowel *o* or *e* between the verb-root and the Past suffix *-de*, as *luf-o-de*, I loved; *styr-e-de*, I stirred; and (*b*) those which had no intervening vowel, as *hýr-de*, I heard.

*Class* (*a*).—The intervening *o* took the form of *e* in Mid. Eng. The A.S. *luf-o-de* thus became *lov-e-de* (three syllables), or *love-de* (two syllables), which in Mod. Eng. (through the loss of the final *e*) became *loved* (one syllable). Hence the real suffix of Weak verbs of this class is not *ed*, but *d*, the *e* being part of the formative stem of the verb itself.[3]

*Class* (*b*).—If the final consonant of the root was voiced, the Past suffix was *-de*. But in verbs that ended in *-nd*, *-ld*, and *-rd*,

---

[1] Skeat's *Princ. Eng. Etym.* series i. pp. 159, 160.

[2] Mr. Sweet in *Short Hist. Eng. Grammar*, ed. 1892, p. 190, § 731, calls *dy-de* a "Weak past." But Brugmann, the German philologist, believes it to be reduplicated. He compares our *do* with the Greek root *thē*, the Ionic imperfect of which was *e-ti-the-a*. This reduplicated form, if we leave out the first and last vowels, gives us a past tense *ti-the*, which is very like A.S. *dy-de*, Old Sax. (of the Continent) *dĕ-da*, and Old High German *tĕ-ta*. The most direct argument for considering it a Strong (redup.) past is that in A.S. itself some texts use *dǽdon* for the plural, whereas if the tense were Weak it would be *dydon*.

[3] Skeat's *Student's Pastime*, pp. 175-178. In fact, the verb was a derivative from the noun *luf-u;* and the *o* in *luf-o-de* takes the place of the final *u* in *luf-u*.

*t* was gradually substituted for *d*, because in such verbs the past tense thus modified could be more rapidly pronounced. Thus we have *send-de*, *send-e*, *sent-e*, *sent*. In the same way we get *build*, *built* (or older *builded*); *gild*, *gilt* (or *gilded*); *bend*, *bent* (or *bended*).

If the final consonant of the root was voiceless, as *f*, *p*, *s*, *t*, *h* (*h* or *gh*), the Past suffix was not *-de*, but *-te* from the first. Hence in Mid. Eng. we have *slip-te*, *skip-te*, *slep-te*, *met-te*, *brough-te*, which in Mod. Eng. appear as *slipped*, *skipped*, *slept*, *met*, *brought*. It is the perversity of English spelling which makes us write *ed* in some cases and *t* in others. The latter is the more phonetic, besides being historically correct.

Verbs with a long root-vowel, as *feed* (A.S. *féd-an*), are very apt to incur a shortening of this vowel, when the suffix *-te* or *-de* is added to them. Thus, *leave* (A.S. *lǽf*-an) formed its Past tense originally in *lǽf-de*, and *féd*-an in *féd-de*. But by the rule given in § 464 (*a*) *féd-de* became shortened (through the accent on the first syllable) to *fĕd-de*, and when the final *e* dropped off, the second *d* became superfluous, and so the Past tense took the form of *fĕd*. Similarly *lǽf-te* became *lĕf-t*.

There is a class of Weak verbs (p. 79) which appear to incur a vowel change when *d* or *t* is added for the Past tense. The change of vowel in these verbs is not of the same kind as that in Strong verbs. In Strong verbs the difference of vowel is the result of *Gradation;* in Weak of *Mutation*. In these it is really *the Present that has changed*, not the Past. In the Present the root-vowel is mutated by the influence of *i* in the Infinitive suffix *-ian*. Thus we have *salde* (I sold), Inf. *sell-an*, through an older form *sal-ian*, and hence the Present tense is *sell*. In the same way we get *tell-an* (tell), *teal-de* (told); *bycg-an* (buy), *bóh-te* (bought); *séc-an* (seek), *sóh-te* (sought); *wyrc-an* (work), *worh-te* (wrought); *thenc-an* (think); *thŏh-te* (thought).

**514. Origin of Suffix "-de."**—It was once believed, and is still widely asserted in books,[1] that the suffix *-d* or *-de* is an abridgment of *did*, the supposed reduplicated Past tense of *do;* so that *loved = love-did*, *lovedst = love-didst*. This theory is now entirely exploded. It was merely a conjecture from the first.

The A.S. suffix *-de* was founded on the form *-da*, which in Gothic, the oldest of the Teutonic languages, was one of the

[1] As, for example, in Mason's *English Grammar*, § 223.

Past suffixes of Weak verbs. We cannot trace the origin of *-de* farther back than this.

In Gothic there were no less than three forms of the suffix of the Past tense of Weak verbs, viz. *-da*, *-ta*, and *-tha*, which in A.S. are represented by *-de*, *-te*, and *-the*.

| | | |
|---|---|---|
| Gothic | nasi-da (I saved) | A.S. neri-de. |
| | brah-ta (I brought) | A.S. bróh-te. |
| | hun-tha (I could) | A.S. cú-ðe. |

The theory that the *-de* came from *did* is inadmissible—(1) because there is no evidence for it; (2) because it does not account for such a Past tense as *bróh-te*, nor yet for such a Past as *cú-the*, which appears as "I couth" in Lowland Scotch; (3) because the A.S. *-de* is traced to an older Gothic form *-da*.

**515. Interchange of Weak and Strong.**—The prevailing tendency in the history of our language has been towards the Weak conjugation in preference to the Strong. This has shown itself in two ways—(*a*) Many Strong verbs have become Weak; and (*b*) Whenever new verbs were or are admitted from foreign sources, or coined from internal ones, they took and take the Weak form. Ben Jonson in his English Grammar calls the Weak class "the common inn to lodge every stranger and foreign guest."[1]

(*a*) The following will serve as examples of Strong verbs which have become Weak:—

| *Pres.* | *Past* (A.S.). | *Pres.* | | *Past* (A.S.). |
|---|---|---|---|---|
| ache | óc (ached) | gnaw | M.E. | gnew (gnawed) |
| burn | bearn (burnt) | laugh | | hlóh (laughed) |
| bring[2] | brang (brought) | melt | | mealt (melted) |
| creep | créap (crept) | sow | | seów (sowed) |
| fare | fór (fared) | suck | | seác (sucked) |
| fold | feóld (folded) | wash | | wósc (washed) |

[1] There was an obvious reason why all foreign verbs should take the Weak, and not the Strong form. The change of the root-vowel peculiar to the Strong conjugation was not possible in any but Teutonic verbs: it was a purely Teutonic process, of which foreign verbs were incapable, because they were foreign. But it was very easy to add a suffix like *-ed* to a foreign stem, and hence this was the mode of conjugation, to which all foreign imports were compelled to conform. The decay of the Strong conjugation may be partly ascribed to the large influx of foreign verbs, all of which were necessarily Weak. The Weak native verbs, reinforced as they were by the Weak foreign ones, set the fashion, and many of our Strong native verbs yielded to its influence.

[2] In A.S. there were two forms of this verb—(1) a Strong verb, *bring*-an, pt. t. *brang;* and (2) a Weak verb, *breng*-an, pt. t. *bróh-te.* Mod. Eng. retains only the Weak past *brought;* and the two presents *bring* and *breng* have melted into one.

The same tendency is seen in verbs, whose recent Weak form has not yet entirely ousted the older Strong:—

| *Pres.* | *Past.* | *Pres.* | *Past.* |
|---|---|---|---|
| climb | clomb, climbed | cleave | clove, cleft |
| crow | crew, crowed | thrive | throve, thrived |
| hang | hung, hanged | | |

(*b*) There are, however, a few examples of verbs originally Weak, which have become Strong either wholly or in part. Verbs that are partly Strong and partly Weak are called **Strong-Weak** or Mixed:—

| *Pres.* | *Past Tense.* | *Past Part.* | *Pres.* | *Past T.* | *Past Part.* |
|---|---|---|---|---|---|
| wear | were | worn | show | showed | shown, showed |
| stick | stuck | stuck | rot | rotted | rotten, rotted |
| dig | dug | dug | stave | stove, staved | staved |
| hide | hid | hid, hidden | | | |
| spit | spat | spat | | | |

*Note* 1.—The verb *rot* is a peculiar case. It is really Weak. The pp. *rotten* is a remnant of a lost Strong verb, and is far older than the Weak past part. *rotted.*

*Note* 2.—Two entirely distinct verbs have become confused in *stick*. This verb in the sense of "stab" was always Strong; in Mid. Eng. its forms were Infin. *stek-en*, Past tense *stak*, Past part. *stek-en.* But "stick" in the sense of "adhere" was originally Weak; A.S. *stic-ian*, Past tense *stic-o-de*, Past part. *stic-o-d.*

*Note* 3.—A similar confusion has occurred in the verb *cleave.* In the sense of "split" this verb was Strong: A.S. *cleóf-an*, pt. t. *cleáf*, pp. *clof-en*, whence we get *cleave, clave, cloven.* In the sense of "stick" "adhere," it was Weak: A.S. *clif-ian* or *cleof-ian*, pt. t. *clif-o-de*, pp. *clif-o-d*, from which we get the forms *cleaved, cleft.*

*Note* 4.—In the verbs *hide* and *spit*, the change of conjugation from Weak to Strong is more apparent than real; for in A.S. we find Infin. *hýd-an*, Past tense *hýd-de;* and Infin. *spitt-an* or *spǽt-an*, Past tense *spǽt-te;* (the alternative form *spit-te* is not found). In Mod. Eng. the final *-te* or *-de* was discarded, because when the *-e* had disappeared, the *t* or *d* became superfluous after *t* or *d* in the stem of the tense. In the case of *hide* the change of conjugation from Weak to Strong appeared to be so complete, that the Past part. *hid* acquired an alternative form *hidden*, which is an undoubted mark of the Strong conjugation.

(*c*) There are four verbs which in Mod. Eng. follow so closely the analogy of other Weak verbs ending in *d* or *t*, that it is convenient now to class them as Weak. But in A.S. they were Strong.

| *Modern English.* | | | *Old English.* | | |
|---|---|---|---|---|---|
| *Pres.* | *Past.* | *Past Part.* | *Pres.* | *Past.* | *Past Part.* |
| (1) Burst | burst | burst | berst-e | bærst, burst-on | borst-en |
| (2) Let (permit) | let | let | lǽt-e | léort | lǽt-en |
| (3) Shed | shed | shed | sceád-e | sceód | scád-en |
| (4) Shoot | shot | shot | sceót-e | sceát, scut-on | scot-en |

In (1) the Plural of the Past tense has evidently supplied the form of the *Present* tense in Mod. Eng. as well as that of the Past part. In (2) the reduplicated Past *léort* (see § 512) has evidently succumbed to the united influence of the stems of the Present tense and Past part., which were identical; so that *lǽtt* was the usual form even in A.S. In (3) the Present tense and Past part. have both yielded to the influence of the Past tense, whose vowel, however, has been shortened from *éo* or *é* to *e*. In (4) the Past tense in both Sing. and Plur. forms has yielded to the influence of the Past Part., while the Present tense has assumed a form different from both by change of accent from *éo* to *eó*.

*Note.*—Two entirely distinct verbs have become confused in *let*. In the sense of "hinder," it was always a Weak verb. In the sense of "permit" it was a Strong verb of the reduplicated class (§ 512).

### 516. Some peculiar Weak Verbs:—

**Teach**: A.S. *tǽc-an, tǽh-te, tǽh-t*. In the Pres. the final guttural, *c* or *k*, has been palatalised to *ch*. In the other two forms it has been changed to *gh*.

**Catch**: from Old Fr. *cach-ier*, conjugated like *lacch-en* (latch), *laughte*, which are now obsolete as verbal forms, though *latch* is still in common use as a noun. The verb *latch* had the same sense as *catch*. This is one of the very few examples of a foreign verb which has undergone a change in its root-vowel as if it were a native one. Cf. *beef, beeves*, the only example of a foreign noun in *f* which has formed its plural in *v* after the manner of native nouns; see § 485 (*a*).

**Clothe**: Northumbrian *cláð*-ian (later *clath*-en), Past tense *clǽð-de*, pp. ge-*clad*-ed. The last has given us the alternative form *clad* for *clothed*.

**Make**: A.S. *mac-e, mac-o-de, mac-o-d*. This verb lost its radical *c* or *k* as early as the thirteenth century. Hence the mod. form *made*.

**Flee**: A.S. *fleón*, Scand. *flý-ja*. The Past tense *fled* is from Scand. *flý-ði*, a Weak past.

**Hang**: there are two chief forms of this verb, one Weak and the other Strong. The Weak form is from A.S. *hang-ian*, Past tense *hang-o-de* (=Eng. *hanged*). This in A.S. was Intransitive. The Strong verb has a very peculiar history. In A.S. there was a verb *hón* for *háhan*, pt. t. *héng*, pp. ge-*hang*-en. In Mid. Eng. the corresponding forms were *hing, hang, hung* (on the analogy of *sing, sang, sung*). In Mod. Eng. the forms are *hang, hung, hung*.

**Say**: A.S. *secg-e*, 3rd Pers. Sing. *seg-eth, sæg-de, sæg-d*. Here the gutturals have been vocalised into *say, said, said*. But the form *say* is derived from such parts of the verb as had only one *g*; it cannot be derived from *secg-an* or *secg-e*. Thus *seg-eð* > *sey-eth* > Mod. Eng. *saith*.

**Lay**: A.S. *lecg-e*, 3rd Pers. Sing. *leg-eth, lecg-de, lecg-d*. As above.

**Buy**: A.S. *bycg-e*, 3rd Pers. Sing. *byg-eth, bóh-te, bóh-t*. Here the guttural *h* (= Mod. Eng. *gh*) has survived in the Past tense and Past Part. The *g* of the stem *byg-* was vocalised, as in *seg-*, *leg-*.

**Went**: originally the Past tense of *wend*.

**Work**: A.S. *wyrc-e, worh-te, worh-t.* The form *wrought* (which is closely allied to *worh-te*) is now less common than the more modern *worked*.

**Think**: A.S. *ðenc-an, ðóh-te, ðóh-t.* (This verb must not be confounded with *ðync-an*, to seem, the base of the Impersonal "me-thinks.")

**517. Present Participle.**—In early Middle English the suffix was *-ende* (Midland), *-inde* (Southern), *-and* (Northern). In the latter part of the twelfth century the suffix *-inge* (borrowed from the so-called Gerund, to be described in § 523) began to be substituted by Anglo-French scribes for the original suffix *-inde*, and the substitution became established in the Southern and Midland dialects by about 1350,—an unfortunate result, which has been the cause of endless confusion between the Pres. part. and the Gerund.

The Northern suffix *-and* was sometimes used archaically in the Tudor period:—

> Glitter-*and*; trench-*and*.—SPENSER.
> Trill-*and* brooks. A stink-*and* brock (badger).—BEN JONSON.

This Northern form of the Pres. part. was adopted from that part of the *Romaunt of the Rose* which was written in a purely Northern dialect, but was wrongly ascribed to Chaucer, because it was placed among poems of which Chaucer was the real author. Chaucer himself never uses *-and*.

The suffix *-and* held its ground much longer in the Northern dialect than *-ende* or *-inde* did in the Midland or Southern. If only it had spread to these dialects, and ousted the bogus form *-ing*, it would have saved much confusion in English grammar.

**518. Past or Passive Participle.**—In Old English this participle, as the student is aware, invariably ended in *-en* in Strong verbs, and in *-t* or *-d* in Weak. We give precedence to *-t*, because that was the Aryan form, and *-d* resulted from it.

(*a*) In *Weak* verbs the final *t* or *d* has remained to this day, unless the final consonant of the root happens to be a dental, in which case the addition of the dental suffix is generally superfluous; as *hit* (Present) *hit* (Past part.). The Past part. suffix *-t* or *-d* is identical with that of Lat. "ama-*t*-us"; see footnote 2 to § 378.

(*b*) In *Strong* verbs the suffix *-en* has in many cases been lost; and even when the suffix was gone, the stem of the Past part.

was not always preserved. The prevailing tendency was for tl Past tense and Past part. to assume the same form, as we see i such a verb as *swing, swung, swung;* contrast with this such verb as *smite, smote, smitten.* The assimilation of the Past ten and Past participle was effected in more ways than one. (1) I some verbs the Past part. has taken the form of the Past tens as *shone* (A.S. *scán*), *held* (A.S. *heóld*), *stood* (A.S. *stód*), *awoke* (A.S *wóc*), *abode* (A.S. *ábád*), which superseded the older Participia forms *scin-en, heald-en, stand-en, wac-en, abid-en.* (2) In othe verbs the Past tense Singular has taken the form of the Pas tense Plural, as *wound, ground, spun, won, bound, found, wrung clung, swung,* which superseded the old Past tenses Singula *wand, grand, span, wan, band, fand, wrang, clang, swang.* I such verbs the Past tense (to take the first example) was—

| *Singular.* | *Plural.* |
|---|---|
| 1st, *wand;* 2nd, *wund-e;* 3rd, *wand.* | *wund-on.* |

The Past tense has been levelled all through to the form of the Plural, the stem of which was the same as that of the Secon person Singular. (3) But in some verbs the *Plural* forms of th old Past tenses had a different stem-vowel from that of the Pas tenses now in use. In such verbs the Past tenses now in us must be ascribed to the influence of the Past participle; as i *shoot, shot, shot* (A.S. *sceót-an, sceát, scot-en*); *steal, stole, stolen* (A.S. *stel-an, stæl* (Sing.), *stǽl-on* (Plur.), *stol-en*); *break, broke broken* (A.S. *brec-an, bræc* (Sing.), *brǽc-on* (Plur.), *broc-en*); *tear tore, torn* (A.S. *ter-an, tær* (Sing.), *tǽr-on* (Plur.), *tor-en*).

(c) The Past part. of Weak and Strong verbs alike was once very frequently preceded by the suffix *ge,* as *ge-cum-en* (come) *ge-fund-en* (found). In Mid. Eng. this prefix was reduced to *i, y,* or *e,* as "*i*-fund-e" (found). In Mod. Eng. only one example remains—"*y*-clept" (called).

> Hail, thou goddess, fair and free,
> In heaven *y*-clept Euphrosyne.—MILTON.

*Note.*—Milton (we do not know on what authority) adds this prefix to a Present participle in the phrase "star *y*-pointing."

**519. Continuous and Perfect Tenses.**—In Old English, as in Modern, the Continuous tenses were formed with the Present participle and the Perfect with the Past, each participle being, of course, preceded by the appropriate Auxiliary verb. Thus as Present and Past Continuous tenses we have in A.S. *Hé is gang-ende* (=he is going); *Hé wæs gang-ende* (=he was going).

In forming, however, the *Perfect* tenses there was one difference between the Old and the Mod. constructions. In Old English, if the verb was *Intransitive*, "is" or "was" or "worth" (which was very common) was the Auxiliary verb used; and if the verb was *Transitive*, "has" or "had" was the Auxiliary. But in Mod. Eng. "has" or "had" is used with Intransitive verbs also; and if "is" or "was" is still used at all, it conveys, according to present idiom, rather a different sense (see § 173).

(*a*) *Intrans.* { Hé *is* ge-cum-en = He is come. (*Sing.*)<br>Wé *sindon* ge-cum-en-*e* = We are come. (*Plural.*) }

The student will observe that in Old Eng. the participle agreed in number and gender with the subject to the verb.

(*b*) *Trans.* { Hé *hæfth* hine ge-fund-enn-e (or ge-fund-en-e).<br>He has him found = has found him. }

Here the student will observe that *hine* in the Accus. case is object to the Trans. verb "has" going before, and that the participle following agrees with it in case, number, and gender.

But in later A.S. the Past participle in this connection became indeclinable; in other words, it ceased to be a participle in the proper sense of the word, and became part of a tense. (On the twofold character of participles, see § 194.)

Hé hæfth hine ge-fund-*en* = He has found him.

This change in the character of the participle paved the way to "have" taking the place of "be" with *Intransitive* verbs no less than with Transitive ones. When "have" became an Auxiliary verb in the strict sense of the word (§ 138), and resigned for that purpose its Transitive sense of possession, there was nothing to prevent its being followed by an Intransitive verb as easily as by a Transitive one.

*Note.*—Three examples have now been given (in the course of this book), in which *have* has usurped the place of *be* in the construction of a sentence or phrase:—

(1) When followed by an *Intransitive* Infinitive; see ch. xx. (2).

I *am* to go, or I *have* to go.

(2) In phrases like "had as lief," "had rather"; see ch. xx. (30).

(3) In forming the *Perfect* tenses of the Intransitive verbs, as is shown in this paragraph (519).

520. **Simple Infinitive.**—The history of this Infinitive may be summed up as follows:—

(1) In Old English the Simple Infinitive was a kind of Abstract noun, formed by adding the suffix *-an* or *-ian* to the root of the verb, as *bind-an*, "the act of binding." It was

commonly used as Subject to a verb, or after certain Auxiliaries and after Intrans. verbs of Incomplete Predication.

(2) In Mid. Eng. the *-an* or *-ian* became *-en* or *-ien* (later *-en*), of which many examples are to be found in Spenser, and a few—very few—in other writers of the Tudor period:—

> Come down and learn the little what
> That Thomakin can *sayne*.—SPENSER.
> Henceforth his ghost
> In peace may pass-*en* Lethe Lake.—SPENSER.
> Thinks all is writ he speak-*en* can.—SHAKSPEARE.
> And with a sigh he ceased
> To *tellen* forth the treachery and the trains.—SACKVILLE.
> The soil that erst so seemly was to *seen*.—SACKVILLE.

In Wycliff the Infin. suffix is for the most part *-e;* in Chaucer *-e* and *-en* are both common. Spenser's use of *-en* was archaic (out of date).

(3) When the final *n* had fallen into disuse and the *e* was becoming mute, writers began to distinguish the Infinitive (which otherwise was likely to be confounded with many other parts of the verb) by placing the preposition "to" before it; and this, for want of something better, was borrowed from the Dative (the so-called Gerundial) Infinitive. The *to* before a Simple Infin. began to be seen about the end of the twelfth century.

(4) The use of "to" went on gaining ground from century to century, till at last it succeeded in restricting the Simple or *to*-less form to the few instances shown above in § 189; but for some time, even so late as the Tudor period, there was a good deal of uncertainty as to whether the "to" should be used or not.

> She tells me she'll *wed* the stranger knight,
> Or never more *to view* nor day nor night.—*Pericles*, ii. 5, 7.
> I would no more
> *Endure* this wooden slavery than *to suffer*
> The flesh-fly *blow* my mouth.—*Tempest*, iii. 1, 62.
> You ought not *walk*.—*Julius Cæsar*, i. 1, 3.
> How long within this wood intend you *stay?*
> *Midsummer Night's Dream*, ii. 1, 138.

(5) The *Noun*-character of the Simple Infin., notwithstanding that the prep. "to" was placed before it, was perceived by old writers, who treated it as a kind of compound noun whenever they placed another prep. before it:—

> Without *to make* any noyse.—CAXTON, *Aymon*, 78.
> He was about (= near) *to die* (= death).—*Mod. Eng.*
> He desired nothing except or but *to succeed* (= success).
> —*Mod. Eng.*

The difference between the two Infinitives, in spite of their identity of form, is well shown in the following:—

I want *to eat* something. (*Simple Infin.—object. to* "want.")
I want something *to eat*. (*Gerund. Infin.—attrib. to* "something.")

**521. Dative or Gerundial Infinitive:—**

(1) What modern grammarians have called the Gerundial Infinitive was, in Old English, merely the Dative case of the Simple Infinitive preceded by the prep. "to"; as *tó cum-enne* (to come), *tó bind-enne* (to bind), which gradually became *to cum-en, to bind-en*, and finally *to come, to bind.*

(2) When the *-en* itself disappeared, as it did in the Transition period between Mid. and Mod. English, there was no difference *in form* between "to come" as a Simple Infin. and "to come" as a Gerundial Infin. In *function*, however, they were as distinct as before, the one being subject to all the duties and liabilities of a noun, and the other to those of an adjective or adverb.

**522. Forms of the Subjunctive Mood.**—From specimens A and B given in § 510 it will be seen that there was no distinction between Weak and Strong verbs in regard to Subjunctive endings. In this mood, as in the Indicative, there were only two tenses that were formed by flexional endings, viz. the Present and the Past. In all persons of the Present tense the ending was *-e* in the Singular number, and *-en* in the Plural. The *-e* was at first syllabic: after becoming non-syllabic and mute, it was dropped altogether, since it was no longer necessary. The *-en* died out also, like the *-en* and *-enne* of the Infinitive, and the *-on* of the Past tense Indicative.

In Mod. English, as in Old, there are no endings in the *Present tense* to distinguish the Second and Third persons from the First. Thus we have "if I *see*, if thou *see*, if he *see*." But in the *Past* tense the Second person has acquired the ending *-st* or *-est*, borrowed from the Second person of the Indicative. The truth really is that the Past Subj. is dead, and the Present is dying.

**523. History of the Gerund.**—In Mod. Eng., if we meet with such sentences as "He was fond of *hunting* foxes," "He was fined for *having lost* his hat," we call "hunting" and "having lost" Gerunds, the one denoting present time, and the other past. This is the accepted name; but it is purely modern, and the form which it denotes has a peculiar history.

(1) The only Gerund in A.S. is what we now call the Gerundial Infinitive; see § 521. It invariably ended in *-ne;* it was invariably a Dative; and was invariably preceded by the preposition *tó* (our modern *to*); as A.S. *tó bind-enne* > Mid. Eng. *tó bind-en* > Mod. Eng. *to bind.* The final *-enne* never took the form of *-inge* or *-ing;* and hence the adoption of the name "Gerund" for the form ending in *-ing* was an encroachment.

(2) The form ending in *-ing* was in A.S. simply a **noun.** It was not part of a verb at all, but a noun pure and simple. The *-ing* or *-ung* (both forms are found in A.S.) was simply a noun-forming suffix, like *-th* in "steal-*th*," or *-r* in "stai-*r*," or *-l* in "aw-*l*," or *-m* in "doo-*m*." It is not correct to call it "a *verbal* noun,"[1] because this name implies that such a word as "bind-*ing*" was part of the conjugation of the verb "bind"; and we are no more entitled to say this than we are to say that "steal-*th*" is part of the verb "steal," or "doo-*m*" a part of the verb "do." The form ending in *-ing* was not a verb or part of a verb, because it was *never* followed by a noun in the *Accusative* case. It was a noun for two reasons—(*a*) it took noun-inflexions, it still takes the plural inflexion *s;* and (*b*) it could be followed by another noun in the *Genitive* case; as,

| | | | |
|---|---|---|---|
| Búton | sceawunge-*e* (Dat.) | ǽnig-*re* (Gen.) | ár-*e* (Gen.).—BEDA, i. 5. |
| Sine | exhibitione | ullius | misericordiæ (*Latin*). |
| Without | showing | (of) any | compassion (*English*). |

That *ár-e* is Genitive is clear from the adj. *ǽnig-re,* since no adj. has an Accus. ending in *-re.* The prep. "of" was not used in early times, because, as long as the Genitive inflexion lasted, it was not required.

(3) It was during the Middle period of English (the Pres. part. having in the meantime taken the form *-inge* instead of *-inde*), that the confusion began. Since the Pres. part. could be followed (as in fact it often was) by a noun in the Accus. case, the noun in *-ing,* having precisely the same form as the Pres. part., *seemed* (through a confusion of ideas in men's minds) to demand an Accusative also, and this led by degrees to the omission of the preposition "*of.*" Hence in Mid. Eng. we find two constructions—(*a*) with the *of,* (*b*) without it:—

[1] Another reason why the name "verbal noun" is unsuitable, is that the suffix *-ing* is not always attached to verb-stems. In "out-*ing*," "off-*ing*," "inn-*ings*," it is attached to adverbs. In "air-*ing*," "ceil-*ing*," "lin-*ing*," "morn-*ing*," "even-*ing*" (A.S. ǽfen-ung) it is attached to nouns. So the name "*verbal* noun" is inaccurate.

(*a*) Wyse in bying *of* vitaille.—CHAUCER, *Prol.* 569.
(Wise in buying of victuals.)
(*b*) Schavinge oure berdes.—MAUNDEVILLE.
(Shaving our beards.)

In example (*b*) the omission of "*of*" seemed to make "oure berdes" in the Accus. case, and this seemed to make "schavinge" a Gerund, that is, a part of the verb "shave." But in point of fact the construction is merely *elliptical;* for "schavinge" is still a pure noun, with the "of" omitted after it, as it is after "board" in the phrase "on board ship."

(4) In the Modern period a new bogus phrase came in. Since "shaving" was believed to be a Gerund, that is, part of the verb "shave," a past form was coined corresponding to the past participle, just as forms like "shaving" corresponded with the present participle. Thus we have such a sentence as—

He was punished for *having broken* a window.

This past form of the so-called Gerund is never followed by "of," as the present is, because it was late in coming; else it would have been.

"The phrase (*having broken*) is now an accepted one, so that the Grammarians in despair have invented, for words thus used, the term *gerund*, under the impression that to give a thing a vague name is the same thing as clearly explaining it. This term, however, should only be employed for convenience, with the express understanding that it refers to a modern usage, which has arisen from a succession of blunders" (Skeat).[1]

### *Auxiliary and Anomalous Verbs.*

**524. To be.**—The conjugation of this verb is made up of parts that are formed from three distinct roots, viz. (1) *es-*, (2) *wes-*, and (3) *béo-*. The first gives the Pres. Indic., the second the Past Indic. and Past Subj., the third the Pres. Subj., the Imper., the Infin., and the Present and Past participles.

**Am**: A.S. *eam* or *eom*, for a theoretical *es-m*, in which the *m* is supposed to have come from *me* (the First personal pronoun). Cf. Lat. *su-m*, Gr. *es-mi*, Sanskrit *as-mi*.

**Art**: A.S. *eart*, for theoretical *es-t*, in which *s* has been changed

---

[1] Skeat's *Princ. Eng. Etym.* series i. p. 260. Sweet accepts this Gerund as an established fact in modern English: "The Mod. Eng. verb is characterised by the development of a gerund" (*Short Hist. Eng. Grammar*, ed. 1892, p. 149). In fact, we cannot now do without the name "gerund," however short its pedigree may be; and we must treat the Gerund as part of the verb, although originally it was simply an abstract noun.

to *r* (as in *was, were*), and the *t* is supposed to have come from *thou*, the Second pers. pron. Cf. the suffix in *shal-t, wil-t, wer-t*.

**Is**, A.S. *is*, for *es, es-t*, in which the *t*, the suffix of the Third pers. Singular, has been lost. Cf. Lat. *es-t*, Gr. *es-ti*, Sanskrit *as-ti*, Germ. *is-t*.

**Are**, for theoretical *es-on*. This came from the Northern dialect, which substituted *ar-on* for A.S. *sind, sind-on*.[1]

*Note.*—Besides the Pres. Indic. formed with the root *es-*, we once had another form of the tense based on the root *be-*.

| | *Sing.* | | *Plur.* | |
|---|---|---|---|---|
| | *A.S.* | *Tud. Eng.* | *A.S.* | *Tud. Eng.* |
| 1. | béo | be | béo-th | be or bin (=be-en) |
| 2. | bi-st | be-est | béo-th | be or bin (=be-en) |
| 3. | bi-th | be | béo-th | be or bin (=be-en) |

*Be-est* thou a spirit of health or goblin damned.—SHAKSPEARE.
As fresh as *bin* the flowers in May.—PEELE.
We *be* twelve brethren.—*Old Testament.*

**Was**: A.S. *wæs*, past tense of the verb *wes-an*; of the Strong conjugation, as is proved by the change of root-vowel, and by the absence of any personal ending from the First and Third persons. See specimen A in § 510.

**Wast**: not established till the fourteenth century. The A.S. form was *wǽr-e*, in which *r* has been substituted for the radical *s* (cf. *art* for *ast*), and *-e* is the correct suffix for the Second pers. Sing. in the Past tense of Strong Verbs. (See specimen A in § 510.) Another form of the Second pers. Sing. was *wert*, formed like *shal-t* and *wil-t*, now obsolete or obsolescent (except in the Subjunctive mood, in which it has been wrongly placed as second person):—

Before the sun, before the heavens thou *wert*.—*Par. Lost.*

**Were**: A.S. *wǽr-on*, where *r* is again substituted for *s*. The difference of the stem-vowel in *was* and *were* has arisen from the fact that in the older stage of our language the stem-vowel of the Past tense Singular differed in gradation from that of the Past tense Plural. (See again specimen A in § 510.)

**Be**, Imperative: A.S. *béo* (Sing.), *béo-th* (Plur.). These superseded the alternative A.S. forms *wes* (Sing.), *wes-ath* (Plur.).

**Be**, Infinitive: A.S. *béo-n*, which superseded the alternative A.S. form *wes-an* in the twelfth century.

**Being**: The A.S. form of the participle was *wes-ende*, which was superseded by the Mid. Eng. form *be-inde*, later *be-inge*. "Being" is also a verbal noun denoting "existence."

**Been**: Mid. Eng. *i-beon*, which superseded A.S. *ge-wes-en*.

**525. Can, dare, shall, may, wot.**—All these verbs were originally Past tenses of Strong verbs, which acquired a

[1] These two words are not so distinct in origin as they look. *Ar-on* (for theoretical *es-on*) and *sind-on* (for theoretical *es-ind-on*) both contain the root *es*. Both, too, have the suffix *-on* (which, however, is usually attached to the plural of *Past* tenses). The *-ind* of *es-ind-on* is another plural suffix; cf. Germ. *sind*, Lat. *sunt*, Sanskrit *sant-i*. For the *-unt* of s-*unt*, cf. Lat. reg-*unt*.

Present signification to compensate them for the loss of their Present tenses. Hence in Old English (as also in Modern) their adopted Present tense is conjugated like the Past of *Strong* verbs, while they have formed new Past tenses according to the *Weak* conjugation. Such verbs have been called **Past-present** (or Preterite-present) verbs.[1] To these we must add *quoth*, which, however, did not form a new Past tense like the rest.

The student will remember (see specimens A and B in § 510) that neither Strong nor Weak verbs have a Third personal suffix in the Past tense, Singular. Hence we have *can, dare, shall, may, wot, quoth* all in the Third person Singular without the suffix *-s*.

In the Second person Singular, however, *can, dare, shall*, and *may* have taken the suffix *-st* or *-t* in lieu of the original Past Suffix *-e*. All other Strong verbs (as is stated in § 511) have done the same. Thus we have *can-st, dar-est, shal-t, may-est.* Similarly in Mid. Eng. the Second person of *wot* was *wos-t*, and in Tud. Eng. *wott-est.* The verb *quoth* has no such form, as it is not used in the Second person.

*Note.*—The omission of *s* in the Third pers. Sing. occurs in the verb **need**, as "He *need* not go," whenever the Infinitive following is not preceded by *to.* But this peculiarity seems to be due to the analogy of the verbs *can, dare*, etc., as *need* was never anything else than a Present tense, and in every part except the Third pers. Sing. Pres. this verb is regularly conjugated as a Weak verb.

**Can**: old Past Indic. *cú-ðe*, coul-d, in which a non-radical *l* has crept in from analogy with *should* and *would.* Cf. the old pp. in *un-cúð*, uncouth, lit. unknown. "Con," to study, is a causal of "can." "Cunning" (=knowing) is a verbal noun formed from *cunn*-an (to know). The same word is also used as an adjective.

**Dare**: The root is *dars.*[2] Hence Past tense *dors-te*, durst; which, however, has often a Present meaning. "Dare" in the sense of "challenge" has formed a new Past tense *dared*, which is also used for *durst*, as "He *dared* not go." The Third Sing. Pres. *dare* is regular, as explained above; but *dares* is used whenever the Infin. following is preceded by "to"; as "He *dare* not go"; "He *dares* to go."

**Shall**: A.S. *sceal* or *scal* in First and Third persons. Past tense *scol-de*, should. In Mod. Eng. "should" very often implies duty; as "you *should* do this." So in Old and Mid. Eng. *sceal* or *scal* sometimes meant "owe." The Second person was *scealt* or *scalt* (shalt).

Hú micel *scealt* ðú ? = How much owest thou ?—*Luke* xvi. 5.

---

[1] These verbs are also called **Strong-Weak**, because they have formed a Weak past tense out of a Strong past tense, the latter having lost its own present form and acquired in place of it a present signification. In this book the name "Strong-Weak" is also given to Mixed verbs like *beat, beat, beaten*, which are strong in some forms and weak in others: see Group III. in § 212.

[2] In Gothic "I dare" was *ik dars*, which in A.S. appears as *ic dearr*, with *rr* for *rz*, Gothic *rs.* The plural in A.S. was *wé durr-on* for *wé durz-on, durs-on.*

**May**: A.S. *mæg*, may; cf. A.S. "dæg," day (the *g* having been vocalised, see § 433). Past tense *meah-te* (Weak past), might.

**Wot**: A.S. *wát*, from which is formed our Present tense *wot*. Past tense *wis-te*, from which we get our Past tense, *wist*; here, as in *mus-t* (§ 527), *s* was substituted for the radical *t*, so as to make a suitable base for the suffix *-te*. *To wit* (=namely) is a Gerundial Infin., A.S. *tó wit-enne*. The Pres. part. appears in "un-witting-ly."

**Quoth.**—This verb answers to A.S. *cwæth*, Past tense of the verb *cweth-an*, to say, and therefore has no *s* in the Third person Singular. *Quoth* is the only form of the verb that is now used; it denotes either present time or past. But it is never used with a plural subject, and never with any person but the First or Third. Its subject is invariably placed after it.

**526. Will.**—This verb resembles those described in the previous paragraph, in having no suffix *-s* in the Third pers. Sing., but from a different cause. "Will" was originally not a Past Indic., but a Past Subjunctive, and this mood, as the student will remember from specimens A and B given in § 510, never took a suffix *-s* for the Third person. With the Past Subj. form Pres. Indic. forms were afterwards mixed, and an Infin. *will-an*. A Weak past was formed, *wol-de* (would), in which the *i* of the base was changed to *o* by the influence of *w*. The phrase *willy-nilly* (A.S. *sam hé will-e, sam hé nill-e*) is elliptical for "whether he *will* or not *will*"; since it expresses a doubt, it is naturally in the Subjunctive mood (see § 186, 4), which recalls the original Subjunctive force of *will*.[1]

**Wil-t.**—Here the *t* is Second personal suffix as in "shal-t," and is due to analogy. "Would" is from Past Indic. *wol-de* (Weak form).

**Won't**=will not. Here we have a trace of the Mid. Eng. *wol*, an alternative form of *wil*.

**527. Ought, must.**—These two verbs are Past-past tenses in form, like *could*, *should*, *would*, *might*, *wist*, but (unlike the verbs just named) they are used in a Present sense, because their Past-present forms are obsolete.

**Ought.**—The obsolete present *áh* was originally a Past tense in the Strong conjugation, like *can*, *dare*, *shall*, *may*, *wot*, *quoth*. From *áh* was formed the Weak past tense *áh-te*, from which we get *ought* in Mod. Eng. This word occurs in Shakspeare in a past sense as equivalent to "owed":—

You *ought* him a thousand pounds.

Our verb *owe*, "to be in debt," is from A.S. *ág-an*: it had a

---

[1] It might be supposed that the *y* of *willy* is a survival of the *e* in the A.S. Subjunctive form *will-e*. But the *e* was lost in the thirteenth century. Probably *willy* arose from *will-I*, and was extended to *will he*.

past part. *ág-en*, from which we get our adj. *own*, as in the phrase "his *own*." From this past part. the Weak verb *ágn-ian* was formed in A.S., from which we get our verb *own*, "to possess."

*Note.*—There is another verb "own," which means "to acknowledge." This is probably also derived from A.S. *ágn-ian*, though it has been doubtfully ascribed to A.S. *unn-an*, to grant. Our modern spelling (perhaps rightly) takes no account of the difference.

**Must.**—The obsolete present *mót* was originally a Past tense in the Strong conjugation, like the obsolete *áh*. From *mót* was formed the Weak past tense *mós-te*, in which *mós* was substituted for *mót* in order to furnish a suitable base for the suffix *-te*. From the Past-past tense *mós-te* we get our modern word *must*.

The old word *mót* has survived in the obsolescent phrase "so *mote* it be" (so be it, amen), in which *mote* is in the Subjunctive mood of *mót*, used in the sense of wish, as the Subjunctive is still sometimes used; see § 186 (2).

**528. Let.**—The verbs *let* in the sense of "hinder" and *let* in the sense of "permit" are quite distinct. The former is A.S. *lett-an*, a Weak verb, derivative of *læt*, late, which had as its Past tense *let-te*, Mod. Eng. *let*. The latter is from A.S. *lǽt-an*, a Strong verb which formed its Past tense in *léort* (Reduplicated, § 512), *léot*, and *lét*, Mod. Eng. *let*. So the two verbs have become confused.

*Let* ("permit") is not a real Auxiliary. But in the forms "*let* me go," "*let* him go," etc., its meaning has been so reduced as to make a periphrastic Imperative in the First or Third person.

**529. Have**: A.S. *habb-an*, a Weak verb, which formed its Past tense in *hæf-de*, later *hed-de* or *had-de*, and its Past part. in *ge-hæf-d*, later *i-haf-d*, or *y-had:* (when the final *e* of the Past tense was lost, there was no use in retaining the *d*). In A.S. the Pres. Indic. Singular was *hæbb-e*, *hæf-st*, *hæf-th*. The loss of the radical *f* gives us *hast*, *hath*. The A.S. short vowel "*æ*" has bequeathed a shortening of the "*a*" in "have," nothwithstanding the final *e*. (*Have* is really a misspelling for *hav.*)

**530. Do.**—This is a Strong verb in the Past part. *ge-dón* (done), and is possibly a Strong verb (of the reduplicated class) in the Past tense also, *dy-de;* see § 512, and footnote. It is Auxiliary only for forming emphatic, negative, and interrogative sentences (§ 172).

In Mid. Eng. it had the sense of *cause;* as it still has in the almost obsolete phrase "I *do* you to wit" = I cause you to know: see ch. xx. (33). It became useful for this purpose, when our language had lost the power of forming Causal verbs, like *raise* from *rise*.

As a pro-verb its use is at least as old as **Chaucer**:—

He slep no more þan *doþ* the nightingale.

**531. Worth.**—A.S. *weorð-an*, Past tense *wearð*, a Strong verb. In Old English it was the verb usually employed as an Auxiliary for forming tenses in the Passive voice.

Now, it survives only in the Third pers. singular Subjunctive, and only in the phrase "Woe *worth* the day."

**Wont.**—A.S. *wun-od*, Past part. of A.S. *wun-ian*, to dwell, to be accustomed to (Weak verb). A second participial suffix *-ed* was added, when the origin of *wont* had been forgotten; so that *wonted* = *won-d-ed*, with two participial suffixes. The word *wont* came by degrees to be used as a noun, as well as a participle.

## Section 5.—The Forms of Adverbs.

**532. Origin of Adverbs.**—The origin of adverbs has been thus described in general terms by Whitney:—"Adverbs (the most ancient and necessary class of indeclinable words or particles) are by origin, in the earliest stage of a language as well as in the latest, forms of declension, *cases of substantives, adjectives, or pronouns.* Both the general classes of adverbs, made by means of apparent adverbial suffixes, and the more regular and obscure single words of kindred meaning and office, which we trace in the earliest vocabulary of the family, are of like derivation."

In the account of adverbs given below, the student will find many facts that bear out the above description of their origin.

### *Adverbs formed by Case-endings of Nouns.*

**533. Genitive Case-ending.**—In Old and Mid. Eng. the suffix *-es* was used for forming adverbs from nouns and adjectives. A few such adverbs have survived; more have become extinct. In Mod. Eng. the prep. "of" has taken the place of the Genitive suffix; as, *of course*, *of necessity*, *of a truth.*

**Extinct.**—Summer-*es*, winter-*es*, dæi-*es* (by day), niht-*es*, will-*es* (willingly), sóþ-*es* (of sooth, truly), hi-*s* þonk-*es* (of his own accord), other-while-*s*.

**Extant.**—Need-*s*, el-*se* (A.S. ell-es), sin-*ce*, then-*ce*, hen-*ce*, when-*ce*, on-*ce* (A.S. *án-es*), twi-*ce*, thri-*ce*, sometime-*s*, alway-*s*, sideway-*s*, lengthway-*s*, the while-*s*(t), again-*s*(t), amid-*s*(t), eftsoon-*s* (archaic), longway-*s*, backward-*s*, wondrou-*s* (a corruption of wonder-*s*).

The Genitival adverb was common in Tudor English :—

Anyway-*s* afflicted or distressed.—*Prayer-book.*
He would have tickled you other gate-*s* (in another way or gate than he did).—*Twelfth Night*, v. 1, 198.
Come a little nearer this way-*s*.—*Merry Wives of Windsor*, ii. 1, 50.
'Tis but early day-*s*.—*Troilus and Cressida*, iv. 5, 12.

The Genitival suffix is sometimes attached to a phrase formed with a noun and the prep. *be* (by) or *a* (on).

Be-time-*s*, be-side-*s*, un-a-ware-*s*, now-a-day-*s*, a-night-*s* (colloquial), a-Sunday-*s* (colloquial).

**534. Dative Case.**—The Dative case-ending in -*um*, Singular or Plural, was used with an adverbial force :—

**Extinct.**—Micl-*um* (much, Sing., from adj. *micel*), lytl-*um* (a little, Sing., from adj. *lytel*), piece-mæl-*um* (piece-meal), Plural.
**Extant.**—Whil-*om* (A.S. hwîl-*um*, at times ; hwîl = while, time), seld-*om* (A.S. seld-*um*, at rare times ; seld = rare). Both Plural.

*Note.*—*At random* is from Old French *à randon*, in violent haste.

**535. Accusative Case.**—This is now called the Adverbial objective ; see § 271 (5). Adverbs were formed from adjectives as well as nouns in this case.

The while (A.S. *þá hwîl-e*), something, somewhat (on *what* see chap. xx. 76), nothing, nowise, noway, yesterday, day and night, straightway, meantime, meanwhile, midway, halfway, home, north, south, east, west, all, enough (A.S. *genoh*).

Many of the Adverbial accusatives have now a Genitive form ; as in *alway-s*, *side-way-s*, *the while-s(t)*, *sometime-s*, etc.

*Note.*—*Sometime* = formerly ; *sometimes* = occasionally.

### *Nouns and Adjectives preceded by Prepositions.*

**536. Prepositional Adverbs.**—Sometimes the prep. is attached to the word as a prefix ; sometimes it stands apart so as to make an adverbial phrase.

**A** = *of: a-kin*, *a*-down (A.S. *á-dún-e*, for "of dune," from a hill), *a*-new, *a*-fresh, *a*-thirst, *a*-clock (now written "o'clock" ; cf. Jack o' lantern).
**A** = *on: a*-bed, *a*-way, *a*-back (also "back"), *a*-gain, *a*-sunder, *a*-foot, *a*-sleep, *a*-live, *a*-head, *a*-breast, etc. Now-*a*-days, un-*a*-wares, *a*-year (= Lat. *per annum*), *an*-on (in one second, immediately).

*Note.*—"*A*" has been substituted for Fr. *en*, in *a-round*, *a-front* ; and for Fr. *à* in *a-part* (à part) and *a-pace* (à pas).

**A**=A.S. *an* or *and*, against: *a*-long (A.S. *and-lang*, over against in length).

**At**: *at* large, *at* length, *at* odds, *at* first, *at* all, *at* once, etc.

**Be** or **by**: *be*-sides, *be*-times, *be*-fore, *be*-yond, *be*-hind, *be*-low, *be*-tween, *by* all means, *by* force, etc.

**In**, **on**: *in* general, *in* future, *in*deed, *in* two, etc. *On* high, *on* trust, *on* purpose, etc.

**Of**: *of* kin, *of* late, *of* old, *of* a truth, *of* necessity, etc.

**Per**, Lat. prep.: *per*chance, *per*force, *per*haps.

**To**: *to*-day (A.S. *tó dæg-e*), *to*-night (A.S. *tó niht-e*), *to*gether, *to* boot, here-*to*-fore.

*Adverbs formed with Suffixes "-ly," "-ling."*

**537. The Suffix "-ly."**—The suffix "-ly" is from A.S. *líc-e*, formed from the adj. *líc* (like). When the final *e* was dropped, *líc-e* was reduced to *líc*, and eventually to *ly*; as *on-ly*, A.S. *ân-líc-e*, *ân-líc*; Mid. Eng. *oon-li*.

*Note.*—If the adjective itself ends in *-ly*, as *kind-ly*, *low-ly*, *sick-ly*, etc., the adverb is usually formed by a phrase, as, *in a kindly way*, *with lowliness*, etc.[1]

This is the commonest mode of forming adverbs, and the suffix "-ly" can be as freely attached to Romanic stems as to Teutonic ones. It can also be attached to Participles, as "knowing-*ly*," "learned-*ly*," "mistaken-*ly*"; and to adjectives formed with a suffix added to nouns, as "play-ful-*ly*," "slav-ish-*ly*."

It has been said that the *-e* of A.S. *líc-e* is the Dative case of the Adj. *líc*. But this cannot be; for adjectives in early A.S. had no such Dative form. For the origin of *líc-e* we must go to Gothic *leik-o*; but what the origin of the *o* may be is unknown.[2]

**The Suffix "-ling" or "-long"**: A.S. *-lung-a* or *-ling-a*, in which the *a* was a Genitive plural case-ending; hence this suffix is of the class explained in § 533.

Side-*ling*, side-*long*; head-*long*.
Dark-*ling*, grove-*ling* (flat on the ground).

*Note.*—The suffix *ling* looks so like the Pres. part., that verbs have been coined from it. "To *grovel*" is now well established. "To *darkle*" is used by Thackeray. "To *sidle* up to a person" is used colloquially.

---

[1] Edgar Allen Poe, however, has *lowlily* to rhyme with *holily*. The first word is adopted for the sake of the rhyme; the second is not open to objection, because *holy* is from A.S. *hálig*. Shakspeare also uses *holily*: "What thou wouldst highly, that wouldst thou *holily*" (*Macbeth*). To avoid the awkwardness of such an adverb as *god-li-ly*, we find the adj. *godly* used as an adverb in New Test.: see *Titus* ii. 12.

[2] Wright's *Gothic Primer*, § 283, p. 124.

**538. Loss of Adverbial Suffix.**—Another Gothic adverbial form was *-u-ba*, as in *hard-u-ba*, which in A.S. (by the loss of *ba*) appears as *heard-e*. The final *-e* in Anglo-Saxon adverbs eventually dropped off. Hence we have several adverbs in Mod. English, which have the same form as adjectives; cf. A.S. *fæst* (adj.), *fæst-e* (adv.) = fast (adj. and adv.).

He speaks *loud*. He works *hard*. Speak *fair*. Come *quick*.
He talks *fast*. The moon shines *bright*. He sleeps *sound*.
*Full* many a year. *Right* along the bank.

Hence from a false analogy adjectives, which could not have taken the suffix *-e*, are used adverbially in Tudor English:—

Which the false man does *easy*.—*Macbeth*, ii. 3, 143.
Thou didst it *excellent*.—*Taming of the Shrew*, i. 1, 89.
Grow not *instant* old.—*Hamlet*, i. 5, 94.
'Tis *noble* spoken.—*Antony and Cleopatra*, ii. 2, 99.

Even so late as Sir W. Scott, we have an adjective used to qualify an adverb:—

Notwithstanding the darkness of the place, Julian succeeded *marvellous* quickly in preparing for his journey.—*Peveril of the Peak*.

### *Pronominal Adverbs.*

**539. Pronominal Adverbs.**—The following table shows how adverbs have been formed from Pronominal and Demonstrative stems:—

| Pron. and Dem. stems. | Place where. | Motion to. | Motion from. | Time. | Manner. | Cause. |
|---|---|---|---|---|---|---|
| who | where | whither | whence | when | how | why, what |
| the | there | thither | thence | then | thus | the |
| he | here | hither | hence | ... | ... | ... |

**Where, there, here**: A.S. *hwǽr*, *ðǽr*, *hér*: "the suffix *r* seems to be due to a Locative case" (Skeat).

**Whither, thither, hither**: A.S. *hwæder* or *hwider*, *ðider*, and *hider*; cf. Lat. ci-*tra* (on this side of), Sanskrit ta-*tra* (to that side). Originally the suffix may have had a comparative force; see comp. suffix *-ther* in § 498 (3). In this view, the *-ther* in *hither*, etc., would mean "more to this place," "in this direction."

**When, then.**—In A.S. there were three pronominal adverbs denoting time, *hwonne*, *ðonne*, and *heon-an*. These are very like the Accusative cases of the corresponding pronouns, and are probably of the same origin. From the last we might have had a modern form *hen*, corresponding to *when* and *then*. But the Mid. Eng. *henne* has been superseded by *now*, which is of the same root as *new*.

**Whence, thence, hence.**—These contain the Genitive suffix *-es*, and answer respectively to A.S. *hwanan*, Mid. Eng. *whenn-es;* A.S. *ðanan*, Mid. Eng. *thenn-es;* A.S. *hinan*, Mid. Eng. *henn-es*. The base is closely allied to the Accusative cases referred to under *when*, *then*.

**Why, how.**—"Why" answers to A.S. *hwí*, the Instrumental case of *hwá*. "How" answers to A.S. *hú*, which is probably only another form of *hwí*.

**Thus** answers to A.S. *ðus*, which is probably another spelling of *ðýs*, the Instrumental case of *ðes*=this.

**The** answers to A.S. *ðý* (Mid. Eng. *the*), the Instrumental case of the Def. art. (or Dem. pron.), used only in such phrases as "*the* more, *the* merrier"=by what degree or on what account more, by that degree or on that account merrier.

**What** answers to A.S. *hwæt*. In Tudor English this word is sometimes used as an Adverbial Interrogative=why.

*What* need we any spur but our own cause?—*Julius Cæsar*, ii. 1.

The compound adverb *some-what* (=slightly) is of common occurrence.

**540.—Compound Pronominal Adverbs.**—The pronominal adverbs shown in § 539 can be compounded (*a*) with prepositions, (*b*) with other adverbs:[1]—

(*a*) *Compounded with prepositions:*—

*There:* therein, thereto, thereat, therefore, therefrom, therewith, thereout, thereon, thereof, thereby, thereabouts.

*Here:* herein, hereto, heretofore, hereat, herewith, hereon, hereof, hereby, hereafter.

*Where:* wherein, whereto, wherefore, whereon.

*Hither:* hitherto.

(*b*) *Compounded with other adverbs:*—

*Where:* wherever, wheresoever, whereas.

*Hence:* henceforth, henceforward.

*Thence:* thenceforth, thenceforward.

*Adverbial Uses of Prepositions.*

**541. Adverbial Uses of Prepositions.**—Most of our prepositions can be used adverbially, and in fact most of them were adverbs originally. The *forms* of prepositions will be shown in the next section. Examples of their adverbial use are given below:—

**About.**—He is walking *about*. *About* forty were present.

**Above.**—He lived in the *above*-named house.

---

[1] It is pointed out, however, in Skeat's *Concise Etymological Dict.* that in these compound forms *there* is not the Locative *ðær*, but *ðære*, the Dative Fem. of the definite article; see below, § 549 (*a*).

**Aft, after.**—Fore and *aft*. He came ten days *after*.
**Before.**—He walked on *before*.
**Behind.**—He was left *behind*.
**By.**—*By* and *by*. They passed *by* on the other side.
**Down.**—He has gone *down* in the world.
**From, fro.**—They are walking to and *fro*.
**In.**—Break *in* the horse. Pull the horse *in*. Give *in* (yield).
**Off.**—He got *off*. They have set *off* (started).
**On.**—Go *on* (go forward). Hold *on* (stop). He got *on* well.
**Over.**—Is there any money *over?* Call *over* (recite) the names.
**To, too.**—Go *to* (let me expostulate). *To* and fro. That was *too* bad.
**Under.**—This medicine will bring the fever *under*.
**Up.**—It is all *up* with us. The time is *up* (exhausted).
**Within.**—You will find him *within* (in the house).
**Without.**—He stood *without*.

*Compound Adverbs or Adverbial Phrases.*

### 542. Compound Adverbs; Adverbial Phrases.

(*a*) *Compounds of "where" and "how":*—else-where, some-where, any-where, every-where, no-where, somehow, any-how.

(*b*) *Adverbial phrases:*—maybe (=it may be, perhaps), howbeit (=however that may be), to wit (=namely), to be sure (=certainly), as it were (=if I may say so).

(*c*) *Adverbs in pairs:*—up and down, to and fro, here and there, hither and thither, in and out, backwards and forwards, now and then, off and on, by and by.

*Miscellaneous Adverbs.*

### 543. Unclassified List.

—There are a few adverbs in common use, which cannot be classified under any of the headings hitherto discussed.

**Ago**: retrospectively from the present time, short for Mid. Eng. *agon*, A.S. *á-gán*, pp. of the verb *á-gán*, to pass or go away. In Mid. Eng. we have the form "ago" as well as the form "agon."

**Ay, aye** (1): spelt as *I* in old editions of Shakspeare. Apparently a corruption of *yea*.

**Aye** (2), (ever): Scand. or Old Norse *ei*, A.S. *á*, *áwa;* Goth. *aiw*, adverb formed from noun *aiws*, an age; cf. Lat. *æv*-um, Gr. *ai*-on; and Gr. adverb *ai*-en=always.

**Ever, never**: A.S. *ǽfre*, *nǽfre*. There is no saying what is the origin of the suffix *re* or *e*. Related to A.S. *áwa*.

**Far**: A.S. *feor*, Mid. Eng. *fer;* cognate with Gr. *per-an*, beyond.

**Fore, forth**: A.S. *fore*, allied to "far," beyond. In composition we have *forthwith*, *henceforth*, *forwards*.

**Ill**, adj., adv., or noun: Scand. *illr*, adj. Not a contracted form of A.S. *yfel* (=evil), adj. or noun, as has been maintained.

**Little**: A.S. *lytel*, adj. *lytl-um*, adv. (with Dative suffix).

**Less**: A.S. *lǽs-sa* (see § 501, II.).

**Much**: A.S. *mycel* (great); Mid. Eng. *muchel*, *muche*.

**Nay**, of Sc. origin, *nei;* Mid. Eng. *nay:* the negative of *aye* (2).

**No** (1): negative adverb, the opposite to "yes." A.S. *ná*, from *ne* (negative particle) and *á*, "ever,"=Scand. or Old Norse *ei*: a doublet of *nay*.

**No** (2): short for *none*, A.S. *nán* (*ne*+*án*, not one). "None" and "no" are both used adverbially, as "*none* the better," "*no* better."

**Not**: a shortened form of "naught" or "nought," from A.S. *ná*, negative particle, and *wiht*, a whit. Hence "naught" means literally "not a whit"; cf. the phrases "not a straw," "not an atom," "not a button," "not a curse" (corrup. of "not a *kers* or cress").

**Now**: A.S. *nú*; cf. Lat. *nu-nc*. See § 539, under When.

**Out**: A.S. *út*, *út-e*, *út-an*, all adverbial, signifying outwards.

**Oft, often**: A.S. *oft*, Mid. Eng. *of-te-n*. A superlative form of comparative "ov-er." In Mid. Eng. we have the form *ofte*, to which an *n* was afterwards added. In Mid. Eng. *-e* was the common adverbial suffix.

**Over**: A.S. *ofer*, a comparative form of Old Aryan *up-a*, the stem of which we see in Eng. "*up*."

**Well**: A.S. *wel*; orig. "agreeably to a wish"; allied to *will*, to desire or be willing.

**So**: from A.S. *swá*; origin uncertain: apparently allied to Lat. *su-us*.

**Yonder**: adverb formed from *yon*, adj., "at a distance." "Yon" is from an old Relative stem, *ya*.

**Ye-a, ye-s**, answer respectively to A.S. *geá* and *gese*. "Yes" is a strengthened form of "yea," and was once supposed to be short for *geá sý*=yea, let it be. But the theory now held is—that the final *s* is due to A.S. *swá*. The stem is traced to the same Relative *ya*. The original sense was "in that way," "just so." Thus *yea*, *yes* are adverbs by etymology.

**Ye-t**, up to the present time, as in the phrase "not yet." Traced to the same root (*ya*) as the two preceding. Cf. Lat. *ja-m*, in which the root is the same.

## SECTION 6.—THE FORMS OF PREPOSITIONS.

**544.** Our prepositions were originally adverbs, which modified verbs, as, "He stood *by*," and served to point out more clearly the direction of the verbal action. By degrees they detached themselves from the verb and came to belong to nouns, furthering the disappearance of case-endings and assuming the peculiar office which they now hold.

Thus "motion to" was originally expressed by the Accusative alone, as it still is in the sentence, "He went home."

In Old English prepositions were followed by certain cases,—the Accusative, Dative, or Genitive. We still say that a preposition governs the Objective case; as *by the man*, *by me*, *by him*.

**545. Simple Prepositions**:—

**At**: A.S. *æt*; cognate with Lat. *ad*, as in "*ad*-jacent."

**By**: Goth. *bi*, which in A.S. was differentiated into the strong or accented form *bi* and the weak form *be.* The former became the preposition "by," and the latter the prefix "be."

**Ere**: before, A.S. *ǽr;* cf. *ear-ly,* from A.S. *ǽr-lic.*

**For**: A.S. *for.*

**From**: A.S. *fram, from;* Scand. *frá;* Mid. Eng. *fra, fro.* Hence the modern adverbial form "fro," as in the phrase "to and *fro.*" The same root is seen in "for," "forth."

**In**: A.S. *in;* cognate with Lat. *in,* Gr. *en.*

**Of, off**: A.S. *of;* cognate with Lat. *ab,* Gr. *ap-o.* Shortened to *a* in "a-down" = of dune (from the hill), and to *o* in "o'clock."

**On**: A.S. *on;* cognate with Gr. *an-a.* Often shortened to *a,* as in "a-breast," "twice *a* day," etc.

> "Farewell, then, lady, *a* God's name," said the king.
> *Peveril of the Peak.*

The A.S. equivalent to "*a* God's name" was "*on* Godes naman." We now say "*in* God's name": but there is no authority for this in Old English.

**Through**: A.S. *ðurh;* cognate with Lat. "*tr*-ans" = across, as in "*trans*-gression."

**Till**: Northern dialect *til,* "to the time when."

**To**: A.S. *tó;* Der. adv. *too.*

**Up**: A.S. *up;* cognate with Lat. *s-ub,* Gr. *h-up-o,* from an old Aryan root "*up-a,*" which appears also in ab-*ove.*

**With**: A.S. *wið,* which often meant "against," as in "*with*-stand."

*Note.*—There are also a few preps. of Romanic origin, which are met with in Mod. Eng.:—

**Per**, through: *per* cent, *per*force, *per* margin, *per*haps.

**Versus**, against: Australian cricketers *versus* Surrey.

**Sans**, Fr. (Lat. *sine*), without:—

*Sans* eyes, *sans* teeth, *sans* taste, *sans* everything.—SHAKSPEARE.

**Maugre**, Fr. (*mal gré,* Old Fr.), in spite of: (rarely used).

**546. Compound and Derivative Prepositions**:—

(*a*) Comparative forms: comparative suffix *-ter,* as in *whe-ther;* or *-er,* as in *long-er*:—

**Af-ter** (adv., prep., conj.): A.S. *æf-ter,* comp. of *af* = of = from. The word "after" denotes "farther off," "more distant" (comp.).

*Note.*—"*Aft*" is not an abridgment of *after.* In *af-t* the *t* is a suffix. Gothic *af-ta.* Cf. "*eft*-soons," "ab-*aft*" (= on by *aft*).

**Near** (adj., adv., and prep.): Scand. *nær,* A.S. *neár,* comp. of A.S. *neáh* = nigh.

**Ov-er**: A.S. *of-er,* comp. of *-ove* in "ab-*ove*" (positive): cognate with Lat. *s-up-er,* and Gr. *h-up-er.* (In A.S. we have "*uf*-an" (adv.), in Goth. *up.*)

**Un-der**: A.S. *un-der.*

(*b*) Prepositions compounded with adverbs or other prepositions:—

**About**: A.S. *á-b-útan,* short for *an-be-útan* = Eng. on-by-out.

**Above**: A.S. *á-b-ufan,* short for *an-be-ufan* = Eng. *on-by-ove* (up).

**Athwart**: Scand. *um þvert*, across; *um*=*on*=*a*, and adv. *þvert*, crossways.

**Before**: A.S. *be-foran*; *be*=by, and adv. *for-an*=in front.

**Behind**: A.S. *be-hindan*; adv. *hind-an*=at the back.

**Beneath**: A.S. *be-neoðan*; adv. *neoð-an*=downwards, from a base *ni*=down.

**Beyond**: A.S. *be-geondan*; adv. *geondan*=on the other side, across. See *yon*, *yonder*, adv., § 543.

**But**: A.S. *b-út-an*, short for *be* or *bi-út-an*=Eng. by-out.

**Throughout**, compound of *through* and the adv. *out*.

**Underneath**, compound of *under* and adv. *neoðan*=neath.

**Unto**, even to.—Not found in A.S. Put for *und-to*, where *to* is the usual prep. The origin of the *und* or *un* is Old Fries. *und*, which means "unto."

(*c*) Prepositions formed from Nouns:—

**Against**: A.S. *ongéan*, which meant *again* (adv.), or *against* (prep.). Origin of A.S. *géan* unknown. "Against" is formed with excrescent *t* from the Genitival adverb *a-yein-es* (Mid. Eng.).

**Across**, cross-wise.—The *a* is short for *on*. Mid. Eng. *cros*, Old Irish *cros*, borrowed from Lat. *cruc-em*, a cross. (This prep. is a hybrid, since the prefix is Teutonic and the noun Romanic.)

**Among, amongst**: A.S. *on mang* (lit. in a mixture or crowd); Mid. Eng. *a-monge*, or in the Genitival form *a-mong-es*, from which "amongst" has been formed with excrescent *t*.

**Beside, besides**.—The origin of these words is not quite the same, and this accounts for the difference of meaning that still attaches to them. "Beside" is from A.S. *be síd-an* ("by the side of"), where *-an* is a Dative suffix of the noun "side." "Besides" has the Genitival suffix *-es*, and was primarily an adverb, as it often is still, in the sense of "in addition." It has also come to be used as a prep. in the sense of "in addition *to*."

**Down**, short for *a-down*: A.S. *of-dúne*, from or off the dune (hill).

**Till**: Scand. *til*, originally a case (perhaps Accus. sing.) of a noun, *tili*, signifying aim or bent. Compound form "*un*-til."

(*d*) Prepositions formed from Adjectives:—

**Along**: A.S. *and-lang*, "over against in length." *A-long-es* (Gen. suffix) and *alongs-t* (with excrescent *t*) were once used.

**Amid, amidst**: A.S. *on-midd-an* (where *-an* is a Dative suffix), in the middle. In Mid. Eng. *amidde* and *amidde-s*, where *-s* is the Genitive suffix, which with excrescent *t* gave *amid-s-t*.

**Anent**, regarding, with reference to: A.S. *an-efen* or *on-efen* (in even). The *t* is excrescent.

**Around** (a hybrid, like "across"): Fr. *en rond*=Eng. *on round* =a-round.

**Below**.—"Low"=Scand. *lágr*, *lág*, "humble," "inferior," low."

**Between**: A.S. *be-twéon-um*, where *twéon-um* is the Dat. plur. of *twéon*, double, twain. Hence "between" is never used when more than *two* persons or things are referred to.

**Betwixt**: A.S. *be-tweoh-s*, where *tweoh*=double, from *twá*, two. The *s* is a Genitive suffix. Mid. Eng. *betwixe*, to which the excrescent *t* was added after the loss of the final *e*.

**Since**, for *sins*, which is short for Mid. Eng. *sithens*, in which the final *s* is the Gen. adverbial suffix. "Sithen" is a modification of A.S. *sið ðám*, "after that." *Sið* was originally an adj. signifying "late"; *ðám* is the Dative neuter of the Dem. pronoun (or Def. article).

**Than**: A.S. *ðænne* or *ðonne*, closely allied to *ðone*, Accus. Masc. of the Def. article. "Than" was frequently written as "then," and was originally the same word.

**Towards.**—The *s* is the Gen. adv. suffix. "Ward" is from A.S. *weord*, inclined, or turned to.

**547. Participial or Verbal Prepositions.**—These were originally Pres. or Past participles used absolutely, sometimes (*a*) with the noun expressed, and sometimes (*b*) with some noun understood.

(*a*) *The noun expressed* (see § 284):—

*Pending* fresh orders = fresh orders *pending* or not yet given.

*During* the summer = the summer (en)*during* or still lasting.

*Notwithstanding* his anger = his anger not-*withstanding* or not preventing it.

All *except* one = all, one being *except(ed)*.

The hour *past* sunset = the hour, sunset having *passed*.

All *save* one = all, one being *safe* (adj. Fr. *sauf*, Lat. *salv-us*) or reserved.

*Note* 1.—"Except" is not the Imperative mood used absolutely, but the Past participle (Lat. *except*-us), to which the Eng. suffix *-ed* has not been added. The participial origin is clear from the French use of the word *except-é*, and from the following passage in Milton:—

> God and his son *except* (being excepted),
> Created thing naught valued he nor shunned.

*Note* 2.—By the rule given in § 269, and repeated in § 284, a noun used absolutely with a participle is in the Nom. case; as in "Fresh orders pending," where "orders" is in the Nom. absolute. But when "pending" becomes a preposition, and "orders" is placed after it as its object, the word "orders" is no longer Nom. but Objective. We still, however, find a Nom. pronoun after *save* or *saved* in Tudor English, and sometimes subsequently; see chap. xx. (61).

> All the conspirators save only *he*.—SHAKSPEARE.
> None save *thou* and thine, I've sworn,
> Shall be left upon the morn.—BYRON.

(*b*) *Some noun understood:* Impersonal absolute (see § 284):—

*Considering* your age, you have done very well.

*Owing* to the long drought, the crops have failed.

Inform me *concerning*, *touching*, or *regarding* this matter.

**548. Phrase Prepositions.**—Two or more words habitually thrown together, and ending with a Simple preposition, may be called Phrase-prepositions or Prepositional phrases:—

By means of; because of; in front of; in opposition to; in spite of; on account of; with reference to; with regard to; for the sake of; on behalf of; instead of; in lieu of; in the place of; in prospect of; with a view to; in the event of, etc.

*Note.*—The phrases "*on this side*" and "*on board*" do not take a Simple prep. after them; as,

*On this side* the river. *On board* the ship.

Similarly the noun "*despite*" can be used as a preposition for the prepositional phrase "in spite of":—

*Despite* his riches, power, and pelf.—SCOTT.

## SECTION 7.—THE FORMS OF CONJUNCTIONS.

**549. Origin of Conjunctions.**—Conjunctions are of comparatively late growth, and have sprung from other parts of speech, especially from pronouns, adjectives, adverbs, and prepositions, or from compounds of these.

Many of our conjunctions are identical in form with adverbs and prepositions, being, in fact, the same words in a different sense or a different connection; and the origin of these has been given already.

The few words remaining are described below:—

(*a*) Co-ordinative conjunctions; for complete list see § 236.

**And**: A.S. *and.* In A.S. it had two meanings—(1) moreover, something added; (2) if. Hence we have the phrase *an if*=if if (a mere reduplication).

But *an if* that evil servant shall say in his heart, etc.—*Matt.* xxiv. 48.

**Both . . . and.**—"Both" is of Scand. origin, *bá-ðir*, dual adjective; Scotch *baith.* Allied to A.S. *bá*, both; cf. Lat. "am-*bo*," Gr. "am-*pho.*" The suffix -*ðir* answers to "they," Nom. plur. of Def. art.

**Also**: compounded of *all* and *so.*

**Either . . . or.**—For "either," see above, § 497. For "or" see below.

**Still** (yet): A.S. *stille,* lit. quietly, even then.

**Therefore**: A.S. *for ðære,* because of that thing or reason, where some feminine noun is understood after *ðære,* the Dative Fem. of Def. art. Another, but less common form, is *therefor.* In A.S. the preposition "for" was spelt sometimes as *for* and sometimes as *fore,* and was followed by a Dative case. *Fore* was also adverbial.

**Nevertheless,** compounded of *never, the* (Instrumental case of Def. art.), and *less.* On the origin of "less," see § 501, II. This word was formerly *natheless,* from A.S. *ná,* not.

**Or,** a contraction of *outher, auther,* the Mid. Eng. forms. These words represent the A.S. *á-hwæþer.* (Observe that "or" is not a doublet of "either," as their derivations are different. "Either" is from *á-gi-*(or *ge-*)*hwæþer:* the mutation of the *á* caused by the *i* in *gi* gives *ǽghwæþer,* out of which came the Mid. and Mod. Eng. *either.* But "or" is from *á-hwæþer* without an intervening *gi* or *ge*; hence the *á* is not mutated, and we get the Mid. Eng. forms *outher*, *auther*, which in Mod. Eng. has been contracted to "or.")

**Yet.**—A.S. *get*, *git*; *get* was probably short for *ge tó*.

(*b*) Subordinative conjunctions; see list in § 238.

**Because**, a hybrid. Eng. *be*=by; Lat. *causa*, a cause.

**As**, a contraction of *also*. A.S. *eál-swá* (quite so).

**Lest**, for fear that, that not. Not connected with "least," but due to A.S. phrase *ðý lǽs ðe*, "for the reason less that" (cf. Lat. *quo minus*). The word *ðý* (for the reason) was dropped, and what remained of the phrase coalesced into "*lest*." *Lǽs*=less (adverb), and *ðe* is the indeclinable relative described in § 507.

**If**: A.S. *gif*, which in other Teutonic languages appears as *ef*, *if*, and also in Mid. Eng. Cf. *op*- in Lat. "*op*-inionem."

**Unless**, if not, except. Formerly written *on lesse*; in the phrase *on lesse that*=in less than, or a less supposition than. Here the *un* of "unless" stands for the prep. "on."

**Though**: A.S. *ðeáh*, *ðéh*, from the Teutonic base *tha*, with suffix -*uh*.

## CHAPTER XXVII.—COMPOUND WORDS.

**550.** When two Simple words are joined together, the word so formed is called a *Compound*; as *ink-pot*, *drinking-water*.

Compound words are subdivided into—

I. **Unrelated**, or those in which the Simple words are not connected together by any grammatical relation. (These have been also called Juxta-positional.)

II. **Related**, or those in which there is some grammatical relation between the component words. (These have been also called Syntactical.)

### Section 1.—Unrelated or Juxta-positional Compounds.

**551.** In all compounds of this class the word that stands *first* defines the one that stands second:—

Thus "*horse-race*" means that kind of race which is run by *horses*, and not by boats or by men or by anything else. But "*race-horse*" means that kind of horse which is used for *racing*, and not for ordinary riding, or for drawing a carriage.

**552. Compound Nouns** can be formed as follows:—

(1) A noun preceded by another noun:—

Oil-lamp, lamp-oil; ear-ring, ring-finger; rail-way, way-side.

(2) A noun preceded by a Gerund:—

Cooking-stove, looking-glass, drinking-water, bathing-place.

*Note.*—The -*ing* is not always used; as in *wash-house*, not *washing-house*; *grind-stone*, not *grinding-stone*, etc.

(3) A noun preceded by an adverb :—

By-word, by-path, under-tone, under-wood, up-land, in-land.

**553. Compound Adjectives** can be formed as follows :—

(1) An adjective preceded by a noun, denoting—

(*a*) *Some point of resemblance* :—

Snow-white (=white like snow), blood-red, coal-black, sky-blue.

(*b*) *Some point of reference* :—

Air-tight (=tight against air), fire-proof, head-strong, heart-broken, book-learned, top-heavy, colour-blind, blood-thirsty.

(*c*) *The cause or source of the quality* :—

Home-sick (=sick for home), purse-proud, heaven-born.

(*d*) *The extent or measure of the quality* :—

Skin-deep (=deep as the skin), world-wide, breast-high, life-long.

(2) A noun (with suffix *-ed*) preceded by a noun :—

Chicken-hearted, hook-nosed, ox-tailed, web-footed, cow-houghed.

(3) An adjective or participle preceded by an adjective :—

Red-hot, dark-brown, bright-blue, dead-alive, luke-warm.

**554. Compound Verbs** can be formed as follows :—

(1) A verb preceded by a noun :—

Hen-peck, brow-beat, top-dress, back-bite, hood-wink, way-lay.

(2) A verb preceded by an adjective :—

Safe-guard, rough-hew, white-wash, rough-shoe, dumb-founder.

## SECTION 2.—RELATED OR SYNTACTICAL COMPOUNDS.

**555. Compound Nouns** can be formed as follows :—

(1) A verb Transitive followed by its Object :—

A tell-tale (one who tells tales), a cut-throat, a pick-pocket.

(2) A verb Transitive (with suffix *-er* or *-ing*) preceded by its Object :—

Shoe-maker, tax-payer ; engine-driving, house-building, etc.

*Note.*—The "*er*" and the "*ing*" are not always used, as in *tooth-pick*, not *tooth-picker* ; *blood-shed*, not *blood-shedding*.

(3) A verb qualified by an adverb :—

(*a*) *When the adverb precedes the verb* :—

An out-turn, an out-look, an out-fit, an up-start, an in-let.

(*b*) *When the adverb is placed after the verb* :—

A run-away, a cast-away, a break-down, a break-up, a fare-well.

*Note.*—Some compounds of this class have two forms ; *set-off* or *off-set* ; *turn-out* or *out-turn* ; *look-out* or *out-look*.

(4) A noun qualified by an adjective :—

A noble-man, a half-penny, a mad-man, a sweet-heart, mid-day.

(5) A noun qualified by a participle :—

(*a*) *Present Participle* :—

Humming-bird, loving-kindness, spinning-top, finishing-stroke.

*Note.*—The "*ing*" is not always used ; as in *screech-owl*, not *screeching-owl* ; *glow-worm*, not *glowing-worm*.

(*b*) *A verb with the force of a Past or Passive participle* :—

Hump-back = humped-back ; lock-jaw = locked-jaw.

(6) A noun qualified by a Possessive noun :—

Sales-man (for sale's-man), bats-man, oars-man, Tues-day, kins-man, herds-man, crafts-man, bees-wax, states-man, sports-man.

*Note* 1.—In some compounds the apostrophe is retained before the *s* :—*stone's-throw, king's-bench, cat's-paw, heart's-ease, land's-end.* The noun *spokes-man* has been formed by a false analogy.

*Note* 2.—The following compounds, since the first noun is not Possessive, are of the Unrelated or Juxta-positional class :—*boat-man, sea-man, oil-man, wood-man, cart-man, plough-man*, etc.

(7) A noun in apposition with a noun or pronoun :—

Washer-woman ; he-goat, she-goat ; man-servant, maid-servant.

556. **Compound Adjectives** can be formed as follows :—

(1) A noun preceded and qualified by an adjective :—

Evil-hearted, hot-headed, long-tailed, one-sided, red-coloured.

(2) A noun as object to the Pres. part. of a Trans. verb :—

A *heart-rending* sight ; a *time-serving* man ; a *soul-stirring* story.

(3) A noun as object to some preposition :—

An *over-land* (over the land) journey ; an *underhand* trick.

557. **Verbs** can be compounded with adverbs :—

(*a*) When the adverb precedes the verb. (Uncommon.)

Back-slide, cross-question, over-awe, under-state, with-hold.

(*b*) When the verb precedes the adverb. This is very common. The two words are written separately ; as *turn out, come on*, etc. (But in *don* (= do on), *doff* (= do off) they are compounded.)

558. **Phrase Compounds.**—Such compounds are sometimes used as nouns, and sometimes as adjectives :—

Forget-me-not (noun) ; hand-and-glove (friends that fit each other as closely as hand and glove) ; man-of-war ; would-be (adj. used for one who intended to be or do something, but was stopped) ; barrister-at-law ; note-of-hand ; ticket-of-leave ; Jack-o'-lantern ; hole-and-corner (adj. clandestine) ; son-in-law ; four-in-hand ; spick-and-span new (lit. spike and spoon new ; new as a nail or spike just made, or a spoon (chip) just cut).

## SECTION 3.—DISGUISED COMPOUNDS.

559. **Agnail**: A.S. *ang-nægl*, a nail or hard knob that gives pain (*ang-*); the modern corrupted form is "hang-nail." See p. 376.

**As**: short for *al-so;* A.S. *eál-swá* (quite so).

**Atone**: *at-one*, to reconcile or make *at one*.

**Auger**: corruption of *nauger;* A.S. *nafu-gár*, from *nafu*, a nave, and *gár*, a piercer. "A nauger" was changed to "an auger."

**Aught**: A.S. *á-wiht*, one whit, anything whatever.

**Back-gammon**: a back-game; A.S. *bæc* (back), *gamen* (game).

**Bandog**: Mid. Eng. *band-dogge*, a dog tied by a band, a watch-dog or ferocious dog.

**Barley**: A.S. *bær-lic*, that which is like *bear* or *bere* (barley). The last syllable has no connection with A.S. *léac*, a plant.

**Bay-window**: a window having a "bay" or recess; not the same word as "bow-window."

**Barn**: A.S. *bere-ern*, a place (A.S. *ærn* or *ern*) for keeping barley.

**Beldam**: a hag. Ironical: Fr. *belle*, beautiful, and *dame*, lady.

**Bilberry**: Scand. *böllr* (a ball), and *bær* (a berry).

**Biscuit**: *bis* (twice, Lat.), and Fr. *cuit*, Lat. *coctus*, cooked.

**Brannew**: for *brand-new*, new from the brand or fire.

**Bridal**: put for *bride-ale*, that is, a bride-feast. A.S. *brýd*, *ealu*.

**Bride-groom**: for *bride-goom;* A.S. *guma*, a man. In Mid. Eng. the Fr. *grome* was substituted for A.S. *guma*.

**Brimstone**: Mid. Eng. *bren-stoon*, burning stone.

**Buck-wheat**: from *beech-wheat*, because the grain resembles the mast of a beech-tree.

**Bulwark**: properly bole-work, from Scand. *bolr*, the stem or trunk of a tree; cf. Fr. *boulevard*.

**Bylaw**: a town-law or municipal law; from Scand. *by*, town. Not compounded with the adverb *by*.

**Cenobite**: one of a brotherhood of monks; Gr. *koinos*, together; *bios*, life.

**Chaffer**: for *cheap-fare*; A.S. *ceáp*, bargain; *far-u*, journey.

**Cobweb**: A.S. *coppa*, a head (only known in the compound *átor-coppa*, a thing with poison in its head, a spider).

**Colporteur**: hawker; Lat. *coll-um* (neck), *port-ator* (carrier).

**Constable**: Old Fr. *conestable*, Lat. *comes stabuli*, count of the stable.

**Coverlet**: Old Fr. *covre*, to cover; and *lit*, Lat. *lectum*, a bed.

**Curfew**: Old Fr. *covre-feu*, a fire-cover.

**Daisy**=day's-eye, A.S. *dæges eáge*.

> That well by reason it men callen may
> The *dayesie*, or else the eye of day.—CHAUCER.

**Dismal**, gloomy: Old Fr. *dis mal*, Lat. *dies mali*, evil days.

**Distaff**: A.S. *distæf* for *dise-* (a bunch of flax) *stæf* (a staff).

**Earwig**: ear-creeper; *wig* from A.S. *wic-ga*, one that runs.

**Eaves-dropper**, one who stands under droppings from the eaves of a house, to listen to what is said inside the room.

**Elbow**: A.S. *el-boga* or *eln-boga*, lit. arm (*eln*), bending (*boga*).

**Fellow**: Scand. *fé-lag-i*, a partner in a *fé-lag*, from *fé*, property (Eng. *fee*), and *lag*, an association or laying together.

**Filibuster**, Span. : a corruption of Eng. *free-booter* ; from Dutch *vrij* (free), and *buit*, booty, plunder.

**Filigree** : formerly spelt as *filigrane; Span. filigrana ; Lat. filum*, a thread, and *granum*, a thread.

**Friday** : A.S. *Frige-dæg*, day of *Frigu* (Love, Venus).

**Fur-long** = furrow-long, the length of a furrow.

**Futtocks**, for *foot-hooks*.

**Gaffer, gammer** : Eng. *grand-father* (hybrid) ; Fr. *grand-mère*.

**Garlic** : A.S. *gár-léac*, spear-leek ; from *gár*, spear.

**Gantlet, gauntlet** (in the phrase "to run the gauntlet"). Confused with *gauntlet*, a glove. The older form was *gantlope*, from Swedish *gat-lopp*, lit. "a gate-leap," where *gate* means street or way. To run the gauntlet is to run down a lane formed by two files of soldiers, who strike the offender as he passes.

**Gospel** : A.S. *gód-spell*, "good story" : trans. of *ev-angelium*.

**Gossamer** : lit. *goose-summer*. The provincial English name is *summer-goose ;* so called from the downy appearance of the film.

**Gossip**, lit. a sponsor in baptism ; *god*, and *sib*, "related."

**Grunsel, groundsill**, threshold ; from *ground* and *sill*.

**Haberdasher** : a seller of small wares ; said to be from Old Fr. *hapertas*, with Eng. suffix *-er* (a hybrid word). But Dr. Murray says "origin unknown."

**Handicap** : hand i' (th') cap ; a mode of drawing lots.

**Handiwork** : here the *i* answers to A.S. *ge* ; as in A.S. *hand-geweorc*. In *handicraft* the *i* has been inserted by analogy.

**Handsel, hansel** : the first instalment of a bargain (Scand.). Lit. *hand-sale*, the conclusion of a bargain by shaking hands.

**Harbinger** : Old Fr. *herberge-our ;* lit. one who goes before to secure a *herberge* (lodging for an army). (See next word.)

**Harbour** (Scand.) : *her-bergi*, army-shelter. Old Fr. *herberge*.

**Hawthorn** : A.S. *haga*, a hedge, and *thorn*.

**Heifer** : A.S. *héah-fore*, from *héah* (high, full-grown), and *fore*, cognate with Greek *poris*, a heifer ; A.S. *fearr*, a bull. See § 479.

**Henchman** : Mid. Eng. *hensman, henchman*, a page ; probably from A.S. *hengst*, a horse, and *man ;* hence lit. "a groom."

**Heyday** : high-day ; Mid. Eng. *hey*, high.

**Hobby-horse** : a horse-shaped toy ; Sc. *hoppe*, a mare.

**Hobnob** : A.S. *hæbban*, to have, and *næbban*, not to have.

**Humbug** : from *hum*, to cajole, and *bug*, a terror.

**Husband** : lit. house-dweller ; Scand. *hús-bóndi*.

**Hussy**, short for house-wife ; A.S. *hús-wíf* (the house-woman).

**Hustings**, properly *husting;* from A.S. *husting*, borrowed from Icelandic *hús-þing*, "house-thing" ; a meeting of the house.

**Icicle** : A.S. *ís-gicel*, from *ís*, ice, and *gicel*, a small piece of ice.

**Kerchief** : Old Fr. *covre-chef*, cover-to-the-head (*chef*).

**Lady** : A.S. *hláf-dige*, loaf-kneader.

**Lammas** : A.S. *hláf-mæsse*, loaf-mass : observed on 1st August.

**Lamprey** : a kind of shell-fish ; lit. a licker of rocks ; Lat. *lamb-ere* (to lick), and *petra* (a rock).

**Leman** : A.S. *léof-man*, dear one, from *leóf*, lief, dear.

**Lichgate** : corpse-gate, from A.S. *líc*, a corpse.

**Limpet** : another form of *lamprey*. See **Lamprey**.

**Livelihood**: Mid. Eng. *livelode*, A.S. *líf* (life), and *lád*, a way.

**Lord**: A.S. *hláf-ord*, probably for *hláf-weard*, a loaf-keeper.

**Lukewarm**: lit. warm-warm; Mid. Eng. *leuk*, *luke*, tepid.

**Malady**, sickness; Lat. *malus*, bad; *habitus*, condition.

**Malaria**: Lat. *mala*, bad; *aria*, air.

**Mermaid**: lake-maid, water-nymph; from A.S. *mere*, a lake.

**Midriff**: A.S. *mid-rif;* from *mid* (middle), and *hrif* (belly).

**Midwife**: from A.S. *mid*, with, and *wíf*, woman; female helper.

**Mildew**: A.S. *mele-deáw*, honey-dew; A.S. *mil*, honey.

**Misletoe**: lit. bird-lime twig; A.S. *mistel* (that which has *mist* or bird-lime), and *tán*, a twig.

**Mulled-ale**: corrupt of *mould-ale*, a funeral feast; cf. *bridal*, or marriage-feast.

**Monday**: A.S. *Mónan-dæg*, day of the moon.

**Narwhal**: the sea-unicorn; lit. corpse-whale, from Icel. *nár* (a corpse), and *hvalr*, a whale; so called from its pallid colour.

**Naught, not**: for *ne aught*. See **Aught.**

**Neighbour**: A.S. *neáh* (nigh), and *búr*, a husbandman.

**Nickname**: lit. an additional name. The *n* has been wrongly attached from *an*; hence "an eke-name" > a nickname.

**Nightingale**: A.S. *nihte-gale*, a singer by night.

**Nostril**: A.S. *nos-þyrl*, nose-thirl, or nose-hole.

**Parboil**: orig. to boil thoroughly; Lat. *per*, and *bullire*. But now "to boil partially," through confusion with *part*.

**Prose**: Lat. *pro* (forward), and *versa* (turned); shortened to *prorsa*, and then to *prosa*, a forward or unembellished speech.

**Puttock**: *put*, a contraction of *poult* or *pullet*, and *hawk;* hence lit. a hawk that seizes pullets.

**Quagmire**: formerly *quake-mire*, a quaking mire.

**Ransack**: Icel. *rann*, a house, and *sæk-ja*, to search.

**Rearmouse**, a bat; A.S. *hrére-mús*, a fluttering or flying mouse.

**Saturday**: A.S. *Sætern-dæg* or *Sæter-dæg*, day of Saturn.

**Scotfree**, free from paying *scot* or *shot*, contribution.

**Sennight**, seven nights, a week.

**Shelter**: A.S. *scild-truma*, a shield-troop, a squadron or guard.

**Sheriff**: A.S. *scír-réfa*, a shire-reeve, officer of the shire.

**Sirloin**: from Old Fr. *sur* (over, upon), and *longe* (loin).

**Sledge-hammer**: lit. a hammer-hammer; A.S. *slecge*, hammer.

**Somersault**: Old Fr. *soubre-soult; soubre* = Lat. *super*, over; *sault* = Lat. *saltus*, a leap.

**Soothsayer**, one who says sooth or truth.

**Squirrel**: Lat. *skiur-ellus*, dim. of Gr. *ski-urus* (shadow-tailed).

**Stalwart**: A.S. *stǽl-wyrðe; stǽl*, foundation, and *wyrðe*, worthy.

**Starboard**: A.S. *stéorbord*, steerboard; the steersman's deck.

**Stark-naked**: Mid. Eng. *start-naked*, lit. "tail-naked."

**Step-child**: A.S. *stéop-cild*, an orphaned child.

**Steward**: A.S. *stí-weard*, keeper of sties and cattlepens.

**Stickleback**, the little fish with stickles (prickles) on its back.

**Stirrup**: A.S. *stig-ráp*, a rope to climb up by.

**Sunday**: A.S. *Sunnan-dæg*, day of the sun.

**Tadpole**, a *toad* nearly all head or *poll*.

**Tantamount**: Lat. *tantus;* Fr. *à mont*, towards the mountain.

**Thursday**: A.S. *Thunres-dæg*, day of Thor or Thunder.

**Topsy-turvy**: orig. *topsy-tervy*. *Top-so-turvy* afterwards altered to *top-side-turvy*, as *up-so-down* was changed to *up-side-down*. *Turvy* means overturned, from A.S. *torfian* (to throw), Mid. Eng. *terven*.

**Trade-wind**, wind of a certain trade, tread, or trend (path).

**Tramway**, a railroad on *trams* (sleepers).

**Tuesday**: A.S. *Tíwes-dæg*, day of Tíw or Mars.

**Twilight**: lit. double (*i.e.* doubtful) light: from A.S. *twi-*, double.

**Valhalla**: Icel. *val-r*, the slain; *hall*, a hall.

**Vinegar**: Fr. *vin* (Lat. *vin-um*), and *egre* (Lat. *acre*, sour).

**Walrus**: Dutch *walrus*; Danish *hval-ros*, a whale-horse.

**Wanton**, undisciplined; A.S. *wan*, lacking; *togen*, disciplined.

**Wassail**: from A.S. *wes hál*, be thou whole or hale.

**Wednesday**: A.S. *Wódnes-dæg*, the day of Woden.

**Wellaway**, an exclamation of sorrow; sometimes corrupted to *welladay*; A.S. *wá lá wá*, woe! lo! woe!

**Whitlow**: a corruption of *quick-flaw*; a flaw in the *quick*.

**Wilderness**, for *wildern*-ness: A.S. *wild* (wild), *déor* (deer, animal).

**Window**: lit. "wind-eye"; Icel. *vindr* (wind), and *auga* (an eye).

**Woman**: A.S. *wif-man*; *wif*, a female, and *mann*, person.

**Woof**: A.S. *ó-wef*, for *on-wef*, lit. web on or across the weft.

**World**: lit. age of man; A.S. *wer*, man; *ældu*, old age.

**Yesterday**, from A.S. *geostra* (yester) and *dæg* (day).

**Zoo-phyte**, animal-plant: Gr. *zoön* (animal), *phuton*, plant.

## Section 4.—Mistaken or Apparent Compounds.

**560. Acorn.**—Not compounded of A.S. *ác* (oak) and *corn*. A.S. *æcern*, fruit of the field; from *æcer*, a field; cognate with Lat. *ager*.

**Blind-fold.**—"Fold" is not connected with "fold," but is a corruption of *feld-en* or *fell-en*, to strike.

**Belfry.**—Not compounded with *bell*. Old Fr. *ber-freit*, of Teutonic origin; *ber* or *berg*, to protect, and *freit*, a place of safety.

**Battle-ment.**—Not from *battle*, but from Fr. *bastile*, a fortress.

**Bondage.**—Not from "bond," but from A.S. *bonda*, a serf.

**Caterpillar.**—Not compounded with *pillar*. Fr. *chate*, a she-cat, and *peleuse* (Lat. *pilosa*), hairy. Old Fr. *chatepeleuse*, a weevil.

**Chincough.**—Not from *chin*, but *chink*=kink, a catch in the breath.

**Counterpane.**—Old Fr. *contre-poinct*, Lat. *culcita puncta*, a quilt punctured or stitched. In older English counterpoint was used:—

Embroidered coverlets or *counterpoints* of purple silk.—North.

**Country-dance.**—This word has been wrongly included among compounds of mistaken origin. It is an English word signifying "rustic dance"; but it was borrowed by the French and misexplained as *contre-danse*, a dance in which the partners stand opposite (*contra*) each other.

**Crayfish.**—Old Fr. *crevisse*; Old High Germ. *crebis*, a crab.

**Curtail.**—Old Fr. *curt-ault*, Lat. *curt-us*, with suffix *-ault*.

**Frontispiece.**—Old Fr. *frontispice*, L. Lat. *fronti-spicium*, a front view.

**Grey-hound**, Sc. *grey* (dog), and *hundr* (hound).

**Gridiron.**—Mid. Eng. *gridire*, Lat. *craticula*. In Mid. Eng. the word for "iron" was *iren* or *ire*. *Gridire* was changed to *gridiron*, because the *ire* was supposed to signify "iron."

**Hand-cuff.**—Apparently for *hand-cops*: *cops* means manacle.

**Hang-nail.**—Not compounded with *hang*. See **Agnail**, § 559.

**Hiccough.**—A misspelling for *hiccock*, dim. of *hic* or *hick*, a catch in the voice imitative of the sound. Cf. "hacking cough."

**Hogshead.**—More correctly *ox-head*. Dutch *oxhoofd*, ox-head.

**Humble-pie.**—Not compounded with *humble*, but *umble*, the entrails of a deer, given as a perquisite to the men who helped in the chase.

**Iron-mould.**—Not compounded with *mould*, but with *mole*, spot.

**Isinglass.**—Dutch *huyzen-blas*, sturgeon-bladder, from which isinglass is made. The *g* after the *n* is intrusive; the *b* before the *l* has been lost.

**Island.**—No connection with Fr. *isle*, Lat. *insula*. A.S. *íg-land*, in which *íg* alone means "island."

**Lanthorn.**—Lat. *lanterna;* misspelt, because *horn* was once used for making the sides of lanterns.

**Lapwing.**—A.S. *hleáp-wince*, "one who turns about in running."

**Lime-house**, a proper name of a place; for *lime-oast*, lime-kiln.

**Loadstone**, a stone that *leads;* A.S. *lád*, a way or course.

**Lute-string.**—Not compounded either with *lute* or *string;* for *lustring*, Fr. *lustrine*, a sort of lustrous silk. Lat. *lustr-are*, to shine.

**Mungoose**, an ichneumon: Indian word *mangús*.

**Mushroom.**—Old Fr. *mouscheron*, an extension of *mousse*, moss.

**Night-mare**, an incubus; A.S. *niht* (night), and *mara* (a crusher).

**Peacock.**—The word *pea* is borrowed from Lat. *pa-vo*, Gr. *ta-os*.

**Pea-jacket.**—Dutch *pij*, a coat of coarse woollen stuff.

**Penthouse.**—Corrupt. of Fr. *a-pentis*, Lat. *appendicium*, appendage.

**Periwig.**—Not compounded with *wig; wig* is itself the short of *periwig*. Fr. *perruque*, from Lat. *pil-um*, hair.

**Pick-axe.**—Mid. Eng. *pikois*, *pikeis*, a mattock; cf. Lat. *spic-a*.

**Policies** (insurance paper).—No connection with *policy*. Gr. *poly* (many), *ptukon* (a fold), a writing in many folds. Late Lat. *polecticum*.

**Porpoise.**—Old Fr. *por-peis*, Lat. *porcus*, pig, and *piscis*, fish.

**Posthumous.**—Not compounded with Lat. *humus*, the ground. A misspelling for *postumus*, "the last," superlative of *post*.

**Primrose.**—Not compounded with *rose*. Mid. Eng. *primerole*, dim. of Late Lat. *prim-ula*, which is itself a dim. of Lat. *prim-a*.

**Rakehell.**—For Mid. Eng. *rakel*, Scand. *reikall*, a vagabond.

**Rein-deer.**—Not compounded with *rein*. Sc. *hreinn*, a deer.

**Rosemary.**—Lat. *ros* (dew), *marinus* (maritime).

**Runagate.**—A corruption of *renegade;* Lat. *re*, again, and *negatus*, denied; one who has denied his faith.

**Sandblind.**—Lit. "half-blind"; A.S. *sám*, half, Lat. *semi*.

**Sangreal.**—Wrongly traced to *sang* (blood), *real* (royal, not real); the word is *san* (holy), *greal* or *grail* (dish). "The Holy Grail."

**Service-tree**, a kind of wild pear. Corruption of Mid. Eng. *serv-es*, plural, A.S. *syrf*, borrowed from Lat. *sorb-us*. Cf. *sorb*-apple.

**Shamefaced.**—For *shame-fast;* cf. "sted-fast": A.S. *sceam-fæst*.

**Slow-worm.**—A.S. *slá-wyrm*, a worm or snake that slays.

**Sovereign.**—Late Lat. *super-aneus;* cf. *foreign*, Lat. *for-aneus*.

**Surcease.**—Fr. *sursis*, pp. of the verb *surseoir;* Lat. *super-sedere*.

**Surround.**—For *sur-ound;* Lat. *super*, over, and *und-are*, to flow.

**Titmouse.**—Scand. *tittr*, little; A.S. *máse*, small bird.

**Touchy.**—Corruption of *tetchy*, from Mid. Eng. *tetch*, a whim.

**Turmoil.**—From Fr. *tremouille*, the hopper of a mill, so called because it is constantly in motion; Lat. *trem-ere*, tremble.

**Uproar.**—Not compounded of *up* and *roar*. Dutch *op-roer*, where *op* means "up," and *roer* means "commotion"; allied to A.S. *hrer-an*, to flutter; cf. **Rearmouse.** "**Roar**" is from A.S. *rár-ian.*

**Wall-eyed**, "with a beam in the eye." Scand. *vagl*, a beam.

**Walnut.**—Not compounded with *wall*, but with A.S. *wealh*, foreign.

**Wiseacre.**—Dutch *wijs-segger*, a wise-sayer.

**Witchelm.**—A.S. *wice*, bending; cf. *wicker*, made of twigs.

**Yeoman.**—Old Fris. *ga-man*, a villager, from *ga*, a village.

## SECTION 5.—HYBRID COMPOUNDS.

*(Compounds made up of words taken from different languages.)*

561. **Arch-fiend**: Gr. *arch* (chief); A.S. *féond* (enemy, hence fiend).

**Bandy-legged**: Fr. *bandé* (bound); Scand. *leggr* (leg).

**Bank-rupt**: Du. *banck* (bench, table); Lat. *rupt-us* (broken).

**Beef-eater**: Fr. *boef*, *bœuf* (beef); Eng. *eater*, one who eats his master's beef; a servant. (The theory which made it a corruption of Fr. *buffetier*, a waiter at a side-board, has been disproved in Skeat's *Student's Pastime*, pp. 157, 158.)

**Black-guard**: Eng. *black* (A.S. *blæc*); Fr. *guard.*

**Cause-way**: Old Fr. *caucie* (Lat. *calciata*), paved; *way* (A.S. *wæg*).

**Foumart**: a pole-cat; A.S. *fúl* (foul); Fr. *marte* (a marten).

**Grandfather, grandmother**: Fr. *grand* (great); Eng. *father, mother.*

**Haut-boy**: Fr. *haut*, high; Dutch *bosch*, wood.

**Heir-loom**: Fr. *heir* (Lat. *her-es*); Eng. *loom* (A.S. *ge-lóma*, a tool).

**Holly-hock**: A.S. *hálig* (holy); Celt. *hoc-ys* (mallow). The flower was indigenous to the Holy Land.

**Inter-loper**: Lat. *inter* (between), and Du. *looper* (runner).

**Kerb-stone**: Lat. *curv-us* (curved), and A.S. *stán* (stone).

**Knight-errant**: Eng. *knight;* Lat. *errant-em* (wandering).

**Life-guard**: A.S. *líf* (life); Fr. *guard.*

**Macadamised**: Gael. *mac* (son); Heb. *Adam;* Greek *-ise* or *-ize*, and Eng. suffix *-d.*

**Mari-gold**: Heb. *Mary;* Eng. *gold:* so called from its colour.

**Nuncheon**: Mid. Eng. *none-schenche*, "noon-drink": Lat. *nona*, ninth hour, noon; and A.S. *scenc-an*, to pour out drink.

**Nut-meg**: A.S. *hnut-a* (a nut); Mid. Eng. *muge*, Lat. *musc-us.*

**Orchard**: A.S. *ort-geard;* from Lat. (*h*)*ort*-us, garden; A.S. *geard*, yard. (The theory which identifies the first syllable with A.S. *wort* is now exploded.)

**Os-trich**: Lat. *avis* (bird); Gr. *struth-ion* (a kind of bird).

**Par-take**, for *part-take*: Lat. *part-em*, Eng. *take* (from Sc. *tac-a*).

**Pas-time**: Fr. *pass*-er, to move onward; A.S. *tím-a* (time).

**Pent-roof**: sloping roof. Fr. *pente*, a slope; A.S. *hróf*, a cabin.

**Piece-meal**: Fr. *piece* (part); A.S. *mǽl* (a portion or time).

**Pur-blind**: orig. *pure-blind*; Lat. *purus*, A.S. *blind.*

**Rigmarole** : Sc. *ragmenni* (coward); Lat. *rotula* (a little wheel, hence *roll*). A coward's roll; a long stupid story.

**Salt-cellar** : A.S. *sealt* (salt); Fr. *salière*, L. *salarium*, saltholder.

**Sorb-apple** : Lat. *sorb-us* (a wild tree); A.S. *æppel* (apple).

**Spike-nard** : Lat. *spic-atus* (spiked); Sanskrit *nalad-a* (nard).

## CHAPTER XXVIII.—TEUTONIC PREFIXES AND SUFFIXES.

**562. Derivatives, Compounds.**—A word derived from *one* Simple word is called a *Derivative;* whereas a word formed by the junction of *two* or more Simple words is called a *Compound.*

Thus *man-like* is a Compound, of which the component words are *man* and *like*. But *man-ly* is a Derivative, because *ly* is not a separate word, but merely a suffix added to the word *man*.

Derivatives are subdivided into two main classes :—

I. **Primary**, when one word is formed out of another by some change in the body of the word.

II. **Secondary**, when a new word is formed by adding some affix (either prefix or suffix) to some given stem.

Thus *men* is a Primary derivative, because it is formed from *man* by vowel-mutation (see § 452); but *man-ly* is a Secondary derivative, because it is formed by adding the suffix *-ly* to the word *man*. Observe, however, that words, whose difference from one another consists of *vowel-gradation*, do not belong to the class of Primary derivatives under any circumstances. Such words are co-radical; that is, one is not derived from another (see § 378, *Note* 3, and § 453). Again, *graze* is a Primary derivative, because this verb is formed from the noun *grass* by changing *ss* to *z;* but *grass-y* is a Secondary derivative, because it is formed by adding the adjective-suffix *-y* to *grass*.

**563. Root, stem.**—The *root* of a word is that essential part of it, which it has in common with a group of cognate words.

Thus from the Teutonic root *bŭg* (Mod. Eng. *bow*) we got *buxom*, lit. *bow-some, i.e.* pliant; *bow*, a weapon (A.S. *boga*); *bight*, a coil of rope (A.S. *byht*). All these are from an Aryan root *bheugh*, which appears in Lat. *fug*-ere, to flee, Gr. *pheug*-ein, to flee, Sanskrit *bhuj*, to bend. See also the Aryan root *pa*, exemplified in *Note* 3 to § 378.

A *stem* is the form assumed by the root, before a suffix is added to it.

Thus in *loved* the root is *lov* (A.S. *luf*), the stem is *lov-e* (A.S. *luf-o*), and the suffix is *-d* (A.S. *-de*). Here *d* is the *derivative* suffix added to the stem *love*, and *-e* is the *formative* suffix, with the help of which the stem *love* is formed. Similarly in the A.S. Infinitive *luf-i-an*, *luf* (as before) is the root, *luf-i* is the stem (consisting of the root combined with the formative suffix *-i*), and *-an* is the flexional or Derivative suffix, which makes the Infinitive. To take one more example :—*stones*. Here *ston* (A.S. *stán*) is the root; the stem is *stán-a* ; *-s* is the (Derivative) Nom. Plural suffix (A.S. *stán-a-s*, Mod. Eng. *stones*).

A stem may therefore be more strictly defined as "a root combined with some formative suffix, to which a derivative suffix can be added."

*Note* 1.—So far as we know, roots never existed as independent words. Thus *luf* (the A.S. root) has never been seen alone. A word is reduced to its root, after all formative and derivative suffixes have been cut off. The root which remains is merely a theoretical form, useful for etymological purposes.

*Note* 2.—Such a word as *luf* is an *English root*,—that is, it is the simplest form to which the word can be reduced in English. It has other forms in other Aryan languages; thus in Sanskrit it has the form *lubh*. The phrase *English root* means "the form that an Aryan root assumes in the English language."

**Prefixes, Suffixes, Affixes.**—A prefix is a particle placed at the beginning of a stem; a suffix is one placed at the end of it. The name "affix" may be given to either.

Prefixes alter the meanings of words, while suffixes alter their functions.

Thus there is a radical difference of meaning between *teach* and *un-teach*, *bid* and *for-bid*, *con-vert* and *sub-vert*, *pro-ceed*, *pre-cede*, and *suc-ceed*.

On the other hand, suffixes form nouns, adjectives, verbs, and adverbs, and hence they change the function of a word, that is, they make it of one part of speech or another. Thus the stem *dark* becomes a noun in *dark-ness*, a verb in *dark-en*, and an adverb in *dark-ling* and *dark-ly*.

## SECTION 1.—TEUTONIC PREFIXES.

**564.** These are either (*a*) Separable, or (*b*) Inseparable.

(*a*) **Separable**, or such as have a separate existence as independent words. Words so formed might be called Compounds; and in fact are so called for convenience in § 555 (3), *a*, *b*. But the name "Compound" is usually restricted to those words of which the component parts are nouns, adjectives, or verbs; whereas the name "Separable prefix" is for the most part restricted to adverbs and prepositions. Words formed with separable prefixes or separable suffixes are a connecting link between Compounds and Derivatives.

**After** (A.S. *æft*, *æfter*) :—*after*-wards, *after*-thought, *after*-life.
**Al-**, **l-** (A.S. *eal*, Eng. *all*) :—*al*-one, *l*-one, *al*-most, *al*-ready, *al*-so.
**At-** (*at*) :—*at*-one, *at*-one-ment, etc.
**By** (A.S. *bi*) :—*by*-path, *by*-word, *by*-way : (on *by*-law, see § 559).

**Fore** (A.S. *fore*, before) :—*fore*-cast, *fore*-tell, *fore*-see, *fore*-head.
**Forth** :—*forth*-coming, *forth*-with.
**Fro** (Scand. *frá*, from) :—*fro*-ward (opp. to *to*-ward).
**In-** (A.S. *in*) :—*in*-to, *in*-sight, *in*-bred, *in*-land, *in*-let, *in*-mate.
**Mis-** (A.S. *mis*, Eng. *miss*, in the sense of wrongly) :—

*With A.S. words and stems* :—*mis*-behave, *mis*-believe, *mis*-deed.
*With stems of Scand. origin* :—*mis*-call, *mis*-hap, *mis*-take.
*With stems of Lat.* or *Fr. origin* (all hybrids) :—*mis*-apply, *mis*-calculate, *mis*-carry, *mis*-conceive, *mis*-conduct, *mis*-construe.

*Note.*—The Lat. prefix *dis-* is sometimes interchanged with Eng. *mis-*. Thus we have *mis*-believe and *dis*-believe, *mis*-trust and *dis*-trust, *mis*-like and *dis*-like.

**Off-** (*of* or *off*) :—*off-ing* (what is seen of the sea at some distance *off* the land), *off*-spring, *off*-shoot, *of*-fal (*off*+fall, what falls off).

*Note.*—It takes the form of *a-*, in *a*-down ; see below under **A**.

**On-** (A.S. *on*) :—*on*-set, *on*-slaught, *on*-to (double preposition).

*Note.*—This prefix appears as *an* in *an*-on (=on one).

**Out-, ut-** (A.S. *út*) :—*out*-let, *out*-cast, *out*-side ; *ut*-ter, *ut*-most.

*Note.*—This prefix gives certain verbs the sense of surpassing :—

*Out*-live, *out*-shine, *out*-run, *out*-vote.

**Over-** (A.S. *ofer*) :—*over*-look, *over*-flow, *over*-due, *over*-coat.

*Note.*—This prefix is often used to denote *excess*, or too much :—

*Over*-eat, *over*-sleep, *over*-eager, *over*-worked.

In the word "*or*-lop," the prefix *or* is a disguised form of *over*.

**Thorough, through** :—*thorough*-fare, *through*-out, *through*-ticket.
**To-** (A.S. *tó*, prep.) :—*to*-day (A.S. *tó* dæg-e, for the day), *to*-morrow.
**Under** (A.S. *under*) :—*under*-bred, *under*-let, *under*-growth.

*Note.*—This prefix also denotes *deficiency*, or too little :—

*Under*-paid, *under*-fed, *under*-valued, etc.

**Up-** (A.S. *up*) :—*up*-start, *up*-shot, *up*-braid, *up*-hold, *upp*-er.
**Wel-, well-** (A.S. *wel*, allied to *will*) :—*wel*-fare, *well*-bred.
**With** (A.S. *with*, against or back) :—*with*-stand, *with*-draw.

*Note.*—In the compound noun "*with*-drawing-room," the prefix *with* has been dropped and the word has become "drawing-room."

*Note.*—To denote bigness, etc., we use *bull*, *horse*, and *tom* :—

**Bull** :—*bull*-dog, *bull*-finch, *bull*-terrier, *bull*-mastiff.
**Horse** :—*horse*-chestnut, *horse*-fish, *horse*-radish, *horse*-leech.
**Tom** :—*tom*-boy (a romping girl), *tom*-fool, *tom*-noddy, *tom*-cat.

(*b*) **Inseparable**, that is, not used as separate words :—

**A-** (*of*) :—*a*-down (A.S. *of-dune*, off a hill or dune), *a*-light (to descend *from*), *a*-fresh, *a*-kin, *a*-new.
**A-** (*on*) :—*a*-foot, *a*-float, *a*-light (adv.), *a*-light (verb, to light *on*).
**A- or an-** (A.S. *and-*, against) :—*a*-long (A.S. *and*-lang, over against in length), *an*-swer (A.S. *and*-swer-ian, to swear or speak back).
**A-** (A.S. *án*, one) :—*a*-ught (á-wiht), n-*a*-ught.
**A-** (A.S. *á*, intensive) :—*a*-rise, *a*-waken, *a*-maze, *a*-rouse, *a*-weary, *a*-shamed, *a*(c)-cursed, *a*(f)-fright, *a*(c)-knowledge.

*Note* 1.—In the three words last named, the A.S. *á* has been confounded with the Lat. suffix *-ad*, which can take the forms *-ac*, *-af*.

*Note* 2.—**An hungred.**—The sentence "He was an hungred" occurs frequently in the Authorised Version of 1611; but in the Revised Version of 1885 it has been changed to "he hungered." The *an* appears to have been substituted for the prefix *a* (A.S. *of*), which was confounded with the Indefinite article. *An hungred*=Mid. Eng. *a-hungred*=Mid. Eng. *of-hungred*. Thus *of*>*o*>*a*>*a*(*n*).

**A-** (*at*, in North. Eng. used for *to*, to express the Gerund):—*a*-do (*much a-do*=much to do), *t*-wit (short for *at*-wit-en, to reproach).

**A-** (A.S. *ge*, Mid. Eng. *i*, *y*):—*a*-ware (A.S. *ge*-wær, Mid. Eng. *i*-war or *y*-war); *a*(f)ford (A.S. *ge*-forth-ian, to further).

**Be-** (by). (1) It forms Trans. verbs:—*be*-calm, *be*-dew, *be*-friend.
(2) It makes Intrans. verbs Trans.:—*be*-moan, *be*-lie, *be*-speak.
(3) It intensifies verbs:—*be*-daub, *be*-smear, *be*-seech (=*be*-seek).
(4) It helps to form nouns:—*be*-hoof, *be*-quest, *be*-half, *be*-hest.
(5) It helps to form adv. or prep.:—*be*-sides, *be*-low, *be*-neath.
(6) It has a privative force in:—*be*-head.

*Note* 1.—In the verb *be*-lieve the *be* has been substituted for *ge* (A.S. *ge*-lýf-an, to *be*-lieve).

*Note* 2.—*Be*-have is a derivative of *have*, with a pronunciation due to *behāviour*, which last simulated a French noun with a French suffix.

**E-** (A.S. *ge*, Mid. Eng. *i*-, *e*-):—*e*-nough (A.S. *ge*-nóg, Mid. Eng. *i*-noh, *e*-nogh).

**E-** (for *a* in Anglo-Fr. *a*-loper, where *a* stands for A.S. *and*, Dutch *ont*, see above **A-**, **an-**):—*e*-lope (akin to *leap*, Dutch *ont*-hlop-en).

**For** (through, thoroughly; related to *from*; distinct from *fore*):—
*Intensive*:—*for*-bear, *for*-lorn, *fr*-et (A.S. *for*-et-an, to eat up).
*Privative and depreciatory*:—*for*-bid, *for*-sake, *for*-get, *for*-swear (swear falsely), *fore*-go (go without, a bad spelling for *for*-go).

*Note.*—In *for*-feit and *for*-close or *fore*-close, the prefix is Romanic.

**Fore** (before): *fore*-tell, *fore*-cast, *fore*-father, *fore*-noon (hybrid).

**Gain** (A.S. *gegn*, against):—*gain*-say (say or speak against).

**I-** (A.S. *ge*):—*i*-wis (A.S. *ge*-wis, Mid. Eng. *y*-wis, or *i*-wis, "certainly"; wrongly written in Mod. Eng. as *I wis*, as if *wis* were a verb), hand-*i*-work (A.S. hand-*ge*-weorc).

**N-** (Indefinite article, *an*, the *n* being wrongly detached):—*n*-ewt (for *an ewt*), *n*-ickname (for *an eke-name*), *n*-ugget (for *an ingot*).

*Note.*—In Shakspeare we find *n-uncle*, *n-aunt*=*mine uncle*, *mine aunt*. The phrase *for the n-once*=*for then once*.

**N-** (A.S. *ne*, negative prefix; cf. Lat. *non*):—*n*-o (A.S. *ná*), *n*-ay (from *ne*+aye), *n*-or (short for A.S. *n*-óther, also spelt as *n-ówther*, *n-áwther*, a contracted form of *n-áhwæðer*), *n*-illy will-y (nill I or he+will I or he), hob-*n*-ob (A.S. *hæbb-en ne hæbb-en*, have or not have).

**Or-** (A.S. *or*-, signifying "out"):—*or*-deal (A.S. *or*-dél, a dealing out, a judgment), *or*-ts (leavings, from A.S. *or*, and *et*-an, to eat).

*Note.*—In the phrase "odds and ends," the *odds* is a Norse spelling of *ords*, beginnings (A.S. *ord*, a point or beginning), not of *orts*.

**Th-** (prefix of 3rd pers. Pro.) :—*th*-e, *th*-is, *th*-at, *th*-ere, *th*-en.

**To-** (A.S. *tó*, intensive prefix) :—*to*-break ("all to-brake his head" = utterly smashed his head : *Judges* ix. 53).

**Twi-** (A.S. *twi*, double) :—*twi*-n, *twi*-ce, *twi*-light, *twi*-ne, *twi*-st.

**Un-** (A.S. *un-*, negative prefix) :—*un*-truth, *un*-told, *un*-ripe.

**Un-** (A.S. *un-*, a verbal prefix, signifying the *reversal* of an action ; akin to A.S. *and-*, "against" ; see above under **A, an**) :—*Un*-tie, *un*-teach, *un*-say (withdraw what has been said), *un*-learn, *un*-lock.

*Note.*—In *un*-loose the *un* is merely intensive.

**Un-** (not in A.S. ; put for *und*, Old Frisian) :—*un*(*d*)-to, *un*(*d*)-til.

**Wan-** (privative, like *un-*) :—*wan*-ton (A.S. *wan*-togen, Mid. Eng. *wan*-towen, untrained). So also *wan*-hope (hopelessness ; obsolete).

**Y-** (A.S. *ge*, Mid. Eng. *i, y*) :—*y*-wis (corrupted to "I wis"), *y*-clept. (Cf. *a-* in *a*-ware, A.S. *ge*-wær, Mid. Eng. *i*-war ; as *e-* in *e*-nough, A.S. *ge*-nóh ; and as *i* in hand-*i*-work, A.S. hand-*ge*-weorc.)

## Section 2.—Suffixes.

### A. *Noun-forming.*

**565. Separable,** or once separable.—Words so formed might, as in the case of words formed with separable prefixes, be called Compounds. They differ from ordinary compounds only in two points—(*a*) the suffixed word is attached to other words so frequently as to constitute *a class*, whereas an ordinary compound stands alone ; (*b*) most of the suffixed words have not completely retained their separate and independent meaning.

*Note.*—In this and the following chapters hybrids are marked with an asterisk. The word "hybrid" is used with various degrees of strictness. In this book, if the stem belongs to one Teutonic language and the suffix to another, the word so formed is not counted as a hybrid. Thus *fellowship* is not counted a hybrid, although *fellow* is Danish and *ship* Saxon. Hybrids are words composed of *heterogeneous* elements, such as Teutonic with Romanic (*hindr-ance*), Teutonic with Greek (*heathen-ism*), Romanic with Greek (*glossary*).

(1) **-craft** (A.S. *cræft*, skill) : sometimes depreciatory :—

Speech-*craft*, *priest-*craft*, witch-*craft*, handi-*craft* (the *i* has been inserted in imitation of "hand-i-work" A.S. *hand-ge-weorc*).

(2) **-dom** (A.S. *dóm*, judgment, jurisdiction ; Eng. *doom*) :—

*Duke-*dom*, earl-*dom*, free-*dom*, *martyr-*dom*, *Christen-*dom*.

*Excluded words* :—

**Seldom** : *seld* = rare, *-om*, Dative Plural suffix (see § 534).
**Random** : Old Fr. *randon*, swiftness, violent haste.

(3) **-fare** (A.S. *faru*, a journey ; from *far*-an, to go) :—

Thorough-*fare*, wel-*fare*, chaf-*fer* (=cheap-fare), war-*fare*.

(4) **-herd** (A.S. *heorde, hirde*, keeper of a *herd*) :—

Shep-*herd*, swine-*herd*, cow-*herd*, neat-*herd*.

(5) **-hood, -head** (A.S. *hád*, state, degree): Abstract:—

God-*head*, maiden-*head*; maiden-*hood*, man-*hood*, *priest-*hood*.

*Excluded word*:—

Livelihood: A.S. *líf-lád*, Mid. Eng. *live-lode*, life-leading.

(6) **-lock, -ledge** (*-lock* is from A.S. *lác* (noun), Mid. Eng. *lok*, play; but *-ledge* is from A.S. *lǽc*-an[1] (verb, to play), Mid. Eng. *lech*-en, Mod. Eng. *-ledge*; cf. verb *ac-know-ledge*):—

Wed-*lock*; know-*ledge*.

(7) **-lock, lic** (A.S. *leác*, a plant; hence Eng. *leek*):—

Hem-*lock*, char-*lock*, house-*leek*, gar-*lic* (spear-plant, *gar*=spear).

*Excluded word*:—

Barley: A.S. *bere*, barley. The *ley* is from *líc*, like.

(8) **-man** (A.S. *mann*, which meant person of either sex). In many words this has taken the place of the old suffix *-ere* or *-er*, denoting agent. In "fish-*er-man*" both suffixes are seen. In "cart-*er*," "cart-*man*," either suffix is seen.

Boat-*man*, *post-*man*, wo-*man* (a corruption of *wíf-man*, that is, a female person), alder-*man* (formed with A.S. *ealdor*, elder, chief).

(9) **-monger** (A.S. *mang-ere*, dealer in mixed or *mingled* goods); sometimes depreciatory:—

Iron-*monger*, coster-*monger*, *ballad-*monger*, *scandal-*monger*.

(10) **-red** (A.S. *rǽden*, rule, counsel, condition):—

Hat-*red*, kin-d-*red* (here the *d* is intrusive; Mid. Eng. *kin-rede*).

(11) **-red** (A.S, *rǽd* or *réd*, rate, reckoning):—

Hund-*red* (from A.S. *hund*=Lat. *cent*-um, a hundred).

(12) **-ric** (A.S. *ríce*, dominion; cf. Lat. *reg*-num, rule):—

*Bishop-*ric* (the only example left).

*Note.*—The *rake* of *drake* is not connected with *ric*; see p. 312.

(13) **-ship** (A.S. *scipe*, form, shape, mode): Abstract suffix:—

Friend-*ship*, hard-*ship*, *author-*ship*, wor-*ship* (for "worth-ship").

*Note.*—"Land-*scape*" was borrowed from Dutch "land-*schap*" in the seventeenth century. Milton uses the word "land-*skip*" (A.S. *scipe*), but not "land-*scape*." *Ship* is the only true form of the suffix. *Scape* is used merely in the art-term "landscape" borrowed from Dutch.

(14) **-son**: a patronymic in the Northern dialect:—

Ander-*son*, Collin-*son*, David-*son*, etc.

(15) **-stead** (A.S. *stede*, a place):—

Home-*stead*, bed-*stead*, in-*stead* of, Hamp-*stead*, Berkham-*stead*.

---

[1] *Lǽc-an* is merely the verb formed by vowel-mutation from the noun *lác*. The earliest form of the verb was *lác-ian*, which by vowel-mutation became *lǽc-an* through the influence of *i*; see § 452.

(16) **-tree** (A.S. *tréow* or *tréo*, sawn timber; Scand. *tré*) :—
Axle-*tree*, roof-*tree*: (cf. "Bound upon the accursëd *tree*").

(17) **-ward** (A.S. *weard*, guardian, keeper) :—
Ste-*ward* (§ 559). Fr. *guard*: van-*guard*, *black-*guard*.

(18) **-wife** (A.S. *wíf*, woman, married or unmarried) :—
Fish-*wife*, mid-*wife* (an attendant woman; A.S. *mid* = with).

(19) **-wright** (A.S. *wyrht-a*, workman; *wyrc*-an, to work) :—
Ship-*wright*, wheel-*wright*, cart-*wright*.

**566. Inseparable.**—These suffixes may have once been independent words, or have been derived from such. But the separate words, if they existed, cannot now be traced.

(20) **-d, -de** (sometimes allied to the weak Past part.) :—

Bloo-*d* (cf. A.S. *blów*-an, to blow or bloom, the blood being the life), bran-*d* (cf. A.S. *brinn*-an, to burn), brea-*d* (fermented flour; cf. A.S. *breów*-an, to brew), broo-*d*, dee-*d* (the thing done), floo-*d* (cf. A.S. *flówan*, to flow).

(21) **-el, -le, -l** (A.S. = *el*), and in compound form **-er-el**.

(*a*) *Diminutive:* **-el, -l, -le, -er-el** :—

Ax-*le*, bund-*le* (A.S. *bund*), freck-*le* (cf. *fleck*, a spot), gir-*l* (cf. *gör* (North Freisic), a child), hov-*el* (A.S. *hof*, a house), cock-*erel* (a young cock), mong-*rel* (a puppy of mixed breed), wast-*rel* (a spendthrift).

(*b*) *Agent, instrument, or result of action:* **-el, -le, -l** :—

Aw-*l* (that which pierces; A.S. aw-*el*), bead-*le*[1] (a proclaimer; cf. A.S. *béod*-an, to bid), beet-*le* (a heavy mallet, a thing that *beats*), beet-*le* (an insect, a thing that *bites*; A.S. *bít*-an, to bite), fow-*l*, nai-*l*, sai-*l*, sou-*l*, tai-*l*, stoo-*l*, swiv-*el*, tack-*le*.

*Peculiar word:*—

**Riddle**: A.S. *rǽdelse* (the *else* is made up of *-el* and *-se*). See § 491.

(22) **-en, -n, -on**, in five different senses :—

(*a*) *Diminutive sense:* **-en** (A.S. *-en*) :—

Maid-*en* (A.S. mægd-*en*), chick-*en* (A.S. cic-*en*, allied to *cocc*, but not a derivative; both of imitative origin).

*Excluded words:*—

**Kitten**: the *-en* is from Fr. suffix *-oun*, Mid. Eng. *kit-oun*.
**Mitten**: from Old Fr. *mitaine*, a winter glove; origin doubtful.
**Mizzen**: from Old Fr. *misaine*, Late Lat. *median*-us.
**Kitchen**: A.S. *cicen*, *cycen*; Lat. *coquina*, a cooking-room.

(*b*) *Feminine suffix* **-en** (A.S. *-en*) :—

Vix-*en* (A.S. fyx-*en*, Fem. of *fox*; on the mutation of *o*, see § 452 (6).

[1] *Beadle* really came to us from Old Fr. *bedel*, a proclaimer or messenger; but this came from a Frankish verb co-radical with A.S. *béodan*.

(*c*) *Agent*: **-en -n, -on**:—

Hav-*en* (that which holds, allied to *have*), mai-*n* (A.S. *mæg*-en, that which *may*), wag-*on* or wai-*n* (that which carries; cf. *weigh*).

(*d*) *Passive sense*, allied to Past part. suffix *-en*:—

Bair-*n* (that which is born), burd-*en* (that which is borne).

(*e*) *Plural suffix*: **-en, -ne, -n** (A.S. *-an*):—

Ox-*en*, childre-*n*, brethre-*n*, ki-*ne*. Archaic: hose-*n*, shoo-*n*.

(23) **-er, -r** (A.S. *-or, -er*): means or result of action:—

Lai-*r* (a thing to *lie* on), stai-*r* (A.S. *stig*-an, to climb); tim-b-*er*, thun-d-*er*, wond-*er*, hung-*er*, ang-*er*, cf. Lat. *ang*-or (Eng. *ang*-uish).

(24) **-er, -ier, -yer, -ar, -or** (A.S. *-ere*, orig a male agent):—

Rid-*er*, *min-*er*, li-*ar*, sail-*or*, *court-*ier*, law-*yer*, London-*er*.

*Note.*—In words like "court-*ier*," "law-*yer*," "saw-*yer*," French influence has been at work. The Fr. *-ier* is from Lat. *-arius*.

*Excluded word*:—

**Begg-ar**: Low Lat. beg-*hard*-us;[1] from which has been formed the verb "beg."

(25) **-ing** (A.S. *-ing*): diminutive and patronymic:—

Wild-*ing* (a wild plant), farth-*ing* (the *fourth* part), trith-*ing* (a *third* part; cf. *Riding* of Yorkshire), k-*ing*, (short for kin-*ing*; A.S. cyn-*ing*, man of noble kin), vik-*ing* (man of a *vik*, creek or bay).

(26) **-ing** (A.S. *-ung* or *-ing*): forms verbal nouns: sometimes attached to nouns and adverbs:—

Learn-*ing*, follow-*ing*, *ceil-*ing*, out-*ing*, off-*ing*, inn-*ings*.

(27) **-kin** (rare in A.S.: Dutch *-ken*): diminutive and patronymic:—

Bump-*kin* or bum-*kin*, fir-*kin* (Dutch, *vier*, four; cf. Eng. *farth*-ing), *nap-*kin*.

Peter-*kin* (hence Per-*kin*), Daw-*kin* (David-*kin*).

*Excluded word*:—

**Welkin**, from A.S. *wolcn-u* (clouds), plural of A.S. *wolcen*, § 490.

(28) **-ling** (double dim., *-el*, *-ing*; see (25) above.

*With nouns.*—Cod-*ling*, duck-*ling*, gos-*ling*, star-*ling*, lord-*ling*.

*Indirectly related to the noun.*—Strip-*ling* (a lad as thin as a *strip*), seed-*ling*, nest-*ling*, *chamber-*lain* (for chamber-*ling*).

*With Adjectives.*—Dar-*ling* (for *dear*-ling), first-*ling*, fat-*ling*.

*With Verbs.*—Ean-*ling* or yean-*ling*, change-*ling*, hire-*ling*.

*With adverbs.*—Under-*ling*, hild-*ing*, short for hinder-*ling*.

---

[1] There is a difference between *Low* Latin and *Late* Latin. Low Latin is a French or Teutonic word turned into Latin,—not true Latin at all: thus *beghardus* was coined from French, and the French word was formed from Teutonic elements. Late Latin is genuine Latin, though late, that is, post-classical, as *subitaneus*, Late Lat. form of *subitus*.

2 C

(29) **-m, -me, -om** (A.S. *-m, -ma ;* cf. Lat. *-mus*) :—

Bes-*om* (A.S. bes-*ma*), bloo-*m* (*blów*-an, to bloom), blo-ss-*om* (*blów*-an, with double suffix *-st* and *-ma ;* A.S. bló-*st-ma*), bos-*om* (A.S. bós-*m*), doo-*m* (A.S. dó-*m*).

*Excluded words :—*

**Beam, broom, harm, dream, foam** ; the *m* is radical.
**Transom**, lintel or cross-beam ; corrupt. of Lat. *transtrum*.
**Ransom**, from Old Fr. form of *redemption*.
**Flotsam, jetsam**, abridgments of Anglo-Fr. *flotteson, jettison*. *Flotteson* is from *floter*, to float, Late Lat. *fluctationem*. *Jettison* is from Late Lat. *jactationem*, goods thrown out of a ship and floating on the water.

(30) **-nd, -and, -end** (Pres. part. ; cf. Lat. *-ant*-em, *-ent*-em) :—

Err-*and* (A.S. ær-*ende*), fie-*nd* (A.S. *féo-n*, to hate), frie-*nd* (A.S. *fréo-n*, to love), tid-*ings* (Southern Eng. tid-*ind*-e), husba-*nd* (Scand. *hús-bó-nd*-i, house-dweller), wi-*nd* (A.S. *wi-nd*, from a root *wa*, cf. Lat. *vent*-us).

(31) **-ness** (A.S. *-nis, -nes, -ness*). This is a compound suffix, divisible into *n-es-s*, in which the *n* belonged originally to some noun-stem, and the *es-s* is supposed to stand for *es-t* or *es-tu ;* see below, No. 34. Abstract suffix, combined as freely with Romanic as with Teutonic stems, and making over 1000 words.

Dark-*ness*, liveli-*ness*, holi-*ness* (A.S. *hálig-nes*), *rigid-*ness*, nothing-*ness*, wilder-*ness* (wild-deer-ness), wit-*ness*.

*Excluded word :—*

**Harness** : Old Fr. *harnois*, equipment ; of the same root as *iron*.

(32) **-ock** (A.S. *-uc ;* but probably the real suffix is *-c*, the *u* being either a separate suffix or part of some stem. In *stir-k*, dim. of *steer*, we have the original suffix *-c* or *-k*). Diminutive.

Bull-*ock*, hill-*ock*, humm-*ock* (dim. of *hump*), butt-*ock* (stem word *bot ;* cf. "*butt*-end"), padd-*ock* (a toad ; stem word *padd-a*), par-*k* (A.S. pearr-*oc*, cf. A.S. *sparr*-an, to enclose), matt-*ock*, shamr-*ock*.

*Excluded words :—*

**Puttock, futtock** (see § 559).
**Bannock**, a cake ; from Gaelic *bonnach*, a cake.
**Cassock**, from Fr. *casaque*, Ital. *casacca*, an outer coat.
**Hammock** : West Ind. *hamaca*.
**Pibroch** : Gael. *piobair* (piper), and *eachd* (merely a suffix = *age*).

(33) **-ow, -w** (A.S. *-u, -we, -wa*) :—

Mead-*ow* (A.S. mǽd-*we*, Dative of *mǽdu*), shad-*ow* (A.S. *sccad-we*, Dat. of *sccadu*), sparr-*ow* (A.S. spear-*wa*, a flutterer ; from root *spar*, to flutter), stra-*w*, de-*w*, sno-*w*, cla-*w*, sto-*w* (a place).

*Excluded words :—*

**Pillow**, Lat. *pulvinus* (A.S. *pyle*, Mid. Eng. *pil-we*).
**Window, elbow** (see § 559).

(34) **-st, -t, -est** (A.S. *-st, -t, -est*) :—

Harv-*est* (A.S. hærf-*est*, autumn), earn-*est* (seriousness; "in earnest"), twi-*st* (*twi*, double), tru-*st* (base *true*), try-*st* (variant of *trust*).

*Excluded word* :—

**Nest** : A.S. *nest*; allied to Lat. *nis-dus*, which has become *nidus*.

(35) **-ster** (A.S. *es-tre*, a compound suffix; cf. Lat. *-as*, and *-ter*, as in "poet-*aster*"). Used in A.S. solely as a Fem. suffix; now denotes trade, etc., often in a depreciatory sense.

Spin-*ster* (the only fem. left), huck-*ster* (orig. fem. of *huck*-er, now spelt as *hawk*-er), song-*ster*, up-hol(d)-*ster*-er (the final "er" is superfluous), rhyme-*ster* (cf. Romanic equivalent "poet-*aster*").

*Excluded words* :—

**Monster** : Lat. *monstrum*, a prodigy or monster.
**Lobster** : A.S. *loppestre*, a corrupt form of *lopust*, Lat. *locusta*.
**Foster** (foster-mother) : A.S. *fóstor*, nourishment.

(36) **-t, -th** (akin to the suffix *-d*; see above, 20) : Abstract :—

*-th* :—bir-*th* (A.S. *ber*-an, to bear), ber-*th* (a variant of "birth"), bro-*th* (A.S. *breów*-an, to brew), grow-*th*, steal-*th*, til-*th*, heigh-*t*, ligh-*t*.

*Note* 1.—The earliest form of the suffix was *-ith*, which by means of the *i* produced the vowel-mutation in *length*, *breadth*, *strength* (from *long*, *broad*, *strong*). See § 452 (6).

*Note* 2.—Another form of this suffix was *-et* (not Diminutive, like the Romanic *-et* in "eagl-*et*"); this appears in the A.S. *þicc-et*, now written *thick-et*.

*Excluded word* :—

**Faith**.—Fr. *feid*, Lat. *fid*-es; *feid* was pronounced *feith* from the beginning; but *d* was used, as there was no symbol for *th* in French.

(37) **-ter, -ther, -der** (A.S. *-dor, -ðer, -der*), agent, action :—

Mo-*ther*, bro-*ther*, rud-*der*, spi(n)-*der* (the insect that spins), slaugh-*ter* (base *slay*; A.S. *slah*-an, to kill), mur-*der* (A.S. mor-*ðor*).

(38) **-y, -ey, -ie** (A.S. *-ig*) : generally Diminutive :—

Bod-*y* (A.S. bod-*ig*), hon-*ey*, Bill-*y*, bird-*ie*, lass-*ie*, ladd-*ie*.

*Excluded words* :—

**Puppy** : Fr. *poupée*, Lat. *pupa*, a girl, doll.
**Lady**, loaf-kneader : A.S. *hláf-dige*; see p. 313.
**Monkey** : Old Ital. *monicchio*, dim. of *mona*, an ape.
**Money** : Mid. Eng. *moneie*, Old Fr. *moneie*, Lat. *moneta*, a mint.
**Valley** : Old Fr. *valee*, Ital. *vallata*, formed like a valley.
**Fairy** : Old Fr. *fae-rie*, from Late Lat. *fata* (with suffix *-ry*), in which the *t* has been lost. It literally meant "enchantment."

(39) **-y** (A.S. *e*, the place of action) :—

Smith-*y* (A.S. smiððe-*e*, a smith's shop), steth-*y* (place for anvil).

*Excluded word* :—

**Lobby** : Low Lat. *lobia*, a gallery or covered way.

B. *Adjective-forming.*

**567. Separable,** or formerly separable :—

(1) **-fast** (A.S. *fæst,* firm, sure) :—

Stead-*fast* (Mid. Eng. stede-*fast,* firm or fast in its stead or place), shame-*faced* (for shame-*fast,* A.S. scam-*fæst,* firm in modesty).

(2) **-fold** (A.S. *feald*) : added to cardinal numbers :—

Two-*fold,* three-*fold,* mani-*fold,* etc.

(3) **-ful** (A.S. *ful,* that is, full) :—

Hope-*ful,* play-*ful,* fear-*ful,* dread-*ful,* *grace-*ful,* *grate-*ful.*

*Excluded words :—*

**Forget-ful :** a mistaken rendering of A.S. *forgit-el.*
**Wake-ful :** a mistaken rendering of A.S. *wac-ol.*

(4) **-less** (A.S. *léas,* loose or free from ; has no connection whatever with the comparative adjective or adverb *less,* but is the Eng. form of the Norse word *loose*).

*With nouns.*—Fear-*less,* hap-*less,* luck-*less,* *sense-*less,* hope-*less,* worth-*less.*

*With verbs* (rare).—*Resist-*less,* *fade-*less,* *cease-*less,* reck-*less.*

(5) **-like** (A.S. *lic,* like or similar).—In older words, the suffix is usually *-ly,*—in more modern ones it is *-like.* For **-ly,** see below, § 568 (21).

God-*like,* life-*like,* war-*like,* business-*like,* *saint-*like* (or saint-*ly*).

(6) **-right** (A.S. *riht*), direction :—

Up-*right,* down-*right.*

(7) **-some, -som** (A.S. *sum,* from the same root (*sama*) as Eng. *same*) :—

(*a*) *With nouns.*—Burden-*some,* trouble-*some,** hand-*some,* toil-*some.*
(*b*) *With adjectives.*—Glad-*some,* ful-*some,* whole-*some,* weari-*some.*
(*c*) *With verbs.*—Irk-*some,* tire-*some,* bux-*om* (A.S. *búg-an,* to bend).

The joyous playmate of the *buxom* breeze.—COLERIDGE.

(8) **-teen** (A.S. *tén,* Eng. *ten*), ten by addition ; **-ty** (A.S. *tig*), ten by multiplication :—

Four-*teen,* fif-*teen,* etc. ; twen-*ty* (A.S. twen-*tig*), thir-*ty,* for-*ty,* etc.

(9) **-ward** (A.S. *weard,* inclined ; A.S. *weorth-an,* to become) :—

Fro-*ward* (A.S. from-*weard*), way-*ward* (away-*ward*), for-*ward.*

(10) **-wart** (A.S. *weorth,* Eng. *worth* or *worthy*) :—

Stal-*wart* (worthy of its *stǽl* or foundation).

(11) **-wise** (A.S. *wís*, knowing, wise):—

Right-*eous* for right-*wise* (wise in what is right); weather-*wise*.

**568. Inseparable:—**

(12) **-d, -ed** (Past participial ending of Weak verbs; A.S. *-d*; cf. Lat. pp. *-tus*: see p. 223, footnote 2):—

Love-*d*, dea-*d*, *place-*d*, col-*d* (cf. Lat. *gel*-u, noun), lou-*d*, wil-*d* (actuated by *will*), wretch-*ed* (made a wretch).

(13) **-el, -le, -l** (A.S. *-ol, -el*):—

Britt-*le* (A.S. *breót*-an, to break), fick-*le* (A.S. ge-*fic*, a fraud), id-*le* (A.S. íd-*el*), ev-*il* (A.S. yf-*el*), fou-*l* (A.S. fú-*l*; cf. Lat. *pu*-tridus), rake-*hell* (a misspelling of M.E. rak-*el*, rash, dissolute; cf. Eng. *rake*, in which the last syllable has been lost).

(14) **-en, -n** (Past participial suffix of Strong verbs):—

Drunk-*en*, hew-*n*, forlor-*n*, op-*en* (that which is *up*).

(15) **-en, -n** (A.S. *-en*, made of, pertaining to; cf. Lat. *-in*-us, as in "sui-*ĭn*-us": cf. A.S. *swín*, swine, § 489, *Note* 3):—

Beech-*en*, wood-*en*, earth-*en*, heath-*en* (man of the *heath*).

(16) **-er, -est** (signs of Comp. and Superl.):—

Hott-*er*, hott-*est*, etc.; be-*st* (short for bet-*est*, bet-*st*).

(17) **-er, -r** (A.S. *-or, -er*): not Comparative:—

Slipp-*er*-y (A.S. slip-*or*, with added *y*), fai-*r* (A.S. fæg-*er*).

(18) **-ern** (allied to "run"; A.S. *irn*-an): direction:—

North-*ern*, south-*ern*, north-*er*-ly (with *n* omitted), south-*er*-ly.

(19) **-ing** (Pres. part. suffix; earliest form *-inde* (Southern dialect), which was superseded by *-inge, -ing*; see § 517):—

Charm-*ing*, astonish-*ing*, middl-*ing* (added to adj. *middle*).

*Note.*—The Pres. participles of Trans. verbs become like real adjectives, when they are not followed by an object:—

It astonishes me = it is astonishing (= wonderful, marvellous) *to* me.

(20) **-ish, -sh, -ch** (A.S. *-isc*; cf. Gr. *-iskos*, Lat. *-iscus*, Fr. *-esque*): diminutive and sometimes depreciative:—

Rom-*ish*, woman-*ish* (fit for a woman, but not fit for a man), *pal-*ish*, redd-*ish*, snapp-*ish* (inclined to *snap*), Fren-*ch* (Frank-*ish*).

(21) **-ly** (an abridged and "inseparable" form of A.S. *-líc*):—

God-*ly* (pious), woman-*ly* (contrast "woman-*ish*"), man-*ly*.

*Note.*—The force of *-ly* in composition with adjectives usually implies "rather," in this point resembling *-ish*:—

Sick-*ly* (rather sick, inclined to be sick), poor-*ly*, clean-*ly*, weak-*ly*.

(22) **-most** (A.S. *mest*, compounded of *-ma* and *-est*; § 498):—

Fore-*most*, in-*most*, ut-*most*, hind-*most*, etc.

(23) **-ow, -w** (A.S. *-we, -u*):—

Call-*ow*, fall-*ow*, mell-*ow*, fe-*w*, ra-*w*, slo-*w*, tr-*ue*.

(24) **-t, -th** (A.S. *-t, -ð*: cf. suffix *-d* under (12):—

*-t*: clef-*t*, ref-*t*, lef-*t*, bough-*t*, swif-*t*, brigh-*t*, ligh-*t*, righ-*t*.
*-th*: un-cou-*th*, sou-*th* (A.S. sú-*ð*, "the *sunned* quarter"), four-*th*.

*Excluded word*:—

**Both**: A.S. *bá*, two; cf. Lat. am-*bo*; *th* means "the," "they."

(25) **-ther** (A.S. *-ðer*, Comparative suffix; see § 498, 3):—

O-*ther*, whe-*ther*, fur-*ther*, ne-*ther*, etc.

*Excluded word*:—

**Rather**: comparative of obsolescent *rathe* (early).

(26) **-y** (A.S. *-ig*):—

Might-*y*, craft-*y*, char-*y* (A.S. cear-*ig*, full of *care*), *flower-*y*, an-*y* (A.S. ǽn-*ig*), naught-*y* (cf. *naught*, from A.S. *ná wiht*=not a whit).

*Excluded word*:—

**Every**: a compound formed of A.S. *ǽfre*, ever, and *ælc*, each.

## C. *Verb-forming.*

**569** (1) **-en, -n** (causal). In A.S. there was a class of causal verbs formed by adding the Infin. suffix *-ian* to a Strong past participle, as "ágn-*ian*" (to own), formed with pp. *ágen*, *ágn*. When the Infin. suffix was lost, no suffix was left but that of **-en** or **-n**. As this had been associated with causal verbs, it became an independent causal suffix, and can now be added to adjectives and even to nouns:—

Bright-*en*, black-*en*; height-*en*, length-*en*; drow-*n*, lear-*n*.

(2) **-k** (frequentative or intensive):—

Hear-*k*, hear-*k*-en, lur-*k* (Scand. *lure*, to lie in wait), scul-*k* (allied to *scowl*), smir-*k* (akin to *smile*, *smir*-en), stal-*k* (A.S. *stæl*, a stem).

*Doubtful word*:—

**Talk**, generally considered to be a frequentative of *tell*, but without authority. In other Aryan languages the root *talc* or *talk* means to interpret. Yet *talk* in English looks like a frequentative of *tell*.

(3) **-se** (A.S. *s*-ian):—

Clean-*se* (A.S. *clǽne*, clean), rin-*se* (base, Scand. *hreinn*, *rein*, pure), clap-*s* (now written *clasp*), grap-*s* (now written *grasp*).

(4) **-sk** (of Scand. origin: *-sk* stands for *sik*, which means self; the suffix is therefore reflexive):—

Ba-*sk* (bathe or warm oneself), bu-*sk* (prepare oneself).

(5) **-le, -el, -l** (chiefly frequentative; sometimes denotes mere continuance, and sometimes has a causal or transitive force):—

*Verbs of imitative origin.*—Babb-*le*, cack-*le*, crack-*le*, chuck-*le*, gabb-*le*, gigg-*le*, gobb-*le*, jang-*le*, jing-*le*, mumb-*le*, ratt-*le*, rumb-*le*, rust-*le*, tatt-*le*, tink-*le*, warb-*le*, whist-*le*.

*Frequentative or continuative.*—Crumb-*le*, drizz-*le*, dwind-*le*, hurt-*le*, hur-*l*, knee-*l*, ming-*le*, wagg-*le*, whirl-*l*, wrest-*le*.

*Transitive or Causal.*—Curd-*le*, jost-*le*, start-*le*, stif-*le*.

*Excluded words*:—

**Tremble**: Fr. *trembler*, Late Lat. *trem-ul-are*. The *b* in *tremble* is intrusive; cf. *hum-b-le*, from Lat. *hum-il-is*.

**Gargle**: Old Fr. *gargouill-er*, to gargle.

**Gurgle**: Ital. *gorgoli-are*, to purl, bubble.

**Grovel, darkle, sidle**: verbs formed from the adverbs *grovling*, *darkling*, *side-long*, which were mistaken for pres. participles. See § 537.

**Broil**: of French origin; *bruiller*, from Old Fr. *bruir*, to roast.

(6) **-er, -r.** This is merely another form of *-el*, *-l*:—

*Verbs of imitative origin.*—Chatt-*er*, clatt-*er*, jabb-*er*, gibb-*er*, patt-*er*, simm-*er*, titt-*er*, twitt-*er*, mutt-*er*, whisp-*er*.

*Other verbs.*—Blust-*er*, clamb-*er*, flick-*er*, glimm-*er*, simp-*er*, whimp-*er*.

(7) **-y** (the *i* of Inf. *-ian*): ferr-*y* (A.S. fer-*ian*), tarr-*y* (Mid. Eng. tar-*ien*).

*Note.*—Verbs of French origin sometimes formed the Infin. in *-ien* in Mid. Eng., as if they had come from Teut. *-ian*. The form *-ien* with the loss of *-en* became *-y*; as Mid. Eng. sal-*ien*, Mod. Eng. sall-*y* (Fr. saill-*ir*, Lat. sal-*ire*); Mid. Eng. mar-*ien*, Mod. Eng. marr-*y* (Fr. *marier*, Lat. marit-*are*).

For Adverb-suffixes, see §§ 533-537.

## CHAPTER XXIX.—ROMANIC PREFIXES AND SUFFIXES.

### SECTION 1.—PREFIXES.

(*Hybrids are marked with an asterisk.*)

**570. Romanic prefixes.**—Latin and neo-Latin (French).

(1) **A-, ab-, abs-** (*from, away*):—

*A*-vert, *ab*-use, *ab*-normal, *abs*-ent, *abs*-tain, *abs*-cond.

(2) **Ad-** (to): *ad-*, *ac-*, *af-*, *ag-*, *al-*, *an-*, *ap-*, *ar-*, *as-*, *at-*, *a-*:—

*Ad*-vice, *ab*-breviate, *ac*-cent, *af*-fable, *ag*-gressor, *al*-lude, *an*-nex, *ap*-pear, *ar*-rears, *as*-sert, *at*-tain, *a*-spect (final *d* being lost).

*Note.*—*A(f)-ford* is from A.S. *ge-forth*-ian; *a(f)-fair* is from a Fr. phrase *à faire*, to do. *Advance*, *advantage* are from Lat. *ab ante*; the *d* is intrusive. *Adventure* is from Fr. *aventure*, with Fr. prefix *a* (from ab), which was needlessly changed into *ad*.

(3) **Ambi-, amb-, am-** (*around*) :—

*Ambi*-dexterous, *amb*-iguous, *amb*-ient, *amb*-ition, *am*-putate.

(4) **Ante-, anti-, ant-** (*before*) :—

*Ante*-cedent, *anti*-cipate, *anci*-ent (with excrescent *t*, from Fr. *anci-en*, Late Lat. *anti-anus*), *ant*-ique, *ant*-ic.

(5) **Bene-** (*well*) :—

*Bene*-fit, *bene*-volent, *bene*-diction, *ben*-ison, *bene*-ficence.

(6) **Bis-, bi-, bin-** (*twice, two*) :—

*Bis*-cuit (Lat. *bis coctus*), *bi*-sect, **bi*-cycle, *bin*-ocular.

(7) **Circum-, circu-** (*around*) :—

*Circum*-spect, *circum*-stance, *circu*-it, *circu*-itous.

(8) **Con-** (*with*) : also *col*-, *com*-, *cor*-, or *co*- (Fr. *coun*-) :—

*Con*-tend, *col*-lege, *com*-mend, *cor*-rect, *co*-gnate, *coun*-sel.

(9) **Contra-, contro-, counter-** (through Fr. *contre*, against) :—

*Contra*-dict, *contro*-versy, *countr*-y, *contr*-ol (for *counter*-roll).

*Note.*—In the word "en-counter," *counter* appears a stem, to which *en*- is prefixed.

(10) **De-** (*down, away from, astray, reversal, intensive*) :—

**De** (*down*) : *de*-scend, *de*-grade, *de*-crease, *de*-spair, *de*-jected.
**De** (*away from*) : *de*-part, *de*-duce, *de*-duct, *de*-camp, **de*-tach.
**De** (*astray*) : *de*-viate, *de*-lirious, *de*-bauch, *de*-lude, *de*-face.
**De** (*reversal*) : *de*-odorise, *de*-plete, *de*-cipher, *de*-merit.
**De** (*intensive*) : *de*-liver, *de*-clare, **de*-file, *de*-fend, *de*-fraud.

*Note.*—"De" (*down*) is sometimes used as the opposite to "ad" (*up*) : *de*-preciate, *ap*-preciate ; *de*-scend, *a*-scend ; *de*-clivity, *ac*-clivity. Sometimes it is used as the opposite to *in*- or *en*- : *de*-crease, *in*-crease ; *de*-throne, *en*-throne ; *de*-camp, *en*-camp ; *de*-cline, *in*-cline.

(11) **Demi-** (*half*) : *demi*-god, *demi*-official, *demi*-quaver.

(12) **Dis-, di-** ; **dif-** before words beginning with *f* :—

**Dis-** (*asunder, aside*) : *dis*-tract, *dis*-member, *dis*-miss, *dis*-perse.
**Dis-** (*intensive*) : *dis*-annul, *dis*-sever, *di*-minish, *di*-rect.
**Dis-** (*oppositive* or *negative*) : con-fident, *dif*-fident ; facility or faculty, *dif*-ficulty ; ease, *dis*-ease ; please, *dis*-please.
**Dis-** (*reversal*) : enchant, *dis*-enchant ; illusion, *dis*-illusion ; enfranchise, *dis*-franchise.

(13) **Duo-, du-,** Fr. **dou-, deu-, do-** (*two*) :—

*Duo*-decimal, *du*-et, *dou*-ble, *deu*-ce, *do*-zen (O. Fr. *do*-saine).

(14) **Ex-, e-** (*off, out*) : appears as *ef*-, when followed by *f* :—

*Ex*-ample, *ex*-alt, *e*-lapse, *e*-normous, *ef*-fort, *ef*-fect.

*Note.*—*Ex* may denote loss of office ; as, **ex*-king, *ex*-empress.

(15) **Extra-** (*exter-ā*, Fem. Abl. of *exter*-us), **exter-** :—

*Exter*-nal, *exter*-ior, *extr*-eme, *extra*-vagant, *extr*(*a*)-aneous.

(16) **For-** (O. Fr. *for-*, Lat. *foris*, out of doors):—

*For*-feit (Lat. *foris* factum), *for*-close (misspelt as *fore*-close).

(17) **In-**: Fr. **en-, em-**; becomes *il-*, *im-*, *ir-*:—

*In*-ject, *il*-lustrate, *im*-pute, *ir*-rigate, *en*-tice, *em*-ploy.

*Note* 1.—Double spellings:—*in*-close, *en*-close; *in*-dorse, *en*-dorse; *in*-twine, *en*-twine; *in*-circle, *en*-circle; *in*-sure, *en*-sure.

*Note* 2.—Prefixed to a noun or adjective, it makes Trans. verbs:—

**En*-dear, *en*-rich, *en*-large, **en*-slave, *en*-title, **em*-body, *im*-peril.

*Note* 3.—The Fr. form *en-* must not be confounded with the Greek *en-*, as in the word "*en*-cyclical."

(18) **In-** (not): can become *il-*, *im-*, *ir-*, *i-*:—

*In*-firm, *il*-literate, *im*-pious, *ir*-regular, *i*-gnorance.

*Note.*—The Lat. *in-* and the Eng. *un-* are equivalent; hence some words are spelt both ways: *in*-frequent or *un*-frequent, *in*-cautious or *un*-cautious, *in*-stable or *un*-stable, *in*-apt or *un*-apt.

(19) **Ind-, indi-** (Old Lat. *indo*, within; cf. Gr. *endon*):—

*Ind*-igent, *indi*-genous.

(20) **Infra-** (*infer-â*, Fem. abl. of *infer*-us), **infer-**:—

*Infer*-ior, *infer*-nal.

(21) **Inter-**, Fr. **entre-, enter-** (*between, among*):—

*Inter*-preter, *inter*-est, *intel*-lect, *enter*-tain, *enter*-prise.

(22) **Intro-, intra-** (*within*):—

*Intro*-duce, *intro*-spection, *intra*-tropical, *intr*-insic.

(23) **Juxta-** (*close by*): *juxta*-position.

(24) **Male-, mali-**, Fr. **mal-** (*badly*):—

*Male*-factor, *male*-volence, *mali*-gnant, *mal*-ice, *mal*-ady.

(25) **Mis-** (from Lat. *minus*, badly; distinct from Eng. *mis-*):—

*Mis*-adventure, *mis*-chief, *mis*-chance, *mis*-creant, *mis*-nomer.

(26) **Ne-, neg-** (not): *ne*-farious, *ne*-uter; *neg*-otiate, *neg*-lect.

(27) **Non-** (not): *non*-sense, *non*-entity, *non*-age, *non*-descript.

*Note.*—"Non" is less emphatic than "in-" or "un-"; the former is merely *negative*, denoting the absence of something; the latter is *positive*, and denotes the presence of some opposite quality. Compare *non*-religious with *ir*-religious (profane), *non*-Christian with *un*-Christian (heathenish), *non*-famous with *in*-famous (disreputable), *non*-professional with *un*-professional (unworthy of the profession).

But in some words the *non* has become emphatic; as *non*-sense (rubbish), *non*-entity (one not worth noticing).

(28) **Ob-** (*against*): older form *obs-*: hence **os-**:—

*Ob*-tuse, *ob*-ject, *oc*-cur, *of*-ficer, *op*-press, *os*-tensible, *o*-mit.

(29) **Pene-** (almost): *pen*-ultimate, *pen*-insula.

(30) **Per-**, Fr. **par-** (through); can become *pel-* :—

*Per*-form, **per*-haps, *pel*-lucid, *par*-don, *par*-lous (Shaks.).

*Note.*—*Per*, like the Teutonic *for*, sometimes passes from the notion of *thoroughness* to that of going *too far* or going *in a wrong direction* :—

*Per*-vert, *per*-sist, *per*-jure, *per*-fidy, *per*-ish, *per*-dition.

(31) **Post-** (*after*) : *post*-script, *post*-date, *post*-pone.

(32) **Por-** (O. Lat. *port* ; cf. Eng. *forth*) : *por*-tend, *pol*-lute.

(33) **Pos-** (Lat. *potis* ; cf. des-*pot*) : *pos*-sible, *pos*-sess.

(34) **Pre-** (Lat. *præ*, before) : *pre*-caution, *pre*-pare, *pre*-dict.

(35) **Preter-** (beyond) : *preter*-natural, *preter*-ite.

(36) **Pro-**, Fr. **pour**, whence *por-*, *pur-* (*before*, *instead of*) :—

*Pro*-fession, *pro*(d)-igal, *pour*-tray, *por*-trait, *pur*-vey, *pur*-pose.

(37) **Quad-**, **quadr-**, **quart-** (Lat. *quatuor*, *quart*-us, four, fourth) :—

*Quadr*-angle, *quadr*-ant, *quar*-antine (Lat. *quadraginta*, forty).

(38) **Quasi** (*as if*, *in pretence*) : *quasi*-judge (a sham judge).

(39) **Quondam** (*formerly*) : *quondam*-judge (a former judge).

(40) **Quinque** (*five*), **quintus** (*fifth*) :—

*Quinqu*-ennial (five-yearly), *quintu*-ple, *quint*-essence.

(41) **Red-** (*back*, *again*), **re-** (before consonants) :—

*Re*-course, *re*-act, **re*-new, **re*-set, *red*-eem, *red*-undant.

*Note.*—A hyphen after *re* gives the prefix the emphatic sense of *again* :—

Recover (get back), re-cover (cover again) ; redress (set right), re-dress (dress again) ; rejoin (answer), re-join (join again, return to).

(42) **Retro-** (*back* or *backwards*) :—

*Retro*-cession, *retro*-grade, *retro*-spection, *retro*-version.

(43) **Sed-** (*apart from*), **se-** (before consonants) :—

*Se*-clude, *se*-parate, *se*-crete, *se*-cure, *se*-duce, *se*-cede, *sed*-ition.

(44) **Semi-** (*half* ; cf. *demi-*) : *semi*-circle, **semi*-colon.

(45) **Sine-** (*without*) : *sine*-cure (pay without care or work).

(46) **Sub-** (*under*) : *suc-*, *suf-*, *sug-*, *sum-*, *sup-*, *sur-*, *sus-*, *su-* :—

*Sub*-ject, *suc*-cour, *suf*-fice, *sug*-gest, *sum*-mon, *sup*-pose, *sur*-reptitious, *sus*-pend, *su*-spect (root, *spec*-ere, *spect*-us, to see).

*Note* 1.—Prefixed to an adjective it means *rather* (cf. Eng. suffix *-ish*) : *sub*-acid, *sub*-tropical, *sub*-tepid (= warm-*ish*).

*Note* 2.—Prefixed to a noun, it denotes subordination :—

*Sub*-judge, *sub*-committee, *sub*-deputy, *sub*-division.

*Note* 3.—Prepositional force : *sub*-terranean, *sub*-marine.

(47) **Subter-** (*under*) : *subter*-fuge.

(48) **Super-**, Fr. **sur-** (*above, over, beyond*):—

*Super*-lative, *sur*-charge (*over*-charge), *sur*-face, *sur*-vive.

*Note.*—In the sense of "very," as *super*-fine = very fine. In the sense of excess, as *super*-fluous.

(49) **Trans-**, **tra-** (*across*):—

*Trans*-mit, *tran*(s)-scend, *tra*-verse, *tra*-ffic, *tra*-dition, *tra*-itor.
*Prepositional force.*—*Trans*-Atlantic, *trans*-continental.

(50) **Tri-**, Fr. **tre-** (*three, thrice*):—

*Tri*-angle, *tri*-ad, *tri*-colour, *tri*-vial, *tre*-ble, *tre*-foil.

(51) **Ultra-** (*beyond, excessively*):—

*Prepositional* ("beyond"): *ultra*-montane, *ultra*-marine.
*Qualifying* ("excessively"): *ultra*-radical, *ultra*-liberal.

(52) **Vice-**, Fr. **vis-** (*instead of*): *vice*-roy, *vis*-count.

**571. Disguised Prefixes**: through French influence. (For the difference between *Late* Lat. and *Low* Lat. the student is referred to the footnote in p. 385.)

**Ab-**: *av*-aunt (Lat. *ab ante*), *v*-an-guard (Fr. *av*-ant-warde), *adv*-ance, *adv*-antage (the last two with an intrusive *d*).

**Ad-**: *ex*-cise (Dutch *aksiis*, corruption of Old Fr. *assise*, a tax), *a*-lert (Fr. *alerte, à l'erte*, on the watch; *a* stands for Lat. *ad*), *af*-fair (Fr. *à faire*, something to do).

**Ante-**: *an*-cestor (Old Fr. *an*-cessour, Lat. *ante*-cessor).

**Bi-**: *ba*-lance (Fr. *ba*-lance, Lat. *bi*-lancem, having two scales).

**Con-**, **co-**: *cu*-stom (Late Lat. *con*-suetumen), **cur*-ry (O. Fr. *con*-roi), *co*-ver (Lat. *co*-operire), *co*-venant (Old Fr. *con*-venant), *co*-unt (Lat. *com*-putare), *co*-unt (noun, Lat. *com*-item), *co*-uch (Lat. *col*-locare), *co*-st (Lat. *con*-stare), *co*-il and *cu*-ll (Lat. *col*-ligere), *co*-stive (Lat. *con*-stipatus), *cou*-sin (Lat. *con*-sobrinus), *cu*-rfew (O. Fr. *co*-vre-feu, covering of fires), *ke*-rchief (O. Fr. *co*-vre-chef, covering to the head).

**De-**: *di*-stil (Lat. *de*-stillare).

**Dis-**, **di-**: *des*-cant, *des*-sert (the last course at dinner), *de*-feat, *de*-fy, *de*-luge, *s*-pend (Lat. *dis*-pendere), *s*-tain (for *dis*-tain), *de*-bark (Fr. *des*-barquer).

**Ex-**, **e-**: *a*-mend (but *e*-mendation), *af*-fray (Low Lat. *ex*-frediare), *a*-fraid (pp. of *affray*), *as*-tonish (Lat. *ex*-tonare), *es*-cape (Lat. *ex* cappâ, out of one's cape), *es*-planade (Lat. *ex*-planata), *es*-cort (Lat. *ex*-correctus), *es*-cheat (Old Fr. *es*-chet, pp. of *es*-cheoir, Lat. *ex*-cadere), *es*-say (Lat. *ex*-agium, a trial of weight), *is*-sue (Lat. *ex*-ire), *s*-ample (Lat. *ex*-emplum), *s*-carce (Lat. *ex*-cerptus), *s*-corch (Lat. *ex*-cortic-are, take off bark or rind), *s*-courge (Lat. *ex*-coriata, flayed off), *s*-ombre (*ex* umbrâ, from the shade), *s*-camp (Old Fr. *es*-camper), *s*-camper (run away), *s*-luice (Lat. *ex*-clusa), *s*-cour (*ex*-curare), *s*-ewer (*ex*-aquaria), *s*-prain (Lat. *ex*-primere), *s*-quare (Lat. *ex*-quadrare; so also *s*-quadron).

**Extra-**: *stra*-nge (Lat. *extr*(*a*)-aneus, external).

**Intra-**: *entr*-ails (Old Fr. *entr*-ailles, Late Lat. *intr*(*a*)-alia).

**In-** (*in*): *an*-oint (Lat. *in*-unctus), *am*-bush (Low Lat. *im*-boscare) *en*-tail (Fr. *en*-tailler, to cut into).

**In-** (*not*): *en*-emy (Lat. *in*-imicus, hence *in*-imical).

**Juxta-**: *joust* (Late Lat. *juxt*-are), **jost*-le (freq. of *joust*-en).

**Male-**: *mau*-gre (in spite of, Fr. *mau*=male, *gré*=gratum).

**Non-**: *um*-pire (older form *num*-pire, Old Fr. *non*-per, peerless; *a numpire* was changed to *an umpire*).

**Per-**: *pil*-grim (Ital. *pell*-egrino, Lat. *per*-egrinus), *par*-don (Lat *per*-don-are), *par*-son (Lat. *per*-sona).

**Post-**: *pu*-ny or *puis*-né (Old Fr. *puis*-né, *post*-natus, born after).

**Pre-**: *pre*-ach (Lat. *præ*-dicare), *pro*-vost (Lat. *præ*-positus, one placed in authority), *pr*-ize, *pr*-ison (Lat. *pre*-hensum).

**Pro-**: *pr*-udent (short for Lat. *pro*-videntem, one who looks before)

**Re-**: *re*(*n*)-der (Fr. *ren*-dre, Lat. *red*-dere), *r*-ally (Fr. *r*-allier, Lat *re*+alligare, to bind together), *r*-ansom (Old Fr. *ra*-enson, Lat. *red* emptionem), *ru*-nagate (corrupt form of *re*-negade, Lat. *re*-negatus).

**Retro-**: *rear*-guard (older spelling *rere*-ward), *rere*-dos.

**Se-**: *s*-ober (Lat. *se*, apart; *ebrius*, intoxicated), *s*-ure (a short form of *se*-cure (Lat. *se*-curus).

**Semi-**: *sin*-ciput (lit. half the head, the fore part of the head).

**Sub-**: *su*-dden (Late Lat. *sub*-itaneus, Old Fr. *so*-dain), *so*-journ (Late Lat. *sub*+diurn-are, to stay, Old Fr. *so*-journ-er), *s*-ombre (*sub* umbra, under the shade; but see above under **Ex**).

**Supr-**: *sopr*-ano, *sover*-eign, *sovr*-an (Late Lat. super-*aneus*), *su*-zer ain (Late Lat. *sur*-ser-anus, Lat. *su*-rsum, upwards).

**Trans-**: *tres*-pass, *tre*-ason, *tres*-tle (Late Lat. *trans*-tellum, dim of *trans*-trum), *tranc*-e (Fr. *trans*-e, Lat. *trans*-itum, a passing away)

**Tri-**: *tra*-mmel (Fr. *tra*-mail, Lat. *tri*+macula, a net).

**Ultra-**: *outr*(*a*)-age (Old Fr. *oltr*-age, excessive violence).

## Section 2.—Suffixes.

(*Hybrids are marked with an asterisk.*)

### A. *Noun-forming.*

**572.** (1) **-ace** (Lat. *-atio*, *-acia*, *-atium*; Fr. *-ace*, *-asse*):—

Popul-*ace*, terr-*ace*, pinn-*ace*, grim-*ace*, men-*ace*, pal-*ace*, sp-*ace*.

*Excluded word*:—

**Place**: Fr. *place*, Lat. *platea*, Gr. *plateia*, Fem. adj., "broad."

(2) **-ade** (Lat. *-ata*, Fem. of *-atus*; Span. *-ada*; Fr. *-ade*):—

Balustr-*ade*, colonn-*ade*, brig-*ade*, crus-*ade*, *block-*ade*.

*Imitations.*—Orange-*ade*, ginger-*ade*, lemon-*ade*.

*Disguised.*—Ball-*ad* (Fr. ball-*ade*), cust-*ard* for crust-*ade*.

*Naturalised words.*—Arm-*ada* (Spanish), son-*ata* (Ital.).

*Excluded word*:—

**Cockade**: Fr. coqu-*arde* (Fem. form of suffix *-ard*).

(3) **-ado** (Lat. *-atus*, Masc.; Span. *-ado*, Masc.; *-ada*, Fem. but in English *-ado* was sometimes wrongly put for Fem. *-ada*):—

Desper-*ado*, bastin-*ado* (for Fem. bastin-*ada*), torn-*ado* (for Fem. torn-*ada*), brav-*ado* (for Fem. brav-*ada*).

(4) **-age** (Lat. -*aticum*, Late Lat. -*agium*, Fr. -*age*):—

*Collective.*—Foli-*age*, plum-*age*, *bagg-*age*, herb-*age*, assembl-*age*.
*Abstract.*—Cour-*age*, *bond-*age*, *till-*age*, *pilot-*age*, vassal-*age*.
*Place of action*, etc.—Hermit-*age*, *cott-*age*, parson-*age*, vill-*age*.
*Result of action.*—*Break-*age*, *leak-*age*, *age* (L. Lat. æt-*aticum*).
*Cost of action.*—*Broker-*age*, post-*age*, *cart-*age*, carri-*age*.
*Agent.*—Sav-*age* (Lat. silv-*aticus*, Fr. *sauvage*, a man of the woods), host-*age* (Late Lat. obsid-*aticus*).

*Imitations*:—

Langu-*age*, cabb-*age*, bever-*age*, surplus-*age*, saus-*age*.

*Excluded words*:—

**Hemorrhage**: the final *age* is here part of the root of a Greek verb.
**Selvage**, lit. "self-edge," from Old Dut. *self-egge*.
**Presage**: the final -*age* is part of the Lat. root *sag-ire*, to perceive.
**Spinage**, or **spinach**: Lat. spin-*aceus*, a herb with prickly leaf.
**Rage**, a variant of *rave*, Lat. *rab*-ies. But "outrage" has the suffix *age* + Lat. *ultra*, beyond, Fr. *outr-*: outr-*age*.

(5) **-al, -als** (Lat. -*alia*, Neut. Plur.); hence the suffix -*als* is made a plural in English. But the Lat. -*alia* gradually became -*aille* in French, which is a Fem. Singular suffix; and this became -*al* or -*le* in English. Thus we have Late Lat. batt-*alia*, Old Fr. bat-*aille*, Mid. Eng. bat-*ail*, Mod. Eng. batt-*le*:—

Victu-*als*, nupti-*als*, *bestow-*al*, tri-*al*, puzz-*le* (formerly spelt *opposayle*, *apposaile*, and *apposelle*; lit. that which *poses* or *puzzles*),[1] can-*al* (hence chann-*el*), minstr-*el* (Old Fr. *menestral*, Lat. *ministralis*), capit-*al* (hence catt-*le*, chatt-*els*), hospit-*al* (hence hot-*el*, host-*el*, and the now almost obsolete spitt-*le*, spit-*al*), jew-*el* (Lat. joc-*ale*).

*Excluded words*:—

**Vassal**: Low Lat. vass-*allus*, a form of *vassus*, a servant.
**Wassail**, A.S. *wes hál* = be hale, words used in drinking wine.
**Burial**, A.S. *byrgels*, a tomb, Mid. Eng. *buriel*. See § 491.

(6) **-an, -ain, -on, -en** (Lat. -*anus*, -*aneus*; Fr. -*ain*, -*en*):—

Public-*an*, de-*an* (Lat. dec-*anus*), Wesley-*an*, capt-*ain*, sext-*on* (for sacrist-*an*), *ward-*en*, *guard-(i)*an*, scriv-*en*-er (L. Lat. scrib-*anus*).

*Note.*—Peas-*ant* (O.F. pais-*an*), anci-*ent* (Late Lat. anti-*anus*), pheas-*ant*,—in all these words the final *t* is excrescent. Sover-*eign* is a misspelling of Old Fr. sover-*ain*, Late Lat. super-*aneus*; cf. for-*eign*, Late Lat. for-*aneus*.

(7) **-ance, -ence** (Lat. -*antiam*, -*entiam*; French -*ance*):—

Arrog-*ance*, *hindr-*ance*, *guid-*ance*, obedi-*ence* (Fr. obeis-*ance*).

(8) **-ancy, -ency.**—A more modern form of -*ance* and -*ence*:—

Brilli-*ancy*, vac-*ancy*, emerg-*ency*, constitu-*ency*.

---

[1] Skeat's *Student's Pastime*, ed. 1896, p. 131.

(9) **-and, -end** (Lat. *-andum, -endum*, Fr. *-ande* or *-ende*) :—

Divid-*end*, leg-*end*, vi-*and* or via-*ands* (Lat. viv-*enda*), preb-*end* ary, prov-*ende*-r (with intrusive *r*), lav-*ende*-r.

*Excluded words* :—

**Stipend**, from Lat. stipend-*ium*, where the *end* is part of th stem.

**Errand, husband** : both Teutonic, see § 566 (30).

(10) **-ant, -and, -ent** (Lat. *-antem, -entem* ; Fr. *-ant*) :—

Merch-*ant*, *ped-*ant*, brig-*and*, *tru-*ant*, stud-*ent*, tang-*ent*.

*Excluded words* :—

**Peas-ant**, from Old Fr. pais-*ant* or pais-*an*, another form of pag-*an*
**Pheas-ant** : Lat. Phasi-*ana* avis, the bird of the river Phasis.

(11) **-ar** (Lat. *-aris, -are*) : originally an adj. suffix :—

Schol-*ar*, pill-*ar*.

(12) **-ard, -art** (Low Lat. *-ardus*, from Teut. *hart* ; Old Fr *-ard* or *-art*) : depreciatory, or implying some kind of excess :—

Drunk-*ard*, cow-*ard* (O. Fr. cou-*ard*, a hare ; Lat. *cauda*, a tail named from the bob-tailed hare), wiz-*ard* (=witt-ish-*ard*).

*Disguised.*—Cock-*ade* (Fr. coqu-*arde*), cost-*er*-monger (for cost-*ard* an apple), duff-*er* (dowf-*art* ; from *dowf*, stupid), begg-*ar* (Low Lat. beg-*hard*-us ; see § 566, 24).

*Excluded words* :—

**Lizard** : Lat. *lacerta*, Fr. *lézard*, Mid. Eng. *lesarde*.
**Orchard** = *ort* + *yard*, "garden-garden" (see § 561, **Orchard**).
**Boulevard** : a corruption of *bulwark* (see § 559, **Bulwark**).
**Custard**, for *crustade* ; Old Fr. *croustade* (a pie made of crust).
**Leopard** = *leo* + *pardus*, a lion-pard.
**Steward** : A.S. *sti-weard*, keeper of sty or pen (§ 559, **Steward**).
**Bustard**, formerly *bistarde*, Lat. *avis tarda*, a slow bird.
**Hazard** : Span. *azar*, the die ; the *d* is excrescent.
**Gizzard** : Mid. Eng. *gis-er*, with excrescent *d*.
**Stalwart** : Mid. Eng. *stal-worth*, foundation-worthy (§ 559).
**Sweetheart**, modern form of Mid. Eng. *swete herte*, sweet heart.
**Rampart**, Old Fr. *rempar*, Lat. *re* (again) + *im* + *par*-are.
**Spikenard**, for *spiked-nard*, nard furnished with spikes.

(13) **-ary, -aire, -air, -ar, -er, -eer, -ier, -or** (Latin *-arius*, Fr *-aire, -ier, -er*) : denotes agent or person :—

Lapid-*ary*, Janu-*ary*, doctrin-*aire*, cors-*air*, vic-*ar*, arch-*er* (arcu-*arius*), butl-*er* (for bottl-*er*), millin-*er* (from *Milan*), volunt-*eer*, *crochet-*eer*, sold-*ier* (Lat. solid-*arius*, a mercenary), farr-*ier* (ferr-*arius*), chancell-*or*.

*Notes on peculiar words* :—messeng-*er*, scaveng-*er*, passeng-*er*,—in all these the *n* is intrusive : the orig. spellings were *messag-er*, etc. Cf. intrusive *n* in "nightingale" for A.S. "nihte-gale," p. 374.

Practit-*ion-er*, parish-*ion-er*, scriv-*en-er*,—in all these the final *-er* was unnecessary. "Practic-*ian*" and "parish-*ian*" were once used like "optic-*ian*." "Scriv-*en*-er" is from Late Lat. scrib-*anus*, a writer.

"Sorc-*er*-*er*": a second *er* added to Fr. sorc-*ier*, Lat. sort-i-*arius*.

"Squire," from Lat. scut-*arius* (one who has armorial bearings).

*Excluded words*:—

**Burgl-ar**, for burgl-*or*, Low Lat. *burgul-ator*; see below (46).

**Li-ar**: the suffix *-ar* is a disguised form of Teutonic *-er*.

**Begg-ar**: the suffix *-ar* is a disguised form of *-ardus* (Low Lat. *beg-hard-us*, *beghardus*); see § 566 (24).

(14) **-ary**, **-ier**, **-ar**, **-er** (Lat. *-ari-us*, *-a*, *-um*; Fr. *-iere*):—

Libr-*ary*, arm-*ory* (for arm-*ary*), chandel-*ier*, cell-*ar*, garn-*er* (variant of gran-*ary*), ew-*er* (aqu-*aria*, a water-vessel).

*Excluded words*:—

**Boundary**, corruption of bound-*er-y*.

**Attainder, remainder, rejoinder,**—in these words the final *-er* represents the final -re of the French Infinitive; as, attaind-*re*.

(15) **-arian** (double suffix, Lat. *-ari* + *anus*): denotes agent:—

Libr-*arian*, *gramm-*arian*, latitudin-*arian*, veget-*arian*.

(16) **-aster** (double suffix, *-as-ter*, allied to Teut. *-es-tre*): forms diminutive nouns in a depreciatory sense.

Poet-*aster*, ole-*aster* (the wild and inferior olive), critic-*aster*.

*Excluded word*:—

**Disaster** = evil star, from *dis* and *astrum*, a star.

(17) **-ate** (from the Latin suffixes shown below):—

(*a*) From *-atus*, *-ata*, Masc. or Fem. of Pass. Part):—

Advoc-*ate*, cur-*ate*, candid-*ate*, reneg-*ade* (hence runag-*ate*).

(*b*) From *-atum* (Neut. of Pass. Part.):—

Postul-*ate*, f-*ate*. (*Chemical terms*: nitr-*ate*, hydr-*ate*, etc.)

(*c*) From *-atem* (Accus. of nouns ending in *-as*):—

Prim-*ate*, magn-*ate*, potent-*ate*.

(*d*) From *-atus* (Fourth declension of Latin nouns):—

Consul-*ate*, magistr-*ate* (orig. the office, now the holder), st-*ate*.

*Excluded word*:—

**Apostate**: Gr. apo-*stat*-es, one who abandons his creed.

(18) **-cre**, **-chre** (Lat. *-crum*):—

Lu-*cre*, sepul-*chre* (Mid. Eng. sepul-*cre*). (*Imitat.* massacre.)

(19) **-cule**, **-cle** (Lat. *-culus*, *-cula*, *-culum*, Fr. *-cle*): a double Diminutive suffix, consisting of *-cu* + *-lus*):—

Reti-*cule*, un-*cle* (from Lat. avun-*culus*), gridd-*le* (Lat. crati-*culum*).

*Excluded words*:—

**Chronicle**, from Greek root: Old Fr. *chronique*. The *l* is intrusive.

**Icicle** = Anglo-Saxon *is* + *gicel*, a bit of ice; see § 559, p. 378.

(20) **-cy, -sy, -acy** (Lat. *-tia*).

Abstract nouns in *-acy* are formed from concrete ones in *-ate*:—

Magistr-*ate*, magistr-*acy*; prel-*ate*, prel-*acy*; cur-*ate*, cur-*acy*.

By degrees *-acy*, *-cy*, and *-sy* became independent suffixes:—

Pap-*acy*, *idiot-*cy*, *bankrupt-*cy*, *diploma-*cy*, ministrel-*sy*.

(21) **-ee, -ey, -y** (Masc. *ātus*, Fr. *-é*, or Fem. *-āta*, Fr. *-ée*):—

(1) *-ātus* (pp.): bail-*ee*, deput-*y*, attorn-*ey*, all-*y* (allig-*atus*).

*Imitations*: devot-*ee*, absent-*ee*, refug-*ee*, grand-*ee*, trust-*ee*.

(2) *-ātus* (4th Declension): duch-*y* (duc-*atus*), count-*y* (comit-*atus*), clerg-*y* (cleric-*atus*), treat-*y* (tract-*atus*).

(3) *-āta*, Fr. *-ée*:—jur-*y*, countr-*y*, journ-*ey*, arm-*y*, jell-*y*.

*Excluded words*:—

**Guarantee**: Old Fr. garant-*ie*, Fem. part. of garant-*ir*.
**Bull-y** (Old Low Germ.); bull-*aert*, a noisy fellow.
**Repartee**: Fr. repart-*ie*, Fem. part. of repart-*ir*.
**Enemy**: O. Fr. *enemi*, Lat. *inimicus* (for the loss of *c*, see § 417).

(22) **-el, -le, -l, -elle** (Lat. *-ellus* or *-illus, -a, -um*): Diminutive suffix. (Cognate with A.S. suffix **-el**):—

Lib-*el*, timbr-*el*, pann-*el*, mod-*el*, chap-*el*, pai-*l* (Lat. pat-*ella*), mant-*le*, mant-*el*, *shamb-*les*, gao-*l* (dim. of Lat. *gabia*), bagat-*elle*, fem-*ale* (Old Fr. fem-*elle*, Lat. fem-*ella*), umbr-*ella*.

*Note.*—In the words par-*c-el*, dam-*s-el*, vermi-*c-elli*, and violon-*c-ello*, we have two diminutive suffixes, *-c* and *-el*, *-elli* or *-ello*. Par-*c-el* = parti-*c-ella*; dam-*s-el* = domini-*c-elle*. For suffix *c*, see above (19).

(23) **-el, -le, -ele** (Lat. *-ela*: an Abstract suffix):—

Quarr-*el* (Lat. quer-*ela*), sequ-*el*, tut-*el*-age, client-*ele*, cand-*le*.

(24) **-en** (Lat. *-enus*, *-ena*, *-enum*, adjectival):—

Ali-*en*, ven-*om* (disguised from Lat. ven-*enum*), chai-*n*, cat-*ena*.

(25) **-eny, -iny** (Lat. *-inium*, *-inia*):—

Larc-*eny* (latroc-*inium*), ignom-*iny* (ignom-*inia*).

(26) **-ern** (Lat. *-erna*):—

Tav-*ern*, cav-*ern*, lant-*ern*, cist-*ern*.

*Excluded words*:—

**Lectern**: from Late Lat. *lectrinum*, a reading-desk.
**Postern**: Old Fr. post-*erle*, Lat. post-*erula*, a little back door.
**Slattern**, an untidy woman; of Scand. origin.
**Pastern**, Old Fr. past-*uron*; this joint was so called because a horse at *pasture* was tethered by the *pastern*.

(27) **-ess** (Late Lat. *-issa*, Fr. *-esse*): feminine suffix:—

Poet-*ess*, count-*ess*, *godd-*ess*, *shepherd-*ess*, etc.

(28) **-ess** (Lat. *-ensis*, as in Carthageni-*ensis*):—

*Burg-*ess*, *marq-*ess* or *marqu-*is* (governor of a march).

(29) **-et, -ot, -ette, -let** (French *-et*, Fem. *-ette*. The form *-let* consists of two suffixes, *-l* and *-et*): Diminutive suffix:—

Pell-*et*, *helm-*et* (A.S. *helm*, a covering), *owl-*et*, bull-*et*, chari-*ot*, piv-*ot* (dim. of *pipe*), statu-*ette*, *brook-*let*.

*Without diminutive force*:—*arm-*let*, *neck-*let*, cors-*let*.

*Excluded words*:—

**Com-et**: from Lat. com-*cta*, long-haired.
**Cover-let** is from Old French covre-*lit*, a *bed*-cover.
**Out-let** means a letting out (compound of the verb *let*).
**Magnet**: Lat. *magnetem* (lapidem) loadstone.
**Gauntlet**, misspelt for *gatlopp*; see § 559 under **Gauntlet**.
**Racket** or raquet, a battledore: Arab. *rahat*.
**Trivet**: A.S. *trefet*, from Lat. *tripod*-em.

(30) **-ic, -k, -ch, -ge** (Lat. *-icus*, *-ica*, *-icum*; Greek *-ikos*):—

Fanat-*ic*, rust-*ic*, mus-*ic*, fabr-*ic*, por-*ch* (Lat. port-*icus*), for-*ge* (Lat. fabr-*ica*), sil-*k* and ser-*ge* (Lat. ser-*icum*), *cler-*k* (Lat. cler-*ic*-us).

*Disguised suffix*.—Enemy (Lat. inim-*icus*, though O. Fr. *enem-i*).

(31) **-ice, -ish** (Lat. *-ix*, *-icem*, often combined with *-tr*):—

Pum-*ice*, rad-*ish* (from rad-*ix*, *-icem*), cocka-*tr-ice*, cica-*tr-ice*.

*Feminine suffixes*.—Testa-*tr-ix*, execu-*tr-ix*, etc.

(32) **-ice, -ise, -esse** (Lat. *-itius*, *-itia*, *-itium*, *-ities*):—

Nov-*ice*, solst-*ice*, fin-*esse*, serv-*ice*, just-*ice*, pent-*house* (corruption of O. Fr. apent-*is*; see § 560 under **Penthouse**), exerc-*ise*, prow-*ess*, rich-*es* (Fr. rich-*esse*, mistaken for an Eng. Plural, see § 491).

*Excluded words*:—

**Pract-ice**: of Greek origin, through Fr. pract-*ique*.
**Advice**: through Old Fr. *à vis*, according to my opinion.
**Pumice**: Lat. pum-*icem*, a pumice-stone.
**Bodice** (stays): corruption of bod-*ies*, plural of *body*. See § 490.
**Caprice**: from Ital. capr-*iccio*, a whim; Fr. *caprice*.
**Crevice**: Old Fr. crev-*asse*, Lat. crep-*acem*.
**Ælm-esse** (A.S.): Mid. Eng. alm-*es*, Mod. Eng. alm-*s*, Gr. *el-e-e-mos-y-ne*, hence adj. *eleemosynary*. See § 491.
**Burgess**, **marquis**; see these words under (28).

(33) **-il, -ile, -le** (Lat. *-illus*, *-illa*, *-illum*; Span. *-illo*):—

Pup-*il* (dim. of Lat. pup-*us*, a boy), sea-*l* (sig-*illum*), ais-*le* (Lat. ax-*illa*), imbec-*ile*, quadr-*ille*, bac-*illus*, peccad-*illo*.

*Note*.—The suffix *-il* is sometimes formed from the double diminutive form *-ic-ulus*, *-a*, *-um*.

Pen-*c-il* (Lat. peni-*c-ulus*), per-*il* (Lat. per-*ic-ulum*, danger).

*Excluded words*:—

**Postil**: probably an abridgment of *post illa verba*.
**Devil**: Greek *diabolos*, A.S. *deóful* or *deófol*.
**Missile**: Lat. *miss-il-e*, an arrow or lance; Lat. suffix *-ile*.
**Foss-il**: Lat. *foss-il-e*, that which may be dug out.

(34) **-ine, -in** (Lat. *-inus*, *-ina*, *-inum*; Fr. *-ine*):—

Libert-*ine*, bullet-*in*, quin-*ine*, pilgr-*im* (Ital. pellegr-*ino*), cous-*in* (Fr. cous-*in*, Low Lat. cos-*inus*, short form of consobr-*inus*, the child of a mother's sister ; wrongly traced to Lat. *consanguineus*).

*Excluded words :—*

**Paraffine**, Lat. *parum + affinis :* not allied to alkali.
**Sardine**, a small kind of fish. From *Sardin-ia*, the island.

(35) **-in**, Lat. *-inem* (Accus. of *-o*) :—

Marg-*in* (Lat. marg-*inem*), orig-*in*, virg-*in*.

(36) **-ion, -on** (Lat. *-ionem*, Accus. of *-io*) : Abstract suffix :—

Un-*ion*, opin-*ion*, fract-*ion*, *starv-at-*ion*.

Double forms : "popular" and "learned" ; see § 417.

| *Learned.* | *Popular.* | *Learned.* | *Popular.* |
|---|---|---|---|
| Poti-*on* | pois-*on*. | Orat-*ion* | oris-*on*. |
| Redempt-*ion* | rans-*om*. | Venat-*io* (L.) | venis-*on*. |
| Rat-*io* | reas-*on*. | Prehens-*io* (L.) | pris-*on*. |
| Lect-*ion* | less-*on*. | Comparat-*io* (L.) | comparis-*on*. |
| Sat-*io* (L.) | seas-*on*. | Fus-*ion* | fois-*on*. |
| Benedict-*ion* | benis-*on*. | Ars-*io* (Late Lat.) | ars-*on*. |
| Maledict-*ion* | malis-*on*. | | |

(37) **-ito** (Span. diminutive) :—

Musqu-*ito* (a little fly, Lat. *musca*, a fly), negr-*ito* (small negro).

(38) **-ive, -iff** (Lat. *-ivus*, Fr. *-if*) : generally Active :—

Fugit-*ive*, conservat-*ive*, nat-*ive*, mot-*ive*, plaint-*iff*, bail-*iff*.
*Passive sense :—*capt-*ive* (a prisoner), cait-*iff*, miss-*ive* (a letter).
*Excluded word :—***olive**, from Lat. *oliva*.

(39) **-lence** (Lat. *-lentia*) : compounded of *l* and *entia* (ence) :—

Pesti-*lence*, vio-*lence*, viru-*lence*, turbu-*lence*, corpu-*lence*.

(40) **-me, -m** (Lat. *-men*, Fr. *-me* ; cf. Greek *-ma*) :—

Cri-*me*, char-*m* (Lat. car-*men*), real-*m* (regali-*men*), cost-*ume* and cust-*om* (Late Lat. consuet-*umen*, Old. Fr. cost-*ume* and cust-*ume*).

(41) **-ment** (Lat. *-mentum* = *-men* + *-tum ;* French, *-ment*) :—

Conceal-*ment*, *fulfil-*ment*, judg-*ment*, pay-*ment*, *rai-*ment*.
*Excluded word :—*

**Parchment** : *Pergamen-us* from *Pergamus*, with excrescent *t*.

(42) **-mony** (Lat. *-monium*, *-monia*, Fr. *-moine*) :—

Acri-*mony*, testi-*mony*, sancti-*mony*, matri-*mony*, patri-*mony*.

(43) **-o** (Lat. *-um* or *-us*, Ital. and Spanish *-o*) :—

Studi-*o* grott-*o*, incognit-*o* (unknown, Pass. part. *in-cognit*-us).
*Excluded words :—*

**Farrago**, a medley or hotch-pot : Latin noun in Nominative case.
**Lumbago**, pain in the loins : similar to the above.
**Curio** : short for "curiosity."

**Limbo**: the original phrase was *in limbo* (in the borders of hell).
**Embryo**, formerly *embryon*, of Greek origin.
**Echo, halo, hero**: Greek words; the *o* belongs to the Gr. noun.
**Memento**: Imperative mood of Lat. verb *memini*.
**Innuendo** (misspelt as *inuendo*): Lat. gerund = by giving a nod.
**Folio, quarto, duodecimo, proviso**,—all are Latin Ablatives.

(44) **-on** (Lat. *-onem*, Accus. of *-o*; also Lat. *-onus*, *-ona*):—

Fel-*on*, li-*on*, simpl-et-*on*, marchi-*on*-ess, kitt-*en* (Fr. kit-*oun*), burd-*en* (refrain of a song; Fr. bourd-*on*, Low Lat. burd-*onem*).

*Excluded words*:—

**Gammon**, nonsense: A.S. *gamen*; hence Eng. *game*.
**Surgeon**, of Gr. origin: *chir-urge-on* = hand-worker.
**Horizon**: Gr. Pres. part., "the bounding or limiting" circle.
**Gnomon** (index of a dial): naturalised Greek word.
**Colon** (a clause; hence a stop-mark): naturalised Greek word.
**Skeleton**: naturalised Greek word, "a dried body."
**Pentagon, hexagon**, etc.: of Greek origin; pentag-*on*-os, etc.
**Cannon**: of Gr. origin through French *canon*, orig. a gun-barrel.
**Canon** (lit. rule): a naturalised Greek word.
**Nuncheon**, a "noon-drink"; see above § 561.
**Luncheon**, of Scand. origin; perhaps for *lunchin(g)*; *lunch* means lump, a piece of bread.

(45) **-oon, -one, -on** (Fr. *-on*, Ital. *-one*): augmentative:—

Ball-*oon* (a large ball), flag-*on* (a large flask), tromb-*one*.

*Excluded words*:—

**Baboon**: Low Lat. *babewynus* (A.D 1295), Fr. *babouin*.
**Monsoon** (a trade wind); of Arab. origin; *mausim*, a season.
**Shalloon** (light woollen stuff): from *Chalons*, a town in France.
**Lampoon**: from the exclamation *lampons*, let-us drink.
**Cyclone**: Gr. *kukl-ōn*, present participle, "circling."

(46) **-or, -our, -eur, -er, -eer** (from Latin suffixes named below). These denote agent or person:—

(*a*) From Lat. *-or*, Old Fr. *-our*, Mid. Fr. *-eur*, denoting agent:—

Act-*or*, auth-*or* (Lat. auct-*or*), *warri-*or*, troubad-*our*, amat-*eur*.

(*b*) From Lat. *-ator*. In Old French the *t* was weakened, and then finally dropped, as in *emper-eor*, *sauv-eor* (hence English savi-*our*):—

Emper-*or* (imper-*ator*), engin-*eer* (ingeni-*ator*), lev-*er* (lev-*ator*), burgl-*ar* for burgl-*or* (Low Lat. burgul-*ator*).

*Excluded words*:—

**Attaind-er, rejoind-er, remaind-er.**—Here the final *-er* represents the French Infinitive ending *-re*, as "attaind-*re*."

(47) **-or, -our, -eur** (Lat. *-or*, Old Fr. *-our*, Mod. Fr. *-eur*): these denote Abstract *qualities* or *states*, and must not be confounded with the preceding:—

Err-*or*, langu-*or*, fav-*our*, *behavi-*our*, grand-*eur*, haut-*eur*.

*Excluded words:—*

**Neighbour** = nigh + bour, a near husbandman; A.S. *búr, gebúr.*
**Scissors,** not from Lat. *scind-ere,* to cut (*sciss-or,* a cutler); but from Old Fr. cis-*oires,* shears; plural of *cisel,* chisel.
**Armour,** from Lat. *armatura;* see below under (55) -ure.

(48) **-ory, -or, -our, -er** (Lat. *-orius, -a, -um,* Fr. *-oire*):—

Dormit-*ory,* signat-*ory,* mem-*oir,* mirr-*or* (Late Lat. mirat-*orium*), parl-*our* (Low Lat. parlat-*orium*), count-*er* (computat-*orium*).

*Excluded word:—*

**Arm-ory,** for arm-*ary,* Lat. arm-*arium,* place for keeping arms.

(49) **-ry, -ery** (French *-rie* or *-erie,* formed by the addition of the Abstract suffix *-ie* (see below under (56) **-y**) to the French ending *-(i)er.* In English also the final *y* was associated with the personal suffix *-er,* as in fish-*er-y.* In such words, therefore, *-ery* is a hybrid suffix:—

Machine-*ry,* statione(r)-*ry* (articles dealt in by a station-*er*), slave-*ry,* *trick-*ery,* *husband-*ry,* *cemet-*ery,* *collie-*ry* (collie(r) + *ry*), poet-*ry,* fai-*ry* (lit. enchantment; O. Fr. *fae,* a fay).

(50) **-t** (Lat. *-tus, -ta, -tum,* Pass. part.):—

Fac-*t* (hence fea-*t*), counterfei-*t,* frui-*t* (cf. usufruc-*t*), join-*t.*

*Peculiar word:—*

**Ink:** Old Fr. *enque,* Lat. *encaust*-um, Gr. *encaust*-on, "burnt in."

(51) **-ter, -tre** (Lat. *-trum,* Gr. *-tron*):—

Clois-*ter,* thea-*tre,* lus-*tre,* spec-*tre,* scep-*tre,* fil-*ter,* mons-*ter.*

*Excluded words:—*

**Goitre,** a swelling on the throat; Lat. *guttur,* a throat.
**Disaster:** Lat. *astr*-um; cf. Eng. *star.*

(52) **-tude** (Lat. *-tudo, -tudineon*): Abstract suffix:—

Longi-*tude,* forti-*tude,* apti-*tude* (hence atti-*tude*), multi-*tude.*

(53) **-ty** (Lat. *-tas, -tatem,* Fr. *-té*): chiefly Abstract:—

Cruel-*ty,* frail-*ty,* dain-*ty* (O. Fr. dain-*tie,* Lat. digni-*tatem*).

(54) **-ule, -le** (Lat. *-ulus, -ula, -ulum,* Fr. *-le*). Diminutive.

Pill-*ule,* circ-*le,* rol-*l* Lat. rot-*ula*), chapt-*er* (Fr. chapit-*re,* Lat. capit-*ulum*), poster-*n* (Lat. poster-*ula* porta; Old Fr. *poster-le* or poster-*ne,* a little back door).

*Excluded words:—*

**Kennel,** from Mid. Eng. ken-*el,* Old Fr. chen-*il,* Lat. can-*ile.*
**Principle, manciple:** L. *principium, mancipium;* with *l* inserted.

(55) **-ure** (Lat. *-ura,* Fr. *-eur*):—

Cult-*ure,* *seiz-*ure,* capt-*ure,* apert-*ure,* fig-*ure,* furnit-*ure,* us-*ury* (Lat. us-*ura*), arm-*our* (Lat. armat-*ura,* Old Fr. arm-*eure*), tent-*er* (properly tent-*ure,* from Lat. tent-*ura,* a stretching frame).

*Excluded words:*—

**Leis-ure**, **pleas-ure**, from French Infinitives, lois-*ir*, plais-*ir*.
**Treas-ure** is from Fr. trés-*or*, Lat. thes-*aurus*, from Greek.
**Sinecure**, Lat. *sine curâ*, without care.
**Cynosure**, Gr. *kunos oura*, the tail of the Lesser Bear.
**Epicure**, Gr. *Epikouros*, the name of a philosopher.
**Debenture**, from the phrase *debentur mihi*, "they are due to me."

(56) **-y** (from the Lat. suffixes named below); on the *-y* suffix derived from *-ate* and equivalent to *-ee*, see (21).

(*a*) From *-ia*, French *-ie*:—
Famil-*y*, abb-*ey* (L. Lat. abbat-*ia*), *jealous-*y*, Ind-*ia*, Arcad-*y*.

(*b*) From *-ium*:—
Stud-*y*, augur-*y*, remed-*y*, jo-*y* (Lat. gaud-*ium*), od-*ium*.

(*c*) From *-ies*:—
Progen-*y*, compan-*y* (Late Lat. compan-*ies*, taking food together).

*Excluded words*:—

**Daisy**, from Anglo-Saxon *dæges éage*, the eye of day.
**Jeopardy** = Old Fr. *jeu parti*, a divided game; hence a risk.
**Enemy** = Old Fr. *enem-i*, Lat. *inim-icus*; see (30).

## B. *Adjective-forming.*

573. (1) **-able** (Lat. *-abilis*): see below under **-ble**.

(2) **-aceous** (Lat. *-aceus*), made of:—

Farin-*aceous*, argill-*aceous*, sapon-*aceous* (soapy).

*Disguised*:—cuir-*ass* (noun: Lat. cori-*aceus*, made of *corium*, leather). Crev-*ice* (noun: Old Fr. crev-*asse*, Late Lat. crep-*acea*).

(3) **-acious** (Lat. *-ax*, *-ac-is*): the *-is* becomes *-ious*:—

Ten-*acious*, loqu-*acious*, mend-*acious*, ver-*acious*, cap-*acious*.

*Note.*—From *-ox*, *-ocis*, we get:—Prec-*ocious*, atr-*ocious*.

(4) **-al** (Lat. *-alis*, Fr. *-al* or *-el*), sometimes added to *ic*:—

Vit-*al*, *ephemer-*al*, parti-*al*, *com-*ic-al*, *dramat-*ic-al*.

(5) **-an**, **-en**, **-ain**, **-ane** (Lat. *-anus*, Fr. *-ain*, *-en*):—

Pag-*an*, mea-*n* and mizz-*en* (Late Lat. medi-*anus*), sull-*en* (Late Lat. sol-*anus*), Rom-*an*, cert-*ain*, mund-*ane*, hum-*ane*.

*-ean*: the *-anus* in Latin was sometimes preceded by *æ* or *e*:—

Hercul-*ean*, subterran-*ean*, Europ-*ean*, Chald-*ean*, Pythagor-*ean*.

(6) **-arian**, compounded of *-ary* + *-an*; see **ary** under (10):—

Unit-*arian*, agr-*arian*, humanit-*arian*, antiqu-*arian*, sect-*arian*.

(7) **-aneous** (Lat. *-aneus*):—

Cut-*aneous*, extr-*aneous*, instant-*aneous*, for-*eign* (Late Lat. for-*aneus*), sover-*eign* (Late Lat. super-*aneus*).

(8) **-ant**, **-ent** (Lat. *-antem*, *-entem*, Pres. part.; Fr. *-ant*):—

Arrog-*ant*, brilli-*ant*, poign-*ant* (Lat. form pung-*ent*), abs-*ent*.

(9) **-ar** (Lat. *-aris*, Fr. *-ier* or *-aire*) :—

Sol-*ar*, lun-*ar*, famili-*ar*, regul-*ar*, singul-*ar*, vulg-*ar*, schol-*ar*.

(10) **-ary, -arious** (Lat. *-arius*, Fr. *-aire*) :—

Contr-*ary*, necess-*ary*, ordin-*ary*, greg-*arious*, prec-*arious*.

(11) **-ate, -atic** (Lat. *-atus*, *-aticus*); see (30) **-t** and (18) **-ic.**

(12) **-ble** (Lat. *-plex*, Fr. *-ple*), fold :—

Dou-*ble* (du-*plex*), tre-*ble* (=Fr. and Eng. tri-*ple*=Lat. tri-*plex*).

(13) **-ble, -able, -ible, -uble** (Lat. -bilis, with *-a*, *-i*, or *-u*). Of these **-able** has become an independent suffix of extensive use :—

Laud-*able*, * eat-*able*, ed-*ible*, manage-*able*, sol-*uble*, * sale-*able*.

*Excluded word* :—

Humble, from Lat. hum-*ilis*; with inserted *b*.

(14) **-esc-ent** (Pres. part. of verbs in *-esc-o*): inceptive :—

Qui-*escent*, conval-*escent*, evan-*escent*, incand-*escent*, efferv-*escent*.

(15) **-ese, -ens**-ic (Lat. *-ensis*, Old Fr. *-eis*) :—

Chin-*ese*, for-*ens*-ic, amanu-*ensis*, court-*eous* (O. Fr. curt-*eis*).

(16) **-esque** (Lat. *-iscus*, Fr. *-esque*); orig. Diminutive :—

Grot-*esque*, pictur-*esque*, burl-*esque*, arab-*esque*, statu-*esque*.

(17) **-et** (Old Fr. *-et*, Ital. *-etto*) :—Dulc-*et*, russ-*et*.

(18) **-ic, -ique** (Lat. *-icus*, *-iquus*, Fr. *-ique*) :—

Publ-*ic*, domest-*ic*, rust-*ic*, Kelt-*ic*, ant-*ique*, obl-*ique*, un-*ique*.

*Compound suffix* -at-ic :—Aqu-*atic*, lun-*atic* (noun), fan-*atic* (noun).

(19) **-id** (Lat. *-idus*, Fr. *-ide*) :—

Ac-*id*, pall-*id*, morb-*id*, viv-*id*, rig-*id*, plac-*id*, liv-*id*, ferv-*id*.

*Note.*—In French the suffix sometimes disappears, as Lat. *nit-idus*, Fr. *net*, Eng. *neat*. Sometimes the suffix is changed into *-e*, as Lat. *pall-idus*, Old Fr. *pall-e*, Eng. *pal-e*.

(20) **-ile, -il, -eel, -le, -el** (Lat. *-ilis*; Fr. *-ile*) :—

Frag-*ile*, fra-*il*, gent-*eel*, gent-*ile*, gent-*le*, hum(b)-*le*, cru-*el*.

*Note.—Depreciatory*: infant-*ile*=child-*ish*; serv-*ile*=slav-*ish*.

(21) **-ine, -in** (Lat. *-inus*, Fr. *-ine*) :—

Div-*ine*, infant-*ine* (not depreciatory, like "infant-*ile*").

(22) **-ior** (Latin Comparative suffix, unchanged in English) :—

Pr-*ior*, super-*ior*, infer-*ior*, jun-*ior*, sen-*ior*, etc.

(23) **-ive** (Lat. *-ivus*, Fr. *-if*; hence bail-*iff*, noun) :—

* Talkat-*ive*, rest-*ive* (Lat. *re*+*sto*, resist), nat-*ive* (hence na-*ive*).

(24) **-lent** (Lat. *-lentus* or *-lens*, *-lentem*) :—

Pesti-*lent*, corpu-*lent*, opu-*lent*, escu-*lent*, vio-*lent*.

*Excluded words :—*

**Malevolent, benevolent, insolent** must be divided etymologically as malevol-*ent*, benevol-*ent*, insol-*ent ;* the *l* is part of the root.

(25) **-me** (Lat. Superlative suffix *-mus;* cf. A.S. *ma*, § 498, 4) :—

Pri-*me*, extre-*me*, supre-*me*.

(26) **-monious** (Lat. *-monius*) :—

Queri-*monious*, sancti-*monious*, cere-*monious*.

(27) **-ory, -orious** (Lat. *-orius*, Fr. *-oire*) :—

Dilat-*ory*, compuls-*ory*, cens-*orious* (cf. *-erious*, in delet-*erious*).

*Note.*—In labori-*ous*, the suffix is *-ous ; ori* is part of the stem.

(28) **-ous, -ose** (from Lat. suffixes (*a*) and (*b*) named below) :—

(*a*) Lat. *-osus*, Fr. *-eux :—*

Glori-*ous* peril-*ous* (parl-*ous* in Shakspeare), adip-*ose* (Lat. *adip-em*, fat).

(*b*) Lat. *us :—*

Tremend-*ous* (Lat. tremend-*us*), ardu-*ous*, posthum-*ous* (postum-*us*).

As an independent suffix *-ous* is added to stems, which had no connection with Lat. *-osus* or *-us :—*

(*a*) *Adject.-stems :—*felicit-*ous*, atroci-*ous*, expediti-*ous*, efficaci-*ous*.
(*b*) *Noun-stems :—*joy-*ous*, lusci-*ous* (corruption of lust-i-*ous*), *up-roar-i-*ous*, pite-*ous*, *hazard-*ous*, *treacher-*ous*, *murder-*ous*.

*Excluded words :—*

**Righteous**, Mid. Eng. *right-wis* = wise in what is right.
**Gorgeous** : Old Fr. *gorgias*, brilliant.
**Court-eous** = Old Fr. *curt-eis ; -eis* represents the Lat. *-ensis*.
**Wondrous**, corruption of the Mid. Eng. Genitival adverb *wond-ers*.

(29) **-ple** (Lat. *-plex*, Fr. *-ple ;* see above under (13) **-ble**) :—

Sim-*ple*, tri-*ple* (= tre-*ble*), quadru-*ple*, sup-*ple*, du-*plex*, com-*plex*.

*Note.*—In "sing-*le*" the *-le* is short for *-ule* from Lat. *-uli*.

(30) **-t, -ate, -ete** or **-eet, -ite, -ute.**—These are the English equivalents of Lat. *-tus*, *-atus*, *-etus*, *-itus*, *-utus*, all of which are Pass. participial suffixes. The suffix *-ate* (cf. the parallel case of **-able**) has become an independent suffix :—

*-t* (here *-e* for *-us* is not required for the pronunciation) :—
Exact, exempt, elect, abrupt, blest, abject, devout, content.
*-ate*, etc. : orn-*nate*, affection-*ate*, compl-*ete*, defin-*ite*, destit-*ute*.

(31) **-und, -ond** (Lat. *-undus*, Fr. *-ond*) :—

Morib-*und*, joc-*und*, rot-*und* or ro-*und*, sec-*ond*, vagab-*ond*.

(32) **-urn** (Lat. *-urnus*, which like *-ish* signified *slightly*) :—

Tacit-*urn*, aub-*urn* (Late Lat. *alb-urnus*).

(33) **-y** (Lat. *-ivus*, Anglo-French *-if*) :—

*Hast-*y*, *joll-*y*, mass-*y*, test-*y*, touch-*y* (for tetch-*y*, freakish).

*Adverb suffixes.*—There are no adverbial suffixes of Latin origin, but adjectives ending in *-ble* form adverbs in *-bly*, as *horrible*, *horribly*, on the analogy of the Teutonic adverbial suffix *-ly*.

### C. *Verb-forming.*

**574.** (1) **-ate** (Lat. *-atus*, Pass. participle) :—

Agit-*ate*, moder-*ate*, captiv-*ate*, gradu-*ate*, accentu-*ate*, vaccin-*ate*.

(2) **-er** (from Fr. Infin. *-re* or *-ir*, Lat. *-ere*) :—

Rend-*er* (Fr. rend-*re* or *-er*, Lat. redd-*ere*).

(3) **-esce** (Lat. *-esco*), inceptive :—

Efferv-*esce*, coal-*esce*, acqui-*esce*, efflor-*esce*.

(4) **-fy** (Lat. *-ficare*, Fr. *-fier*).—Makes Causal verbs :—

Magni-*fy* (to make great), signi-*fy*, simpli-*fy*, modi-*fy*, terri-*fy*.

(5) **-ish** (Fr. *-iss*, from Lat. inceptive *-esc*, "flor-*esc*-entem") :—

Establ-*ish*, garn-*ish*, publ-*ish*, van-*ish*; pun-*ch* (short for pun-*ish*).

(6) **-y** (Fr. *-i* in the Infin. *-i-er*; cf. A.S. *-i* in the Infin. *-i-an*: see above § 569 (7).

Marr-*y* (Fr. mar-*i*-er), sall-*y* (Fr. saill-*i*-r), carr-*y* (O. Fr. car-*i*-er).

## CHAPTER XXX.—GREEK PREFIXES AND SUFFIXES.

### SECTION 1.—PREFIXES.

**575. A-, an-, am-** (*not, without*; like English *un-*) : *an*-archy, *an*-æsthetic, *an*-ecdote, *an*-odyne, *an*-onymous, *a*-theism, *a*-pathy.

**Allo-** (other, different) : *allo*-pathy, *all*-egory.

**Amphi-** (*about, on both sides*) : *amphi*-theatre, *amphi*-bious.

**Ana-, an-** (*up to, again*) : *ana*-chronism, *ana*-tomy, *ana*-logy.

**Anti-, ant-** (*against*) : *anti*-podes, *anti*-type, *anti*-thesis, *ant*-arctic.

**Apo-, aph-** (*from*) : *apo*-logy, *apo*-state, *apo*-strophe, *aph*-orism.

**Arch-, archi-, arche-** (*chief, head*) : *arch*-heretic, *arch*-bishop.

**Auto-, auth-** (*self*) : *auto*-graph, *auto*-car, *auto*-maton, *auto*-nomy.

**Cata-, cath-, cat-** (*down*) : *cata*-ract, *cath*-edral, *cat*-echism.

**Dia-** (*through*) : *dia*-meter, *dia*-logue, *dia*-dem, *dia*-gonal, *dia*-lysis. Disguised in *dea*-con (Gr. *dia*-konos), *de*-vil (Gr. *dia*-bolos).

**Dis-, di-** (*in two*) : *dis*-syllable, *di*-glott, *di*-phthong, *di*-lemma.

**Dys-** (*ill*) : *dys*-peptic, *dys*-entery.

**Ec-, ex-** (*out, from*) : *ex*-odus, *ex*-orcise ; *ec*-stasy, *ec*-clesiastic.

**En-** (*in*) : *en*-thusiasm, *en*-demic, *en*-caustic, *en*-cyclical, *en*-ergy, *em*-piric, *em*-porium, *em*-pyrean, *em*-phasis, *el*-lipsis, *en*-comium.

**Endo-** (*within*) : *endo*-gamous, *endo*-genous.

**Epi-, eph-, ep-** (*upon*) : *epi*-gram, *ep*-och, *epi*-taph, *eph*-emeral.

**Eu-, ev-** (*well*) : *eu*-phony, *eu*-phemism, *eu*-logy, *ev*-angelist.

**Eso-,** (*within*) : *eso*-teric.

**Exo-** (*without*) : *exo*-teric, *exo*-tic, *exo*-gamous.

**Hemi**- (*half*): *hemi*-sphere, *hemi*-stitch. (Disguised in *me*-grim, Gr. *hemi*-cranion, half the skull.)

**Hepta**-, **hept**- (*seven*): *hepta*-gon, *hept*-archy.

**Hetero**- (*different*): *hetero*-dox, *hetero*-geneous.

**Hexa**- (*six*): *hexa*-meter, *hexa*-gon.

**Homeo**- (*similar*): *homeo*-pathy.

**Homo**-, **hom**- (*same*): *homo*-geneous, *hom*-onym.

**Hyper**- (*above*, *too much*): *hyper*-bole, *hyper*-critical, *hyper*-borean.

**Hypo**-, **hyph**- (under): *hypo*-crite, *hypo*-thesis, *hyph*-en.

**Meta**-, **meth**-, **met**- (*after*): *meta*-phor, *meth*-od, *met*-eor.

**Mono**-, **mon**- (*single*): *mono*-graph, *mon*-astery (*min*-ster), *mon*-k.

**Palin**- (*again*): *palin*-ode, *palim*-psest.

**Pan**-, **panto**- (*all*): *pan*-theist, *pan*-orama, *panto*-mime.

**Para**-, **par**- (*beside*): *para*-phrase, *par*-ody, *para*-lysis (*pa*-lsy).

*Note.*—The Greek *para* is quite distinct from *para* in *para*-chute, *para*-pet, *para*-sol. These are from Fr. *parer*, to guard against.

**Penta**- (five): *penta*-meter, *penta*-teuch, *penta*-polis, *penta*-gon.

**Peri**- (*around*): *peri*-meter, *peri*-phrasis, *peri*-od, *peri*-gee.

**Poly**- (*many*): *poly*-syllable, *poly*-theist, *poly*-glot.

**Pro**- (*before*): *pro*-gramme, *pro*-logue, *pro*-phet, *pro*-blem.

**Pros**- (*towards*): *pros*-ody, *pros*-elyte.

**Pseudo**-, **pseud**- (*false*): *pseudo*-critic, *pseud*-onym.

**Syn**- (*with*): *syn*-thesis, *syn*-agogue, *sym*-pathy, *syl*-lable, *sy*-stem.

**Tele**- (*afar*): *tele*-graph, *tele*-phone, *tele*-gram.

**Tetra**- (*four*): *tetra*-gon, *tetra*-hedron, *tetr*-arch, *tra*-pezium.

**Tri**- (*thrice* or *three*): *tri*-pod, *tri*-syllable, *tri*-gonometry.

**U**- (*not*, properly *ou*): *u*-topia (the land of no-where).

## SECTION 2.—SUFFIXES.

(*Hybrids are marked with an asterisk.*)

### A. *Noun-forming.*

576. (1) -ac (Gr. *-akos*, an adjective suffix in Greek):—

Mani-*ac*, demoni-*ac*.

(2) -ad, -id (Gr. *-as*, Genitive *-ad-os*; *-is*, Genitive *-id-os*):—

Ili-*ad*, Dry-*ad*, mon-*ad*, myri-*ad*, dec-*ade*, Æne-*id*, Nere-*id*.

*Excluded word*:—

**Druid**, from Celtic *druidh*, a soothsayer.

(3) -ant (Gr. *-anta*):—

Gi-*ant*, eleph-*ant*, adam-*ant*.

(4) -asm (Gr. *-asmos*): chiefly Abstract:—

Enthusi-*asm*, pleon-*asm*, phant-*asm* (other form, phant-*om*).

(5) -ast (Gr. *-astes*), agent:—

Enthusi-*ast*, gymn-*ast*, iconocl-*ast*, encomi-*ast*.

*Excluded word*:—

**Bombast**: Pers. *bandash*, carded cotton well blown out.

(6) **-e** (Greek suffix unchanged), syllabic *ĕ*:—

Epitom-*e*, catastroph-*e*, acm-*e*, apostroph-*e*.

(7) **-ic, -ics** (Gr. *-ikos*, *-ica*, Neut. Plur.):—

Cler-*ic* or cler-*k*, cyn-*ic*, scept-*ic*, etc.; log-*ic*, mus-*ic*; phys-*ics*, eth-*ics*.

*Note* 1.—The Latin *-ian* is added to *-ic* to denote agent:—

Optic-*ian*, physic-*ian*, statistic-*ian*, politic-*ian*.

*Note* 2.—The adjective suffix *-al* is added to *-ic*:—

Optic-*al*, physic-*al*, statistic-*al*, sceptic-*al*, critic-*al*, etc.

*Excluded word*:—

**Antics**: the stem *antic* is from Lat. *antiqu*-us, ancient.

(8) **-ine** (Gr. *-in-e*, Fr. *-ine*): hero-*ine* (Gr. *he-ro-i-ne*, four syll.).

(9) **-isk, -esque** (Gr. *-iskos*, Fr. *-esque*): Diminutive:—

Aster-*isk*, basil-*isk*, obel-*isk*.

(10) **-ism** (Gr. *-ismos*): Abstract:—

Bapt-*ism*, *de-*ism*, *heathen-*ism*, *Roman-*ism*, *Cockney-*ism*.

*Note.*—*Wittic-ism* has two Gr. suffixes attached to a Teut. stem, viz. *-ic* (adj.) and *-ism* (noun). Perhaps this has been suggested by such a word as *cynic-ism*.

(11) **-ist** (Gr. *-istes*): the concrete counterpart to *-ism*:—

*Art-*ist*, dramat-*ist*, pap-*ist*, *optim-*ist*, *nihil-*ist*.

(12) **-ite, -it** (Gr. *-ites*):—

Israel-*ite*, erem-*ite* or herm-*it*, anchor-*ite* or *-et*, dynam-*ite*.

*Excluded word*:—

**Favour-ite**, the fem. of the French adjective *favori*.

(13) **-m, -mme** (Gr. *-ma*):—

The-*me*, progra-*mme*, cli-*me* (Gr. *cli-ma*, *cli-mat-os*), cli-*mate*.

*Excluded words*:—

**Anthem**: Gr. *anti-phona*, Anglo-Saxon *antefn*, later *antem*.
**Phantom**: corruption of Gr. phant-*asm*, Old Fr. fant-*osme*.
**Balsam, balm**: in these the *m* is part of the stem.

(14) **-oid** (Gr. *eid*-os, form or kind, preceded by *o*):—

Anthrop-*oid*, negr-*oid*, metall-*oid*, musc-*oid* (moss-like), tabl-*oid*.

(15) **-on** (Greek *ŏn*, unchanged):—

*Naturalised words*:—Phenomen-*on*, criteri-*on*, automat-*on*, col-*on*, skelet-*on*.

(16) **-on** (Greek *ōn*, unchanged):—

Gnom-*on*, horiz-*on*, surge-*on*, can-*on*.

(17) **-ot** (Gr. *-otes*): denotes agent or title:—

Zeal-*ot*, *patri-*ot*, idi-*ot*, Iscari-*ot*, Cypri-*ot*.

(18) **-sy, -se** (Gr. *-sis*): chiefly Abstract:—

Drop-*sy*, pal-*sy*, eclip-*se*, ba-*se*.

*Excluded word*:—

**Minstrelsy**, a misspelling for minstrel-*cy*, with Lat. suffix *-cy*.

(19) **-t, -te** (Gr. *-tes*, *-te*, Lat. *-ta*):—

Prophe-*t*, plane-*t*, poe-*t* (Gr. or Lat.), die-*t*, aposta-*te*, come-*t*.

(20) **-tre, -ter** (Gr. *-tron*, Lat. *-trum*):—

Cen-*tre*, me-*tre*, me-*ter*, phil-*tre*, diame-*ter*, thea-*tre*, scep-*tre*.

(21) **-y** (Gr. *-ia*, Lat. *-ia*): chiefly Abstract:—

Monarch-*y*, academ-*y*, energ-*y*, agon-*y*, dyspeps-*ia*, hydrophob-*ia*.

*Imitation*:—orthodox-*y* (from Gr. ortho + dox-*a*).

(22) **-ysm** (Gr. *-usmos*):—

Catacl-*ysm*, parox-*ysm*.

### B. *Adjective-forming.*

**577.** (1) **-ac** (Gr. *-akos*):—

Demoni-*ac*, Syri-*ac*, *ili-*ac*.

(2) **-ic** (Gr. *-ikos*, similar to the Lat. *-icus*):—

Authent-*ic*, lacon-*ic*, empir-*ic*, climat-*ic*, spasmod-*ic*, opthalm-*ic*.

The Greek *-ic* is often compounded with the Latin *-al*:—

Period-*ic*, period-*ical*; polit-*ic*, polit-*ical*; cyn-*ic*, cyn-*ical*.

(3) **-astic** (Gr. *-astikos*, the adjective of *-ast* with added *-ic*):—

Pleon-*astic*, sarc-*astic*, bomb-*astic*, enthusi-*astic*, fant-*astic*.

(4) **-istic** (Gr. *-istikos*, the adj. of *-ist*): *al* is sometimes added:—

Patr-*istic*, eulog-*istic*, evangel-*istic*, *lingu-*istic*, *egot-*istic*-al.

### C. *Verb-forming.*

**578.** **-ize, -ise** (Gr. *-izein*, Fr. *-iser*).—Should be spelt with *s*, since this suffix came to us through French: see p. 262, note 1.

*Human-*ise*, *Anglic-*ise*, botan-*ise*, Gorgon-*ise* (Tennyson).

## CHAPTER XXXI.—SUMMARY OF RESULTS IN PREFIXES AND SUFFIXES.

**579. Hybrids.**—As a general rule Teutonic affixes are added to Teutonic stems, Romanic to Romanic, and Greek to Greek.

But all these prefixes and suffixes have now become naturalised in English, and hence many Derivative words are of mixed origin. Such words are called Hybrids or half-breeds, § 565, *Note*.

(*a*) Teutonic stems with Romanic prefixes :—

*En*-dear, *en*-snare, *per*-haps, *demi*-god, *re*-call, *counter*-work.

(*b*) Teutonic stems with Romanic suffixes :—

Starv-*ation*, stream-*let*, godd-*ess*, lusci-*ous*, scrimm-*age*, drink-*able*, fern-*ery*, block-*ade*, atone-*ment*, talkat-*ive*, forbear-*ance*, bond-*age*.

(*c*) Romanic stems with Teutonic prefixes :—

*Under*-estimate, *un*-deceive, *be*-siege, *a*-cross, *after*-piece, *over*-turn.

(*d*) Romanic stems with Teutonic suffixes :—

False-*hood*, priest-*craft*, quarrel-*some*, bishop-*ric*, rapid-*ly*, merci-*ful*, duke-*dom*.

*Note* 1.—On hybrid *compounds*, see list in chap. xxvii. § 561.
*Note* 2.—For a hybrid *suffix*, see **-ery**, as "fish-*er-y*," § 572 (49).

**580. Comparative Results.**—The comparative results of what is shown in chaps. xxviii.-xxx. are exemplified below :—

(*a*) Affixes denoting a *moderate* degree of some quality :—

**-ish**, Teut.: black-*ish* (rather black), sweet-*ish* (rather sweet).
**-ly**, Teut.: clean-*ly*, sick-*ly*, elder-*ly*, weak-*ly*.
**Sub-**, Rom.: *sub*-acid (rather acid), *sub*-tropical (almost tropical).

(*b*) Suffixes denoting a *high* degree of some quality :—

**-ful**, Teut.: *plenti-*ful*, wonder-*ful*, *taste-*ful*, truth-*ful*.
**-ous**, **-ose**, Rom.: verb-*ose*, numer-*ous*, fam-*ous*, odi-*ous*.

*Note.*—The equivalence of these two suffixes is shown by the pairs of words in which they appear. Thus we have : *plenti-*ful*, plente-*ous*; *beauti-*ful*, beaute-*ous*; *bounti-*ful*, bounte-*ous*; *piti-*ful*, pite-*ous*; *joy-*ful*, joy-*ous*; *grace-*ful*, graci-*ous*.

(*c*) Prefixes signifying the undoing of something done :—

**Un-**, Teut.: *un*-bolt, *un*-tie, *un*-lock, *un*-fold.
**Dis-** or **di-**, Rom.: *dis*-mount, *dis*-appear, *dis*-arm.
**De-**, Rom.: *de*-throne, *de*-camp, *de*-tach, *de*-odorise.

(*d*) Prefixes and Suffixes denoting a negative :—

**Un-**, Teut.: *un*-happy, *un-safe, *un*-ready.
**-less**, Teut.: hap-*less*, law-*less*, hope-*less*.
**N-**, Teut.: *n*-one, *n*-ever, *n*-either, *n*-or.
**Dis-**, **di-**, Rom.: *dis*-quiet, *dif*-ficult, *dif*-fident, *dis*-honour.
**In-**, Rom.: *in*-human, *ir*-regular, *im*-moral, *il*-legible.
**Ne-**, **neg-**, **non-**, Rom.: *ne*-farious, *neg*-lect, *non*-sense.
**A-** or **an-**, Greek: *a*-pathy, *an*-archy, *am*-brosial.

(*e*) Suffixes indicating the Feminine gender :—

**-ster**, Teut.: spin-*ster*.
**-en**, Teut.: vix-*en*.
**-ess**: Rom.: lion-*ess*, temptr-*ess*, tigr-*ess*.

(*f*) Prefixes indicating something bad :—

**Mis-**, Teut. (from *miss*) : *mis*-take, *mis*-deed, *mis*-hap.
**Male-**, mal-, Rom. : *male*-factor, *mal*-treat.
**Mis-**, Rom. (from *minus*) : *mis*-use, *mis*-fortune.
**Dys-**, Greek : *dys*-entery, *dys*-pepsia.

(*g*) Prefixes indicating something good :—

**Well-**, Teut. : *wel*-fare, *wel*-come, *well*-being.
**Bene-**, Rom. : *bene*-volent, *bene*-fit, *bene*-diction.
**Eu-**, Greek : *eu*-phemism, *ev*-angelist, *eu*-phony.

(*h*) Suffixes denoting diminutives, endearment, or contempt :—

*Teutonic* :—

**-el, -le, -erel** : kern-*el*, padd-*le*, dott-*erel*.
**-en** : maid-*en*, chick-*en*.
**-ing** : wild-*ing*, sweet-*ing*.
**-ling** : dar-*ling*, strip-*ling*, weak-*ling*, under-*ling*.
**-kin** : bump-*kin*, manni-*kin*, lamb-*kin*, fir-*kin*.
**-ock** : hill-*ock*, bull-*ock*, humm-*ock*, padd-*ock*.
**-y, -ie** : bird-*ie*, dogg-*y*, lass-*ie*, Charl-*ey*, Johnn-*y*.

*Romanic* :—

**-aster** : poet-*aster*, pil-*aster*.
**-ule, -le** : pill-*ule*, sched-*ule* ; circ-*le*, chasub-*le*.
**-cule, -cle** : animal-*cule*, mole-*cule* ; parti-*cle*, pinna-*cle*.
**-el, -le, -l, -elle** : parc-*el*, kett-*le*, vea-*l*, bagat-*elle*.
**-et, -ot, -ette, -let** : bill-*et*, ball-*ot*, statu-*ette*, *brook-*let*.
**-ito** : mosqu-*ito*, negr-*ito*.

*Greek* :—

**-isk** : aster-*isk*, obel-*isk*.

(*i*) List of Suffixes forming Abstract Nouns :—

*Teutonic* :—

**-craft** : witch-*craft*, *priest-*craft*, handi-*craft*.
**-dom** : free-*dom*, *martyr-*dom*, *pope-*dom*, *duke-*dom*.
**-hood, -head** : maiden-*head*, likeli-*hood*.
**-lock, -ledge** : wed-*lock*, know-*ledge*.
**-red** : hat-*red*, kind-*red*.
**-ric** : *bishop-*ric*.
**-ing** : learn-*ing*, hunt-*ing*, etc.
**-ness** : dark-*ness*, nothing-*ness*.
**-ship** : friend-*ship*, wor-*ship*, owner-*ship*, *citizen-*ship*.
**-t, -th** : heigh-*t*, sigh-*t* ; tru-*th*, dear-*th*, etc.
**-ter, -der** : laugh-*ter*, slaugh-*ter*, mur-*der*.

*Romanic* :—

**-age** : cour-*age*, hom-*age*, umbr-*age*, *bond-*age*.
**-al** : refus-*al*, tri-*al*, arriv-*al*, surviv-*al*.
**-ance, -ence, -ancy, -ency** : dist-*ance*, prud-*ence*, const-*ancy*, urg-*ency*.
**-ate** : consul-*ate*, noviti-*ate*, patriarch-*ate*.
**-cy, -sy, -acy** : secre-*cy*, minstrel-*sy*, prel-*acy*.
**-ice, -ise, -ess, -es** : serv-*ice*, franch-*ise*, prow-*ess*, rich-*es*.

**-ion** : relig-*ion*, suspic-*ion*, fash-*ion*, fact-*ion*.
**-lence** : opu-*lence*, viru-*lence*, corpu-*lence*.
**-ment** : judg-*ment*, enjoy-*ment*, attach-*ment*.
**-mony** : acri-*mony*, parsi-*mony*, matri-*mony*.
**-or, -our, -eur** : err-*or*, fav-*our*, grand-*eur*.
**-ry, -ery** : *husband-*ry*, *trick-*ery*.
**-tude** : lassi-*tude*, forti-*tude*.
**-ty** : cruel-*ty*, authori-*ty*.
**-ure** : cult-*ure*, *seiz-*ure*, nat-*ure*, verd-*ure*.
**-y** : perfid-*y*, luxur-*y*, master-*y*, infam-*y*.

*Greek* :—

**-asm, -ism** : sarc-*asm*, *optim-*ism*.
**-ic, -ics** : log-*ic*, eth-*ics*.
**-sy, -se** : drop-*sy*, apocalyp-*se*.
**-y** : monarch-*y*, energ-*y*, sympath-*y*.

(*j*) List of Suffixes denoting agent or person :—

*Teutonic* :—

**-man** : boat-*man*, wo-*man*, midship-*man*, fisher-*man*.
**-el, -le** : bead-*le*, cripp-*le*, scoundr-*el*.
**-er, -ier, -yer, -ar, -or** : rid-*er*, cloth-*ier*, law-*yer*, li-*ar*, sail-*or*.
**-ster** : huck-*ster*, -malt-*ster*, trick-*ster*, rhyme-*ster*.
**-ter, -ther, -der** : mo-*ther*, fa-*ther*, sis-*ter*, daugh-*ter*, spi-*der*.
**-nd** : fie-*nd*, frie-*nd*, wi-*nd*, husba-*nd*.

*Romanic* :—

**-an, -ain, -on, -en, -ian** : public-*an*, capt-*ain*, citiz-*en*, sext-*on*, guard-*ian*.
**-ant, -ent** : merch-*ant*, tru-*ant* ; stud-*ent*, presid-*ent*.
**-ard, -art** : *wiz-*ard*, Spani-*ard*, *bragg-*art*.
**-ary, -aire, -ar, -er, -eer, -ier, -or** : statu-*ary*, million-*aire*, vic-*ar*, arch-*er*, volunt-*eer*, cash-*ier*, chancell-*or*.
**-ate, -ee, -ey, -y** : candid-*ate*, *trust-*ee*, attorn-*ey*, deput-*y*.
**-ine, -in** : libert-*ine*, gobl-*in*.
**-on** : fel-*on*, glutt-*on*, mas-*on*, sculli-*on*.
**-or, -our, -eur, -er** : aggress-*or*, troubad-*our*, amat-*eur*, preach-*er*.

*Greek* :—

**-ac** : mani-*ac*, demoni-*ac*.
**-ast** : enthusi-*ast*, inconocl-*ast*.
**-ic** : heret-*ic*, scept-*ic*, crit-*ic* (cf. Lat. lunat-*ic*).
**-ist** : psalm-*ist*, anarch-*ist*, the-*ist*.
**-ite, -it** : cosmopol-*ite*, erem-*ite*, Jesu-*it*.
**-ot** : zeal-*ot*, patri-*ot*, Cypri-*ot*.

(*k*) List of Adjective Suffixes that convey a Passive sense :—

**-d, -ed, -t,** Past part. Teut. : love-*d*, kill-*ed*, brough-*t*.
**-able, -ible, -uble,** Rom. : laud-*able*, ed-*ible*, sol-*uble*.

(*l*) List of Adjective Suffixes conveying an active sense :—

**-ing,** Pres. part. Teut. : astonish-*ing*, amus-*ing*.
**-ive,** Rom. : recept-*ive*, amat-*ive*, curat-*ive*.
**-ory, -orious,** Rom. : illus-*ory*, cens-*orious*.
**-erious,** Rom. : delet-*erious*.

(*m*) List of Suffixes having a depreciatory force :—

*Teutonic for forming Nouns* :—
**-craft** : *priest-*craft*, *state-*craft*, witch-*craft*.
**-ling** : hire-*ling*, ground-*ling*, under-*ling*, world-*ling*, weak-*ling*.
**-monger** : *ballad-*monger*, *crotchet-*monger*, *grievance-*monger*.
**-erel, -rel** : mong-*rel*, dogg-*erel*, dott-*erel*, *wast-*rel*.
**-ster** : trick-*ster*, young-*ster*, rhyme-*ster*.
*Romanic for forming Nouns* :—
**-ard** : cow-*ard*, *drunk-*ard*, *slugg-*ard*, dot-*ard*.
**-aster** : poet-*aster*, critic-*aster*.
*Teutonic for forming Adjectives* :—
**-ish** : Rom-*ish*, woman-*ish*, child-*ish*, baby-*ish*, upp-*ish*, *slav-*ish*.
*Romanic for forming Adjectives* :—
**-ile** : puer-*ile* (=child-*ish*), infant-*ile* (=baby-*ish*), serv-*ile* (=slav-*ish*).

(*n*) List of Suffixes having an augmentative force :—

*Teutonic* :—
**-le** (frequentative verb) : dabb-*le*, grumb-*le*, wagg-*le*, etc.
**-er** (freq. verb) : sputt-*er*, be-spatt-*er*, wand-*er*, etc.
*Romanic* :—
**-ard** (excess to a fault) : *blizz-*ard*, *lagg-*ard*, *drunk-*ard*.
**-oon, -one** (augment. noun) : ball-*oon*, bass-*oon*, tromb-*one*.

(*o*) List of Suffixes denoting patronymics :—

*Teutonic* :—
**-ing** : Vik-*ing*, k-*ing* (A.S. cyn-*ing*), Brown-*ing*, Mann-*ing*.
**-son** : Ander-*son*, Collin-*son*, David-*son*.
**-kin** : Peter-*kin* (hence Per-*kin*), Sim-*kin* (Simon-*kin*), Wil-*kin*-s.

(*p*) List of Prefixes and Suffixes by which Transitive Verbs can be formed from an Adjective or Noun :—

**Be-**, Teut : *be*-friend, *be*-calm, *be*-numb, *be*-little.
**-en**, Teut. : dark-*en*, length-*en*, hast-*en*, lik-*en*.
**-se**, Teut. : clean-*se*, rin-*se*, glimp-*se*.
**-le**, Teut. : start-*le* (start), jost-*le* (joust), stif-*le* (stiff).
**In-, en-**, Rom. : *im*-peril, *en-dear, *em- or *im*-bitter.
**-fy**, Rom. : magni-*fy*, modi-*fy*, stupe-*fy*.
**-ise** or **-ize**, Greek : *human-*ise*, *brutal-*ise*, *galvan-*ise*.

(*q*) Suffixes denoting Collection or Place. All Romanic.

**-ade** : arc-*ade* (collection of arches), colonn-*ade*, *balustr-*ade*.
**-age** : foli-*age*, plum-*age*, *bagg-*age*, *lugg-*age*, equip-*age*.
**-ary** : *gloss-*ary*, ros-*ary*, libr-*ary*, gran-*ary*.
**-ory** : invent-*ory*, consist-*ory*, fact-*ory*, dormit-*ory*.
**-ry, -ery** : tenant-*ry*, gent-*ry*, caval-*ry*, machin-*ery*.

**581.**—*Latin and Greek equivalent Prefixes* :—

| | | | | | |
|---|---|---|---|---|---|
| Ambi- (L.) | amphi- (G.) | on both sides. | Semi- (L.) | hemi- (G.) | half. |
| Ab- (L.) | apo- (G.) | from. | Super- (L.) | hyper- (G.) | above. |
| Ex- (L.) | ec- (G.) | out of. | Sub- (L.) | hypo- (G.) | under. |
| In- (L.) | en- (G.) | in, into. | Pro- (L.) | pro- (G.) | before. |
| Indo- (L.) | endo- (G.) | within. | Tri- (L.) | tri- (G.) | thrice. |

**582. The same Affix from different Sources.**—Sometimes we find a suffix or prefix that has one form and spelling, but comes from more than one source. The following are the principal examples:—

(1) **mis-** (Teut. *miss*, wrongly): *mis*-deed, *mis*-hap, *mis*-take.
,, (Rom. *minus*, less, badly): *mis*-count, *mis*-chief, *mis*-nomer, etc.

(2) **a-** (Teut.): *a*-down (for *of*), *a*-foot (for *on*), *a*-long (for *and*), *a*-*ught* (for *án*), *a*-rise (for *á*), *a*-do (for *at*), *a*-fford (for *ge*).
,, (Rom.): *a*-vert (for *a*), *a*-spect (for *ad*), *a*-mend (for *e*).
,, (Gr. *a*, not): *a*-pathy, *a*-theism, *a*-mnesty, etc.

(3) **-en** (Teut. *-en*): maid-*en* (dim.), vix-*en* (fem.), hav-*en* (agent), burd-*en* (pass. sense), ox-*en* (plur.), beat-*en* (pass. part.), wood-*en* (adj.), bright-*en* (Trans. verb).
,, (Rom.): ali-*en* (for *-enus*), kitch-*en* (for *-ina*), mizz-*en* (for *-anus*), kitt-*en* (for *-oun*, Fr. kit-*oun*).

(4) **-ther** (Teut.): mo-*ther* (agent, for *-der*), fur-*ther* (comp. *-ther*), hi-*ther* (adverbial *-der* or *-ther*).

(5) **-ish** (Teut. *-isc*): pal-*ish*, woman-*ish*, peev-*ish*, etc.
,, (Rom.): rad-*ish* (noun, for *-icem*), pun-*ish* (verb, for Lat. *-esc*, Fr. *-iss*).

(6) **-red** (Teut.): hat-*red* (for *rǽden*, rule), hund-*red* (for *rǽd*, rate).

(7) **-lock** (Teut.): wed-*lock* (for *lác*, sport), hem-*lock* (for *leác*, plant).

(8) **-ing** (Teut.): learn-*ing* (noun, for *-ung* or *-ing*), learn-*ing* (pres. part., for *-inde*).

(9) **-le** (Teut.): freck-*le* (dim.), bead-*le* (agent), britt-*le* (adj.), crumb-*le* (freq. verb).
,, (Rom.): catt-*le* (for *-alia*), cast-*le* (for *-ellum*), cand-*le* (for *-ela*), ais-*le* (for *-illa*), circ-*le* (for *-ulus*), humb-*le* (for *-ilis*).

(10) **-ling** (Teut.): seed-*ling* (double dim. for *-el* + *-ing*), dark-*ling* (adv. for *-linga*).

(11) **-er** (Teut.): timb-*er* (for *-er*, *-or*), rid-*er* (for *-ere*, agent), hott-*er* (comp. for *-er*, *-or*), bitt-*er* (positive for *-er*, *-or*), chatt-*er* (freq. verb).
,, (Rom.): arch-*er* (for *-arius*), lev-*er* (for *-ator*), tent-*er* (for *-ura*), attaind-*er* (for Fr. Inf. *-re*), rend-*er* (verb, for *-re*, Fr. Inf.).

(12) **-y** (Teut.): dadd-*y* (dim. for *-ig*), smith-*y* (for *-e*, place of action), might-*y* (adj., for *-ig*), ferr-*y* (verb, for the *i* in *-ian*, Inf. suffix).
,, (Rom.): deput-*y* (for *-atus*), jell-*y* (for *-ata*), enem-*y* (for *-icus*), famil-*y* (for *-ia*), stud-*y* (for *-ium*), progen-*y* (for *-ies*), joll-*y* (for *-ivus*, Fr. *-if*), sall-*y* (verb, for *i* in Fr. Inf. *-ir*).
,, (Greek): energ-*y* (for *-eia*).

(13) **-ure** (Rom.): capt-*ure* (for *-ura*), leis-*ure* (for Fr. Inf. *-ir*).

(14) **-ly** (Teut.): man-*ly* (adj. for *-lic*), fit-*ly* (adv., for *lic-e*).

(15) **-ate** (Rom.): cur-*ate* (for *-atus*), postul-*ate* (for *-atum*), prim-*ate* (for *-atem*), st-*ate* (for *-atus*, 4th declens.), agit-*ate* (verb, from *-atum*).

(16) -ar (Teut.): li-*ar* (for *-ere*, agent).
,, (Rom.): schol-*ar* (for *-aris*), vic-*ar* (for *-arius*), cell-*ar* (for *-arium*).
(17) -ble (Rom.): dou-*ble* (for *-plex*), fee-*ble* (for *-bilis*).
(18) -or (Teut.): sail-*or* (for *-ere*, agent).
,, (Rom.): chancell-*or* (for *-arius*, agent), act-*or* (*-or*, agent), emper-*or* (for *-ator*, agent), err-*or* (*-or*, abstract), mirr-*or* (for *-orium*, place), super-i-*or* (comp.).
(19) -on (Teut.): wag-*on* (borrowed from Dutch).
,, (Rom.): sext-*on* (for sacrist-*an*, Lat. *-anus*), pois-*on* (for *-ionem*, Lat. pot-*ionem*), li-*on* (for *-onem*), patr-*on* (for *-onus*), matr-*on* (for *-ona*).
,, (Greek): phenomen-*on* (for *ŏn*), surge-*on* (for *ōn*).

## CHAPTER XXXII.—BILINGUALISM, DOUBLETS, GRIMM'S LAW, VERNER'S LAW.

583. **Bilingual Character of English.**—One of the most notable peculiarities of English is the bilingual or double character of its vocabulary; § 398. Thus Romanic and Teutonic words of the same, or of almost the same, meaning frequently go in pairs; nouns of Teutonic origin are provided with adjectives of Romanic origin; or the same noun has two adjectives, one Teutonic and the other Romanic. A few examples will now be given in illustration of this point:—

(i) *Words in pairs.*

| *Teut.* | *Rom.* | *Teut.* | *Rom.* |
|---|---|---|---|
| Abode | domicile | Brow | front |
| Answer | reply, respond | Build | construct |
| Ask | inquire | Building | edifice |
| Begin | commence | Burial | funeral |
| Belief | faith | Bury | inter |
| Bemoan | deplore | Buy | purchase |
| Bent | curved | Calling | vocation |
| Blunder | error | Clasp | embrace |
| Boldness | fortitude | Clothes | vestments |
| Bright | radiant | Cold | frigid |

(ii) *Romanic Adjectives to Teutonic Nouns.*

| *Teut.* | *Rom.* | *Lat. word.* | *Teut.* | *Rom.* | *Lat. word.* |
|---|---|---|---|---|---|
| Cat | feline | *felis* | Eye | ocular | *oculus* |
| Church (Gr.) | ecclesiastical | *ecclesia* (Gr.) | Foe | hostile | *hostis* |
| Cow | vaccine | *vacca* | Fox | vulpine | *vulpis* |
| Dog | canine | *canis* | Gospel | evangelical | *evangelium* |
| Ear | auricular | *auris* | Head | capital | *capit-is* |
| Egg | oval | *ovum* | Hearing | audible | *audi-o* |

| *Teut.* | *Rom.* | *Lat. word.* | *Teut.* | *Rom.* | *Lat. word.* |
|---|---|---|---|---|---|
| Horse | equine | *equus* | Sight | visible | *vis-um* |
| Husband | marital | *maritus* | Son | filial | *fili-us* |
| Island | insular | *insula* | Daughter | filial | *fili-a* |
| Light | lucid | *luc-is* | Sun | solar | *sol-is* |
| Lip | labial | *labium* | Spring | vernal | *ver-is* |
| Mankind | human | *homo* | Stream | fluvial | *fluvi-us* |
| Moon | lunar | *luna* | Tongue | lingual | *lingua* |
| Mouth | oral | *or-is* | Tooth | dental | *dent-is* |
| Name | nominal | *nomin-is* | Tree | arboreal | *arbor-is* |
| Nose | nasal | *nas-us* | Wheel | rotatory | *rotat-um* |
| Ox | bovine | *bov-is* | Wife | conjugal | *conjug-is* |
| Sea | marine | *mar-e* | Husband | conjugal | *conjug-is* |
| Sheep | ovine | *ov-is* | Womb | uterine | *uter-us* |
| Side | lateral | *later-is* | | | |

(iii) *Two Adjectives to the same Noun.*

| *Teut. noun.* | *Teut. adj.* | *Rom. adj.* | *Lat. noun.* |
|---|---|---|---|
| Blood | bloody | sanguinary | *sanguin-is* |
| Body | bodily | corporeal | *corpor-is* |
| Brother | brotherly | fraternal | *frater* |
| Burden | burdensome | onerous | *oner-is* |
| Child | childish | puerile | *puer* |
| Cloud | cloudy | nebular | *nebula* |
| Day | daily | diurnal | *dies* |
| Earth | earthly | terrestrial | *terra* |
| Father | fatherly | paternal | *pater* |
| Fear | fearful | timorous | *timor* |
| Fire | fiery | igneous | *ignis* |
| Flesh | fleshly | carnal | *carn-is* |
| Friend | friendly | amicable | *amic-us* |
| Frost | frosty | glacial | *glacies* |
| God | godlike | divine | *div-us* |
| Hand | handy | manual | *man-us* |
| Heart | hearty | cordial | *cord-is* |
| Heaven | heavenly | celestial | *cœl-um* |
| Home | homely | domestic | *domus* |
| Kind | kindly | generic | *gener-is* |
| King | kingly | regal | *reg-is* |
| Knight | knightly | equestrian | *eques* |
| Life | lively | vital | *vita* |
| Milk | milky | lacteal | *lact-is* |
| Mother | motherly | maternal | *mater* |
| Night | nightly | nocturnal | *noct-is* |
| Room | roomy | spacious | *spatium* |
| Skin | skinny | cutaneous | *cutis* |
| War | warlike | bellicose | *bellum* |
| Water | watery | aqueous | *aqua* |
| Will | wilful | voluntary | *voluntas* |
| Woman | womanly | feminine | *femina* |
| | womanish | effeminate | |
| World | worldly | mundane | *mundus* |

(iv) *Verbs in pairs.*

| | |
|---|---|
| Back up (support) a claim. | Bring on (cause) a debate. |
| Bear out (substantiate) a charge. | ,, up (educate) a child. |
| Beat off (repel) an attack. | ,, forward (produce) facts. |
| Block up (obstruct) a passage. | Buy back (redeem). |
| Blot out (obliterate) a word. | Call over (recite) the names. |
| Blow out (extinguish) a candle. | ,, off (divert) attention. |
| Break up (dissolve) a meeting. | ,, in (invite) a doctor. |
| Breathe out (exhale). | ,, up (recollect) a matter. |
| Bring under (reduce) a fever. | ,, forth (evoke) applause. |
| ,, forth (produce) fruit. | Cast out (expel) from society. |
| ,, out (elicit) facts. | ,, down (dejected) with grief. |
| ,, out (publish) a book. | ,, off (discarded) clothes. |
| ,, in (introduce) a custom. | ,, aside (reject) facts. |
| ,, to (resuscitate) a patient. | Clothe (dress). |

DOUBLETS.

**584. Doublet defined.**—Words derived from the same original elements, but differing in form and generally differing in meaning, are called *doublets.*

**585. Origin of Doublets.**—Doublets have arisen from various causes:—

(*a*) Our semi-vowel *w* was seldom sounded in French; so it was usually changed to a *g* or *gu*:—

Wile, guile; ward, guard; wise (manner), guise.

(*b*) Words of Romanic or Greek origin frequently appear in two different forms, one "Popular" and the other "Learned" (see § 417):—

Abridge, abbreviate; aggrieve, aggravate; allow, allocate; amiable, amicable; antic, antique; appraise, appreciate; benison, benediction; chance, cadence; challenge, calumny, etc.

(*c*) Substitution of one letter for another (§ 434):—

Fabric, forge; boss, botch; locust, lobster; deck, thatch; aptitude, attitude; cask, casque; prune, plum; servant, serjeant; ant, emmet; sect, sept; wrap, lap; porridge, pottage, etc.

(*d*) *Metathesis*, or change of place among consonants (§ 436):—

Granary, garner; wight, whit; scarp, scrap; task, tax; ask, ax (vulgar); thrill, thirl; gabble, jabber (here *r* is substituted for *l*).

(*e*) Palatalisation, or the substitution of a palatal consonant for a guttural (§ 438):—

Bank, bench; dike, ditch; kirk, church; trickery, treachery; gaud, joy; gabble, jabber; gig, jig; lurk, lurch; disc, dish, desk, dais; etc.

(*f*) A change of inner vowel:—

Brown, bruin; shock, shake; these, those; dune, down; grove, groove ; hale, whole ; load, lade ; lust, list ; truth, troth ; cavalry, chivalry ; clause, close ; custom, costume ; one, an ; assay, essay.

(*g*) Excision of an initial letter or syllable :—

Adamant, diamond ; engine, gin ; defence, fence ; appeal, peal ; history, story ; affray, fray ; etiquette, ticket ; ensample, sample ; estrange, strange, etc.

(*h*) Interchange of words from cognate roots :—

Name, noun ; barb, beard ; beaker, pitcher ; knot, node ; foam, spume ; corn, horn ; eatable, edible ; brother, friar, etc.

*Grimm's Law, Verner's Law.*

**586. Purport of Grimm's Law.**—Grimm's Law does not belong to historical English grammar, but to comparative Aryan philology ; and therefore a very brief notice of it will be given in this book.[1] It is altogether beyond the reach of those who are unacquainted with Sanskrit, Latin, and Greek on the one side and High German on the other.

The purport of this law is to show (1) the shiftings of Mute consonants (see § 431) from the classical languages (Sanskrit, Greek, Latin) to the Low German, of which English is one ; and (2) from the Low German to the High German. The second has no connection at all with the etymology of English words, but concerns only those students who have mastered High German and desire to trace its descent from English or Low German. Even the first does not give the etymology of English words, but merely shows how they are allied to kindred Aryan words that have sprung from some common Aryan root.

The law may be roughly shown in the following table : here Class. = Classical, L.G. = Low German, and H.G. = High German.

| | Class. | L.G. | H.G. | Class. | L.G. | H.G. | Class. | L.G. | H.G. |
|---|---|---|---|---|---|---|---|---|---|
| 1. Dental . . | d > | t > | th | t > | th > | d | th > | d > | t |
| 2. Labial . . | b > | p > | ph | p > | ph > | b | ph > | b > | p |
| 3. Guttural . . | g > | k > | kh | k > | kh > | g | kh > | g > | k |
| Mnemonic letters. | S | H | A | H | A | S | A | S | H |

[1] Mr. Sweet omits the subject altogether in his *Short Historical English Grammar*, and gives his reasons for so doing in the preface :—" Some

In stating this law its original author (Grimm) made two mistakes. He supposed (*a*) that the second shifting took place at the same time as the first, whereas in point of fact it was developed much later, since High German grew out of Low, and did not begin to exist till after the commencement of the eighth century; (*b*) that the second shifting was as perfectly carried out as the first, whereas in point of fact the second shifting was not complete even in the Dentals and Labials, and did not occur at all in the Gutturals.[1]

In the above scheme the symbol > means "becomes"; thus the Class. *d* becomes *t* in Low German; and the Low German *t* becomes (or rather is supposed to become) *th* in High German. S denotes the *Soft* (or voiced) consonants, H the *Hard* (or voiceless), A the Aspirated. Any one who has mastered the classification of consonants given in § 432, will easily remember Grimm's Law with the help of the three mnemonic words SHA, HAS, ASH. It will further help the student to understand and remember the Law, if he will pay attention to the fact that the only consonants to which it relates are the pairs of *Mutes* or *Stops* shown in § 431.

1. *Dental Series.*—SHA: Lat. **d***uo* > Eng. **t***wo* > High Germ. **z***wei.* (Observe that here the High Germ. letter is *z* = *ts*, which is substituted for *th*, *t* with a spirant (*s*) being used instead of the *t* with an aspirate; sometimes the Eng. **t** shifts to **ss**, as in Eng. *wa***t***er*, Germ. *wa***ss***er.*) || HAS: Lat. **t***res* > Eng. **th***ree* > High Germ. **d***rei.* (Another very simple example is Lat. **t***u*, Eng. **th***ou*, High Germ. **d***u.*) || ASH: Gr. **th***ugater*, Eng. **d***aughter*, High Germ. **t***ochter.*

*Note* 1.—In the combination *st* the classical *t* is not shifted to *th* in Teutonic: thus we have Lat. st-are, Gr. i-st-emi, Eng. st-and, Germ. st-ehen.

*Note* 2.—Sometimes a real shifting takes place, but is disguised; as in Lat. *sua*(d)-*vis*, Eng. *swee***t**, High Germ. *süss.*

2. *Labial Series.*—SHA: Lat. (*s*)*lu***b***ricus*, Eng. *sli***p**, High Germ. *schleifen.* || HAS: Lat. **p***edem*, Eng. *foot*, High Germ.

---

still plead for the retention of Grimm's Law on the ground of its being so interesting and having such a stimulating effect on pupils. The answer to this is, By all means teach it then, but teach it as an extra, not as a part of English grammar, any more than you would include French, Latin, or Greek etymology in English grammar."

[1] Skeat's *Primer of English Etymology*, p. 83. It occurred only in Old High German forms that are no longer in use; as in O.H.G. *chinni*, Mod. Germ. *kinn* (chin).

*fuss.* (Observe, the Low Germ. *ph* or *f* does not really shift to a High Germ. *b*, neither does the *t* of *foot* shift to High Germ. *th*, but to *ss.*) || ASH: Lat. *frater*, Eng. *brother*, Old High Germ. *pruoder* (which in Mod. High Germ. appears as *bruder*, in spite of Grimm's Law): Lat. *flo*, Eng. *blow*, High Germ. *blüh-an.*

3. *Guttural Series.*—(In this series, there is no shifting from Low Germ. to High, but only from Class. to Low Germ.) SHA: Lat. *genu*, Eng. *knee.* || HAS: Lat. *centum* (for *kentum*), Eng. *hundred.* (Here observe the real shifting is from *k* to *h*, and not from *k* to *kh.*) || ASH: Gr. *cholē*, Eng. *gall.*

*Note.*—In all instances the Teutonic *h* is found in lieu of the *kh* which seems to be suggested by Grimm's Law; cf. *cornu*, horn; *cord-is*, heart; *cent-um*, hundred, etc. Owing to difficulty of pronunciation the Teutonic languages discarded *kh.*

**587. Verner's Law.**—This law is intended to supplement Grimm's Law, by accounting for the apparent exceptions to it. It shows that classical *t*, *p*, *k*, when preceded by an *originally unaccented* vowel, shifted one step further than is explained by Grimm. Thus the *t* in Lat. *citra* did not stop at *th*, but shifted a step further to *d*, as in A.S. *hider* (to this place). Similarly the *t* in *pater* did not stop at *th*, when it passed into Low German, but shifted a step further to *d*, as in A.S. *fæder* (not *fæðer*, though in Mod. Eng. *d* has again become *th*). In strict accordance with Grimm's Law, owing to the stress thrown on the first vowel, *t* shifted regularly to *th* in Lat. *frater*, Eng. *brother.*

*Note.*—In the word *mother* there seems to be an exception to Grimm's Law, which Verner's Law fully explains: Lat. *mater*, A.S. *módor.*[1] But in Mod. Eng. the *d* appears as *th.* Perhaps the *d* was changed to *th* on the analogy of *brother.* Or it may have been due to dialectal influence.

The same law explains how the voiceless *s*, after being voiced to *z*, passed into *r.* Thus from the root *as* (to be) we get *are* instead of *ase* for the Third person Plural, and from the root *wes* we get *were* instead of *wese.* Another example is *rear*, a Causal verb formed from the base *rís-an*, to rise. From this

---

[1] The student must understand that the mark ′ placed over the *o* in A.S. *módor* does not denote that this vowel is pronounced with an accent or stress, but merely that the sound of the vowel is prolonged. The accent was originally on the last syllable *dor*, and the *mó*, though prolonged, was unaccented. Moreover, the accent was shifted back on to the former syllable before A.S. was committed to writing. Verner's Law only refers to a primitive accent, in very early times.

base we have the Sc. *reis-a*, to raise (in which the *s* remains), and the A.S. *rǽr-an* (for *rǽs-an*), to rear.

In Lat. *gena*, A.S. *cinn* (sounded as *kin*), the shifting is in accordance with Grimm's Law; but A.S. *cinn* has become *chin* by palatalisation. Similarly in Gr. *phḗg-os*, Lat. *fāg-us*, A.S. *bóc*, the shifting is in accordance with the Law; but in Mod. Eng. we have not only *book*, but also a mutated form *beech*, in which the *ch* is due to palatalisation.

---

## QUESTIONS ON HISTORICAL ENGLISH.

Collected in the order of their occurrence from London Matriculation Papers set since 1879 up to June 1897,—18 years. The month and year are noted against each question :—

1. Show the position of English among allied Teutonic languages. What consonantal changes have been observed to prevail between cognate words in English and any other of these languages? (Jan. 1879.)

2. What is a vowel? What vocalic sounds exist in modern English? Show particularly how they are all expressed by means of the six Roman vowels. (Jan. 1879.)

3. From what languages and at what dates have we received the following words?—*orange, receive, street, bosh, boom, chintz, kiln, fetish, die* (verb), *armadillo, concatenation, chess, chagrin, pool, carouse.* (Jan. 1879.)

4. Account for the letters in italics in—nam*e*, thes*e*, thos*e*, passe*n*ger, sover*eig*n, we*t*test, ci*t*ies, potato*e*s, scept*re*, s*c*eptic, hand*i*work, right*e*ous, tom*b*, cou*l*d, o*u*r. (Jan. 1879.)

5. What cases had nouns formerly in English? What traces still remain of them? Which of them still formally exist? Of how many of them can the force still be expressed by the simple form of the word without a preposition? (Jan. 1879.)

6. What were the ancient forms of the Fem. gender of nouns? What traces of them remain? How have they been supplanted? Discuss the meaning and origin of the termination *-ster.* (Jan. 1879.)

7. Classify adjectives irregularly compared. Give the positive and superlatives of *more, farther, former, utter, hinder, less, rather, further, latter, nearer;* and tell what you know of the history of each. (Jan. 1879.)

8. What part is taken by the verb *have* in conjugating English verbs? Explain the process by which *have* came to be so used, and discuss the following :—

(*a*) I *have* a letter.
(*b*) I *have* written a letter.
(*c*) I *have* come to post it.
(*d*) The post *is* gone.
(*e*) I *have* to go, whether I like it or not. (Jan. 1879.)

9. Classify adverbs (*a*) as to the ideas they express; (*b*) as to their origin. (Jan. 1879.)

10. What are *verbal prepositions?* Give six examples, and show how they came to be used prepositionally. (Jan. 1879.)

11. Show how we came by the Possessive case in *'s*, and by the Plural in *s*. Tell what you know about nouns forming their plurals in *-en*. (June 1879.)

12. Account for the following past tenses of verbs:—*loved, caught, ate, sang*. Tell what you know of the forms *ought* and *must*. (June 1879.)

13. Distinguish between the Classical and the Teutonic elements in English. Point out the several times and ways in which words of Latin (not French) origin have been introduced into the language. (Jan. 1880.)

14. What letters are called mutes, and how are they subdivided? Tell the substance of Grimm's Law. (Jan. 1880.)

15. Describe the several ways of indicating sex in English nouns, including an explanation of the words *woman, lady, vixen, seamstress, mistress, bridegroom, widower, drake*. (Jan. 1880.)

16. Account for the separate forms *two* and *twain*, and for the words *ten, eleven, twelve, hundred, thousand, first, second, dozen, score, fortnight*. (Jan. 1880.)

17. Explain the difference between the two forms of conjugation by telling what you know about the history of each form. (Jan. 1880.)

18. Discuss the inflexions of the verbs *may, make, have, will, do*. (Jan. 1880.)

19. Make a table showing the relationship of English to the other languages of the Indo-European or Aryan family. (June 1880.) Can you name any special peculiarities of the Teutonic group?

20. Indicate some of the most important facts in the history of our alphabet, and account as far as you can for the order in which its letters follow one another. (June 1880.)

21. Describe and account for the loss of inflexions in English nouns, with especial reference to the inflexions that remain. (June 1880.)

22. Write a few notes on the past and present forms of the Subjunctive mood in English verbs, and the present use of the Subjunctive mood. (June 1880.)

23. Explain the following terms applied to the structure of words:—*root, stem, primary derivative, secondary derivative, compound word*.

Apply your explanation to the words *song, bait, batch, suds, thicket, spider, farthing, landscape, knowledge, wedlock, hemlock, eyry, along, gossip, waylay, walking-stick*. (June 1880.)

24. At what different periods has a French element been introduced into our language? Give examples of French words introduced in the several periods mentioned. (Jan. 1881.)

25. What is meant by *runes?* Tell whatever you know concerning any runic letters admitted into the English alphabet. (Jan. 1881.)

26. What is meant by *English roots?* What letter-changes from the English root have occurred in the following words:—*each, thunder, speak, crumb?* (Jan. 1881.)

27. Define the term "Grammatical gender." What was the original force of the suffix in *hunter* and *maltster?* Give other examples. Account for the gender now ascribed to Sun and Moon, and what were their genders in Old English? (Jan. 1881.)

28. Mention any English nouns that form their plurals by processes generally obsolete, and describe the processes. Which of the following are genuine plurals, and how do you account for the forms that are not such :—*alms, summons, banns, sessions, costs, eaves, weeds, riches, dice*? (Jan. 1881.)

29. What is the original meaning of the term *case*, and what does it now mean in English Grammar? Of what *lost* case-endings are the traces still discernible in our language? (Jan. 1881.)

30. Discuss the words italicised in the following :—

> Long *ago* we were *wont* to let plain *living* accompany high *thinking*.
>
> *Methinks* you *might* have spoken, but you *durst* not.

(Jan. 1881.)

31. Explain the forms *worse, next, first, farthest, furthest*. (June 1881.)

32. Explain the origin and the present use of the words *what, which, whether*. (June 1881.)

33. We write *he thinks*; why do we not write *he musts*? Illustrate your answer by reference to some other verbs. (June 1881.)

34. Define a *root*, and an *English root*. What are *hybrids*? Mention any hybrids that are generally recognised as good English. (Jan. 1882.)

35. What vowel-sounds were the letters *a, e, i, o, u* originally intended to represent? Point out the letter changes that have taken place in the following words :—*gossip, number, tyrant, fee*. (Jan. 1882.)

36. What is the real power of the Genitive case? Explain the following forms :—*their, golden*, for Christ *his* sake. (Jan. 1882.)

37. Derive *score, dozen, hundred, eleven*. How are distributive numerals expressed in English? Give the first three ordinal English adverbs. (Jan. 1882.)

38. What pronouns were originally used, where Relatives are now employed in our language? Explain the forms—*yours truly; to-morrow*; I and the lad will go *yonder; the* more, *the* merrier. Define Reflexive pronouns. (Jan. 1882.)

39. Give examples of a prepositional and a pronominal adverb,—of an adverb formed by the Genitive Singular of a substantive, and of a preposition formed by the past participle of a verb. Why are interjections not to be reckoned as parts of speech? Derive *well-a-day, alas*. (Jan. 1882.)

40. What is meant by *Diminutives* and *Augmentatives*? Enumerate, and illustrate by examples, the suffixes most commonly used in English in the formation of such words, and of patronymics. (Jan. 1882.)

41. How many vowel-sounds are used in spoken English? What are they? How many diphthongs are used in written English? What are they? (June 1882.)

42. Use the words *book, but, thou, be, who, why, enough, feet, ought, knew, best*, as examples of some means of distinguishing words in modern English, that belonged to the language in its earliest Teutonic form. (June 1882.)

43. Explain the formation of the words—*dean, sexton, vinegar, biscuit, tile, orchard, livelihood, allow, isle, island*, and add a few comments on the phonetic changes illustrated by their history. (June 1882.)

44. Tell the history of the Possessive case in English, and define the present limits of its use. (June 1882.)

45. Tell what you know of the origin and structure of the English alphabet. (Jan. 1883.)

46. Account for the suffix or inflexion in each of the following words:—*chicken*, *oxen*, *vixen*, *beeves*, *pennies*, *pence*, *spinster*, *widower*, *gander*, *drake*. (Jan. 1883.)

47. Explain as fully as you can the superlative forms *inmost*, *next*, *best*, *least*, *last*, *first*, and the comparative forms *nearer* and *worse*. (Jan. 1883.)

48. "You *ought* him a thousand pound." Explain this use of the word *ought*; show how we came by the two forms *own* and *owe*; account also for the forms *durst*, *quoth*, *methinks*. (Jan. 1883.)

49. Show that the following words were originally compound nouns:—*barn*, *orchard*, *stirrup*. Tell what you know of the Teutonic suffixes used in the forming of abstract nouns. (Jan. 1883.)

50. With what languages of Europe is English in its origin most closely connected? What exactly is its relation to Latin? What to French? (June 1883.)

51. Explain the term *Anglo-Saxon*. What objections are there to it? What terms have been proposed in its stead? Give reasons for its retention. (June 1883.)

52. Mention any words that have been added to our language in the nineteenth century. (June 1883.)

53. Discuss the plural form *children*. Write down some nouns that have no special form to express plurality, and account for them. Is it correct to speak of *a two-foot rule*? (June 1883.)

54. Examine the forms—*lesser*, *worse*, *foremost*, *elder*, *farther*. Derive *next*, *last*, *best*, *further*, *rather*. (June 1883.)

55. Mention some verbs that, being originally preterites, have come to be used as presents. Can you account for such a usage? (June 1883.)

56. Tell what you know of the origin of each of the following words, with comment upon any fact in the history of English that it might serve to illustrate:—*Avon*, *Chester*, *Grimsby*, *cloister*, *minster*, *cherry*, *beef*, *nuisance*, *cousin*, *potion*, *poison*. (Jan. 1884.)

57. Discuss each of these plural forms—*leaves*, *oxen*, *kine*, *men*, *brethren*; also the forms—*news*, *means*, *pains*, *riches*, *eaves*, *summons*. (Jan. 1884.)

58. Which form do you prefer to use—"He *dare* not," or "He *dares* not"? What is to be said on behalf of each form? Explain the forms *willy-nilly*, *won't*, *to wit*. (Jan. 1884.)

59. Explain with reference to their origin the use of the words *own* and *owe* in "I *own* a pound," "I *owe* a pound," "I *own* I *owe* a pound." Explain the verbs in the question "How *do* you *do*?" (Jan. 1884.)

60. What various sounds has the letter *a* in Mod. English? How does it come to have so many? Which of them is the oldest? (June 1884.)

61. Show as definitely as you can the influence of Norman-French on our grammar. (June 1884.)

62. Explain how it is that we have such forms as *Sunday* and *Monday* alongside of such forms as *Wednesday* and *Thursday*. Also how it is we say *Lady-day* and not *Lady's-day*. (June 1884.)

63. Derive the words *lady*, *madam*, *sir*, *husband*, *woman*, *bachelor*, *lass*, *cousin*, *uncle*, *archbishop*. (June 1884.)

64. Name the main sources which have contributed to form *modern* English, and state the period at which the influence of each has been chiefly felt. (Jan. 1885.)

65. Explain the origin of the suffixes in the following words:—*shadow, hillock, holy, busy, farthing, darling, worship, favour, burgess, ceremony, enemy, homage, terrace.* (Jan. 1885.)

66. What is the etymology of the following words:—*under, over, every, eleven, twenty, least, near?* (Jan. 1885.)

67. What traces are there in English of a Perfect formed by reduplication? Can you show by what process reduplication has disappeared? (Jan. 1885.)

68. Give the etymology of the following pronouns, and show how their use has varied:—*this, that, what, which, whose.* (Jan. 1885.)

69. What explanation has been given of the suffixes which mark the past tense in Weak verbs? (Jan. 1885.)

70. Distinguish between the terms *cognate* and *derived* as applied to words. Mention some words cognate with *bear* (the verb), and some derived from it. (June 1885.)

71. What is meant by a *letter?* Give some account of the letter *c* and its uses. What various sounds are represented in English by the letter *u?* (June 1885.)

72. Discuss the forms—*brethren, seamstress, indices, fisherman, cherry, kind, swine, cherubim, riches, uttermost.* (June 1885.)

73. Mention some usages in which *am* as an auxiliary has been ousted by *have.* (June 1885.)

74. Show clearly that English in its origin and basis is a Teutonic language. Also say by what other Teutonic languages it has been affected and influenced since its coming into this island. (Jan. 1886.)

75. Mention the various times and ways in which Latin has increased our vocabulary through the medium of the Romance languages. (Jan. 1886.)

76. What is meant by *organs of speech?* How would you define a *vowel?* how a *diphthong?* How many more vowel-sounds has English than vowels? (Jan. 1886.)

77. In what various ways are the letter *g* and the combination *gh* pronounced in English? How do there come to be various ways? (Jan. 1886.)

78. Can you explain the italicised letters in the following words?—child*r*en, wou*l*d, cou*l*d, agains*t*, gen*d*er, vi*c*tuals, frontisp*ie*ce, crayfis*h*, mi*c*e. (Jan. 1886.)

79. Give half a dozen instances of words of which the present spelling obscures the etymology. How did such spelling come into fashion? (Jan. 1886.)

80. State the force or forces of the suffixes *-ster, -ism, -let, -some, -ard, -ish.* (June 1886.)

81. What is the origin of the *d* in the preterite of *love?* What of the *d* in its past participle? Explain the forms—*had, made, left, built, clad, methinks.* (June 1886.)

82. When is *dare* inflected in the 3rd Sing. Pres. Indicative? Can you cast any light on the forms *durst, wist, wrought, sold, sought, ago?* (June 1886.)

83. Mention some cognates of *better, nether, among, noun.* (June 1886.)

84. Give examples of all the various sounds of *a* in our language; also those of *ough* and of *ch*. (Jan. 1887.)

85. Is the difference in usage between *each* and *every* justified by their etymology? Why should you not say, "Neither of the ten suited me"? What alternative form of expression is there to, "That is mine and nobody else's"? Which do you think is to be preferred? (Jan. 1887.)

86. Explain and illustrate the terms *synthetic* and *analytic* as applied to languages. By which would you describe the English language as it now is? (June 1887.)

87. Distinguish between the Teutonic and the Romance elements of the English vocabulary; and write two short sentences, one containing no words of Romance origin, the other none of Teutonic. Which is the easier sentence to write, and why? (June 1887.)

88. Classify the consonantal letters. What is meant by Grimm's Law, and to which group does it apply? How would you class the letter *h*? (June 1887.)

89. State some differences as regards verbal forms, case-endings, and suffixes, between the English of the fourteenth century and that of the present day? (June 1888.)

90. Illustrate the influence which the classical element has had upon modern English directly, and through the medium of the Romance languages. (June 1888.)

91. Several words are found to be common to the dialect of Scott and Chaucer. Can you account for this? (June 1888.)

92. Account for the formation of the following auxiliary verbs:—*may, am, will, could, ought, might, hast, must*. (June 1888.)

93. Chaucer has been called "the well of English undefiled." Discuss this with reference to the growth of English in Chaucer's time. (June 1888.)

94. Give the derivation of the following words:—*alive, dead, many, alert, entail, result, heresy, ideal, knife, key, bury, rather, king, lady*. (June 1888.)

95. Explain the suffixes of the following words:—*kingdom, every, seemly, business, farthing, hardship, piecemeal, nostril, gospel, orchard, namesake*. (June 1888.)

96. Discuss the use and abuse of technical terms. Whence do we chiefly obtain them? (June 1888.)

97. Give a complete list of English possessive pronouns, stating in regard to each its origin and the period when it first came to be used. (Jan. 1889.)

98. State the different forms that have been employed for marking comparison in adjectives, and explain the origin and exact import of the most usual forms. (Jan. 1889.)

99. What traces of reduplication can you adduce in the tense formations of verbs in English (Old and Modern). (Jan. 1889.)

100. Show the different usages of the following words, and account for these by their derivations:—*alight, burden, broil, wind, blow, race*. (Jan. 1889.)

101. Give the original and the derivative meaning of each of the following words:—*cynical, puny, trivial, agony, pagan, villain, heathen, economy, tally*. (Jan. 1889.)

102. Give, as concisely as you can, equivalents of Saxon origin for the

following words :—*frustrate, eliminate, elucidate, desiderate, prevaricate, identical, eradicate, corroborate, reciprocal, internecine.* (Jan. 1889.)

103. Explain exactly the following, commenting upon anything which is archaic in usage :

(*a*) Truly and indifferently to minister justice.
(*b*) Let him pursue his course without let or hindrance.
(*c*) Prevent us in all our doings.
(*d*) In good sooth.
(*e*) Vouchsafe us thy help. (Jan. 1889.)

104. From what sources do we principally obtain our naval, agricultural, and political terms ? Illustrate your answer by instances. (Jan. 1889.)

105. What languages have existed, or do still exist, in the British Isles ? (June 1889.)

106. Tell all you know of the development of the English language down to the Norman Conquest, and show how the Norman Conquest affected it. (June 1889.)

107. Tell all you know of *my* and *mine*, of *me* and *thee*, and of *his, hers, its.* (June 1889.)

108. What is meant by the Laws of Speech ? Mention any of the ways in which they have affected our language. (June 1889.)

109. From what other sources besides Latin and the Romance languages have we borrowed words ? Show that our vocabulary is constantly being enlarged ? (Jan. 1890.)

110. Discuss these phrases :—*Next Lady-day, for conscience sake, a friend of mine, the Emperor of Germany's accession, the Queen's rebels, for John his sake.* (Jan. 1890.)

111. What adjectives have we to the nouns *parish, cat, horse, alms, church, bishop* ? (Jan. 1890.)

112. Discuss the etymology of the following words :—*also, axe, could, only, songstress, such, testator, twain, vixen, whichever.* (June 1890.)

113. Show the marks of distinction between Weak and Strong verbs in Old and Modern English. (June 1890.)

114. Show how frequently in English the pronunciation of a word does not correspond with its orthography. How would you account for such discrepancies ? (Jan. 1891.)

115. How many sounds has the symbol *a* in English ? Also in what other ways can the sound it has in *hate* be expressed ? (Jan. 1891.)

116. From what other parts of speech are Adverbs formed, and what is the function of Adverbs ? Can you cast any light on the forms *darkling, whilom, piecemeal, afterwards* ? (Jan. 1891.)

117. Show how the languages of the Celts and the Danes have at different times affected the English tongue ? (June 1891.)

118. Show how at different times foreign words have become a part of the English tongue ? What is meant by an acclimatised foreign word in English ? (June 1891.)

119. Discuss the forms—*less, lesser ; worse, worser ; inmost, innermost.* (June 1891.)

120. Discuss the etymology of *our* and *ours, their* and *theirs, who* and *what, why* and *which.* (June 1891.)

121. Show how in word-building Prefixes alter the meanings of words,

and Suffixes their functions. Cite six derived words with English, six with Latin, six with Greek, and six with French Suffixes. (June 1891.)

122. What languages had already been talked in this island, or were being talked in it, when the Anglo-Saxon Conquest took place? Were they in any way akin to the dialects spoken by the Angles and Saxons? (Jan. 1892.)

123. Why is the speech of the peasants in Yorkshire so different from that of the peasants in Devonshire? and why are they both so different from the English of Literature? (Jan. 1892.)

124. Explain the terms *letter*, *vowel*, *accent*, *guttural*, *sibilant*. What two different pronunciations has the combination *th*? How many has the combination *ough*? (Jan. 1892.)

125. Give ten instances in which distinction of sex is denoted by words of quite separate origin, and explain in some at least of them why it is so? (Jan. 1892.)

126. Parse and annotate the italicised words in—

(*a*) He *must* go.
(*b*) He *ought* to have gone.
(*c*) He *ought* to go.
(*d*) He *need* not go.
(*e*) He *dare* not go.

And discuss: *Methinks; I wis; quoth he; so mote it be; this will never do.* (Jan. 1892.)

127. What are the adverbs answering to the adjectives *shy*, *far*, *fast*, *kindly*, *lowly*? Explain the forms *betimes*, *whilom*, *erewhile*, *piecemeal*, *ashore*. (Jan. 1892.)

128. Give as large a list as you can of Classical words which found their way into our language before the Norman Conquest, and point out how they were probably introduced. (June 1892.)

129. Mention ten words that have come to us from Italian, five from Dutch, five from Hebrew, and ten from modern French. (June 1892.)

130. Discuss the etymology and usage of the masculine possessive *his*, and the neuter possessive *its*. (June 1892.)

131. What are *doublets*? Show with illustrations in what various ways they have arisen in English. (Jan. 1893.)

132. State what you know of the history of every word in the present question, noting any peculiarities in the form or significance of each. (Jan. 1893.)

133. Trace the origin of the words—*priest*, *curate*, *bard*, *minstrel*, *soldier*, *fellow*, showing what light each throws upon the character of the intercourse to which its adoption in English was due. (Jan. 1893.)

134. State with illustrations anything you know about the effects of accent in English. (Jan. 1893.)

135. Mention as many as you can of the derivatives or cognates of *two*. (Jan. 1893.)

136. Write a short history of the 2nd personal pronouns (Singular and Plural) with regard to changes both in form and usage. (Jan. 1893.)

137. Give a concise account of the formation of Adverbs. Is there anything anomalous in the words *godly* and *goodly*? (Jan. 1893.)

138. Distinguish derivatives and compounds, and comment on the formation of the following:—*witticism*, *oddity*, *non-plussed*, *wondrous*, *bridal*, *lawyer*. (Jan. 1893.)

139. How do we find names for the new things that from time to time

have to be expressed in words, *e.g.* for new games, new inventions, new political or social ideas? Give instances. (June 1893.)

140. Explain why the pronunciation and even the language of the peasantry, in various parts of the country, are so distinctly different, giving a few specimens. (June 1893.)

141. What other permissible spellings are current of the following words —*inflection, programme, rhyme, era, mediæval, apothegm?* What is to be said for or against them? (June 1893.)

142. Show carefully how Grimm's Law, or any apparent exception to it, is illustrated by the following words:—*stand, father, third, sweet.* (Jan. 1894.)

143. State briefly what you know of the origin and history of each word in the following sentence:—"Meanwhile the great rhetorical fabric gradually arose. He revised, erased, strengthened, emphasised, with indefatigable industry." (Jan. 1894.)

144. What phases of English are illustrated by the plurals—*men, shoes, these presents, sheep, mathematics?* (Jan. 1894.)

145. Illustrate, from the names for the different parts or contents of a house, the characteristic differences between the Roman and the English element in the vocabulary. (Jan. 1894.)

146. Describe the principal sources of apparent irregularity in the conjugation of Strong verbs in modern English. Comment on the forms "I have *struck*," "the sun has *shone*," "I *shot*." (Jan. 1894.)

147. Illustrate the formation of Adverbs from cases of nouns and adjectives. (Jan. 1894.)

148. Distinguish between Compounds and Derivatives, and illustrate your distinction from the words—*orchard, flood, nest, bridal.* (Jan. 1894.)

149. Under what circumstances do words go out of use? (Jan. 1894.)

150. Give examples (not more than three under each head)—(1) of writers who have contributed to fix the literary language; (2) of writers who, since its establishment, have written in dialects. (Jan. 1894.)

151. What exactly do you understand by the statement that two languages are "related"? How would you describe the relationship of modern English to French, Greek, Welsh, Danish, and the English spoken by King Alfred respectively? (June 1894.)

152. In what various ways, besides borrowing from foreign languages, may the vocabulary of a language be increased? Give examples. (June 1894.)

153. Give an account of the vowel-sounds now used in educated English (using some phonetic notations, if possible, but illustrating your symbols by words in which the corresponding sounds occur.) (June 1894.)

154. Point out the inflexions in *then, than, win, there, whence, why, seldom,* and show how far their force is traceable in the present meaning of these words. (June 1894.)

155. Comment on the marks of comparison in the following, and point out which of them are, in modern usage, true comparatives: *worser, former, nearer, latter, inferior, elder, other.* (June 1894.)

156. Explain the forms of the first *four* ordinal numbers. (June 1894.)

157. From what sources have we the suffix *-y?* Explain its occurrence in the words—*duchy, flowery, body, jelly, jolly.* (June 1894.)

158. Mention other English words cognate with *cadence, hospital, tradition, quiet, potion, pauper,* stating what you know of the origin of each. (June 1894.)

159. Enumerate and account for the chief anomalies of modern English spelling. (Jan. 1895.)

160. Write etymological notes on the following words: *forlorn, alms, thunder, livelihood, went, pagan, alchemy, bask, Monday, island.* (Jan. 1895.)

161. What is meant by *gender* in grammar? Enumerate the various ways of indicating *gender* in English. Comment on *gander, tapster, vixen, bridegroom, songstress.* (Jan. 1895.)

162. Classify English adjectives according to (i.) their functions, and (ii.) their terminations. From what sources have we the suffix *-ous?* Explain its occurrence in *conscious, glorious, wondrous, courteous, righteous.* (Jan. 1895.)

163. Trace, as fully as you can, the history of the inflexions of the 3rd pers. Pronoun, Singular and Plural. (Jan. 1895.)

164. Discuss the origin of the Relative Pronouns, and distinguish their use in modern English. What equivalents are there in English for the Relative? Give illustrative sentences. (Jan. 1895.)

165. Account for the following forms:—*told, sought, caught, could, must, wot, are, went, ought, hight.* (Jan. 1895.)

166. Tabulate the Pronominal Adverbs, and explain their formation. (Jan. 1895.)

167. State what you know of the history of any *six* words in the following sentence:—"No man hardly is so savage, in whom the receiving kindnesses doth not beget a kindly sense." (June. 1895.)

168. Give some account of the Scandinavian element in English. (June 1895.)

169. Classify the vocalic *sounds* (not letters) in English, denoting each by means of some word in which it occurs. (June 1895.)

170. Distinguish *accent* and *emphasis,* and illustrate the part played by the first in the history of English words. (June 1895.)

171. Illustrate the influence of the social and political institutions of the Normans on the English vocabulary. (June 1895.)

172. Account clearly for the differences between a *compound* and (1) a *derivative,* (2) two words in syntactical connection, with instances. (June 1895.)

173. Analyse each of the following expressions with its component parts, and explain how its syntactical function arose:—*lest, therefore, therefor, nevertheless, besides, anent.* (June 1895.)

174. Explain the terms—*auxiliary, past-present, strong-weak,* as applied to certain classes of verbs. (June 1895.)

175. Give a short account of the origin of adverbs. (June 1895.)

176. State the source or sources of the suffixes *-ate, -ish, -ling, -y,* with instances of each. How far do they serve to distinguish different parts of speech? (June 1895.)

177. Comment on the spelling of the following words:—*broad, once, doubt, could, whose, right.* (June 1895.)

178. Illustrate the chief varieties of Doublets. (June 1895.)

179. Explain carefully what is meant by calling English a Teutonic language. (Jan. 1896.)

180. Give some account of the influence of Christianity on the English vocabulary. (Jan. 1896.)

181. Write etymological notes on the following words:—(i.) *anthem*; (ii.) *chicken*; (iii.) *eleven*; (iv.) *fairy*; (v.) *gossip*; (vi.) *island*; (vii.) *rhyme*; (viii.) *righteous*; (ix.) *songstress*; (x.) *wanton*. (Jan. 1896.)

182. Write a short history of *-s* as the sign of the plural in English. (Jan. 1896.)

183. (i.) Enumerate and illustrate the chief methods of forming compound nouns; (ii.) Give three instances of monosyllabic words which are in reality compounds. (Jan. 1896.)

184. Discuss the inflexions in the following:—*him*, *their*, *hers*, *why*, *once*, *whilom*; give another example in each case. (Jan. 1896.)

185. Illustrate and explain the different uses of (i.) the Infinitive, and (ii.) the various verbal forms in *-ing*. Tell the history of *-ing* as the ending of the present participle. (Jan. 1896.)

186. Account for the decay of Strong verbs in English. Give one instance of the Strong past participle used merely as an adjective, and one instance of its use as an adverb. Explain these forms—*fell*, *brought*, *sold*, *taught*, *wert*, *wrought*. (Jan. 1896.)

187. How many tenses are there in an English verb? What is meant by saying that there is no future tense in the English language? (Jan. 1896.)

188. From what sources have we the prefix *a-*, and the suffix *-y*? (Jan. 1896.)

189. Classify prepositions according to their origin. Explain *but*, *between*, *except*. (Jan. 1896.)

190. What is meant by the distinction between "learned" and "popular" *borrowed words*? Under what circumstances have Latin words (not French) at various times been borrowed in English? Refer in answer to the above distinction. (June 1896.)

191. Show, if possible with a table, what vocalic sounds are used in ordinary spoken English. (June 1896.)

192. Write down (i.) *six* illustrations of Grimm's Law; (ii.) *six* apparent exceptions to it, commenting upon the latter. (June 1896.)

193. Give the force of the suffixes which occur in the following words, commenting upon any anomaly in the form or meaning of each:—*witness*, *childhood*, *girdle*, *lawyer*, *gosling*, *rookery*. (June 1896.)

194. Show accurately how the following cognate words are distinguished, and also how they are connected in meaning:—*corps*, *corpse*; *gage*, *wage*; *diamond*, *adamant*; *cage*, *cave*; *dish*, *desk*, *disc*, *dais*; *priest*, *presbyter*. (June 1896.)

195. Give two examples each of (i.) Strong verbs which have become weak; (ii.) Weak that have become Strong; (iii.) Strong participles that have been assimilated to the preterite (past tense); (iv.) Strong preterites that have been assimilated to the participle. (June 1896.)

196. Explain and illustrate the laws or principles involved in the formation of the following words:—*causeway*, *book-learned*, *hindmost*, *thirteen*, *piecemeal*, *darkling*. (June 1896.)

197. Show summarily in what various ways adverbs have been formed in English. (June 1896.)

198. Give a summary of the various ways in which the vocabulary of a language may be enlarged, with illustrations from English. (June 1896.)

199. Give a brief account of the process of inflexional levelling in English. (Jan. 1897.)

200. Trace the history of the 3rd Personal Pronoun, singular and plural. (Jan. 1897.)

201. Differentiate the following both as regards usage and origin:—*further*, *farther*; *later*, *latter*; *older*, *elder*; *outer*, *utter*; *foremost*, *first*. (Jan. 1897.)

202. Account clearly for the present and past tense forms of the chief Auxiliary verbs. Explain the modern use of *shall* and *will*. (Jan. 1897.)

203. Classify the Weak verbs, and explain the following forms:—*taught*, *sold*, *sought*, *fed*, *felt*. (Jan. 1897.)

204. Annotate the following statement:—Words, originally other parts of speech, are sometimes used as conjunctions. (Jan. 1897.)

205. Explain the force and origin of the following suffixes:— *-ship*, *-en*, *-ly*, *-ness*, *-y*. Give instances. (Jan. 1897.)

206. Explain carefully what is meant by (i.) Anglo-Saxon; (ii.) Anglo-French; (iii.) Hybrids. (Jan. 1897.)

207. Enumerate the principal Indo-European languages, and indicate, by description or diagram, how English is related to Italian, Sanskrit, Dutch, Erse. (June 1897.)

208. At what periods have Latin words been largely borrowed? Give six examples from living English of words so borrowed at each period, and show what class of the vocabulary was at each period chiefly affected by such borrowing. (June 1897.)

209. Illustrate the borrowing of words either from Celtic or from Scandinavian sources into English. (June 1897.)

210. Give a short account of existing case-forms in English, and also of some which no longer survive as cases. (June 1897.)

211. Explain the italicised letters in the following words:—a*d*vantage, s*c*ent, de*b*t, frontispi*e*ce, cou*l*d, ancien*t*. (June 1897.)

212. What peculiarities, of form or meaning, in the expression of relations of number, are illustrated by the following?—*score*, *triple*, *hundred*, *first*, *second*, *million*. (June 1897.)

213. Trace the origin of *who*, *which*, and *that*, as relative pronouns, and define their usage in modern English. (June 1897.)

214. Distinguish the origin of the suffix *y* in the following words:—*jury*, *body*, *jolly*, *army*, *wordy*, *jelly*. (June 1897.)

215. Explain carefully what is meant by the past-present or strong-weak verbs, giving the reason for each name. (June 1897.)

216. Explain the structure and meaning of the following:—*each*, *every*, *any*, *about*, *either*, *or*. (June 1897.)

217. In what different ways are adverbs formed in English? (June 1897.)

# APPENDIX I.—PROSODY AND POETRY.

**588. Prosody** (Gr. *pros-odia*, lit. a song sung to an instrument) treats of the laws of metre. It might be called "the grammar of verse."

**Rhythm** (Gr. *rhuthmos*, measured flow or motion) is "the musical flow of language." This is produced for the most part by a well-balanced recurrence of pauses and accents.

Rhythm has been elsewhere defined "a principle of proportion introduced into language."[1] This definition is practically equivalent to our own, though perhaps it scarcely gives enough prominence to *sound*. It is only a practised reader who can perceive "the proportion of language" without reading the composition aloud.

Rhythm is not confined to verse. It is quite as necessary to an orator as to a poet; and there is scarcely any kind of prose, of which the attractiveness is not increased by the recurrence of pauses and accents at suitable intervals.

**Rime** (A.S. *rim*, "number," misspelt as *rhyme* from a supposed connection with Gr. *rhuthmos*) is a repetition of the same sound at the *ends* of two or more lines. The effect of rime, however, is not produced, unless the lines succeed one another immediately or near enough for the resemblance of sound to strike the ear. Monosyllabic rimes are always accented.

*Note* 1.—A rime is usually of *one* syllable. But rimes can also be in two or more syllables, provided that the first syllable is accented and the rest are unaccented; as, *motion, ocean; behaviour, saviour*. Double rimes are called in French, and sometimes in English, female or feminine, while a single rime is called a male. Double and treble rimes are more commonly used in comic poetry:—

> To hear them rail at honest *Sunderland*,
> And rashly blame the realm of *Blunderland*.—POPE.

*Note* 2.—A monosyllabic rime is *perfect* under three conditions: (1) the vowel or vowels, whatever the spelling may be, must produce precisely the same effect on the ear; (2) if any consonant or consonants *follow* the riming vowel or vowels, these (whatever the spelling may be) must produce precisely the same effect; (3) the consonant that *precedes* the rime must, to prevent monotony, pro-

[1] Abbott and Seely's *English Lessons for English People*, p. 143.

duce a *different* effect on the ear. Thus *hair* and *fair* are perfect rimes, because the three conditions just stated are all satisfied. But *bear* and *fear* are not perfect rimes, because the vowel-sounds, though not very different, are not quite the same. Again, *fare* and *af-fair* are not perfect rimes, because the riming vowel is preceded by the same consonant. Again, ap-*peased*, re-*leased* are not perfect rimes, because the final consonants in the former have the sound of *zd*, while those in the latter have the sound of *st*.

When the rime is dissyllabic or polysyllabic, every syllable except the first must begin with the same consonant; cf. *Sunderland*, *Blunderland*, un-*fortunate*, im-*portunate*.

**Assonance** (Lat. *ad* + *sonant-ia* verba).—This term is applied to words which rime in the vowel or vowels, but not in the consonant or consonants following. It is therefore a very imperfect kind of rime; as, *slumber*, *blunder*; *same*, *cane*.

**Alliteration** (Lat. *ad* + *litera*).—When two or more words begin with the same vowel, or the same consonant, or the same syllable, this is called alliteration. It is *initial* riming as distinct from *end*-riming.

*Ruin* seize thee, *ruthless* king!—GRAY.

*Note.*—All our earliest poetry was alliterative. The last great specimen of such poetry in our literature is *Piers the Plowman*, by William Langland, born in A.D. 1332. The poem is written in lines of ten to twelve syllables. The following is a specimen:—

In a *s*omer *s*eson, when *s*oft was the *s*onne,
I *sh*ope me in *sh*roudës, as I a *sh*ope were.

**Cæsura** (a Latin word denoting "a cut"). In Latin prosody this meant the "cut" or division of a foot somewhere near the middle of the line, the cut being followed by a pause of the voice in reading the line aloud. In English prosody cæsura means merely the *pause* of the voice, by which lines of eight or more syllables are usually divided, when they are read aloud; and this pause may occur either at the end or in the middle of a foot. (For the meaning of "foot" see below, § 590.) Rhythm greatly depends on the position of the cæsura.

In the following example the figure against each line shows the number of feet (with or without a half foot) preceding each cæsura. When a comma or other stop occurs in the same place as the cæsura, the rhythm of the line is helped by the sense; but a pause or cæsura can be made independently of punctuation, if the rhythm of the line is improved thereby. Sometimes a line has no cæsura; that is, neither the rhythm nor the sense of the line require that any pause should be made in reading or repeating the line aloud:—

3½ Of man's first disobedience ‖ and the fruit
3 Of that forbidden tree, ‖ whose mortal taste
Brought death into the world and all our woe
2½ With loss of Eden, ‖ till one greater Man
1½ Restore us ‖ and regain the blissful seat,
2 Sing, Heavenly Muse, ‖ that on the secret top, etc.
MILTON.

Observe that monotony is avoided and the rhythm of the lines enhanced by varying the place of the cæsura.

Observe also that the third line does not need any cæsura.

**589. Metre** (Gr. "measure") is "rhythm reduced to law." It depends on two factors:—

(*a*) The accentuation of syllables.

(*b*) The number of *accented* syllables to a line.

*Note.*—Quantity means the amount of time required for pronouncing a syllable distinctly. In Latin prosody syllables were subdivided by quantity into Long and Short. In English versification, however, quantity is of no importance excepting so far as it affects accentuation. It is entirely subordinated to accent.

Then tore' | with blood'- | y tal'- | on the' | rent plain'.—BYRON.

Here the short syllable *the* is made as long as possible for the sake of giving it an accent, and the long syllable *rent* is made as short as possible for the sake of removing its accent.

**590.** A specific combination of accented and unaccented syllables is called a **foot**. The number of syllables to a foot may be either two or three, but it cannot be less than two or more than three, and *one of these must be accented.*

(*a*) An **Iambus** consists of one unaccented and one accented syllable. This is the commonest of all our feet.

Ap-pear', be-sides', at-tack', sup-ply'.

(*b*) A **Trochee** consists of one accented and one unaccented syllable. Not so common as the Iambus.

Ho'-ly, up'-per, grand'-eur, fail'-ing.

(*c*) An **Anapæst** consists of two unaccented syllables followed by an accented one. Rather uncommon.

Col-on-nade', re-ap-pear', on a hill'.

(*d*) A **Dactyl** consists of one accented syllable, followed by two unaccented ones. Very rare.

Mes'-sen-ger, mer'-ri-ly, prop'-er-ty, in'-fa-mous.

*Note* 1.—A fifth kind of foot is sometimes added, called an **Amphibrach**, consisting of an accented syllable between two unaccented ones; as *re-venge'-ful, a-maz'-ing.* The following line from Campbell may be quoted as an example:—

There came' to | the beach' a | poor ex'-ile | of E'-rin.

It would be easy, however, to subdivide the line into anapæsts by making the first foot an Iambus, which is common in anapæstic metre :—

There came′ | to the beach′ | a poor ex′- | ile of E′-rin,

in which *Erin* is a double rime.

But the following lines contain amphibrachs, which cannot be resolved into anapæsts :—

Most friend′-ship | is feign′-ing,
Most lov′-ing | mere fol′-ly ;
Then heigh′-ho | the hol′-ly,
This life′ is | most jol′-ly.—SHAKSPEARE.

*Note* 2.—A sixth kind of foot, long and consisting of two accented syllables, is sometimes added. In Latin prosody this foot is called a **Spondee.** But in English prosody no such foot is recognised, since theoretically there cannot be more than one accent to an English foot. Sometimes, however, two accented syllables are placed together for the artificial purpose of making the sound of the line suggestive of the sense :—

When A′- | jax strives′ | *some* rock's′ | *vast* weight′ | to throw′,
The line′ | *too* la′- | bours and′ | the words′ | *move* slow′.

*Note* 3.—The names of all the feet are derived from Greek. *Iambus* means "aiming at," "attacking," so called because this foot was first used in Satire. *Trochee* means "running," so called because it is a rapid measure. *Dactyl* means "finger," so called because this foot, like a finger, consists of one long followed by two shorts. *Anapæst* means "thrown back," because this foot is a dactyl reversed. *Spondee* means "pertaining to libations," so called because, when libations were poured out, slow and solemn melodies were used. *Amphibrach* means "short at both sides," so called because this foot consists of one long syllable enclosed by two short ones.

**591.** To **scan** a line (Lat. *scan*-d-ere, to climb) is to divide it into its several feet, and say *what kind* of feet they are, and *how many* of them there are. Lines of two feet are called *dimeters;* of three, *trimeters;* of four, *tetrameters;* of five, *pentameters;* of six, *hexameters.* In Tennyson's *Locksley Hall* we have an example of *octometers* (8 feet). In scanning a line the following precautions should be noted :—

(*a*) The number of feet to a line depends on the number of *accented* syllables, not on the total number of syllables (§ 589).

(*b*) An accented monosyllable at the beginning of a line is sometimes made to do duty for an entire Iambic foot :—

*Stay*′, | the king′ | hath thrown′ | his war′- | der down′.—SHAKS.
(*Iambic pentameter*, 5 feet.)

(*c*) In the Trochaic and Dactylic metres, an accented monosyllable at the end of a line counts as an entire foot, though in the former this foot is short of one unaccented syllable, and in the latter of two :—

Life′ is | but′ an | em′-pty | dream′.—LONGFELLOW.
(*Trochaic tetrameter*, 4 feet.)

Com′-rades, | leave′ me | here′ a | lit′-tle, | while′ as | yet′ 'tis | ear′-ly | morn′.—TENNYSON (*Trochaic octometer*, 8 feet.)

Mer′-rily, | mer′-rily | shall′ I live | now′,
Un′-der the | blos′-som that | hangs′ on the | bough′.—SHAKS.
(*Dactylic tetrameter*, 4 feet.)

(*d*) Metres are not always perfectly carried out. In an Iambic line the first foot is sometimes a Trochee instead of an Iambus. In the Anapæstic metre, Iambic feet are sometimes put for Anapæsts, and this in any part of the line :—

Daugh′-ter | of God′ | and man′, | ac-com′- | plished Eve′.—MILTON.
(*Iambic pentameter*, 5 feet.)

Not a drum′ | was heard′, | not a fu′- | neral note′.
(*Anapæstic tetrameter*, 4 feet.)

(*e*) In scanning a line, two short syllables coming together can be counted as one for the sake of the metre :—

Wing″d with | red light′- | ning and′ | impet′- | *uous* rage′,
The mul′- | ti-tud′- | *inous* sea′ | incarn′- | adine′.

(*f*) Two open vowels belonging to different words can be slurred, so as to be fused together and pronounced as one :—

Impressed′ | th*e* efful′- | gence of′ | his glo′- | *ry a*bides′.
By her′- | ald's voice′ | explained′ ; | the hol′- | *low a*byss′,
Abom′- | ina′- | b*le, u*nut′- | tera′ | b*le, a*nd worse′.
T*o i*nsult′ | the poor′ | or beau′- | ty in′ | distress′.
May I′ | express′ | th*ee u*nblamed, | since God′ | is light′.

**592. Blank Verse.**—"Blank" means unrimed. This is much used in Epic and Dramatic verse, and generally in Iambic pentameters. This is the noblest of all verse. It is the most difficult to write effectively, though it seems the easiest.

See example of Epic blank verse quoted from *Paradise Lost* in §588 under Cæsura.

In Longfellow's *Hiawatha* we have a solitary example of blank verse in Trochaic tetrameters:—

Then′ the | lit′-tle | Hi′-a- | wa′-tha
Learned′ of | ev′-ery | bird′ the | lan′-guage.

Occasionally we have blank verse in Dactylic dimeters :—

Can′-non to | right′ of them,
Can′-non to | left′ of them,
Can′-non in | front′ of them.—TENNYSON.

Some attempts have been made to introduce Classical (Latin

and Greek) metres into English; but they have not been successful. This is a third kind of blank verse. The best examples of Latin hexameters are Longfellow's *Evangeline* and Kingsley's *Andromeda*:—

> This' is the | for'-est pri- | mev'-al, the | mur'-mu-ring | pines',
> and the | hem'-lock.—LONGFELLOW.

*Special Metres.*

**593. The Heroic Couplet.**—In this metre lines consisting of five Iambic feet rime together in pairs.

This is called "Heroic" because it has been much used in translating Epic or Heroic poetry; as in Dryden's translation of Virgil, and Pope's translation of Homer.

This metre is sometimes varied by a triplet, in which the third line (called an Alexandrine) can have *six* Iambic feet instead of five:—

> The sacred lake of Trivia from afar,
> The Veline fountains, and sulphureous Nar,
> Shake at the baleful blast, the signal of the war.—DRYDEN.

**594. The Sonnet.**—Borrowed from Italy. It consists of fourteen Iambic pentameters. The first eight lines (called the octave), have usually three rimes amongst them, which occur in no fixed order. The last six lines (called the sestette) have also three rimes, of which the last two are always a couplet, and the other four usually alternate.

The subject of a sonnet is usually either reflective or amatory. The word *sonnet* is derived from Ital. *sonetto.*

**595. Ottava Rima.**—Borrowed from Italy. Each stanza consists of eight Iambic pentameters. The letters *a*, *b*, *c* show the system of riming. (The word *ottava* means "octave.")

> *a* 'Tis sweet to hear the watch-dog's honest bark
> *b* Bay deep-mouthed welcome as we near our home;
> *a* 'Tis sweet to know there is an eye will mark
> *b* Our coming, and look brighter when we come;
> *a* 'Tis sweet to be awakened by the lark,
> *b* Or lulled by falling waters; sweet the hum
> *c* Of bees, the voice of girls, the song of birds,
> *c* The lisp of children and their earliest words.—BYRON.

**596. The Spenserian Stanza.**—Called Spenserian from its originator, Spenser, who used it in writing *The Faery Queen.*

> *a* Roll on', | thou deep' | and dark'- | blue O'- | cean, roll,
> *b* Ten thou'- | sand fleets' | sweep o'- | ver thee' | in vain:
> *a* Man marks' | the earth' | with ru'- | in; his' | control
> *b* Stops with' | the shore'; | upon' | the wa'- | tery main
> *b* The wrecks' | are all' | thy deed'; | nor doth' | remain

c A shad'- | ow of' | man's rav'- | age save' | his own,
b When for' | a mo'- | ment like' | a drop' | of rain
c He sinks' | into' | thy depths' | with bub'- | bling groan,
c Without' | a grave', | unknelled', | uncof'- | fined, and' | unknown.
BYRON.

The ninth and last line, which in this metre always consists of six feet instead of five, is called an Alexandrine, like the third line in heroic triplets, § 593.

**597. The Metre of "In Memoriam."**—This consists of a four-line stanza in which each line contains four Iambic feet, the fourth line riming with the first, and the third with the second. This metre was not, as is often supposed, originated by Tennyson. It was used by Sandys in his metrical paraphrase of the Psalms, A.D. 1636:—

What profit can my blood afford,
When I shall to the grave descend?
Can senseless dust thy praise extend?
Can death thy living truth record?—*Psalm* cxxx.

(Quoted from Skeat's *Student's Pastime*, p. 347, No. 424.)

**598. Stanzas** (Ital. *stanza*, Old Ital. *stantia*, so called from the stop or pause at the end of it). All stanzas are in rimed, not in blank, verse.

A stanza of three lines is called a **Triplet**, as in Tennyson's *Two Voices*, in which each line consists of an Iambic tetrameter; the third line is not an Alexandrine.

Whatev'- | er cra'- | zy sor'- | row saith',
No life' | that breathes' | with hu'- | man breath'
Has ev'- | er tru'- | ly longed' | for death'.

A stanza of four lines is called a **Quatrain** (Fr. *quatre*, Lat. *quatuor*, four). Of such stanzas the most common examples are —(1) the **Ballad** metre, as in *Chevy Chase;* and (2) the **Elegiac** metre, as in Gray's *Elegy*. In both of these the rimes alternate: —in the former a tetrameter with a trimeter; in the latter a pentameter with a pentameter. The stanza used in *In Memoriam* is another kind of quatrain; see § 597.

A stanza of six lines is called a **Sextant**, in which the rimes may occur in the following orders:—(1) *a, b, a, b, a, b;* (2) *a, a, b, c, c, b;* (3) *a, b, a, b, c, c.*

A stanza of eight lines is called an **Octave**; but it is best known under the name of Ottava Rima (Ital. sounded as *ottāva reema*, Lat. *octavus*, eighth); see § 594.

A stanza of nine lines is the Spenserian; see § 596.

*Poetic Diction.*

**599. Prose, Poetry.**—Poetry (from Gr. *poiēt-es*, an originator) is distinguished from prose (Lat. *prosa*, for *prorsa* or *pro-versa*, turned forward, rapid, unchecked) not only by the possession of metre, but by certain peculiarities of diction and of thought. The most prosaic matter may be expressed in the most prosaic language, and yet in the most perfect metre; the metre does not make either the matter or the language poetical.

> Something had happened wrong about a bill,
> Which was not drawn with sound commercial skill;
> So, to amend it, I was told to go
> And seek the firm of Clutterbuck and Co.—CRABBE.

**600. Poetic Diction.**—The chief peculiarities are the following:—

(1) *The use of archaic or less common words.*—Poetry pays little or no attention to changes in current speech. At the same time it likes to distinguish itself from prose. It therefore avoids common words, and retains words that were used by former poets, after they have gone out of general use:—

**Nouns.**—Poetry often uses *swine* for *pigs; swain* for *peasant* or *husbandman; billow* for *wave; main* for *sea* or *ocean; maid* or *damsel* for *girl; nuptials* for *marriage; vale* for *valley; steed* or *charger* for *horse; ire* for *anger; woe* for *sorrow* or *misery; thrall* for *distress*, etc.

**Adjectives.**—Poetry often uses *lone* or *lonesome* for *lonely; drear* for *dreary; dread* for *dreadful; intrepid* or *dauntless* for *brave; rapt* for *delighted; hallowed* for *holy; baleful* for *pernicious*, etc.

**Adverbs.**—Poetry often uses *scarce* for *scarcely; haply* for *perhaps; sore* for *sorely; oft* for *often; erst* or *whilom* for *formerly; of yore* or *of old* for *in ancient times; scantly* for *scantily; anon* for *at once*, etc.

**Verbs.**—Poetry often uses the older forms of past tenses in preference to the modern or Weak ones; as *wrought* for *worked; bade* for *bid; begat* for *begot; clove* for *cleft; crew* for *crowed; drave* for *drove; throve* for *thrived; clomb* for *climbed; stove* for *staved; clad* for *clothed.*

**Conjunctions.**—Poetry often uses *what though* or *albeit* for *although; ere* or *or ere* for *before; nathless* for *nevertheless; an if* for *if.*

(2) *Omission of words required by Prose.*—Two purposes are served by such omissions: the metre is preserved, and the diction is made less like that of prose:—

| Example | Omitted |
|---|---|
| The brink of (the) haunted stream | *Article.* |
| Creeping like (a) snail unwillingly to school | *Article.* |
| (He) who steals my purse steals trash | *Noun or Pronoun.* |
| Lives there (the man) who loves his pain? | *Noun or Pronoun.* |
| For is there aught in sleep (that) can charm the wise? | *Relative as Subject to a Verb.* |
| 'Tis distance (that) lends enchantment to the view | *Relative as Subject to a Verb.* |

| | |
|---|---|
| Mean though I am, (I am) not wholly so . . | Finite Verb. |
| Happy (is) the man, whose wish and care, etc. . | |
| To whom thus Adam (spoke) . . . . . | |
| Soldier rest, thy warfare (being) o'er, etc. . . | *Participle.* |
| My ramble (being) ended, I returned . . . | |
| He knew himself (how) to sing . . . . . | *Conjunction.* |
| Permit (that) I marshal thee the way . . | |
| He mourned (for) no recreant friend . . . . | *Preposition.* |
| Through the dear might of Him that walked (on) the waves . . . . . . . . . | |
| Despair and anguish fled (from) the struggling soul | |

(3) *Change in the regular order of words.*—The same two purposes are hereby served as before.

(*a*) Adjective placed after its noun, instead of before it:—

> Or where the gorgeous East with richest hand
> Showers on her kings *barbaric* pearl and gold.—MILTON.

(*b*) Subject placed after its verb, and object before it:—

> No *hive* hast *thou* of hoarded sweets.

(*c*) Preposition placed after its noun instead of before it:—

> Where echo walks steep hills *among*.

(*d*) Infinitive placed before the finite verb, instead of after it:—

> When first thy sire *to send* on earth,
> Virtue, his darling child, designed.—GRAY.

(*e*) Adverb placed before its verb, instead of after it:—

> *Up* springs from yonder tangled thorn
> A stag more white than mountain snow.—SCOTT.

(*f*) Complement placed before its verb, instead of after it:—

> *Grieved* though thou art, forbear the rash design.

(4) *Use of adjectives or participles for clauses.*—One of the aims of poetry is to say as much as possible in the fewest possible words: hence an adj. or part. is made to do duty for a clause.

> (*a*) He can't combine each well-*proportioned* part.

That is, he cannot make the different parts proportionate to each other, and then combine them into a symmetrical whole.

> (*b*) From his *slack* hand the garland wreathed for me
> Down dropped, and all the faded roses shed.

Here "slack" stands for "which had become slack."

> (*c*) From *loveless* youth to *unrespected* age
> No passion gratified except her rage.

Her youth was devoid of love, the peculiar grace of youth; and her old age was devoid of respect, the peculiar privilege of age; all through life the one predominant passion was her evil temper.

*Note.*—In paraphrasing poetry into prose one of the first things to be done is to convert such adjectives or participles as those quoted above into verbs, adding such Relatives or Conjunctions as may be necessary.

(5) *Use of ornamental epithets not required by the sense:*—

The breezy call of *incense-breathing* morn,
  The swallow twittering from its *straw-built* shed,
The cock's shrill clarion, and the echoing horn
  No more shall rouse them from their lowly bed.—GRAY.

*Note.*—In paraphrasing poetry, such epithets, if they are repeated at all, should be thrown into the background, as they are out of place in prose composition, and tend to encumber the sense.

(6) *A freer use of figurative language.*—See the Figures of Speech in Appendix II.

*The different kinds of Poetry.*

**601. Epic.** From Gr. *epik-os*, *epos*, a word, speech, or tale. Heroic legends told in metrical language were originally recited, not written; hence such poems were called "words."

"The epic poem treats of one great complex action, in a grand style, and with fulness of detail."—T. ARNOLD.

**Lyric.** From Gr. *lurik-os*, adapted to the lyre. Short rapid poems in irregular metre. Such poems are often called *Odes* (Gr. literally "songs").

**Dramatic**, the poetry of the stage. From Gr. *dramatik-os*, that which pertains to action or acting.

*Note.*—Thus in the name "Epic," the idea of recitation is prominent; in "Lyric," the music; and in "Dramatic," the acting.

**Pastoral.** From Lat. *pastor*, a shepherd. The poetry of rural life.

**Didactic.** From Gr. *didaktik-os*, instructive. Instruction on some technical or moral subject, set forth in verse and embellished as far as possible with poetic ornament.

**Satire.** From Lat. *satira*, "a dish of mixed foods." Poetry which exposes and censures the faults of persons or communities.

Added to these there is **Descriptive** poetry, such as Thomson's *Seasons;* **Elegiac** poetry (from Gr. *elegos*, a lament), as Wolfe's *Burial of Sir John Moore;* the poetry of **Romance** or **Legend**, as Macaulay's *Lays of Ancient Rome*, or Scott's *Lady of the Lake;* **Ballad** poetry, as *Chevy Chase.*

## APPENDIX II.—FIGURES OF RHETORIC.

A FIGURE of rhetoric is a deviation from the ordinary use of words, with a view to increasing their effect.

(1) **Simile** (Lat. *similis*, like): a formal expression of the likeness said to exist between two different objects or events:—

> Errors, *like* straws, upon the surface flow;
> He that would search for pearls must dive below.

(2) **Metaphor** (Gr. transference): an informal or implied simile:—

> Experience is the *lamp* by which our feet are guided.

(3) **Personification**: the ascription of mind and will to inanimate things:—

> *Weary* wave and *dying* blast
> *Sob* and *moan* along the shore;
> And all is peace at last.

(4) **Fable, Parable, Allegory**: a description of one event under the image of another. These are the same at bottom, but a parable is more serious than a fable, and an allegory is a parable carried to a greater length. The aim of all is to enforce some prudential or moral truth by a story, in which a personification or series of personifications is maintained to the end. In fables the lower animals are personified as men.

*Note.—Fable* is from Lat. *fabula*, a story. *Parable* is from Gr. *parabolê*, a comparison. *Allegory* is from Gr. *allegoria*, a description of one thing under the image of another.

(5) **Metonymy**: lit. "a change of name" (Gr. *meta*, change, *onoma*, name): to describe a thing by some *accompaniment* instead of naming the thing itself:—

> The *crown* (=king) would not yield to the *mitre* (=priest).

(6) **Syn-ec-do-ché** (Greek): "the understanding of one thing by means of another," as in the following examples:—

| | |
|---|---|
| All *hands* (=men) at work . . | (part for whole). |
| The smiling *year* (=season) . . | (whole for part). |
| He acted *the lord* (=lordly character) | (concrete for abstract). |
| A *justice* (=judge) of the peace . . | (abstract for concrete). |
| The *marble* (=statue) speaks . . | (material for thing made). |

(7) **Euphemism** (Gr. *eu*, well, *phemismos*, speaking): the describing of something disagreeable or offensive in agreeable or non-offensive terms:—

> That statement was purely an effort of imagination (*i.e.* a lie).

*Note.*—Euphemism must not be confounded with *Euphuism*, an affected, high-flown style assumed as a mark of good breeding (Gr. *Euphues*, "well-born," the title of a book by Lyly, a contemporary of Shakspeare, who made his hero talk in this style, and wrote in the same style himself).

(8) **Climax** (Gr. ladder): a series of representations that succeed one another in an ascending order of impressiveness:—

It is an *outrage* to *bind* a Roman citizen; to *scourge* him is an *atrocious crime;* to *put him to death* is almost a *parricide;* but to *crucify* him, what shall I call it?

(9) **Anticlimax** or **bathos** (Gr. depth): a ludicrous descent from the more impressive to the less impressive:—

Here thou, great Anna, whom three realms obey,
Dost sometimes *counsel* take, and sometimes *tea.*—POPE.

(10) **Interrogation**: an emphatic mode of affirming or denying something by means of asking a question:—

Who is here is so base that would be a bondman? Who is here so rude that would not be a Roman?—SHAKSPEARE.

(11) **Antithesis** (Gr. *anti*, against, *thesis*, placing): placing words in contrast to each other:—

A *friend* exaggerates a man's *virtues*, an *enemy* his *crimes.*

(12) **Epigram** (Gr. *epi*, on, *gramma*, writing): a tersely expressed combination of ideas that might seem to be contradictory, or are rarely thought of together:—

Art lies in concealing art (*Ars est celare artem*).—*Latin Proverb.*
By *merit* raised to that *bad* eminence.—MILTON.
A past that was never present.—GROTE.

(13) **Irony** (Gr. dissimulation): praise intended for blame:—

And Brutus is an *honourable* man.—SHAKSPEARE.

(14) **Litotes** (Gr. extenuation): the use of a negative before a noun or adjective to indicate a strong affirmative in the opposite direction:—

He is no dullard (decidedly clever).

(15) **Apostrophé** (Gr, *apo*, away, *strophé*, turning): addressing some absent person, as if he were present, or some inanimate thing (concrete or abstract), as if it were living:—

O Luxury! thou curst by heaven's decree,
How ill exchanged are joys like these to thee!—GOLDSMITH.

(16) **Prosopopœia** (also called Vision, from Gr. *prosōpon*, face, *pœia*, making): describing the past or future as if it were present, the imaginary as if it were real:—

Is this a dagger that I see before me?—SHAKSPEARE.

*Note.*—The Historic present (see § 349, *e*) exemplifies this figure.

(17) **Onomatopœia** (Gr. *onomat-os*, name, *pœia*, making): the use of words that suggest the sense by their sound. See p. 438, *Note* 2 :—

> Rend with tremendous sound your ears *asunder*,
> With *gun*, *drum*, *trumpet*, *blunderbuss*, and *thunder*.

(18) **Circumlocution, Periphrasis** (Gr. *peri*, around = *circum*; *phrasis*, speaking = *locutio*): a roundabout way of describing anything;—an aid to euphemism, if such aid is wanted:—

> He resembled *the animal that browses on thistles* (= an ass).
> His *prominent feature* (nose) like an eagle's beak.—WORDSWORTH.

(19) **Hyperbolé** (Gr. exaggeration): not always a fault:—

> They were swifter than eagles and stronger than lions.—*Old Test.*

## APPENDIX III.—SYNONYMS.

FOR a definition of synonym, see p. 216.

(1) **Adoration, worship.**—The former gives prominence to the outward act; the latter to devotional feeling.

(2) **Allude, refer.**—We *refer* to a thing that has been specified, or is just going to be specified. We can *allude* to a thing by implication, without specifying it at all.

(3) **Aid, help.**—We *aid* a man, when we add our efforts to his own, as in raising a ladder against a wall. We *help* him, when we give him something that he requires, as by throwing him a rope to save him from drowning.

(4) **Apparent**, what seems to be; **evident**, what is and cannot be otherwise.

(5) **Aware, conscious.**—*Aware* of something external to oneself; *conscious* of one's own thoughts and feelings. "He was *aware* of the enemy's designs, and *conscious* of his inability to cope with them."

(6) **Confess, admit.**—We *confess* a fault; *admit* an error.

(7) **Couple, pair.**—Except in the phrase "a married couple," a *couple* means two things not matched: cf. "a *couple* of horses," "a *pair* of horses."

(8) **Delightful, delicious**: as "*delightful* music," "*delicious* fruit." What pleases the lower senses is delicious; what pleases the higher ones is delightful.

(9) **Discover, invent.**—We *discover* some fact or law that existed before, but was unknown. We *invent* some new device or contrivance, that did not exist before. *Discovery* belongs to science; *invention* to art.

(10) **Distinguish, discriminate.**—We *distinguish* sounds into high and low. We *discriminate* them as being either high or low, when we hear them.

(11) **Habit, custom.**—*Habit* is the tendency of *mind*, on which custom or customary *action* depends. A *habit* of industry leads to the *custom* of keeping punctual hours.

(12) **Imagination, fancy.**—*Imagination* is the faculty by which we mentally realise effects before they are produced. *Fancy* is the more playful exercise of the same faculty; and hence the word sometimes degenerates into the sense of whim or freak: "That is mere *fancy*."

(13) **Import, meaning.**—*Import* is the actual sense of a word; *meaning* is the sense intended by the speaker, which might not tally with the actual sense or real import.

(14) **Liberty, freedom.**—*Liberty* implies previous restraint: "He set his slaves at *liberty*." *Freedom* implies absence of restraint at the time: "He is *free* to go where he likes."

(15) **Patient, passive.**—*Patient* means absence of anger or complaint; *passive* means absence of resistance.

(16) **Part, portion.**—*Part* is a fraction of a whole; *portion* is a part allotted: "The estate was divided into four *parts*, and each heir received his *portion*."

(17) **Perpetual, eternal.**—The former is the weaker of the two.

(18) **Politician, statesman.**—The first is a self-seeker who makes a trade of politics. The second is one who in his political capacity consults the general good.

(19) **Stop, stay.**—A man may *stop* at a house and *stay* inside it for the night. The one implies arrested motion; the other implies a halt where motion has been arrested already.

(20) **Strict, severe.**—A man may be *strict* in observing rules, and *severe* in punishing the breach of them.

(21) **Unlikely, improbable.**—*Unlikely* applies chiefly to the future; *improbable* to the present and past. We say a thing is unlikely, but not improbable, to happen.

## APPENDIX IV.—CHANGES OF MEANING.

One important branch in the history of a language is to trace the changes of meaning that some of its words have undergone in the course of their literary use.[1] The changes can be classified as follows:—(*a*) Elevation of meaning; (*b*) degradation of meaning; (*c*) narrowing of meaning; (*d*) widening of meaning; (*e*) shifting to some side-meaning, which gradually ousts the original, as in *x*, *xy*, *y*.

### (*a*) *Elevation of Words.*

**Amiable** (Lat. *amabilis*); once denoted physical beauty.
So *amiable* a prospect.—HERBERT.

**Babe, baby**; once denoted a doll or puppet.
The *baby* of a girl.—SHAKSPEARE (*Macbeth*).

**Brave**; once denoted brilliant, gaudy.
Sweet rose, whose hue angry and *brave*.—HERBERT.

**Companion**; once a term of contempt; a low fellow.
*Companion*, hence!—SHAKSPEARE (*Julius Cæsar*, iv. 3).

**Delicate**; once used in a bad sense; luxurious, voluptuous.
Haarlem is a very *delicate* town.—EVELYN.

**Emulation**; once used in the sense of an evil passion,—envy.
Such factious *emulations* shall arise.—SHAKSPEARE.

**Feminine**; once in the sense of womanish; now, womanly.
The *feminine* son of a brave father.—HOLLAND.

**Generous**; once noble only in birth; now noble in character.
The *generous* and gravest citizens.—SHAKSPEARE.

**Liberal**; once free in a bad sense; unscrupulous.
A profane and *liberal* counsellor.—SHAKSPEARE.

**Mountaineer**; once used in the sense of freebooter.
No savage fierce, bandit, or *mountaineer*.—MILTON.

**Prestige**; once used in the sense of illusion.
The sophisms of infidelity and the *prestiges* of imposture.
WARBURTON.

**Popularity**; once the practice of courting popular applause.
Indicted for *popularity* and ambition.—HOLLAND.

**Spinster**; could once denote a woman of bad life.
Many would never be indicted *spinsters*, were they spinsters indeed.—FULLER.

### (*b*) *Degradation of Words:* much more numerous than (*a*).

**Animosity**; once, spiritedness or courage; now, resentment.
A man of *animosity* and courage.—HALES.

**Artificial**; could once mean artistic, with the sense of natural.
*Artificial* strife
Lives in these touches, livelier than life.—SHAKSPEARE.

**Base**; once, humble, low, without being depraved.
A peasant and *base* swain.—BACON.

---

[1] Out of the 156 illustrative sentences quoted in this Appendix nearly all are from Webster's *English Dictionary*, a few are from the author's own reading, and a few more, about 20 in number, from Trench's *Select Glossary*.

**Brat**; once, a child in a favourable sense.
Oh Abraham's *brats*, oh brood of blessed seed.—GASCOIGNE.

**Censure**; once, merely opinion; now, blame.
Take each man's *censure*, but reserve thy judgment.
SHAKSPEARE.

**Conceit**; once, any kind of notion; now, vanity.
A *conceit* of somewhat ridiculous.—BACON.

**Counterfeit**; once, to imitate without any sinister purpose.
Christ doth not set forth this unrighteous steward for us to *counterfeit*.—TYNDALE.

**Demure**; once modest without affectation.
Sober, steadfast, and *demure*.—MILTON.

**Doleful dumps**; once used seriously; now, in a comic sense.
The pensive court in *doleful dumps* did rue.—FULLER.

**Egregious**; once, remarkable; now, remarkably bad.
Wiclif's *egregious* labours are not to be neglected.—MILTON.

**Formal**; once, essential, real, pertaining to the form (essence).
The *formality* (essence) of the vow lies in the promise made to God.—STILLINGFLEET.

**Fulsome**; once, simply full; now, full *ad nauseam*, sickening.
His lean, pale corpse grew *fulsome*, fair, and fresh.—GOLDING.

**Garble**; once, to pick out the good and reject the bad; as "to garble spices."

**Gossip**; once, a sponsor in baptism; now, a mischief-maker.
A lady invited to be a *gossip*.—SELDEN.

**Gross**; once, great; now, coarse.
A *gross* body of horse under the Duke.—MILTON.

**Idiot**; once, uneducated, simple-minded.
Christ was received of *idiots* and the simple sort.—BLOUNT.

**Imp**; once, a child; now, a goblin or little fiend.
The tender *imp* was weaned.—FAIRFAX.

**Insolent**; once, unusual; now, insulting.
If any should accuse me of being new or *insolent*.—MILTON.

**Knave**; once, merely a boy or servant; now, a rascal.
Fortune's *knave*, a minister of her will.—SHAKSPEARE.

**Libel**; once, a bill or indictment; now, a false charge.
A *libel* of forsaking (a bill of divorce).—WYCLIFF.

**Libertine**; once, free-thinker; now, free-liver.
Our modern *libertines*, deists, and atheists.—A.D. 1711.

**Lust**; once, eager desire; now, carnal or other evil passion.
My *lust* to devotion is little.—BISHOP HALL.

**Maudlin** (contr. of *Magdalene*); once, penitent, sorrowful in a good sense.

**Mere**; once, pure; now used in a depreciatory sense.
Our sorrows would be *mere* and unmixed.—TAYLOR.

**Minion**; once, favourite; now, an unworthy favourite.
Brave Macbeth, like Valour's *minion*.—*Macbeth*, i. 2, 32.

**Naughty**; once used of adults; now only of children.
So shines a good deed in a *naughty* world.—SHAKSPEARE.

**Obsequious**; once, obedient in a good sense; now, servile.
*Obsequious* to his orders, they bear him hither.—ADDISON.

**Officious**; once, helpful, dutiful; now, meddlesome.
Yet not to earth are these bright orbs *officious*.—MILTON.

**Plausible**; once, commendable; now, specious, disingenuous.
Which made a *plausible* bishop seem to be Antichrist.—HACKET.

**Portly**; once, stately; now, bulky, corpulent.
He bears him like a *portly* gentleman.—SHAKSPEARE.

**Prejudice**; once, prejudgment in a neutral sense, foresight.
Naught might hinder his quick *prejudice*.—SPENSER.

**Puny**; once, younger, junior; now, paltry, insignificant.
If *punies* or freshmen neglect Aristotle.—JACKSON.

**Rascal**; once, a man of the common sort; now, a scoundrel.
The heads of clans with their several *rascalities* (=retainers, followers).—JACKSON.

**Resentment**; once, reciprocal feeling; now, angry feeling.
They declared their *resentment* of his services.
*Council Book*, 1651.

**Retaliation**; once, requital in a neutral sense; now, revenge.
He sent word to the duke that his visit should be *retaliated*.—HERBERT.

**Sad**; once, serious, settled; now, sorrowful.
Ripe and *sad* courage.—CHAUCER.

**Sensual**; once, appealing to any outward sense; now, carnal.
Pleasing and *sensual* rites and ceremonies.—BACON.

**Silly**; once, timely; then, innocent; now, simple, foolish.
The *silly* (innocent) virgin strove him to withstand.
SPENSER.

**Tawdry** (*St. Awdry*); once, fine and showy; now, trashy and vulgar.

**Tempt**; once, to put to the test; now, to entice to evil.
God did *tempt* Abraham.—*Old Testament*.

**Tinsel**; once, a silver or gold texture; now, paltry finery.
Under a duke, no man to wear cloth-of-gold *tinsel*.—A.D. 1551.

**Umbrage**; once, a shadow; now, offended feeling.
That opinion carries no *umbrage* of reason.—WOODWARD.

**Uncouth** (lit. *unknown*); once, rare and elegant; now, inelegant.
Harness . . . so *uncouth* and so rich.—CHAUCER.

**Varlet**; once, a groom, stripling; now, a term of contempt.
My gentle *varlet* has come in.—MALORY.

**Vassalage**; once, *valorous* service rendered by a vassal.
For all forgotten is his *vassalage*.—CHAUCER.

**Vilify**; once, to hold cheap; now, to abuse.
I do *vilify* your censure (hold your opinion cheap).—BEAUMONT AND FLETCHER.

**Wiseacre**; once, a sage or wise man; now, always ironical.
Pythageras became a mighty *wiseacre*.—LELAND.

**Wizard**; once, a sage or wise man; now, a sorcerer.
The star-led *wizards* haste with odours sweet.—MILTON.

(c) *Words that have narrowed their meaning.*

**Amuse**; once, to occupy the mind with anything, not merely mirth.
He *amused* his followers with idle promises.—JOHNSON.

**Brook**; once, to use in any way; now, only to tolerate.
Let us *bruik* the present hour.—*Scotch Ballad.*

**Carpet**; once, any kind of covering, not only of floors.
The subject came upon the *carpet* (table-cloth, *i.e.* it was brought before the meeting; see p. 213 (80)).

**Disease**; once, discomfort of any kind; now, sickness.
So all that night they passed in great *disease.*—SPENSER.

**Duke**; once, captain or leader; now, only a title.
Theseus, *duke* of Athens.—SHAKSPEARE.

**Harness**; once, equipment of any kind, as "die in *harness.*"
At least we'll die with *harness* on our back.—SHAKSPEARE.

**Knuckle**; once, joint of any kind; now, only a finger.
She kneeled down sadly with weary *knuckles.*—GOLDING.

**Manure**; once it could denote moral improvement.
*Manure* thyself, then; to thyself be improved.—DONNE.

**Mediterranean**; once, of land as well as sea.
Cities as well *mediterranean* as maritime.—HOLLAND.

**Repeal**; once, to recall or cancel anything; now, only a law.
Repelling sorrows and *repealing* gladness.—SYLVESTER.

**Starve**; once, to die from any cause; now, only from hunger.
Thus *starved* the mighty Hercules.—CHAUCER.

**Vermin, worm**; once, a crawling animal of any length.
The crocodile is a dangerous *vermin.*—HOLLAND.
When Cerberus perceived us, the great *worm*,
His mouth he opened and displayed his tusks.—LONGFELLOW.

**Voyage**; once, any kind of journey (Lat. *viaticum*).
So steers the prudent crane
Her annual *voyage* borne on winds.—MILTON.

**Wife**; once, woman; now, married woman.
On the green he saw sitting a *wife.*—CHAUCER.

(d) *Words that have widened their meaning.*

**Assure**; once, to betroth; now, to make certain in any sense.
To me, sad maid, he was *assured.*—SPENSER.

**Chest**; once, coffin; now, a strong box (Lat. *cista*).
He dieth and is *chested.*—HAWES.

**Harbinger**; once, one who prepared *harbour* (*herberge*, Old Norse) for another by going on first; now, simply a forerunner.
A gentleman expostulated with a *harbinger*, who had prepared him a very ill room.—BACON.

**Help**; once, to heal; now, to assist in any sense.
The true calamus *helps* coughs.—GERARDE.

**Institute**; once, to teach; now, to establish in any sense.
If children were early *instituted*.—DR. MORE.

*Note.*—We still call an Arts School a Technical *Institute*.

**Maker**; once, a poet; now, a maker of anything.
We Englishmen have met well with the Greeks in calling a poet a *maker*.—SIDNEY.

**Misery**; once, avarice; now, wretchedness of any kind.
He will die in *misery* and niggardliness.—BROWNE.

**State**; once, a republican,—now any kind of,—government.
Well, monarchies may own religion's name,
But *states* are atheists in their very fame.—DRYDEN.

(*e*) *Words that have shifted their meaning.*

**Abandon**: (1) to cast out, expel; (2) relinquish.
That he might *abandon* them from him.—UDALL.

**Abuse**: (1) to deceive, cf. *disabuse*; (2) revile.
Their eyes *abused* by a double object.—TAYLOR.

**Allow**: (1) to praise, cf. Lat. *laud*-em; (2) permit.
Ye *allow* the deeds of your fathers.—*Luke* xi. 48.

**Angry**: (1) red, ruddy; (2) incensed.
Sweet rose, whose hue *angry* and brave.—HERBERT.

**Awkward**: (1) contrary, untoward; (2) ungainly, clumsy.
*Awkward* wind. *Awkward* casualties.—SHAKSPEARE.

**Battle**: (1) battalion; (2) combat.
The king divided his army into three *battles*.—BACON.

**Bombast**: (1) cotton-wadding; (2) inflated diction.
A candle with a wick of *bombast*.—LUPTON.

**Boor**: (1) a cultivator; (2) a country bumpkin.
The Dutch farmers in South Africa are still called *Boors*.

**Buxom**: (1) yielding, pliable; (2) blithe and pretty.
The joyous playmate of the *buxom* breeze.—COLERIDGE.

**By-and-by**: (1) immediately; (2) some time afterwards.
When persecution ariseth, *by-and-by* he is offended.—*Matt.* xiii. 21.

**Cheer**: (1) face, countenance; (2) repast.
Be of good *cheer*.—*New Test.* All dreary was his *chere*.—CHAUCER.

**Christendom**: (1) baptism; (2) the Christian world.
Sins will wash off the water of *christendom*.—TYNDALE.

**Churl**: (1) a rustic labourer; (2) a surly, ill-bred man.
Let men of cloth bow to the stalwart *churls*.—EMERSON.

**Copy**: (1) the original to be copied; (2) the copy itself.
What is sent to be printed is still called the *copy*.

**Danger**: (1) jurisdiction; (2) risk.
You stand within his *danger*, do you not?—SHAKSPEARE.

**Defend**: (1) to prohibit, to forbid; (2) to protect.
Which God *defend* that I should wring from him.—SHAKSPEARE.

**Defy**: (1) to renounce, discard; (2) challenge.
For thee I have *defied* my constant mistress.—BEAUMONT AND FLETCHER.

**Depart**: (1) to separate; (2) to go away.
Till death us *depart* (now changed to *do part*).—*Prayer-Book.*

**Discourse**: (1) the faculty of inference; (2) conversation.
Since he hath made us with such large *discourse*,
Looking before and after.—MILTON.

**Disoblige**: (1) to release from an obligation; (2) to fail in conferring one.
*Disobliged* from payment.—TAYLOR.

**Document**: (1) unwritten warning; (2) written evidence.
They were stoned to death as a *document* to others.—RALEIGH.

**Ebb**: (1) shallow, *adj.*; (2) the outflow of the tide.
Cross the stream where it is *ebbest.*—*Proverb.*

**Elephant**: (1) ivory; (2) the animal.
Of silver, gold, and polished *elephant.*—CHAPMAN.

**Feature**: (1) the whole; (2) a part, an aspect.
So scented the grim *feature*, and upturned
His nostril wide into the murky air.—MILTON.

**Firmament**: (1) foundation; (2) sky.
Custom is the *firmament* of the law.—TAYLOR.

**Forlorn hope**: (1) vanguard (Dutch *verloren hoop*, lost band); (2) a hopeless case.
Our *forlorn* of horse marched within a mile of the enemy.
CROMWELL.

**Garland**: (1) a king's crown; (2) a wreath of flowers.
Corona regis, quæ vulgariter *garlanda* dicitur.—MATTHEW OF PARIS.

**Gist**: (1) resting-place (Lat. *jacet*); (2) main point.
These quails have their set *gists.*—HOLLAND.

**Harvest**: (1) autumn; (2) the fruits of autumn.
At *harvest*, when corn is ripe.—TYNDALE.

**Husband**: (1) rustic, ploughman; (2) husband.
The painful (laborious) *husband* ploughing up his ground.
HAKEWILL.

**Imp**: (1) engrafted shoot; (2) child in a bad sense, goblin.
Of feeble trees there comen wretched *imps.*—CHAUCER.

**Indifferent**: (1) impartial, the same to all; (2) unconcerned.
Truly and *indifferently* to minister justice.—*Prayer-Book.*

**Ingenuity**: (1) ingenuousness, sincerity; (2) cleverness.
Openness and *ingenuity* in contracts.—TAYLOR.

**Kind**: (1) natural, pertaining to its kind; (2) loving.
It becometh sweeter and loseth the *kind* taste.—HOLLAND.

**Lace**: (1) a snare, noose (Lat. *laqueus*); (2) lace.
Vulcanus hath caught thee in his *lace.*—CHAUCER.

**Legacy**: (1) commission, appointed task; (2) bequest.
My *legacy* wherefore I am sent into the world.—TYNDALE.

**Livery** (short for *delivery*): (1) food allowance for horses; (2) dress uniform of men-servants.
*Liverye* is allowance of horse meate.—SPENSER.

**Lumber**: (1) a pawnshop (orig. Lombard); (2) goods not in use.
They put all their plate in *lumber* (pawn).

**Medley**: (1) conflict; (2) mixture, confusion.
The *medley* was hard fought between them.—HOLLAND.

**Mess**: (1) a quartette; (2) distribution of food (lit. by fours).
Where are your *mess* of sons to back you now?—SHAKSPEARE.

**Miscreant**: (1) unbeliever (Lat. *minus credent-em*); (2) a wicked wretch.
Thou oughtest to constrain *miscreants* to keep the faith.—RIVERS.

**Obnoxious**: (1) liable, answerable (persons); (2) objectionable (things).
Lawyers are *obnoxious* to their particular laws.—BACON.

**Occupy**: (1) to lay out money; (2) to take possession of.
*Occupy* till I come.—*Luke* xix. 13.

**Overture**: (1) an opening; (2) a proposal.
The cave's inmost *overture*.—CHAPMAN.

**Palliate**: (1) to hide a fault; (2) to make excuses for one.
They never hide or *palliate* their vices.—SWIFT.

**Pester**: (1) to crowd; (2) to annoy.
All rivers and pools *pestered* with fishes.—HOLLAND.

**Plantation**: (1) colony, settlement; (2) plantation of tea, etc.
While these *plantations* were forming in Connecticut.—TRUMBULL.

**Race**: (1) root of a plant (Lat. *radic-em*); (2) lineage.
A *race* of ginger.—SHAKSPEARE.

**Reduce**: (1) bring back, restore; (2) bring down, lower.
And to his brother's house *reduced* the wife.—CHAPMAN.

**Restive**: (1) backing (Lat. *re-stare*); (2) eager to go forward.
*Restive* or *resty*, drawing back instead of going forwards.—PHILLIPS.

*Note.*—Cf. the phrase "the horse turned *rusty*" (for *resty*).

**Sad**: (1) steadfast, serious-minded; (2) mournful.
Lady Catherine, a *sad* and religious woman.—BACON.

**Secure**: (1) without fear or anxiety; (2) safe, without danger.
Men may *securely* sin, but safely never.—BEN JONSON.

**See**: (1) seat (Lat. *sed-es*) of a king's power; (2) of a bishop's.
Jove laughed at Venus from his sovereign *see*.—SPENSER.

**Sight**: (1) a multitude; (2) a spectacle.
A wonderful *sight* of flowers.—GOWER.

**Staple**: (1) chief market-place; (2) chief commodity.
Alexandria was the *staple* of the Indian trade.

**Suspect**: (1) to respect; (2) to regard with suspicion.
The tyrant did not *suspect* the dignity of an ambassador.—NORTH.

**Symbol**: (1) a contribution; (2) a token.
They paid their *symbol* in a war or in a plague.—TAYLOR.

**Tarpaulin**: (1) sailor, jack tar; (2) tarred palling, *i.e.* tarred canvas.
To landsmen these *tarpaulins* seemed a strange and half-savage race.—MACAULAY.

**Thews**: (1) qualities of mind, manners; (2) muscles.
Evil speeches destroy good *thewes*.—WYCLIFF.

**Trade**: (1) the path we *tread;* (2) buying and selling.
The *trade*-winds, *i.e.* the winds of certain seasons.

**Treacle**: (1) antidote against venomous bites; (2) treacle.
Christ is *treacle* to every harm.—MORE.

**Tree**: (1) timber as used by carpenters; (2) living tree.
Jesus whom they slew and hanged on a *tree.—Acts* x. 39.

**Union**: once a pearl in which all the best qualities were united. *Onion* is so called from its likeness to such pearls.

If pearls be white, great, round, smooth, and weighty, our dainties and delicates here call them *unions*.—HOLLAND.

**Vivacity**: (1) longevity; (2) sprightliness.

The *vivacity* of some of these pensioners is little less than a miracle: they live so long.—FULLER.

### (*f*) *Words once used for males as well as females.*

(Cf. *flirt*, still used for both sexes.)

**Coquet** (masc.), *coquette* (fem.). You are *coquetting* to a maid of honour.—SWIFT.

**Hag.** That old *hag*, Silenus.—GOLDING.

**Girl** (child). A boy was called a knave-*gerl* in Mid. Eng.

**Hoyden** (doublet of *heathen*). Shall I argue with this *hoyden*, at *his* opportunities in the larder?—MILTON.

**Maid.** Sir Gelehad is a *maid* and sinner never.—MALORY.

**Man**, person; hence *wife-man*, woman.

**Muse.** So may some gentle *Muse*
With lucky words favour my destined vow,
And as *he* passes turn, etc.—MILTON'S *Lycidas*.

**Termagant.** This terrible *termagant*, this Nero.—BALL.

**Witch.** Thy master is a rare man; they say he's a *witch*.—BEAUMONT AND FLETCHER.

(*g*) There is a large number of words sprung from the same root, but differently spelt and rather differently formed, which once had the same, but have since differentiated their meanings. Some of the following pairs are doublets:—

Achievement, hatchment.
Artisan, artist.
Benefice, benefit.
Caitiff, captive.
Cattle, chattels.
Chivalry, cavalry.
Convince, convict.
Demerit, merit.
Diamond, adamant.
Drench, drown.
Drift, drove.
Fact, feat.
Handsome, handy.
Heathen, hoyden.
Ingenuousness, ingenuity.
Lively, living.
Needful, needy.
Novelist, innovator.
Polite, polished.
Propriety, property.
Prune, preen.
Punctual, punctilious.
Queen, quean.
Sensual, sensuous.
Spice, species.
Taint, tint.
Virtuous, virtual.

## APPENDIX V.—NOTE BY PROFESSOR SKEAT.

### NAMES OF VOCALIC SOUNDS IN MODERN ENGLISH.

THE difficulty of understanding and explaining the vocalic sounds in Modern English is chiefly due to the unfortunate names by which we denote the symbols *a*, *e*, *i*, *o*, and *u*.

For example, the symbol *ā* (long *a*) was used in Latin, and in all languages (including A.S.) which employed the Latin alphabet, to denote the sound of the *a* in *path* or *father;* and nearly all foreign languages still employ this symbol for the same purpose; and the *name* which they give to the symbol is still pronounced in such languages as it always has been; *i.e.* the name is sounded like the modern English *ah* (*a* in *path*, *al* in *calm*, and even (in many parts of Southern England) as *ar* in *cart*).

But the change in the vocalic sounds of Modern English, as compared with those of Middle English, is so great, that none of the present vowel-names are at all suitable for the symbols used to represent them. The names of the symbols *a*, *e*, *i*, *o*, *u* can only, at the best, be intelligently employed to denote the *long* vowels or diphthongs, and it is remarkable that only one out of the whole set still represents a pure long vowel, viz. *e* (*ee*). The names of the remaining symbols, viz. *a*, *i*, *o*, *u*, are all so pronounced as to form diphthongs. Even the name of the vowel *e* is misleading; for it denotes a sound which in Latin, and in a large number of languages which employ the Latin symbols, is denoted by (long) *i*. Indeed, we actually employ the symbol *i* ourselves, in order to represent the sound to which we now give the name of *e;* viz. in words derived from modern French, such as *unique*, *machine*, *glacis*, *quinine*, *pique*, and several others.

It follows, from the above explanation, that the vowel-names are wholly inappropriate for the symbols. The convenience of having names which are really appropriate for them is so obvious, that it is worth while for every English child to *know* them, in order that he may be able to distinguish what sounds are being discussed. All philologists are agreed that the only *appropriate* names for the symbols *a*, *e*, *i*, *o*, *u* (all supposed long) are the names which the Romans themselves gave them.[1] These names are represented, respectively, by the following sounds:—

1. The symbol *a* was called *ah;* *i.e.* it had the sound of E. *a* in *father*, or of *al* in *calm*.

2. The symbol *e* was called *eh;* *i.e.* it had the sound of the *e* in *vein;* for it must be particularly noted that the *ei* in *vein* is a diphthong, composed of long *e* (*eh*) followed by a slight glide (denoted by *i*) such as is heard at the end of the word *they*, in which it is denoted by the final *y*. Or we may say that the *e* was sounded like Fr. *é* in *été*.

---

[1] The Roman names for their letters of the alphabet are given in Postgate's *New Latin Primer* as follows:—Ah, Beh, Keh (*i.e.* C), Deh, Eh, ef, Geh, Hah, ee, Kah, el, em, en, Oh, Peh, Coo (Q), er, ess, Teh, oo (U, V), ix (X), ypsīlon, Zēta.

3. The symbol *i* was called *ee*; *i.e.* it had the sound of E. *ee* in *seem*, or of E. *i* in *unique*.

4. The symbol *o* was called *o*, the *o* being purely pronounced, as in the German word *so*. The E. *o* in *so* is not the same sound, being in fact impure; for it not only expresses the German *o*, but is followed by a slight after-sound, like a faint utterance of the Eng. *u* in *full*. This after-sound is expressed by *w* in the case of the word *know*, pronounced as (nou).[1] The Englishman who pronounces the German *so* as if it were spelt *zo* in English, can immediately be detected as being no German; his *z* for *s* is right enough, but the sound which he gives to the *o* is peculiarly and unmistakably his very own.

5. The symbol *u* was called *u*, as in E. *rule*, a sound which English usually represents by *oo*, as in *doom*, *loose*, *cool*, *soon*.

If the reader who has mastered the above facts will now reconsider the names of the English so-called "long vowels," he will begin to realise what the English vowel-names really imply.

1. The English symbol *a* is *now* called by a name resembling the very sound of *a* in the word *name*. This sound is precisely that of the *ei* in *vein*; *i.e.* the E. *a* in *name* is really a diphthong, such as in French is composed of the Latin *e*, followed by a glide which may be represented by a short *i*. Hence, in phonetic writing, the sound is represented by (ei).

2. The English symbol *e* is now called by a name which is pronounced like E. *ee* in *seem*, or E. (and Fr. and foreign) *i* in *unique*. It is a pure vowel, and was denoted in Latin by *ī*, which is often written *ī* by grammarians in order to express its length. Hence, in phonetic writing, the sound may be represented by (ii), the *i* being repeated to indicate length.[2]

3. The English symbol *i* is now called by a name which is pronounced somewhat like the *ai* in Isaiah, but with the former element a little shorter and less distinct. It may approximately be denoted by (ai), though the symbol (əi) is perhaps better. The meaning of the symbol (ə) is given below.

4. The English symbol *o* is now called by a name which is pronounced like E. *ou* in *soul* or *ow* in *know*. It really consists of a German long *o*, followed by a slight (u), where (u) denotes the *u* in *full*. Hence its phonetic symbol is (ou); though this is only approximate, unless we remember that the *o* is stressed, and the *u* is slight.

5. The English symbol *u* is now called by a name which is pronounced like the word *yew*, or the *u* in *duke*. The former element is the glide or semi-vowel which we usually denote by *y*, denoted in phonetics by (j); *i.e.* the German *j* in *ja*, or by (i). The latter element is the sound of long *u* in *rule*. Hence the phonetic symbol is (juu) or (iuu); where the repetition of (u) denotes that the latter element is long.

---

[1] All pronunciations which are denoted by true phonetic symbols are enclosed, as here, between brackets.

[2] The latter element is apt to pass into a glide; hence some write (ij), where the (j) represents the German *j* as in *ja*, or E. *y*. The glide is well heard in a word like *seeing* (sijing).

Recapitulating the above results, we see that, when we utter the names of the symbols *a, e, i, o, u,* we really utter sounds which, in older English, in Latin, and in most Continental languages, would rather be expressed by such symbols as (ei), (ii), (ai), (ou), and (iuu) or (iū). The accent falls on the former element in the case of the diphthongs which we denote by *a, i, o;* and on the latter element in the case of the diphthong which we denote by *u*. Only one of the symbols, viz. *e*, denotes a pure vowel; and even here, the sound meant is that of the *i* in *unique*.

When we apply their usual names to the short vowels, *i.e.* to the symbols *a, e, i, o, u,* as in the words *cat, bed, it, not, full,* it is obvious that, here again, the mere names are utterly inapplicable to the sounds intended. It follows that the English vowel-names are altogether useless for denoting sounds, unless in every case an example is given of the way in which the sound is written; and for this purpose the example given must be an entire word, having an invariable pronunciation. It would, obviously, be a great help to have a *true* name for every one of the *sounds* of the English vowels and diphthongs; and the following list may be taken as giving a *sufficient* approximation to the desired result.[1] The twenty vocalic sounds of the English language are these:—

**A.** Four sounds frequently denoted by the symbol *a;* one short and three long.

(1) Short: a sound between French *a* and French *e*. Name: short *æ*, pronounced "short *æ*," where by *æ* is meant the sound of *a* in *cat*, as heard in the South of England. In order to produce this sound, think of *cat*, and then sound the vowel *only*, omitting *c* and *t*. Phonetic symbol (æ). Sound: that of *a* in *cat* (kæt).

(2) Long. Name: long *æ*, pronounced "long *æ*." Phonetic symbol (ae). Sound: that of *a* in *Mary* (maeri). This vowel occurs by itself only before a trilled *r* (*i.e.* an *r* followed by a vowel in the same or the next word). With an untrilled *r*, as in *care, bare,* it helps to form a diphthong, being followed by the sound numbered 18. That is, *care, bare* (before a consonant) are pronounced as (kaeə, baeə).

(3) Long. Name: diphthongal *ei*, pronounced "diphthongal *eh-ee*." Phonetic symbol (ei). Sound: that of *a* in *mate* (meit).

(4) Long. Name: long *aa*, pronounced "long *ah*." Phonetic symbol (aa). Sound: that of *a* in *path* (paath), *father* (faadhə). (There is no "short *ah*." The vowel formerly so pronounced has passed into the sound numbered 18.)

**E.** Two sounds commonly denoted by the symbol *e;* one short and one long.

(5) Short. Name: short *eh*, pronounced "short *eh*." Phonetic symbol (e). Sound: that of *e* in *bed* (bed).

---

[1] In other words, we can only speak clearly, so as to be always understood, if we give *foreign* names to the symbols. Unless this be done, it is impossible to emerge from chaos. And it must be remembered, that the pronunciation here spoken of is that of Southern and Midland English, that of the higher classes in London. In the North, the *a* of *cat* is often sounded as the Italian *a* in *matto*, and the *u* of *but* as the Southern English *u* in *full*.

(6) Long. Name: long *e*, pronounced "long *ee*." Phonetic symbol (ii). Sound: that of *i* in *unique*, or of *é* in *mete* (miit).

**I.** Two sounds commonly denoted by *i*; one short and one long.

(7) Short. Name: short *e*, pronounced "short *ee*." Phonetic symbol (i). Sound: that of *i* in *bit* (bit).

(8) Long. Name: diphthongal *ai*, pronounced "diphthongal *ah-ee*." Phonetic symbol (ai). Sound: that of *i* in *bite* (bait). Also written (bəit), meaning that the (a) is indistinct.

**O.** Three sounds commonly denoted by *o*, with which may be associated the sound of *aw* in *hawk*, seldom written with *o*, except in a few words, such as *off*, *soft*, *frost*.

(9) Short. Name: short *au*, pronounced "short *au*." Phonetic symbol (o). Sound: that of *o* in *not* (not).

(10) The unaccented *o* in *omit* (o'mit·), the phonetic symbol for which is written as (o') by Miss Soames, to indicate that the *o*, if not sounded as No. 18, is nearly pure, the element (u) being scarcely noticeable. It is, of course, quite different from the (o) in *not*, being a close *o* instead of an open one. Name: the unaccented *o*.

(11) Long. Name: long *au*, pronounced "long *au*." Phonetic symbol (ao). Sound: that of *aw* in *hawk* (haok), or *au* in *naught* (naot), or of *o* in *frost* (fraost).

(12) Long. Name: diphthongal *o*, pronounced "diphthongal *oa*." Phonetic symbol (ou). Sound: that of *oa* in *boat*, or *o* in *note* (bout, nout); also written (ow), as (bowt, nowt). The (u) is more distinct at the end of a word.

**OO.** Two sounds commonly denoted by *oo*; one short and one long.

(13) Short. Name: short *oo*; pronounced "short *oo*." Phonetic symbol (u). Sound: that of *oo* in *book* (buk), or *u* in *full* (ful).

(14) Long. Name: long *oo*; pronounced "long *oo*." Phonetic symbol (uu). Sound: that of *oo* in *boot* (buut).

(15) **U.** The diphthongal sound to which we give the name of *u*. Phonetic symbol (iuu) or (juu); as in *duke* (djuuk) or (diuuk).

(16) The diphthong *oi*; pronounced *oi*; composed of Nos. 11 and 7. Phonetic symbol (oi); as in *toil* (toil).

(17) The diphthong *ow*; pronounced as *ow* in *now*; composed of Nos. 4 and 13. Symbol (au); as in *now* (nau).

Three obscure vowel-sounds, the first of which only occurs in *unaccented* syllables.

(18) Name: the unaccented obscure vowel. Phonetic symbol (ə); called "turned *eh*," or (colloquially) "turned *ee*." Example: the final *a* in *China* (chainə).

(19) Name: the long obscure vowel. Similar to the preceding in sound, but long, and only occurring in accented syllables. Phonetic symbol (əə); called "double turned *eh*." Example: the *ur* in *turn* (təən).

(20) Name: the unrounded *u*. Phonetic symbol (ɐ), called "turned *ah*." Example: the *u* in *cut* (kɐt).

Hence there are eight short vowels (æ, e, i, o, o', u, ə, ɐ); six long vowels (aa, ae, ii, ao, uu, əə); and six diphthongs (ei, ai, ou, iuu, oi, au).

*Note.*—As "turned *ah*" is rather troublesome to print, there is no *great* objection to using the same symbol as in No. 18. For though the sounds are not quite the same, the fact that No. 20 only occurs in *accented* syllables always distinguishes it, *in practice*, from No. 18, which only occurs in *unaccented* syllables. Hence we may write *cut* as (kət). Miss Soames uses the symbol (œ), but it is liable to confusion with (æ).

It has already been said that the name *a* (ei) is very inappropriate, inasmuch as the symbol *a* originally meant the sound of *ah*. It is worth notice, on the other hand, that the sound of the *a* in *name* is so far from being always represented by the symbol *a*, that it can be represented in *twenty* different ways. Examples are: *fate, pain, pay, dahlia, vein, they great, eh, gaol, gauge, champagne, campaign, straight, feign, eight, played, obeyed, weighed, trait, halfpenny.*

# I. INDEX OF SUBJECTS.

*The references are to pages.*


ABSOLUTE participle, 7, 124, 129
Impersonal, 7, 129
Imperative, 7, 68
Infinitive, 7, 68, 69, 129
case, 149
construction, 213
Abstract nouns, defined, 10
used as Proper, 11
used as Common, 10
expressed by Common, 160, 161
expressed by Adjective, 163
expressed by Gerund, 11, 73
expressed by Infinitive, 11, 67, 68
suffixes, 413
Accent, defined, 301
in Teutonic words, 301-304
in Romanic words, 304-308
Accidence, defined, 213
Accusative case, adverbs, 359
Active and Passive, 55
Active verb in Passive sense, 56
Adjective, defined, 2, 25
kinds of, 26
verbal, 5, 70
comparison of, 30-33, 163, 164, 326-330
used as nouns, 161-163
substitutes for, 30
two uses of, 29, 30
loss of inflexions, 322, 323
Adjective-clause, 30, 113
Adjective substituted for adverb, 126
Adjective suffixes :—
Teutonic, 388-390
Romanic, 405-407
Greek, 411
Adjuncts, to Subject, 104
to verb of Predicate, 106
Adverb, defined, 3, 87
kinds of, 89-91
two uses of, 92, 93, 126, 127
sentence qualified by, 88
qualifying prepositions, 88, 175-177
qualifying conjunctions, 88
comparison of, 91, 92
functions of, 87-89
position of, 173-175
forms of, 358-364
object to preposition, 93
substitute adverbs, 90
Adverb-clause, 114-116
Adverbial objective, 125, 359
adjuncts to Predicate, 106
suffixes *-ly*, *-ling*, 360
loss of suffix, 361
Adverbs compounded with :—
nouns, 89, 370
Adverbs compounded with :—
verbs, 92
origin of, 358
unclassified list of, 363, 364
Adversative conjunctions, 97
Affixes, comparative results, 412-415
the same from different sources, 416, 417
Agent, suffixes, 414
Alexandrine, 440, 441
Allegory, 445
Alliteration, 436
Alternative conjunctions, 97
Amphibrach, 437
Analysis, various applications, 214
Analysis of sentences :—
simple, 102-106
compound, 106-109
complex, 110-118
Anapæst, 437
Anglo-French scribes, 292
dialect, 257
Anglo-Saxon, origin of name, 230
periods of, 231
alphabet, 266, 267, 291, 292
Anomaly, 214
Antecedent :—
to Demonstrative pronoun, 37
to Relative pronoun, 42
understood, 42
Anticlimax, Bathos, 446
Antithesis, 446
Apheresis, 308
Aphesis, 308
Apocope, 308
Apostrophe, figure of speech, 446
Apostrophe in punctuation, 136
Apostrophes, omission of, 16, 136
Apposition, 5, 6, 124, 125, 214
Archaism, 214
Articles, origin of, 4, 159
idiomatic use of, 160, 161
Aryan languages, 222
Assertive sentences, 1
Assimilation, 214
Assonance, 436
Asterisk, 138
Attributive :—
use of adjectives, 30
use of adverbs, 92
use of participles, 129
use of Infinitives, 30, 129
adjuncts (to Subject), 104
"Au" sound, 287
Augmentative suffixes, 415
Auxiliary verbs, defined, 46, 53
list of, 54
conjugated, 81-84

Borrowings, miscellaneous, 262-265
Brackets in punctuation, 137

Cæsura, 436
Cardinals, old forms of, 323, 324
Case, in Old Eng., 314
in Mod. Eng., 16-18
Case-endings, Possessive, 315
Causal use of Intransitive verbs, 51
Causal verbs, formation of, 291, 390, 415
Celtic borrowings, 247, 248
Circumlocution, 447
Clause, defined, 2
Noun-clause, 110-112
Adjective-clause, 113, 114
Adverb-clause, 114-116
Climax, 446
Cognate object, 50, 51, 150
Cognate words, 223, 290
Collective nouns, 9
suffixes, 415
Colon in punctuation, 134-136
Comma in punctuation, 131-134
Commas, inverted, 131
Common gender, 15
Common nouns, 9
other nouns used as, 9, 10
Comparatives, irregular, 32
Latin, 33
which have lost their force, 164
pairs of, distinguished, 165
Comparison of adjectives, 30-33, 164, 326-330
adverbs, 91, 92
Complement defined, 6, 47, 49
forms of, 47
Subjective, 50
Objective, 50
position of, 50
Complex sentences, 110-116
Compound words, Related, 370, 371
Unrelated, or Juxtapositional, 369, 370
disguised, 372-375
mistaken, 375-377
hybrid, 377, 378
sentences, 106, 107
Concord, 180
Concrete nouns, 8, 10
Conjugation of verbs, 75-80, 337, 338
Conjunction, defined, 3, 95
Co-ordinative, 96, 97
Subordinative, 97-101
Conjunctions, uses of, 189-193
forms of, 368, 369
Consonants, classified, 268
how sounded, 269-272
voiced and voiceless, 272, 273
vocalised, 273, 274
substitution of, 274
assimilation of, 275
metathesis, 275
Continuative use of "who," 43, 113
Continuous forms of tense, 58, 348, 349
Contracted sentences, 108
Cumulative conjunctions, 96, 97

Dactyl, foot, 437
Danish influence, 237, 238
borrowings, 248, 249
Dash in punctuation, 137
Dative case, uses of, 149
Absolute, 149
Infinitive, 351
case-endings, 314, 315, 359
Defective, defined, 45, 214
Definite article, 160
Demonstrative adjectives, 28, 325
pronouns, 37-41
Depreciatory suffixes, 415
Derivative suffix, 378
Derivatives, 223, 378
Primary, 378
Secondary, 378
Descriptive adjectives, 26
Diæresis, 138
Dialect, 214
Dialects of Old English, 227
of Mid. English, 232
decay of, 246
Diminutive suffixes, 413
Direct object to verb, 47
Disguised prefixes, 395, 396
compounds, 372-375
Distributive adjectives, 29, 326
phrases, 159
Double Parts of Speech, 5
object to verbs, 47
Feminines, 15, 310
comparisons, 327
Doublets, defined, 419
origin of, 419, 420
Doubt, in Subjunctive mood, 65
Dutch borrowings, 250

"Ea" diphthong, 288
Ellipsis of verbs or clauses, 214
Emphasis, 301
English language, stages of change, 226, 227
bilingual character, cause, 242
bilingual character, examples, 417-419
English, origin of name, 225
verbs from Lat. ones, 255
Epigram, 446
Etymology, defined, 214
Euphemism, 445
Euphony, 214
Euphuism, 446
Exclamation, how expressed, 162
Exclamatory sentence, 1

Fable, defined, 445
Factitive verbs, 6, 47
Familiar "your" and "my," 146
Feminines, in *ess*, 310, 311
foreign, 14, 310
Figure of speech, defined, 445
Finite verbs and moods, 4, 57, 58, 62, 63, 66
First Personal pronouns, 35, 330-332
Foot defined, 437, 438
Foreign Plurals, 20, 21
Feminines, 14, 310

Formative suffix, 378
Forms of adverbs, 358-364
of prepositions, 364-368
of conjunctions, 368, 369
of subject, 6, 104, 111
of object, 6, 46, 111
French and English, struggle, 239
influence on Eng. Gram., 240
influence on Eng. Vocab., 241
borrowings, 255-261
phrases, 213
Frisian origin of Mercian, 228
Full stop, 136
Future tense :—
Indefinite, 61, 167, 168
Perfect, 167

GENDER, in Mod. Eng., 12-15
in Old Eng., 309, 310
of personified things, 15
Genitive or Possessive, meanings, 147
Personal use, 148
case-endings, 315, 316, 358, 359
German borrowings, 264
Low and High, 224
Gerund, history of, 351-358
double part of speech, 5, 73, 74
distinct from verbal noun, 74
preceded by a Possessive, 74
followed by objects, 74
used as adjective, 30, 125
Gerundial Infinitive, 68, 69, 129, 351
Gerundive use of Participles, 74, 130, 212, 213
Government of words, 130
Grammar, defined, 214
Greek prefixes, 408, 409
suffixes, 409-411
plurals, 21
borrowings, 261, 262
Grimm's Law, 420-422

HEROIC couplet, 440
triplet, 440
"His" for apostrophe *s*, 316
Historical present, 166
Homonym, 215
Hybrids, 377, 378, 382, 411, 412
Hyperbole, Exaggeration, 447
Hyphen, 137

IAMBIC foot, 437
Idiom, 215
Illative conjunctions, 97
Imperative, uses of, 62, 63
sentences, 1
Impersonal verbs, 87, 154
absolute, 129
Impropriety, defined, 215
Incomplete predication :—
Factitive verbs, 6, 47
Intransitive verbs, 49
Indefinite article, 28, 159, 160
adjectives, 27, 28, 158, 324, 325
pronouns, 40, 41
tenses, 58-60
Indicative mood, 58-62

Indirect :—
object to verb, 47
Infinitive, two kinds of, 66-69, 128, 129
the Indefinite form, 168
the Perfect form, 169
after Relative pronouns, 170
after Relative adverbs, 170
Inflexion, defined, 215
Initial *h*, 275, 276
Interchange of Strong and Weak verbs, 344-346
Interjection, examples, 101, 102
defined, 3, 101
Interjectional phrases, 102
Interrogation :—
in punctuation, 136
figure of speech, 446
Interrogative adverbs, 90, 91
sentences, 1, 167, 168
Interrogative pronouns, modern forms, 44, 45
old forms, 334-336
Intransitive verbs, 7, 46, 49-52
with complement, 7, 49
in causal sense, 51
Irony, 446
Irregular comparisons, 328-330
Italian borrowings, 262, 263

LANGUAGES first spoken in Britain, 221
still spoken in Britain, 223
Late French, 259-261
Latin plurals, 21
comparatives, 33
borrowings, 251-255
and Gr. equivalent prefixes, 415
Litotes, figure of speech, 446
Low German origin of English, 225
Lowland Scotch, 234, 246

MATERIAL, nouns of, 10
used as common, 10
Mercian dialect, 227-230
Metaphor, defined, 445
Metonymy, defined, 445
Metre, defined, 437
Middle Eng., character of, 232
Midland dialect, 234-236
sub-dialects, 236
periods, 236
Mixed or Strong-Weak verbs, 78
Mixed comparisons, 327, 328
Mod. Eng. characteristics, 243
subdivisions, 245
Modes of expressing comparison, 326, 327
Moods, four kinds of, 57
Multiplicatives, 27, 324
Multitude, nouns of, 9, 21

NAMES of vocalic sounds, 457-461
Neologism, defined, 215
Nominative case, 123, 124
Norman Conquest, 238
Note of Exclamation, 136
Interrogation, 136
Northern dialect, 233, 246
Northumbrian dialect, 227

Notional verbs, 53
Noun, defined, 2, 8
  kinds of, 8
  verbal, 74
  Infinitive, 67, 68
  used as adjective, 30, 125
Noun-clause, 6, 12, 110-112
Nouns, substitutes for, 12
Number, of Nouns, 18-25, 316-322
Number and Person, 57, 127, 128
Numeral adjectives, 27, 28, 323, 324

"OA," diphthong, 288
Object, position of, 46, 47
  omission of, 48
Objective case, 124, 125
Objective complement, 50
Objects to verbs, five kinds, 56, 74, 124, 125
"Of," followed by a Possessive, 147, 148
"Of," in the sense of apposition, 177
Old Eng. compared with Mod., 281
Onomatopœia, 447
Optative sentence, 1, 65
Ordinals, old forms of, 324
Origin of suffix *-de*, 343, 344
Ottava Rima, 440

PAIRS of English and Latin words, 417-419
Palatalisation, 276, 277
Parable, figure of speech, 445
Parenthesis, 69, 137
Paronym, defined, 215
Parsing, defined, 215
Parsing chart, 121-123
Participles, double character, 5, 70
  three uses of, 129
  forms of, 69
  meanings implied in, 72
  old forms of Present, 347
  old forms of Past, 347, 348
Parts of a verb not finite, 5
Parts of Speech, defined, 2-4
  same word as different, 118-121
Passive voice, 55, 56
Past Indefinite, uses of, 166
  Perfect, uses of, 166, 167
Past or Pass. participle, 347, 348
Perfect tenses, old forms, 349
Periphrasis, 447
Personal pronouns, mod. forms, 34-37
  old forms, 330-334
Personification, 11, 15, 17, 445
Philology, defined, 215
Phonetics, 216
Phrase, defined, 2
  adverbial, 7
  prepositional, 8
  conjunctional, 8, 189
  interjectional, 8, 102
  absolute participial, 8, 106, 124
  distributive, 159
Pleonasm, 216
Plural endings in Old Eng., 316, 317
Plurals, how formed, 18-21
  special sense of, 22, 23
Plurals, double, 20
  foreign, 20, 21
  two to one noun, 22
  true, used as Singulars, 24
  without a singular, 25
Plurals in *-ves*, 317
  by mutation, 318
  in *-en* or *-ne*, 318
  double, 319
  with no change of form, 320, 321
  that have become Singulars, 320, 321
Poetic diction, 442-444
  license, 216
Poetry, kinds of, 444
Popular and Learned, 256, 257
Portuguese borrowings, 264
Positive degree, 31, 163, 164
Possessive case :—
  of nouns, 16-18, 315
  of pronouns, 35, 36, 311, 312
  double, 36
  before a gerund, 74
  syntax of, 124
  omission of *s*, 16, 17
Predicate, defined, 1, 104
  parts of, 105
Predicative, use of :—
  adjectives, 30, 125
  Gerundial Infinitive, 69
  adverbs, 92, 127
  participles, 129
Prefixes :—
  Teutonic, 379-382
  Romanic, 391-396
  Greek, 408, 409
  Latin and Greek equivalents, 415
  disguised Romanic, 395, 396
Preposition, defined, 3, 93
  Noun-clause as object, 94, 111
  adverb as object, 93
  phrase as object, 94
  omission of object, 94
  disguised, 94
  forms of, 364-367
  compared, 180, 181
  participial, 181
  relations denoted by, 177-180
  nouns followed by, 182, 183
  adjectives followed by, 183-185
  verbs followed by, 185-188
  adverbs followed by, 188, 189
Prepositional phrase, 8, 367, 368
  verbs, 52
  adverbs, 359, 360
Present Indefinite, uses of, 166
  Perfect, uses of, 166
Principal and Auxiliary verbs, 53
  clause, 110
Pronominal adverbs, 361, 362
Pronoun, defined, 2, 33
  kinds of, 34
  syntax of, 126
  old forms of, 330-336
Proper adjectives, 26
  nouns, 8
  used as Common nouns, 9
Prosody, defined, 435

Prosopopœia, 446
Pro-verb, 83
Purity, 216
Purpose, conjunctions of, 98, 171, 172

QUALITY :—
  Nouns of, 10, 11
  Adjectives of, 26
  Adverbs of, 90
Quantity :—
  Adjectives of, 26
  in prosody, 437

REDUPLICATED past, 341
Reflexive pronouns :—
  forms of, 36, 37
  omitted after Transitive verb, 48, 49
  object to Intransitive verb, 51
Related or Syntactical compounds, 370, 371
Relative or Conjunctive pronouns, 41-43
  old forms, 334-336
  adverbs, 91
Restrictive use of Relatives, 43, 113
Retained object, 55
Rhythm, defined, 435
Rime, perfect, 435
  female, 435
Root, defined, 378

SCANNING, 438
Semicolon, 134
Sentence, defined, 1
  five kinds of, 1
Sequence of tenses :—
  after Past tense, 170, 171
  after any other tense, 171
  after conjunctions of purpose, 171, 172
  after conjunctions of comparison, 172, 173
Shifting of Long Vowel sounds, 283-286
Simile, defined, 445
Simple adverbs, 89-90
  Infinitives, 66, 67, 128, 129, 349-351
Singulars that have become Plurals, 321
Singulars, true, 24
Slang, 216
Solecism, 216
Sonnet, 440
Southern dialect, decline of, 233
Spanish borrowings, 263
Spellings, history, 291-295
  summary, 296-301
Spenserian stanza, 440
Spondee, 438
Stanzas, 441
Stem, defined, 378, 379
Strong and Weak in Old Eng., 337-341
Strong conjugation, 76-78, 338
Strong verbs classified, 341
Strong-Weak verbs, 78, 345, 355
Style, 216
Subject, defined, 1
  various forms of, 16, 104
Subjective complement, 50
Subjunctive mood, forms, 63, 64
  uses, 64-66
Subordinate clause, 110
Subordinative conjunctions, 97-101
Substitute-adverbs, 90
Substitute-verb, 83
Substitutes for nouns, 12
  for adjectives, 30
Suffixes :—
  Teutonic, 382-391
  Romanic, 396-408
  Greek, 409-411
  hybrid, 412
Superlative degree :—
  adjectives, 31, 164, 326-330
  adverbs, 91, 92
Supposition expressed by :—
  Imperative, 63
  Subjunctive, 65
Syllabic division, 308, 309
Syncope, 308
Synecdoche, 445
Synonym, 216
  examples, 447, 448
Syntax, defined, 216
Synthesis, defined, 216

TAUTOLOGY, 216
Technology, 217
Tense, three kinds of, 58
  four forms of each kind, 58
Tenses, Indicative—forms, 58-62
  uses of, 166-168
Teutonic languages, 224
  characteristics of, 223
"Thou" supplanted by "you," 150, 151
Transitive verbs, defined, 6, 45
  how made Intransitive, 48, 49
  with Double object, 47
  formed by suffixes, 415
Trochee, foot, 437
Two Singulars with Plural verb, 128

VERBAL nouns, 74, 75
Verb and Subject, 57, 127, 128
Verb, defined, 2
  kinds of, 45
  conjugation of, 75-80, 337-341
  Impersonal, 87
  in pairs, Teutonic and Romanic, 419
Verbiage, 217
Verbs, in Old Eng., 336, 337
Verner's Law, 422, 423
Vocalic sounds, 277-281
  classification of, 282, 283
  names of, 457-461
Voice, Active and Passive, 55, 56
Voiced and Voiceless consonants, 272, 273
Vowel-lengthening by *e*, 283
  mutation, 288, 289
  gradation, 290, 291

WEAK verbs, classified, 342, 343
Wessex dialect, 228
Words, denoting sex, 311-314
  in pairs, Teutonic, Romanic, 417-419
  changed in meaning, 449-456

"YE" supplanted by "you," 150

# II. INDEX OF SELECTED WORDS AND PHRASES

*The references are to pages.*


a (*art.*), 28, 118, 160, 325
a (*prefix*), 118, 359, 360, 380, 381
a few, 156
a great meinee, 157
a little, 155
a many, 156, 157
abbess, 311
about, 365
above, 365
across, 366
advice, 401
affect, 213
after, 365, 379
against, 177, 366
ago, 363
alackaday, 101, 102
alas, 101
all, 118, 175, 324, 379
all of them, 193
alms, 24, 321, 401
along, 366
also, 368
am, 81, 353
am, have, 194, 349
amid, amidst, 366
among, 180, 366
an, 287, 325
an hungred, 381
an if, 194
and, 194, 368
and all, 194
and so on, 209
anent, 366
anon, 287, 359
anthem, 410
antics, 410
any, 118, 155, 158, 325
anything but, 200
apostate, 399
are, 230, 237, 354
armour, 404
armoury, 404
around, 366
art (*verb*), 353
as, 42, 118, 192, 195, 196, 336, 369
as thee, as me, 195
as to, 195, 213
as usual, 196
as well as, 189
at, 178, 180, 360, 364, 379, 381
at best, 196
at ten years old, 196
athwart, 366
atone, 287, 379
attainder, 399, 403
away, 196
aye, 190, 363

baboon, 403
bachelor, 311
baize, 320
balsam, balm, 410
bannock, 386
barley, 383
be (*verb*), 54, 81, 353, 354
be (*prefix*), 360, 381
because, 369
been, 354
before, 366
beggar, 385, 398, 399
behind, 366
being, 354
below, 366
beneath, 366
beside, 180, 366
besides, 180, 366
better, best, 119, 328
between, 180, 366
betwixt, 366
beyond, 366
bid fair to, 196
bitch, 312
bite, bait, 291
blink, blench, 291
bodice, 320, 401
bombast, 409
both, 119, 193, 323, 390
both . . . and, 189, 368
boulevard, 398
boundary, 399
bow (*verb*), 201
boy, 311
breeks, breeches, 319
brethren, 20, 22, 319
bridal, 372
bridegroom, 314
broil, 391
brother, 311, 422
buck, 311
bullock, 312, 386
bully, 400
burgess, 400, 401
burglar, 399, 403
burials, 321, 397
bustard, 398
but, 43, 95, 119, 193, 366
but he, 196
but what, 197
buy, 346
by, 178, 180, 360, 364, 379
by far, 93
by thousands, 197

came to pass, 198
can, could, 84, 355
can but, 198
can, ken, 291
cannon, 403
caprice, 401
cassock, 386
catch, 346
cherry, 321
chess, 321
children, 20, 319
chronicle, 399
clink, clench, 291
clothe, 346
cock, 312
cockade, 396
colon, 403
colt, 312
come, go, 198
comet, 401
concerning, 367
considering, 367
countess, 312
courteous, 407
coverlet, 401
crevice, 401
curio, 402
custard, 398
cyclone, 403
cynosure, 405

daisy, 372, 405
dam, madam, 313
dare, 85, 198, 355
darkle, 360, 391
debenture, 405
dependent on, 199
devil, 401
disaster, 399, 404
do, 55, 83, 342, 357
doe, 311
dog, 312
doubt but, 200

down, 366
dozen, 324
drake, 312
drink, drench, 291
druid, 409
duchess, 311
duck, 312
duodecimo, 403
during, 181, 367
durst, 198, 355

e (*prefix*), 381, 395
each, 29, 326
each other, 159
earl, 312
eaves, 24, 321
echo, 403
eight, 323
either, neither, 29, 119, 326, 368
either . . . or, 368
eldest, oldest, 165, 289, 328
eleven, 323
else, 119, 358
embryo, 403
empress, 311
enemy, 400, 405
enough, 119, 324, 381
epicure, 405
-er, -est, 326
ere, erst, 329, 365
errand, 398
even, 200
ever, never, 368
ever so, 205
every, 29, 326
ewe, 318
except, 367
excuse, 200
exploit, 213

fairy, 387
faith, 387
fall, fell, 291
far, farther, 165, 329, 363
far from, 200
fare, ferry, 291
farrago, 402
father, 312
favourite, 410
few, 156, 324
filly, 312
first, 165, 324, 329
first importance, 201
five, 323
flee, 346
flotsam, 386
folio, 403
foot, 20, 318
for, 178, 181, 365, 381
for to, 170
fore, further, 165, 329, 363
foremost, 165, 329
forth, 329, 363
fossil, 401
four, 323
fourth, 324

friar, 312
from, 179, 180, 365
furthermost, 327
futtock, 378, 386

gaffer, gammer, 312
gammon, 408
gander, 312
gargle, 391
gauntlet, 378, 401
gentleman, 312
girl, 311
gizzard, 398
gnomon, 403
goitre, 404
good-bye, 102
good-looking, 201
goose, 20, 312, 318
gorgeous, 407
governess, 311
grovel, 360, 391
guarantee, 400
gurgle, 391

had as lief, 201, 349
half, 119, 325
halo, 403
hammock, 386
hang, 346
harness, 386
have, 54, 81, 357
have, am, 194, 349
hazard, 398
he, her, 37, 332, 333
he to deceive me, 202
heifer, 312
hemorrhage, 397
hen, 312
hence, 362
her, hers, 333
here, 361
hero, heroine, 310, 403, 410
hight, 87, 342
him, 333
hinder (*adj.*), 329
hindermost, 327, 329
his, 316, 333
hither, 361
horizon, 403
horse, 312
how, 362
how do you do? 202, 213
humble, 406
hundred, 324, 383
husband, 312, 373, 398

I (*pron.*), 330
I beg to, 203
I do you to wit, 202
I take it, 203
I was given to, etc., 203
I wis, 381
icicle, 399
if, 191, 369
if you like, 203
ilk, 325

ill, 363
in, 180, 360, 365
in God's name, 365
ink, 404
innermost, 327, 330
inuendo, 403
in respect of, 203
in that, 203
in thorough, etc., 204
is, 354
it, its, 37, 38, 154
it is, it was, 41, 155
it is I, 41, 155
it's me, 204, 213

jeopardy, 405
jetsam, 386

kennel, 404
kettle, 289
kine, 20, 319
king, 313
kitchen, 384
kitten, 384

laches, 322
lackadaisical, 102
lad, lass, 313
lady, 312, 313, 387
lampoon, 403
last, latest, 165, 328
last importance, 201
lay (*verb*), 346
lectern, 400
leisure, 405
leopard, 398
less, least, 204, 328, 363
lesser, 204
lest, 192, 369
let, 55, 84, 357
liar, 399
lie, lay, 291
limbo, 403
little, 119, 155, 325, 328, 363
livelihood, 383
lizard, 398
lobby, 387
lobster, 387
lord, 313
luncheon, 403

-ma, 327
magnet, 401
maid, 311
make, 346
mamma, 313
man, 313, 318
manciple, 404
many, 156, 328
many a, 156
marchioness, 311
mare, 312
marquis, 400, 401
maugre, 365
may, 54, 84, 356
me, 330

mean, means, 162
memento, 403
methinks, 87, 204
million, 324
milter, 318
mine, my, 36, 331
minnow, 321
minster, 290
minstrelsy, 411
miss, mistress, 311
missile, 401
mistaken, 210
mitten, 384
mizzen, 384
money, 387
monk, 312
monkey, 387
monsoon, 403
monster, 287
more, most, 326, 328
more than, 204
mote, 357
mother, 312
mouse, 20, 318
much, 120, 324, 328, 363
murderess, 311
must, 85, 357
mutual friend, 205
my, 331

n (*prefix*), 331
natheless, 368
nay, 189, 363
near, 120, 328, 365
need, 86, 355
needs, 86, 120, 358
neighbour, 374, 404
nephew, niece, 313
nest, 387
nethermost, 327, 329
never so, 205
next, 165, 328
nine, 323
no, 90, 205, 324, 364
no more, 205
none, 39, 205, 206, 324
not, 364
not only, 189
notwithstanding, 367
now, 364
nun, 312
nuncheon, 377, 408
nurse, 311

odds and ends, 206
of, off, 178, 360, 365
oft, often, 364
on, 179, 365
one, ones, 39, 40, 120, 158, 286, 323
one another, 159, 206
one more and, 206
only, 120, 174, 175, 287
or (*prefix*), 381
or (*conj.*), 190, 207, 363
or ere, or ever, 207
orchard, 377, 398

other, 29, 257, 325
other than, 158, 207, 325
ought, 84, 356
our, 330
ours, 36, 330, 332
out, outer, 329, 364
out and out, 207
out of temper, 208
outer, utter, 165
outlet, 401
outrage, 397
over, 364, 365
owing to, 367
own, 36, 151, 332, 357

papa, 318
paraffine, 402
parchment, 402
past, 367
pastern, 400
peas, 22, 321
peasant, 398
pending, 367
penny, pence, 319
pentagon, 403
per, 360, 365
phantom, 409, 410
pheasant, 398
pibroch, 386
pillow, 386
place, 396
please, 208
pleasure, 405
postern, 400
postil, 401
practice, 401
presage, 397
prevent, 208
principle, 404
proviso, 403
pumice, 401
puppy, 387
puttock, 374, 386

quail, quell, 291
quarto, 403
queen, 313
quoth, 86, 356

racket, 401
rage, 397
ram, 318
rampart, 398
random, 359, 382
ransom, 386, 402
rather, 390
rejoinder, 399, 403
remainder, 399, 403
repartee, 400
riches, 24, 321
riddles, 321, 384
righteous, 407
rise, raise, rear, 291

same, 28, 43, 237, 325
sans, 365
sardine, 402

save he, 208, 367
say, 346
scissors, 404
score, 324
second, 324
seldom, 359, 382
self, 86, 151
selvage, 397
seven, 323
several, 208, 324
shall, should, 54, 82, 167, 168, 355
shalloon, 408
she, 37, 333
shortly, briefly, 208
sidle, 360, 391
since, 120, 180, 367
sinecure, 405
sink, 291
sir, sire, 313
sister, 311
sit, set, 201
six, 323
sixpence, 319, 321
skates, 321
skeleton, 403
slattern, 400
sledge, 321
sloven, slut, 313
smallpox, 321
so, 39, 364
so and so, 209
so as to, 209
so kind as to, 209
so mote it be, 357
so much for, 210
so so, 209
solidarity, 213
some, 155, 158, 324
somehow, 209
sometimes, 359
somewhat, 211
son, daughter, 313
songster, songstress, 310
sorcerer, -ess, 310, 311
sow, 311
spawner, 313
spikenard, 398
spinage, 397
spinster, 311
stag, hind, 311
stallion, 312
stalwart, 398
steward, 374, 398
still (*adv.*), 368
stipend, 398
such, 39, 120, 158, 325
summons, 24, 322
sundry, 324
surgeon, 403
swain, nymph, 313
sweetheart, 398
swine, 311, 320
swoop, sweep, 291

tapster, 310, 313
teach, 346

ten, 323
-ter, -ther, 327
than, 94, 120, 367
thank you, 210
that, 38, 39, 42, 44, 120, 153, 325
that's him, 204
that will do, 202
the (*art.*), 28, 120, 153, 160, 162, 163, 325
the (*adv.*), 90, 120, 325, 362
the other day, 158, 210
the window gives, 213
their, theirs, 36, 237, 334
them, 237, 334
themselves, 152
then, 361
thence, 362
there, 361
therefore, 368
these, those, 38, 325
these presents, 161
they, 40, 237, 332, 334
thicket, 387
thine, 36, 331
think, 347
third, 324
thirteen, 324
this, 38, 39, 157, 325
this much, 210
thither, 361
thou, 331
though, 193, 369
thousand, 324
three, 323
through, 365, 366
thus, 362
thy, 331
till, 237, 365, 366
to, 66, 170, 350
to be sure, 211
to boot, 211
too, 66, 170, 365, 385
tooth, 20, 318
touching, 367
touchy, 407
towards, 367
trace, 320
transom, 386
treasure, 405
tremble, 391
trivet, 401
truce, 320
twelve, 324
twenty, 324
two, 286, 323

uncle, aunt, 313
under, 365, 366
unless, 369
unto, 366
up, 365
upon the carpet, 213
uppermost, 327
utter, 165, 329
uttermost, 327, 329

valley, 387
vassal, 397
versus, 365
vixen, 14, 310, 384

was, wast, were, 354
wassail, 397
welkin, 321, 385
well, 190, 364
welladay, 102
went, 347
wether, 313
what, 42, 121, 153, 336, 362
what not, 211
what was, 211
what with, 211
when, 361
whence, 362
where, 361
whether, 45, 336
which, 44, 153, 336
while, 191
whilom, 359
whither, 361
who, whose, whom, 42, 153, 212, 286, 335, 336
whole, 325
why, 362
widow, 14, 310, 314
wife, 309, 312
will, 54, 82, 167, 168, 356
window, 386
wit, 86, 356
with, 179, 180, 365
without saying, 213
wizard, witch, 313
woman, 313
wondrous, 359, 407
wont, 87, 358
won't, 356
work, wrought, 347
worse, worst, 328
worth (*verb*), 86, 358
wot, wist, 356
write you, 212

y (*prefix*), 382
yclept, 87, 382
ye, 331
yea, yes, 190, 364
yes, 90
yet, 364, 369
yon, yonder, 157, 325, 364
your, yours, 36, 331, 332

zounds, 102

THE END